PRACTICAL MEASUREMENTS FOR EVALUATION IN PHYSICAL EDUCATION

by

Barry L. Johnson
Northeast Louisiana State College

Jack K. Nelson
Louisiana State University

Illustrated by
Dwight C. McLemore

Burgess Publishing Company

426 South Sixth Street • Minneapolis, Minn. 55415

PHYSICAL EDUCATION CONSULTANT TO THE PUBLISHER:

Eloise M. Jaeger
Chairman, Department of Physical Education for Women
University of Minnesota

FOREWORD

One measure of the progress being made in a profession is to be found in the quantity and the quality of the literature produced in the various areas of concern in that profession over a period of time. With respect to the areas of measurement and evaluation in physical education, it would be accurate to say that while the quantity of books published to date has not been large, the quality, for the most part, has been high. This speaks well for our profession since it indicates a focus upon excellence rather than mass in production.

Progress in the areas of measurement and evaluation in physical education will be reflected in our literature in the opinion of the writer:

FIRST – To the degree that the publications give evidence that those who write have used the best of the known and proven tools and techniques as a basis for the creative and innovative approaches which they themselves have made to improve our testing, measuring, and evaluating procedures.

SECOND – When new publications reflect the importance of the concept that those who measure and evaluate must be both efficient practitioners and reflective students of measurement and evaluation.

THIRD – When new publications give clear evidence that the Research Approach to measuring and evaluating is essential to progress in these areas.

FOURTH – When the authors of new books show that they realize the importance of supplying adequate materials in the publications to aid the student-in-training as well as the teacher-on-the-job to understand how to use the data gathered through testing and measuring in evaluating student progress through physical education.

FIFTH – When new publications re-affirm the importance of measurement in the area of elements which appear to be basic to effective movement and performance in a wide variety of physical education activities.

SIXTH – When new publications clearly indicate that measurement of knowledge and attitudes regarding physical education and sound experience are of primary importance.

SEVENTH – When the publication reveals the fact that, while the authors realize the inadequacies and shortcomings of many of the available tools and techniques now being used in measuring and evaluating in physical education, they have faith and confidence in the concept "that if something exists it can be measured" and so if we continue our efforts to successfully identify and understand the many "somethings" that still challenge and provoke us in our research efforts we shall eventually be able to accurately measure and evaluate with reference to these items.

It is my considered judgment that careful examination of this book will in light of the criteria indicate above – and other criteria well worth using – establish the fact that we are making substantial progress in our profession in the areas of measurement and evaluation.

J. W. Kistler
University of Connecticut
Storrs, Connecticut

PREFACE

Recently there has been a surge of interest in the *how* and *why* of movement technique. With greater emphasis now being placed on learning fundamental movement skills and abilities in physical education classes, there is a definite need for a better understanding of how to measure and evaluate physical skill performance in an economical and practical manner. Moreover, there has been a continued interest in the promotion of physical fitness; desirable social qualities, interests and attitudes; and the presentation of important facts from our *body of knowledge*. Thus, the teacher who attempts to stress each major objective must also attempt to measure progress toward the accomplishment of such objectives if the program is to be effective.

Keeping the above points in mind, it is the purpose of this book to:

1. Develop within the prospective physical education teacher a greater understanding and appreciation of the need and the application of tests and measurements in the evaluation process.

2. Offer several practical and economical tests in each of the subject areas which can be used by the average physical education teacher in a typical school situation.

3. Discuss the various qualities and present brief summaries of pertinent research findings, and to identify problems that arise in isolating and measuring the particular abilities.

To become effective in any endeavor, one must know where he is going and have some means of knowing how well he has achieved his goals. Therefore, it is the hope of the authors that the readers of this book, whether they are undergraduate or graduate students or teachers in the field, will develop an attitude of evaluation that transcends the mere utilization of tests and measurements. The theme of this book is that it is the person that is doing the evaluating, not the test or measuring device, that is the key to successful evaluation. A test that has high validity and reliability coefficients is worthless if it is not administered and interpreted correctly.

Many of the tests that are included in this book were selected from those that have been published, while a few have been devised by the authors, and still others are modifications of earlier tests. Obviously, there are other good tests in many of the areas in addition to the ones we have chosen. Tests requiring expensive equipment were excluded. Consequently, the reader must not be lulled into complacency with the idea that the tests in this book are the only ones, nor that they are perfect by any means.

We hope that in our discussion more questions will be raised than answered, and that the reader will critically appraise each test and seek ways of improving them or designing new ones.

B.L.J.
J.K.N.

ACKNOWLEDGMENTS

The authors wish to express their appreciation to their former measurements teachers who have influenced the writing of this book: Dr. Ted Powers, Baylor University; Dr. H. Harrison Clarke, University of Oregon; and Dr. J. W. Kistler, University of Connecticut.

Fellow associates and graduate assistants who were especially helpful in gathering data and establishing norms are listed as follows: Mr. John Nipper, Mr. Robert Boudreaux, Mr. Ted Nadeau, Dr. I. F. Waglow, Dr. John Leach, and Mr. Jeff Fitch. We are also indebted to Miss Suzette Neubig and Mrs. Jack Nelson (Alice) for work above and beyond normal duty as typists.

This section would not be complete without a special note of thanks to Dr. George T. Walker, President of Northeast Louisiana State College; Dr. Glenn F. Power, Dean of Instruction; Dr. T. E. Holtzclaw, Former Dean of Education; Dr. H. T. Garner, Dean of Education; and Mr. Alva Huffman, Chairman of Health and Physical Education for their cooperation and assistance during the writing of this book. The authors are also especially grateful to the many fine students of Northeast Louisiana State College and Louisiana State University who served as guinea pigs for the experiments and tests conducted for this publication.

Last, but not least, the authors wish to express their sincere appreciation to Dr. Eloise Jaeger for her keen insight and valuable suggestions concerning the content and organization for this book.

TABLE OF CONTENTS

Chapter I

ORIENTATION TOWARD MEASUREMENT AND EVALUATION IN PHYSICAL EDUCATION

The physical educator must be skilled in evaluation processes. The objectives that have been set forth by the physical education profession, such as development of organic efficiency and neuromuscular skills, social and emotional adjustment, and improved mental performances are indeed worthy goals and certainly ambitious ones. The evaluation of progress in achieving these objectives requires knowledge and skills in different areas of human behavior.

Probably the most common misconception concerning evaluation in physical education is that it is employed only in the process of grading. Certainly grading is an important matter and one that has been discussed and debated copiously. Chapter XII is devoted to this topic. Yet, despite its prominence it is by no means the only, nor the most important, reason for possessing an adequate knowledge of evaluation techniques.

Basic Terms

Before we explore more fully other purposes for evaluation, it seems appropriate to identify and discuss the following basic terms:

Test — A test is a form of questioning and/or measuring used to assess retention of knowledge and capability, or to measure ability in some physical endeavor.

Measurement — Measurement is an aid to the evaluation process in that various tools and techniques are used in the collection of data.

Evaluation —Evaluation transcends mere measurement in that basically subjective judgments are based upon the data collected in the measurement process. Such judgments may aid us in determining the extent to which we are accomplishing our objectives.

Research —Research is used to designate those careful investigations conducted to extend knowledge, or to further explore and verify that which has already been explored.

From the above we can see that a test is merely one form of measurement, while measurement itself involves all the tools which may be employed in the collection of data. Examples of various tools of measurement would include achievement scales, rating scales, various instruments (for determining time, distance and amount), and score cards.

In order to make an intelligent evaluation of a program, one must know the desired objectives of the program, know which tools are most effective for the collection of data about the program, and make unbiased judgments concerning educational significance.

Research has to rely on scientifically constructed measuring instruments in order to reach a satisfactory conclusion. Thus, tests and measuring instruments are basic tools of research, and the measurements course should be thought of as one of the prerequisites to

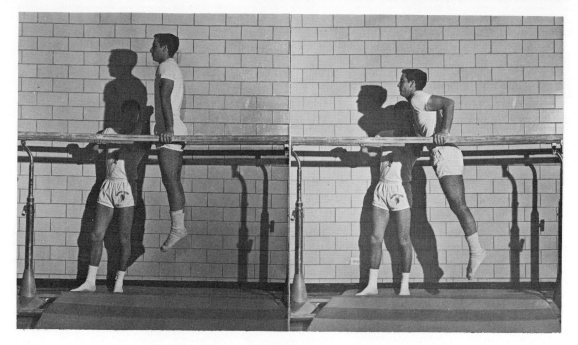

FIGURE 1 - 1

Dip Test — A Test of Muscular Endurance

research. It should also be pointed out that it is through research that the physical educator is able to determine effective means of measurement and evaluation. Consequently, each area compliments the other.

The Need for Measurement in the Evaluation Process

There are many reasons for employing tests and measurements. Moreover, once the data has been collected, the interpretation and utilization of the information may have varied application. To be more specific, a test that is given for the purpose of improving the learning process may be put to further use by the teacher in grading and/or in interpreting the program to pupils, administrators, teachers, and other interested groups.

Some of the reasons for the utilization of tests and measurements in the evaluation process are to:

1. Motivate students when there appears to be a leveling off of interest in the instruction. Tests also help the teacher to end the unit of instruction with a high level of interest.
2. Help the teacher assess students' performances.
3. Help students evaluate their own knowledge and/or skills in various physical activities.
4. Enable the teacher to objectively measure improvement by testing before and after the unit of instruction.
5. Assist the teacher in pin-pointing the limitations as well as the strong points in a program.

6. Aid the teacher in evaluating different methods of instruction.
7. Provide a means for determining the better performances within a group and to gain insight as to the potential ability of others.
8. Provide a basis for the classification of players and teams for practice and competition.
9. Diagnose needs in relation to body mechanics, fitness, and motor skills.
10. Help establish age, sex, and grade level norms for use within a school or school district as well as for comparison with national norms.
11. Determine status and changes in status brought about by physical education for public relations purposes.
12. Collect data for research.
13. Help determine the relative values of sports activities in terms of meeting desired objectives.
14. Determine the needs of individuals within the program and the extent to which educational objectives have been accomplished.
15. Enable the teacher to evaluate his own teaching effectiveness.

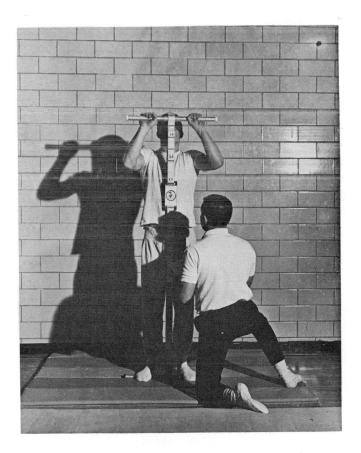

FIGURE 1 - 2

Iso-scale and Kit-Measurement of Static Strength

Principles of Tests and Measurements in Evaluation

Success in a program of evaluation is of a greater certainty when sound principles are understood and followed. When the following principles are adhered to, greater depth and meaning is given to the total physical education program.

As a Means to an End

Measurement and evaluation should be considered as a means to an end and not as ends in themselves. Testing just for the sake of testing is not only a waste of time, but an actual obstruction in the total educational process. When measurements are conducted, there should be a guiding purpose for which the resulting data may be used. Therefore, measurement and evaluation are the means by which we accomplish the task of developing well-adjusted and physically educated students.

Related Objectives

Measurement should be conducted for the purpose of evaluating the outcomes of physical education in the light of educational objectives. Examples of common objectives in physical education are listed as follows:

1. Development of physical fitness and organic efficiency
2. Neuromuscular skill development
3. Improved social and emotional adjustment
4. Development of knowledges and understandings

If we are serious about our objectives, we must attempt to evaluate in each of the above areas to determine the status, needs, and effectiveness of our programs.

Determining Needs

Measurement must aid in determining the needs of the individual and the group. Measurements provide the teacher with opportunities to evaluate needs and then gear the physical education program toward the aim of satisfying the needs of each individual or group.

Determining Value of Equipment, Materials, and Methods

Measurement should provide a special service to the evaluation process in the physical education program that seeks aid in improving teaching methods and in determining the worth of physical education equipment and materials. Through repeated measurements, it is possible to identify and eliminate inferior equipment and materials as well as abandon certain methods which tend to make the physical education program inferior.

Measurement is Broader than Tests Alone

The program which employs only tests is a limited program in physical education. The test is only one form of measurement in our field; and, therefore, physical educators should consider many types of measurement for use in the evaluation process.

Objective and Subjective Measurement

There is considerable advantage to be gained in having a number of objective measures in the evaluation program, particularly in the process of awarding grades. Students,

FIGURE 1 - 3

Bass Stick Test — A Measure of Static Balance

parents, and administrators understand objective measures more readily, and, consequently, they are more easily defended. However, the physical education teacher can never divorce himself from subjective evaluation, nor should he even try. It is a simple fact that certain performances require qualitative, rather than quantitative, evaluation. However, the physical education teacher should be alert to the fact that when subjective measurement is called for, every effort should be made to make his subjective evaluation as objective as possible. It is commonly accepted that no amount of objective measurement will replace sound judgment, nor is there anything wrong with subjective judgment when the tester is qualified to evaluate the quality being measured. In a sports skill such as tennis or basketball, for example, there are no objective tests which can measure all the factors involved in actual competition. Some qualities are more accurately measured than others, and, therefore, the validity coefficient will vary accordingly. If a test item is capable of being measured easily, such as in units of time or distance, it should have high validity. On the other hand, if it is hard to measure, as in the case of a stunt on a trampoline, or an attitude assessment, then a lower validity coefficient is acceptable.

Instruction and Practice Normally Precedes Testing

Unless the performance test is designed to measure educability or initial status, it should normally follow a period of instruction and practice to insure safety and familiarity with the test items. In those cases where instruction and practice interfere with the purpose of the test, it must be made certain that the directions for each test item are quite clear and that performance hazards are eliminated.

Conducted in a Professional Manner

Measurements programs should be conducted in a professional and unbiased manner. Testing conditions must be exactly alike for all students within the group to insure fairness and validity, since it is quite evident that a change in conditions produces different results. Thus, if we attempt to motivate one student during a test, we should attempt to motivate them all in order to get unbiased results. This also implies that test directions be explicit and that they be rigidly followed to insure accurate scores. Where possible, well-trained and experienced testers should direct comprehensive measurements programs, and it is, of course, essential for research.

Consideration of the Whole Individual and His Environment

Evaluation of measurements data should be interpreted in terms of the whole individual in relation to his environment. A student who has done exceptionally well for several months, but suddenly begins to do poorly due to circumstances beyond his control, should be evaluated on a different basis as opposed to students whose performance has been consistent throughout the semester. Similarly, a student who does poorly on a skill test, who is obviously a better performer than the test indicates, should not be condemmed for one day's performance. The better the teacher is able to get to know his students, the more effectively he will be able to evaluate.

Functioning Soundly Within School Grading Policies

The physical education evaluation program must make every attempt to function soundly within the grading policies of the school and on an equal basis with other subjects. In defending the use of physical education grades (in the four basic activity classes) toward the cumulative scholastic average at his university, a Dean of Education* stated that there is considerable agreement on the importance of health and physical fitness to success in life; and, therefore, failure to use such grades in computing academic averages would cross the institution's stated purpose of helping students in *the full development of their talents and personalities.*

---

*Robert E. May, "A Dean of Education Speaks . . ." *JOHPER*, September, 1965.

Chapter II

A BRIEF HISTORICAL OVERVIEW IN THE AREAS OF PHYSICAL EDUCATION TESTS AND MEASUREMENTS

Introduction

A review of the literature that deals with tests and measurement in physical education reveals that valuable contributions have been made by numerous individuals as well as by various organizations. Many different types of tests have been developed, and a vast number of measuring instruments have been employed ranging from the simple yardstick to the complex electrical equipment used in physiological testing. The brief history presented below includes some of the important contributions in specific testing areas.

Age, Height, Weight, and Body Types

Most of our earliest research studies were concerned with measurement in this area. For example, in 1860 Cromwell completed a study on the growth of school children for ages eight to eighteen and discovered that boys were shorter and lighter than girls during the approximate ages of eleven to fourteen. He noted that after fourteen the boys became taller and heavier and continued their growth longer than girls.[1] In 1861 Edward Hitchcock of Amherst began collecting data from measurements in this area, and he is generally recognized as the leading figure in anthropometric testing between the years of 1860 to 1880.[5] In 1878 D. A. Sargent began a measurements program at Harvard University and compiled considerable data on students. These data were published some fifteen years later in the form of percentile tables which indicated standards based on anthropometric and strength measures for both men and women at different years of college life.[36] In 1902 D. W. Hastings undertook a study of the growth of the human body from the fifth to the twenty-first birthday and later published a manual based upon his findings.[36] Other contributions made in this area include: (1) McCloy's Classification Index[23] based upon age, height, and weight; (2) Wetzel's Grid Technique[40] which used age, height, and weight measures to plot and evaluate growth and development on a grid with seven physique channels; (3) Pryor's Width-Weight Tables[31] which used the width of the pelvic crest and the width of the chest and standing height in determining normal weight; and (4) Meredith's Height-Weight Chart[28] which identifies normal and abnormal growth patterns. Concerning the establishment of body types, the following contributors should be mentioned: Kretschmer,[21] one of the earliest workers in this field, classified individuals into asthenic (thin type), athletic (muscular type), and pyknic (fat type) categories and attempted to relate body type to personality; Sheldon,[37] influenced by Kretschmer, refined his system of classification and began a life's work of studying the ramifications of somatotypes. His three basic components were termed ectomorphy (characterized by leanness), mesomorphy (characterized by muscular hardness), and endomorphy (characterized by heavy softness); Sills[39] introduced a fourth somatotype called omomorphy, which is characterized by a V-type build with large shoulders and chest and small hips and legs; Cureton[13] devised a simple physique rating scale that could be used by the non-expert in establishing the general physique type based on a subjective rating of external fat, muscular, and skeletal development.

Power Measurement

Although power performances have been measured in athletic events through the centuries, it was not given a great deal of attention by physical educators until after Sargent's publication in 1921 of *The Physical Test of a Man.*[33] Then McCloy,[25] working with Sargent's vertical jump test, found satisfactory correlations with the total point score of the following track and field events: 100 yard dash, running high jump, standing broad jump, and eight pound shot put. Other noteworthy contributors to knowledge in this area were Capen[9] and Chui,[10] who conducted studies revealing the importance of strength gains in increasing velocity; and Bovard and Cozens,[6] who designed the leap meter for measuring vertical jump power. Recently, Glencross[17] has experimented in this area in an attempt to develop and validate tests of power. The names and contributions of other researchers in power measurement may be found in Chapter VI.

Agility Measurement

Agility measurement as a specific area does not have a long or extensive background. However, contributions made in this area include the following: (1) Royal H. Burpee's test of agility (known as the Burpee Test or the squat thrust test); (2) McCloy's scholarly endeavors in the area of motor ability, which included agility measurement;[26] and (3) the analysis of agility tests by Young,[41] Gates and Sheffield,[16] and Sierokowski.[38]

General Motor Ability Measurement

Sargent pioneered testing in the area of general motor ability in the 1880's for the purpose of assessing athletic ability in men. In 1901 Sargent developed a test consisting of six simple exercises which were to be executed in a thirty minute period without rest. Several years later Meylan of Columbia University developed a comprehensive physical ability test which included running, jumping, vaulting, and climbing.[5] In 1924 J. H. McCurdy served as chairman of the National Committee on Motor Ability Tests which established a number of such tests. In 1927 David K. Brace developed his famous Brace Motor Ability Test for the purposes of classification and measuring achievement. McCloy suggested that Brace's test was basically a motor educability test, and after much research McCloy in 1931 revised the Brace test in an attempt to increase its validity as a measure of motor educability. This revision is now known as the *Iowa Brace Test.* In 1932 the *Johnson Motor Educability Test,* named after the originator of the test battery, Granville Johnson, was designed for the purpose of sectioning classes into homogeneous groups. Since the publication of his test, research has revealed that it has predictive value as a general motor educability test, particularly as far as predicting success in learning tumbling skills.[26] Other contributions to this area of measurement include: (1) Kenneth Hill's motor educability test for Junior High School boys; (2) Aileen Carpenter's study of motor ability and motor capacity; and (3) Arthur Adam's Sports type Motor Educability Test. McCloy combined size, maturity, power, motor educability, and large muscle speed into a general motor capacity test which sought to assess innate potential in the area of motor ability. This was undoubtedly the most comprehensive effort to predict potential for physical achievement in a similar fashion to the way intelligence tests are used. A number of other motor ability tests have been devised, but space does not permit adequate discussion here. This area of measurement is covered in Chapter VIII.

Balance Measurement

Balance measurement is another area that does not have a long or extensive background. Ruth Bass is probably the most widely known contributor in this area with her practical tests of static and dynamic balance which were published in 1939. Other researchers who have made contributions in this area are Anna Espenschade, Thomas Cureton, Thomas P. Whelan, and Robert F. Lessl. The names and contributions of other researchers in balance measurement may be found in Chapter IX.

Kinesthetic Perception

Numerous studies have been conducted which have attempted to measure and evaluate different forms of kinesthetic perception. The study of kinesthesis has posed a special enigma to physical educators due to its acknowledged importance in physical performance and its elusiveness in resisting measurement, and even definition. Special mention should be made of M. Gladys Scott for her work in this area. Other researchers who have made significant contributions are Bass, Henry, McCloy, Russell, Slater-Hammel, Wiebe, Witte, and Young. Other contributions may be noted in Chapter X.

Flexibility Measurement

In 1941 T. K. Cureton, Jr. presented several practical flexibility tests which have been widely used in the profession. Later McCloy modified the scoring of several of the tests in order to take into account different body segment measurements. Other physical educators who have devised tests of flexibility are M. Gladys Scott, Esther French, Katherine Wells, and Evelyn Dillon. Perhaps one of the most significant contributions toward scientific measurement of flexibility measurement was Jack Leighton's modification of the goniometer. Leighton's instrument is known as the Flexometer and has shown high reliability in establishing the range of motion of various parts of the body. Other contributions in the area of flexibility measurement are referred to in Chapter XI.

Rhythm and Dance Measurement

This area of measurement has been plagued by a lack of experimentation for the development of objective and practical tests. While the well-known Seashore tests have been extensively used in research, they have not been found to be practical for physical education measurement.. Moreover, objective instruments for measuring rhythm have been devised, but are not feasible for the average teacher's use. However, special mention should be made of the following test constructors for presenting tests which can be useful to teachers of rhythm and dance: (1) I. F. Waglow, (2) Eloise Lemon and Elizabeth Sherbon, and (3) Dudley Ashton. Other contributors to this area of measurements may be found in Chapter XII.

Speed and Reaction Time Measurement

Numerous studies have been conducted in physical education, psychology and other fields which have investigated various facets of reaction time and speed of movement. Psychologists have been primarily concerned with response measurement as it relates to learning, whereas physical education researchers have been mainly concerned with methods of improving speed of movement and reaction time and how these factors influence physical performance. Although there are a number of variables that affect measurement of speed and reaction time, such as motivation, set, sensory discrimination, and practice, the measuring devices are generally quite precise. Consequently, many studies on this topic have been reported, and it is difficult to identify specific individuals as being leading researchers in this area. Speed and reaction time measurement and research findings in this area may be found in Chapter XIII.

Strength Measurement

Sargent provided the chief impetus for strength measurement during the early years of our profession. It was during this period that the dynamometer and the spirometer were developed and utilized for testing in Sargent's Intercollegiate Strength Test.[5] The Universal Dynamometer, developed in 1894 by J. H. Kellogg, was used to test the static or isometric strength of a large number of muscles. Then in 1915, E. G. Martin developed a resistance strength test to measure the strength of muscle groups with a flat-faced type spring balance.[5] In 1925 F. R. Rogers refined the inter-collegiate strength test, and proved its validity as a measure of general athletic ability. Rogers also created the physical fitness index (the PFI) including in it a new statistical technique for determining norms of physical achievement. He later showed how his PFI program could be adapted to the physical needs of the individual. McCloy developed a strength test that he felt was an improvement over the Rogers Strength Test in terms of administration, scoring and validity. McCloy's test left out the lung capacity test which he did not consider to be a strength measure.[26] It might also be noted at this time that chin-ups and dips, which were items in Sargent's, Rogers', and McCloy's strength tests, were not exclusively strength items, but were muscular endurance items as well. Thus, only the following three items of these early strength tests were pure measures of strength: (1) back strength, (2) leg strength, and (3) grip strength. In 1928, Edwin R. Elbel, while working on the Master's degree at Springfield College, found that strength could be increased by short static (isometric) contraction exercises. However, interest in isometric exercises seemed to remain dormant for the next two decades. In fact, it was not until 1953, when the startling results of Hettinger and Muller's experiments on isometric strength training were published, that a new era in strength training began. As mentioned previously, static strength testing was not new, as evidenced by the early use of the dynamometer and the comprehensive measurement of strength by H. Harrison Clarke with the tensiometer. This instrument was originally designed to measure aircraft cable tension, but was adapted [1] Clarke to measure strength of various muscle groups.

Muscular Endurance Measurement

The history of muscular endurance measurement closely parallels that of muscular strength testing. Hitchcock and Sargent compiled extensive data on muscular endurance of the arms and shoulders of college men in the latter half of the nineteenth century.[5] In 1884 Mosso, an Italian physiologist, invented the ergograph and helped establish the relationship between physical condition and muscular activity. Mosso also pointed out that the body's ability to do work depends upon adequate nutrition, and that fatigue of one set of muscles affects others as well.[8] In 1922 an adaptation of Mosso's ergograph made it possible to study successive muscular contractions on a smoke drum. H. Harrison Clarke and other researchers have conducted a number of studies on the Kelso-Hellebrandt ergograph using larger muscle groups than were used with the earlier ergograph of Mosso's. Test items such as chin-ups and dips that combine both strength and endurance have been utilized as either strength measures or muscular endurance measures or both on many physical fitness tests, strength tests, and motor ability tests. The measurement of strength and muscular endurance will be covered in depth in later chapters.

Cardiovascular Endurance

In 1905 Ward C. Crampton[12] developed a rating scale to obtain data on the general physical condition of a person by observing changes in the cardiac rate and arterial pressure on assuming the erect position from a lying down position. Five years later McCurdy[27] published a study out of which evolved a test of physical condition based on the change of heart rate from the reclining to the erect position. Several investigators reported tests of physical efficiency in 1914.[8] Meylan and Foster employed somewhat similar measures to determine the heart's reaction to exercise, and J. H. Barach devised a test utilizing several physiological measures to determine an index of efficiency. Two years later Barringer constructed a test which was designed to demonstrate a delayed rise in blood pressure of the physically unfit following exercise. In 1920 Schneider[35] reported findings concerning a rather comprehensive test which had been used to assess fatigue and physical condition. The test had been employed to determine the physical state of aviators in World War I by the Air Force.[5] In 1925 Campbell published a test involving breath holding and recovery after exercise. This preliminary study later developed into the *Campbell Pulse Ratio Test* and the *Tuttle Pulse Ratio Test*. The author of the latter test, W. W. Tuttle at the State University of Iowa, conducted a considerable amount of cardiovascular research during the 1930's.[5] In 1943 the Harvard Step Test[7] was developed by Lucien Brouha and Associates to determine the general capacity of the body to adapt and recover from work. The work consisted of stepping up and down on a bench at a prescribed cadence. Pulse rate was taken at set intervals after exercise. This test has been extensively used in testing and research programs. In addition to McCurdy, Brouha, and Tuttle, other outstanding contributors to knowledge in cardiovascular measurement have been Cureton, Clarke, Henry, Larson, Karpovich, and McCloy to name but a few. In recent years cardiovascular research and measurement have become somewhat more sophisticated with the increased use of machines in determining the behavior of the circulatory and respiratory systems under various test conditions. Cardiovascular endurance measurement is discussed in Chapter XVI.

Physical Fitness Measurement

Physical fitness has always been one of the foremost goals of physical education. The measurement of physical fitness and methods of developing fitness have been topics of national concern through the years. The medical doctors who constituted the early leadership in the profession were initially attracted to physical education because of their interest in physical fitness. It was mutual interest in physical fitness and other physical measurements that prompted the meetings leading to the formation of our national organization, now known as the American Association for Health, Physical Education and Recreation (AAHPER). A great deal of credit must be given to the Turner societies in the 1800's for promoting an interest in the development and maintenance of physical fitness through gymnastic exercise programs. The Turners were mainly German immigrants who had fled to the United States in the 1840's because of political pressures in Europe. Turnvereins were established throughout much of the east and the midwest. These societies took advantage of every opportunity to sell their programs of gymnastics and physical fitness to the schools. As a result of their efforts gymnastics and developmental exercises made up the greater part of the physical education programs around the nation until the early 1900's. Increasing popularity of team games and lighter recreational type activities then began to crowd out the more formal physical development programs. The draft statistics in World War I brought national attention to be focused on a need for increased physical fitness of the American youth. Consequently, the states passed laws making physical education mandatory in the schools. The natural play movement spearheaded by Wood and Hetherington and others brought about a decrease in emphasis on physical fitness in the 1920's and 1930's. Again, a world war generated national concern over the need for physical fitness. During World War II the Army, the Navy, and Air Force established their own physical fitness test batteries, and considerable research was done in this area. After the war the nation relaxed again only to be jarred awake by the startling results of the Kraus-Weber test in which American children were shown to be decidedly inferior to European children in this test of minimum muscular fitness. As a result, in 1956 President Eisenhower established the President's Council on Youth Fitness which was to focus national attention on the need for physical fitness programs in the schools. In 1958 the AAHPER Youth Fitness Test was developed for boys and girls (in grades 5-12) with national norms. In 1965 the AAHPER Youth Fitness Test was revised again under the direction of Paul A. Hunsicker, and new national norms were established. This test, which can be administered indoors or outdoors with practically no equipment, represents a major accomplishment by the AAHPER. There are many tests by physical fitness that have been constructed and standardized by various individuals in different sections of the country. The reader is referred to Chapter XVII for further discussion of physical fitness measurement.

Sports Skill Measurement

One of the earliest reported sports skills tests were the Athletic Badge Tests devised in 1913 by the Playground and Recreation Association of America. The test items pertained to the sports of volleyball, tennis, baseball, and basketball. In 1918 Hetherington developed tests for the California decathlon which made use of a graduated score plan.[5] In 1924 Brace reported a six item skill test in basketball,[5] and a year later Beall[2] completed an experimental study in tennis to determine a battery of tests for that sport. Increasing interest in testing of sports skills was evident in the 1930's, and throughout the following thirty years many fine tests were proposed, developed, and utilized by physical educators. However, for many years there had been an often expressed need for nationally standardized tests. This lack of national standards had been frequently cited as one of physical education's biggest failings. In response to this need AAHPER initiated a sports skills test project in 1959 to determine standards for at least 15 sports activities. This project began under the direction of the Research Council of AAHPER, with David K. Brace serving as test consultant and Frank D. Sills as Chairman. The tests and norms have made it possible to more effectively evaluate skill performance, bring about greater motivation, and improve teaching. References and further contributions for this area of measurement may be found in Chapter XVIII.

Posture Measurement

The earliest contributions made in this area of measurement were in the form of records and anthropometric charts by Hitchcock, Sargent, J. W. Seaver, Luther H. Gulick, Thomas D. Wood, Delphine Hanna, and others. During the 1930's and 1940's a great deal of interest was shown in developing methods of measuring and evaluating posture. Studies were presented which reported the use of such instruments as the Cureton-Gunby conformateur, Korbs' comparograph, the posturemeter, the scoliometer, x-rays, pedograph, photography, and rating scales. Difficulty in devising practical, objective instruments for assessing posture, plus the lack of definite criteria as to what good posture should entail for different individuals, resulted in a drop in the number of reported studies on the topic in the 1950's. Nevertheless, articles on posture have continued to appear in the professional literature, which indicates that there has not been a lessening of concern as to the importance of good posture.

Social Qualities Measurement

McCloy focused attention on the measurement of social qualities by physical educators in an article which appeared during the first year of publication of the Research Quarterly.[24] In 1936 O'Neel[30] and Blanchard[3] published separate behavior rating scales for use in physical education. Despite the reluctance of this area to yield to objective measurement, there has been an imposing number of studies published and new measuring instruments reported in the last thirty years. Physical educators have long recognized that continuous attempts should be made to measure social qualities if development in this area is to be one of physical education's objectives. The work of J. L. Moreno[29] and Helen Jennings[20] in sociometric measurement has been of great value to physical educators as well as to counselors and other teachers. The late Charles C. Cowell[11] made splendid contributions in this area in physical education. Considerable progress has been made in attitude assessment, and such names as Carlos Wear, Barbara Drinkwater, and others have been prominent in this area.

Knowledge Measurement

Among the earliest published sports knowledge test was a basketball knowledge test published by J. G. Bliss[4] in 1929. Since that date numerous sports knowledge tests have been constructed and published in the professional literature. Unlike other subject areas standardized tests have not been available on a commercial basis, and, consequently, physical educators have had to prepare thier own or locate tests from the literature to duplicate. Outstanding contributors to the literature in the area of sports knowledge tests have been Esther French,[15] Catherine Snell, Katherine Ley,[22] Gail Hennis,[18] Rosemary Fisher,[14] and Jack Hewitt.[19] References and further contributions for this area of measurement may be found in Chapter XXI.

Concluding Statement

The quantity and quality of research in physical education has continued to improve, which is to be expected. This is certainly not meant to imply any criticism of the early researchers. On the contrary, physical education has been extremely fortunate to have had such excellent and inspiring leadership in the areas of research and tests and measurements. As in any profession, students must profit from the experiences of their professors and strive to improve upon the work of those who have gone before.

It has been observed that scientific endeavors in all fields have had rather crude beginnings. To confirm this phenomenon we need only recall the primitive practices in the history of medicine, the simple, awkward designs of the early automobiles, and the hilarious first attempts of men to fly. Yet, when one considers the tremendous advances that have been made in these fields in the last quarter of a century, the prognosis for progress in evaluation in physical education should indeed be encouraging. Physical education is a relatively new field. This is attested to by the fact that many of the persons named in this chapter as being early leaders in the area of tests and measurements are still active today.

We must guard against complacency and discouragement. The history of tests and measurements in physical education reveals that in some areas no further research efforts have been reported for twenty or thirty years. It is imperative that we continue to seek new and better ways of measuring those traits which we have already had some success in measuring, and, at the same time, make renewed and vigorous efforts to assess those qualities which heretofore have baffled attempts at measurement.

With new and more precise measuring devices, improved methods of analyzing data, increased emphasis on research in graduate study, combined with the fact that more persons are seeking advanced degrees, the future indeed looks bright.

BIBLIOGRAPHY

1. Baldwin, Bird T., *Physical Growth and School Progress,* Washington, D.C.: Bureau of Education Bulletin No. 10, 1914, p. 143.

2. Beall, Elizabeth, "Essential Qualities in Certain Aspects of Physical Education with Ways of Measuring and Developing Same," (Unpublished Master's thesis, University of California, 1925).

3. Blanchard, B. E., "A Behavior Frequency Rating Scale for the Measurement of Character and Personality in Physical Education Classroom Situations," *Research Quarterly,* Vol. 6, May 1936, pp. 56-66.

4. Bliss, J. G., *Basketball,* Philadelphia: Lea & Febiger, 1929.

5. Bovard, John F., and others, *Tests and Measurements in Physical Education,* Philadelphia: W. B. Saunders Company, 1950.

6. Bovard, J. F., and F. W. Cozens, *The "Leap Meter," An Investigation into the Possibilities of the Sargent Test as a Measure of General Athletic Ability,* Eugene: University of Oregon Press, 1928.

7. Brouha, Lucien, "The Step Test: A Simple Method of Measuring Physical Fitness for Muscular Work in Young Man," *Research Quarterly,* 14:31-35, March, 1943.

8. Burton-Opitz, R., "Tests of Physical Efficiency," *American Physical Education Review,* 27:153-159, April, 1922.

9. Capen, Edward K., "The Effect of Systematic Weight Training on Power, Strength, and Endurance," *Research Quarterly,* 21:83-93, May, 1950.

10. Chui, Edward, "The Effect of Systematic Weight Training on Athletic Power," *Research Quarterly,* 21:188-94, October, 1950.

11. Cowell, Charles C., "Validating an Index of Social Adjustment for High School Use," *Research Quarterly,* Vol. 29, March, 1958, pp. 7-18.

12. Crampton, Ward C., "A Test of Condition," *Medical News,* LXXXVIII: 529, September, 1905.

13. Cureton, Thomas K., *Physical Fitness Appraisal and Guidance,* St. Louis: The C. V. Mosby Company, Inc., 1947.

14. Fisher, Rosemary B., "Tests in Selected Physical Education Service Courses in a College," (Microcarded Dissertation, State University of Iowa, 1950), p. 72.

15. French, Esther, "The Construction of Knowledge Tests in Selected Professional Courses in Physical Education," *Research Quarterly,* 14:406-424, 1943.

16. Gates, Donald D., and R. P. Sheffield, "Tests of Change of Direction as Measurements of Different Kinds of Motor Ability in Boys of the Seventh, Eighth, and Ninth Grades," *Research Quarterly,* 11:136-147, October, 1940.

17. Glencross, Dennis J., "The Nature of the Vertical Jump Test and the Standing Broad Jump." *Research Quarterly,* 37:353-359, October, 1966.

18. Hennis, Gail M., "Construction of Knowledge Tests in Selected Physical Education Activities for College Women," *Research Quarterly,* 27:301-309, October, 1956.

19. Hewitt, Jack E., "Hewitt's Comprehensive Tennis Knowledge Test," *Research Quarterly,* 35:147-155, May, 1964.

20. Jennings, Helen, *Sociometry in Group Relations,* American Council on Education, 1948, 1959.

21. Kretschmer, E., *Physique and Character,* New York: Harcourt Brace and Company, Inc., 1925.

22. Ley, Katherine L., "Constructing Objective Test Items to Measure High School Levels of Achievement in Selected Physical Education Activities," (Microcarded Dissertation, University of Iowa, 1960), p. 25.

23. McCloy, Charles H., "Athletic Handicapping by Age, Height, and Weight," *American Physical Education Review,* 32:635-42, November, 1927.

24. _____, "Character Building through Physical Education," *Research Quarterly,* 1:41, October, 1930.

25. _____, "Recent Studies in the Sargent Jump," *Research Quarterly,* Vol. 3, May, 1932, p. 235.

26. McCloy, Charles H., and Norma D. Young, *Tests and Measurements in Health and Physical Education,* New York: Appleton-Century Crofts, Inc., 1954.

27. McCurdy, J. H., "Adolescent Changes in Heart Rate and Blood Pressure," *American Physical Education Review,* 15:421, June, 1910.

28. Meredith, Howard V., *Physical Growth Records for Boys and Physical Growth Records for Girls,* Washington, D.C.: National Education Association.

29. Moreno, J. L., "Who Shall Survive? A New Problem to the Problem of Human Relationships," Washington: Nervous and Mental Disease Publishing Company, 1934.

30. O'Neel, E. W., "A Behavior Frequency Rating Scale for the Measurement of Character and Personality in High School Physical Education Classes for Boys," *Research Quarterly,* Vol. 7, May, 1936, p. 67.

31. Pryor, Helen B., *Width-Weight Tables,* Stanford University: Stanford University Press, 1940.

32. Reilly, Frederick J., *New Rational Athletics for Boys and Girls,* Boston: D. C. Heath & Company, p. 191.

33. Sargent, D. A., "The Physical Test of a Man,' *American Physical Education Review,* 26:188-94, April, 1921.

34. _____, "Twenty Years Progress in Efficiency Tests," *American Physical Education Review,* 18:452, October, 1913.

35. Schneider, E. C., "A Cardiovascular Rating as a Measure of Physical Fatigue and Efficiency," *Jr. American Medical Association,* LXXIV:1507, May, 1920.

36. Seaver, Jay W., *Anthropometry and Physical Examination.* Meriden, Conn.: Curtis-Way Company, 1909, pp. 14-15.

37. Sheldon, W. H., and others, *The Varieties of Human Physique,* New York: Harper and Brothers, 1940.

38. Sierakowski, Frances, "A Study of Change of Direction Tests for High School Girls," (Master's thesis, State University of Iowa, 1940).

39. Sills, Frank A., "A Factor Analysis of Somatotypes and Their Relationship to Achievement in Motor Skills," *Research Quarterly,* 21:424-37, December, 1950.

40. Wetzel, Norman C., "Physical Fitness in Terms of Physique, Development, and Basal Metabolism," *Journal of American Medical Association,* 116:1187-95, March, 1941.

41. Young, Kathryn E., "An Analytic Study of the Tests of Change of Direction," (Master's Thesis, State University of Iowa, 1937).

Chapter III

BASIC STATISTICAL TECHNIQUES

Introduction

One of the essential steps in evaluation is to be able to analyze and present the products derived from tests and measurements. The prospective teacher is continually admonished to refrain from testing merely for the sake of testing. The physical educator can spend hours carefully and skillfully measuring, but without the ability to organize and analyze the data, the information cannot be interpreted and effectively used to evaluate the program. This then brings us to the subject of statistical analysis.

Mention of the word *statistics* usually brings about a shudder of fear or revulsion on the part of the prospective teacher. There may be a number of reasons for this attitude — a poor background in mathematics, being intimidated by the terminology and formulae, etc. — but whatever the reason, it is an unfortunate situation. When faced with that part of teacher preparation that includes statistics, the reluctant student grits his teeth and endures the daily assignments and struggles through the quizzes. He firmly resolves that he will never, by choice, encounter the subject again; nor will he use the wretched computations in his teaching. Thus, he enters the field minus a very valuable tool of his trade.

With the recalcitrant student in mind, we will attempt to present this portion of the evaluation process as simply and as practicable as possible. We will use what has often been called the *cookbook* approach wherein the teacher need not understand the derivation of the formulae, which may be likened to the ingredients. Instead, he merely follows the steps to achieve the end product. The authors would be among the first to agree that the researcher and specialist in tests and measurements should have a rather extensive background in statistics. However, it goes without saying that the teacher in the field does not possess this background, and thus the most important thing is that he should be able to use, with confidence, some basic statistical tools that are required for effective evaluation.

The Frequency Distribution

After the data have been collected, the scores are normally placed in a column either in random order or arranged from high to low. If the number of scores is quite small, probably the latter is the most logical method of organization. But when the number of scores is large, with many students having identical scores, then the task of arranging them in order becomes much more time-consuming. In this situation it usually is more feasible to construct a frequency distribution with step intervals.

A step interval is merely a small range of scores, such as scores from 96 to 100. In this case the size of the step interval is 5. In other words all students who had scores of 96, 97, 98, 99, or 100 are placed in this interval. The next step interval below this would be from 91 to 95, and the next from 86 to 90, and so on. It can be readily seen that once the scores are placed in a step interval, they lose their individual identities. Consequently, when scores are put in step intervals, they are called *grouped data.*

There are several points that should be brought out regarding the use of a frequency distribution with grouped data.

1. Although there is no hard and fast rule, the <u>number</u> of step intervals ordinarily should be between 10 and 20. This is primarily determined by the number of students and the <u>range</u> of the scores, which is the difference between the highest and lowest score (plus one). In most instances, one could plan on having somewhere between 12 and 16 step intervals.

2. The <u>size</u> of the step interval is mainly governed by the size of the scores. For instance, if the scores are back strength measures using a dynamometer, the step intervals would most likely be large. Thus, typical step intervals might be 300-314, 315-329 and so on upward, with each interval containing 15 scores. On the other hand if the scores were pull ups, for example, the size of the step interval would be quite small, perhaps 0-1, 2-3, 4-5, and so forth.

    The size of the step interval can be automatically determined when one arbitrarily affixes the number of step intervals. For example, if the spread of scores is from 11 to 85, the range is 75 (Highest-Lowest +1). If the teacher should elect to have 15 step intervals, then the size of each interval would be 5 ($75 \div 15 = 5$).

3. The size of each step interval in a frequency distribution must be the same. To illustrate, you could not have one step interval of 96-100, and the next one below it, 90-95, because one interval contains 5 scores (96, 97, 98, 99, 100), while the other interval has 6 (90, 91, 92, 93, 94, 95).

4. The top and bottom step intervals must contain the highest and lowest scores, respectively. It should be noted that in the step interval 96-100, the highest score need not be 100. It could be any of the numbers encompassed by the interval; the same would hold true for the bottom interval in that the lowest score of the interval does not have to be the smallest actual score. Establishing the step intervals is merely a matter of choice and convenience.

5. The actual limits of any step interval extend from .5 below through .4 above the values which are written. In the interval 96-100, the actual lower limit is 95.5 and the upper limit is 100.4. Thus, all scores included in the range of 95.5-100.4 are placed in this interval. A score of 100.5 would belong in the next interval above. The above rule holds true even if the interval contains only one number. For example, a score of 1 includes all values from .5 through 1.4.

6. Since all scores lose their individual identities when placed in a step interval, it is assumed then that all scores contained in the interval are evenly distributed throughout the interval. Continuing with this assumption, the most representative value for any step interval would be its mid-point. To calculate the mid-point one must remember the actual limits of the interval as described above. Consequently, the mid-point of the interval 96-100 is 98, which was computed by adding one-half the size of the step interval to the lower limit of that interval. In this case the size of the interval is 5 and the lower limit is 95.5. So one-half of 5 is 2.5 which, when added to 95.5, equals 98. Similarly, the mid-point of the interval 110-125 would be 109.5 + 1/2 of 16 (size of interval), or 109.5 + 8 = 117.5.

The points made about frequency distribution will be illustrated in the following example.

<u>Example</u> 3-1. The numbers below represent scores obtained by 60 college men in floor push-ups. They are listed in random order with no attempt made to arrange them in any definite order, such as from high to low. The high and the low score each are starred.

30	20	22	13	28	27
17	18	22	27	24	20
12	47	37	35	17	21
41	32	53*	5*	25	15
36	25	26	31	25	34
24	12	20	26	38	28
25	9	6	27	32	30
18	31	16	15	10	16
26	38	29	29	17	23
30	34	42	37	27	25

<u>Step 1</u>: The first step in organizing and analyzing these scores is to prepare a frequency distribution. To do so one must locate the highest score and the lowest score to determine the range. After examining the data carefully, it is seen that 53 is the highest number and that 5 is the lowest. The range is 53 - 5 = 48 + 1 = 49.

<u>Step 2</u>. The number of step intervals and the size of each is now to be decided. It may be recalled that the number of step intervals should normally be somewhere between 10 and 20. The size of each step interval is determined by the units of measurement and, of course, by the number of intervals decided upon. There are several ways to approach this step, and because of this it can be quite confusing to the novice. This should not be difficult because it is mainly a matter of choice and, perhaps, trial and error on the part of the teacher.

Keeping in mind that most of the time the number of intervals will most efficiently be 12 to 16, one can proceed by trying some of these numbers to see what effect they will have on establishing the size of the intervals. Dividing 12 into the range of 49 results in 4.08; 13 into 49 is 3.77; 14 into 49 is 3.5; 15 into 49 is 3.27, and 16 into 49 is 3.06. One can readily see that a step interval of 3 to 5 will result in 12 to 16 step intervals. The size of the step interval is almost always rounded off to a whole number for ease of handling.

<u>Step 3</u>. Now that the approximate size and number of step intervals has been determined, it is simply a matter of arranging the score units into the frequency distribution. Suppose that the teacher selects 4 as the size of the step interval. He may begin at the top or at the bottom of the scores just as long as the highest score is contained in the top interval and the lowest score is located in the bottom interval. Arbitrarily he chooses to begin at the bottom with an interval of 4-7, which thus includes scores of 4, 5, 6, and 7. The resulting frequency distribution containing 13 step intervals is presented as column A in Table 3-1.

To illustrate that the arrangement of the frequency distribution is mostly a matter of choice and convenience, the same data are shown in Table 3-1 with a step interval of 3 and a step interval of 5 in Distributions B and C, respectively. With 3 as the size of the step interval there are 17 step intervals, and with 5 as the size of the interval there are 10 step intervals. Consequently, although it would not be wrong to choose either 3 or 5 as the size of the step interval, the selection of a step interval of 4 appears to be the most appropriate.

TABLE 3 - 1

Frequency Distributions of the Same Data Utilizing Three Different Sizes of Step Intervals

Frequency Distribution A (Size of S.I.=4)			Frequency Distribution B (Size of S.I.=3)			Frequency Distribution C (Size of S.I.=5)		
Step Interval	Tally	f	Step Interval	Tally	f	Step Interval	Tally	f
52-55	I	1	51-53	I	1	50-54	I	1
48-51		0	48-50		0	45-49	I	1
44-47	I	1	45-47	I	1	40-44	II	2
40-43	II	2	42-44	I	1	35-39	͵Ш I	6
36-39	͵Ш	5	39-41	I	1	30-34	͵Ш IIII	9
32-35	͵Ш	5	36-38	͵Ш	5	25-29	͵Ш ͵Ш ͵Ш	15
28-31	͵Ш IIII	9	33-35	III	3	20-24	͵Ш ͵Ш	10
24-27	͵Ш ͵Ш IIII	14	30-32	͵Ш II	7	15-19	͵Ш IIII	9
20-23	͵Ш II	7	27-29	͵Ш II	7	10-14	IIII	4
16-19	͵Ш II	7	24-26	͵Ш ͵Ш	10	5- 9	III	3
12-15	͵Ш	5	21-23	͵Ш	5			N = 60
8-11	II	2	18-20	͵Ш	5			
4- 7	II	2	15-17	͵Ш II	7			
		N = 60	12-14	III	3			
			9-11	II	2			
			6- 8	I	1			
			3- 5	I	1			
					N = 60			

Step 4. After the frequency distribution is prepared, the teacher simply returns to the list of raw scores and proceeds to enter each score into the proper step interval. The first score on the list is 30, and it is thus tallied in the 28-31 step interval (assuming that Distribution A is to be used). The next score is 17, and it is placed in the 16-19 interval and so on throughout the whole list of scores. This merely requires care in that a score(s) is not omitted.

The tally marks are later transposed into totals for each interval, thereby forming the frequency (f) column. A check is made when the numbers in this column are added to make sure the total number (N) is 60.

Measures of Central Tendency

Thus far the raw scores have been organized to the extent that they have been arranged from high to low in step intervals. Yet for the most part the series of scores still do not yield much information. Granted, the teacher can see at a glance which are the high scores, the low scores, and where most of the students placed. But the main purpose of the frequency distribution is to present the scores to facilitate analysis.

One of the first questions any student asks upon seeing his own score is, "What was the average?" He asks this completely unaware that he is now dealing in statistics. He merely wants to know how he stands in relation to the rest of the group. Despite the fact that he has not had the privilege of taking a formal course in statistics, he knows from his past school experiences that there usually are a few high scores, a few low scores, and that most tend to cluster in the middle. The *average* tells him how most of the class did. This then is a measure of central tendency. It is a single score which best represents all the scores. The three basic measures of central tendency are the mean, the median, and the mode.

The Mean.   The mean is simply the arithmetic average. It can be computed by adding all the scores and then dividing by the number of scores involved. It is by far the most commonly used measure of central tendency, and, for the most part, the most reliable. The main weakness of the mean is that, with a small sample, extreme scores have a misleading effect. For example, in the following group of scores the mean is 10, and it is representative of the group.

$$
\begin{array}{c}
X \\
12 \\
11 \\
10 \\
9 \\
\underline{8} \\
\Sigma X^* = 50
\end{array}
\qquad
\text{Mean} = \frac{\Sigma X}{N} = \frac{50}{5} = 10
$$

However, if we add an extreme score such as 30 to the above group of scores, the mean changes considerably.

$$
\begin{array}{c}
X \\
30 \\
12 \\
11 \\
10 \\
9 \\
\underline{8} \\
\Sigma X - 80
\end{array}
\qquad
\text{Mean} = \frac{\Sigma X}{N} = \frac{80}{6} = 13.3
$$

*The symbol Σ, which is the Greek letter sigma, means summation. The X stands for scores, thus the ΣX means the sum of scores.

The mean of 13.3 is not representative of the group since it is higher than every score but one. Although this example may in itself be a bit extreme, it is hoped that it illustrates the point that one should always consider the number of cases and <u>look</u> at the data rather than blindly trusting statistics.

The method of computing the mean employed above will not suffice with grouped data. A technique which is appropriate, called the *short method,* will be described later in the chapter.

The Median. The median is that point at which 50 percent of the scores lie above and below it. In other words it is the mid-point, or 50th percentile. Using the scores that were shown in the above discussion of the mean, the principal advantage of the median can be demonstrated. In the first illustration the median score is 10, which is the same as the mean.

12
11
(10)
9
8

It is easily obtained in this case by locating the middle score. In some instances it is a point rather than an actual score, as is illustrated by the second example.

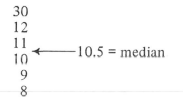

30
12
11
10 ←———— 10.5 = median
9
8

The main advantage of the median should now be evident: the addition of extreme scores has relatively little effect.

When the scores are arranged from high to low, the median is easily obtained and can be utilized as a quick and ready average. When the data are grouped, the task of locating the median is not so easy and is mostly used in that case when percentiles are wanted. This procedure will be shown later.

The Mode. This measure of central tendency is defined as the score which occurs the most frequently. It is a very rough measure and is used for description more than for any exact analysis. For example, the word mode is sometimes used in describing fashions; it simply indicates what most people are wearing. When scores are ungrouped, the teacher needs merely to locate the score (or scores, for there may be more than one mode) that appears the most number of times. Because there may be more than one mode, it is the least reliable of the three measures of central tendency that are generally used. When the data follows a typical normal curve, the mean, the median, and the mode will fall in the same place.

Computation of the Mean, the Median, and the Mode from Grouped Data

It has been pointed out before that when scores are placed in step intervals in a frequency distribution, they lose their individual identities. This, then, requires some adjustments when one desires to locate specific points such as the mean, the median, the mode, percentiles, etc.

Calculation of the Mean from Grouped Scores

The method commonly used to calculate the mean with grouped data is called the *short method*. Although it probably will not seem like a short method at all to someone doing this procedure for the first time, it is actually quite simple. It merely involves an estimate as to where the mean lies, and then a correction is applied to locate the actual mean.

The data from Distribution A, Table 3 - 1, involving the number of push-ups scored by 60 college men, is reproduced in Table 3 - 2 to illustrate the short method of computing the mean.

Step 1: The first step is to estimate where the mean lies. There is no set rule in making the estimate; ordinarily one selects a step interval near the center of the distribution and, usually, which contains the largest number of scores. However, a correction factor is to be applied; therefore, there is no penalty for making a *poor* estimate.

In this sample problem the estimate or assumed mean was chosen to lie in the 24 - 27 interval. The assumed mean is taken to be the mid-point of that interval. It should be recalled that the location of the mid-point of an interval is figured by adding one-half the size of the step interval to the lower limit of the interval. In this case the mid-point is

$$23.5 + \frac{1}{2} \times 4 = 25.5$$

and this is entered as the assumed mean (AM).

Step 2: After the interval containing the assumed mean has been indicated, the correction factor must be determined. To do this the step intervals above and below the assumed mean interval are numbered as to their deviation from the assumed mean. To illustrate, the step interval 28 - 31 is 1 deviation above the assumed mean interval; step interval 32 - 35 is 2 deviations above; step interval 20 - 23 is -1 deviation below, and so on until column d is completed.

Step 3: Since the deviation column is in terms of step intervals, the number of scores in each interval must be taken into account. Consequently, the values in column f are multiplied by their respective deviations above and below the assumed mean. Naturally, the step intervals below the assumed mean have negative value, thus the entries in the fd column below the assumed mean must have negative signs.

Step 4: The next step is simply to obtain the algebraic sum of the fd column. To do this the positive numbers are added, then the negative values are added and the difference is determined. In this sample problem the positive fd values totaled 54 and the negative fd values totaled -55, resulting in the sum of the fd column (Σfd) to be -1. Because the positive and negative values were nearly identical, it indicates that our estimate of where the actual mean lies was quite accurate. Since the negative values exceeded the positive, it shows that the actual mean lies slightly beneath the assumed mean, which was 25.5 (the mid-point of the interval 24 - 27). If the positive fd values should exceed the negative values, it would indicate that the estimate was too low.

Step 5: The next step in determining the correction factor to be applied to the assumed mean is to take into account the number (N) of scores and the size of each step interval (i). Dividing 60(N) into the Σfd (-1), the result is -.02 (rounded off to two places). This is then multiplied by the size of the step interval to complete the calculation of the correction. Since it is negative, it is subtracted from the assumed mean, and the actual mean is found to be 25.42.

TABLE 3 - 2

Calculation of the Mean from Grouped Scores

Scores in Step Intervals	f	d	fd	
52 - 55	1	7	7	
48 - 51	0	6	0	
44 - 47	1	5	5	
40 - 43	2	4	8	
36 - 39	5	3	15	
32 - 35	5	2	10	
28 - 31	9	1	9	
				(54)
24 - 27	13	0	0	
20 - 23	8	-1	-8	
16 - 19	7	-2	-14	
12 - 15	5	-3	-15	
8 - 11	2	-4	-8	
4 - 7	2	-5	-10	
				(-55)
	N = 60		$\Sigma fd = -1$	

$$M = AM + \left(\frac{\Sigma fd}{N} \times i \right) = 25.5 + \left(\frac{-1}{60} \times 4 \right) = 25.5 + (-.02 \times 4) =$$

$$25.5 - .08 = 25.42$$

M = Mean
AM = Assumed Mean
Σfd = Sum of frequency $\times$ deviation columns
N = Number of scores
i = Size of step interval
c = Correction factor, or $\frac{\Sigma fd}{N}$

Calculation of the Median from Grouped Scores

The median can be found in grouped data by the use of a cumulative frequency column and interpolation within the step interval. In this case the number of scores is 60, and thus the median, or mid-point, is the 30th score.

To count into the distribution to locate the 30th score, we begin at the bottom of the frequency distribution and progressively add the total number of scores that are included up through each step interval. This is shown in Table 3-3.

The bottom interval (4 - 7) has 2 scores, so 2 is entered in the cumulative frequency column; the next interval has also 2 scores in it, making a total of 4 scores up through that interval (8 - 11). Thus 4 is the entry in the *Cum f* column opposite that interval. The next entry is 4 + 5 = 9; the next 9 + 7 = 16, etc. up to the interval containing the 30th score. The completion of the cumulative frequency column was not necessary for the calculation of the median. It will be used later in determining percentiles.

Counting into the distribution it can be seen in Table 3 - 3 that there are 24 scores below the interval 24 - 27. There are 37 scores below the 28 - 31 interval; therefore, the 30th score lies somewhere in the 24 - 27 interval. However, there are 13 scores in that interval and only 6 are needed for the 30th score (24 below interval, 30 - 24 = 6). Since the step interval itself encompasses 4 possible raw scores, this too must be included in the interpolation. Therefore, 6/13 of the size of the interval, 4, is located in that interval by adding it to the exact lower limit of the interval, which is 23.5. The resulting calculations reveal the median to be 25.34. This value is quite close to the value obtained for the mean, which indicates that the sample fairly well approximates the normal curve.

Calculation of the Mode from Grouped Scores

When the mode is taken from a frequency distribution, it is merely as an approximation of the true mode. This approximation would be the same as the true mode only if the N were very large and the scores followed the exact pattern of the normal curve. The formula for determining the mode from grouped data is

$$\text{Mode} = 3 \text{ Median} - 2 \text{ Mean}$$

If we apply this formula to the sample data, the mode is 25.18. Ordinarily, a rough estimate of the mode is obtained by using the mid-point of the step interval containing the greatest number of scores.

In summary, the mean, the median, and the mode may be obtained using ungrouped scores or when the data are in frequency distributions. In the sample problem that was used to illustrate the methods of calculation, all three of the measures of central tendency were found to be at 25 push-ups.

Percentiles

The physical educator frequently has occasion to use percentiles. Many standardized tests present their norms in this manner, and, generally speaking, the student is fairly well oriented in the interpretation of percentiles.

A percentile score informs the student as to what proportion of the group scored below him. For example, a percentile rank of 80 means that 80 percent of the people taking that particular test had scores lower than that and 20 percent had higher scores. When percentiles are used, scores from different tests can be compared to show how a student scored in relation to the others on each test.

The method of calculating the median from a frequency distribution can be used to determine percentiles. In Table 3 - 3 the calculations for certain percentile points are

TABLE 3 - 3

Calculation of the Median and Percentiles from Grouped Scores

Score	f	Cum f			
52-55	1	60	Median $= \dfrac{N}{2} = \dfrac{60}{2} = 30$		
48-51	0	59			
44-47	1	59	$23.5 + \dfrac{6}{13} \times 4 = 25.34$		Rounded Off
40-43	2	58	P_{10}	10% of 60 = 6	$11.5 + \dfrac{2}{5} \times 4 = 13.10\ (13)$
36-39	5	56	P_{20}	20% of 60 = 12	$15.5 + \dfrac{3}{7} \times 4 = 17.22\ (17)$
32-35	5	51	$P_{25\ (Q_1)}$	25% of 60 = 15	$15.5 + \dfrac{6}{7} \times 4 = 18.94\ (19)$
28-31	9	46	P_{30}	30% of 60 = 18	$19.5 + \dfrac{2}{8} \times 4 = 20.50\ (20)$
24-27	13	37	P_{40}	40% of 60 = 24	$23.5 + \dfrac{0}{13} \times 4 = 23.50\ (23)$
20-23	8	24	$P_{50\ (Mdn)}$	50% of 60 = 30	$23.5 + \dfrac{6}{13} \times 4 = 25.34\ (25)$
16-19	7	16	P_{60}	60% of 60 = 36	$23.5 + \dfrac{12}{13} \times 4 = 27.18\ (27)$
12-15	5	9	P_{70}	70% of 60 = 42	$27.5 + \dfrac{5}{9} \times 4 = 29.74\ (30)$
8-11	2	4	$P_{75\ (Q_3)}$	75% of 60 = 45	$27.5 + \dfrac{8}{9} \times 4 = 31.06\ (31)$
4-7	2	2	P_{80}	80% of 60 = 48	$31.5 + \dfrac{2}{5} \times 4 = 33.10\ (33)$
			P_{90}	90% of 60 = 54	$35.5 + \dfrac{3}{5} \times 4 = 37.90\ (38)$

shown. One merely counts up the cumulative frequency column to find the interval which contains the desired score. Then the proportion of the scores that is needed is computed, and that value is added to the lower limit of the interval. Needless to say, any percentile point, such as P_{23}, P_{67}, P_{41}, etc. could be found in the same way. P_{25} is called the first quartile (Q_1) and P_{75} is the third quartile (Q_3). Quartiles are very often used as cut-off points for screening purposes.

A principal weakness of percentiles is that they assume equal distance between score units. However, in the normal curve the scores are clustered around the middle, and, consequently, a small change in scores results in a rather large change in percentile points. Likewise, a relatively large change in score is needed to produce a change in percentile rank at the ends of the scale. This weakness is largely overcome by the use of T-scores and other standard scores mentioned in the following section.

T-Scores

In addition to percentiles the adept physical education teacher has other tools available to him by which he can make different test scores comparable. Many of the measurements taken by physical educators are in different units. There may be scores recorded in seconds as in a 50 yard dash, or in feet as in the softball throw, or in repetitions, as in sit-ups. The physical educator measures strength in pounds; he records the number of times a student volleys a tennis ball off a wall; he scores the vertical jump in inches; he charts the zone in which a golf ball lands; he uses written test scores, ratings, game scores, and various and sundry other units of measurement.

The combining of scores from separate tests has often posed a difficult problem for teachers who lack the knowledge, or the desire, or both to transform raw scores into percentiles, or some form of standard score. Of the latter there are a number of scales including z-scores, T-scores, stanines, the Hull scale, and others. The most common one is the T-scale.

The T-scale converts raw scores to normalized standard scores with a mean of 50 and a standard deviation of 10. Before an illustration of the steps involved in preparing a T-scale is given, it is necessary to first briefly discuss the concept of the normal curve and standard deviation.

The Normal Curve. The normal curve, which has been alluded to several times in this chapter, is a theoretical distribution based on probability. It is bell-shaped and perfectly balanced (Figure 3 - 1) because it is based on an infinite number of cases.

Many human qualities are distributed in this manner because they follow the laws of chance. In other words heredity, environment, social conditions, and other factors produce traits in a frequency of occurrence that follows the laws of probability, or chance. Our concept of what is *normal* or *average* is based on this phenomenon. For example, in a given population of 10 year old boys of a particular race and location, you will find some very short, some very tall, and most about the same size. The same is true for strength, speed, neuromuscular skills, mental ability, and other traits.

Standard Deviation. The standard deviation is one of several measures of variability. Standard deviation means the spread or scatter of scores around the mean. The range is also a measure of variability, although it is a rather rough measure.

Measures of variability augment measures of central tendency in providing information about a group of scores. It was stated earlier that one of the first questions a student asks concerning a test is to find out the average. A second question is, "What is the highest (or lowest) score?" The student has learned in his school experience that the range tells him how the scores varied and, consequently, more about his performance in relation to the class.

The standard deviation is a much more precise measure of variability than the range, and it is frequently employed in research studies. It may be thought of as a unit of distance along the baseline of the normal curve. In a normal distribution one standard deviation above and below the mean encompasses the middle 68.26% of the scores (Figure 3 - 1). Plus and minus two standard deviations include approximately 95% of the scores; and plus and minus three standard deviations account for over 99% of the distribution.

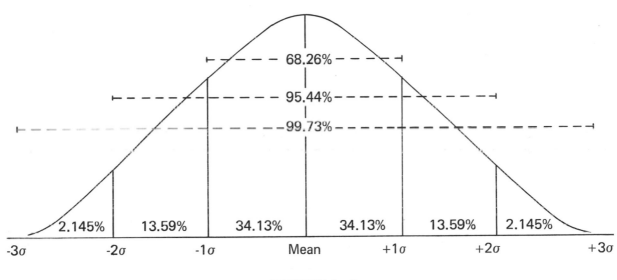

FIGURE 3 - 1

The Normal Probability Curve

The standard deviation is a useful tool for tests and measurements people. Unfortunately, it is rarely used because at first glance it appears to be a complicated statistical procedure. If the standard deviation is large, it means that the scores are widely scattered; if the standard deviation is small, it indicates that the scores are grouped closely around the mean.

Calculation of the standard deviation is necessary in transforming raw scores to T-scores in the method shown in Table 3 - 4. The first three columns are familiar since they were needed in obtaining the mean.

One more column is added, called the fd^2 column. The values are easily computed simply by multiplying the numbers in the d column by the values in the fd column. When this is accomplished, it makes all the values in the column positive.

Next, the column is totaled and substituted into the formula. It should be noted that the $\frac{\Sigma fd}{N}$ value is the correction factor that was utilized in calculating the mean. The reason it is used here is the same as when the mean was computed: an assumed mean was employed, thereby making it necessary to correct for the estimate.

The standard deviation of the push-up scores in this sample problem was found to be 9.56. Presuming that this group approximated the normal probability curve, this would

TABLE 3 - 4

Calculation of Standard Deviation from Grouped Scores

Scores	f	d	fd	fd^2
52-55	1	7	7	49
48-51	0	6	0	0
44-47	1	5	5	25
40-43	2	4	8	32
36-39	5	3	15	45
32-35	5	2	10	20
28-31	9	1	9 (54)	9
24-27	13	0	0	0
20-23	8	-1	-8	8
16-19	7	-2	-14	28
12-15	5	-3	-15	45
8-11	2	-4	-8	32
4- 7	2	-5	-10 (-55)	50
	N = $\overline{60}$		Σfd = $\overline{-1}$	Σfd^2 = $\overline{343}$

$$(\Sigma\text{fd} = -1)$$

$$SD = i\ \sqrt{\frac{\Sigma\text{fd}^2}{N} - \left(\frac{\Sigma\text{fd}}{N}\right)^2} = 4 \times \sqrt{\frac{343}{60} - \left(\frac{-1}{60}\right)^2} =$$

$$4 \times \sqrt{5.72 - (.02)^2} = 4 \times \sqrt{5.72 - .0004} =$$

$$4 \times \sqrt{5.72} = 4 \times 2.39$$

$$9.56$$

mean that 68.26% (roughly two-thirds) of the subjects scored 25.42 (the mean), plus or minus 9.56 push-ups. In other words, two-thirds of the class performed between 16 and 35 push-ups.

The "Long" (But Simpler) Method of Calculating The Mean and Standard Deviation

Despite the advantages of working with grouped data, the various steps involved often invite confusion and may actually defeat the intended purposes of speed and convenience. As was pointed out in the beginning of the chapter, the student frequently leaves the tests and measurements (or introductory statistics) class with a vast sense of relief and with what could be described as considerable trepidation insofar as functional knowledge is concerned. He has tried so hard to memorize the steps in constructing the frequency distribution, and to insert numbers into the various formulae in order to do his assignments and pass the tests, that he has failed to grasp the significance of the procedures. He has, in many respects, created a mountain out of a molehill.

Thus, when he is engaged in teaching and would like to establish norms or combine scores of unlike units of measurement into composite scores, etc. he is faced with a dilemma. He is very reluctant to consult his old class notes (if he has even kept them) because by now he has the conviction firmly implanted in his mind that the procedures involved in constructing step intervals, mid-points of the intervals, guessing at a mean and then correcting for it, and so on are much too complicated and time-consuming. Yet, in actual practice, the factor of time is not such a formidable obstacle if the steps involved are simple, and especially if the teacher has access to an office adding machine. Hence, the so-called long (but simple) method is offered for the teacher who may identify with the person described above.

For ease of presentation the number of scores in the example will be limited. In Table 3 - 5 the scores are ungrouped in that they have not been arranged in any specific order or organized into groups of scores.

The steps are as follows:

Step 1: Add the scores and divide by the number of students. This, of course, is the mean. $\dfrac{\Sigma X}{N}$

Step 2: Each score is then squared. When the numbers are large, it is usually easier to consult a table of squares. This column is totaled and recorded as the ΣX^2.

Step 3: The necessary data can now be inserted into the formula

$$SD = \sqrt{\frac{\Sigma X^2}{N} - M^2}$$

and the standard deviation is then computed.

In effect, with this method we are assuming the mean to be zero and then we apply a correction factor. A more direct way of obtaining the standard deviation would be to subtract each score from the mean, square each deviation, obtain the sum, and the formula would simply be as follows:

$$SD = \sqrt{\frac{\Sigma d^2}{N}}$$

However, this method is quite laborious, often dealing with decimals, and is generally more time-consuming. Consequently, most people prefer using the whole numbers as described in the foregoing section and shown in Table 3 - 5.

Calculation of T-Scores

The T-scale can be constructed by several methods. The T-score value for any specific raw score can be determined by the following formula

$$\text{T-score} = 50 + \frac{10}{SD} (X - \bar{X})$$

where SD is the standard deviation of the raw scores, X is the specific score in question, and $\bar{X}$ is the mean of the group of scores. To illustrate, suppose a student made a score of 94 on a test in which the mean was 80 and the standard deviation 20. Substituting in the formula we have

$$T = 50 + \frac{10}{20} (94 - 80) = 50 + .5(14) = 50 + 7 = 57$$

Consequently, any T-score could be computed in this way.

However, another approach that we feel offers a relatively easy and expedient method of establishing a T-score table from a collection of raw scores is described below. The steps are described using the push-up scores that were featured in previous calculations.

Step 1: Compute the mean and standard deviation for the data (See Table 3 - 3, and 3 - 4). Generally speaking, the larger the number of scores the teacher has accumulated, the more reliable the T-scale will be. It is also imperative that accurate measurements are taken and that the testing procedures and conditions are identical for all the subjects.

Step 2: Multiply the standard deviation by 5 and divide the resulting number by 50. In the example the SD was 9.56, thus $\frac{9.56 \times 5}{50}$ = .96.

Step 3: Construct a table of numbers from 1 to 100. Place the mean of the raw scores opposite the number 50 on the table.

Step 4: Next, the value obtained in Step 2 (.96) is added to the mean, and each subsequent number to represent T-scores 51 to 100

$$(i.e., T_{51} = 25.42 + .96 = 26.38; \ T_{52} = 26.38 + .96 = 27.34, \text{ etc.})$$

Conversely, the constant is subtracted from the mean and each number thereafter to determine T-scores 49 to 0

$$(i.e., \ T_{49} = 25.42 - .96 = 24.46; \ 24.46 - .96 = 23.50, \text{ etc.})$$

Step 5: The scores should be rounded off in order to correspond to the actual raw scores. The teacher can then construct a T-scale such as is shown in Table 3 - 6.

The physical education teacher should periodically revise his T-scale. As more scores are accumulated, the mean and standard deviation should be computed again to verify their accuracy; and, if warranted, a new T-scale should be constructed. The T-scale should not be expected to change markedly once it has been established with a sufficient number of observations. The physical educator would be remiss, however, if he did not continue to inspect and evaluate his norms, just as he should regularly evaluate his total tests and measurements program.

TABLE 3 - 5

Calculation of the Mean and Standard Deviation
from Ungrouped Scores

X	X^2
12	144
8	64
7	49
16	256
6	36
2	4
20	400
10	100
8	64
1	1
4	16
10	100
8	64
6	36
2	4
$\Sigma X = 120$	$\Sigma X^2 = 1338$

$$M = \frac{\Sigma X}{N} = \frac{120}{15} = 8$$

$$SD = \sqrt{\frac{\Sigma X^2}{N} - M^2} =$$

$$\sqrt{\frac{1338}{15} - (8)^2} =$$

$$\sqrt{89.20 = -64} =$$

$$\sqrt{25.20} = 5.02$$

$N = 15$

$\Sigma X = 120$

$\Sigma X^2 = 1338$

$M^2 = 64$

It should be pointed out that in the normal probability curve, plus and minus 3.5 standard deviations encompass nearly all the cases. The T-scale extends plus and minus 5 standard deviations from the mean. Consequently, T-scores for a distribution that closely approximates the normal curve may be expected to range from 85 to 15. This may give rise to some confusion on the part of the student in comprehending what is high and what is low. For this reason some educators prefer the Hull scale rather than the T-scale. The Hull scale includes 3.5 standard deviations above and below the mean. Thus, there is more liklihood that scores will be found in the upper and lower ends of the scale. Regardless of the scale that is used, the solution lies in the proper interpretation of scores to each student.

The Hull scale can be computed in the same way as the T-scale; the only difference is that the standard deviation is multiplied by 3.5, instead of 5, in calculating the rate to add to and subtract from the mean.

T-scores, and other standard scores, represent an invaluable tool for the teacher. Their application for grading purposes will be discussed in Chapter XXII. Besides grading, T-scores may be used in the construction of a test battery, in establishing a profile assessing performance in various areas, and for any of the many occasions in which one wants to compare scores from different types of tests.

Correlation

The authors feel that the statistical techniques presented thus far will suffice for most practical purposes of analyzing and interpreting data. It has already been acknowledged that a thorough understanding of statistics is needed for the specialist in tests and measurements, and is absolutely essential for the research worker. While it is conceivable that the average physical education teacher might have occasion to use such statistical techniques as comparison of means, analysis of variance, covariance, multiple correlation, etc. such concepts were considered to be beyond the scope of this text.

However, one further statistical tool will be discussed briefly, which is, correlation. Occasionally, the worker in tests and measurements will want to ascertain the degree of relationship between two traits or abilities. Moreover, an understanding of correlation is necessary in determining validity, reliability, and objectivity as steps in test construction, and in evaluating a test already published.

A brief explanation of the nature of correlation may be in order before we proceed to describe two methods of computing it. The range of correlation is from -1.00, which is perfect negative correlation, through 0 to +1.00, which represents perfect positive correlation.

Positive correlation means that a small score in one trait accompanies a small score in the other; and a high score in one is associated with a high score in the other. For example, a positive correlation between strength and endurance would mean that those persons with the greatest strength have the most endurance.

Negative correlation is when a large score in one trait is found with a small score in the other, and vice versa. To illustrate, if body weight and push-ups were found to be negatively correlated, it would mean that the heavier students did fewer push-ups, and, conversely, the lighter subjects performed more push-ups.

The distinction between negative correlation and no correlation must be emphasized. This is a common error in interpretation. No correlation means that there is no real relationship between two variables. In the two illustrations above, no correlation would mean that strength is not related to endurance, and that push-up performance is not related to body weight. In other words, a person of high strength may score high, low, or

TABLE 3 - 6

Construction of a T-Scale

T-Score	Raw Score	T-Score	Raw Score	T-Score	Raw Score
100	73	75	49	50	25
99	72	74	48	49	24
98	71	73	47	47	23
97	70	72	46	46	22
96	69	70	45	45	21
94	68	69	44	44	20
93	67	68	43	43	19
92	66	67	42	42	18
91	65	66	41	41	17
90	64	65	40	40	16
89	63	64	39	39	15
88	62	63	38	38	14
87	61	62	37	37	13
86	60	61	36	36	12
85	59	60	35	35	11
84	58	59	34	34	10
83	57	58	33	33	9
82	56	57	32	32	8
81	55	56	31	31	7
80	54	55	30	30	6
79	53	54	29	29	5
78	52	53	28	28	4
77	51	52	27	27	3
76	50	51	26	26	2

Mean = 25 (25.42 rounded off)

average in endurance, and heavy students may score as many push-ups as light ones, and so on. On the other hand, a negative correlation is just as important as a positive correlation; the only difference being in the direction of the relationship. Perfect correlations, either +1.00 or -1.00, are almost never found in actual practice. The problem of interpreting coefficients of correlation, as to what is high, low, and average, is sometimes difficult. The number of subjects involved directly determine how high the coefficient must be to reach statistical significance. But this in itself is misleading because a relatively *low* correlation can be statistically significant if the number of subjects is large.

Probably one of the most important factors regarding the size of the coefficient has to do with the purpose for which the correlation is computed. For example, a coefficient of correlation of .65 may be considered quite high when a specific measurement such as leg strength is correlated with performance in a particular sport. On the other hand, a coefficient of .65 is quite low when the correlation is between the scores made on the odd and even numbered questions on a written examination. Certain arbitrary rankings as to what correlations are considered to be high, average, and low are sometimes given. The following scale is an example of interpretation of coefficients of correlation in general terms.

$$r = .00 \ldots\ldots\ldots\ldots\ldots\ldots \text{ no relationship}$$
$$r = \pm.01 \text{ to } \pm.20 \ldots\ldots\ldots \text{ low relationship}$$
$$r = \pm.20 \text{ to } \pm.50 \ldots\ldots\ldots \text{ slight to fair relationship}$$
$$r = \pm.50 \text{ to } \pm.70 \ldots\ldots\ldots \text{ substantial relationship}$$
$$r = \pm.70 \text{ to } \pm.99 \ldots\ldots\ldots \text{ high relationship}$$
$$r = \pm 1.00 \ldots\ldots\ldots\ldots \text{ perfect relationship}$$

Such rankings are of course merely rough guides and, as was stated above, their worth is dependent upon the purposes for which the computation was done. For instance, for demonstrating reliability of a test, a coefficient of correlation of at least .80 is desired, and preferably higher. Methods of establishing test reliability will be discussed in Chapter IV.

In essence, if the purpose is to predict future performance of an individual, then the coefficient of correlation must be much higher than if the purpose is to just establish a relationship between two traits. However, this leads to another misconception concerning the characteristics of correlation. The misconception, which can be rather dangerous, is to assume that a correlation shows causation. Suppose that a rather high correlation is found between physical fitness and scholastic achievement. The conclusion might erroneously be made that academic achievement results from being physically fit. Although there may be some causation present, the correlation itself does not support this assumption. In any correlation there may be several other factors which are actually responsible for both performances. In the above example a more absurd interpretation would be that gains in scholastic achievement would result in improved physical fitness.

One of the several ways of interpreting coefficients of correlation is by means of the coefficient of determination.* In this method one merely squares the r and the resulting r^2 represents the proportion of the variance in one variable that can be accounted for by the other variable. To illustrate, suppose that the coefficient of correlation between the X

*Henry E. Garrett, *Statistics in Psychology and Education.* 5th ed. New York: Longmans, Green and Co., 1958, p. 179.

variable, speed, as measured by a sprint, and the Y variable, agility, as measured by a shuttle run, was r = .80. Then r^2 = .64. This is interpreted as indicating that 64% of the variance in the agility score was accounted for by the variability in the speed score. This method points out rather strongly that a high coefficient of correlation is needed to reveal a marked degree of association. An r of .30 indicated only 9% association, for example, and an r of .40 only 16%. On the other hand, when the r is very high, the degree of association is also high. To illustrate, an r of .97 indicates that 94% of the variability of one variable is accounted for by the variance in the other variable.

One further precaution should be mentioned regarding correlation. One should not interpet a coefficient of correlation as a percentage of perfect relationship. This is often done, probably because coefficients of correlation are usually reported in hundredths. In any event, this results in gross misunderstanding. While it is beyond the scope of this book to go into a discussion of the meaning of statistical significance, it should be emphasized that an r of .50 is not half as large as an r of 100; nor that an r of .75 is merely three times larger than a coefficient of correlation of .25. By using the coefficient of determination (r^2), it can be seen that an r of 1.00 is four times as strong as a correlation of r = .50; and an r of .75 is nine times as large as an r of .25.

Calculation of Correlation by the Product-Moment Method

The product-moment method (technically referred to as the Pearson Product-Moment Correlation Coefficient) will be illustrated first using a small number of ungrouped scores. Following this, the product-moment method will be employed using grouped data arranged on a scattergram.

Product-Moment Method of Correlation with Ungrouped Data

In Table 3 - 7, the push-up scores (X) and fitness index scores (Y) from the Harvard Step Test are shown for 15 students. The following steps describe the procedures for determining the relationship between push-up performance and cardiovascular fitness by the product-moment method of correlation. The symbol for the product-moment coefficient of correlation is r.

Step 1: Compute the mean for each set of scores. The mean for push-ups ($\overline{X}$) is found to be 22 and 73 for the step test scores ($\overline{Y}$).

Step 2: Each score in column X is subtracted from the mean ($\overline{X}$) and entered in column x. Similarly, the scores in column Y are subtracted from $\overline{Y}$ to form column y.

Step 3: Each value in columns x and y are squared and entered as x^2 and y^2, respectively. The sum for each column is obtained, (Σx^2 = 734, Σy^2 = 1714).

Step 4: The xy column represents the product-moment values. These indicate the distance that each student lies in relation to the mean of each set of scores. These values are found by multiplying x times y. Note that there is a column for positive cross-products and a column for negative values. The algebraic sum of these two columns is then found (Σxy = 777). If the column of negative cross-products were higher, it would indicate a negative correlation.

Step 5: The obtained values are now substituted into the formula, and the coefficient of correlation is determined (r = .69).

TABLE 3 - 7

Calculation of the Coefficient of Correlation for Ungrouped Scores
by the Product-Moment Method

Student	Push-up X	Step Test Y	x	y	x^2	y^2	xy (+)	xy (-)
1	28	84	6	11	36	121	66	
2	23	74	1	1	1	1	1	
3	13	57	-9	-16	81	256	144	
4	16	63	-6	-10	36	100	60	
5	17	80	-5	7	25	49		-35
6	24	72	2	-1	4	1		-2
7	25	70	3	-3	9	9		-9
8	26	65	4	-8	16	64		-32
9	10	59	-12	-14	144	196	168	
10	33	91	11	18	121	324	198	
11	25	73	3	0	9	0		
12	20	60	-2	-13	4	169	26	
13	18	73	-4	0	16	0		
14	16	83	-6	10	36	100		-60
15	36	91	14	18	196	324	252	
N=15	$\Sigma X=330$	$\Sigma Y=1095$			$\Sigma x^2=734$	$\Sigma y^2=1714$	915	-138
	$\overline{X}= 22$	$\overline{Y}= 73$					$\Sigma xy=777$	

$$r = \frac{\Sigma xy}{\sqrt{(\Sigma x^2)(\Sigma y^2)}} = \frac{777}{\sqrt{(734)(1714)}} = \frac{777}{\sqrt{1,258,076}} = \frac{777}{1122} = .69$$

NOTE: Another method may be used with ungrouped data which is actually less laborious, but it utilizes a more imposing looking formula. This method is to assume the means to be zero and to use the raw scores and then a correction factor. It uses the same principle as was outlined in calculating standard deviation from ungrouped data. The formula is

$$r = \frac{N(\Sigma XY) - (\Sigma X)(\Sigma Y)}{\sqrt{N(\Sigma X^2) - (\Sigma X)^2}\sqrt{N(\Sigma Y^2) - (\Sigma Y)^2}}$$

As illustrated, Table 3 - 8 shows the body weights and the scores (in seconds) for the flexed-arm hang test for 10 girls, 12 years of age. In calculating the coefficient of correlation by this method, each score is squared, the cross-product of the X and Y scores are computed, and the resulting totals of each column are inserted into the formula.

In this case a high negative correlation is obtained. This indicated that the heavier girls were not able to hang as long on the bar as the lighter girls. In other words, the greater the body weight the poorer the performance on this test.

TABLE 3 - 8

Calculation of Coefficient of Correlation for Ungrouped Scores
Using Deviations Taken From Zero (AM=O)

Student	Weight X	Score Y	X^2	Y^2	XY
A	80	35	6400	1225	2800
B	117	10	13689	100	1170
C	96	19	9216	361	1824
D	85	22	7225	484	1870
E	92	25	8464	625	2300
F	100	15	10000	225	1500
G	130	5	16900	25	650
H	125	8	15625	64	1000
I	93	15	8649	225	1395
J	88	20	7744	400	1760

N= 10 $\quad \Sigma X = 1006 \quad \Sigma Y = 174 \quad \Sigma X^2 = 103{,}912 \quad \Sigma Y^2 = 3734 \quad \Sigma XY = 16{,}269$

$$(\Sigma X)^2 = 1{,}012{,}036 \qquad (\Sigma Y)^2 = 30{,}276$$

$$r = \frac{N(\Sigma XY) - (\Sigma X)(\Sigma Y)}{\sqrt{N(\Sigma X^2)-(\Sigma X)^2} \; \sqrt{N(\Sigma Y^2)-(\Sigma Y)^2}} \qquad r = \frac{10(16269) - (1006)(174)}{\sqrt{10(103{,}912)-(1006)^2} \; \sqrt{10(3734)-(174)^2}}$$

$$r = \frac{162{,}690 - 175{,}044}{\sqrt{27{,}084} \; \sqrt{7064}} = \frac{-12{,}354}{13{,}860} = -.89$$

Product-Moment Method of Correlation with Grouped Data

The procedures just described are suitable for a small number of scores, and/or when the teacher can use a desk calculator. However, the teacher may elect to group the scores rather than utilize the longer process. In this case the scores for each variable are arranged into frequency distributions and the individual scores are tallied in cells of a scattergram. (See Figure 3 - 2.)

The steps for computing the product-moment coefficient of correlation with grouped data are outlined below. The familiar push-up scores will be correlated with the Harvard Step Test performance of these 60 college men. (See Appendix A for raw scores.)

Step 1: Arrange frequency distributions for both sets of data. One set of scores becomes the X variable, the other the Y variable. The X variable's step intervals run from low on the left to high on the right. The step intervals for Y are arranged from low on the bottom to high on the top. (Note: in this example the number of step intervals and the size of the step intervals happen to be the same. This need not be, although it is desirable to have approximately the same number of step intervals for each variable.)

Step 2: Lines are drawn from top to bottom and side to side setting off each variable's step intervals and, consequently, forming cells. Each student's push-up and step test scores are tallied in the appropriate cell in the upper left hand corner. For example, the first student on the list did 30 push-ups and had a score of 81 on the Harvard Step Test. His tally was placed in the cell for the 28-31 interval across and the 80-83 interval coming down.

Step 3: An assumed mean is chosen for each variable, and these intervals are set apart by heavy lines, forming a cross on the scattergram. In this example the step-interval 68-71 was chosen·for the step test data (X variable); and the 24-27 interval for the push-up scores (Y variable) was selected as in the previous examples.

Step 4: The f, d, and fd columns are established as described earlier in the chapter. The correction factor for each variable (cx and cy) are found with the formulae $\frac{\Sigma fdx}{N}$ and $\frac{\Sigma fdy}{N}$.

Step 5: The fd^2 column is computed and totaled for each distribution, and the standard deviations (σx and σy) are calculated. Note that the size of the intervals is not used in establishing the standard deviations.

Step 6: The product-moment values are now determined in order to make the necessary entries in the xy column. In each cell that has one or more tally marks, the distance that the cell lies from the two assumed means is multiplied by the number of scores in that cell. To illustrate, for the cell that intersects the 60-63 interval down and the 36-39 interval across, the distance is calculated in terms of deviation units as follows: it is 3 step intervals above the assumed mean for push-ups (Y variable), and it is -2 intervals from the assumed mean for the X variable. Thus, the product-moment of the cell alone is

$$3 \times (-2) = -6$$

and, since there are 2 tally marks in it, the cell's total value, which is circled, is -12.

It can be seen that by multiplying deviations from the two assumed means, each of the four quadrants of the scattergram has a positive or negative value. The upper right and lower left quadrants are positive, and the upper left and lower right quadrants are negative. Consequently, by looking at the pattern formed by the tally marks on a scattergram, one can determine the direction and roughly estimate the size of the correlation.

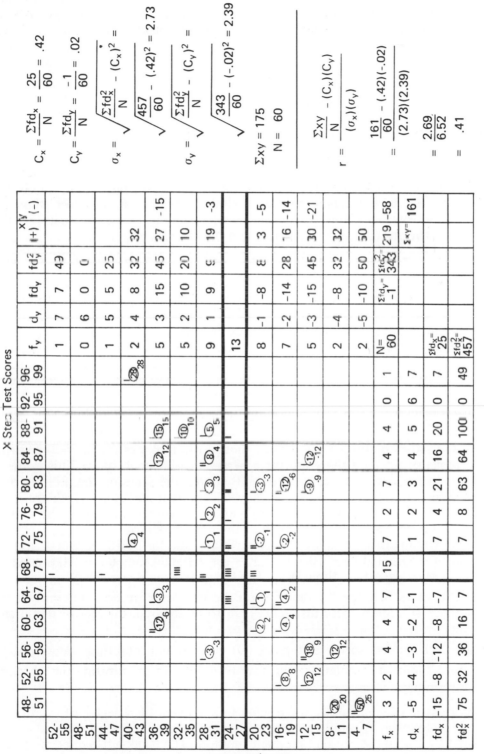

FIGURE 3 - 2

Product-Moment Method of Correlation Using Scattergram

Step 7: The *xy* column is made up of all the product-moment values, both positive and negative. The algebraic sum is found and is entered in the formula as Σxy. All the information is now available to complete the formula for the product-moment correlation coefficient with grouped data.

$$r = \frac{\dfrac{\Sigma xy}{N} - (cx)(cy)}{(\sigma x)(\sigma y)}$$

Calculation of Correlation by the Rank-Difference Method

Another method of establishing the relationship between two variables is the Rank-Difference Method. This is a convenient tool for teachers who want to obtain a quick measure of relationship between two sets of scores involving a small number of subjects. This method uses the rank that each student attains on each test; then the relationship is established in terms of the degree of difference between rankings. The symbol for this coefficient is the Greek rho (ρ), and the formula is

$$\rho = 1 - \frac{6x\Sigma D^2}{N(N^2 - 1)}$$

The steps involved in computing the correlation coefficient by this method will be illustrated by the data presented in Table 3 - 9. In this example a teacher has devised a skill test in badminton, and he wishes to establish the validity (the degree to which the test measures what it is supposed to measure) of his test. The students have completed a round-robin tournament in badminton and have been ranked according to their order of finish in the tournament. The teacher reasons that if his test is valid, those persons who were the most successful in the tournament should score the highest on the skill test, and the losers the lowest. He administers his test and ranks the students from first to last. For purposes of illustration, only 15 subjects are used.

Step 1: Rank the scores on both tests. Notice that in the rankings for the skill test that there are two ranks of 3.5, and there are three persons with a rank of 10. This is due to duplicate scores. In the first instance two students scored the same on the skill test and, therefore, deserved the same rank. However, they take up two positions, which are 3 and 4. An average is computed ($3 + 4 = 7 \div 2 = 3.5$), and both students are given the rank of 3.5. Four places have been accounted for now, so the next rank is 5.

Similarly, three students had identical scores which took up positions 9, 10, and 11. An average is again computed ($9 + 10 + 11 = 30 \div 3 = 10$), and the rank of 10 is assigned to each. The next rank after these three is 12. The last rank should equal N.

Step 2: The differences between the rankings on the two tests are now determined and entered in column "D". Since these differences are to be squared, the plus or minus sign is not important.

Step 3: Square each number in the difference (D) column and total these values (ΣD^2).

Step 4: The coefficient of correlation can now be found by substituting the obtained values into the formula.

In the hypothetical example above the teacher found a very high degree of validity for this skill test in badminton. It should be pointed out that the relationship could also have been established by use of the product-moment method. The Rank-Difference method is quick and simple, but it becomes impractical with a large number of scores.

TABLE 3 - 9

Calculation of Coefficient of Correlation Using the
Rank-Difference Method

Subject	Rank in Skill Test	Rank in Tournament	D	D^2
1	1	1	0	0
2	2	3	1	1
3	3.5	2	1.5	2.25
4	3.5	5	1.5	2.25
5	5	4	1	1
6	6	9	3	9
7	7	6	1	1
8	8	7	1	1
9	10	10	0	0
10	10	8	2	4
11	10	11	1	1
12	12	15	3	9
13	13	13	0	0
14	14	12	2	4
15	15	14	1	1
N = 15				36.50

$$p = 1 - \frac{6 \times \Sigma D^2}{N(N^2 - 1)}$$

$$= 1 - \frac{6 \times 36.50}{15(15^2 - 1)}$$

$$= 1 - \frac{219}{15 \times 224}$$

$$= 1 - \frac{219}{3360}$$

$$= 1 - .07$$

$$p = .93$$

Selected References

Freund, John E., *Modern Elementary Statistics*. 3rd ed. Englewood Cliffs, New Jersey: Prentice-Hall, Inc., 1967.

Garrett, Henry E., *Statistics in Psychology and Education*. 5th ed. New York: Longmans, Green and Co., 1958.

Snedecor, George W., *Statistical Methods*. 5th ed. Ames, Iowa: The Iowa State University Press, 1956, 1967.

Spiegel, Murray R., *Outline of Theory and Problems of Statistics*. New York: Schaum Publishing Company, 1961, 1962.

Underwood, Benton J., Carl P. Duncan, Janet T. Spence, and John W. Cottom, *Elementary Statistics*. New York: Appleton-Century-Crofts, Inc., 1954.

Wert, James E., Charles O. Neidt, and J. Stanley Ahmann, *Statistical Methods in Education and Psychological Research*. New York: Appleton-Century-Crofts, Inc., 1954.

Chapter IV

TEST EVALUATION AND CONSTRUCTION

In order for the physical education teacher to effectively evaluate tests that are available for use in his program, he should have some knowledge concerning the construction of tests. Included in the procedures for test construction are the criteria by which a test may be judged. It is also believed that this information will enable the teacher to acquire confidence in his efforts to establish tests of his own.

Basic Concepts in Test Evaluation

As in any area of specialization, it is necessary to have a basic understanding of the terms that are used. Four of the most basic concepts involved in test construction and evaluation are validity, reliability, objectivity, and norms.

Validity refers to the degree to which a test measures what it was designed to measure. To the beginner in the field of tests and measurements this concept may seem so basic that it scarcely deserves mention. Nevertheless, many tests are found to be rather weak in this most basic consideration. Probably every student has had the unnerving experience of being given a test which seems to pertain to some course other than the one in which he is enrolled. In such cases the test fails in content validity by not being related to the material that has been covered in the course.

Another example of poor testing is in the case of the student who can beat everyone in the badminton class, but whose grade is lowered because he does poorly on one skill test (which consisted of bouncing a bird off a wall). In this instance the teacher, in his zeal to employ objective measures, has overlooked their main function — which is to supplement other means of evaluation. In addition to the teacher's misuse of the test, the test itself did not represent an accurate measure of a person's ability to play badminton. We should hasten to say that, in many cases, vollying tests demonstrate high validity. The point we were attempting to make in the above example was that the test constituted a somewhat artificial setting, and it touched upon only a small facet of the game.

Obviously, then, in order for a test to be valid, a critical analysis must be made as to the nature of the activity, and the skills and special abilities that are involved. It should be emphasized that the selected skills should be basic and fairly general regardless of the position one plays on the team. Other desirable characteristics of a test which will have a bearing on its validity are discussed later in the chapter.

Reliability may be thought of as the repeatability of a test. A student's score should not differ markedly on repeated administrations of the same test. Some measures require exact duplication in order to be considered reliable, while other measures are allowed more leeway. For example, a scale would not be acceptable at all if it did not give the same reading each time a specified weight was placed upon it. On the other hand one would scarcely expect a student to obtain the exact same score on a golf test in which he hits balls into numbered circles. In the latter example there are too many factors involved which would tend to reduce the probability of identical scores.

It should be evident that reliability and validity are interrelated, although it is certainly possible to have one without the other. To illustrate, suppose that a physical education teacher wishes to measure leg strength. Using a gauge and belt arrangement, he is able to obtain an accurate measure of force exerted by the legs. However, the angle at which the leg extension test is performed is very difficult to determine. Consequently, although the teacher obtains an accurate (and valid) measure of a particular student's leg lift at the specified angle, he may find that there is considerable variation in his scores on subsequent tests because of the difficulty in establishing the correct angle — resulting in a low reliability coefficient.

Furthermore, when he tests a group of students for leg strength, his inability to establish the same angle for everyone results in an invalid measure of the group's leg strength at the desired position.

Similarly, a test can be reliable and yet not valid. Suppose that in an attempt to isolate and measure leg strength a teacher has the students push upward on a bar that is placed on their shoulders and attached to a dynamometer. Regardless of the fact that he obtains consistent (reliable) scores on repeated tests, the amount that each student can lift is limited by the amount of weight that the back can support. Consequently, the strength of the legs, which is much greater than that of the back, is not being isolated, and this results in an invalid measure of leg strength.

There are many factors which can affect the reliability of a test. Obviously, if there is an appreciable time lapse between test administrations, learning, forgetting, or changes in condition may influence performance. The circumstances and environment in which the test is given may also produce inconsistent results. The teacher should be alert to the possible influences of such factors as standardization and clarity of directions, time of day, presence of spectators, the mood of the student, motivation (or the lack of it), fatigue, and the student's general state of health.

Objectivity of a test pertains primarily to the clarity of the directions for administering and scoring the test. High objectivity is when different teachers can give a test to the same individuals and obtain approximately the same results. Naturally, we are assuming that the testers are equally competent.

Objectivity and reliability are related but are, nevertheless, distinct concepts. A stop watch is a highly reliable device for measuring the time it takes for a student to run 440 yards. Yet, if the directions are not clear as to when to start the watch — at the sound of the gun or upon seeing the smoke, etc. — then there is an increased liklihood for error. Moreover, if there are no standardized procedures for scoring, some testers will record scores to the nearest one-half second, others to the nearest tenth of a second, and so on. Thus, a reliable measuring device does not guarantee objectivity.

Norms are values considered to be representative of a specified population. A test that has accompanying norms is definitely preferred to one that does not. They provide information for the student and the teacher to enable them to interpret the student's score in relation to the scores made by other individuals in the same population. An understanding of what constitutes the "same population" is necessary in order to intelligently use norm tables.

Norms are usually based on age, grade, height, weight, or various combinations of these characteristics. In norm tables for physical performance there are separate scales for boys and girls; in written tests this distinction is usually not made. The important factor is that the interpretation of norm tables is done in light of the specific group from which the norms were compiled. For example, a standing broad jump of eight feet would not be impressive at all if done by a college athlete; whereas, it would indeed be an outstanding achievement if performed by a 10-year-old boy.

In order to evaluate performance in relation to a set of norms, one must first evaluate the adequacy of the norms. There are several factors that should be considered.

1. The number of subjects that were used in establishing the norms should be sufficiently large. Although sheer numbers do not guarantee accuracy, generally speaking the larger the sample the more likely it will approximate the population.

2. The norms should represent the performance of the population for which the test was devised. It would not be appropriate to compile norms from a select group, such as physical education majors, to represent all college students in a physical performance test. Similarly, the user of norms should not evaluate the performance of his students on the basis of norms designed for a different population.

3. The geographical distribution that the norms represent should be taken into account. Considerable variation in performance is often found among students in different geographical locations. For the most part local norms are of more value to the teacher than are national norms.

4. The clarity of the directions for test administration and scoring is definitely involved in the evaluation of the accompanying norms. Obviously, if the testing and scoring procedures utilized by the teacher are not identical to those employed by the testers who compiled the norms, then the norms themselves are worthless.

5. Norms are only temporary and must be periodically revised. Certain traits, characteristics, and abilities of children today differ from those of children a number of years ago. Consequently, the date in which the norms were established should be considered and weighed accordingly.

FIGURE 4 - 1

Shuttle Run Test — A Test of Agility

Additional Criteria for the Selection and Evaluation of Tests

In addition to the basic concepts of validity, reliability, objectivity, and norms, there are several other features that should be considered in selecting and evaluating tests. These will be presented in the form of questions that one might ask before selecting a particular test to use as part of his evaluation program.

1. *Is the test easy to administer?* Ease of administration involves many things including time, equipment, space, number of testers needed, etc. These will be taken up separately, but this one basic question is an example of the whole being greater than the sum of the parts. The administrative feasibility of a test extends to the attitude that the tester, and certainly the students, have toward that particular test. There are some physical fitness tests, for example, that are so rigorous that some students actually become ill, and many others suffer from soreness for days afterwards. In such a case as this, the test could have high validity, reliability, and objectivity coefficients; it could possess any number of desirable test characteristics, such as economy of time, space, equipment, etc.; but it would still be unacceptable. Thus, ease of administration encompasses the entire realm of administrative considerations, including attitude, in relation to the contribution that the test can make to the program.

2. *Does the test require expensive equipment?* A formidable item to consider in any school testing program is cost. There is no doubt that with unlimited resources elaborate instruments, machines, and electronic devices could be applied to measure human performance with great precision. In reality, however, the physical education budget rarely permits the purchase of expensive equipment that is only applicable to a specific test. Some tests must be excluded for exactly this reason. One of the outstanding features of the AAHPER Youth Fitness Test is that it requires almost no equipment. Occasionally, a teacher may have to compromise to some extent by selecting a test having less accuracy than another but requiring less equipment.

3. *Can the test be administered in a relatively short period of time?* A perpetual problem that confronts most physical educators is the numerous encroachments upon his class time. Recognizing this, most authorities recommend that tests and measurements programs should consume no more than ten percent of the total instructional time. Therefore, any single test battery must be evaluated in terms of economy of time as well as of money.

   Economy of time can be a very important factor in test selection, and often the teacher is faced with a dilemma. In order for a test to meet the demands of validity and reliability, a sufficient number of trials must be given which may consume more time than the teacher wishes to spend. Attempts to compromise, by reducing the number of test items and/or trials, usually result in a serious loss in validity and reliability, thereby reducing the intended worth of the test. The problem is compounded in short activity units where time for instruction and practice is at a premium.

4. *Can the test be used as a drill during practice sessions?* Although this feature of a test is not always desirable, it can offer a partial solution to the problem stated above concerning economy of time as well as of other test criteria. For example, the more familiarity the students have with a test, the less time is needed to explain the administration and scoring procedures. In addition, practice of the test also serves to reduce the sometimes misleading effects of insight into the nature of the test, which may cause a rather pronounced rise in scores in the middle or latter portions of the test.

If the test is a measure of skill and represents the actual abilities that are required in the activity, then it would seem that its use as a form of practice would be logical and desirable. This line of reasoning is based on the principle of content validity — in other words, one should be tested on what is practiced. On the other hand if the test is artificial and the student practices more for the test than the total activity in question, then, of course, this is not to be condoned.

5. *Does the test require several trained testers?* Since some test batteries contain a number of individual test items, in the interest of time it is almost imperative that more than one person be called upon to administer the test. Furthermore, some test items require more skill and experience to administer than others. This requires training and practice. If more than one person is going to be giving the same test, objectivity coefficients should be established. In cases where one person will be the only one handling a particular measurement, then reliability should also be demonstrated.

Besides the training and practice that are involved, the utilization of several testers requires considerable planning and organization. Naturally, arrangements must be made to have the testers available at the proper time; pre-test meetings are usually required; and various other details of coordination need to be accomplished.

Thus far it would appear that tests that call for several testers are undesirable. It should be quickly pointed out that there are times when tests of this nature are of immense value. One such instance is when large-scale, comprehensive evaluation is advocated, as is sometimes done for physical fitness testing at various times during the school year. Generally, placement and screening tests are most effectively administered in this way.

To summarize, whenever the abilities that are to be measured necessitate the use of several test items, or when a particular test item requires a specialist to administer it, then the utilization of trained testers is not only expedient but necessary. On the other hand the teacher who must evaluate his students in various activities ordinarily does not have other staff members or trained assistants available; thus he must bear this in mind in his selection of tests. While the use of students as testers may be profitable to the student testers as well as the teacher, there are times when this is not administratively feasible nor desirable.

6. *Can the test be easily and objectively scored?* Certainly this criterion has been mentioned or alluded to a number of times in the foregoing discussion. Nevertheless, there is a need for further comment regarding this feature of a test. Specifically, one should consider the following factors: (a) whether or not a test requires another person to act as an opponent, a thrower, a server, etc.; (b) whether or not the students can test and score themselves during practice sessions; and (c) whether or not the scores adequately distinguish among different levels of skill.

The first consideration, concerning the role of another individual involved in the performance of the testee, represents somewhat of a paradox in the construction of a performance test. In most sports the skill of the opponent definitely has a direct bearing on an individual's performance. In activities such as tennis, badminton, handball, volleyball, football, to name but a few, the quality of the performance of a player is relative to the skill of the opponent. In other sports such as golf, archery, bowling, and others, a person's performance can be immediately assessed by his score alone (playing conditions being equal for everyone, of course). Therefore, in many activities a performance test simply cannot take into account the influence that is rendered by the competitive situation.

Recognizing this restriction, the makers of performance tests have attempted to isolate the skills that are involved and measure them independently. However, if the isolated skills call for the services of another individual, either acting as an opponent or a teammate, then, of course, objectivity is reduced. To illustrate, in an attempt to duplicate the actual activity, it may be desirable to have someone serve the shuttlecock to the person being tested on the high *clear* stroke; or to have someone pitch to a student being tested on batting; or to have someone run a pass pattern to test an individual's skill at passing a football. In these cases it is obvious that the skill of the other individual could greatly affect the testee's score. This is not to say that tests of this type are inferior. On the contrary, if the other person is sufficiently skilled and his performance is constant for each subject, this can be a very effective and efficient method of evaluation. This individual might very well be the teacher, but of course there are some problems that arise in planning and organizing a testing arrangement such as this, and there are the factors of sufficient number of trials and fatigue on the part of the teacher.

In striving to avoid the influence of another person and preserve high objectivity, there is the danger of creating an artificial situation. Having a student hit a softball from a batting tee and bounce the ball himself before stroking in tennis are examples of situations which are not found in the actual game conditions. This, then, is the paradox inherent in performance test construction — scientific precision versus gamelike conditions.

A second consideration in scoring a test is whether or not the students can test and score themselves. Although this feature of a test is not always applicable, it is usually of considerable importance when the test is to be used as a teaching aid. For instance, a wall volley drill in tennis might be employed as a regularly scheduled exercise and rainy day activity for developing proficiency in the basic strokes. It also might be one of the measuring devices used in evaluation. In this situation the students could benefit from self-testing throughout the course in providing them with a record of progress, and, at the same time, blocking the possible negative effects of confronting a unique test situation at the end of the unit.

A third aspect of scoring that should be considered relates to the precision with which test scores can differentiate among persons of different abilities. This consideration overlaps with so many other characteristics of testing that it will only be mentioned briefly here. Tests that stress speed are sometimes prone to encourage poor form. Some wall volley tests are examples of this in that an individual may be able to achieve a higher score by standing very close and using mainly wrist action rather than the desired stroking movement.

In some tests the units of measurement are not fine enough to reflect various levels of ability. A classic example is an agility test in which the student scores a point each time he crosses a center line as he runs from one side of the court to the other. Because of the distance involved and the limited opportunity to earn points, most of the scores are identical within a range of about three points. Other examples would include test items scored on a pass-or-fail basis, and tests using targets with widely spaced point values.

Related to the above are tests which are designed to measure the accuracy of the individual in hitting a ball, a shuttlecock, etc., into particular scoring zones on a court. Several tests employ a rope or string placed above the net, or at other spots on the floor, to separate the skilled player who correctly places the shot from the *sloppy* performer who might hit the same scoring zone but with a poor shot that would be unsuccessful against an actual opponent. Similarly, attention should be given to the probable action of a real opponent in marking the zones on a playing court. For instance, areas that are just barely out-of-bounds should be given some point value if it is logical that the opponent would not let a ball (or shuttlecock, etc.) land in that area for fear that it might fall good. In addition, it should be assumed that the more highly skilled players will deliberately hit shots that land close to boundary lines, as these are ordinarily the hardest to return. Therefore, it does not seem appropriate that a good player should be penalized — to the extent that he receives no points — for barely missing on what would probably be a good shot in an actual game.

One might argue that in an actual game a player does, in fact, receive no score for hitting just barely out-of-bounds. It would be pointless to debate this issue, or to attempt to list situations when point values should or should not be awarded. The important consideration is that the physical education teacher evaluates the method of scoring in light of the test's purposes and in accordance with the students' level of proficiency.

7. *Is the test challenging and meaningful?* Of vital importance to the success of any testing program is the attitude with which the students approach the tests. Generally speaking, most students like to be tested. The challenge of the task, the information that is derived, and the curiosity and competitive nature of the individual are some of the factors which operate to produce a favorable testing situation. Needless to say, students also can learn to dread tests for any number of reasons. Sometimes an individual feels unduly threatened by a test in which he is made to feel inferior and an object of ridicule. In other instances a student may feel inadequately prepared, or he may place too much importance on the results. In still other circumstances a student may regard the test as being unfair, too strenuous, too easy, or perhaps meaningless.

Therefore, the physical educator should seek to capitalize on the positive motivating properties that are generally inherent in physical performance tests. The tests and the conditions in which they are given should be carefully considered with regard to student enjoyment. This is a time when the physical education teacher has an excellent opportunity to establish a favorable teacher-student relationship through encouragement and individual attention.

The test itself must be challenging. To do this it must offer sufficient latitude in scoring to accommodate large differences in ability. A disadvantage of a test such as pull-ups is that there are almost always students in a class who cannot do a single pull-up, and, therefore, receive a score of zero. Similarly, a test should allow opportunity to record improvement. Referring again to pull-ups, a student may have improved during the course to the point where he could just about pull himself up to chin level, which for that student might represent a significant gain in strength; but he still receives a zero. At the other extreme, there are some tests that have a performance ceiling and make no provision for better scores after a particular level has been attained.

Related closely to the challenging aspect of a test is the degree to which it is meaningful. Performance tests should involve the actual skills that are used in the activity; and the skills should be measured as much as possible in game-like situations. A softball test in which the student is asked to catch a ball that is thrown out of a second-story window can hardly be considered realistic. Granted that it would have built-in validity since it does involve the catching of a softball. However, it would seem rather difficult for a teacher to convince a student that his ability to play softball was being assessed in such an *un-game-like* situation. Doubly hard might be the task of interpreting the efficacy of the physical educator's evaluative techniques to the public who observe students attempting to catch balls thrown out of a window.

Test selection, then, must couple scientific considerations with common sense. There can be no substitute for good judgment. The physical educator must be constantly alert to the needs and interests of his students as they pertain to tests and measurements as well as to the program of which they are a part.

FIGURE 4 - 2

Bridge-up Test — A Test of Flexibility

Steps in Test Construction

When published tests are either not available or not exactly suitable for the physical educator's particular situation, it becomes necessary to construct his own test. Although it is not imperative that a teacher read books on tests and measurements in order to simply devise a test for his own use, it does require skillful analysis and technical training to construct a test that is scientifically sound. Moreover, many teachers are reluctant to try their hand at formulating tests because they lack confidence in their ingenuity and in their knowledge of test construction.

The following steps are suggested to guide the physical educator in devising a physical performance test that will adhere to the criteria of validity, reliability, and other basic principles.

Step 1: <u>Analysis of the game or physical qualities in question in order to determine the skills or factors that are to be measured.</u> This, of course, necessitates a thorough understanding of what is involved in the physical performance that is being evaluated. A mere listing of the components of the activity is insufficient. One must be able to determine the relative importance of each component. Naturally, some abilities involving strategy and reaction to an opponent are ordinarily not considered in this analysis because of the difficulty in measuring those qualities.

Step 2: <u>Selection of test items that measure the desired qualities.</u> Unquestionably, this is one of the most crucial steps in the entire test construction procedure. The items must be chosen with regard to their importance as well as their propensity to be measured accurately.

The test items may be selected from other established tests; they may be chosen through the utilization of a jury of experts; or they may be determined arbitrarily by the physical educator after analyzing the performance in question. If the test pertains to a sport, the test item should conform as much as possible to the actual game situation and not be taken out of context. If the test is for physical fitness or motor ability, the test item should not favor persons of a particular size and penalize others unless body size is meant to be a factor in the performance, such as the fact that obesity is not compatible with physical fitness.

The test items generally should stress good form as well as the main scoring criteria. It has been observed that in some tests the student can achieve a higher score by using an unorthodox style rather than the prescribed form.

The literature contains numerous test items that have been used for measuring various components of physical fitness. In this case the test maker might choose test items in accordance with their compliance with some established criteria. These criteria might entail restrictions as to time, equipment, space, or other considerations pertinent to one's local situation.

It must be remembered that any test item is only a sample of the total performance or quality. This concept must be thoroughly understood by the teacher when formulating the test and especially when evaluating the results. In devising the test items care must be taken to isolate as much as possible the desired ability. If the test situation is too complicated, the results may be misleading. This is particularly true when a test item is to be used for diagnostic purposes. To illustrate, if the teacher is attempting to measure arm and shoulder girdle strength, a test item such as the shot put would not be suitable because of the uncontrolled variables of past experience and technique. On the other hand test makers sometimes make the mistake of isolating a skill or trait to such an extreme that the test item becomes meaningless.

Step 3: <u>Establish the exact procedures for the administration and scoring of the test.</u> In accomplishing this obvious step the physical educator must resort to a certain amount of trial and error. The best laid plans on paper may be totally inoperable in practice. Furthermore, the directions for testing and scoring may appear to be perfectly clear when the test is tried on only one or two subjects. However, marked revisions may be necessary after giving the test to a number of people due to differences in the way the directions may be interpreted, or perhaps due to unanticipated levels of performance.

The clarity and simplicity of directions have a direct bearing on the reliability and objectivity of a test. The test maker should strive to establish procedures that facilitate the administration of the test both from the standpoint of the tester and the testee. Validity is also obviously impaired if the student does not fully understand the directions.

Step 4: Determine the reliability of each test item. A reliability coefficient can be obtained for each test item by giving the test twice to the same group of subjects and correlating the scores on the first test with the scores on the second test. Some considerations involved in accomplishing this step are suggested below.

1. The subjects that are selected for testing should of course be representative of the population for whom the test is intended.

2. In establishing the score value that is to be used to indicate the performance of each subject for each of the two test administrations, care should be taken to obtain an appropriate measure. In other words a sufficient number of trials should be given, the test directions should be made perfectly clear, and ample opportunity should be afforded each person to become accustomed to the test itself. These suggestions have been mentioned before, but it is important that they be considered.

   A further consideration relating to the number of trials given has to do with the type of performance that is being measured. If the test item is a measure of skill, then more trials need to be given than if the test involves an all-out effort such as for the vertical jump test or for a strength test. In either case the average score (as opposed to best score) is considered to be the most reliable measure to use.

3. The reader is referred to Chapter III for discussion of correlation and factors to consider in the interpretation of a specific coefficient of correlation. Test makers generally recommend that a test should have a reliability coefficient of at least .70 to be acceptable. Naturally, the higher the coefficient the better. Some authorities feel that a correlation coefficient of at least .85 should be required in order to satisfy the criterion of reliability. Certainly one should not expect perfect correlation due to the normal variations in performance noted in individuals from one time to the next.

   Low reliability coefficients ordinarily call for revisions in the test item or its elimination. Sometimes just allowing more trials will greatly improve the reliability. Some types of physical performance are much harder to measure reliably than others. Tests of kinesthesis, for example, generally are notoriously lacking in reliability due to the nature of the test items.

   One final admonition for teachers who are judging tests based on coefficients of reliability, validity, and objectivity is that these values mean nothing if the person using the test is not a competent tester. A particular test can be highly reliable when administered by one person, but completely unreliable if it is given by a careless or untrained tester. It is also certainly possible for a skilled, conscientious person to obtain a higher reliability coefficient than that which is published.

Step 5: Compute the objectivity of each test item. This step is accomplished by having two competent testers administer the test item to the same individuals. Correlation is again employed to determine the extent of agreement between the different test administrators. Most of the considerations that were discussed regarding reliability are applicable here. Needless to say, objectivity is directly related to the skill and integrity of the testers as well as to the clarity and simplicity of the instructions and scoring procedures of the test.

Step 6: Establish validity. This procedure in test construction may be approached in several ways. The test maker may wish to use more than one method or a combination of methods. The most common procedures utilized in establishing validity are enumerated as follows:

1. The students' performance on the homemade test can be correlated with their scores made on a previously validated test. If a high correlation is obtained, the test maker can claim that his test is valid. It should be obvious, however, that this procedure has certain weaknesses. In the first place the validity coefficient only demonstrates the degree to which the new test coincides with the other test; consequently, it can only be shown to be as valid as the older test, never more valid. This last point is especially noteworthy because in the majority of cases, a person is prompted to devise a new test in order to improve upon the present evaluation tools.

2. If the test in question is designed to measure performance in an activity such as tennis, badminton, handball, etc., it can be effectively validated by correlating the scores on the test with the results of a round-robin tournament. If it is valid, the persons placing highest in the tournament should score highest on the test, the poorest players should have the lowest scores, and so on through the different levels of ability.

3. In some activities, such as team sports, round-robin tournaments are not feasible. However, a comparable validating procedure can be employed by utilizing the ratings of experts as the criterion to which the performance on the test is correlated. The experts must be selected with care, but at the same time it is not necessary to obtain the services of nationally known figures for this purpose. To illustrate, if the test pertains to performance in basketball, the varsity basketball coaches could certainly be considered qualified to rate basketball skills, provided ample opportunity is allowed for observing each student. In addition, scales must be devised that are suitably graduated in order to differentiate between various levels of ability. For example, specific point values are usually given for arbitrary standards of performance, such as 5 for excellent; 4, good; 3, average; 2, etc. If several judges are used, the average rating is ordinarily correlated with the score made on the performance test. Judges' ratings can also be utilized in validating individual activities as well as team sports.

4. Another approach which is quite similar to the method just described involves comparison of persons of known levels of ability on their test performance. In this method individuals are assigned to different groups which supposedly represent different degrees of proficiency. The formation of the groups may be done through ratings by competent judges, such as a coach rating his varsity players, his junior varsity players, his freshmen, et cetera; or, it may be accomplished by simply selecting whole groups of performers on the basis of their status as a group. For instance, the varsity may be assumed to represent the highest level of ability, the junior varsity next, the freshmen next, intramural players next, and, finally, perhaps physical education students just beginning the activity. After the test has been administered to all the subjects, the test performances of the different groups are then compared to determine the degree to which the test differentiated among the assumed levels of ability. A variation of the same approach involves the use of a number of teams that are considered to represent different degrees of skill based on their order of finish in a tournament or conference standings. It can be readily seen that there is bound to be some erroneous assumptions as to the various levels of ability due to upsets, unusual circumstances, and the indistinguishable clustering effect that is found at the middle of any performance scale which conforms to normal distribution.

FIGURE 4 - 3

Flexed Arm Hang — A Test of
Static Muscular Endurance

5. The last method of determining validity that will be presented here involves the use of a composite score of all the test items in the battery as the performance criterion. Frequently, physical fitness tests are established in this manner. The scores for the various test items that were selected as measures of the basic components are converted to standard scores and are then added. This total is assumed to represent physical fitness, or motor ability, or sports skill, or whatever is being tested. Then each test item is correlated with the criterion (total score) and with each of the other items. Multiple correlation can then be employed to select the test battery which is composed of the test items that correlate highest with the criterion and lowest with one another. The latter is necessary because a test item that correlates highly with another one is considered to be measuring the same thing, and is therefore superfluous. Consequently, if two test items are found to be highly related, the one that correlates highest with the criterion would be selected.

   If there are a considerable number of test items, this process can select the least number of items to comprise the test battery. Regression equations can also be used to predict what an individual would do on the total performance based on his scores on the selected items.

6. The basic procedures just described above can be used to establish the validity of each test item in any battery. In cases where the composite score is not considered appropriate, the items can be correlated with judges' ratings, tournament standings, established tests, etc. to determine the validity of each item. The items should then also be intercorrelated to eliminate duplication.

Step 7: Revise the test in light of the findings of the steps just described; and finalize the written instructions for administering and scoring the test.

Step 8: Construct norms. A large number of subjects who are representative of the population for whom the test was intended, should be given the test and their scores recorded. The scores can then be converted to percentiles or T-scores (or whatever suitable score form is wanted). Norms for each test item should be prepared, and usually norms for the composite or total score is also desirable.

Summary

Much more could be said about test construction and test selection and evaluation. In fact, an entire book could be devoted to this area. Certainly it represents the very essence of the tests and measurements program. Separate coverage could be accorded the construction of written tests, attitude scales, social adjustment inventories, and other measuring tools. It was simply not within the scope of this book to do so. The interested reader is referred to other sources that pertain to knowledge of test construction, the devising of attitude scales, and other measuring tools. The primary consideration in evaluating any test, and the basic steps in constructing a test of any type, are the same.

The underlying message of this chapter, and in fact the theme of the entire book, pertains to the intelligent application of tests and measuring tools. An evaluating device can only be valid, reliable, and objective if it is utilized properly. Norms yield worthwhile information only when the tests are administered and scored in the same way for each individual, and only when the individuals are from the same population. With these thoughts in mind we are ready to turn our attention to the discussion and presentation of some practical measurements for evaluation in specific areas in physical education.

Selected References

Clarke, H. Harrison, *Application of Measurement to Health and Physical Education,* 4th ed. Englewood Cliffs, New Jersey: Prentice-Hall, Inc., 1967.

Garrett, Henry E., *Statistics in Psychology and Education,* 5th ed. New York: Longmans, Green and Co., 1958.

Lien, Arnold J., *Measurement and Evaluation of Learning,* Dubuque, Iowa: Wm. C. Brown Company Publishers, 1967.

Mathews, Donald K., *Measurement in Physical Education,* 3rd ed., Philadelphia: W. B. Saunders Company, 1968.

Smith, Fred M. and Sam Adams, *Educational Measurement for the Classroom Teacher,* New York: Harper & Row, Publishers, 1966.

Weiss, Raymond A., and M. Gladys Scott, "Construction of Tests," Chapter 8. *Research Methods in Health, Physical Education, and Recreation,* 2nd ed. Washington, D.C.: American Association for Health, Physical Education and Recreation, 1959.

Chapter V

AGE, HEIGHT, WEIGHT AND BODY TYPE MEASUREMENT

Anthropometric measurements have been a part of physical education since its inception in this country. The earliest research was in the area of anthropometry with the emphasis on changes in muscle size brought about through exercise. The modern physical educator is often assigned the task of measuring height and weight of students. These measures, like any of the other measures taken in school, should be used and not merely recorded and then ignored.

The question is frequently raised, "What do you do with such measures?" "You certainly can't grade on whether a student grows or not." It is indeed true that growth does not constitute a valid criterion upon which a student is graded. However, height, weight, and certain anthropometric measures, used in conjunction with other pertinent data, do represent potentially valuable information. This chapter will consider the utilization of these measures under three general headings: classification indexes, the assessment of normal growth and nutrition, and body build classification, otherwise called somatotyping.

Classification Indexes

Physical educators have long realized that the performance of boys and girls is greatly influenced by such factors as age, height, weight, and body structure. It is also acknowledged that persons of the same age will vary considerably in body size and shape; that individuals of the same height will differ greatly in body weight; that persons may weigh the same, but the relative proportion of muscle, fat, and bone will be anything but equal. It is obvious, then, that no single measure by itself is satisfactory for the purposes of classifying students into homogenous groups.

Our school system in the United States is based primarily on a single classification, age. A child starts to school at a specified age, and if he makes satisfactory progress, he advances a grade each year. The main objection to this system lies in the known differences in maturity within a given chronological age. Clarke[6] tested boys within two months of their 10th birthday and reported differences in skeletal maturity ranging from 8 years and less to 12 years and more. Certainly, it is unfair to expect a boy who is at a maturation level of 8 years to compete equally with a boy of 12 years. Yet we continually do this as long as our only classification index is chronological age.

The assessment of skeletal age, or physical maturity, by X-ray is, of course, not practical for the school situation. Therefore, the physical educator must use other devices if he wishes to classify students into homogenous groupings. Two of the most commonly used classification devices have been the McCloy Classification Index and the Neilson and Cozens Classification Index. Both systems utilize a combination of age, height, and weight.

Before the various classification indices and age-height-weight tables are presented, it may be pertinent to briefly discuss some points that should be considered in measuring height and weight. These measures are so common that occasionally the examiner tends to be too lax and inaccuracies result. Remember that practice and attention to detail are as important here as in any measurement if the results are to have real value.

Measurement of Height. In measuring height the only equipment and materials necessary are a flat surface against which the subject stands, a measuring tape or marked surface, and an object to place on the subject's head that forms a right angle to the wall or a backboard. If a wall is used, it should not have quarter round or wainscotting so that the subject can stand against it with heels, buttocks, upper back, and back of the head making firm contact.

For permanent mounting the markings can be painted on the wall or backboard. Most classification devices and nutritional status instruments call for height measured to the nearest ¼ of an inch. Therefore, the scale should be marked in these units. However, for greater versatility and application it is recommended that a parallel scale be prepared reading in centimeters.

Frequently, weight scales have stadiometers attached consisting of a sliding calibrated rod with hinged top piece. These sometimes are found to be unsatisfactory in cases where the top piece is loose and fails to make a right angle, or when the rod sticks or perhaps is too loose.

The subject should be measured without shoes. It has been suggested that standing with the back against a support helps the subject to stretch to his full height. The chin is tucked in slightly and the head is held erect. The object used to form a right angle to the backboard is pressed firmly onto the subject's head. Care should be taken so that the upper surface is horizontal and not tilted, and also that this pressure does not cause the subject to slump or alter his position. Finally, the subject bends his knees slightly when he steps away so as not to disturb the angle before the height is recorded.

Measurement of Weight. Generally speaking, scales based on the lever system are more reliable than the spring scales. Both types, however, require periodic inspection and rather delicate handling.

The subject to be weighed should be wearing a minimum amount of clothing, such as only gym shorts. While it may be more accurate for the subjects to be weighed in the nude, it is often not practical nor desirable. Actually, no appreciable accuracy is lost if the amount of clothing is kept consistent. Consistency is the key to all measurements. The subject should be weighed at the same time of day and to the same degree of accuracy — usually the nearest half pound. Smithells and Cameron[39] point out that hair styles may cause variations in weight, and that it is somewhat incongruous that hair is pressed down and thus, in a sense, not counted in height measurement, but it is included in body weight.

The teacher should attempt to control the weighing situation so that there is minimal embarrassment on the part of the students. With experience the teacher can acquire the knack of predicting the body weight of students as they step to the scale. This facilitates the process by eliminating much trial and error with regard to jiggling the scale's sliding weights back and forth.

The McCloy Classification Index[25]

Despite their limitations age height and weight have been found to correlate highly with valid criteria of competition. Therefore, McCloy believed that, because of their convenience and validity, they should be utilized for classification purposes. On the bases of a statistical study McCloy established three indexes with the following weightings for age, height, and weight:

(For high school)	Classification Index I	20(age in yrs.) + 6(ht. in inches) + weight in lbs.
(For college)	Classification Index II	6(ht. in inches) + weight in lbs.
(For elementary grades)	Classification Index III	(10 X age in yrs.) + weight in lbs.

McCloy, in recommending the different indices for different age levels, found that age ceased to make a contribution at 17 years and that height was not an important factor at the elementary level.

Table 5 - 1 presents the proposed divisions for McCloy's Classification Indices for elementary, junior high, high school, and college.

TABLE 5 - 1

Divisions for the McCloy Classification Indices*

Classification Index—Elementary School
Range 515-875

Class	For a small group	Class	For a larger group
A	800 and over	A	800 and over
B	770	B	775
C	740	C	750
D	710	D	725
E	680	E	700
F	650	F	675
G	620	G	650
H	619 and under	H	625
		I	600
		J	599 and under

* C. H. McCloy and N. D. Young, *Tests and Measurements in Health and Physical Education.* 3rd edition. New York: Appleton-Century-Crofts, Inc. 1954. p. 59. Reprinted by permission of Appleton-Century-Crofts, Division of Meredith Corporation.

TABLE 5 - 1 (continued)

Classification Index—Junior High School
Range 540-900

Class	
A	875 and over
B	845
C	815
D	785
E	755
F	725
G	695
H	665
I	664 and under

Classification Index—High School
Range 685-955

Class	For a small group	Class	For a larger group
A	890 and over	A	900 and over
B	860	B	875
C	830	C	850
D	800	D	825
E	770	E	800
F	740	F	775
G	739 and under	G	750
		H	725
		I	724 and under

TABLE 5 - 1 (continued)

Class	For a small group	Class	For a larger group
\multicolumn{4}{c}{Classification Index—College Range 700-975}		

Class	For a small group	Class	For a larger group
A	910 and over	A	925 and over
B	890	B	900
C	860	C	875
D	830	D	850
E	800	E	825
Γ	799 and under	Γ	800
		G	775
		H	750
		I	749 and under

The Neilson and Cozens Classification Index[32]

Neilson and Cozens developed two Classification Indices based on age, height, and weight. However, their second index is the one commonly employed. Its formula is as follows:

Classification Index = 20(age in yrs.) + 5.55(ht. in inches) + weight in lbs.

It can be seen that this formula is very similar to McCloy's Classification Index I. As a matter of fact an r of .98 has been obtained between the two indices which indicates that either index could be used.

The Neilson and Cozens Classification Index can be quickly and easily determined by consulting a table. The teacher simply finds the exponent value for each of the variables of height, age, and weight. After adding the three exponents the class, in the form of a letter A, B, C, etc., is established. For the elementary and junior high school students eight classes (A through H) are given. For high school only three classes (A, B, and C) are determined. The *AAHPER Youth Fitness Manual* presents norms based on the Neilson and Cozens Classification Index as well as norms based on age only. The differences in a student's percentile scores on the test items when based on age only and the Classification Index are illustrated in the chapter on physical fitness tests, Chapter XVII.

Table 5 - 2 shows the chart for finding the Classification Index for elementary and junior high school boys and girls.

Example: A sixth grade boy is 12 years, 4 months of age, stands 58 inches tall and weighs 90 pounds. The exponent for his age is seen to be 5, the exponent for his height is 8, and for his weight, 6. The sum of exponents is 5 + 8 + 6 = 19. Therefore, this boy's classification is Class C.

TABLE 5 - 2

The Neilson and Cozens Classification Chart for Elementary and Junior High School Boys and Girls*

Exponent	Height in inches	Age in years	Weight in pounds
1	50 to 51	10 to 10-5	60 to 65
2	52 to 53	10-6 to 10-11	66 to 70
3		11 to 11-5	71 to 75
4	54 to 55	11-6 to 11-11	76 to 80
5		12 to 12-5	81 to 85
6	56 to 57	12-6 to 12-11	86 to 90
7		13 to 13-5	91 to 95
8	58 to 59	13-6 to 13-11	96 to 100
9		14 to 14-5	101 to 105
10	60 to 61	14-6 to 14-11	106 to 110
11		15 to 15-5	111 to 115
12	62 to 63	15-6 to 15-11	116 to 120
13		16 to 16-5	121 to 125
14	64 to 65	16-6 to 16-11	126 to 130
15	66 to 67	17 to 17-5	131 to 133
16	68	17-6 to 17-11	134 to 136
17	69 and over	18 and over	137 and over

Sum of exponents	Class	Sum of exponents	Class
9 and below	A	25 to 29	E
10 to 14	B	30 to 34	F
15 to 19	C	35 to 38	G
20 to 24	D	39 and above	H

* N. P. Neilson and F. W. Cozens, *Achievement Scales in Physical Education Activities for Boys and Girls in Elementary and Junior High Schools.*   New York: A. S. Barnes & Company, Inc. 1934.

Growth and Nutritional Status Measurement

Many attempts have been made to establish standards for assessing normal growth, desirable body weight, and nutritional status. Tables are available for both sexes at different age levels. Of course, those tables which attempt to take into account differences in body structure are generally more reliable than charts based only on height. Even so, one should exercise reasonable judgment in using such tables because of their inherent limitations. The tables do not differentiate among individuals on the basis of muscular development and relative proportion of muscle and fat. For example, in one table of desirable weights for adult man, the most that a six foot man with a large frame should weigh was slightly over 180 pounds.

Nevertheless, age-height-weight tables are of value if used properly. Bogert[2] presents numerous age-height-weight charts as well as comparative descriptions of persons suffering from malnutrition and good nutrition. The descriptions include the appearance of the skin, hair, muscular development, posture, and other characteristics including sleeping habits, appetite, and disposition

The Wetzel Grid[44]

One of the most extensively used devices for plotting and evaluating growth in the last quarter century has been the Wetzel Grid. This chart and record form was developed by Wetzel on the principle that normal, healthy development proceeds in an orderly manner in keeping with an individual's natural physique. Therefore, the child serves as his own standard of comparison.

Although upon first appearance the Grid gives the impression of being complicated, it actually is quite easy to use. The validity of the Grid in detecting growth failures and nutritional disturbances has been well documented. For references see *Don't Take Growth for Granted* by Robert M. Grueninger, PHD.

Nine general body types were designated by Wetzel. These are identified on the chart by the corresponding channels A_4, A_3, A_2, A_1, M, B_1, B_2, B_3, B_4. The M channel represents the average or medium build; along with A_1 and B_1 it forms a central group of *good physical status*. Channels A_2 and A_3 represent stocky builds. The majority of A_4's are obese. Channels B_2, B_3 and B_4 reflect increasing degrees of thinness, respectively. The procedures for using the Grid are as follows:

1. The child's height and weight are recorded and then plotted, thus placing a child in a particular physique channel on the left side of the chart (panel A). The corresponding developmental level is also read off from the horizontal lines crossing the physique channels and then entered in the table. For in the example shown in Figure 5 - 1; the boy's height is 52½ inches and his weight 61 pounds, yielding a point on the border of B_1 and B_2 at level 76.
2. It should be emphasized that the first plotting reveals very little in terms of *quality of growth*. The successive plottings are of primary importance in indicating the character of growth progress. All plots should be checked for accuracy; in case of notable irregularity weight and height should be re-measured.
3. The child's developmental level is then plotted against age (panel B) e.g. level 76 at age 9.
4. The next measurement, in this instance, is six months later. Height and weight are again plotted, on the channel system and the developmental level in panel B at 9 years 6 months.

5. Subsequent plottings build up the channel and auxodrome trends. These are to be interpreted in relation to the background Grid standards of direction and speed of physical development thereby revealing the *quality of individual growth.*

6. Interpretation of a child's advancement in panel B is made by referring to the curved age schedules, or auxodromes. The standard of reference for determining whether a child is *normal, advanced, or retarded* in development is the 67 per cent auxodrome. To illustrate how this may be used, the "X" on panel B shows a child, aged 10 years at developmental level 100. This child would be considered one and one-half years advanced in development, since the standard auxodrome does not cross the 100 level until the age of 11½ years.

7. The dotted-line curves in panel B (for girls) are seen to level off sooner than the solid line (for boys). This is because of the fact that girls ordinarily mature at an earlier age.

8. Although one shouldn't expect the plotted lines to stay exactly along a particular channel or auxodrome, it has been found that healthy growth and development are remarkably precise, channelwise, as well as along an auxodrome. In the example in Figure 5 - 1 the boy's growth and development is progressing in a very satisfactory manner.

9. Any child who deviates markedly from his normal channelwise progress or from his own auxodrome should be investigated. Children in A_4 (obese) should be observed closely and children in B_2 and to the right of the 67 per cent auxodrome should be carefully watched also. In his early work with the Grid, Wetzel was able to identify 95 per cent of the children that had been rated as poor or borderline by physicians.

10. The last two columns are for estimating basal metabolism and daily caloric requirements. Although these standards were announced almost 30 years ago they, nonetheless, correspond with current NRC *recommended allowances.*

Meredith Height-Weight Chart[28]

After much study of growth records of children at various age levels, Meredith was able to construct a zone classification system for height and weight for boys and girls 4 to 18 years of age. The charts that were prepared for convenient use by the classroom teacher contain curved zones for height and weight upon which the child's growth progress can be plotted. There are five zones for height: tall, moderately tall, average, moderately short, and short. Similarly, there are five zones for weight: heavy, moderately heavy, average, moderately light, and light. The height zones are at the top of the chart and the weight zones are at the bottom.

When the height and the weight of the child are plotted at the appropriate age column, an immediate check is available to see whether the child's height and weight are in similar zones. It is normally to be expected that a child who is moderately short will be light, and a child who is tall will be heavy, and so on. When the zones are dissimilar, then it should be determined whether the child's physique accounts for the dissimilarity; for example, if the child is naturally tall and slender or short and stocky, etc. If this is not the case, then further examination is made for possible health problems such as malnutrition, obesity, and illness. Moreover, as successive plottings are made, growth patterns can be observed. It is expected that a child's height and weight will essentially parallel one another in that they will proceed along their same zones. Any marked deviation from one zone to another is usually cause for referral.

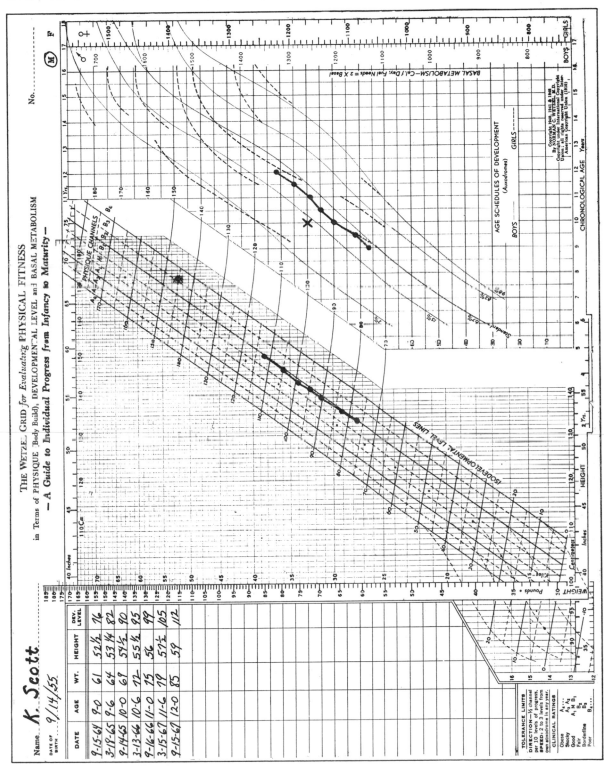

FIGURE 5 - 1. The Wetzel Grid (Courtesy of Normal C. Wetzel, M.D. and NEA Service, Inc.,

The ACH Index[14]

The ACH Index was developed as a means for screening children in the elementary grades (ages 7 to 12) in need of referral for medical examination with regard to nutritional status. Franzen and Palmer reported that over 10,000 school children had been involved in determining the most significant anthropometric measures for assessing the amount of soft tissue in relation to skeletal build.

Seven measures were selected: hip width, chest depth, chest width, height, weight, arm girth, and subcutaneous tissue over the biceps muscle. It was recognized that these measurements are quite time-consuming and require considerable skill. Consequently, a shorter battery was selected from these measures that could be used effectively for screening purposes. These measures are (1) arm girth, (2) chest depth, and (3) hip width.

Franzen and Palmer recommended that the Index be used in either of two ways. It could be employed to screen one-fourth of the children for further measurement. These children would then be given the rest of the seven measures. In this manner the authors report that 90 per cent of the children would be selected that would have been identified by giving all seven measures to the entire group of children. Another way of using the ACH Index is to set the standards so that a tenth of the group is selected for further measurement. Although some extreme cases may be missed, Franzen and Palmer maintain that it is superior to the age-height-weight method, and the speed and simplicity of the measurements justify this system for use in the school situation. The measurement procedures are as follows:

Arm Girth

1. The child flexes his dominant arm. A skin pencil is used to mark the highest point on the biceps.
2. The child flexes so that the tips of the fingers are touching the shoulder. The girth of the arm at the marked site is measured by a gulick tape to the nearest tenth of a centimeter. In measuring this girth, as in any girth measure, the tape is pulled tight enough so that it is smooth but not producing an indentation in the skin. The tape is crossed to get the point of reading.
3. The child relaxes his arm, letting it hang by the side of his body, and the girth is again measured and recorded.

Chest Depth

1. A wooden caliper is placed firmly against the chest and back at a point just above the nipple line and just below the angle of the scapula, respectively.
2. Two measures are taken: after normal inspiration, and after normal expiration.
3. The measurement is to the nearest tenth of a centimeter.

Hip Width

1. The wooden caliper is pressed against the widest part of the hips at the greater trochanters.
2. The measurement is read to the nearest tenth of a centimeter.

Scoring

1. The two arm-girth measures are added, and this figure is subtracted from the total of the two chest-depth measures.
2. From Table 5 - 3 the child's hip width is located, and the corresponding minimum difference between arm-girth and chest-depth is found.
3. If the measured difference is equal or less than the figure in the table, the child is referred for further examination.

TABLE 5 - 3

The Ach Index of Nutritional Status*
(ages 7-12)

Boys		Girls	
Width of Hips	Minimum Difference between Arm Girth and Chest Depth	Width of Hips	Minimum Difference between Arm Girth and Chest Depth
Below 20.0	0.0	Below 20.0	.5
20.0-20.4	0.0	20.0-20.4	1.0
20.5-20.9	.4	20.5-20.9	1.6
21.0-21.4	1.0	21.0-21.4	2.1
21.5-21.9	1.6	21.5-21.9	2.6
22.0-22.4	2.2	22.0-22.4	3.0
22.5-22.9	2.7	22.5-22.9	3.4
23.0-23.4	3.3	23.0-23.4	3.8
23.5-23.9	3.8	23.5-23.9	4.2
24.0-24.4	4.2	24.0-24.4	4.5
24.5-24.9	4.7	24.5-24.9	4.8
25.0-25.4	5.1	25.0-25.4	5.1
25.5-25.9	5.6	25.5-25.9	5.4
26.0-26.4	6.0	26.0-26.4	5.6
26.5-26.9	6.3	26.5-26.9	5.8
27.0-27.4	6.7	27.0-27.4	6.0
27.5-27.9	7.0	27.5-27.9	6.1
28.0-28.4	7.3	28.0-28.4	6.2
28.5-28.9	7.6	28.5-28.9	6.3
29.0 over	7.9	29.0 over	6.4

Pryor Width-Weight Tables[35]

Pryor developed weight tables based on chest and hip widths in addition to height, age, and sex. In this way an attempt was made to take into account differences in body structure. After extensive study with different anthropometric measurements on boys and girls over a period of years, Pryor found the width of the iliac crest to be the most important and least variable measurement.

* Raymond Franzen and George Palmer: The *ACH Index of Nutritional Status*. New York, American Child Health Association, 1934.

Tables have been prepared for each sex for ages one through forty. The subject's age is recorded to the nearest year. The subject's weight and height are measured to the nearest pound and inch, respectively. Calipers are used for the hip and chest width measures. These calipers can be easily made by taking a meter stick and making and attaching wooden arms to slide along the stick. The hip width is measured with the calipers pressed firmly against the iliac crest; the chest width is measured with the calipers held against the chest at the level of the nipples with no pressure applied. Both measures are to the nearest tenth of a centimeter.

There are three sets of tables for the different sex and age levels depending upon whether the subject's chest is found to be classified as narrow, medium, or broad. Using the appropriate set of tables, the proper weight can be determined according to the subject's height and hip width. While these tables have been considered to be a definite improvement over the conventional age-height-weight tables, they still do not adequately allow for variations in physique and muscle-fat distribution. The tables should probably be revised. Hamilton[18] observed that many of the junior high school girls in her study classified as overweight or underweight by the Pryor tables did not give this appearance. The fact that children are taller and heavier at an earlier age today may account for this observation, since the tables were developed approximately thirty years ago.

Body Build Classification (Somatotyping)

The association of certain body builds with personality and behavior patterns, health problems, and physical performance has long been recognized. Most of us have rather stereotyped notions of what the typical fat person is like, the skinny person, and the person who is *all muscle.* This concept that a man behaves as he does because of what he is represents the foundation of somatotyping.[45]

William H. Sheldon is without doubt the foremost name in the field of somatotyping. He, in turn, was influenced by the work of Kretschmer and others before him. Sheldon and his co-workers[38] concluded that while there are three basic body types, people have varying amounts or degrees of all three. The three primary components are called endomorphy, mesomorphy, and ectomorphy.

Endomorphy is characterized by roundness of body parts with concentration in the center. This is the pear-shaped individual with a large abdomen, round head, short neck, narrow shoulders, fatty breasts, short arms, wide hips, heavy buttocks and short, heavy legs.

Mesomorphy is evidenced by rugged musculature and large bones. The mesomorph has prominent facial bones, a rather long but muscular neck, wide sloping shoulders, muscular arms and forearms, broad chest, heavily muscled abdomen, low waist and narrow hips, muscular buttocks, and powerful legs.

Ectomorphy is characterized by small bones, with linearity and fragility predominating. The ectomorph has a large forehead, small facial bones, a long skinny neck, narrow chest, round shoulder with winged scapulae, long slender arms, flat abdomen, inconspicuous buttocks, and long, thin legs.

In determining the body build classification, or somatotype, the individual is scaled from 1 to 7 in each component. The somatotype is thus given in a three-number sequence in which the first number represents the endomorphic component; the second, mesomorphy, and the third, ectomorphy. An extreme endomorph would be classified as a 7-1-1; an extreme mesomorph is a 1-7-1; and an extreme ectomorph is a 1-1-7.

Most people are dominated by two components. The lesser of the two is usually employed as the adjective in describing the somatotype. For example, a 2-6-4 would be described as an ectomorphic mesomorph, and a 5-4-2 would be a mesomorphic endomorph, etc.

Accurate somatotyping for research purposes requires a great amount of training and practice. The specifications and instructions for taking the photographs and the steps and procedures in the somatotyping process are given in detail in Sheldon's *Atlas of Men*.[37] Briefly, they are as follows: The subject is photographed, preferably in the nude, from three views — front, side, and back. In order to minimize any changes in body position a revolving pedestal is used. The subject's height and weight are carefully measured, and the ponderal index is then determined. The ponderal index is the height divided by the cube root of weight ($Ht./\sqrt[3]{wt.}$). It is the maximal achieved mass over surface area; in other words, it indicates the person's position in relation to ectomorphy. The higher the ponderal index, the more the subject tends toward ectomorphy. A table is consulted showing the possible somatotypes for the obtained ponderal index, and photographs are used for comparative reference.

Recently, Sheldon has refined the somatotyping process by making it more objective through the computation of a trunk index. A planimeter is utilized to measure the abdominal and thoracic trunk area on the photograph. Tables have been developed in which the combination of ponderal index, trunk index, and height enable the researcher to accurately identify the subject's somatotype. These tables have not yet been incorporated into the *Atlas*.

Simplified Somatotype Assessment

Willgoose.[45] presents a rather comprehensive discussion of somatotyping, its implications, and applications. In his discussion he suggests a method of somatotyping that, while not meant to be as accurate as Sheldon's process, has more practical application for the physical education teacher.

The teacher rates the subject on the primary component on the 1 to 7 scale. Next, he rates the secondary and then the third components in the same manner. The ponderal index is calculated by using the nomograph shown in Figure 5 - 2. In using the nomograph the teacher places a ruler on the scale so that it connects the subject's height and weight. The point at which the ruler intersects the middle column is the ponderal index.

The teacher may then consult Sheldon's *Atlas of Men* and study the charts of possible somatotypes given for the particular ponderal index. The final step is to refer to the many pictures of somatotypes and confirm the somatotype classification. Willgoose maintains that even without the *Atlas* or the ponderal index one can estimate somatotypes accurately enough for use in the school situation.

This prompts an obvious question — of what practical value is somatotyping to the physical education teacher? The answer may not be so obvious. First of all, it would not be practical to consume blocks of class time for the sole purpose of somatotyping students. On the other hand it can be done quite efficiently on a scheduled individual-observation basis. What we are referring to here is a plan in which the teacher makes it a point to observe a particular student(s) each day. Through careful observation the teacher is able to gain valuable information about each student as to his motor performance, his strengths and weaknesses, and his social adjustment and personality, as well as his posture

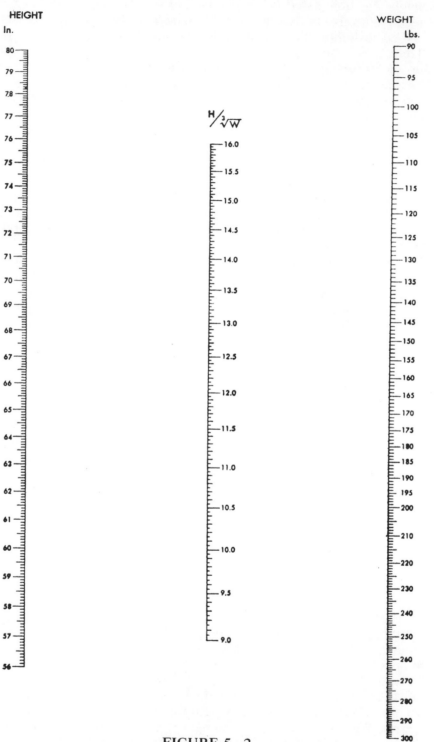

FIGURE 5 - 2

Nomograph for Ponderal Index[45]

and his somatotype. This, of course, is not meant to sound like a one-shot proposition. It would be continuous throughout the year, thereby affording the teacher an opportunity to observe each student in various situations. The main advantage of such a plan is that it insures that the teacher will consciously study every person in the class, rather than just noticing the loud ones, the students who misbehave, and the good and the bad performers.

Thus, the real value of somatotyping lies in its contribution toward a better understanding of the individual. Better understanding in turn enables the teacher to better meet the needs of each student. The mesomorph's energetic need for physical exercise, excitement, and adventure; the endomorph's inclination toward social activities and relaxing recreational games; and the ectomorph's tendency to shy away from team sports and group activities, all present a challenge to the physical educator. The discerning teacher who is able to anticipate the sensitivity of the ectomorph and the endomorph in situations where their physiques and poor physical abilities are apt to evoke ridicule, can make a great contribution toward making friends instead of enemies for physical education.

The physical educator and the coach can effectively utilize a knowledge of somato-typing along with physical performance measures in predicting potential athletic ability. Since most people are mixtures rather than extremes in a single component, the teacher and coach who are skilled in identifying body structure characteristics will be most likely successful in predicting abilities and channeling students into activities best suited for their needs, interests, and capabilities.

Problems Associated with Height and Weight Measurement and Body Build Classification

Undoubtedly, the major problem in the area of height and weight and body type classification systems is not in their use, but rather in their misuse. One only has to look around and it becomes evident that people come in all shapes and sizes. Some individuals seem to be all legs with very small trunk and arms. Others have massive shoulders, arms, and chest and almost puny legs. Still others appear to be evenly proportioned. To judge them all on the same standard, as for example, to decide whether each is overweight or underweight on the basis of a single factor such as height, is indeed ludicrous.

Growth charts such as the Wetzel Grid and the Meredith graphs can be valuable tools if employed wisely. Obviously, one must recognize that there are wide differences among individuals in height, weight, and body build that are still within the limits of normal growth and maturation. The real value of these devices lies in the recommended emphasis that should be placed on changes in growth patterns detected by the successive plottings. The other recommended feature about these charts is that the child should be evaluated in relation to his own growth pattern rather than be compared favorably or unfavorably with someone else, or by some arbitrary standard.

A major criticism of age-height-weight tables is that even though some allow for differences in body framework, they do not account for differences in proportion of muscle, fat, and bone. Some attempts have been made to account for these differences, such as by using the ACH Index, the weight formula developed by Cureton[10] and studies in which the specific gravity of the body is calculated in determining body composition.[4] However, specific gravity poses another problem with regard to the reliability of skinfold and girth measurements, and certainly in terms of the amount of time required to obtain accurate measurements.

Among the various measures that have been taken and used to indicate nutritional status are chest width, chest depth, chest circumference, bi-iliac hip width, trochanteric hip width, shoulder width, knee width, thigh girth, upper and lower arm girths, wrist girth, and ankle and calf girths. Fat measures are frequently taken at the abdomen, the side, the chest, the back, and the thighs. The length of the body and body segments have been measured to determine standing height, lying height, sitting height, arm length, arm span, leg length, forearm length, hand width and finger span. There are numerous other anthropometric measurements that have been studied. It is to be recalled that Sargent's profile chart for appraising the physical development of college men contained forty-four anthropometric measurements.

Anthropometry is a science requiring much knowledge and skill, and especially practice. It is this fact that poses the biggest problem for the use of such measurements by the physical educator. Even in laboratory situations researchers have trouble obtaining repeatable readings. The use of a flesh marking pencil is of considerable value in taking successive measurements within a short period of time. But when measurements are taken days, weeks, or months later, the location of the exact body site must be repeated all over again. Even a difference of several hours can affect nearly all such measurements due to diurnal variation in hydration, etc.

The basic purpose of classification indices is to allow for more equal competition. They are founded on the premise that older, taller, and heavier children should be stronger and more physically mature than children who are smaller and younger. While this is generally true, it should be obvious that these indices are not infallible. Here again body build is an important factor. An endomorph would surely not be an *equal* for a mesomorph of the same age, height, and weight. Wear and Miller[42] suggested that students of excess weight usually are doubly penalized in physical performance tests. First, they must perform while carrying the excess weight, and secondly, his classification index is higher than a lighter student of comparable age and height. Therefore, he has to do more in order to achieve a similar percentile rank. Perhaps this may serve to stimulate the student to shed excess pounds. On the other hand it may have negative motivational effects insofar as making his task seem almost hopeless.

A Brief Summary of Research Findings
Concerning Age, Height, Weight, and Body Type

Kistler[21] reported a correlation of .81 between McCloy's Classification Index and selected track and field events. A lower relationship (r = .57) was obtained between certain sports skills and the McCloy Index. In separate studies Miller found both the Wetzel Grid[29] and the Neilson and Cozens Index[30] to effectively equate college men according to body size.

Wear and Miller[42] studied the relationship of physique and developmental level, as determined by the Wetzel Grid, to performance in fitness tests of junior high school boys. They found subjects who were medium in physique and normal in development to be the best performers, and the subjects of heavy physiques to be the poorest in performance. Bookwalter and others[3], utilizing the Wetzel Grid, also found the obese to be the poorest performers among the elementary school boys, whereas the thin boys of average size out-performed those boys of medium physique. With high school boys as subjects Bartell[1] found those subjects classified by the Wetzel Grid as having medium builds to perform better than the slender and obese subjects in McCloy's General Motor Capacity, General Motor Ability, and Motor Quotient tests.

In the Medford Growth Study, Clarke and other investigators have utilized the Wetzel Grid as one of the many measures used in this longitudinal study. Clarke and Petersen[9] compared athletes with non-athletes in elementary and junior high school boys as to Wetzel physique channel ratings and found no significant differences. Weinberg[43] obtained significant correlations between Wetzel physique channels and anthropometric and strength tests. He also found a high relationship between Wetzel's developmental level and weight.

Solley[40] was unable to find significant differences among boys classified by the Wetzel developmental ratio as accelerated, average, and retarded with regard to coordination tests. In another study Solley[41] observed that the physiques of children in grades 1-8 undergo many changes over a five year period. More variability was evident as grade level increased.

Gross and Casciani[17] utilized data from over 13,000 students to determine the value of age, height, and weight as a classification device for the AAHPER Youth Fitness test. They reported that in all four groups — senior high school girls, junior high school girls, senior high school boys, and junior high school boys — the factors of age, height, and weight had practically no value, singly or in combination, as classifiers for the seven test items. In other words each group could be considered as a homogeneous group with respect to the effects of these factors on the fitness measures. Pierson and O'Connell[33] reported that grip strength of college men, college athletes, recruit policemen, and policemen was significantly related to body weight, but not to height or age. Espenschade[13] investigated the relationships of age, height, and weight to the performances of boys and girls on performance tests. Low correlations were found between performances and height and weight when age was held constant. The author recommended the use of age alone as a basis for the development of test norms.

Somatotype ratings and anthropometric measurements were studied by Hebbelinck and Postma[19] as to their relationship to performances on motor fitness tests. Generally, the correlations between body measurements and motor performance were low. The subjects classified as mesomorphs were superior in all motor fitness tests except the 60 yard dash, and the ecto-mesomorphs excelled the endo-mesomorphs except in the shot put event. Garrity,[15] in a study involving college women, found a general tendency for the subjects classified as mesomorphic ectomorphs to perform in a more efficient manner on physical fitness tests. The ectomorph-endomorph group was consistently low in all test items.

Laubach and McConville[23] reported low correlations between flexibility and anthropometric measurements and between somatotype and flexibility. A high, negative relationship was obtained between body fat and flexibility. Somatotype components were found to correlate highly with the anthropometric measurements employed in the study. In a later study the same authors reported many significant correlations between strength and anthropometric measurements. The only somatotype component found to correlate significantly with muscle strength was mesomorphy[24].

Piscopo[34] established norms and compared skinfold and other measurements of 647 Italian, Jewish, and Negro preadolescent boys. Some of the following results were revealed: (1) the largest skinfold measurements and upper arm girth, thigh girth, and bi-iliac diameter measurements were found within the Jewish group, followed by the Italian and Negro groups, respectively; thigh girth approximately doubled upper arm girth measurements in all three groups; high correlations were found between skinfold sites within each group; high correlations were found between skinfold and weight, but low correlations were found between skinfold and height. Lane and Mitchem[22] reported anthropometric differences between Negro and white male university students and found the Negro group to have less buoyancy than the white subjects. In another study pertaining to buoyancy Howell and others[20] obtained significant correlation between all buoyancy measures and specific gravity, and between buoyancy measures and body fat.

Dempsey[11] subjected a small group of obese and non-obese men to a vigorous exercise program. He observed that overweight subjects experienced significant losses of body weight, body fat, and an increase in muscular mass. Neither fat nor weight loss, however, was dependent upon the initial degree of obesity. In another study Dempsey[12] employed a multiple regression analysis of height, weight, and body fat data on treadmill performance. He found body fat, fat-free body weight, and relative weight to account for a significant amount of the total variance in step test performance. Burt and others[5] did not find a significant relationship between recalcified plasma clotting times and any of the following variables: physical fitness, body fat, age, height, or weight.

Malina and Johnston[27] studied age, sex, and maturity differences in the composition of the upper arm. They found fat in the upper arm to be the best predictor of weight in both sexes. Sex differences in the composition of the upper arm were found to arise essentially at adolescence due to the loss of fat in boys. Gordon[16] developed and validated an instrument designed to assess muscle firmness or tone. The instrument, called a myotonometer, was found to be reliable, and it differentiated between normal and flaccid muscles.

Studies utilizing x-ray to determine skeletal maturity have been reported from time to time in the literature. Especially prominent have been those studies conducted as a part of the Medford Growth Study. Clarke and Harrison[8] found the more physically mature group to have a higher mean in all cases where differences in physical and motor traits were significant. A greater difference was observed between mean body weights at all ages than for any other test variable. The greatest differences between means were found at 15, 12, and 9 years of age, in that order. Clarke and Degutis[7] compared skeletal ages and selected physical and motor measures with the pubescent development of 10, 13, and 16 year old boys. Physical maturation was most effectively differentiated by pubescent assessment at 13 years of age, but it was not as sensitive as was skeletal age. Rarick and Oyster[36] found skeletal maturity to be of little consequence in explaining individual differences in strength and motor proficiency of second grade boys. Of the four physical maturity indicators utilized, chronological age was the most important with regard to variance in strength scores.

Mitchem and Arsenault[31] reviewed the studies reported in the *Research Quarterly* from 1940 to 1960 for the purpose of evaluating the techniques, the anatomical sites, and the instruments used in taking anthropometric measurements. They concluded that there was a definite need for standardization in this area. Furthermore, they recommended that a standardized anthropometric methodology should be established by the profession, that this methodology be published and then followed by regional workshops.

BIBLIOGRAPHY

1. Bartell, Joseph A., "A Comparison Between Body Build and Body Size with Respect to Certain Sociophysical Factors Among High School Boys," (Microcarded Doctoral Dissertation, University of Pittsburgh, 1952).

2. Bogert, L. Jean, *Nutrition and Physical Fitness,* 6th ed., Philadelphia: W. B. Saunders Co., 1954; 8th ed., 1966.

3. Bookwalter, Karl W., and others, "The Relationship of Body Size and Shape to Physical Performance," *Research Quarterly,* 23:271-279, October, 1952.

4. Brozek, J., and A. Keys, "The Evaluation of Leanness-Fitness in Man: Norms and Interrelationships." *British Journal of Nutrition,* 5:194-206, 1951.

5. Burt, John J., Carl S. Blyth, and Herman Rierson, "Body Fat, Blood Coagulation Time, and the Harvard Step Test Recovery Index," *Research Quarterly,* 33:339-342, October, 1962.

6. Clarke, H. Harrison, *Application of Measurement to Health and Physical Education,* 4th ed., Englewood Cliffs, New Jersey: Prentice-Hall Inc., 1967. p. 79.

7. _____ , and Ernest W. Degutis, "Comparison of Skeletal Age and Various Physical and Motor Factors with the Pubescent Development of 10, 13, and 16 Year Old Boys," *Research Quarterly,* 33:356-368, October, 1962.

8. _____ , and James C. E. Harrison, "Differences in Physical and Motor Traits Between Boys of Advanced, Normal, and Retarded Maturity, *Research Quarterly,* 33:13-25, March, 1962.

9. _____ , and Kay H. Petersen, "Contrast of Maturational, Structural, and Strength Characteristics of Athletes and Nonathletes 10 to 15 Years of Age," *Research Quarterly,* 32:163-176, May, 1961.

10. Cureton, Thomas K., *Physical Fitness Appraisal and Guidance,* St. Louis: The C. V. Mosby Co., 1947, Chapter 5.

11. Dempsey, Jerry A., "Anthropometrical Observations on Obese and Nonobese Young Men Undergoing a Program of Vigorous Physical Exercise," *Research Quarterly,* 35:275-287, October, 1964.

12. _____ , "Relationship Between Obesity and Treadmill Performance in Sedentary and Active Young Men," *Research Quarterly,* 35:288-297, October, 1964.

13. Espenschade, Anna S., "Restudy of Relationships Between Physical Performances of School Children and Age, Height, and Weight," *Research Quarterly,* 34:144-153, May, 1963.

14. Franzen, Raymond, and George Palmer, *The ACH Index of Nutritional Status,* New York: American Child Health Association, 1934.

15. Garrity, H. Marie, "Relationship of Somatotypes of College Women to Physical Fitness Performance," *Research Quarterly,* 37:340-352, October, 1966.

16. Gordon, Alan H., "A Method to Measure Muscle Firmness or Tone," *Research Quarterly,* 35:482-490, December, 1964.

17. Gross, Elmer A., and Jerome A. Casciani, "Value of Age, Height, and Weight as a Classification Device for Secondary School Students in the Seven AAHPER Youth Fitness Tests," *Research Quarterly,* 33:51-58, March, 1962.

18. Hamilton, Xandra L., "The Effects of Isometric and Isotonic Endurance Exercises on the Development of Cardiovascular Efficiency of Eighth Grade Girls Classified According to Initial Cardiovascular Efficiency and Weight," (Unpublished Doctoral Dissertation, Louisiana State University, 1966).

19. Hebbelinck, Marcel, and Johan W. Postma, "Anthropometric Measurements, Somatotype Ratings, and Certain Motor Fitness Tests of Physical Education Majors in South Africa," *Research Quarterly,* 34:327-334, October, 1963.

20. Howell, Maxwell L., J. Moncrieff, and W. R. Morford, "Relationship between Human Buoyancy Measures, Specific Gravity, and Estimated Body Fat in Adult Males," *Research Quarterly,* 33:400-404, October, 1962.

21. Kistler, Joy W., "A Comparative Study of Methods for Classifying Pupils," *Research Quarterly,* 5:42-48, March, 1934.

22. Lane, Elizabeth C., and John C. Mitchem, "Buoyancy as Predicted by Certain Anthropometric Measurements," *Research Quarterly,* 35:21-28, March, 1964.

23. Lauback, Lloyd L., and John T. McConville, "Relationships between Flexibility, Anthropometry, and the Somatotype of College Men," *Research Quarterly,* 37:241-251, May, 1966.

24. _____ , "Muscle Strength, Flexibility, and Body Size of Adult Males," *Research Quarterly,* 37:384-392, October, 1966.

25. McCloy, C. H., *The Measurement of Athletic Power.* New York: A. S. Barnes & Co., 1932.

26. _____, and Norma D. Young. *Tests and Measurements in Health and Physical Education,* 3rd ed., New York: Appleton-Century-Crofts, Inc., 1954, p. 59.

27. Malina, Robert M., and Francis E. Johnston, "Significance of Age, Sex, and Maturity Differences in Upper Arm Composition," *Research Quarterly,* 38:219-230, May, 1967.

28. Meredith, Howard V., "A Physical Growth Record for Use in Elementary and High Schools," *American Journal of Public Health,* 39:878-885, July, 1949.

29. Miller, Kenneth D., "The Wetzel Grid as a Performance Classifier with College Men," *Research Quarterly,* 22:63-70, March, 1951.

30. _____ , "A Critique on the Use of Height-Weight Factors in the Performance Classification of College Men," *Research Quarterly,* 23:402-416, December, 1952.

31. Mitchem, John C., and Barbara Kay Arsenault, "An Evaluation of Anthropometric Studies Appearing in the *Research Quarterly* from 1940-1960," *Research Quarterly,* 37:438-439, October, 1966.

32. Neilson, N. P., and Frederick W. Cozens, *Achievement Scales in Physical Education Activities for Boys and Girls in Elementary and Junior High Schools.* New York: A. S. Barnes & Co., Inc., 1934.

33. Pierson, William R., and Eugene R. O'Connell, "Age, Height, Weight, and Grip Strength," *Research Quarterly,* 33:439-443, October, 1962.

34. Piscopo, John, "Skinfold and Other Anthropometrical Measurements of Preadolescent Boys from Three Ethnic Groups," *Research Quarterly,* 33:255-264, May, 1962.

35. Pryor, Helen B., *Width-Weight Tables,* Stanford University, California: Stanford University Press, 1940.

36. Rarick, G. Lawrence, and Nancy Oyster, "Physical Maturity, Muscular Strength, and Motor Performance of Young School-Age Boys," *Research Quarterly,* 35:522-531, December, 1964.

37. Sheldon, William H., *Atlas of Men.* New York: Harper & Brothers, 1954.

38. _____ , S. S. Stevens, and W. B. Tucker, *The Varieties of Human Physique,* New York: Harper & Brothers, 1940.

39. Smithells, Philip A., and Peter E. Cameron, *Principles of Evaluation in Physical Education,* New York: Harper & Brothers, Publishers, 1962.

40. Solley, William H., "Ratio of Physical Development as a Factor in Motor Co-ordination of Boys Ages 10-14," *Research Quarterly,* 28:295-304, October, 1957.

41. _____ , "Status of Physique, Changes in Physique, and Speed in the Growth Patterns of School Children, Grades 1-8," *Research Quarterly,* 30:465-478, December, 1959.

42. Wear, C. L., and Kenneth Miller, "Relationship of Physique and Developmental Level to Physical Performance," *Research Quarterly,* 33:615-631, December, 1962.

43. Weinberg, Herbert A., "Structural, Strength and Maturity Characteristics as Related to Aspects of the Wetzel Grid for Boys Nine Through Fifteen Years of Age," (Microcarded Doctoral Dissertation, University of Oregon, 1964).

44. Wetzel, Norman C., *The Treatment of Growth Failure in Children,* Cleveland, NEA Service, Inc., 1948.

45. Willgoose, Carl E., *Evaluation in Health Education and Physical Education,* New York: McGraw-Hill Book Company, Inc., 1961, Chapter 13.

Chapter VI

THE MEASUREMENT OF POWER

Power may be identified as the ability to release maximum force in the fastest possible time, as is exemplified in the vertical jump, the broad jump, the shot put, and other movements against a resistance in a minimum of time.

The measurement of power in physical education has recently become controversial enough to warrant recognition of two types of such measurement. The two types are identified as follows:

Athletic Power Measurement. This type of measurement is expressed in terms of the distance through which the body or an object is propelled through space. Such tests as the Sargent jump, broad jump, and medicine ball put are both practical and common tests of athletic power. While such tests involve both force and velocity, other factors also influence testing results. However, the factors of force and velocity are not measured as such; thus, only the resultant distance (inches or feet) is recorded in athletic power measurement.

Work-Power Measurement. In measuring power for research purposes, special efforts are usually made to eliminate extraneous movements, thus placing maximum effort on the specific muscle group to be studied. Then the result is usually based on computations of work (force × distance) or power (work/time). Examples of this type of measurement are vertical power jump,[26] power lever, [29] modified vertical power jump (work),[26] and the vertical arm pull (work).[35]

Athletic power tests are quite practical for the majority of schools and have been widely used in physical fitness and motor ability testing programs. New tests, the modified vertical power jump (work) and the vertical arm pull (work), have also been developed for practical use in physical education programs and for research. Because power includes the important factors of strength and speed of movement, it may become confused with those types of tests. However, strength tests are concerned only with the force exerted or the number of pounds successfully lifted, and speed tests are concerned with the amount of time taken to cover a specified distance or the distance covered in a specified amount of time. In power tests the distance, force, and time factors should be specified while the resistance is usually either body weight or a specified number of pounds. The sixty yard dash, which has been used as a test of power, has caused confusion on this point. However, since this test is more characteristic of speed, the authors do not consider it as an adequate test of power.

Uses of Power Tests

Several ways by which power tests are utilized in physical education classes are listed as follows:
1. As a factor in physical fitness and motor ability tests.
2. As a means to motivate students to improve their status within the class.
3. As a measure for determining achievement and grades when improvement in athletic power is a specific objective in a physical activity class.
4. As a means to indicate an individual's potential for varsity athletics.

Practical Tests of Athletic Power

Several practical tests of athletic power in terms of time, equipment, and cost are presented on the following pages:

Vertical Jump (Sargent Chalk Jump)[17]

Objective: To measure the power of the legs in jumping vertically upward.

Age Level: Satisfactory for ages 9 through adulthood.

Sex: Satisfactory for both boys and girls.

Reliability: Has been reported as high as .93.

Validity: A validity of .78 has been reported with the criterion of a sum of 4 track and field event scores.

Equipment and Materials: A yardstick, several pieces of chalk, and a smooth wall surface of at least 12 feet from the floor are required.

Directions: The performer should stand with one side toward a wall, heels together, and hold a one inch piece of chalk in the hand nearest to the wall. Keeping the heels on the floor, he should reach upward as high as possible and make a mark on the wall. The performer then jumps as high as possible and makes another mark at the height of his jump.

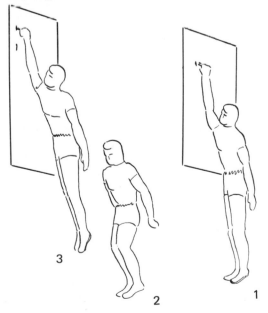

FIGURE 6 - 1 Vertical Jump Test

<u>Scoring</u>: The number of inches between the reach and the jump marks measured to the nearest half of an inch is the score. Three to five trials are allowed and the best trial is recorded as the score.

<u>Additional Pointers</u>: (1) A double jump or a "crow hop" should not be permitted upon take-off. (2) The chalk should not be extended any further than necessary beyond the finger tips to make the standing and jumping marks. (3) The reliability and validity of the test can be slightly improved if the performer practices the jump until it is correctly executed before being tested.

TABLE 6 - 1[49]

Vertical Jump Scoring Table*

	100	90	80	70	60	50	40	30	20	10	0
Boys and Girls 9-10-11	16	15	14	12	11	10	9	7	4	2	0
Boys 12-13-14	20	18	17	16	14	13	11	9	5	2	0
Girls 12-13-14	16	15	14	13	12	11	10	8	4	2	0
Boys 15-17	25	24	23	21	19	16	12	8	5	2	0
Girls 15-17	17	16	15	14	13	11	8	6	3	2	0
Men 18-34	26	25	24	23	19	16	13	9	8	2	0
Women 18-34	14	13	13	12	10	8	6	4	2	1	0

Source: Harold T. Friermood, "Volleyball Skills Contest for Olympic Development," Berne, Indiana: *The 1967 Annual Official Volleyball Rules and Reference Guide of the U.S. Volleyball Association*, pp. 134-135.

* Raw scores are located in the chart in accordance with age and sex, and percentile scores are located across the top.

Standing Broad Jump[1]

Objective: To measure the athletic power of the legs in jumping forward.

Age Level: Ages 10 through college.

Sex: Satisfactory for both boys and girls.

Reliability: Has been reported as high as .963.

Validity: A validity of .607 has been reported for this test when a pure power test was used as the criterion.

Equipment and Materials: Either a mat or the floor may be used for this test. Marking material (tape or chalk) is needed for the starting line along with a tape measure to mark off increments of distance along the landing area.

Directions: With the feet parallel to each other and behind the starting mark, the performer bends the knees and swings the arms and jumps as far forward as possible.

Scoring: The number of inches between the starting line and the nearest heel upon landing is the score. Three trials are permitted, and then the best trial is recorded as the score.

Additional Pointers: (1) If the performer falls backwards upon landing, the measurement is made between the starting line and the nearest part of the body touching the landing surface. (2) The jump should be practiced until the movement can be executed correctly, since validity and reliability can be improved thereby.

3   2   1

FIGURE 6 - 2

Standing Broad Jump

TABLE 6 - 2A

Standing Broad Jump for Boys[1]

Percentile Scores Based on Age/Test Scores in Feet and Inches

Percentile	Age								
	10	11	12	13	14	15	16	17	coll.
100th	5' 8"	10' 0"	7'10"	8' 9"	8'11"	9' 2"	9' 1"	9' 8"	9' 6"
95th	6' 1"	6' 3"	6' 6"	7' 2"	7' 9"	8' 0"	8' 5"	8' 6"	8' 5"
90th	5'10"	6' 0"	6' 4"	6'11"	7' 5"	7' 9"	8' 1"	8' 3"	8' 2"
85th	5' 8"	5'10"	6' 9"	6' 9"	7' 3"	7' 6"	7'11"	8' 1"	7'11"
80th	5' 7"	5' 9"	6' 1"	6' 7"	7' 0"	7' 6"	7' 9"	8' 0"	7'10"
75th	5' 6"	5' 7"	6' 0"	6' 5"	6'11"	7' 4"	7' 7"	7'10"	7' 8"
70th	5' 5"	5' 6"	5'11"	6' 3"	6' 9"	7' 2"	7' 6"	7' 8"	7' 7"
65th	5' 4"	5' 6"	5' 9"	6' 1"	6' 8"	7' 1"	7' 5"	7' 7"	7' 6"
60th	5' 2"	5' 4"	5' 8"	6' 0"	6' 7"	7' 0"	7' 4"	7' 6"	7' 5"
55th	5' 1"	5' 3"	5' 7"	5'11"	6' 6"	6'11"	7' 3"	7' 5"	7' 4"
50th	5' 0"	5' 2"	5' 6"	5'10"	6' 4"	6' 9"	7' 1"	7' 3"	7' 3"
45th	5' 0"	5' 1"	5' 5"	5' 9"	6' 3"	6' 8"	7' 0"	7' 2"	7' 1"
40th	4'10"	5' 0"	5' 4"	5' 7"	6' 1"	6' 6"	6'11"	7' 0"	7' 0"
35th	4'10"	4'11"	5' 2"	5' 6"	6' 0"	6' 6"	6' 9"	6'11"	6'11"
30th	4' 8"	4'10"	5' 1"	5' 5"	5'10"	6' 4"	6' 7"	6'10"	6'10"
25th	4' 6"	4' 8"	5' 0"	5' 3"	5' 8"	6' 3"	6' 6"	6' 8"	6' 9"
20th	4' 5"	4' 7"	4'10"	5' 2"	5' 6"	6' 1"	6' 4"	6' 6"	6' 7"
15th	4' 4"	4' 5"	4' 8"	5' 0"	5' 4"	5'10"	6' 1"	6' 4"	6' 5"
10th	4' 3"	4' 2"	4' 5"	4' 9"	5' 2"	5' 7"	5'11"	6' 0"	6' 2"
5th	4' 0"	4' 0"	4' 2"	4' 5"	4'11"	5' 4"	5' 6"	5' 8"	5'10"
0	2'10"	1' 8"	3' 0"	2' 9"	3' 8"	2'10"	2' 2"	3' 7"	4' 2"

Source: AAHPER, Youth Fitness Test Manual, Revised, Washington, D.C., 1966, pp. 37, 65.

TABLE 6 - 2B

Standing Broad Jump for Girls[1]

Percentile Scores Based on Age/Test Scores in Feet and Inches

Percentile	Age								
	10	11	12	13	14	15	16	17	coll.
100th	7' 0''	7'10''	8' 2''	7' 6''	7' 4''	7' 8''	7' 5''	7' 8''	7'10''
95th	5' 8''	6' 2''	6' 3''	6' 3''	6' 4''	6' 6''	6' 7''	6' 8''	6' 6''
90th	5' 6''	5'10''	6' 0''	6' 0''	6' 2''	6' 3''	6' 4''	6' 4''	6' 3''
85th	5' 4''	5' 8''	5' 9''	5'10''	6' 0''	6' 1''	6' 2''	6' 2''	6' 1''
80th	5' 2''	5' 6''	5' 8''	5' 8''	5'10''	6' 0''	6' 0''	6' 0''	5'11''
75th	5' 1''	5' 4''	5' 6''	5' 6''	5' 9''	5'10''	5'10''	5'11''	5'10''
70th	5' 0''	5' 3''	5' 5''	5' 5''	5' 7''	5' 9''	5' 8''	5'10''	5' 8''
65th	5' 0''	5' 2''	5' 4''	5' 4''	5' 6''	5' 7''	5' 7''	5' 9''	5' 7''
60th	4'10''	5' 0''	5' 2''	5' 3''	5' 5''	5' 6''	5' 6''	5' 7''	5' 6''
55th	4' 9''	5' 0''	5' 1''	5' 2''	5' 4''	5' 5''	5' 5''	5' 6''	5' 5''
50th	4' 7''	4'10''	5' 0''	5' 0''	5' 3''	5' 4''	5' 4''	5' 5''	5' 4''
45th	4' 6''	4' 9''	4'11''	5' 0''	5' 1''	5' 3''	5' 3''	5' 3''	5' 3''
40th	4' 5''	4' 8''	4' 9''	4'10''	5' 0''	5' 1''	5' 2''	5' 2''	5' 2''
35th	4' 4''	4' 7''	4' 8''	4' 8''	5' 0''	5' 0''	5' 0''	5' 0''	5' 0''
30th	4' 3''	4' 6''	4' 7''	4' 6''	4' 9''	4'10''	5'11''	5' 0''	4'11''
25th	4' 2''	4' 4''	4' 5''	4' 6''	4' 8''	4' 8''	4'10''	4'10''	4'10''
20th	4' 0''	4' 3''	4' 4''	4' 4''	4' 6''	4' 7''	4' 8''	4' 9''	4' 8''
15th	3'11''	4' 1''	4' 2''	4' 2''	4' 3''	4' 6''	4' 6''	4' 7''	4' 7''
10th	3' 9''	3'11''	4' 0''	4' 0''	4' 1''	4' 4''	4' 4''	4' 5''	4' 5''
5th	3' 6''	3' 9''	3' 8''	3' 9''	3'10''	4' 0''	4' 0''	4' 2''	4' 1''
0	2' 8''	2'11''	2'11''	2'11''	3' 0''	2'11''	3' 2''	3' 0''	2' 3''

Source: AAHPER, Youth Fitness Test Manual, Revised, Washington, D.C., 1966, pp. 30, 64.

Two-Hand Medicine Ball Put (6 lbs.)

<u>Objective</u>: To measure the power of the arms and shoulder girdle.

<u>Age Level</u>: Ages 12 through college.

<u>Sex</u>: Satisfactory for boys and girls.

<u>Reliability</u>: An r of .81 was found for college girls while an r of .84 was found for college men.

<u>Validity</u>: An r of .77 was obtained by correlating distance scores with scores computed by the power formula. However, angle of release was not figured in the correlation, although it is a definite limiting factor affecting the validity!

<u>Equipment and Materials</u>: A six-pound medicine ball, marking material (chalk or tape), small rope, chair, and a tape measure are needed for this test.

<u>Directions</u>: From a sitting position in a straight back chair, the performer holds the ball in both hands with the ball drawn back against the chest and just under the chin. He then pushes the ball upward and outward for maximum distance. The rope is placed around the performer's chest and held taut to the rear by a partner in order to eliminate rocking action during the push. The performer's effort should be primarily with the arms.

<u>Scoring</u>: The distance of the best of three trials measured to the nearest foot is recorded as the score. One practice trial may be taken before scoring.

<u>Additional Pointers</u>: (1) Each of three trials should be taken in succession. (2) Distance is measured from the forward edge of the chair to the point of contact of the ball with the floor.

FIGURE 6 - 3

Two-Hand Medicine Ball Put

TABLE 6 - 3

T-Score Norms for Medicine Ball Put
for College Men and Women*

College Men		College Women	
T-Score	Raw Score	Raw Score	T-Score
85	25	15	85
80	24	14	80
75	23	13	75
70	22	12	70
65	20	11½	65
60	19	11	60
55	18	10	55
50	16	9	50
45	15	8	45
40	14	7½	40
35	12	7	35
30	11	6	30
25	10	5	25
20	9	4	20

*Based on 325 scores secured from physical education classes at Northeast Louisiana State College, Monroe, La.

*Based on 175 scores secured from physical education classes at Northeast Louisiana State College, Monroe, La.

WORK-POWER TESTS

Vertical Arm Pull Test (Work)[35]

Objective: To measure the power of the arms and shoulder girdle in a vertical rope pull.

Age Level: Ages 14 through college.

Sex: Satisfactory for boys only.

Reliability: An r of .94 was found for this test.

Validity: An r of .76 was found when the work score (ft. lbs.) was correlated with the vertical power pull (work/time).

Objectivity: An r of .99 indicated a high degree of objectivity.

Equipment and Materials: A climbing rope, marking tape, a tape measure, and weight scales are required for this test. Students are required to dress in shorts, light shirt, and no shoes.

Directions: Record the performer's weight and then have him assume a sitting position on a chair or bench (seat level at least 15" off of the floor) and grasp as high up the rope as possible without raising the buttocks from the chair or bench seat. Concerning the grasp, the hand of the preferred arm should be just above the opposite hand. The tester should place a piece of marking tape around the rope just above the uppermost hand. The performer should then pull (without letting the feet touch the floor) and reach as high up the rope as possible and grasp and hold the rope until the tester can again place a piece of marking tape above the uppermost hand. The tester should allow each performer three trials and disregard any trial where the feet touch the floor during the pull. On the third trial, say "This is your last pull. Try to beat your last two pulls."

Scoring: Using the score of the best pull (distance between the two tape marks) calculate as follows:

$$\frac{\text{Distance of pull} \times \text{body weight}}{12} = \text{foot pounds}$$

Additional Pointers: (1) The tester must have marking tape ready to immediately place above the uppermost hand as it grasps the rope. (2) The performer should be instructed to vigorously pike (flex) the hips as he makes the pull. (3) The performer may close his legs in around the rope following his pull and grasp (but not before the uppermost hand makes its grasp). (4) The rope should hang directly downward so that it touches the front edge of the chair between the legs of the performer.

FIGURE 6 - 4

Vertical Arm Pull Test (Work)

TABLE 6 - 4A

T-Score Norms for Vertical Arm Pull Test (Work)*

College Men					
T-Score	Raw Score	T-Score	Raw Score	T-Score	Raw Score
90	536	63	369	36	203
89	529	62	363	35	197
88	523	61	357	34	191
87	517	60	351	33	185
86	511	59	345	32	178
85	505	58	338	31	172
84	499	57	332	30	166
83	492	56	326	29	160
82	486	55	320	28	154
81	480	54	314	27	148
80	474	53	308	26	141
79	468	52	302	25	135
78	462	51	295	24	129
77	466	50	289	23	123
76	449	49	283	22	117
75	443	48	277	21	111
74	437	47	271	20	104
73	431	46	265	19	98
72	425	45	258	18	92
71	419	44	252	17	86
70	412	43	246	16	80
69	406	42	240	15	74
68	400	41	234	14	68
67	394	40	228	13	61
66	388	39	221	12	55
65	382	38	215	11	49
64	375	37	209	10	43

*Based on 150 scores secured from physical education classes at Northeast Louisiana State College, Monroe, La.

TABLE 6 - 4B

T-Score Norms for Vertical Arm Pull Test (Work)*

High School Boys					
T-Score	Raw Score	T-Score	Raw Score	T-Score	Raw Score
90	473	66	324	42	176
89	467	65	318	41	170
88	461	64	312	40	163
87	454	63	306	39	157
86	448	62	300	38	151
85	442	61	293	37	145
84	436	60	287	36	139
83	430	59	281	35	132
82	423	58	275	34	126
81	417	57	269	33	120
80	411	56	262	32	114
79	405	55	256	31	108
78	399	54	250	30	101
77	392	53	244	29	95
76	386	52	238	28	89
75	380	51	231	27	83
74	374	50	225	26	77
73	368	49	219	25	70
72	362	48	213	24	64
71	355	47	207	23	58
70	349	46	201	22	52
69	343	45	194	21	46
68	337	44	188	20	39
67	331	43	182		

*Based on 200 scores secured from physical education classes at Ouachita Parish High School, Monroe, La.

Vertical Power Jump (Work)[26]

Objective: To measure pure power of the legs in jumping vertically upward.

Age Level: Ages 10 through college.

Sex: Satisfactory for both boys and girls.

Reliability: Has been reported as high as .977 for college men.

Validity: Has been reported as high as .989 with the vertical power jump (horse-power) as the criterion with college men.

Equipment and Materials: A jump board marked off in half inches, chalk dust, and weight scales are required for the test. The subject must be dressed in shorts, light shirt, and no shoes.

Directions: Record the performer's weight and then have him assume a standing position facing sideways to the jump board, the preferred arm behind the back (hand grasping top of shorts at the back), and the other arm raised vertically with the hand turned outward and fingers extended. Holding the described position, the performer should stand as tall as possible on the toes so that the height of the extended middle finger of the raised arm can be recorded. Chalk dust is then placed on the middle finger, and the performer adopts a full squat position with head and back erect and body in balance. The performer is then told to jump as high as possible (using only the legs) and to touch the board at the top of the jump. The tester must watch and disregard any jump in which balance or position is lost. The tester should record the height of the chalk mark on the jump board. Each performer is allowed three trials. On the last trial the tester should say, "This is your last jump. Try to beat your last two jumps." (See Fig. 6 - 5.)

Scoring: (See Table 6 6.) Using the measure of the best jump (difference between the reaching height and jumping height), calculate the following formula:

$$\frac{\text{Distance} \times \text{body weight}}{12} = \underline{\hspace{2cm}} \text{ foot lbs.}$$

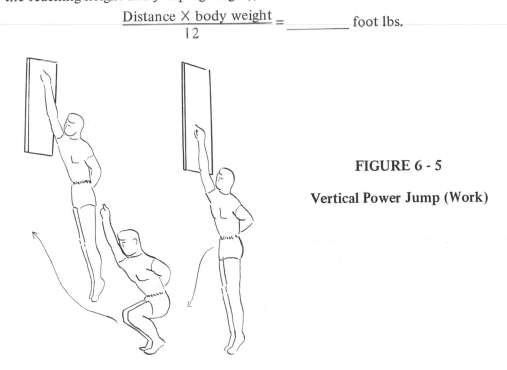

FIGURE 6 - 5

Vertical Power Jump (Work)

TABLE 6 - 5

T-Score Norms for Vertical Power Jump (Work)*

College Men

T-Score	Raw Score	T-Score	Raw Score	T-Score	Raw Score
80	328	59	222	38	116
79	323	58	217	37	111
78	318	57	212	36	105
77	313	56	207	35	99
76	308	55	202	34	95
75	303	54	197	33	90
74	298	53	192	32	85
73	293	52	186	31	80
72	288	51	181	30	75
71	283	50	176	29	70
70	278	49	171	28	65
69	273	48	166	27	60
68	267	47	161	26	55
67	262	46	156	25	50
66	257	45	151	24	45
65	252	44	146	23	40
64	247	43	141	22	35
63	242	42	136	21	30
62	237	41	131	20	25
61	232	40	126		
60	227	39	121		

*Based on 125 scores secured from physical education classes at Northeast Louisiana State College, Monroe, La.

TABLE 6 - 6

T-Score Norms for Vertical Power Jump (Work)*

College Women					
T-Score	Raw Score	T-Score	Raw Score	T-Score	Raw Score
85	155	63	108	41	62
84	153	62	106	40	59
83	151	61	104	39	57
82	148	60	102	38	55
81	146	59	100	37	53
80	144	58	98	36	51
79	142	57	95	35	49
78	140	56	93	34	47
77	138	55	91	33	45
76	136	54	89	32	42
75	134	53	87	31	40
74	131	52	85	30	38
73	129	51	83	29	36
72	127	50	81	28	34
71	125	49	78	27	32
70	123	48	76	26	30
69	121	47	74	25	28
68	119	46	72	24	26
67	117	45	70	23	23
66	115	44	68	22	21
65	112	43	66	21	19
64	110	42	64	20	17

*Based on 100 scores secured from physical education classes at Northeast Louisiana State College, Monroe, La.

TABLE 6 - 7

T-Score Norms for Vertical Power Jump (Work)*

High School Girls

T-Score	Raw Score	T-Score	Raw Score	T-Score	Raw Score
85	138	64	100	43	61
84	136	63	98	42	60
83	134	62	96	41	58
82	132	61	94	40	56
81	130	60	92	39	54
80	129	59	90	38	52
79	127	58	89	37	51
78	125	57	87	36	49
77	123	56	85	35	47
76	121	55	83	34	45
75	119	54	81	33	43
74	118	53	80	32	42
73	116	52	78	31	40
72	114	51	76	30	38
71	112	50	74	29	36
70	110	49	72	28	34
69	109	48	71	27	32
68	107	47	69	26	31
67	105	46	67	25	29
66	103	45	65		
65	101	44	63		

*Based on 100 scores secured from physical education classes at Ouachita Parish High School, Monroe, La.

Problems Associated with Power Testing

Several of the problems associated with power testing are listed as follows:

1. Vigorous activity prior to jumping performance tests seems to have a significantly negative effect upon performance. Therefore, more consideration should be given to rest for participants prior to jumping performance.[42,43,44,51]

2. Practice and coaching tips seem to affect the reliability and validity of athletic power tests due to the improved use of extraneous movements rather than of an actual increase in power itself. Thus, it seems necessary to either eliminate the extraneous movements, or practice them until all movements are executed correctly before recording scores.

3. The level of motivation must be controlled so that all students are tested under the same conditions. The conditions which are usually considered standard are a knowledge of results, tested in the presence of peers, and the avoidance of cheering and other unusual circumstances.

4. The common tests of athletic power (vertical jump, broad jump, medicine ball put, etc.) are inadequate for use in experimental research since learning to perform could be misinterpreted as increased power. Therefore, such tests as the vertical power jump and the power lever should be used since extraneous movements have been eliminated.

5. There is a need for norms at all grade levels for both boys and girls on certain power tests. The norms for several tests presented in this chapter were based on the scores of local high school and college students.

Findings and Conclusions from Power Measurement and Research

Power has been measured and studied in various ways. For example, it has been studied by the following methods: (1) Athletic power method where extraneous movements are not eliminated,[8,13,21,38,46,50] (2) Work-power method where extraneous movements are eliminated,[7,26,27,28,29,30,31,32,48] and (3) motion photography where recordings of force, distance, and time were collected to calculate power based on its mechanical principle.[18,23,25,36]

Studies have shown that systematic weight training can improve athletic power performance.[12,16,19,24] However, Muller[41] concluded that strong muscles do not necessarily indicate better performance. Since dynamic (isotonic) training was found to be effective in improving athletic power performance, it was theorized that static (isometric) training might equally be as effective. However, several studies failed to obtain gains in jumping performance to accompany static strength increases[52,45,5,3] at the end of training programs, although other studies have found that isometric training improved both strength and speed performance, the two important factors in power performance.[39,15,34,40,17] Obviously, studies are in conflict concerning the effectiveness of isometrics because of variations in testing or training procedures. In isometric training it is important that a measuring device be used each day so that subjects will know how hard they are straining, and it is important to train subjects at the angles where the greatest force is needed in power performance. Otherwise, mediocre results are more than likely to occur.

Several studies have shown that previous activity such as basketball[43] and swimming [42,43,44,51] have a negative effect upon jumping tests. Therefore, rest prior to athletic power jump tests should be considered if optimum results are to be achieved.

In studying age, height, weight, and power, the following findings have been reported:

1. The Sargent Jump was found to be a better means of classifying girls for individual athletic performance, since age, height, and weight alone were found to be of little value for such classification.[2]

2. Power measures were not found to increase or decrease with the increased age and growth of Junior High girls enrolled in ungraded classes.[10]

3. Power was found to increase during the early years until the approach of middle age, after which there was a decline in power performance.[20]

A number of studies were concerned with the relationship of strength and speed to power. The results of such studies are listed as follows:

1. Two studies found static strength[22,6] and dynamic strength[6,37] significantly related to leg power, thus indicating strength as an important variable in power measurement.

2. Several studies indicated that speed was significantly related to power and that it was more important than strength in athletic performance.[13,14,21]

Concerning physical activities McCloy[38] found the Sargent jump significantly related to the total point score of select track and field events, and Bushey[11] found a significant relationship between vertical jump scores and modern dance performance.

BIBLIOGRAPHY

1. AAHPER, *Youth Fitness Test Manual,* Washington, D.C.: AAHPER, 1965, p. 20.

2. Adams, Eleanore Groff, "The Study of Age, Height, Weight, and Power as Classification Factors for Junior High School Girls," *Research Quarterly,* 5:95-100, May, 1934.

3. Ball, Jerry R., and others, "Effects of Isometric Training on Vertical Jumping Ability," *Research Quarterly,* 35:234, October, 1964.

4. Barrow, Harold M., and Rosemary McGee, *A Practical Approach to Measurement in Physical Education,* Philadelphia: Lea & Febiger, 1964, pp. 147-148.

5. Berger, Richard A., "Effects on Dynamic and Static Training on Vertical Jumping Ability," *Research Quarterly,* 34:423, December, 1963.

6. _____ , and Joe M. Henderson, "Relationship of Power to Static and Dynamic Strength," *Research Quarterly,* 37:9, March, 1966.

7. Bilodeau, E. A., "Decrements and Recovery from Decrements in a Single Work Task with Variations in Force Requirements at Different States of Practice," *Journal of Exp. Psychol.,* 44:96-100, 1952.

8. Bovard, J. F., and F. W. Cozens, *The "Leap Meter," an Investigation into the Possibilities of the Sargent Test as a Measure of General Athletic Ability,* Eugene: University of Oregon Press, 1928.

9. Burley, Lloyd R., and Roy Anderson, "Relation of Jump and Reach Measures of Power to Intelligence Scores and Athletic Performances," *Research Quarterly,* 28:28-34, March, 1955.

10. _____ , Helen C. Dobell, and Betty J. Farrell, "Relations of Power, Speed, Flexibility, and Certain Anthropometric Measures of Junior High School Girls," *Research Quarterly,* 32:443-448, December, 1961.

11. Bushey, Suzane R., "Relationship of Modern Dance Performance to Agility, Balance, Flexibility, Power, and Strength," *Research Quarterly,* 37:313, October, 1966.

12. Capen, Edward K., "The Effect of Systematic Weight Training on Power, Strength, and Endurance," *Research Quarterly,* 21:83-93, May, 1950.

13. Carpenter, Aileen, "A Critical Study of the Factors Determining Strength Tests for Women," *Research Quarterly,* 9:26, December, 1938.

14. _____ , "Strength, Power, and Femininity as Factors Influencing the Athletic Performance of College Women," *Research Quarterly,* 9:120-127, May, 1938.

15. Chui, E. F., "Effects of Isometric and Dynamic Weight-Training Exercises Upon Strength and Speed of Movement," *Research Quarterly,* 35:246-257, 1964.

16. _____ , "The Effect of Systematic Weight Training on Athletic Power," *Research Quarterly,* 21:188-194, October, 1950.

17. Clarke, David F., "The Effect of Prescribed Exercise on Strength, Speed, and Endurance in Swimming the Crawl Stroke," (Microcarded Master's Thesis, Central Michigan University, Mount Pleasant, Michigan, 1965).

18. Cureton, T. K., "Elementary Principles and Techniques of Cinematographic Analysis," *Research Quarterly,* 10:3-24, May, 1939.

19. Darling, Donald E., "A Comparative Study to Determine the Effect of Heel Raises and Deep Knee Bend Exercises on the Vertical Jump," (Microcarded Master's Thesis, Springfield College, Springfield, Massachusetts, 1960).

20. Dawson, Percy M., "The Influence of Aging on Power and Endurance in Man," *Research Quarterly,* 16:95-101, May, 1945).

21. DiGiavanna, Vincent, "The Relation of Selected Structural and Functional Measures of Success in College Athletics, *Research Quarterly,* 14:213, May, 1943.

22. Eckert, Helen M., "Linear Relationships of Isometric Strength to Propulsive Force, Angular Velocity, and Angular Acceleration in the Standing Broad Jump," (Microcarded Doctoral Dissertation, University of Wisconsin, Madison, 1961).

23. Fletcher, J. G., and others, "Human Power Output: "The Mechanics of Pole Vaulting," *Ergonomics,* 3:30, 1960.

24. Garth, R. P., "A Study of the Effect of Weight Training on the Jumping Ability of Basketball Players," (Unpublished Master's Thesis, State University of Iowa, 1954).

25. Gerrish, P. H., *A Dynamic Analysis of the Standing Vertical Jump,* New York: Columbia University, 1934.

26. Glencross, Dennis J., "The Measurement of Muscular Power; A Test of Leg Power and a Modification for General Use," (Microcarded (Ed. B.), University of Western Australia, Perth, 1960).

27. _____ , "The Measurement of Muscle Power on Evaluation of the Validity of Existing Measures of Muscle Power Used in Physical Education," (Microcarded Master's Thesis, University of Western Australia, Perth, 1963, p. 196).

28. _____ , "The Nature of the Vertical Jump Test and the Standing Broad Jump," *Research Quarterly,* 37:353-359, October, 1966.

29. _____ , "The Power Lever: An Instrument for Measuring Muscle Power," *Research Quarterly,* 37:202, May, 1966.

30. Gray, R. K., K. B. Start, and D. J. Glencross, "A Test of Leg Power," *Research Quarterly,* 33:44-50, March, 1962.

31. _____ , and others, "A Useful Modification of the Vertical Power Jump," *Research Quarterly,* 33:230-235, May, 1962.

32. _____ , K. B. Start, and A. Walsh, "Relationship Between Leg Speed and Leg Power," *Research Quarterly,* 33:395-400, October, 1962.

33. Hofmann, James A., "A Comparison of the Effect of Two Programs of Weight Training on Explosive Force," (Microcarded Master's Thesis, South Dakota State College, Brookings, 1959, p. 48).

34. Johnson, Barry L., "A Comparison of Isometric and Isotonic Exercises Upon the Improvement of Velocity and Distance as Measured by a Vertical Rope Climb Test," (Unpublished Master's Thesis, Louisiana State University, 1964).

35. _____ , "The Establishment of a Vertical Arm Pull Test (Work)," *Research Quarterly,* 40: at Press, March, 1969.

36. Koepke, C. A., and L. S. Whitson, "Power and Velocity Developed in Manual Work," *Mech. Eng.,* 62:383-389, 1940.

37. McClements, Lawrence C., "Power Relative to Strength of Leg and Thigh Muscles," *Research Quarterly,* 37:71, March, 1966.

38. McCloy, C. H., "Recent Studies in the Sargent Jump," *Research Quarterly,* 3:35, May, 1932.

39. Meadows, P. E., "The Effect of Isotonic and Isometric Muscle Contraction Training on Speed, Force, and Strength," (Microcarded Doctoral Dissertation, University of Illinois, Urbana, 1959, pp. 93-95).

40. Michael, Charles E., "The Effects of Isometric Contraction Exercise on Reaction and Speed of Movement Times," (Unpublished Doctoral Dissertation, Louisiana State University, Baton Rouge, 1963, p. 61).

41. Muller, E. A., "The Regulation of Muscular Strength," *Journal Assoc. Phy. & Ment. Rehabilit.,* 11:41-47, 1957.

42. Nelson, Dale O., "Effect of a Single Day's Swimming on Selected Components of Athletic Performance," *Research Quarterly,* 32:389-393, October, 1961.

43. _____ , "Effects of Swimming and Basketball on Various Tests of Explosive Power," *Research Quarterly,* 33:586, December, 1962.

44. _____ , "Effect of Swimming on the Learning of Selected Gross Motor Skills," *Research Quarterly,* 28:374-378, December, 1957.

45. Newlin, Bruce, "The Relation of Isometric Strength to Isotonic Strength Performance," (Unpublished Master's Thesis, University of California, 1959).

46. Sargent, D. A., "The Physical Test of a Man," *American Physical Education Review,* 25:188-194, April, 1921.

47. Sargent, L. W., "Some Observations in the Sargent Test of Neuro-Muscular Efficiency," *American Physical Education Review,* 29:47-56, 1924.

48. Start, K. B., and others, "A Factorial Investigation of Power, Speed, Isometric Strength, and Anthropometric Measures in the Lower Limb," *Research Quarterly,* 37:553-558, December, 1966.

49. United States Volleyball Association, *The 1967 Annual Official Volleyball Rules and Reference Guide,* Berne, Indiana: USVBA Printer, 1967, pp. 134-135.

50. Van Dalen, Deobold, "New Studies in the Sargent Jump," *Research Quarterly,* 11:114, May, 1940.

51. Whitaker, R. Russell, "Effect of Swimming on the Learning of Selected Gross Motor Skills When the Skills and Swimming are Performed on the Same Day," (Unpublished Master's Thesis, Utah State University, 1960).

52. Wolbers, Charles P., and Frank D. Sills, "Development of Strength in High School Boys by Static Muscle Contraction," *Research Quarterly,* 27:446-450, November-December, 1956.

Chapter VII

THE MEASUREMENT OF AGILITY

Introduction

Agility may be defined as the physical ability which enables an individual to rapidly change body position and direction in a precise manner. Agility is an important ability in many sports activities as exemplified in a fast game of badminton by two experienced players, or as exemplified by the trampolinist executing a triple twisting back somersault. By the proper use of tests which rate high in validity and reliability, it is possible for the physical education teacher to determine which individuals in class are most agile and which ones need work in agility in order to better perform the particular activity.

Uses of Agility Tests

Several ways by which agility tests are utilized in physical education classes are listed as follows:

1. As an element for predicting potential in different sports activities.
2. As a measure for determining achievement and grades when agility improvement is a specific objective in the teaching unit.
3. As a factor in general motor ability tests and physical fitness tests.
4. As a means to evaluate results obtained from activities and methods of instruction. For example, if you were to measure agility before and after a unit of instruction in weight training, you could evaluate weight training as to whether it is beneficial or not in agility improvement.

Practical Tests of Agility

Tests of agility which are practical in terms of time, equipment, and cost are presented on the following pages.

Burpee Test (or Squat Thrust)*

Objective: To measure the rapidity by which body position can be changed.
Age Level: Ages 10 through college.
Sex: Satisfactory for both boys and girls.
Reliability: Has been reported as high as .921.
Validity: With the criterion of general athletic ability, an r of .553 has been reported for boys and .341 for girls.

*To the best of the author's knowledge this test was first presented by Royal H. Burpee and first checked for reliability and validity by C. H. McCloy.

Equipment and Materials: Stop watch or wrist watch with a second hand.

Directions: (See Figure 7 - 1.) From a standing position (1) bend at the knees and waist and place the hands on the floor in front of the feet, (2) thrust the legs backward to a front-leaning rest position, (3) return to the squat position, and (4) rise to a standing position. From the signal "go" repeat this movement as rapidly as possible until the command "stop" is given.

Scoring: The test is scored in terms of the number of parts executed in 10 seconds. For example, squatting and placing the hands on the floor is one, thrusting legs to the rear is two, returning to squat-rest position is three, and returning to the standing position is four. (See Table 7 - 1.)

Penalty: There is a one point penalty for the following faults: (1) If the feet move to the rear before the hands touch the floor, (2) if there is excessive sway or pike of the hips in the rearward position, (3) if the hands leave the floor before the feet are drawn up in position number three, and (4) if the stand is not erect with the head up.

Start   1   2

3   4

FIGURE 7 - 1

Burpee Test (or Squat Thrust)

TABLE 7 - 1

T-Score Norms for Burpee (Squat Thrust) Test

College Men		College Women		High School Girls
T-Scores — Raw Scores		T-Scores — Raw Scores		Raw Scores
80 — 35		95 — 31		31
77 — 34		91 — 30		30
75 — 33		88 — 29		29
72 — 32		84 — 28		28
69 — 31		80 — 27		27
67 — 30		77 — 26		26
64 — 29		73 — 25		25
62 — 28		69 — 24		24
59 — 27		66 — 23		23
57 — 26		62 — 22		22
54 — 25		58 — 21		21
51 — 24		55 — 20		20
49 — 23		51 — 19		19
46 — 22		47 — 18		18
44 — 21		44 — 17		17
41 — 20		40 — 16		16
38 — 19		37 — 15		15
36 — 18		33 — 14		14
33 — 17		29 — 13		13
31 — 16		25 — 12		12
28 — 15		22 — 11		11
25 — 14		18 — 10		10
23 — 13		14 — 9		9
20 — 12		11 — 8		8
18 — 11				Temporary norms based on a limited number of girls in a high school physical education class.
15 — 10				
Based on the scores of 100 college men at Northeast Louisiana State College, Monroe, La.		Based on the scores of 100 college women at Northeast Louisiana State College, Monroe, La.		As modified from Mary E. O'Connor and T. C. Cureton, "Motor Fitness Tests for High School Girls," *Research Quarterly*, 16: 302-314 (Dec., 1944).

Side Step Test*

Objective: To measure the rapidity by which lateral movement can be made and changed to the opposite direction.

Age Level: Ages 10 through college.

Sex: Satisfactory for both boys and girls.

Reliability: Has been reported as high as .89.

Validity: Has been reported as high as .70.

Equipment and Materials: Marking tape and a stop watch or wrist watch with a second hand.

Directions: (See Figure 7 - 2.) From a standing position astride the center line, (1) the performer sidesteps on the signal "go" to the right until his foot has touched or crossed the outside line. (2) He then sidesteps to the left until his left foot has touched or crossed the outside line to the left. (3) He repeats these movements as rapidly as possible for ten seconds.

Scoring: A one foot tick mark should be placed between the center line and each outside line to facilitate the spreading of scores. Each trip from the center line across a marker counts as one. For example, moving to the right the performer crosses a tick mark for one point, the outside marker for two, back across the tick mark for three, across the center marker for four, across the left tick mark for five, across the outside marker for six, and so on until he hears the signal to stop at the end of ten seconds. (See Table 7 - 2.)

Penalty: There is a one point penalty for each time one foot is crossed over the other and for each failure to get the proper foot on or across the outside marker.

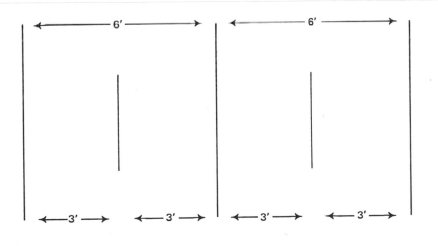

FIGURE 7 - 2

Side Step Test

*This test is the author's modification of the sidestep test proposed by H. D. Edgren in the March, 1932, issue of the *Research Quarterly*.

TABLE 7 - 2

T-Score Norms for Side Step Test

College Men			College Women		
T-Scores	—	Raw Scores	T-Scores	—	Raw Scores
80	—	31	80	—	25
78	—	30	76	—	24
76	—	29	72	—	23
73	—	28	68	—	22
70	—	27	63	—	21
67	—	26	60	—	20
63	—	25	56	—	19
60	—	24	52	—	18
57	—	23	48	—	17
54	—	22	44	—	16
51	—	21	40	—	15
47	—	20	36	—	14
44	—	19	32	—	13
41	—	18	28	—	12
38	—	17	24	—	11
34	—	16	20	—	10
31	—	15	16	—	9
28	—	14	12	—	8
25	—	13			
22	—	12			
18	—	11			
15	—	10			

Based on the scores of 100 college men at Northeast Louisiana State College, Monroe, La.

Based on the scores of 100 college women at Northeast Louisiana State College, Monroe, La.

Dodging Run*

Objective: To measure the agility of the performer in running and changing direction.

Age Level: Ages 10 through college.

Sex: Satisfactory for both boys and girls.

Reliability: Has been reported as high as .934 for boys and .802 for girls.

Validity: Has been reported as high as .820 with a criterion of the sum of T-scores in 16 tests of agility for boys.

Equipment and Materials: Marking tape, 4 chairs, and a stop watch.

Directions: (See Figure 7 - 3.) The performer starts behind the starting line on the signal "go" and runs a "figure 8" course around each chair and returns in the same pattern until he crosses the starting line.

Scoring: The score for each performer is the length of time required (to the nearest tenth of a second) to complete the course. (See Table 7 - 3.)

Penalty: The performer receives one tenth of a second penalty for each chair touched.

Additional Pointers: (1) Stress importance of not touching chairs. (2) Stress importance of running as hard as possible across the finish line. (3) Marking tape should be used to designate the starting and finishing line.

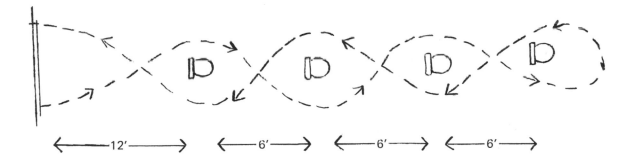

FIGURE 7 - 3

Dodging Run

*D. P. Gates and R. P. Sheffield, "Tests of Change of Direction as Measurement of Different Kinds of Motor Ability in Boys of the 7th, 8th, and 9th Grades," *Research Quarterly*, 11:136-147, October, 1940.

TABLE 7 - 3

T-Score Norms for Dodging Run
(Scores are recorded to the nearest 1/10 of a sec.)

Junior High School Boys (7th & 8th Grade)		
Raw Scores — T-Scores	Raw Scores — T-Scores	Raw Scores — T-Scores
8.1 — 73	10.0 — 57	11.9 — 41
8.2 — 72	10.1 — 56	12.0 — 40
8.3 — 71	10.2 — 55	12.2 — 39
8.4 — 70	10.4 — 54	12.3 — 38
8.6 — 69	10.5 — 53	12.4 — 37
8.7 — 68	10.6 — 52	12.5 — 36
8.8 — 67	10.7 — 51	12.6 — 35
8.9 — 66	10.8 — 50	12.8 — 34
9.0 — 65	10.9 — 49	12.9 — 33
9.2 — 64	11.1 — 48	13.1 — 32
9.3 — 63	11.2 — 47	13.2 — 31
9.4 — 62	11.3 — 46	13.3 — 30
9.5 — 61	11.4 — 45	13.5 — 29
9.6 — 60	11.6 — 44	13.6 — 28
9.8 — 59	11.7 — 43	13.7 — 27
9.9 — 58	11.8 — 42	13.8 — 26

*Based on the scores of 100 subjects from East Baton Rouge Parish Schools, Baton Rouge, Louisiana.

Quadrant Jump*

Objective: To measure the agility of the performer in changing body position rapidly by jumping.

Age Level: Ages 10 through college.

Sex: Satisfactory for both boys and girls.

Reliability: An r of .89 was found for this test when the best of two trials administered on different days was correlated.

Validity: Face validity was accepted.

Equipment and Materials: Marking tape, and a stop watch or wrist watch with a second hand.

Directions: (See Figure 7 - 4.) The performer begins behind the small starting tick mark and jumps both feet into one, then into 2, 3, 4, and back to 1 again. The pattern is continued until the signal "stop" is given.

Scoring: The score for each performer is the number of times the feet land in a correct zone in ten seconds. The best score of two trials is recorded as the test score. (See Table 7 - 4.)

Penalty: There is a ½ point penalty for each time the feet land on a line or in an improper zone.

Additional Pointers: (1) The two cross lines should each be 3' long. (2) One assistant should count the number of jumps and a second assistant should count the number of errors. The ½ point errors should then be totaled and subtracted from the number of jumps. (3) A performer who stops or who could obviously do better should be retested. (4) Each zone may be identified by tick marks with marking tape.

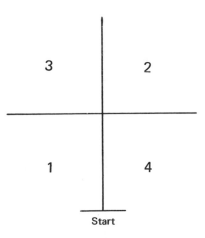

FIGURE 7 - 4

Quadrant Jump

*This test is the author's modification of a similar one once demonstrated by a colleague in a measurements class.

TABLE 7 - 4

T-Score Norms for Quadrant Jump

College Men			College Women		
T-Scores	—	Raw Scores	T-Scores	—	Raw Scores
80	—	33	80	—	35
78	—	32	79	—	34
76	—	31	77	—	33
74	—	30	75	—	32
72	—	29	73	—	31
69	—	28	71	—	30
67	—	27	69	—	29
65	—	26	67	—	28
63	—	25	65	—	27
61	—	24	63	—	26
59	—	23	61	—	25
57	—	22	59	—	24
55	—	21	57	—	23
53	—	20	55	—	22
51	—	19	53	—	21
49	—	18	51	—	20
47	—	17	49	—	19
45	—	16	47	—	18
42	—	15	45	—	17
40	—	14	43	—	16
38	—	13	41	—	15
36	—	12	39	—	14
34	—	11	37	—	13
32	—	10	35	—	12
30	—	9	33	—	11
28	—	8	31	—	10
26	—	7	29	—	9
24	—	6	27	—	8
22	—	5	24	—	7
20	—	4	22	—	6
			20	—	5

Based on the scores of 124 subjects at Northeast Louisiana State College, Monroe, La.

Based on the scores of 150 subjects at Northeast Louisiana State College, Monroe, La.

Right-Boomerang Run[8]

    Objective: To measure the agility of the performer in running and changing direction.
    Age Level: Ages 10 through college.
    Sex: Satisfactory for both boys and girls.
    Reliability: Has been reported as high as .93 for boys and .92 for girls.
    Validity: Has been reported as high as .82 for boys and .72 for girls using the sum of T-scores for 16 and 15 tests of agility, respectively, as the criterion.
    Equipment and Materials: One jumping standard or chair for the center station, four Indian clubs or small similar objects for the outside stations, one stop watch, and marking tape.
    Directions: (See Figure 7 - 5.) Upon hearing the signal "Go," the performer runs to the center station making a quarter right turn and continues through the course as shown in Figure 7 - 5.
    Scoring: The score is determined by the time taken to complete the course. Time is recorded to the nearest tenth of a second. (See Table 7 - 5.)
    Penalty: There is a one tenth of a second penalty for each object touched at the various stations.
    Additional Pointers: (1) Stress running as hard as possible across the finish line. (2) Stress importance of not touching the object at each station. (3) Retest a performer when it is obvious that he could have done better. (4) Allow the students to jog through it once to become familiar with the pattern.

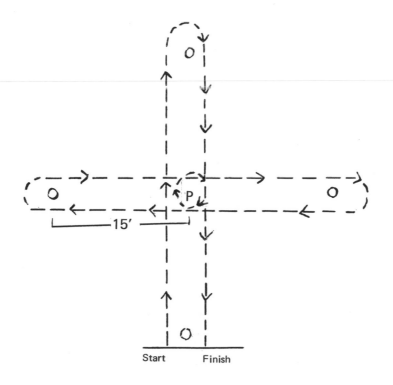

FIGURE 7 - 5

Right-Boomerang Run

TABLE 7 - 5

T-Score Norms for Right-Boomerang Run
(Scores are recorded to the nearest 1/10 of a sec.)

Junior High School Boys (7th & 8th Grade)					
Raw Scores	— T-Scores	Raw Scores	— T-Scores	Raw Scores	— T-Scores
10.9	— 72	13.0	— 55	15.2	— 38
11.0	— 71	13.1	— 54	15.3	— 37
11.1	— 70	13.3	— 53	15.5	— 36
11.2	— 69	13.4	— 52	15.6	— 35
11.3	— 68	13.5	— 51	15.7	— 34
11.4	— 67	13.7	— 50	15.9	— 33
11.6	— 66	13.8	— 49	16.0	— 32
11.7	— 65	13.9	— 48	16.1	— 31
11.8	— 64	14.0	— 47	16.3	— 30
12.0	— 63	14.2	— 46	16.4	— 29
12.1	— 62	14.3	— 45	16.5	— 28
12.2	— 61	14.4	— 44	16.6	— 27
12.4	— 60	14.6	— 43	16.8	— 26
12.5	— 59	14.7	— 42	16.9	— 25
12.6	— 58	14.8	— 41	17.0	— 24
12.7	— 57	14.9	— 40	17.2	— 23
12.9	— 56	15.1	— 39	17.3	— 22

Based on the scores of 100 subjects from East Baton Rouge Parish Schools, Baton Rouge, Louisiana.

L.S.U. Agility Test*

Objective: To measure the agility of the performer in running, dodging, changing directions and scrambling to his feet from the lying position.

Age Level: Ages 10 through college.

Sex: Satisfactory for both boys and girls.

Reliability: Using the average of two trials on each of two successive days, a reliability coefficient of .89 was obtained with college men.

Validity: The coefficient between this test and the Scott-French obstacle course was found to be .95.

Equipment and Materials: A badminton court (no net), five chairs, a light stick at least 6 feet long, a mat approximately 6' X 9', a stop watch, and chalk or marking tape are needed.

Directions: (See Figure 7 - 6.) The subject lies on his back with feet back of the end line. Upon the signal "go," the performer scrambles to his feet, runs to the left of the first chair, to the right of the second, to the left and around the third chair angling toward the mat and the stick, which is supported by two chairs. The performer scrambles under the stick, gets to his feet and runs to touch his hand behind the doubles service court end line, returns to touch the floor beyond the short service line, repeats the above two floor touches, and races to cross the end line.

Scoring: The score is from the time the signal "go" was given until the subject crosses the finish line. Time is recorded to the nearest tenth of a second. No penalty is assessed for knocking the stick off the chairs. Two trials are given with a short rest in between trials. Score is the average of the two trials.

Penalty: There is a one tenth of a second penalty for touching any of the first three chairs.

Additional Pointers: (1) Allow the subjects to jog through the course to familiarize themselves with the test. Especially stress the circling of the chair and the number of floor touches. (2) Knee guards may be of value if they are available. (3) Stress the point that they must lie flat until the starting signal is given. (4) Retest anyone who gets confused or falls down. (5) Testing in small groups on a rotating basis allows for adequate rest between the two trials.

---

*This test is a modification of the Scott-French Obstacle Race.[21] It was devised to facilitate the testing of a large number of subjects by making possible the use of badminton courts as testing stations. The test requires almost no markings other than those on a badminton court.

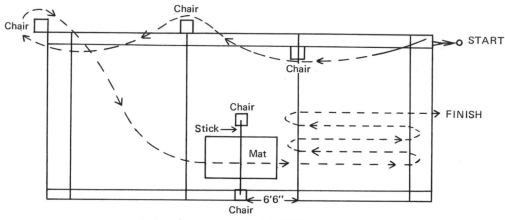

(Crossbar is approximately 18" high)

FIGURE 7 - 6

LSU Agility Test

TABLE 7 - 6

T-Score Norms for the L.S.U. Agility Test
(Scores are in seconds)

College Men					
Raw Scores	— T-Scores	Raw Scores	— T-Scores	Raw Scores	— T-Scores
12.9	— 77	13.8	— 59	14.7	— 41
13.0	— 75	13.9	— 57	14.8	— 39
13.1	— 73	14.0	— 55	14.9	— 37
13.2	— 71	14.1	— 53	15.0	— 35
13.3	— 69	14.2	— 51	15.1	— 33
13.4	— 67	14.3	— 49	15.2	— 31
13.5	— 65	14.4	— 47	15.3	— 29
13.6	— 63	14.5	— 45	15.4	— 27
13.7	— 61	14.6	— 43	15.5	— 25

*Based on the scores of 100 subjects from physical education classes at Louisiana State University, Baton Rouge, La.

Problems Associated with Agility Testing

Concerning agility testing there are several problems and limitations which exist in the laboratory situation. They are listed as follows:

1. The surface area and the type of foot wear seem to have a definite bearing on the scoring ability of students in certain tests such as the obstacle run[21] and the sidestep test. Perhaps this problem could be overcome by using a non-slip surface and by requiring all students to either go bare-footed or wear the same type shoes.
2. It requires considerable time to administer certain agility tests to large groups. The obstacle run[21] is a case in point. Although the time factor should not prohibit the use of the test when there are several testers present and students can be divided into rotating groups, there is a need for some experimentation to bring about a faster administration.
3. Too many of the tests concerning agility involve running ability, or the ability to change body position rapidly as initiated by the legs. In the opinion of the writer there is a need for more tests which make use of various body parts.
4. Several of the agility tests do not scatter scores widely enough to give a definite distinction between good and poor performance. Thus, further efforts are needed to overcome this problem.
5. The sidestep test possibly gives the taller student an unfair advantage, since he has to take fewer steps to cross the side lines than the shorter student. Perhaps this could be overcome by varying the side lines from the center line in accordance with each subject's height.
6. There is a shortage of norms for tests of agility at the elementary, junior high, and senior high school levels.

Findings and Conclusions From Agility Measurement and Research

In the past it was generally believed that agility was almost entirely dependent upon one's heritage; however, measurement and research revealed that it could be improved through practice, training, and instruction.[2,18,4,12]

Seils,[22] in testing primary grade children, found a moderately high positive correlation between physical growth and agility performance in boys and girls. Espenschade[7] noted that both boys and girls increase in agility performance up to 14 years of age, after which girls seem to decline while boys rapidly gain in agility performance.

Concerning body types there is general agreement among investigators that endomorphs (fatty types) have the least potential of the somatotypes concerning performance in agility.[23,6,19,3] However, some disagreement exists concerning whether mesomorphs (muscular types) are superior to ectomorphs (thin types). While Sills[23] found the mesomorphs superior, Bookwalter[3] noted that thin boys of average size perform better than medium physique boys of average size. Moreover, Solley[24] found no significant evidence to support the claim that boys who are big for their age or small for their age may be expected to perform better or worse on agility items.

Numerous investigators have indicated the importance of agility as a factor in the prediction of motor ability and/or sports ability.[13,8,5,9,14,10,15] Agility seems to be fundamental to skill in certain sports activities.[1,17,20] Mohr and Haverstick[16] found significant associations between volleying skill in volleyball and agility, while Hoskins,[9] Lehsten,[14] and Johnson[10] found agility important to basketball performance.

For many years physical educators and coaches generally felt that muscular development associated with weight training was harmful to skill co-ordination. However, in recent years investigators have elicited results which indicate that progressive resistance exercises tend to affect favorably the co-ordination of performers.[4,11,18]

BIBLIOGRAPHY

1. Beise, Dorothy, and Virginia Peasely, "The Relation of Reaction Time, Speed, and Agility of Big Muscle Groups to Certain Sports Skills," *Research Quarterly,* 18:133-142, March, 1937.

2. Bennett, Colleen L., "Relative Contributions of Modern Dance, Folk Dance, Basketball, and Swimming to Motor Abilities of College Women," *Research Quarterly,* 27:256-257, October, 1956.

3. Bookwalter, Karl W., et al, "The Relationship of Body Size and Shape to Physical Performance," *Research Quarterly,* 23:279, October, 1952.

4. Calvin, Sidney, "Effects of Progressive Resistive Exercises on the Motor Coordination of Boys", *Research Quarterly,* 30:387, December, 1959.

5. Carruth, Wincie Ann, "An Analysis of Motor Ability and its Relationship to Constitutional Body Patterns of College Women," (Unpublished Doctoral Dissertation, New York University, New York, 1952).

6. Cureton, Thomas K., "Body Build and a Framework for Interpreting Physical Fitness and Athletic Performance," *Research Quarterly,* 12:301-330, March, 1941.

7. Espenschade, Anna, "Development of Motor Co-ordination in Boys and Girls," *Research Quarterly,* 18:3043, March, 1947.

8. Gates, D. P., and R. P. Sheffield, "Tests of Change of Direction as Measurement of Different Kinds of Motor Ability in Boys of the 7th, 8th, and 9th Grades," *Research Quarterly,* 11:3,136-147, October, 1940.

9. Hoskins, Robert N., "The Relationships of Measurements of General Motor Capacity to the Learning of Specific Psycho-Motor Skills," *Research Quarterly,* 5:63-72, March, 1934.

10. Johnson, L. William, "Objective Basketball Tests for High School Boys," (Unpublished Master's Thesis, University of Iowa, 1934).

11. Kurt, Charles P., "The Effect of Weight Training on Hand-Eye Coordination, Balance, and Response Time," (Microcarded Master's Thesis, State University of Iowa, 1956, p. 26).

12. Lafuze, Marion, "A Study of the Learning of Fundamental Skills by College Freshman Women of Low Motor Ability," *Research Quarterly,* 22:149-157, May, 1951.

13. Larson, Leonard, "A Factor Analysis of Motor Ability Variables and Tests, with Tests for College Men," *Research Quarterly,* 12:499-517, October, 1941.

14. Lehsten, Nelson, "A Measure of Basketball Skills for High School Boys," *The Physical Educator,* 5:103-109, December, 1948.

15. McCloy, Charles H., "Blocks Test of Multiple Response," *Psychometrika,* 7:165-169, September, 1942.

16. _____ , and Norma D. Young, *Tests and Measurements in Health and Physical Education,* Appleton-Century-Crofts, Inc., New York, 1954, p. 78.

17. Mohr, Dorothy R., and Martha L. Haverstick, "Relationship between Height, Jumping Ability and Ability to Volleyball Skill," *Research Quarterly,* 27:74, March, 1956.

18. Moseley, J. W., A. Hairaedian, and D. N. Donelson, "Weight Training in Relation to Strength, Speed, and Co-ordination," *Research Quarterly,* 24:308-315, October, 1953.

19. Perbis, Joyce A., "Relationships Between Somatotype and Motor Fitness in Women," *Research Quarterly,* 25:84, March, 1954.

20. Rarick, Lawrence, "An Analysis of the Speed Factor in Simple Athletic Events," *Research Quarterly,* 8:89, December, 1937.

21. Scott, Gladys, M., and Esther French, *Measurement and Evaluation in Physical Education,* Wm. C. Brown Co., Dubuque, Iowa, 1959.

22. Seils, L. G., "Agility-Performance and Physical Growth," *Research Quarterly,* 22:244, May, 1951.

23. Sills, Frank, "The Relationship of Extreme Somatotypes to Performance in Motor and Strength Tests," *Research Quarterly,* 24:223-228, May, 1953.

24. Solley, Wm. H., "Ratio of Physical Development as A Factor in Motor Coordination of Boys Ages 10-14," *Research Quarterly,* 28:295-303, October, 1957.

Chapter VIII

THE MEASUREMENT OF
GENERAL MOTOR ABILITY

A measure of general motor ability would theoretically represent all the factors that enter into various types of physical performance. Not only would this be beyond the scope of any one test, but by and large, research has failed to find generality of motor skills. Nevertheless, physical educators have continued to speak in terms of general athletic ability and have sought ways of measuring it.

It is not our intention to enter into the argument of specificity vs. generality, but merely to present some of the test batteries that have been frequently used as measures of general motor ability. The skills that are measured are presumably basic motor skills, which are involved in a variety of athletic events, but which do not include highly specialized skills.

Typical test items include measures of speed, power, agility, hand-eye coordination, and balance. Although reaction time is recognized as a separate factor, it has not been measured as such in general motor ability, but rather it has remained combined with speed. Other test items which are sometimes included are strength and endurance, although they more properly belong classified as physical fitness factors. It is recognized that these factors may be improved with practice, but essentially they are considered relatively stable. Despite the fact that most studies have found motor ability to be task specific, perhaps more generality would be found with sufficient practice. In other words if a person possesses considerable ability in basic skills that are thought to underlie motor performance, and are represented by the test items in the general motor ability tests, then he should perform well in a variety of physical tasks if given enough practice to overcome initial inhibitions and to establish the specific neuromotor patterns. Cratty[13] has proposed an interesting three-level theory of perceptual-motor behavior that is pertinent to this topic.

Uses of General Motor Ability Tests

Although more research is indicated as to the efficacy and predictability of general motor ability tests, the following uses have been suggested:
1. As a means for preliminary classification of students into homogeneous groups.
2. As a tool for diagnosis of weaknesses in particular areas of motor performance.
3. As a form of motivation in which the students are able to assess their own status and note improvement.
4. As one of a number of measures for prognostic purposes.
5. As a test of physical achievement.

Tests of General Motor Ability

Carpenter Motor Ability Test[9,10]

Objective: To measure general motor ability in primary school children.

Age Level: Grades 1, 2 and 3.

Sex: Boys and Girls.

Validity: Utilizing a criterion of total points on a battery of events, a multiple correlation of .84 was obtained for girls and .82 for boys.

Reliability: No figures given.

Equipment and Materials: One gymnasium mat, a measuring tape, a 4 lb. shot, and a set of scales are needed for the test items composing the battery.

BROAD JUMP. (Same as the standing broad jump presented in Chapter VI.)

SHOT PUT

Directions: The subject stands at the rear of the shot put circle with a four pound shot held in the fingers and cradled at the junction of the neck and shoulder. When ready, the performer moves toward the center of the ring with gliding hops on the rear leg, and then thrusts the shot away from the body at approximately a forty-five degree angle. It should be emphasized that it is a put, not a throw, and that it is a foul to step out of the circle. One warm-up is allowed, and then the best of three trials is scored.

Scoring: The distance from the front of the circle to the middle of the indentation made by the shot is measured to the nearest foot.

Safety: Precautions must be taken to keep the throwing area absolutely clear. Assistants who are marking each throw must be warned to stay well out of range while a subject is throwing. After each throw the retriever must roll the shot back, or better still, carry it back to the circle. Sufficient warm-up should be allowed.

Additional Pointers: (1) Tongue depressers make good markers. The subject's name can be quickly written on a stick when the subject reports to the throwing circle. (2) One assistant should be assigned to watch where the shot lands and immediately mark it while another assistant stops the rolling shot. (3) The subject's stick should not be moved if he or she obviously has a longer throw on a previous trial. (4) Three or four subjects can be tested at a time quite efficiently. Subject A throws, the shot is retrieved then Subject B throws, and so on until all three or four subjects have had their first trial. Then Subject A takes his second trial, etc. If more than four or so are throwing, there is too much time between trials for each subject. (5) After the group of three or four students have had their last trial, measurements should be taken so that their sticks can be removed before the next group begins their trials. (6) In taking the measures one assistant holds the end of the measuring tape at the inside edge at the front of the circle. Another assistant or the instructor then moves in an arc, placing the tape down at each stick, and calling out the name and distance to be recorded.

Body Weight: The subject's weight is recorded to the nearest pound.

Total Battery Scoring: Two equations were developed by multiple regression equations to predict general motor ability for boys and girls.[10] The equations for the general motor ability scores are as follows:

Boys: GMAS = Standing Broad Jump + 2.5 shot put + .5 weight
Girls: GMAS = Standing Broad Jump + 1.5 shot put + .05 weight

Norms based on the above equations are not available. However, a *Physical Efficiency Index*[9] was developed using the same test items with the following equations:

Boys: .1 Broad Jump + 2.3 Shot Put – Weight
Girls: .5 Broad Jump + 3 Shot Put – Weight

The norms for this test are based upon McCloy's Classification Index, (10 × age) + (wt.), which is intended for children at the elementary school level. The Classification Index is then weighted to establish the individual norms, as shown below:

Girls' Norm: .2549 C.I. – 27.91
Boys' Norm: .3009 C.I. – 64.60

The *Physical Efficiency Index* or *PEI* is found by multiplying the motor ability score by 100, then dividing by the individual's norm. The normal *PEI* is 100, which is interpreted to mean that the boy or girl possesses a sufficient level of motor ability for his or her size and age. A *PEI* greater than 100 means the child is superior in motor ability; conversely, a *PEI* that is less than 100 indicates inferior motor ability for that child's age and body size. Norms for this test are shown in Tables 8 - 1 and 8 - 2 for boys and girls, respectively.

TABLE 8 - 1

Carpenter's Motor Ability Test for First Three Grades (Boys)*

	0	1	2	3	4	5	6	7	8	9
600	115.94	116.24	116.54	116.84	117.14	117.44	117.75	118.05	118.35	118.65
590	112.93	113.23	113.53	113.83	114.13	114.44	114.74	115.04	115.34	115.64
580	109.92	110.22	110.52	110.82	111.13	111.43	111.73	112.03	112.33	112.63
570	106.91	107.21	107.51	107.82	108.12	108.42	108.72	109.02	109.32	109.62
560	103.90	104.20	104.51	104.81	105.11	105.41	105.71	106.01	106.31	106.61
550	100.90	101.20	101.50	101.80	102.10	102.40	102.70	103.00	103.30	103.60
540	97.80	98.19	98.49	98.79	99.09	99.39	99.69	99.99	100.29	100.59
530	94.88	95.18	95.48	95.78	96.08	96.38	96.68	96.98	97.28	97.59
520	91.87	92.17	92.45	92.77	93.07	93.37	93.67	93.97	94.28	94.58
510	88.86	89.16	89.46	89.76	90.06	90.36	90.66	90.97	91.27	91.57
500	85.85	86.15	86.45	86.75	87.05	87.35	87.66	87.96	88.26	88.56
490	82.84	83.14	83.44	83.74	84.04	84.35	84.65	84.95	85.25	85.55
480	79.83	80.13	80.43	80.73	81.04	81.34	81.64	81.94	82.24	82.54
470	76.82	77.12	77.42	77.73	78.03	78.33	78.63	78.93	79.23	79.53
460	73.81	74.11	74.42	74.72	75.02	75.32	75.62	75.92	76.22	76.52
450	70.81	71.11	71.41	71.71	72.01	72.31	72.61	72.91	73.21	73.51
440	67.80	68.10	68.40	68.70	69.00	69.30	69.60	69.90	70.20	70.50
430	64.79	65.09	65.39	65.69	65.99	66.29	66.59	66.89	67.19	67.50
420	61.78	62.08	62.38	62.68	62.98	63.28	63.58	63.88	64.19	64.49
410	58.77	59.07	59.37	59.67	59.97	60.27	60.57	60.88	61.18	61.48
400	55.76	56.06	56.36	56.66	56.96	57.26	57.57	57.87	58.17	58.47

* Aileen Carpenter, "Strength Testing in the First Three Grades," *Research Quarterly*, Vol. 13, No. 3 (October 1942), page 332.

TABLE 8 - 2

Carpenter's Motor Ability Test for First Three Grades (Girls)*

	0	1	2	3	4	5	6	7	8	9
600	125.03	125.28	125.54	125.79	126.05	126.30	126.56	126.81	127.07	127.32
590	122.48	122.74	122.99	123.23	123.50	123.76	124.01	124.26	124.52	124.78
580	119.93	120.19	120.44	120.70	120.95	121.21	121.46	121.72	121.97	122.23
570	117.38	117.64	117.89	118.15	118.40	118.66	118.91	119.17	119.42	119.68
560	114.83	115.09	115.34	115.60	115.85	116.11	116.36	116.62	116.87	117.13
550	112.29	112.54	112.79	113.05	113.30	113.56	113.81	114.07	114.32	114.58
540	109.74	110.00	110.25	110.50	110.76	111.01	111.27	111.52	111.78	112.03
530	107.19	107.44	107.70	107.95	108.21	108.46	108.72	108.97	109.23	109.48
520	104.64	104.89	105.15	105.40	105.66	105.91	106.17	106.42	106.68	106.93
510	102.09	102.34	102.60	102.85	103.11	103.36	103.62	103.87	104.13	104.38
500	99.54	99.79	100.05	100.30	100.56	100.81	101.07	101.32	101.58	101.83
490	96.99	97.25	97.50	97.76	98.01	98.27	98.52	98.78	99.03	99.29
480	94.44	94.70	94.95	95.21	95.46	95.72	95.97	96.23	96.48	96.74
470	91.89	92.15	92.40	92.66	92.91	93.17	93.42	93.68	93.93	94.19
460	89.34	89.60	89.85	90.11	90.36	90.62	90.87	91.13	91.38	91.64
450	86.80	87.05	87.30	87.56	87.81	88.07	88.32	88.58	88.83	89.09
440	84.25	84.50	84.76	85.01	85.27	85.52	85.78	86.03	86.29	86.54
430	81.70	81.95	82.21	82.46	82.72	82.97	83.23	83.48	83.74	83.99
420	79.15	79.40	79.66	79.91	80.17	80.42	80.68	80.93	81.19	81.44
410	76.60	76.85	77.11	77.36	77.62	77.87	78.13	78.38	78.64	78.89
400	74.05	74.30	74.56	74.81	75.07	75.32	75.58	75.83	76.09	76.34

* Aileen Carpenter, "Strength Testing in the First Three Grades," Research Quarterly, Vol. 13, No. 3 (October 1942), page 331.

Barrow Motor Ability Test[3]

Objective: To measure motor ability for purposes of classification, guidance, and achievement.

Age and Sex: College men, junior and senior high school boys.

Validity: Twenty-nine test items measuring eight factors were administered to 222 college men. Through multiple correlation and regression equations two test batteries were established. The first test contained six items which yielded an R of .950 with the criterion. This figure was the total score from the twenty-nine items. The shorter test battery, containing three items (which are included in the six-item battery), was found to have an R of .920 with the criterion.

Reliability: Using the test-retest method, reliability for each test item was computed. Objectivity was also established by having two persons score each subject on each test item. The test item, the motor ability factor it represents, reliability coefficient, objectivity coefficient, and the correlation of that item with the criterion are presented in Table 8 - 3.

TABLE 8 - 3

Test Item Data for the Barrow Motor Ability Test for College Men

Test Item	Factor*	Reliability	Objectivity	Correlation with Criterion
Standing Broad Jump	Power	.895	.996	.759
Softball Throw	Arm-Shoulder Coord.	.928	.997	.761
Zig Zag Run	Agility	.795	.996	.736
Wall Pass	Hand-eye Coord.	.791	.950	.761
Medicine Ball-Put	Strength	.893	.997	.736
60-Yard Dash	Speed	.828	.997	.723

*Balance and flexibility were also identified as motor ability factors, but no test item for either factor was found to have a high enough coefficient of correlation with the criterion to be included in the final battery.

Equipment and Materials: The equipment and space needed for the six test items are as follows: (1) Standing Broad Jump: A mat 5′ × 12′ and a measuring tape if the mat is not marked off. (2) Softball Throw: Several 12″ inseam softballs, a target area of about 100 yards. A football field marked off in five yard intervals is ideal for this test. (3) Zig Zag Run: Stop watch, 5 standards or obstacles, and space enough to accommodate the 16′ × 10′ course. (4) Wall Pass: Regulation basketball, stop watch, wall space. (5) Medicine Ball-Put: Space approximately 90′ × 25′ and tape measure. (6) 60-Yard Dash: Stop watch, whistle, smooth surface at least 80 yards long with start and finish lines.

STANDING BROAD JUMP. (Same as the standing broad jump presented in Chapter IV.)

SOFTBALL THROW

Directions: The subject is allowed three trials in which he attempts to throw the softball as far as possible. A short run is allowed, but the subject must not step over the restraining line.

Scoring: The best of three trials is recorded. Distance is measured to the nearest foot.

Safety: Students who are assisting with marking and measuring of the throws must be warned to keep their eyes on the ball when it is thrown. The subject should not be allowed to throw until the field is clear. Adequate warm-up should be provided.

Additional Pointers: (1) Student helpers can be utilized effectively in marking each throw, measuring and retrieving the balls. If a football field is used, markers can be prepared, reading in feet, and placed at each 5-yard line. (2) One of the student helpers should be assigned to immediately run and stand at the spot at which the ball lands while another brings the subject's marker. A decision can then be made whether the subject has a better throw. (3) Measuring from the nearest 5-yard line facilitates the process as opposed to the use of a tape measure from the point of the throw.

ZIG ZAG RUN.

Directions: The student begins from a standing start on the command to go. He runs the prescribed pattern shown in Figure 8 - 1 as quickly as he can without grasping or moving the standards. Three complete circuits are run. The stop watch is started when the command to go is given and stopped when the subject crosses the finish line.

Scoring. The elapsed time to the nearest tenth of a second is recorded. If the student should grasp or move a standard, run the wrong pattern, or otherwise fail to follow the directions, he should run again after a suitable rest period.

Safety: The subjects should wear proper fitting shoes with good traction to avoid blisters and slipping. Other students should be kept well away from the perimeter of the obstacle course and, especially, away from the finishing area. Sufficient warm-up should be allowed.

Additional Pointers: (1) The instructor should demonstrate the pattern of the course and stress the point that three complete circuits are to be made. (2) The students should be allowed to jog through the course. (3) If any student believes he can improve his score he should be given another trial after he has rested.

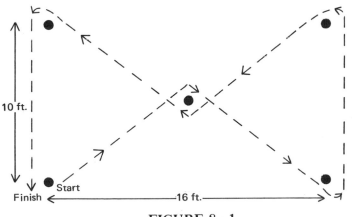

FIGURE 8 - 1

Pattern for Zig Zag Run in Barrow Motor Ability Test

WALL PASS

Directions: The subject stands behind a restraining line that is drawn 9 feet from the wall. On the signal to begin he passes the ball against the wall in any manner he chooses. He attempts to catch the rebound and pass it again as many times as possible for fifteen seconds. For the pass to be legal, both of the subject's feet must remain behind the restraining line. If he should lose control of the ball, he must retrieve it and return to the line and continue passing.

Scoring: The score is the number of times the ball hits the wall in the fifteen seconds.

Safety: There are no special safety hazards with this test.

Additional Pointers: (1) The teacher should consider the possible variations in the cases where a subject loses control of the ball. He may wish to standardize the distance behind the subject by having students line up to block the ball, or have a wall of rolled mats, etc. (2) The teacher should stress the fact that the subject must maintain control of the ball and that he won't be thrown a new ball if he misses the rebound.

SIX-POUND MEDICINE BALL PUT

Directions: The subject stands between two restraining lines which are fifteen feet apart. He then attempts to propel the medicine ball out as far as possible without stepping on or over the restraining line. He should hold the ball at the junction of his neck and shoulder and thrust it away from his body at an angle of approximately forty-five degrees. He is given three throws.

Scoring: The best of three throws is recorded. The distance is computed to the nearest foot. A throw in which the subject commits a foul is not scored. However, if all three trials are fouls, he should try until he makes a fair put.

Safety: The same safety considerations should be followed as were presented for the shot put event in the Carpenter Test.

Additional Pointers: (1) Two students are needed at all times to assist in marking and measuring the throws. It is helpful to also have a student assigned to retrieve the ball. One student should quickly run to the exact spot where the ball lands while another comes to mark (or measures) it. (2) Any of several plans could be followed in measuring the individual throws. Since the test is conducted on the gymnasium floor, small pieces of tape could be used to quickly mark each of the three throws. Then the tape measure could be brought in to measure the best of the three trials. (3) Another approach is to leave the tape stretched out from the restraining line and then measure each throw. One disadvantage to this method is that each throw must be recorded unless, of course, the succeeding throw(s) is not as far. The tape should be swung in an arc in order to be sure that the distance from the point of the throw to the spot of landing is obtained. (4) Still another method is to have arcs marked on the floor 5 or 10 feet apart. In this way the measuring tape would not have to be as long, and it may facilitate testing. (5) The tester may wish to dust the ball with powdered chalk before each throw in order to obtain the exact point of landing. This procedure is ordinarily not too practical because of the time consumed and the necessity of continually wiping off the marks.

The 60-YARD DASH

Directions: The subject starts from a standing position on the signal to go and runs as rapidly as possible to the finish line. One trial is given.

Scoring: The score is recorded in seconds to the nearest tenth of a second. The time begins when the command "go" is given. In 60 yards there should be no appreciable time lag due to the relative speed of sound versus the speed of light.

Safety: The most important safety precaution has to do with pulled muscles. The teacher should make it a point to provide a thorough warm-up. The other safety features concern footwear, running surface, and adequate space beyond the finish line. Additional Pointers: (1) The timer should be stationed parallel to the finish line to make sure he obtains an accurate score. (2) The starter should standardize the preparatory commands such as "Ready," "Get Set," "Go." If an arm signal is employed for starting, the movement of the arm must be practiced to synchronize it with the verbal command to "Go."

Scoring for Total Battery: A regression equation utilizing weighted standard scores is provided to determine the total General Motor Ability Test (G.M.A.S.) score. The equation is as follows:

$$\text{G.M.A.S.} = 2.2 \text{ (standing broad jump)} + 1.6 \text{ (softball throw)} + 1.6 \text{ (zig zag run)} + 1.3 \text{ (wall pass)} + 1.2 \text{ (medicine ball put)} + 60\text{-yard dash.}$$

Barrow recommends that the users of the test establish their own norms. In the original source the author offered the following norms based on a sample of college students and a group of physical education majors.

TABLE 8 - 4

General Motor Ability Test Scores for College Men

P. E. Majors			Non-Majors	
Six-Items	Three-Items		Six-Items	Three-Items
586 Up	197 Up	Excellent	550 Up	185 Up
534-585	180-196	Good	481-549	163-184
480-533	161-179	Average	410-480	138-162
428-479	143-160	Poor	341-409	116-137
427 Down	142 Down	Inferior	340 Down	115 Down

Barrow adapted his motor ability test to include junior and senior high school boys.[4] Using the three-item indoor battery consisting of the standing broad jump, medicine ball put, and zig zag run, norms are presented for grades 7 through 11 as well as for college men. It should be remembered that this shortened version loses very little in predictive power when compared to the six-item test. The small loss is compensated for by the tremendous increase in administrative economy. It is also significant to point out that the order of testing is unimportant, which enables the teacher to employ three testing stations.

The norms for college men are shown in Table 8 - 5. The norms for boys in grades 7 through 11 for each test item are presented in Tables 8 - 6, 8 - 7, and 8 - 8.

TABLE 8 - 5

T-Scores for College Men

T-Score	Standing Broad Jump (Inches)	Zig Zag Run (Seconds)	Medicine Ball Put (Feet)	T-Score
80	113 Up	20.8 Up	58 Up	80
75	109-112	21.6-20.9	55-57	75
70	105-108	22.4-21.7	52-54	70
65	101-104	23.2-22.5	48-51	65
60	97-100	23.9-23.2	45-47	60
55	93-96	24.7-24.0	42-44	55
50	89-92	25.5-24.8	39-41	50
45	85-88	26.3-25.6	35-38	45
40	81-84	27.1-26.4	32-34	40
35	77-80	27.8-27.2	29-31	35
30	73-76	28.6-27.9	26-28	30
25	69-72	29.4-28.7	23-25	25
20	68 Down	29.5 Down	22 Down	20

TABLE 8 - 6

Standing Broad Jump T-Scores for High School and Junior High School Boys

Grade	7	8	9	10	11	
T-Score						T-Score
80	90 Up	97 Up	103 Up	105 Up	112 Up	80
75	86-89	92-96	98-102	101-104	107-111	75
70	82-85	88-91	93-97	97-100	103-106	70
65	77-81	83-87	88-92	92-96	97-102	65
60	73-76	78-82	83-87	88-91	93-96	60
55	69-72	73-77	79-82	83-87	88-92	55
50	65-68	69-72	74-78	79-82	83-87	50
45	61-64	64-68	69-73	75-78	78-82	45
40	56-60	59-63	64-68	71-74	74-77	40
35	52-55	54-58	59-63	66-70	69-73	35
30	48-51	50-53	54-58	62-65	64-68	30
25	44-47	45-49	49-53	58-61	59-63	25
20	43 Down	44 Down	48 Down	57 Down	58 Down	20

TABLE 8 - 7

Zig Zag Run T-Scores for High School and Junior High School Boys

Grade	7	8	9	10	11	T-Score
T-Score						
80	20.1 Down	17.8 Down	20.2 Down	21.6 Down	21.5 Down	80
75	21.4 - 20.2	19.5 - 17.9	21.3 - 20.3	22.7 - 21.7	22.6 - 21.6	75
70	22.7 - 21.5	21.2 - 19.6	22.4 - 21.4	23.8 - 22.8	23.7 - 22.7	70
65	24.0 - 22.8	22.8 - 21.3	23.5 - 22.5	24.8 - 23.9	24.7 - 23.8	65
60	25.2 - 24.1	24.5 - 22.9	24.6 - 23.6	25.8 - 24.9	25.8 - 24.8	60
55	26.5 - 25.3	26.2 - 24.6	25.7 - 24.7	26.9 - 25.9	26.8 - 25.9	55
50	27.8 - 26.6	27.8 - 26.3	26.8 - 25.8	27.9 - 27.0	27.8 - 26.9	50
45	29.0 - 27.9	29.5 - 27.9	27.9 - 26.9	28.9 - 28.0	28.9 - 27.9	45
40	30.3 - 29.1	31.2 - 29.6	29.0 - 28.0	29.9 - 29.0	29.9 - 29.0	40
35	31.6 - 30.4	32.8 - 31.3	30.1 - 29.1	31.0 - 30.0	31.0 - 30.0	35
30	32.8 - 31.7	34.5 - 32.9	31.2 - 30.2	32.1 - 31.1	32.0 - 31.1	30
25	34.1 - 32.9	36.2 - 34.6	32.3 - 31.3	33.1 - 32.2	33.0 - 32.1	25
20	34.2 Up	36.3 Up	32.4 Up	33.2 Up	33.1 Up	20

TABLE 8 - 8

Medicine Ball Put T-Scores for High School and Junior High School Boys

Grade	7	8	9	10	11	T-Score
T-Score						
80	43 Up	45 Up	49 Up	50 Up	54 Up	80
75	38-42	43-44	46-48	47-49	51-53	75
70	35-37	40-42	44-45	44-46	48-50	70
65	33-34	37-39	41-43	42-43	46-47	65
60	30-32	34-36	38-40	39-41	43-45	60
55	27-29	31-33	35-37	37-38	40-42	55
50	25-26	28-30	32-34	34-36	37-39	50
45	22-24	25-27	29-31	32-33	34-36	45
40	19-21	23-24	27-28	29-31	31-33	40
35	17-18	20-22	24-26	27-28	28-30	35
30	14-16	17-19	21-23	24-26	25-27	30
25	12-13	14-16	18-20	22-23	22-24	25
20	11 Down	13 Down	17 Down	21 Down	21 Down	20

Scott Motor Ability Test.[35,36]

<u>Objective</u>: To measure general motor ability in order to determine the individual needs of students and to assist in the sectioning of classes.

<u>Age and Sex</u>: College women and high school girls.

<u>Validity</u>: Two test batteries were devised through the use of subjective ratings of sports ability, skill items common to sports, the McCloy general motor ability test items for girls, and a composite score made up of the above criteria.

Validity was established for each test battery. The criterion that was used was a composite score comprised of ratings by experts, T-scores from a variety of sport skills, and an achievement score composed of three fundamental activities. Validity coefficients of .91 and .87 were found for Battery 1 and Battery 2, respectively. (See Table 8 - 9 for validity coefficients for each test item.)

<u>Reliability</u>: The reliability coefficients for individual test items ranged from .62 to .91. (See Table 8 - 9 for reliability coefficients for each test item.)

TABLE 8 - 9

Validity and Reliability Data
for Scott Motor Ability Test Items[37]

Test Item	Validity	Reliability
1. Basketball Throw	.79 when correlated with the McCloy general motor ability test, total points scored from running, throwing, and jumping, and .78 with composite criterion of total points, other sport items, and subjective ratings.	An r of .89 on successive trials with 200 University of Iowa women.
2. Dash	Utilizing the same criteria as the basketball throw, r's of .71 and .62 were obtained, respectively.	.62 with 88 University of Iowa women.
3. Wall Pass	Using the same criteria as above, coefficients of .47 and .54 were found, respectively.	.62 with 188 college women, .75 for 185 high school girls.
4. Broad Jump	Using same criteria as above, the coefficients were .79 and .78, respectively.	.79 for 252 college women, .92 for 144 high school girls.
5. Obstacle Race	When correlated with the longer, but similar test, an r of .94 was found. The older test used the same criteria as described above, and the coefficients were .65 and .58, respectively.	.91 when taken on two successive days.

Test Battery 1 is made up of the following test items: the basketball throw, dash, wall pass, and broad jump.

Test Battery 2 has three items: basketball throw, broad jump, and obstacle race. This battery is much easier to administer and may be preferable because of this factor. It differs very little from the larger battery in validity. Scott has found it to be accurate in predicting rate of achievement in physical education skills, and it has been used effectively for screening purposes in locating individuals needing special help in motor ability development.

Equipment and Materials: (1) Basketball Throw: Three or four regulation basketballs, (although one could suffice), measuring tape. Chalk or tape is desirable to mark off the floor. (2) Dash: Stop watch and whistle. Tape or chalk or other marking materials are also needed. (3) Wall Pass: Regulation basketball, stop watch, and unobstructed wall space. (4) Broad Jump: Gymnasium mat, measuring tape (or mat marked in inches), beat board (or 2-foot solid board). (5) Obstacle Race: Stop watch, jump standard, a 6-foot cross bar and supports, and chalk or tape for marking.

BASKETBALL THROW

Directions: This test is intended to measure arm and shoulder girdle strength and coordination. The subject attempts to throw the basketball as far as she can without stepping on or across the restraining line. The student has three trials. The directions emphasize that no demonstration should be given. Any technique of throwing is allowed, but the teacher is not to specify any particular one.

Scoring: The distance from the restraining line to the spot where the ball lands is measured to the nearest foot. The best of the three trials is used as the score for this event.

Safety: There are no particular hazards connected with this test. Sufficient warm-up should be provided, and the throwing area should be kept clear of traffic. On each trial the student should not be allowed to throw until the marker and scorer are ready.

Additional Pointers: The students can be utilized to help with the testing as they proceed from one station to another. One student should be utilized as a spotter to work the landing point while another is utilized to watch for fouls at the throwing line.

DASH

Directions: On the command to go the student starts running down the lane as fast as possible until the whistle blows. The student does not have to stop on the whistle, but simply slows down and stops at her own pace. The student should be told that the running time will be 4 seconds, and only one trial is given. The student stands behind the starting line in any position she wishes.

Scoring: The running course is marked and numbered in one-yard zones. The zone in which the student was at the sound of the whistle is quickly marked by an assistant. The distance in yards is then noted and recorded as the score for this event.

Safety: There are several factors that should be considered with regard to safety. Pulled muscles and other injuries can easily occur without adequate warm-up. Another precaution the teacher must take is to provide ample space at the end of the course to accommodate a gradual stop. Without sufficient space it is not only a safety hazard, but it will affect the validity of the test as well if the performer starts to slow down prior to the whistle.

Adequate footwear is another factor that should be insisted upon by the teacher in the interests of safety (and again validity). Of course, all obstructions must be removed from the running lane. The width of the lane itself should be at least 4 feet, and additional space along the sides of the lane should be kept clear.

Additional Pointers: (1) The first ten yards need not be marked off in one-yard intervals. The numbers can either be painted (or chalked) on the floor, or cards can be prepared and placed along the side of the running lane. The latter is preferable since it has to be done only once and the cards can then be used again. (2) More than one student can be tested at the same time if provisions are made for judges. If this procedure is followed, the judges must be impressed with the importance of keeping her eyes on her assigned runner. The judges must guard against the tendency to watch to see who is ahead. At the sound of the whistle each judge should run out and stand on the spot at which her assigned runner was when the whistle sounded. (3) The tester must be careful not to glance up at the runner(s) and thereby let the watch run past the 4 seconds.

WALL PASS. (Same as wall pass test previously presented in the Barrow motor ability test.)

BROAD JUMP. (Same as for the standing broad jump test previously presented in Chapter VI.)

OBSTACLE RACE

Directions: This test was modified from the earlier form.[36] It was designed to measure speed, agility, and general body coordination. The student starts in a back-lying position on the floor with her heels at the starting line. When given the command to go, she scrambles to her feet and runs to the first square that is marked on the floor (see Figure 8 - 2). She must step on this square, and on each of the next two squares, with both feet. She then runs twice around the jump standard and proceeds to the crossbar, gets up and runs to the end line, touches it with her hand, runs back to line F, touches it, runs and touches the end line, back to line F, then sprints across the end line. One trial is given.

Scoring: The stop watch is started when the signal to go is given and stopped when the student sprints across the end line. The score is the number of seconds, to the nearest tenth of a second, that is required to complete the course.

Safety: As is true in all speed and agility tests, the subject's footwear is an important consideration. Another possible source of injury is the part of the test in which the student must crawl or roll under the crossbar. This sometimes results in a scraped knee, and the teacher might consider the use of knee guards for this test. The crossbar itself should be made of very light material so as not to pose any danger when it is knocked down. The teacher should keep onlookers well away from the course boundaries, and particularly away from the finishing area. Adequate warm-up should be provided.

Additional Pointers: (1) It is suggested that all the class be given the directions at the same time in order to avoid needless repetion. (2) The teacher should walk through the test and make sure the students understand what is meant by stepping with both feet in the squares. It is not necessary to call the student back if the toe or heel is not completely inside the square. (3) It should not be considered a foul if the subject happens to bump and dislodge the crossbar as she passes under it. (4) The student cannot grasp the jump standard as she runs around it. (5) The teacher should emphasize the method of circling the jump standard and also stress the number of times the student must touch behind the end line and line F, as this procedure can result in some confusion if not thoroughly understood. (6) It is suggested that two timers and watches could be utilized to reduce the testing time. In this arrangement the second girl is started when the first girl finishes circling the jump standard.

Norms: T-scales are available for each test item and for the composite scores (G.M.A.) for each test battery for high school girls and college women. These norms are presented in Tables 8 - 10 and 8 - 11.

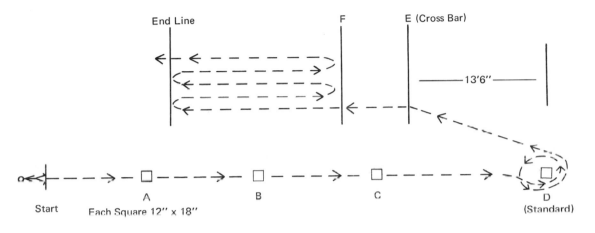

FIGURE 8 - 2

Obstacle Race for Scott Motor Ability Test

Two methods are suggested for computing the composite score. One method is to obtain an average T-score by adding the T-score values for the three or four tests given and dividing this sum by the appropriate number. For example, on Test Battery 1, a high school girl has the following T-scores: 45 for the basketball throw, 55 for the dash, 52 for the wall pass, and 48 for the broad jump. The mean of these T-scores is thus 50, which indicates that the student's overall performance on this test battery was exactly average.

Another method is to utilize the regression equation for the appropriate test battery, as follows:

Test Battery 1 (4 items) .7 (basketball throw) + 2.0 (dash)
+ 1.0 (wall pass) + .5 (broad jump)

Test Battery 2 (3 items) 2.0 (basketball throw) + 1.4 (broad jump)
− (obstacle race)

To illustrate, a college girl has the following raw scores on the 3-item test battery:

Basketball Throw	47 feet
Broad Jump	72 inches
Obstacle Race	20.6 seconds

The raw scores are multiplied by their proper weightings and the products added, as follows:

$$2.0(47) + 1.4(72) - 20.6 = 174.2$$

This value is then found to represent a T-score of 63, which indicates that this girl is considerably above average in motor ability.

TABLE 8 - 10

T-Scales For High School Girls
On Scott Motor Ability Test[37]

T-Score	Wall Pass (410)*	Basketball Throw (Ft.) (310)*	Broad Jump (In.) (287)*	4 Sec. Dash (Yd.) (398)*	Obstacle Race (Sec.) (374)*	T-Score
80	16	71				80
79			96			79
78						78
77	15	68	94	27		77
76		66			18.5-18.9	76
75		65				75
74		64	92			74
73	14	63				73
72		61				72
71		59	90	26		71
70		55	88		19.0-19.4	70
69	13	54				69
68		52	86	25		68
67		51			19.5-19.9	67
66		50				66
65		49				65
64		48	84	24	20.0-20.4	64
63	12	47				63
62		46	82		20.5-20.9	62
61			80			61
60		45		23		60
59		44	78		21.0-21.4	59
58	11	43				58
57		42	76		21.5-21.9	57
56		41				56
55		40	74	22		55
54					22.0-22.4	54
53		39				53
52	10		72			52
51		37			22.5-22.9	51
50		36		21		50

TABLE 8 - 10 (cont.)

T-Score	Wall Pass (410)*	Basketball Throw (Ft.) (310)*	Broad Jump (In.) (287)*	4 Sec. Dash (Yd.) (398)*	Obstacle Race (Sec.) (374)*	T-Score
49		35	70			49
48			68		23.0-23.4	48
47		34	66			47
46	9	33			23.5-23.9	46
45		32	64	20		45
44		31			24.0-24.4	44
43			62			43
42		30			24.5-24.9	42
41	8	29	60	19		41
40		28				40
39			58		25.0-25.4	39
38		27	56			38
37	7		54		25.5-25.9	37
36		26			26.0-26.4	36
35			52	18	26.5-26.9	35
34		25	50		27.0-27.4	34
33						33
32		24	47		27.5-27.9	32
31	6	23				31
30			44		28.0-28.4	30
29		22		17	28.5-28.9	29
28					29.0-29.4	28
27		21			29.5-29.9	27
26			40		30.0-30.4	26
25	5	20				25
24				16	30.5-31.9	24
23		19	36		31.5-32.4	23
22				15	32.5-24.9	22
21		16				21
20	4			14	35.0-36.0	20

* Indicates the number of subjects on which the scale is based.

TABLE 8 - 11

T-Scales for College Women on Scott Motor Ability Test

T-Score	Basketball Throw	Passes	Broad Jump	Obstacle Race	T-Score
85	75	18	86	17.5-17.9	85
84					84
83	71	17		18.0-18.4	83
82					82
81		16	85		81
80	70	15			80
79	69			18.5-18.9	79
78	68	14	84		78
77	67		83		77
76	66				76
75	65		82	19.0-19.4	75
74	64		81		74
73	62		80		73
72	61	13	79	19.5-19.9	72
71	59				71
70	58		78	20.0-20.4	70
69	57		77		69
68	56		76		68
67	55		75	20.5-20.9	67
66	54	12	74		66
65	52				65
64	51		73	21.0-21.4	64
63	50		72		63
62	48		71	21.5-21.9	62
61	47				61
60	46		70		60
59	45	11	69	22.0-22.4	59
58	44		68		58
57	43		67	22.5-22.9	57
56	42				56
55	41		66	23.0-23.4	55
54	40		65		54
53	39		64	23.5-23.9	53
52	38	10	63		52
51	37			24.0-24.4	51

TABLE 8 - 11 (cont.)

T-Score	Basketball Throw	Passes	Broad Jump	Obstacle Race	T-Score
50	36		62		50
49	35		61	24.5-24.9	49
48			60		48
47	34		59	25.0-25.4	47
46	33		58		46
45	32	9	57	25.5-25.9	45
44	31				44
43			56	26.0-26.4	43
42	30		55		42
41			54	26.5-26.9	41
40	29		53	27.0-27.4	40
39	28	8	52		39
38				27.5-27.9	38
37	27		51	28.0-28.4	37
36	26		50		36
35			49	28.5-28.9	35
34	25		48	29.0-29.4	34
33			47	29.5-29.9	33
32		7	46	30.0-30.4	32
31			45	30.5-30.9	31
30	24		44	31.0-31.4	30
29			43	31.5-31.9	29
28	23		42	32.0-32.4	28
27	21		41	32.5-32.9	27
26		6	40	33.0-33.4	26
25	20		39	33.5-33.9	25
24			38	34.0-34.4	24
23		5	37	34.5-34.9	23
22			36		22
21	19			35.0-35.4	21
20					20
19			35	35.5-35.9	19
18					18
17	18	4			17
16					16
15					15
14				43.5-43.9	14
13			30	45.5-45.9	13

Latchaw Motor Achievement Tests for Fourth, Fifth, and Sixth Grade Boys and Girls.[24,25]

Objective: To measure general motor achievement.

Age and Sex: Fourth, fifth, and sixth grade girls and boys.

Validity: Face validity was accepted for each test.

Reliability: The reliability coefficients for the individual test items ranged from .77 to .97. Students from twenty elementary schools in two states were tested.

Equipment and Materials: The special equipment and the space needed for each of the test items are: (1) Basketball Wall Pass: Stop watch, regulation basketball, tape or marking equipment, and wall space to accommodate a target that is 8 feet long, 4 feet high, and drawn 3 feet from the floor. Restraining line is 8 feet long and 4 feet from wall. (See Figure 8 - 3.) (2) Volleyball Wall Volley: Stop watch, regulation volleyball, and a target identical to basketball wall pass test (Figure 8 - 3). (3) Vertical Jump: Forty-eight one-inch cloth strips, cut so that when suspended from a horizontal bar, the longest strip is 5 feet from the floor and each succeeding one is one inch shorter, with the shortest strip being 8 feet 11 inches from the floor. Forty-eight pennies are needed so that the bottom of each strip is weighted to provide even hanging. (4) Standing Broad Jump: A mat and measuring tape unless mat is marked in inches. (5) Shuttle Run: Stop watch, floor markings, as follows: two 1/2 inch lines parallel to each other and 20 feet apart. The lines are at least 20 feet long. The test requires space to permit the 20 foot shuttle run as well as an equal distance to allow for slowing down after crossing the finish line. (6) Soccer Wall Volley: Stop watch, regulation soccer ball, marking material, and wall and floor space to accommodate a wall target 4′ × 2½′ and a 4′ × 2½′ floor area. (See Figure 8 - 4.) (7) Softball Repeated Throws: Stop watch, regulation softball (12-inch inseam), marking material and wall and floor space to accommodate a wall target 10 feet high and 5½ feet wide with the bottom of the target 6 inches above the floor. A 5½ foot square is marked as the throwing area, 9 feet from the wall. A backstop 15 feet behind throwing area should be 12 feet long and at least 2½ feet high (Figure 8 - 5).

BASKETBALL WALL PASS

Reliability:	Boys, Grade 4 = .91	Girls, Grade 4 = .94
	Grade 5 = .84	Grade 5 = .89
	Grade 6 = .78	Grade 6 = .83

Directions: The student must stand behind the restraining line which is 4 feet from the wall. When the teacher gives the signal to begin, the student throws the ball against the wall inside the target as many times as possible in 15 seconds. The ball must be thrown from behind the restraining line in order to count, and it must hit completely inside the target. Balls which touch the line do not count. The student does not have to catch the ball first in order for it to be a successful hit. In other words he could catch it in the air, on the bounce, or have to run to retrieve it before he throws. If he loses control of the ball, he must recover it himself. A 10 second practice period is allowed, then two 15 second trials are given.

Scoring: The score is the number of correct hits in the 15 second period. The best of the two trials is recorded as the score.

Safety: There are no particular safety hazards connected with this test. The area should be kept free from traffic and obstacles which might be in the way of a subject who loses control of the ball.

Additional Pointers: (1) Make sure that the subject understands that he must hit inside the target area, and he must throw from behind the line. (2) It should also be stressed that he doesn't have to catch the ball in the air on the rebound, and that if he loses it, he must retrieve it as quickly as possible, since the time keeps running (3) It makes for much easier testing if the person keeping the time does not have to simultaneously count hits and watch for faults.

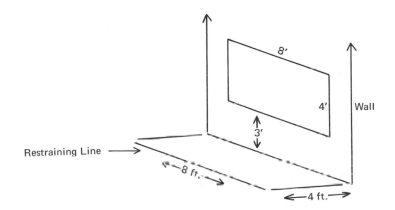

FIGURE 8 - 3

**Wall and Floor Markings for Basketball Wall Pass
and Volleyball Wall Volley Tests**

VOLLEYBALL WALL VOLLEY
<u>Reliability</u>:   Boys, Grade 4 = .85   Girls, Grade 4 = .88
                      Grade 5 = .89   Grade 5 = .92
                      Grade 6 = .91   Grade 6 = .93

<u>Directions</u>: On the signal to begin the subject throws the ball (from behind the restraining line) against the wall. He then must hit it as it bounces off the wall so that it hits inside the target. He must hit from behind the restraining line, and if the ball gets away, he must recover it. Anytime that he must start again, he may throw the ball against the wall and then continue to hit it. Balls that are thrown or *carried* are not counted, nor are balls which hit the lines of the target. One 10 second practice test is given, then the subject has four 15-second trials.
<u>Scoring</u>: The best of the four trials is counted, with the score being the number of legal hits inside the target.
<u>Safety</u>: Same as in basketball wall pass.
<u>Additional Pointers</u>: (1) The teacher should be sure to explain the difference between a hit and a throw, or *carry*. (2) Other procedures are the same as the basketball wall pass.

VERTICAL JUMP. (Same as for vertical jump presented in Chapter VI, except cloth strips are used and unlimited trials are allowed.)

STANDING BROAD JUMP. (Same as for the standing broad jump test previously presented in Chapter VI.)

SHUTTLE RUN

Reliability: Boys, Grade 4 = .89   Girls, Grade 4 = .84
                    Grade 5 = .89   Grade 5 = .85
                    Grade 6 = .89   Grade 6 = .79

Directions: The student stands behind the starting line with one foot against the line. On the command to go he runs to the other line and places at least one foot on the line. He then returns to the other side, touches that line with at least one foot, returns, and so on back and forth until three round trips have been completed. He thus finishes by crossing the same line at which he started. The student is stopped if at any time he does not at least touch one of the lines. He may step beyond a line, of course. If he is stopped, he is given no score for the trial and after a short rest is tested again. If he fails again to follow directions, he is given a score of zero for that trial. Two trials are given in this test.

Scoring: The better of two trials is taken as the score for this test, measured in seconds to the nearest tenth of a second.

Safety: All subjects should be required to wear suitable shoes to prevent injury to their feet. Warm-up is recommended, and the area should be kept clear beyond both lines, and especially at the finish line.

Additional Pointers: (1) Spotters at both ends could be assigned to watch for foot faults; however, the tester can usually do the timing, watching and recording quite easily by himself in such a small area. (2) When the student sprints across the end line at the finish of the race, the timer should be parallel to that line in order to get the most accurate score. (3) If subjects are tested in pairs, the factor of fatigue can be well handled by testing student A, then B, then A again, and finally B. Short rest periods between the two trials are thus provided without any lag in the testing. (4) If a large number of students are to be tested, chalk is unsuitable for marking the lines as it rubs off. White washable tempera paint is recommended.

SOCCER WALL VOLLEY

Reliability: Boys, Grade 4 = .82   Girls, Grade 4 = .77
                    Grade 5 = .89   Grade 5 = .83
                    Grade 6 = .88   Grade 6 = .77

Directions: The subject stands behind the restraining line, which is an extension of one foot on either side of the 4-foot line on the floor area farthest from the wall. He places the ball at any place he chooses behind the line. When the teacher gives the signal to begin, the subject kicks the ball toward the wall in an attempt to hit inside the target. When the ball rebounds from the wall, the student attempts to kick it again inside the target. If the ball gets away from the student, he must recover it and bring it back into position to kick again. When the student is attempting to retrieve the ball, that is within the 4' × 2½' floor area between the restraining line and the wall, he may not use his hands. However, if he must recover a loose ball outside that area, he is allowed to use his hands. To be counted, all kicks must be made from behind the restraining line, and the ball must be completely within the target area without touching any line. A practice period of 15 seconds is allowed, then four 15-second trials are given.

Scoring: The number of legal kicks in a 15-second trial is counted, and the best of the four trials is used as the score. A penalty of 1 point is deducted for each time a subject touches the ball with his hands while in the rectangular floor area.

Safety: All subjects should wear shoes, and the area should be kept unobstructed.

Additional Pointers: (1) While a kick made from within the 6′ × 2½′ floor area is not counted as a legal score, the student may certainly kick a ball from within this area and then kick the ball on the rebound from behind the restraining line. In this way the student can recover the ball quickly and not use his hands. This point should be stressed. (2) The suggestions that were mentioned for the basketball wall pass and volleyball wall volley also apply for this item. In all three events the teacher may wish to regulate the degree of ball control loss. For example, if there is a large open area behind the subject, the student could not hope to recover a loose ball and return before the trial was over. Therefore, the teacher may wish to standardize it by having the students who are waiting to be tested stand in a line at a prescribed distance in back of the restraining line. Then, if the student loses control, the line of students could allow the ball to hit them, and be kept from rolling far, but they must not do anything to help or hinder the performer.

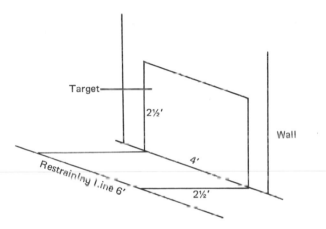

FIGURE 8 - 4

Wall and Floor Markings for Soccer Wall Volley Test

SOFTBALL REPEATED THROWS
Reliability: Boys, Grade 4 = .82   Girls, Grade 4 = .80
                      Grade 5 = .81   Grade 5 = .82
                      Grade 6 = .85   Grade 6 = .85

Directions: The student may stand anywhere within the 5½ foot square throwing area. On the command to go he throws the ball at the target with an overhand throwing motion. He attempts to catch the ball as it rebounds in the air, or on the bounce, so that he may throw it again as many times as possible in 15 seconds. Each ball must be thrown from within the throwing area in order to be legal, and the ball must strike the wall completely within the target boundaries. Balls that hit the target lines do not count. If the student loses control of the ball, he must retrieve it as quickly as possible, rush back to the throwing area, and continue throwing. A practice period of 10 seconds is provided, and then two 15 second trials are given.

Scoring: The better score of the two 15 second trials is recorded. The score is the number of correct throws in the 15 second period.

Safety: All persons should be kept well away from the target area. The entire testing area from the wall to the backstop and with ample lateral distance should be kept free of obstructions and people.

Additional Pointers: (1) The backstop may be a rolled mat, an ordinary table turned on its side, or an actual wall. (2) A wall volley test with a softball quickly softens and alters the shape of the ball. This, of course, can influence subsequent performance, and it should be considered when administering the test. The tester may wish to bring out new balls periodically or rotate them in some manner. At any rate it can be expensive, but with children of this age it is not nearly as serious a problem as with older students.

Norms: Norms are available in the form of T-scores and percentile scores for each of the seven tests. The T-scales provide for separate norms for boys and girls at the fifth grade level. These norms are presented in Tables 8 - 12 and 8 - 13.

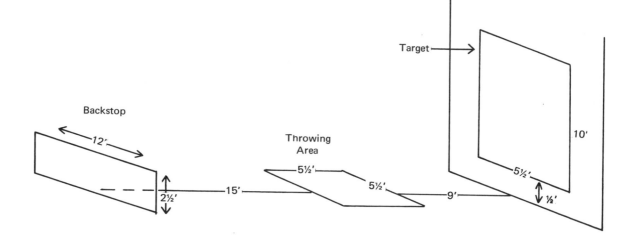

FIGURE 8 - 5

Wall and Floor Markings for Softball Repeated Throws Test

TABLE 8 - 12

Latchaw Achievement Scales for Fifth Grade Boys*

T-Scores	Basketball Wall Pass	Volleyball Wall Volley	Vertical Jump	Standing Broad Jump	Shuttle Run	Soccer Wall Volley	Softball Repeated Throws	Percentile
75	27 / 26		17"	6'3"	11.2	16		99
70	22	20	16	6-2	11.4	15	14	97
65	21 / 20	19 / 17	15	6-0 / 5-8	11.5 / 11.8	14 / 13 / 12	13 / 12	92
60	19 / 18	14 / 13 / 11	14 / 13	5-3	12.2	11	11	81
55	17 / 16	10	12	5-0	12.5	10	10	69
50	15	8	11	4-3	12.8	9	9	50
45	14 / 13	7 / 6 / 5	10	4-5	13.3	8	8	30
40	12 / 11	4	9	4-0	13.7	7	7	15
35	10 / 9	3	8	3-9	14.0		6	6
30	8		7	3-8	14.8			2
25	6	2		3-7	15.9 / 15.1	5	5	1

*Modified for economy of space. By permission of author and M. Gladys Scott and Esther French, *Measurement and Evaluation in Physical Education*. Dubuque, Iowa: Wm. C. Brown Company, 1959.

TABLE 8 - 13

Latchaw Achievement Scales for Fifth Grade Girls*

T-Scores	Basketball Wall Pass	Volleyball Wall Volley	Vertical Jump	Standing Broad Jump	Shuttle Run	Soccer Wall Volley	Softball Repeated Throws	Percentile
75	20	18	16	5'8"	11.6	15	10	99
70	19	17, 13, 12	15	5-7	11.8	14, 13	9	97
65	18, 17	11	14, 13	5-4	12.2	12, 11		92
60	16, 15	9, 8, 7	12	4-10	12.5	10		81
55			11	4-5	13.0	9	8	69
50	14	6, 5	10	4-1	13.4	8	7	50
45	13, 12	4		3-10	13.5, 13.7	7		30
40	11, 10, 9	3	9, 8	3-8, 3-7	14.0, 14.1, 14.4	6	6	15
35	8, 7	2	7	3-3	14.5	5		6
30	6	1		2-11	15.1	4	5, 4	2
25			6	2-8	15.9, 16.0		3	1

*Modified for economy of space.

Other Tests of Motor Ability

Space does not permit the description of other general motor ability tests. Brief mention is made here of some of these. The reader is referred to the individual references for test descriptions and norms.

McCloy[27,29] devised tests which were described as being measures of general motor achievement. These tests included track and field events and strength tests. The test items for boys consisted of pull-ups, a 50- or 100-yard dash, running or standing broad jump, running high jump, and a shot-put or basketball throw for distance, or baseball throw for distance. For girls the items were modified pull-ups, a dash, a broad jump, and a throw. Through the use of his tables the General Motor Ability Score (GMAS) is obtained with the following formulae for boys and girls:

$$\text{GMAS (Boys)} = .1022 \text{ (total track and field points)} + .3928 \text{ (chinning strength)}$$

$$\text{GMAS (Girls)} = .42 \text{ (total track and field points)} + 9.6 \text{ (number of chins)}$$

Cozen's General Athletic Ability Test[12] has been used for measuring motor ability of college men for a number of years. Through a study of forty activities seven tests were selected. The test items are dips, baseball throw for distance, football punt for distance, bar snap, standing broad jump, dodging run and quarter-mile run. These items, which were selected as measuring the elements of general motor ability, are weighted and totaled. Then, through the use of a classification scale which takes into account body size, the score for the test battery is interpreted as superior, above average, average, below average, and inferior. The validity and reliability coefficients have been very high. The principal disadvantage to this test is the space and time requirements for administration.

Larson[23] developed a motor ability test for college men through factor analysis which has both an indoor and an outdoor form. The indoor test battery includes a dodging run, chinning, dipping, vertical jump, and the bar snap. The outdoor test has the baseball throw for distance, bar snap, chinning, and the vertical jump. The raw scores are converted to T-scores which are weighted and totaled in order to be used for classification. High validity and reliability have been reported.

The Humiston Motor Ability Test[19] was devised to measure the present status in motor ability for college women for the primary purpose of classifying them for intramurals and physical education. It contains seven test items consisting of a dodging run, sideward roll on a mat, climb over a box, turn around in a circle, and run between two barriers, throwing of a basketball over a rope and catching it, and 60-foot sprint. These items are arranged in the form of an obstacle course set upon a gymnasium floor. The items must be executed in sequence and the score is the elapsed time to the nearest tenth of a second.

The Newton Motor Ability Test for high school girls was developed by Powell and Howe.[32] The test is made up of three items: the standing broad jump; a hurdle race in which the girl jumps over five 15-inch hurdles, runs around an Indian club and back over the hurdles; and a scramble, which involves getting to her feet from a supine position and running to tap a bell twice, then returning to the starting position, clapping her hands twice on the floor, and, finally, repeating the task until the fourth double tap of the bell. The authors recommend that the test be given again on successive days and an average taken for each item in order to increase reliability.

Motor Educability

The term motor educability was coined to mean the facility with which an individual is able to learn new motor skills. It has been thought of as being somewhat comparable to an intelligence test, except that it pertains to the physical aptitude of the individual. Of course, everyone recognizes that the mental ability of the person cannot be separated and is obviously intrinsically involved in the perception of the motor skill item that is to be tested. (See Chapter II for Historical Points on Motor Educability.)

Generally speaking, the validity of the tests of motor educability has not been impressive. Perhaps validity relates to the over-all problem of finding generality in motor performance. There definitely seems to be a need for more research in this area if physical educators are to continue to speak of general motor abilities. It might be that a different approach to the problem is in order. Possibly, instead of seeking stunts or tasks which are not easily improved by practice — the uncovering of which have not been too successful — researchers should allow practice and then measure motor educability in relation to the speed with which the student is able to master the skill. Henry[17] employed this practice in establishing learning scores while holding initial skill constant.

Another approach might be to have the student practice one skill, then be tested on a different but similar skill, and then measure the rapidity or ease of learning motor skills through transfer.

For the physical educator who may wish to incorporate motor educability testing in his program, or who may wish to investigate this area further, the Iowa-Brace, the Johnson-Metheny, and the Adams Sports-type tests are briefly described here.

Iowa-Brace Test[28,29]

Test 1. One foot — touch head.

Stand on the left foot. Bend trunk forward and place both hands on the floor. Raise the right leg and stretch it backward. Touch the head to the floor and return to standing position without losing the balance. It is a failure: (1) not to touch the head to the floor, and (2) to lose the balance and touch the right foot on the floor or move the left foot.

Test 2. Side leaning rest.

Sit down on the floor with the legs straight and the feet together. Put the right hand on the floor behind you. Pivot to the right and assume a side leaning-rest position. Hold this position with the weight on the right hand and the right foot (left arm raised) for five counts. It is a failure: (1) not to assume the correct position, and (2) not to hold the position for five counts.

Test 3. Grapevine.

Standing with both heels together, bend down and extend both arms down between the knees and around behind the ankles. Hold the fingers together in front of the ankles without losing the balance. Hold for five seconds. It is a failure: (1) to fall over, (2) not to touch the fingers of both hands together, and (3) not to hold the position for five seconds.

Test 4. One knee balance.

Turn to the right. Kneel down on one knee. Raise other leg from the floor, arms stretched out at the side, and maintain balance for five counts. It is a failure: (1) to touch the floor with any part of the body other than the one leg and knee, and (2) to fall over.

Test 5. Stork stand.
Stand on left foot. Hold the bottom of right foot against the inside of the left knee. Place the hands on the hips. Close the eyes and hold this position for ten seconds without shifting the left foot about on the floor. It is a failure: (1) to lose the balance, (2) not to keep the right foot against the knee, and (3) to open the eyes or remove hands from the hips.

Test 6. Double heel click.
Jump upward and clap the feet together twice and land with the feet apart (any distance). It is a failure: (1) not to click the feet together twice, and (2) to land with the feet touching each other.

Test 7. Cross leg squat.
Fold arms across chest. Cross the feet and sit down cross-legged. Then get up without unfolding the arms or having to move the feet about to regain balance. It is a failure: (1) to unfold arms, (2) to lose the balance, and (3) to not be able to get up.

Test 8. Full left turn.
Stand with the feet together. Jump upward and make a full turn to the left, landing on approximately the same spot. Do not lose the balance or move the feet after they hit the floor. It is a failure: (1) not to make a full turn, and (2) to move the feet after landing.

Test 9. One knee — head-to-the-floor.
Kneel on one knee with the other leg raised behind the body, but not touching the floor, the arms raised out at the side, shoulders level. Bend forward and touch the head to the floor, then raise the head from the floor and return to kneeling position without losing the balance. It is a failure: (1) to lose the balance, (2) to touch the floor with the raised leg or any other part of the body before completing the stunt, and (3) not to touch the head to the floor.

Test 10. Hop backward.
Stand on either foot. Close the eyes and take five hops backward. It is a failure: (1) to open eyes, and (2) to touch the floor with other foot.

Test 11. Forward hand kick.
Jump upward. Swing the legs forward and bend forward so as to touch the toes with both hands before landing. Keep the knees straight. It is a failure: (1) not to touch both feet in the air, and (2) not to keep knees straight (they must not bend more than 45 degrees).

Test 12. Full squat — arm circles.
Take a full squat position. Raise arms out to the sides at shoulder level. Wave the arms so that each hand makes a circle about one foot in diameter while jiggling up and down at the same time. Continue for ten counts. It is a failure: (1) to move the feet, (2) not to jiggle up and down, (3) not to move hands in circles, and (4) to lose balance and fall.

Test 13. Half turn jump — left foot.
Stand on the left foot and jump making a one-half turn to the left. Keep the balance. It is a failure: (1) to lose the balance, (2) to fail to complete the half turn, and (3) to touch the floor with the right foot.

Test 14. Three dips.
Take a front leaning-rest position (up position for push-ups). Bend the arms, touching the chest to the floor, and push up again, so arms are fully straight. Do this three times in succession. Do not touch the floor with the legs or abdomen. It is a failure: (1) not to push up three times, (2) not to touch chest to the floor, and (3) to touch the floor with any part of the body other than the hands, feet, and chest.

Test 15. Side Kick.

Swing the left foot sideways to the left while jumping upward with the right leg. Clap the feet together in the air and land with the feet apart. The feet should clap together at a point outside of the left shoulder. It is a failure: (1) not to swing the leg enough to the side, (2) not to clap the feet together in the air at a point outside of the left shoulder, and (3) not to land with the feet apart.

Test 16. Kneel, jump to feet.

Kneel on both knees. The toes must be extended out behind and not curled under. Swing the arms and jump to the feet. Do not rock back and curl toes, or lose the balance after landing. It is a failure: (1) to have the toes curled and rock back on them, and (2) not to execute the jump, and not to stand still on both feet.

Test 17. Russian dance.

Squat and stretch one leg forward. Perform a Russian dance step by extending the opposite leg out while hopping and retracting the other. Do this twice so that each leg is extended and retracted two times. The heel of the forward foot may touch the floor. The heel of the retracted foot should hit under hip each time. It is a failure: (1) to lose the balance, and (2) not to do the stunt twice with each leg.

Test 18. Full right turn.

Stand with both feet together. Jump up and make a full turn to the right, landing on about the same spot. Do not lose the balance upon landing causing the feet to move. It is a failure: (1) not to make a full right turn and land facing in the original direction, and (2) to lose the balance and have to move the feet after they touch the floor.

Test 19. The top.

Sit with knees bent. Slide arms between the legs and under and behind the knees and grasp the ankles. Roll rapidly around to the right with the weight first over right knee, then right shoulder, then on back, then left shoulder, left knee; then in sitting position. You should be facing in the opposite direction from where you started. From that position repeat the same roll and finish facing in the same direction from which the test was started. It is a failure: (1) to lose the grasp of the ankles, and (2) not to complete the circle.

Test 20. Single squat balance.

Squat down on either foot, hands on hips. Stretch the other leg forward and lift heel off the floor. Hold this position for five counts. It is a failure: (1) to remove the hands from the hips, (2) to touch the floor with the extended foot, and (3) to lose the balance before the five seconds have elapsed.

Test 21. Jump foot.

Hold the toes of either foot in the opposite hand. Jump upward so that the free foot jumps over the foot that is held. Do not let go of the foot. It is a failure: (1) to let go of the foot that is held, and (2) not to jump through the loop made by the foot and arm.

In this test the students are paired and score one another. It is suggested that double lines are formed about ten feet apart with the students spaced about eight feet from one another. Each student has a pencil and score card. Scoring is on a pass or fail basis with two trials allowed. If the person does it correctly on the first trial, he receives 2 points. If he fails on the first trial, he immediately tries again and, if successful, receives 1 point. If he fails on this attempt he receives a zero. No practice is allowed.

Each stunt is explained and demonstrated. One line of students performs the first five stunts; the other line then performs all ten stunts, after which the first line performs the second five stunts. A perfect score is 20. The batteries for the different grade levels for boys and girls are shown in Table 8 - 14. The numbers indicate the number of the stunt as enumerated and described above. The T-scale for the grade levels for boys and girls is presented in Table 8 - 15.

TABLE 8 - 14

Iowa-Brace Test Batteries

BOYS					
Elementary (Grades 4-6)		Junior High School (Grades 7-9)		Senior High School (Grades 10-12)	
1st half	2nd half	1st half	2nd half	1st half	2nd half
10	2	1	2	1	3
4	3	14	3	11	14
13	7	13	12	16	15
11	16	19	16	5	17
8	17	6	17	20	21

GIRLS					
Elementary (Grades 4-6)		Junior High School (Grades 7-9)		Senior High School (Grades 10-12)	
1st half	2nd half	1st half	2nd half	1st half	2nd half
10	1	2	1	3	2
18	3	12	13	11	18
8	16	15	11	7	16
19	15	19	16	17	9
11	6	17	20	19	20

TABLE 8 - 15

T-Score Table for Iowa-Brace Test

Test Score Points	BOYS			GIRLS		
	Elementary	Jr. High	Sr. High	Elementary	Jr. High	Sr. High
20	69	66	71	67	64	71
19	66	63	65	65	61	66
18	63	60	60	62	58	63
17	60	57	56	60	56	60
16	57	54	53	58	53	57
15	54	51	50	56	50	55
14	51	48	47	54	47	53
13	48	45	44	52	45	51
12	45	42	41	50	43	49
11	43	39	38	48	41	47
10	41	36	35	45	39	45
9	39	34	33	42	37	43
8	37	32	31	39	35	41
7	35	30	29	36	32	39
6	33	28	--	33	30	37
5	31	26	--	30	26	34
4	29	24	--	28	--	32
3	27	22	--	26	--	30
2	25	20	--	24	--	28
1	23	19	--	--	--	--

Johnson-Metheny Test[30]

A canvas, 15 feet long, is marked as shown in Figure 8 - 6. In the middle of the canvas a lane, 24 inches wide, is divided into 10 equal sections. Every other line is 3 inches wide; the narrow lines are ¾ inch wide. The centers of the lines are 18 inches apart. A ¾ inch line is then drawn down the center of the 24 inch lane, running the length of the canvas. The canvas should be placed over a mat with the ends and sides tucked under so that the canvas is stretched taut. Of course, the lines could be painted or chalked directly on a mat.

The four test items are described on the following pages. For measuring girls only the first three items are used. The numbers in parentheses refer to the number of the test item in the original Johnson test battery.

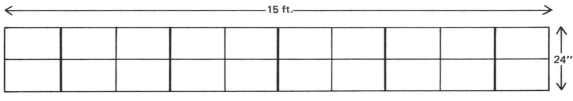

FIGURE 8 - 6

Canvas Markings for Johnson-Metheny Test

Front-roll Test (5).
The subject starts from a standing position at one end of the 24 inch lane. He performs one front roll within the limits of the first half of the lane; he then does another front roll within the limits of the second half of the lane. Each roll is worth 5 points. Points are deducted as follows: (a) For each roll two points are deducted if the subject strays beyond the left boundary and a similar penalty is imposed if he overreaches the right boundary. (b) One point is deducted for each roll if the subject does not complete the roll within the designated half of the lane. (c) Five points are deducted for failure to perform a true roll. If the subject fails on the first attempt, he is allowed to try a second roll in the last half of the lane.
Back-roll Test (7).
The subject starts from the end of the 24 inch lane and performs two back rolls. One roll is done within the first half of the lane; the other roll is performed within the second half of the lane. The scoring is the same as in the front-roll test.
Jumping-half-turn Test (8).
Standing on the first 3 inch line the subject jumps upward and executes a half turn in either direction, landing on the second 3 inch line. He is now facing the starting line. He then jumps upward making a half turn in the opposite direction from which the first jump was done. He proceeds in this manner, alternating directions of the turns, until he has completed four jumps. Perfect execution is worth ten points. Two points are deducted for each jump in which the subject does not land on the line with both feet, or if he should turn in the wrong direction. Only two points are deducted for each jump.
Jumping-full-turn Test (10).
The subject stands at the end of the lane, jumps upward with feet together, and executes a full turn in either direction while landing in the second section. He then jumps and makes another full turn in the same direction and lands in the fourth section. He continues the length of the mat in this manner. From a possible ten points, two points are deducted if the subject does not land on both feet, or if he fails to land in the designated section, or if he turns too far or not enough, or if he moves his feet upon landing for balance.

Adams Sports-Type Test[1]

Wall Volley Test.

The subject stands behind a line three feet from the wall and attempts to volley a volleyball against the wall above a line drawn 10½ feet above the floor ten times. Regardless of whether he succeeds or fails to volley it ten times, it constitutes one trial. Seven trials are given. A perfect score would be 70.

Lying Tennis Ball Catch.

The subject lies on his back and tosses a tennis ball in the air and catches it with either hand. The ball must go at least 6 feet in the air, and he must maintain the lying position. Ten trials are given. The score is the number of correct tosses. A perfect score would be 10.

Ball Bounce Test.

The subject stands in a circle that is 6 feet in diameter. Holding a softball bat one hand length from the thick end, he attempts to bounce a volleyball on the top end of the bat for ten consecutive bounces. Ball must bounce at least 6 inches on top of bat. Each attempt, whether successful or not, is a trial. Ten trials are given. A perfect score would be 100.

Basketball Shooting Test.

The subject shoots 20 free throws from the foul line. The number of baskets made is the score. A perfect score would be 20.

A regression equation is employed to determine the total score, as follows:

$$\text{Sport Educability Score} = 7.17 \text{ (wall volley)} + 17.28 \text{ (tennis ball catch)} + 2.7 \text{ (ball bounce)} + 19.22 \text{ (foul shooting)}.$$

Norms are presented in Table 8 - 16.

Problems Associated with Motor Ability Testing

The problems that are involved in the testing of general motor ability are primarily the problems that are associated with the testing of the separate qualities which make up the total battery. In other words, if the motor ability test contains measures of agility, balance, power, etc. the same problems are involved that are associated with agility testing, balance testing, power testing, etc. However, the problems are not necessarily additive. Some of the limitations of the individual measures are actually remedied when the tests are used as part of a battery that purports to measure general motor ability. For example, the standing broad jump might be questioned as a strict measure of leg power because of the arm and trunk action. However, for general motor ability, the inclusion of this coordination of the arms, trunk, and legs is desirable.

An obvious problem in motor ability testing is the question of whether or not physical fitness factors should be included in motor ability batteries. Such factors as cardiovascular capacity, strength, muscular endurance, and flexibility are essential to a satisfactory fitness level, whereas power, agility, coordination, reaction time, balance, and speed are factors primarily essential to motor performance and not to physical fitness. The authors have found the criteria set up for this distinction by Johnson and associates* most satisfactory.

---

*Perry B. Johnson and others. *Physical Education – A Problem Solving Approach to Health and Fitness.* Chicago: Holt, Rinehart and Winston, 1966, pp. 20-27.

TABLE 8 - 16

Adams' Test of Sport Type Motor
Educability for College Men

R	S	R	S	R	S
1391 — up	100	910 — 925	71	444 — 460	43
1375 — 1390	99	893 — 909	70	428 — 443	42
1358 — 1374	98	876 — 892	69	411 — 427	41
1342 — 1357	97	860 — 875	68	395 — 410	40
1325 — 1341	96	843 — 859	67	378 — 394	39
1308 — 1324	95	827 — 842	66	361 — 377	38
1292 — 1307	94	810 — 826	65	345 — 360	37
1275 — 1291	93	793 — 809	64	328 — 344	36
1258 — 1274	92	777 — 792	63	312 — 327	35
1242 — 1257	91	760 — 776	62	295 — 311	34
1225 — 1241	90	743 — 759	61	278 — 294	33
1209 — 1224	89	727 — 742	60	262 — 277	32
1192 — 1208	88	710 — 726	59	245 — 261	31
1175 — 1191	87	694 — 709	58	230 — 244	30
1159 — 1174	86	677 — 693	57	212 — 229	29
1142 — 1158	85	660 — 676	56	195 — 211	28
1126 — 1141	84	644 — 659	55	179 — 194	27
1109 — 1125	83	627 — 643	54	162 — 178	26
1092 — 1108	82	611 — 626	53	145 — 161	25
1076 — 1091	81	594 — 610	52	129 — 144	24
1059 — 1075	80	577 — 593	51	112 — 128	23
1042 — 1058	79	561 — 576	50	96 — 111	22
1026 — 1041	78	544 — 560	49	79 — 95	21
1009 — 1025	77	528 — 543	48	62 — 78	20
993 — 1008	76	511 — 527	47	46 — 61	19
976 — 992	75	494 — 510	46	29 — 45	18
969 — 975	74	478 — 493	45	9 — 28	17
943 — 968	73	461 — 477	44	below 9	16
926 — 942	72				

If this distinction is accepted by the majority of the members of our profession, then we can safely state that there is a need for new motor ability tests based on the factors identified above as motor ability factors.

The physical educator must make the decision concerning the efficacy of motor ability tests based on his own particular situation. Obviously, if only a few activities are offered in the program, then testing for purposes of classification should involve tests for those specific activities. On the other hand if a large number and wide variety of activities are taught, then task-specific testing is normally not feasible. In this case, the use of general motor ability tests would appear to be applicable. In all cases the teacher should utilize tests in conjunction with his own knowledge and subjective evaluation of the attitudes and the individual needs and interests of the students.

Findings and Conclusions From General Motor Ability Measurement and Research

Studies related to the topic of general motor ability are so numerous that this brief summary can only be considered as a sampling at best. Furthermore, only studies reported in the literature since 1950 are presented here, although a great deal of research in this area was done prior to that time. In fact, most of the motor ability tests were developed in the thirties and forties. However, the sprinkling of studies that are mentioned here are merely intended to acquaint the reader with some of the current information pertaining to this topic.

Although some of the test makers have proceeded on the assumption that motor ability is basically stable, Lafuze[21] found that general motor ability can be significantly improved through specific practice. Glassow and Krause[16] observed that while changes did occur, individuals tended to remain in the same relative position from year to year. Broer[8] studied the improvement in general motor ability of students of low ability. She concluded that basic instruction is more beneficial than participation in a regular activity program and should precede participation in the regular program. In a somewhat contradictory study Dohrmann[14] concluded that throwing and kicking training programs, performed in addition to the regular physical education programs, did not result in greater improvement in throwing and kicking ability than did the regular physical education program alone.

Some findings that are particularly relevant to the subject of testing and motor ability are those by Smith and Bozymowski,[41] Ryan,[34] and Singer.[39] Smith and Bozymowski concluded that subjects who viewed warm-up as being desirable performed better when warm-up preceded performance in an activity, such as an obstacle race. Subjects who had less favorable attitudes toward warm-up did not improve significantly following warm-up. Ryan studied the relationship between motor performance and arousal and found indications that arousal precedes performance. Singer found that non-athletes performed significantly better on a gross motor task than athletes in the presence of spectators.

Landiss[22] found that of eight activities studied, tumbling, gymnastics, and wrestling appeared most effective in developing those abilities measured in the Larson Test of Motor Ability. In a study with college women Bennett[6] investigated the relative effectiveness of four activities in developing specific and general motor ability. The subsequent ratings were swimming and modern dance first, basketball second, and folk dance third.

Boys were found to be superior to girls on all motor ability-educability tests and practically all physical skills by Smith[40] and Hoffman.[18] Bachman,[2] however, concluded that the rate of learning in large muscle skills was independent of age and sex over the range of 6 to 26 years, and that no sex differences were found in motor learning ability in that age range.

Lockhart and Mott[26] concluded that superior performers benefit by being segregated into homogeneous ability groupings, and that the majority of subjects involved preferred participation in classes composed of persons of similar ability. Walters[42] found that the above average bowlers had higher motor ability scores than the below average bowlers. Roloff,[33] Hoffman,[18] and Phillips and Summers[31]—all found positive realtionships between motor ability tests and kinesthesis. Athletes were found to be superior to non-athletes in performance on test items related to general motor ability and motor capacity by Shelley[38] and by Girolamo.[15] Coleman and others[11] reported a strong positive relationship between motor ability scores and both peer acceptance and social adjustment with boys experiencing learning difficulties.

BIBLIOGRAPHY

1. Adams, Arthur R., "A Test Construction Study of Sport-Type Motor Educability for College Men," (Microcarded Doctor's Dissertation, Louisiana State University, 1954).

2. Bachman, John C., "Motor Learning and Performance as Related to Age and Sex in Two Measures of Balance Coordination," *Research Quarterly,* 32:123-137, May, 1961.

3. Barrow, Harold M., "Test of Motor Ability for College Men," *Research Quarterly,* 25:253-260, October, 1954.

4. _____, *Motor Ability Testing for College Men,* Minneapolis: Burgess Publishing Co., 1951.

5. _____, and Rosemary McGee, *A Practical Approach to Measurement in Physical Education,* Philadelphia: Lea & Febiger, 1964.

6. Bennett, Colleen L., "Relative Contributions of Modern Dance, Folk Dance, Basketball, and Swimming to Motor Abilities of College Women," *Research Quarterly,* 27:253-261, October, 1956.

7. Brace, David K., *Measuring Motor Ability,* New York: A. S. Barnes & Co., 1927.

8. Broer, Marion R., "Evaluation of a Basic Skills Curriculum for Women Students of Low Motor Ability at the University of Washington," *Research Quarterly,* 26:15-27, March, 1955.

9. Carpenter, Aileen, "Strength Testing in the First Three Grades," *Research Quarterly,* 13:328-335, October, 1942.

10. _____, "The Measurements of General Motor Capacity and General Motor Ability in the First Three Grades," *Research Quarterly,* 13:444-465, December, 1942.

11. Coleman, James C., Jack F. Keogh, and John Mansfield, "Motor Performance and Social Adjustment among Boys Experimenting Serious Learning Difficulties," *Research Quarterly,* 34:516-517, December, 1963.

12. Cozens, F. W., *Achievement Scales in Physical Education Activities for College Men,* Philadelphia: Lea & Febiger, 1936.

13. Cratty, Bryant J., "A Three Level Theory of Perceptual Motor Behavior," *Quest,* Monograph VI, Spring Issue, May, 1966, pp. 3-10.

14. Dohrmann, Paul, "Throwing and Kicking Ability of 8-Year-Old Boys and Girls," *Research Quarterly,* 35:464-471, December, 1964.

15. Girolamo, Carmen G., "A Comparison of General Motor Capacity of Athletes and Non-Athletes," (Microcarded Master's Thesis, State University of Iowa, 1956).

16. Glassow, Ruth B., and Pauline Kruse, "Motor Performance of Girls Age 6 to 14 Years," *Research Quarterly,* 31:432-433, October, 1960.

17. Henry, Franklin M., "Evaluation of Motor Learning When Performance Levels Are Heterogeneous," *Research Quarterly,* 27:176-181, May, 1956.

18. Hoffman, Virginia, "Relation of Selected Traits and Abilities to Motor Learning," (Microcarded Doctor's Dissertation, Indiana University, 1955).

19. Humiston, Dorothy A., "A Measurement of Motor Ability in College Women," *Research Quarterly,* 8:181-185, May, 1937.

20. Johnson, Granville B., "Physical Skill Tests for Sectioning Classes into Homogeneous Units," *Research Quarterly,* 3:128-134, March, 1932.

21. Lafuze, Marion, "A Study of the Learning of Fundamental Skills by College Freshmen Women of Low Motor Ability," *Research Quarterly,* 22:149-157, May, 1951.

22. Landiss, Carl W., "Influence of Physical Education Activities on Motor Ability and Physical Fitness of Male Freshmen," *Research Quarterly,* 26:295-307, October, 1955.

23. Larson, Leonard A., "A Factor Analysis of Motor Ability Variables and Tests, with Tests for College Men," *Research Quarterly,* 12:499-517, October, 1941.

24. Latchaw, Marjorie, "Measuring Selected Motor Skills in Fourth, Fifth, and Sixth Grades," *Research Quarterly,* 25:439-449, December, 1954.

25. _____ , and Camille Brown, *The Evaluation Process in Health Education, Physical Education and Recreation,* Englewood Cliffs, N.J.. Prentice-Hall, Inc., 1962, pp. 84-104.

26. Lockhart, Aileene, and Jane A. Mott, "An Experiment in Homogeneous Grouping and Its Effect on Achievement in Sports Fundamentals," *Research Quarterly,* 22:5862, March, 1951.

27. McCloy, C. H., "The Measurement of General Motor Capacity and General Motor Ability," *Supplement to Research Quarterly,* 5:46-61, March, 1934.

28. _____ , "An Analytical Study of the Stunt Type Test as a Measure of Motor Educability," *Research Quarterly,* 8:46-55, October, 1937.

29. _____ , and Norma D. Young, *Tests and Measurements in Health and Physical Education,* 3rd ed., New York: Appleton-Century-Crofts, Inc., 1954, Chapter 17.

30. Metheny, Eleanor, "Studies of the Johnson Test as a Test of Motor Educability," *Research Quarterly,* 9:105-114, December, 1938.

31. Phillips, Marjorie, and Dean Summers, "Relation of Kinesthetic Perception to Motor Learning," *Research Quarterly,* 25:456-468, December, 1954.

32. Powell, Elizabeth, and E. C. Howe, "Motor Ability Tests for High School Girls," *Research Quarterly,* 10:8188, December, 1939.

33. Roloff, Louise L., "Kinesthesis in Relation to the Learning of Selected Motor Skills," *Research Quarterly,* 24:210-215, May, 1953.

34. Ryan, Dean E., "Relationship Between Motor Performance and Arousal," *Research Quarterly,* 33:279-287, May, 1962.

35. Scott, M. Gladys, "The Assessment of Motor Abilities of College Women Through Objective Tests," *Research Quarterly,* 10:63-83, October, 1939.

36. _____ , "Motor Ability Tests for College Women," *Research Quarterly,* 14:402405, December, 1943.

37. _____ , and Esther French, *Measurement and Evaluation in Physical Education,* Dubuque, Iowa: Wm. C. Brown Company, Publishers, 1959, pp. 344-350.

38. Shelley, Morgan E., "Maturity, Structure, Strength, Motor Ability, and Intelligence Test Profiles of Outstanding Elementary School and Junior High School Athletes," (Microcarded Master's Thesis, University of Oregon, 1960).

39. Singer, Robert N., "Effect of Spectators on Athletes and Non-Athletes Performing a Gross Motor Task," *Research Quarterly,* 36:473482, December, 1965.

40. Smith, Jean A., "Relation of Certain Physical Traits and Abilities to Motor Learning in Elementary School Children," *Research Quarterly,* 27:220-228, May, 1956.

41. Smith, Judith L., and Margaret F. Bozymowski, "Effect of Attitude toward Warm-up on Motor Performance," *Research Quarterly,* 36:78-85, March, 1965.

42. Walters, Etta C., "Motor Ability and Educability Factors of High and Low Scoring Beginning Bowlers," *Research Quarterly,* 30:94-100, March, 1959.

Chapter IX

THE MEASUREMENT
OF BALANCE

Introduction

The two types of tests of balance which are in common use in physical education are tests of static balance and tests of dynamic balance. Static balance may be defined as that physical ability which enables an individual to hold a stationary position. On the other hand dynamic balance is the ability to maintain balance during vigorous movement, as in walking a fence or leaping from stone to stone while crossing a brook. There is evidence to indicate that the ability to balance easily, whether statically or dynamically, depends upon the function of the mechanisms in the semi-circular canals; the kinesthetic sensations in the muscles, tendons, and joints; visual perception while the body is in motion; and the ability to coordinate these three sources of stimuli.[1] Balance is an important ability which is used in our every day activities, such as in walking and standing, as well as in most games and sports.

Uses of Balance Tests

Balance tests may be utilized in physical education classes as follows:
1. As a measure for determining achievement when balance improvement is a specific objective in the teaching unit.
2. As an element for assessing potential in gymnastics, diving, and other individual and team activities.
3. As a means of diagnosis to determine whether there has been injury or damage to one or more of the kinesthetic receptors in the body or its parts.
4. As a factor in general motor ability tests.

Practical Tests of Balance

Several practical tests of balance in terms of time, equipment, and cost are presented on the following pages.

Static Balance Tests

Stork Stand

Objective: To measure the static balance of the performer while supported on the ball of the foot of the dominant leg.

Age Level: Ages 10 through college.

Sex: Satisfactory for both boys and girls.

Reliability: An r of .87 was found for this test when the best trial of the initial test was correlated with the best trial of the second test both of which were administered on different days.

Validity: Face validity was accepted for this test.

Equipment and Materials: One stop watch or a wrist watch with a second hand.

Directions: (See Figure 9 - 1.) From a stand on the foot of the dominant leg, place the other foot on the inside of the supporting knee and place the hands on the hips. Upon a given signal raise the heel from the floor and maintain the balance as long as possible without moving the ball of the foot from its initial position or letting the heel touch the floor.

Scoring: The score is the greatest number of seconds counted between the time the heel is raised and the balance is lost on three trials with the preferred foot. (See Table 9 - 1.) Only the highest score is recorded.

Additional Pointers: (1) Students may be tested in pairs, with one performing while the other takes note of how long the performer balanced as the number of seconds are counted off (aloud) by the timer. (2) Students who failed to get started on time are retested. (3) The performer cannot remove his hands from his hips during the test.

FIGURE 9 - 1

Stork Stand

TABLE 9 - 1

T-Score Norms for Stork Stand

College Men				College Women			
T Scores	Raw Scores	T Scores	Raw Scores	T Scores	Raw Scores	T Scores	Raw Scores
80 — 73		57 — 36		90 — 62		63 — 30	
79 — 71		56 — 34		89 — 61		62 — 29	
78 — 70		55 — 32		88 — 60		61 — 28	
77 — 68		54 — 31		87 — 59		60 — 27	
76 — 66		53 — 29		86 — 57		59 — 25	
75 — 65		52 — 28		85 — 56		58 — 24	
74 — 63		51 — 26		84 — 55		57 — 23	
73 — 61		50 — 24		83 — 54		56 — 22	
72 — 60		49 — 23		82 — 53		55 — 21	
71 — 58		48 — 21		81 — 52		54 — 20	
70 — 57		47 — 20		80 — 50		53 — 18	
69 — 55		46 — 18		79 — 49		52 — 17	
68 — 53		45 — 16		78 — 48		51 — 16	
67 — 52		44 — 15		77 — 47		50 — 15	
66 — 50		43 — 13		76 — 46		49 — 14	
65 — 49		42 — 12		75 — 44		48 — 12	
64 — 47		41 — 10		74 — 43		47 — 11	
63 — 45		40 — 8		73 — 42		46 — 10	
62 — 44		39 — 7		72 — 41		45 — 9	
61 — 42		38 — 5		71 — 40		44 — 8	
60 — 41		37 — 4		70 — 38		43 — 6	
59 — 39		36 — 2		69 — 37		42 — 5	
58 — 37		35 — 1		68 — 36		41 — 4	
				67 — 35		40 — 3	
				66 — 34		39 — 2	
				65 — 33		38 — 1	
				64 — 31			

Based on the scores of 99 subjects attending Northeast Louisiana State College, Monroe, Louisiana.

Based on the scores of 114 subjects attending Northeast Louisiana State College, Monroe, Louisiana.

Bass Stick Test (Crosswise)[1]

Objective: To measure the static balance of the performer while supported on a narrow surface on the ball of the foot.

Age Level: Ages 10 through college.

Sex: Satisfactory for both boys and girls.

Reliability: Has been reported as high as .90.

Validity: Has been accepted for its obvious face validity.

Equipment and Materials: (1) Several sticks one inch wide, one inch high, and twelve inches long, (2) a stop watch, or wrist watch with a second hand, and (3) adhesive tape are needed for this test.

Directions: (See Figure 9 - 2.) Arrange several performers in one line and an observer for each performer in an opposite line. Each performer should place the ball of the foot crosswise on the stick and (upon a given signal) lift the opposite foot from the floor holding the balance for as long as possible up to a maximum of 60 seconds. As the timer counts aloud, each observer takes note of how long his performer maintains balance. Have each performer execute the test six times (3 times on right leg and 3 times on left leg).

Scoring: The score for the test is the sum of the times for all six trials. (See Table 9 - 2.)

Additional Pointers: (1) Tape the sticks to the floor. (2) If either the heel or the toe of the performer's supporting foot touches the floor, the observer should terminate the count for that trial. (3) Performers who lose their balance within the first three seconds of a trial should be retested due to a bad start. (4) Although a large number of trials increase reliability, the authors have found that not a great deal of reliability is lost when the subjects are given only three trials on the preferred leg. In the interest of time and application of test results, the instructor might consider shortening this test.

FIGURE 9 - 2

Bass Stick Test Crosswise

TABLE 9 - 2

T-Score Norms for Stick Test Crosswise

College Men				College Women			
T Scores	Raw Scores	T Scores	Raw Scores	T Scores	Raw Scores	T Scores	Raw Scores
79 — 360		56 — 165		84 — 360		60 — 170	
78 — 350		55 — 160		83 — 350		58 — 160	
77 — 340		54 — 150		82 — 340		57 — 150	
76 — 335		53 — 140		80 — 330		56 — 140	
75 — 325		52 — 135		79 — 320		55 — 130	
74 — 315		51 — 125		78 — 310		53 — 120	
73 — 310		50 — 115		77 — 300		52 — 110	
72 — 300		49 — 110		75 — 290		51 — 100	
71 — 290		48 — 100		74 — 280		49 — 90	
70 — 285		47 — 90		73 — 270		48 — 80	
69 — 275		46 — 85		71 — 260		47 — 70	
68 — 265		45 — 75		70 — 250		46 — 60	
67 — 260		44 — 65		69 — 240		44 — 50	
66 — 250		43 — 60		67 — 230		43 — 40	
65 — 240		42 — 50		66 — 220		42 — 30	
64 — 235		41 — 40		65 — 210		40 — 20	
63 — 225		40 — 35		64 — 200		39 — 10	
62 — 215		39 — 25		62 — 190		38 — 5	
61 — 210		38 — 15		61 — 180			
60 — 200		37 — 10					
59 — 190		36 — 5					
58 — 185		35 — 0					
57 — 175							

Based on the scores of 99 subjects attending Northeast Louisiana State College, Monroe, Louisiana.

Based on the scores of 100 subjects attending Northeast Louisiana State College, Monroe, Louisiana.

Bass Stick Test (Lengthwise) [1]
(See Figure 9 - 3.) Same as for previous test, except place the foot on the stick lengthwise. (See Table 9 - 3.)

FIGURE 9 - 3

Bass Stick Test Lengthwise

TABLE 9 - 3

T-Score Norms for Bass Stick Test Lengthwise

College Men				College Women			
T Scores	Raw Scores	T Scores	Raw Scores	T Scores	Raw Scores	T Scores	Raw Scores
60 — 360		41 — 180		61 — 360		41 — 175	
59 — 355		40 — 170		60 — 350		40 — 165	
58 — 345		39 — 160		59 — 335		39 — 155	
57 — 335		38 — 150		58 — 325		38 — 145	
56 — 325		37 — 140		57 — 320		37 — 140	
55 — 315		36 — 130		56 — 310		36 — 130	
54 — 305		35 — 120		55 — 300		35 — 120	
53 — 295		34 — 110		54 — 290		34 — 110	
52 — 285		33 — 100		53 — 280		33 — 100	
51 — 280		32 — 90		52 — 275		32 — 95	
50 — 270		31 — 80		51 — 265		31 — 85	
49 — 260		30 — 70		50 — 255		30 — 75	
48 — 250		29 — 60		49 — 245		29 — 65	
47 — 240		28 — 50		48 — 235		28 — 55	
46 — 230		27 — 40		47 — 230		27 — 50	
45 — 220		26 — 30		46 — 220		26 — 40	
44 — 210		25 — 20		45 — 210		25 — 30	
43 — 200		24 — 10		44 — 200		24 — 20	
42 — 190		23 — 5		43 — 190		23 — 10	
				42 — 185		22 — 5	

Based on the scores of 98 subjects attending Northeast Louisiana State College, Monroe, Louisiana.

Based on the scores of 100 subjects attending Northeast Louisiana State College, Monroe, Louisiana.

Progressive Inverted Balance Test [14] (Long form and short form.)

Objective: To measure the ability to balance in an inverted position. These test items are probably most appropriate for a gymnastics unit or self-testing activities unit.

Age Level: Ages 9 through college.

Sex: Satisfactory for both boys and girls.

Reliability: An r of .82 was found for this test when subjects were tested on separate days.

Validity: Face validity was accepted for this test.

Equipment and Materials: One stop watch and a tumbling mat.

Directions: The inverted balance test consists of five inverted balance stunts. Each is described and illustrated below:

1. Tripod Balance. From a squatting position, place the hands shoulder width apart with the fingers pointing straight ahead. Lean forward bending at the elbows and place the inside of the knees against and slightly above the outside of the elbows.

FIGURE 9 - 4 (A)

Tripod Balance

Continue to lean forward until the feet come off the floor and the forehead rests on the mat. Balance in this position for as many counts as possible up to a maximum of 5 seconds. (See Figure 9 - 4(A).)

2. Tip-Up Balance. Same as for the tripod balance except do not allow the head to rest on the mat, but balance with the face several inches from the floor. (See Figure 9 - 4(B).)

FIGURE 9 - 4 (B)

Tip-Up Balance

3. <u>Head Balance</u>. Place the forehead on the mat several inches ahead of the hands and kick upward one foot at a time and maintain the balance with the back slightly arched, legs straight and together, and toes pointed. Body weight should be primarily on the hands with some weight on the forehead. Balance in this position for as many counts as possible up to a maximum of 5 seconds. To get out of this position push with the hands, duck the head, and roll forward, or step down one foot at a time. (See Figure 9 - 4(C).)

<u>Safety Tip</u>: A partner may grasp the performer's legs and assist him to the proper position before the balance begins.

FIGURE 9 - 4 (C)

Head Balance

4. <u>Head and Forearm Balance</u>. Place the forearms on the mat and bring the hands close enough together for the thumbs and forefingers to form a cup for the head to fit into. Place the back of the head in the cup formed by the thumbs and fingers and kick upward one foot at a time and balance between the tripod support formed by the head and forearms. (See Figure 9 - 4(D).) Balance in this position for as many counts as possible up to a maximum of 5 seconds.

<u>Safety Tip</u>: Same as for the head balance.

FIGURE 9 - 4 (D)

Head and Forearm Balance

5. <u>Handstand</u>. Bend forward and place the hands on the mat about shoulder width apart. Lean the shoulders over the hands and separate the feet so that one foot is ahead of the other. With the eyes looking forward of the finger tips, swing the rear foot upward as the front foot pushes from the mat, and maintain a balanced position with the feet overhead for as many counts as possible up to a maximum of five seconds. (See Figure 9 - 4(E).)

<u>Safety Tip</u>: Same as for the head balance.

FIGURE 9 - 4 (E)

Handstand

<u>Scoring for Long Form</u>: The above balances carry the following weights:

    Tripod — weight of 1
    Tip-Up — weight of 2
    Head Balance — weight of 3
    Head and Forearm — weight of 4
    Handstand — weight of 5

Each balance may be held for a maximum of five points (one point for each second). To figure the total score, multiply the weight of the balance by the number of seconds it was held and then add the five scores together for the final score. The maximum raw score possible is seventy-five points. If a student cannot balance or fails to try a particular balance, his score is 0 for that balance.

<u>Scoring for Short Form</u>: Same as for the long form except that the student chooses only one of the five balances to perform. For example, if a student chose the head balance with a weight of 3 and held the position for 5 seconds, his score would be 15 points. The maximum score possible for the short form test is 25 points.

TABLE 9 - 4

T-Score Norms for Progressive Inverted Balance Test (Long Form)

College Men				College Women			
T Scores	Raw Scores	T Scores	Raw Scores	T Scores	Raw Scores	T Scores	Raw Scores
67 — 75		46 — 36		77 — 75		51 — 37	
66 — 73		45 — 34		76 — 74		50 — 35	
65 — 71		44 — 33		75 — 72		49 — 34	
64 — 69		43 — 31		74 — 70		48 — 32	
63 — 68		42 — 29		73 — 69		47 — 31	
62 — 66		41 — 27		72 — 67		46 — 29	
61 — 64		40 — 25		71 — 66		45 — 28	
60 — 62		39 — 23		70 — 64		44 — 27	
59 — 60		38 — 21		69 — 63		43 — 25	
58 — 58		37 — 20		68 — 61		42 — 24	
57 — 57		36 — 18		67 — 60		41 — 22	
56 — 55		35 — 16		66 — 58		40 — 21	
55 — 53		34 — 14		65 — 57		39 — 19	
54 — 51		33 — 12		64 — 56		38 — 18	
53 — 49		32 — 10		63 — 54		37 — 16	
52 — 47		31 — 9		62 — 53		36 — 15	
51 — 46		30 — 7		61 — 51		35 — 13	
50 — 44		29 — 5		60 — 50		34 — 12	
49 — 42		28 — 3		59 — 48		33 — 11	
48 — 40		27 — 2		58 — 47		32 — 9	
47 — 38		26 — 1		57 — 45		31 — 8	
				56 — 44		30 — 6	
				55 — 43		29 — 5	
				54 — 41		28 — 3	
				53 — 40		27 — 2	
				52 — 38		26 — 1	

Based on the scores of 100 subjects at Northeast Louisiana State College.

Based on the scores of 139 subjects at Northeast Louisiana State College.

Modified Bass Test of Dynamic Balance[1,15]

Objective: To measure the ability to jump accurately and maintain balance during movement and after movement.

Age Level: High School and College.

Sex: Boys and Girls.

Reliability: An r of .75 was found for this test when subjects were tested on separate days.

Validity: Face validity was accepted for this test.

Objectivity: An r of .97 was found when two testers scored twenty-five subjects independently on the test.

Equipment and Materials: The equipment and materials needed are stop watches, ¾" marking tape, and yardsticks. Cut eleven 1" × ¾" pieces of marking tape and tape them in the proper pattern to the floor. (See the proper pattern in Figure 9 - 5.)

Directions: Standing with the right foot on the starting mark, the performer leaps to the first tape mark with the left foot and tries to hold a steady position on the ball of his left foot for as many seconds as possible up to five seconds. He then leaps to the second tape with the right foot, and so on, alternating the feet from tape to tape. He should remain on each tape mark for as many seconds as possible up to a maximum of five seconds, and his foot must completely cover the tape so that it cannot be seen.

Scoring: The score for each mark successfully landed on is five points, and in addition, one point is awarded for each second the balance is held up to five seconds per mark. Thus, a performer may earn a maximum of ten points per marker or a total of 100 pts. for the test. (See Table 9 - 5.)

Penalties: The penalties for this test may be classified into landing errors and balance errors.

Landing errors—The performer sacrifices 5 points for improper landing if he commits any of the following errors:

1. Failing to stop upon landing from the leap.
2. Touching the heel or any other part of the body to the floor other than the ball of the supporting foot upon landing.
3. Failing to completely cover the marker with the ball of the foot.

*The performer is allowed to reposition himself for the five second balance on the ball of the foot after making a landing error.

Balance errors—If the performer commits any of the balance errors below prior to the completion of the five seconds, he sacrifices the remaining points at the rate of one point per second:

1. Touching any part of the body to the floor other than the ball of the supporting foot.
2. Moving the foot while in the balance position.

*When the performer loses his balance, he must step back on the proper marker and then leap to the next marker.

Additional Pointers: (1) The seconds of each balance attempt should be counted aloud for the performer. (2) The landing score and the balance score should be recorded for each marker.

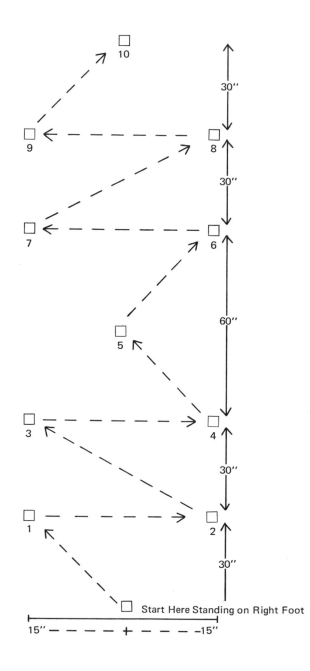

FIGURE 9 - 5

Floor Pattern for Modified Bass Dynamic Test

TABLE 9 - 5

T-Score Norms for Modified Bass Dynamic Test

T-Scores		Raw Scores	T-Scores		Raw Scores
67	—	100	40	—	60
66	—	98	39	—	59
65	—	97	38	—	57
64	—	95	37		56
63	—	94	36		54
62	—	93	35	—	53
61	—	91	34		51
60	—	90	33	—	50
59	—	88	32	—	48
57	—	85	31	—	47
56	—	84	30	—	45
55	—	82	29	—	44
54	—	81	28	—	42
53	—	79	27	—	41
52	—	78	26	—	39
51	—	76	25	—	38
50	—	75	24	—	36
49	—	73	23	—	35
48	—	72	22	—	34
47	—	70	20	—	32
46	—	69	19	—	30
45	—	67	18	—	29
44	—	66	17	—	27
43	—	64	16	—	26
42	—	63	15	—	24
41	—	62	14	—	23

*Based on the scores of 100 college women at East Texas State University, Commerce, Texas.

Dynamic Test of Positional Balance[16]

<u>Objective</u>: To measure the ability to land accurately, and to balance while in various precarious positions.

<u>Age Level</u>: Ages 10 through college.

<u>Sex</u>: Satisfactory for boys and girls.

<u>Reliability</u>: An r of .76 was found for this test when the subjects were scored on separate days.

<u>Validity</u>: Face validity was accepted for this test.

<u>Objectivity</u>: An r of .94 was found when two different testers scored 25 subjects.

<u>Equipment and Materials</u>: The equipment and materials needed are stop watches, tape measures or yardsticks, and marking tape. Cut four 1″ × ¾″ pieces of marking tape and tape them in the proper pattern to the floor. (See the proper pattern in Figure 9 - 5.)

<u>Directions</u>: (1) Standing on the right foot behind the starting mark, the performer leaps to marker A landing on the left foot and balances in a stork stand for as many seconds as possible up to five seconds. (2) The performer leaps from marker A to marker B landing on the ball of the right foot while immediately lowering into a front scale position where the trunk is tilted forward and the nonsupporting leg is raised upward (parallel to floor) in the rear. The arms should be extended horizontally to the sides while the head and chest are held high. The supporting leg should be straight as the balance is held for as many seconds as possible up to five seconds. (3) Return to an upright position on one foot and leap from marker B to marker C landing on the left foot, and lower into a side scale position by leaning to the left side and by lifting the right leg until it is parallel to the floor. The right arm is extended along the side of the body with the hand resting on the thigh while the left arm is extended forward. The head should be leaned close to the extended left arm. Keeping the supporting leg straight, hold the position for as many seconds as possible up to five seconds. (4) Return to an upright position on one foot and leap from marker C back to marker B landing on the ball of the right foot. Maintain a position on the ball of the foot for as many seconds as possible up to five seconds. (5) Lean forward and drop to the floor so that the hands will be resting on each side of marker D. Draw the left leg under the trunk and place the knee on marker D. The performer then balances on the knee as the hands and the opposite leg are lifted from the floor. The balance should be held for as many seconds as possible up to five seconds. (6) Exchange knees and repeat the knee balance on the opposite knee.

<u>Scoring</u>: The score for each marker successfully landed on is five points except for marker D where there is no landing skill involved. There is a total of 20 points possible for correct landings. For balance, one point is awarded for each second that each of the six balances are held. Five seconds is maximum per balance. Thus, a performer may earn a maximum of 30 points for balance. The grand total for the test is fifty points. The best of three trials is recorded as the test score.

<u>Penalties</u>: The penalties for this test may be classified into landing errors and balance errors.

<u>Landing Errors</u>: The performer sacrifices 5 points for improper landings if he commits the following errors: (1) Failing to stop upon landing from the leap. (2) Failing to completely cover the marker with the foot. *The performer is allowed to reposition himself for the five second balance after making a landing error.

<u>Balance Errors</u>: If the performer commits the following errors prior to the completion of the five seconds, he sacrifices the remaining points at the rate of one point per second: (1) Touching any part of the body to the floor other than the point of

support. (2) Moving the foot while in the balance position. *When the performer loses his balance, he must step back on the proper marker and then leap to the next marker. <u>Additional Pointers</u>: (1) The seconds of each balance attempt should be counted aloud for the performer. (2) The landing score and the balance score should be recorded for each marker.

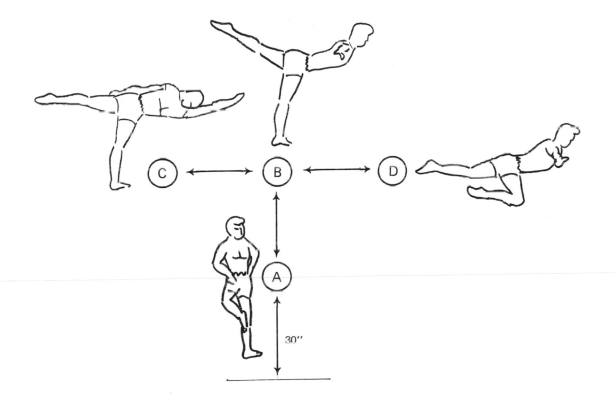

A. Stork Stand with
   eyes open, foot flat.
B. Front Scale. Balance
   on ball of foot.
C. Side Scale.
D. Knee Scale. (Perform
   one for each knee.)

FIGURE 9 - 6

Dynamic Test of Postional Balance

TABLE 9 - 6

T-Score Norms for Dynamic Test of Positional Balance

T-Scores		Raw Scores	T-Scores		Raw Scores
84	—	50	42	—	32
81	—	49	39	—	31
79	—	48	37	—	30
77	—	47	35	—	29
74	—	46	32	—	28
72	—	45	30	—	27
70	—	44	28	—	26
67	—	43	25	—	25
65	—	42	23	—	24
63	—	41	21	—	23
60	—	40	18	—	22
58	—	39	16	—	21
56	—	38	14	—	20
53	—	37	11	—	19
51	—	36	9	—	18
49	—	35	7	—	17
46	—	34	4	—	16
44	—	33	2	—	15

*Based on the scores of 100 college men at East Texas State University.

Modified Sideward Leap Test [24]

Objective: To measure the ability to land accurately, and to balance during and after movement.

Age Levels: Ages 10 through college.

Sex: Satisfactory for both boys and girls.

Reliability: Has been reported between .66 and .88 at various grade levels.

Validity: Has been accepted for its obvious face validity.

Equipment and Materials: The equipment and materials needed for this test are stop watches, tape measures, chalk markers, and several small objects such as the cork heads cut off of old badminton birds.

Directions: (See Figure 9 - 7.) Place a small object on spot B and measure the student's leg from the hip joint to the floor in order to determine the spot on the floor from which the subject will begin his leap. This spot should be the nearest "x" which corresponds most closely in distance to the length of the leg. The performer then places the left foot on the proper X mark and leaps sideward landing on spot A with the ball of right foot. He then immediately leans forward and pushes the small object off of spot B and maintains his balance for five seconds. Each performer executes two trials to the left and two trials to the right.

Scoring: (See Table 9 - 7.) On each trial the performer is awarded five points for covering spot A on the landing, five points for immediately lowering and pushing the cork from spot B (this must be accomplished within 2 seconds from time foot landed on spot A), and one point for each second the balance is held up to five seconds. The total possible score for the four trials is 60 points.

Penalty: (1) If the performer fails to cover spot A with the ball of his foot upon landing, or fails to maintain a steady position, he sacrifices the five points for correct landing; but he may reassume the correct position and immediately lower (within 2 sec.) and push the object from point B or C and continue for the balance of five seconds. (2) If the performer takes longer than two seconds to remove the object from B or C, he sacrifices five points; but he may continue for the balance of five seconds. (3) If the performer loses his balance before the 5 seconds is up, his score for that part of the test is the number of seconds the balance was held.

Additional Pointers: (1) Several patterns should be drawn on the floor so that students can be tested faster. (2) The student should be timed on the five second balance from the time he assumes a steady position on the ball of one foot at spot A. Thus, if it takes him 2 seconds to push the object from B or C, he would have only three seconds left to maintain position. (3) The timer should count the seconds aloud.

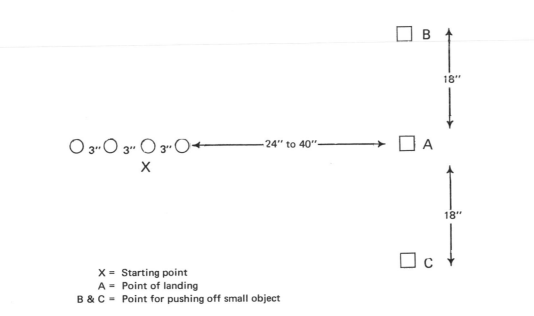

X = Starting point
A = Point of landing
B & C = Point for pushing off small object

FIGURE 9 - 7

Modified Sideward Leap Test

TABLE 9 - 7

T-Score Norms for Modified Sideward Leap Test

College Men				College Women			
T Scores	Raw Scores	T Scores	Raw Scores	T Scores	Raw Scores	T Scores	Raw Scores
60 — 60		37 — 31		64 — 60		38 — 32	
59 — 58		36 — 30		63 — 59		37 — 31	
58 — 57		35 — 29		62 — 58		36 — 30	
57 — 56		34 — 27		61 — 57		35 — 29	
56 — 55		33 — 26		60 — 56		34 — 27	
55 — 53		32 — 25		59 — 55		33 — 26	
54 — 52		31 — 24		58 — 53		32 — 25	
53 — 51		30 — 22		57 — 52		31 — 24	
52 — 49		29 — 21		56 — 51		30 — 23	
51 — 48		28 — 20		55 — 50		29 — 22	
50 — 47		27 — 19		54 — 49		28 — 21	
49 — 46		26 — 18		53 — 48		27 — 20	
48 — 45		25 — 16		52 — 47		26 — 19	
47 — 43		24 — 15		51 — 46		25 — 18	
46 — 42		23 — 14		50 — 45		24 — 17	
45 — 41		22 — 13		49 — 44		23 — 16	
44 — 40		21 — 11		48 — 43		22 — 14	
43 — 38		20 — 10		47 — 42		21 — 13	
42 — 37		19 — 9		46 — 40		20 — 12	
41 — 36		18 — 8		45 — 39		19 — 11	
40 — 35		17 — 7		44 — 38		18 — 10	
39 — 34		16 — 5		43 — 37		17 — 9	
38 — 32		15 — 4		42 — 36		16 — 8	
				41 — 35		15 — 7	
				40 — 34		14 — 6	
				39 — 33		13 — 5	

Based on the scores of 99 subjects at Northeast Louisiana State College.

Based on the scores of 124 subjects at Northeast Louisiana State College.

The Nelson Balance Test *

Objective: To measure both static and dynamic balance in a single test.

Age Level: Ages 10 through college.

Sex: Satisfactory for both boys and girls.

Reliability: Using the average of three trials on a test — retest basis, a coefficient of .89 was obtained.

Validity: The test has face validity as a measure of balance. Moreover, a coefficient of .77 was found when the test was correlated with the combined score of several standard balance measures.

Equipment and Materials: The following equipment and materials are needed: (1) Nine small wooden blocks, 2″ X 4″ X 8″. A ten foot wooden balance beam, 2″ X 4″. The beam is held edgewise by three triangular shaped supports. (See Figure 9 - 8B.) (2) In order to prevent the blocks from sliding or tipping, pieces of rubber are glued to the bottom of each block. This also protects the gymnasium floor. Four of the blocks are painted red, or in some way marked differently. (3) Stop watch, tape measure, and possibly chalk or tape to mark the position of the blocks on the floor.

Directions: Two lines may be drawn 24 inches apart and 20 feet long. The blocks are placed crosswise, the blocks and balance board are positioned as shown in Figure 9 - 8A.

When ready, the subject steps onto the first block on the ball of the left foot. The tester starts the watch and counts aloud "1-2-3-4-5-" to signify five seconds. (This count is repeated as the subject mounts each red block, but not when he mounts others.)

The performer then proceeds along the route indicated in Figure 9 - 8A, leaping from one block to the next, alternating feet each time.

The subject tries to go as fast as he can, but without making mistakes. There are four red - 5 - second - hold - blocks where the subject must balance on one foot while the tester calls out the five seconds. When crossing the balance board, the performer must walk heel-to-toe. In other words he can not cross it by running or in leaps.

Scoring: The score is entirely based on time to the nearest tenth of a second from the start until he steps off the last block.

Penalties: Any time the performer's foot touches the floor, he must get back onto the block at the place at which he fell off and proceed from that point. If the subject should leave one of the "hold" blocks before the five seconds has elapsed, he must return and "hold" for the remaining seconds (i.e., if the subject should leave a red block after 3 seconds, he would have to return and hold for 2 seconds to satisfy the 5 second requirement for the red blocks).

Similarly, if the subject should fall off, or deviate from the heel-toe walk across the balance board, he must return to that point at which the fault occurred and resume the walk across the board.

In all cases the watch continues to run until the end of the last "5 - second - hold" count at the end of the course.

*Jack K. Nelson. "The Nelson Balance Test," Un-published Study, Louisiana State University, Baton Rouge, Louisiana, 1968.

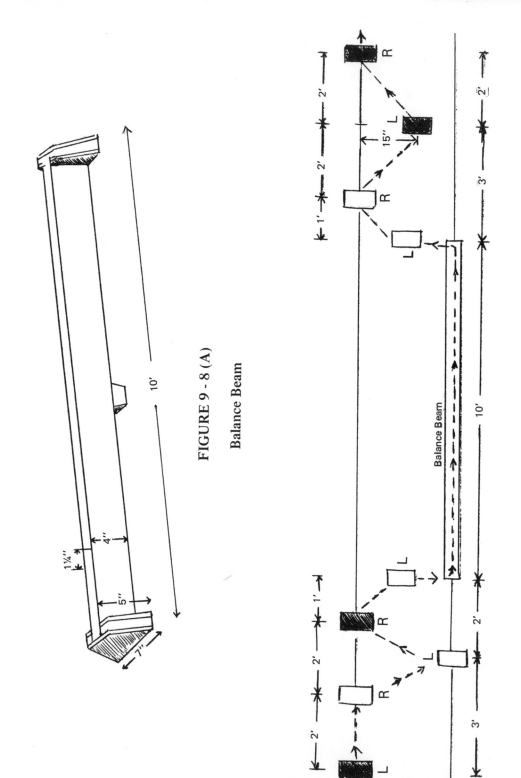

FIGURE 9 - 8 (A)

Balance Beam

FIGURE 9 - 8 (B)

Nelson Balance Test

TABLE 9 - 8

T-Scale for Nelson Balance Test*
(Raw Scores in Seconds)

T Scores	Raw Scores	T Scores	Raw Scores	T Scores	Raw Scores	T Scores	Raw Scores
81 —	22.5	65 —	30.5	49 —	38.5	33 —	46.5
80 —	23.0	64 —	31.0	48 —	39.0	32 —	47.0
79 —	23.5	63 —	31.5	47 —	39.5	31 —	47.5
78 —	24.0	62 —	32.0	46 —	40.0	30 —	48.0
77 —	24.5	61 —	32.5	45	40.5	29 —	48.5
76	25.0	60 —	33.0	44 —	41.0	28 —	49.0
75 —	25.5	59 —	33.5	43 —	41.5	27 —	49.5
74 —	26.0	58 —	34.0	42 —	42.0	26 —	50.0
73 —	26.5	57 —	34.5	41 —	42.5	25 —	50.5
72 —	27.0	56 —	35.0	40 —	43.0	24 —	51.0
71 —	27.5	55 —	35.5	39 —	43.5	23 —	51.5
70 —	28.0	54 —	36.0	38 —	44.0	22 —	52.0
69 —	28.5	53 —	36.5	37 —	44.5	21 —	52.5
68 —	29.0	52 —	37.0	36 —	45.0	20 —	53.0
67 —	29.5	51 —	37.5	35 —	45.5	19 —	53.5
66 —	30.0	50	38.0	34 —	46.0	18 —	54.0

*Tentative norms based on 50 male college students.

Problems Associated with Balance Testing

Several of the problems and limitations associated with the testing of balance are listed and discussed below:

1. Strength seems to have a considerable influence on certain tests of balance. This is especially noticeable in the Bass Stick Tests and the Progressive Inverted Balance Test.
2. Although research reveals controversy on this point, it seems logical to the author that moderate to severe fatigue affects the balance scores of a student. Thus, it would seem logical to conduct balance skills prior to the more strenuous tests that may be given during a testing program.
3. Because of the exact position required (and display of force to get in that position), it may be necessary to allow students as many as 3 trials on certain tests in order to get their best score. This, of course, requires more time.
4. Norms in this area of testing are limited primarily to the college level. There is a need for norms to be constructed at the elementary, junior high, and high school levels for both boys and girls.

5. Since static balance is positional or specific in nature, a student may show up poorly in one aspect of balance and yet be quite proficient in other aspects. Perhaps motor ability tests which include static balance items should have several balance items of similar difficulty from which to choose.

6. Certain balance tests require not only expensive equipment, but also excessive amounts of time to administer. Therefore, the tests presented in this chapter should be of practical value when several stations are set up and students are rotated between stations. Moreover, further attempts should be made to devise inexpensive balance tests for the average school situation.

Findings and Conclusions From Balance Measurement and Research

The author has frequently heard, and inaccurately so, that girls have better balance than boys because of their lower center of gravity. However, in an upright position a female's center of gravity is not enough lower than the male's to overcome the greater strength factor which rests in favor of the male. Moreover, in the inverted position the male assumes the lower center of gravity, plus the fact that he still has the strength factor in his favor. Therefore, the findings of Smith[26] and Hoffman[13] that boys are superior to girls of compatible ages in balance activities seems most logical and valid.

Another fallacy frequently heard is that balance is inherited and that there is very little the average person can do to improve his balance. While the ability to balance may be inherited to a certain extent, it can be significantly improved upon as determined in studies by Espenschade,[7] Lafuze,[17] Smith,[26] Gunden,[12] and Garrison.[9] Furthermore, Espenschade[7] found that balance improved with an increase in chronological age between the ages of 11 and 16 years, but the rate of gain between the ages of 13 and 15 was noticeably retarded among boys.

Concerning mental ability, Hoffman[13] has stated that fast learning groups for each sex and grade tend to be superior to slow learning groups on balance tests.

A number of researchers have reported a positive relationship between static balance and ability in gross motor activity.[3,5,6,7,8,22,28]

Concerning the relationship of balance and kinesthesis, Scott[23] has stated that specific balance tests should be a part of any kinesthesis battery since the balance leap and the balance stick tests were consistently reliable and valid in her study.

In identifying factors of balance, Whelan[27] found four factors which corresponded with the findings of Bass.[1] They were general-static-balance kinesthetic response, vertical semicircular canals, general-ampular-sensivity, and convergence of the eyes. Whelan[27] also found that very little difference existed between the blind and the sighted in balance ability, and that balance ability in the blind probably does not over-compensate for the loss of sight as do other factors such as hearing and touch. Furthermore, Padden[20] found that poor balance groups among deaf students made significantly poorer showings in the ability to orient themselves under water than better balance groups among deaf students when the eyes were blindfolded. However, in Padden's study[20] the groups were not equated in swimming ability, and there is a possibility that lack of experience, and not poor balance, brought about the results.

Some controversy exists among physical educators concerning whether or not fatigue reduces balance control. While Scott and French[24] have maintained that excessive fatigue reduces balance control, Culane[4] has reported that fatigue has no noticeable effect upon balance. However, in the opinion of the authors, it seemed that Culane should have used the terms "slight fatigue" or "warm-up" to specify the degree of fatigue, since the exercises she used were not severe enough to cause "moderate" or "severe" fatigue to the average student. It has been noted by gymnastic coaches and performers that moderate to severe fatigue usually has an adverse effect on static balance. Moreover, Johnson* found that squat thrusts performed for maximum repetition significantly decreased static balance performance as measured by the stork stand (heel up) test.

If balance is of importance in athletic activities, it is logical to assume that athletes would perform better than non-athletes on tests of balance. Lessel[18] found scientific evidence to this effect when he compared college athletes with average college students. Other investigators have found similar results. Slater-Hammel[25] found varsity athletes significantly better than physical education majors, and Reynolds' Balance Test showed that physical education majors were significantly better than liberal arts majors. Mumby[19] found that good wrestlers were somewhat better than poor wrestlers in the ability to balance and to learn to balance. Gross[11] concluded that good swimmers have better dynamic balance than poor swimmers.

Several investigators have attempted to determine the contribution of physical education activities to improvement in balance. Greenlee[10] conducted a study in which a significant relationship was found between dynamic balance and bowling performance. Bennett[2] concluded at the end of 16 weeks of participation that there were no significant differences among the activities of modern dance, swimming, folk dance, and basketball concerning balance as measured by the Bass Leap Test. It should be pointed out, however, that since an initial test was not given before participation, the author was unable to assess the amount of improvement that was made. Consequently, it was not known whether or not initial differences among groups might have masked any differences in improvement in balance brought about by the activities. Gunden[12] found that participation in the physical education activities of basketball, tumbling, tennis, and volleyball resulted in improvement in the balance ability of college women.

*Barry L. Johnson, and others. "The Effect of Fatigue Upon Balance," *Abstracts of Research Papers 1968/AAHPER Convention.* Washington, D.C.: AAHPER, 1968, p. 118.

BIBLIOGRAPHY

1. Bass, Ruth I., "An Analysis of the Components of Tests of Semi-Circular Canal Function and of Static and Dynamic Balance," *Research Quarterly,* 10:33, May, 1939.

2. Bennett, Colleen L., "Relative Contributions of Modern Dance, Folk Dance, Basketball, and Swimming to Motor Abilities of College Women," *Research Quarterly,* 27:261, October, 1956.

3. Carruth, Wincie A., "An Analysis of Motor Ability and Its Relationship to Constitutional Body Patterns," (Micro-carded Doctor's Dissertation, New York University, 1952).

4. Culane, Mary J., "The Effect of Leg Fatigue Upon Balance," (Micro-carded Master's Thesis, State University of Iowa, 1956).

5. Cumbee, Frances J., "A Factorial Analysis of Motor Coordination," *Research Quarterly,* 25:420, December, 1954.

6. _____, and others, "Factorial Analysis of Motor Co-ordination Variables for Third and Fourth Grade Girls," *Research Quarterly,* 28:107-108, May, 1957.

7. Espenschade, A., and others, "Dynamic Balance in Adolescent Boys," *Research Quarterly,* 24:270, October, 1953.

8. Estep, Dorothy O., "Relationship of Static Equilibrium to Ability in Motor Activities," *Research Quarterly,* 28:5, March, 1957.

9. Garrison, Levon E., "An Experiment in Improving Balance Ability Through Teaching Selected Exercises," (Unpublished Master's Thesis, State University of Iowa, 1943).

10. Greenlee, Geraldine A., "The Relationship of Selected Measures of Strength, Balance, and Kinesthesis to Bowling Performance," (Unpublished Master's Thesis, State University of Iowa, Iowa City, 1958).

11. Gross, Elmer A., and Hugh L. Thompson, "Relationship of Dynamic Balance to Speed and Ability in Swimming," *Research Quarterly,* 28:346, December, 1957.

12. Gunden, Ruth E., "The Effect of Selected Sports Acitivies Upon the Balance Ability of College Women," (Micro-carded Master's Thesis, State University of Iowa, 1956).

13. Hoffman, Virginia, "Relation of Selected Traits and Abilities to Motor Learning," (Micro-carded Doctor's Dissertation, Indiana University, 1955).

14. Johnson, Barry L., "A Progressive Inverted Balance Test," (Unpublished Study, Northeast Louisiana State College, Monroe, Louisiana, 1966).

15. _____, and John Leach, "A Modification of the Bass Test of Dynamic Balance," (Unpublished Study, East Texas State University, Commerce, Texas, 1968).

16. _____, and Jeff Fitch, "Dynamic Test of Positional Balance," (Unpublished Study, East Texas State University, Commerce, Texas, 1968).

17. Lafuze, Marion, "A Study of the Learning of Fundamental Skills by College Freshman Women of Low Motor ABility," *Research Quarterly,* 22:156, May, 1951.

18. Lessl, Robert F., "The Development of a New Test of Balance and Its Use in Comparing College Athletes and Average College Students in their Ability to Balance," (Micro-carded Master's Thesis, University of Wisconsin, 1954).

19. Mumby, Hugh H., "Kinesthetic Acuity and Balance Related to Wrestling Ability," *Research Quarterly,* 24:334, October, 1953.

20. Padden, Don A. "Ability of Deaf Swimmers to Orient Themselves When Submerged in Water," *Research Quarterly,* 30:225, May, 1959.

21. Russell, Ruth I., "A Factor Analysis of the Components of Kinesthesis," (Doctor's Dissertation, State University of Iowa, 1954).

22. Scott, M. Gladys, "Motor Ability Tests for College Women," *Research Quarterly,* 14:402, December, 1943.

23. _____, "Measurement of Kinesthesis," *Research Quarterly,* 26:337, October, 1955.

24. _____, and Esther French, *Measurement and Evaluation in Physical Education,* Dubuque, Iowa: W. C. Brown Co., 1959.

25. Slater-Hammel, A. T., "Performance of Selected Groups of Male College Students on the Reynold's Balance Test," *Research Quarterly,* 27:351, October, 1956.

26. Smith, Jean A., "Relation of Certain Physical Traits and Abilities to Motor Learning in Elementary School Children," *Research Quarterly,* 27:228, May, 1956.

27. Whelan, Thomas P., "A Factor Analysis of Tests of Balance and Semicircular-Canal Function," (Micro-carded Doctor's Dissertation, State University of Iowa, 1955).

28. Wiebe, Vernon R., "A Study of Tests of Kinesthesis," (Unpublished Master's Thesis, State University of Iowa, 1951).

29. Witte, Faye, "A Factorial Analysis of Measures of Kinesthesis," (Doctor's Dissertation, Indiana University, 1953).

Chapter X

THE MEASUREMENT OF KINESTHETIC PERCEPTION

Kinesthetic perception, the ability to perceive the position and movement of the body and its joints during muscular action, is often referred to as the sixth sense. In reality, we have many more than just *six senses*; in fact, the sixth sense, or sense of kinesthetic perception, could be considered as several senses within itself. Steinhaus[39] has emphasized the importance of *muscle sense* by declaring that our muscles see more than our eyes. The various senses of kinesthetic perception are located in the muscles, tendons, and joints, and together they supply us with some of the information needed concerning body position and movement. Individuals who can observe a demonstration and perceive the significance of the sequence of movements are able to develop a physical empathy which enables them to learn a movement much faster than others whose kinesthetic ability is not as highly developed. While we must depend upon our proprioceptors in all daily activities, they can be developed and used in intricate skills in such sports as bowling, golf, basketball, diving, and gymnastics. Physical educators have devised several practical tests which the class room teacher may use to determine to some extent the degree to which students have developed their response to proprioceptive *feedback*.

Uses of Kinesthetic Perception Tests

Several ways by which tests of kinesthetic perception are utilized in physical education classes are listed as follows:
1. As a factor in general motor ability tests.
2. As an element in estimating potential in specialized physical activities.
3. As a means for diagnostic or interpretive purposes.
4. As a measure for determining achievement and grades when improvement in kinesthetic perception is a specific objective in a physical activity class.
5. As a means for motivating students to develop an awareness of body position and movement during physical activity.
6. As a form of practice in establishing the *feel* of certain movements.

Practical Tests of Kinesthetic Perception

Since research has revealed that no one single kinesthetic test has a high enough validity coefficient to warrant its use as a single test, it is suggested that several of the practical tests on the following pages be combined into a test battery to provide sufficient validity.

Distance Perception Jump [34]

Objective: To determine the ability of the performer to perceive distance by concentrating on the effort involved in a jump.

Age Level: Ages 10 through college.

Sex: Satisfactory for both boys and girls.

Reliability: A reliability coefficient of .44 was obtained on a test - retest with seventh and eighth grade boys.

Validity: Without the use of the eyes, there is obvious face validity.

Equipment and Materials: The materials needed are yardsticks or tape measures, blindfold material, and chalk or marking tape.

Directions: (See Figure 10 - 1.) The performer is instructed to sense the distance between the two lines without a practice trial. The performer is then blindfolded and instructed to jump from behind one line toward the other line trying to land the heels as close to the line as possible.*

Scoring: (See Table 10 - 1.) The score is the number of inches between the heels and the target line measured to the nearest quarter of an inch. Two trials are totaled for the score. When the heels are not even with each other, measure to or from the heel that is furthest from the target line.

Additional Pointer: Further experimentation with scoring systems is needed, since the reliability of the test as presented above was found quite low.

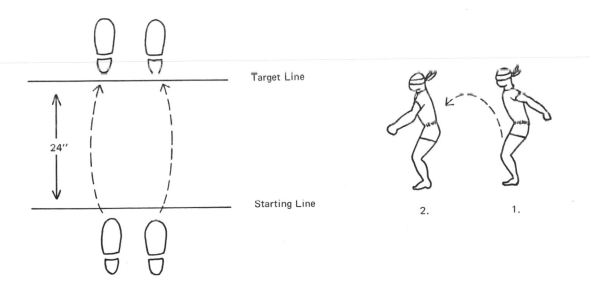

FIGURE 10 - 1

Distance Perception Jump

*A variation of this test is to first allow the subject to jump while using visual reference. Then he is blindfolded to measure whether he can duplicate the *feel* of the movement required for that distance.

TABLE 10 - 1

Excellent, Average, and Very Poor Performance Scores on the Distance Perception Jump Test for Junior and Senior High School Boys

School Level	Very Poor Scores	Average Scores	Excellent Scores
Junior High School	10¼	5½	¾
Senior High School	10¼	5¼	½

*Score deviations are in inches and are based on a limited number of subjects from physical education classes in East Baton Rouge Parish, Baton Rouge, La.

The Shuffleboard Control of Force Test [20]

Objective: To determine the ability of the performer to perceive distance by concentrating on the effort involved in pushing a disc.

Age Level: Ages 10 through college.

Sex: Satisfactory for both boys and girls.

Reliability: An r of .37 was found for college men when test #1 was correlated with test #2 on separate days. For college women, an r of .30 was found using the same procedure.

Validity: Without the use of the eyes, there is obvious face validity.

Equipment and Materials: The equipment and materials needed are cue sticks, discs, chalk markers or tape markers, blindfolds, and a tape measure.

Directions: (See Figure 10 - 2.) Draw the floor pattern shown below on the gym floor with chalk and allow each student three practice trials at the center ten mark. Each student is then blindfolded and allowed ten trials. The score on each trial is announced so that students have a knowledge of results. Several areas may be marked off to save time.

Scoring: (See Table 10 - 2.) The student's score for each of the ten trials is added for the total score. The maximum score is one hundred points for ten trials. Further experimentation with scoring systems is needed, since the reliability of the test was found to be quite low.

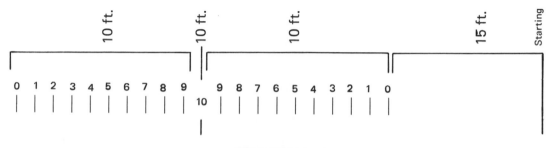

FIGURE 10 - 2

The Shuffleboard Control of Force Test

TABLE 10 - 2

Excellent, Average, and Very Poor Performance Scores
on Selected Kinesthetic Tests (Raw Scores)

Test*	(College Men) (Section A)			(College Women) (Section B)		
	Very Poor Scores	Average Scores	Excellent Scores	Very Poor Scores	Average Scores	Excellent Scores
1. Shuffle-Board Test	40-50	65-75	90-100	30-40	60-70	80-90
2. Kinesthetic Obstacle Test	30-40	65-75	95-100	40-50	70-80	95-100
3. Pedestrial Test of Size	8½ 10¼	3½ 3¾	1 1¾	8¼ 10	3½ 4	0 1
4. Pedestrial Vertical Space	5½ 9	2¼ 2¾	0 ½	6½ 8½	2½ 3	0 ½

*Sources:

1. Based on 100 scores as submitted by Roosevelt Johnson, N.L.S.C., Monroe, La. — Based on 100 scores as submitted by Dalton LeBlanc, N.L.S.C., Monroe, La.

2. Based on 100 scores as submitted by Barbara Borgivest, N.L.S.C., Monroe, La. — Based on 91 scores as submitted by Dorothy Washington, N.L.S.C., Monroe, La.

3. Based on 100 scores as submitted by Ivory Smity, N.L.S.C., Monroe, La. — Based on 104 scores as submitted by Mary George, N.L.S.C., Monroe, La.

4. Based on 48 scores as submitted by John Hall, N.L.S.C., Monroe, La. — Based on 48 scores as submitted by John Hall, N.L.S.C., Monroe, La.

Kinesthetic Obstacle Test [18]

Objective: To measure ability to predict position during movement without the use of the eyes.

Age Level: Ages 10 through college.

Sex: Satisfactory for both boys and girls.

Reliability: An r of .30 was found for college women when test #1 was correlated with test #2. For men, an r of .53 was found using the same procedure.

Validity: Without the use of the eyes, there is obvious face validity.

Equipment and Materials: The equipment and materials required are twelve chairs (or similar objects), material for blindfolds, chalk markers or a tape marker, and tape measures.

Directions: Arrange twelve chairs in accordance with the floor pattern shown in Figure 10 - 3 on the following page. Each performer is allowed one practice trial walk through the course without a blindfold and one walk through the course blindfolded for a score.

<u>Scoring</u>: The performer scores ten points for each station he successfully clears without touching. There are ten stations for a maximum score of one hundred points. (See Table 10 - 2.)

<u>Penalty</u>: (1) There is a ten point penalty for touching any part of the body against any part of a chair. When such a penalty occurs, the performer is directed to the center line and one step ahead of the station where the penalty occurred. (2) There is a five point penalty for each occurrence of getting outside of the line or pattern of the chairs. Upon such occurrences, the performer is directed back into the center of the pattern at the nearest point from which he went astray.

<u>Additional Points</u>: (1) The dotted line merely shows the ideal walking path and need not be drawn on the floor. (2) The two outside lines are boundary lines and should be indicated on the floor. (3) Further experimentation with scoring systems is needed, since the reliability of the test was found to be quite low.

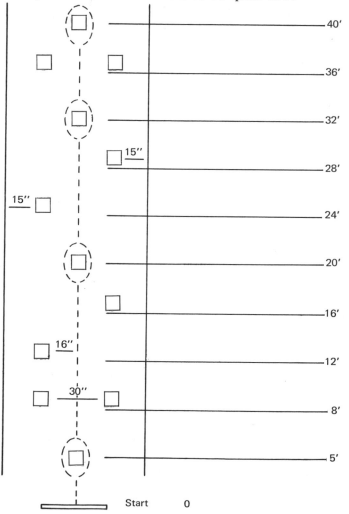

FIGURE 10 - 3

Kinesthetic Obstacle Test

Pedestrial Kinesthesis Test of Size [46]

Objective: To measure the ability to position the feet a prescribed distance.

Age Level: Ages 10 through college.

Sex: Satisfactory for both boys and girls.

Reliability: Has been reported as high as .90 when the split half correlation was stepped up by the Spearman Brown formula; however, when test #1 was correlated with test #2 as performed on separate days, r's of .17 and .19 were found for boys and girls, respectively. Further study of reliability is obviously needed.

Validity: With the eyes closed, there is obvious face validity.

Equipment and Materials: Several yardsticks should be provided since students may work in pairs or groups on this test.

Directions: (See Figure 10 - 4.) The student should stand erect with the eyes closed and the heels touching, and then separate the heels so that the medial sides of the heels are twelve inches apart. The student should mentally concentrate on the length of a twelve inch ruler before each of three trials.

Scoring: The deviation from the preferred score of 12 inches is measured with a yardstick to the nearest one-fourth of an inch. The total amount of deviation for the three trials is the score. (See Table 10 - 2.)

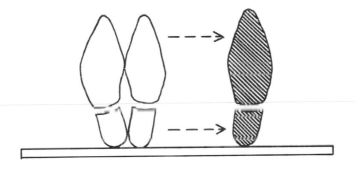

FIGURE 10 - 4

Pedestrial Kinesthesis Test

Pedestrial Kinesthetic Test of Vertical Linear Space [46]

Objective: To measure ability to determine a specified vertical distance by dependence upon the kinesthetic sense.

Age Level: Ages 10 through college.

Sex: Satisfactory for both boys and girls.

Reliability: Has been reported as high as .83 when a split half correlation was stepped up by the Spearman-Brown formula; however, when test #1 was correlated with test #2 as performed on separate days, r's of .50 and .54 were found for boys and girls, respectively. Further study of reliability is needed.

Validity: With the eyes closed, this test has obvious face validity.

Equipment and Materials: The materials needed are several yardsticks, blindfold material, and either chalk markers or tape markers.

Directions: (See Figure 10 - 5.) A line is drawn on a wall fourteen inches above the floor, and the performer is instructed to place the bottom edge of his shoe sole on top of and parallel with the line. Several stations should be set up to save time during testing.

Scoring: The deviation from the line on the wall is measured with a yardstick to the nearest one-fourth of an inch. Each of three trials are totaled for the score. (See Table 10 - 2.)

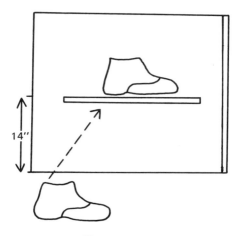

FIGURE 10 - 5

Pedestrial Kinesthesis Test of Vertical Linear Space

Horizontal Linear Space Test [46]

Objective: To measure the kinesthetic ability to determine a specific position along a horizontal line.

Age Level: Ages 10 through college.

Sex: Satisfactory for both boys and girls.

Reliability: On a test-retest correlation, r's of .48 and .33 were found for junior high boys and senior high boys, respectively. Further study of reliability is needed.

Validity: Without the use of the eyes the test has obvious face validity.

Equipment and Materials: The required materials are yardsticks, blindfold material, and tape. Several stations may be set up to save time.

Directions: (See Figure 10 - 6.) Tape the yardstick horizontally to a wall in front of the seated subject at a height that is at approximately eye level for the height of the average student. The subject is instructed to look at the eighteen inch mark and sense its position. Without a practice trial, the subject is blindfolded and instructed to point to the mark indicated.

Scoring: (See Table 10 - 3.) The deviation from the desired mark is recorded to the nearest quarter of an inch on each of three trials. The deviations are then totaled for the score.

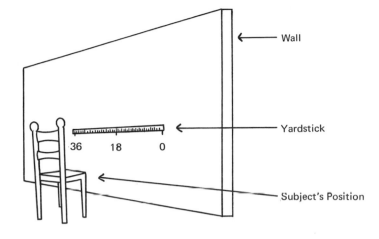

FIGURE 10 - 6

Horizontal Linear Space Test

TABLE 10 - 3

**Excellent, Average, and Very Poor Performance Scores
on the Horizontal Linear Space Test for
Junior and Senior High School Boys**

School Level	Very Poor Scores	Average Scores	Excellent Scores
Junior High School	5¾	3¾	¾
Senior High School	6	4	1

*Score deviations are in inches and are based on a limited number of subjects from physical education classes in East Baton Rouge Parish, Baton Rouge, La.

Vertical Linear Space Test [46]

Objective: To measure the kinesthetic ability to determine a specific position along a vertical line.

Age Level: Ages 10 through college.

Sex: Satisfactory for both boys and girls.

Reliability: Test-retest correlations for junior and senior high school boys ranged between .21 and .30. Further study of reliability is needed.

Validity: With the eyes closed this test has obvious face validity.

Equipment and Materials: The materials needed are yardsticks, blindfolds, and tape. Several stations may be set up to save time.

Directions: (See Figure 10 - 7.) Tape the yardstick vertically to a wall in front of the seated subject at a height where the 16″ mark is about eye level for the average student. The subject is instructed to look at the 16″ mark and sense its position. Without a practice trial the subject is blindfolded and instructed to point to the mark indicated.

<u>Scoring</u>: The deviation from the desired mark is recorded to the nearest quarter of an inch on each of three trials. The deviations are then totaled for the score. (See Table 10 - 4.)

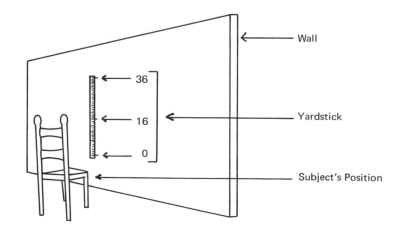

FIGURE 10 - 7

Vertical Linear Space Test

TABLE 10 - 4

**Excellent, Average, and Very Poor Performance Scores
on the Vertical Linear Space Test for Boys
in Grades Seven through Ten**

Grade Level	Very Poor Scores	Average Scores	Excellent Scores
Seventh	4	2¼	1
Eighth	4½	2	¾
Ninth	3¾	1¾	¾
Tenth	2¾	1½	¾

*Score deviations are in inches and are based on a limited number of subjects from physical education classes in East Baton Rouge Parish, Baton Rouge, La.

Bass Kinesthetic Stick Test (Lengthwise) [49]

Objective: To measure the kinesthetic ability to maintain balance on a small narrow surface.

Age Level: Ages 10 through college.

Sex: Satisfactory for both boys and girls.

Reliability: Test — retest correlations for junior and senior high school boys were found to be .21 and .20, respectively. Further study of reliability is needed.

Validity: With the eyes closed this test has obvious face validity.

Equipment and Materials: The equipment and materials needed are stop watches, several sticks cut to one inch by one inch by twelve inches, tape, and blindfolds. Several stations may be set up to save time.

Directions: (See Figure 9 - 3.) The subject is instructed to place his dominant foot lengthwise on a balance stick and to raise his opposite foot from the floor to see how long he can maintain his balance. Each subject is given one preliminary trial and is then blindfolded for the test. The subject is timed from the moment he raises his opposite foot from the floor until balance is lost.

Scoring: The score is recorded to the nearest one-half second. (See Table 10 - 5.)

TABLE 10 - 5

Excellent, Average, and Very Poor Performance Scores
on the Bass Kinesthetic Stick Test (Lengthwise)
for Junior and Senior High School Boys

School Level	Very Poor Scores	Average Scores	Excellent Scores
Junior High School	3	9	15
Senior High School	3½	10	16

*Scores are in seconds and are based on a limited number of subjects from physical education classes in East Baton Rouge Parish, Baton Rouge, La.

Bass Kinesthetic Stick Test (Crosswise) [49]

This test is the same as the previous test except the ball of the dominant foot is placed crosswise on the stick. The scoring is exactly the same as on the previous test. The reliability for the test with junior and senior high school boys was .33 and .68, respectively, when scores were correlated from a test-retest on separate days. (See Table 10 - 6.)

TABLE 10 - 6

Excellent, Average, and Very Poor Performance Scores
on the Bass Kinesthetic Stick Test (Crosswise)
for Junior and Senior High School Boys

School Level	Very Poor Scores	Average Scores	Excellent Scores
Junior High School	3½	7½	12
Senior High School	4	8	12½

*Scores are in seconds and are based on a limited number of subjects from physical education classes in East Baton Rouge Parish, Baton Rouge, La.

Problems Associated with Kinesthetic Perception Testing

Several of the problems and limitations associated with the testing of kinesthetic perception in the laboratory situation are listed as follows:

1. Many investigators have failed to recognize the influence of tactual stimulation involved in the more traditional tests of kinesthesis.[35] For example, Chernikoff[4] has pointed out that when a subject exerts force against a scale, body contact produces tactual stimulation. Moreover, when the subject is blindfolded and is required to move a body part to a designated point in space, the tester commonly moves the subject's body part in the preliminary trial, and this also produces tactual stimulation. However, Slater-Hammel[35] has stated that in spite of this limitation, an intriguing type of human response has become available for study. He later investigated the use of muscle potential changes as a measure of kinesthetic perception without the influence of tactual stimulation and found the technique to be promising.[36]

2. Since certain kinesthetic perception tests require not only expensive equipment, but also an excessive amount of time to administer, further attempts should be made by students and teachers to devise inexpensive kinesthetic tests for the average school program. Also, many kinesthetic tests (including those in this chapter) which have been used are still in the exploratory stage, and are of questionable reliability and validity. However, concerning validity, Henry[13] stated that a test in which *muscle sense* is the only possible cue for a successful response should be acknowledged as a valid test of some aspect of kinesthetics. Concerning reliability, investigators frequently show kinesthetic tests to be reliable by using the split half technique when stepped up by the Spearman-Brown formula, but then they recommend a different scoring system when testing other than for reliability. In checking such recommended scoring systems by the test-retest method on separate days, the authors and their assistants found considerably lower r's. Thus, there is a need for further experimentation to establish reliable scoring systems which will also be practical for use.

3. Since most writers on the topic of kinesthesis suggest that it is specific rather than general, it would seem appropriate to devise tests of kinesthesis with that thought

in mind. For example, if a coach is trying to emphasize *touch* in basketball goal shooting, he might experiment with having a player shoot blindfolded. After each shot the performer receives verbal feedback and then tries to adjust by *feel.* The use of skill tests while blindfolded as a form of practice in certain activities may have considerable value in trying to establish consistency of performance such as in *grooving* a golf swing. Needless to say, common sense must prevail; nevertheless, there may be merit in this procedure.

4. Norms for kinesthetic tests are quite limited, and thus there is a need for the establishment of norms at different grade levels for the various tests of kinesthesis.

Findings and Conclusions From Kinesthetic Perception Measurement and Research

Early studies have given some indication of the place of kinesthesis in learning. For example, one study pointed out that kinesthesis does not directly help learning, since rats with a sectioned cervical cord did not need kinesthetic aid in learning and perfecting a maze habit, and that learning on the basis of kinesthesis alone was impossible.[17] Hozik[16] also worked with rats, but found that kinesthetic perception was important in at least some types of learning. He found kinesthesis essential to the smooth flowing of movements, which assures this function only in conjunction with other types of stimuli and only after learning has begun on the basis of the other stimuli.

Phillips[29] has indicated that both psychologists and coaches seem to agree, based on *a priori* knowledge, that kinesthesis is necessary for superior motor performance. He further pointed out that several studies[36,26,21,46] indicated a tendency for the skilled performer of a specific activity to score higher than the less skilled performer on kinesthetic tests; however, such studies are not as conclusive as one might expect.

Various researchers have related kinesthesis to motor performance,[12,26,28,29,32,37,40,41,44,49] motor learning,[5,6,23,25,30,32,44] and certain psychological and physiological factors[1,3,5,13,15,31,38,43] For the most part, such relationships were found to be low, but positive.

In measuring kinesthetic reaction time, Slater-Hammel[35] concluded that reaction time to a stimulus which involved the subject's arm being moved was significantly shorter than reaction time to a visual stimulus for all students tested.

Although many tests of kinesthetic perception are still in the exploratory stage and have caused concern among investigators on the question of validity, some tests of kinesthesis have been validated at least to some extent.[5,13,34,40]

After studying tests and conducting research in the area of kinesthetic perception, several investigators have concluded that there is no general kinesthetic ability, but rather that there are probably numerous specific factors involved.[7,34,38,46]

Two studies revealed that differences between boys and girls in kinesthetic perceptivity were not significant.[36,48] Recent test results compiled by the authors further supported the above studies.

Concerning activity groups and sports activities, the following findings have been reported:

1. Among groups taking kinesthetic perception tests, differences were recorded in favor of athletes.[21,35,46] Moreover, varsity athletes, physical education majors, and music majors were found to have significantly shorter reaction time to the feeling of arm movement than liberal arts majors.[35]

2. No appreciable relationships have been established between kinesthesis and gymnastics,[44] bowling,[12] and basketball[41] ability. However, Mumby[26] reported that ability to maintain constant muscular pressure under a changing dynamic condition was significantly related to ability in wrestling as subjectively rated by wrestling instructors.

BIBLIOGRAPHY

1. Ball, R. V., "Objective Measurement of Emotional Instability; Study of Kinesthetic Motor Learning Among a Group of Juvenile Delinquents," *Journal of Applied Psychology,* 9:226-245, 1929.

2. Bass, Ruth I., "Analysis of the Components of Tests of Semi-circular Canal Functions and of Static and Dynamic Balance, *Research Quarterly,* 10:33-52, May, 1939.

3. Brown, J. S., and others, "The Accuracy of Positioning Reactions as a Function of Direction and Extent." *American Journal of Psychology,* 61:167-182, 1948.

4. Chernikoff, R., and F. V. Taylor, "Reaction Time to Kinesthetic Stimulation Resulting from Sudden Arm Displacement," *Journal of Experimental Psychology,* 43:1-8, 1952.

5. Clapper, Dorothy Jean, "Measurement of Selected Kinesthetic Responses at the Junior and Senior High School Levels," (Microcarded Master's Thesis, University of Iowa, 1954).

6. Coady, C., "The Effects of Applying the Principles of Kinesthesis in Teaching Golf Skills to College Women." (Unpublished Master's Thesis, Indiana University, Bloomington, 1950).

7. Cratty, Bryant J., "Comparison of Learning a Time Motor Task with Learning a Similar Gross Motor Task Using Kinesthetic Cues," *Research Quarterly,* 33:220, May, 1962.

8. Davis, Rex Stuart, "Placement of Selected Tumbling and Balance Stunts in the Elementary School Physical Education Program" (Microcarded Master's Thesis, Washington State University, 1951).

9. Denenberg, V. H., "A Simplified Method of Measuring Kinesthetic Reaction Time," *American Journal of Psychology,* 66:309-311, 1953.

10. Ellfeldt, Lois, and Eleanor Matheny, "Movement and Meaning: Development of a General Theory," *Research Quarterly,* 29:264-273, October, 1958.

11. Felton, Elvira Amela, "A Kinesiological Comparison of Good and Poor Performers in the Standing Broad Jump," (Microcarded Master's Thesis, University of Wisconsin, Madison, 1960).

12. Greenlee, Geraldine A., "The Relationship of Selected Measures of Strength, Balance, and Kinesthesis to Bowling Performance, (Microcarded Master's Thesis, State University of Iowa, Iowa City, 1958).

13. Henry, F. M., "Dynamic Kinesthetic Perception and Adjustment," *Research Quarterly,* 24:176-187, May, 1953.

14. Hicks, W. E., "Reaction Time for the Amendment of a Response," *Quarterly Journal of Experimental Psychology,* 1:175-179, 1949.

15. Holway, A. W., and Jurnich, L. M., "On the Discrimination of Minimal Differences in Weight Lifting. A Theory of Differential Sensitivity," *Journal of Psychology,* 4:309-332, 1937.

16. Honzik, C. W., "Role of Kinesthesis in Maze Learning." *Science,* 84:373, 1936.

17. Ingebritsen, O. C., "Maze Learning After Lesion in the Cervical Cord," *Journal Comp. Psychology,* 14:279-294, 1932.

18. Johnson, Barry L., "A Kinesthetic Obstacle Test," (Unpublished Study, Northeast Louisiana State College, Monroe, September, 1966).

19. _____ , "A Study of Selected Kinesthetic Tests," (Unpublished Study, Northeast Louisiana State College, Monore, September, 1966).

20. _____ , "The Shuffle Board Control of Force Test," (Unpublished Study, Northeast Louisiana State College, Monroe, September, 1966).

21. Kerr, W. H., and J. D. Weinland, "Muscular Perceptivity as a Trade Test," *The Journal of Applied Psychology,* 17:550-558, 1933.

22. Lafuze, Marion, "A Study of the Learning of Fundamental Skills by College Freshmen Women of Low Motor Ability," *Researh Quarterly,* 22:149-157, May, 1951.

23. Linsay, D., "Relationship Between Measures of Kinesthesis and the Learning of a Motor Skill," (Unpublished Master's Thesis, University of California, 1952).

24. McCloy, Charles Harold, "A Preliminary Study of Factors in Motor Educability," *Research Quarterly,* 11:28-40, May, 1940.

25. McGrath, J. W., "The Relative Importance of Kinesthetic and Visual Cues in Learning a Hand-Eye Coordination Skill," (Unpublished Master's Thesis, University of California, Berkely, 1944).

26. Mumby, H. Hugh, "Kinesthetic Acuity and Balance Related to Wrestling Ability," *Research Quarterly,* 24:334, October, 1953.

27. Nichols, Anne, "The Psychomotor Factors that are Associated with Ability to Play Superior Golf," (Unpublished Master's Thesis, State University of Iowa, 1935).

28. Norrie, M. L., "The Relationship Between Measures of Kinesthesis and Motor Performance," (Unpublished Master's Thesis, University of California, 1952).

29. Phillips, Bernath Eugene, "The Relationship Between Certain Phases of Kinesthesis and Performance During the Early Stages of Acquiring Two Perceptuo-Motor Skills," (Microcarded Master's Thesis, Pennsylvania State College, 1941).

30. Phillips, Marjorie, and Dean Summers, "Relation of Kinesthetic Perception to Motor Learning," *Research Quarterly,* 25:456-469, December, 1954.

31. Roffel, G., "Visual and Kinesthetic Judgements of Length," *American Journal of Psychology,* 48:331-334, 1936.

32. Roloff, Louise L., "Kinesthesis in Relation to the Learning of Selected Motor Skills," *Research Quarterly,* 24:210-217, May, 1953.

33. Russell, Ruth, "A Factor Analysis of the Components of Kinesthesis," (Microcarded Doctor's Dissertation, University of Oregon, Eugene, 1962).

34. Scott, M. Gladys, "Tests of Kinesthesis," *Research Quarterly,* 26:324-241, October, 1955.

35. Slater-Hammel, A. T., "Comparisons of Reaction-Time Measures to a Visual Stimulus and Arm Movement," *Research Quarterly,* 26:470-479, December, 1955.

36. _____ , "Measurement of Kinesthetic Perception of Muscular Force with Muscle Potential Changes," *Research Quarterly,* 28:153-159, May, 1957.

37. Slocum, Helen M., "The Effect of Fatigue Induced by Physical Activity on Certain Tests in Kinesthesis," (Microcarded Doctoral Dissertation, State University of Iowa, Iowa City, 1952, pp. 39-40).

38. Start, K. B., "Kinesthesis and Mental Practice," *Research Quarterly,* 35:316-319, October, 1964.

39. Steinhaus, Arthur H., "Your Muscles See More than Your Eyes," *JOHPER,* 37:38, September, 1966.

40. Stevens, M., "The Measurement of Kinesthesis in College Women'" (Unpublished Doctoral Dissertation, Indiana University, Bloomington, 1950).

41. Taylor, William J., "The Relationship Between Kinesthetic Judgement and Success in Basketball," (Unpublished Master's Thesis, The Pennsylvania State College, 1933).

42. Vince, M. A., "Corrective Movements in a Pursuit Task," *Quarterly Journal of Experimental Psychology,* 1:85-103, 1948.

43. Weber, C. O., "The Properties of Space and Time in Kinesthetic Field of Force," *American Journal of Psychology,* 38:597-606, 1927.

44. Wettstone, Eugene, "Tests for Predicting Potential Ability in Gymnastics and Tumbling," *Research Quarterly,* 9:115-125, December, 1938.

45. Wiebe, Vernon R., "A Factor Analysis of Tests of Kinesthesis," (Microcarded Doctoral Dissertation, State University of Iowa, Iowa City, 1956, pp. 66-67).

46. _____ , "A Study of Tests of Kinesthesis," *Research Quarterly,* 25:222-227, May, 1954.

47. Witte, Fae, "Relation of Kinesthetic Perception to a Selected Motor Skill for Elementary School Children," *Research Quarterly,* 33:476, October, 1962.

48. _____ , "A Factorial Analysis of Measures of Kinesthesis," (Microcarded Doctoral Dissertation, Indiana University, 1953).

49. Young, Olive G., "A Study of Kinesthesis in Relation to Selected Movements," *Research Quarterly,* 16:277, May, 1945.

Chapter XI

THE MEASUREMENT
OF FLEXIBILITY

When we speak of flexibility, we are referring to the ability of an individual to move the body and its parts through as wide a range of motion as possible without undue strain to the articulations and muscle attachments. Flexibility measurements include flexion exercises (where the angle of the body and its articulations are decreased through movement) and extension exercises (where the angle of the body and its articulations are increased through movement). Since the degree of flexibility in various joints of the same individual may differ greatly, it is considered as a specific ability of the joint involved. By the proper use of standard instruments and tests, it is possible to determine which individuals (and which joints of the body) have the greatest flexibility. Examples of standard instruments used are the goniometer and the Leighton Flexometer,[19] while examples of practical tests are the trunk flexion and trunk extension tests. Although flexibility correlates rather low with some motor abilities, it is usually considered to be an important factor in certain activities as exemplified by the diver as he flexes and extends in the air; or by the swimmer as he executes the butterfly stroke with the dolphin-fish-tail kick. Since it is difficult to determine how much flexion-extension is good or bad for an individual, the coach and student must evaluate the degree needed in each specific joint in terms of ease of performance and safety in the activity or part of the body that is involved. Flexibility is also usually mentioned when one is describing physical fitness. A loss in flexibility is frequently noticed as being one of the first signs of getting *out of shape.*

Uses of Flexibility Tests

Several ways by which flexibility tests are utilized in physical education classes are listed as follows:
1. As a factor in general motor ability tests and physical fitness tests.
2. As a means to determine potential in certain sports activities.
3. As a means for determining achievement and skill grades when flexibility improvement is a specific objective in the teaching unit.
4. As a means to diagnose the extent of a previous injury or the cause of poor posture.

Practical Tests of Flexibility

The Leighton Flexometer[19] and the electrogoniometer* are usually regarded as the most accurate instruments for the measurement of flexibility; however, the tests

---

*Marlene Adrian, Charles M. Tipton, and Peter V. Karpovich, *Electrogoniometer Manual,* Springfield, Mass.: Physiological Research Laboratory, Springfield College, 1965.

presented below may be satisfactorily used in those schools which do not have such equipment.

The Modified Sit and Reach Test [34,14]

Objective: To measure the flexion of the hip and back as well as the elasticity of the hamstring muscles.

Age Level: Ages 10 through college.

Sex: Satisfactory for both boys and girls.

Reliability: An r of .92 was found when scores recorded on two separate days were correlated.

Validity: Face validity was accepted for this test.

Equipment and Materials: The only materials needed are several yardsticks. Several testing stations may be set up to save time.

Directions: The subject assumes a sitting position on the floor with the legs extended at right angles to a line drawn on the floor. The heels should touch the near edge of the line and be about five inches apart. A partner's feet are used to brace the performer's feet so that on the reach the heels will not slip over the line. The performer should *bob* forward 3 times and then reach with both hands as far forward as possible on the yardstick and hold. (See Figure 11 - 1.)

Scoring: A yardstick is placed between the legs of the performer so that it rests on the floor with the 15″ mark resting on the near edge of the heel line. The score is the farthest point reached on the yardstick by the finger tips. Measure to the nearest quarter of an inch. (See Table 11 - 1.) The yardstick should be taped to the floor to insure a constant position. Powdered chalk may be used on the finger tips to help identify the farthest point reached. The best score of 3 trials is recorded as the test score.

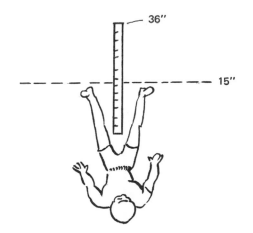

FIGURE 11 - 1

Sit and Reach Test

TABLE 11 - 1

T-Score Norms for Sit and Reach Test

College Men			College Women		
T-Scores	—	Raw Scores	T-Scores	—	Raw Scores
80	—	32	80	—	27
78	—	31	78	—	26
76	—	30	74	—	25
74	—	29	71	—	24
72	—	28	68	—	23
70	—	27	65	—	22
68	—	26	62	—	21
65	—	25	59	—	20
63	—	24	55	—	19
61	—	23	52	—	18
59	—	22	49	—	17
57	—	21	46	—	16
55	—	20	43	—	15
53	—	19	40	—	14
50	—	18	36	—	13
48	—	17	33	—	12
46	—	16	30	—	11
44	—	15	27	—	10
42	—	14	23	—	9
40	—	13	21	—	8
38	—	12	18	—	7
35	—	11			
33	—	10			
31	—	9			
29	—	8			
27	—	7			
25	—	6			
23	—	5			
20	—	4			

Based on the scores of 97 subjects   Based on the scores of 125 subjects
at N.L.S.C., Monroe, La.   at N.L.S.C., Monroe, La.

Bridge Up [14]

Objective: To measure the extension of the spine.

Age Level: Ages 10 through college.

Sex: Satisfactory for both boys and girls.

Reliability: An r of .96 was found when the best of two scores were recorded on separate days.

Validity: Face validity was accepted for this test.

Equipment and Materials: The materials needed are several yardsticks or tape measures, and chalk. Several stations should be set up for testing in order to save time.

Directions: From a supine position on the floor or mat, extend the hips upward by arching the back and walk the hands and feet as close together as possible. (See Figure 11 - 2.)

Scoring: (See Table 11 - 2.) Measure the distance between the finger tips and the heels to the nearest quarter of an inch. Keep in mind that the lesser the distance, the better the score. Allow two trials with the best trial being recorded as the score.

Additional Pointers: (1) Be sure that each student has the feet flat on the floor before measuring. (2) Make a chalk mark at the edge of the heels and the finger tips when they are at their closest point; and then measure the distance between the chalk marks.

FIGURE 11 - 2

Bridge Up

TABLE 11 - 2

T-Score Norms for Bridge-Up

College Men				College Women			
T-Scores	Raw Scores	T-Scores	Raw Scores	T-Scores	Raw Scores	T-Scores	Raw Scores
73	0	48	22	70	0	45	18
72	1	47	23	69	1	43	19
71	2	46	24	68	2	42	20
69	3	44	25	67	3	40	21
68	4	43	26	65	4	39	22
67	5	42	27	64	5	37	23
66	6	41	28	62	6	36	24
65	7	40	29	61	7	35	25
64	8	39	30	59	8	33	26
63	9	38	31	58	9	32	27
62	10	37	32	56	10	30	28
60	11	35	33	55	11	29	29
59	12	34	34	53	12	27	30
58	13	33	35	52	13	26	31
57	14	32	36	51	14	24	32
56	15	31	37	49	15	23	33
55	16	30	38	48	16	22	34
54	17	29	39	46	17	20	35
52	18	27	40				
51	19	26	41				
50	20	25	42				
49	21						

Based on the scores of 96 subjects at N.L.S.C., Monroe, La.

Based on the scores of 125 subjects at N.L.S.C., Monroe, La.

Shoulder Elevation [5]

Objective: To measure the ability to elevate the shoulders.

Age Level: Ages 10 through college.

Sex: Satisfactory for both boys and girls.

Reliability: Has been reported as high as .85.

Validity: Face validity was accepted for this test.

Equipment and Materials: The materials needed are several yardsticks or tape measures, several light sticks 2′ long, and chalk. Several testing stations may be set up to save time.

Directions: The performer assumes a prone position with the arms straight and about shoulder width apart. He grasps the stick and then raises it upward as high as possible while keeping the chin on the floor and the elbows and wrists straight. (See Figure 11 - 3.)

Scoring:[23] The tester measures the distance from the bottom of the stick to the floor on 3 trials. The best measurement is then multiplied by 100, and the product is divided by arm length. The arm length is measured by taking the distance between the acromion process and the upper surface of the stick which is being held as the arms hang downward. (See Table 11 - 3.)

Additional Pointer: Some performers are so flexible that they can move the stick beyond the highest vertical point; however, the measurement should be taken at the highest vertical point.

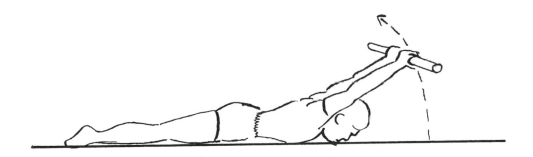

FIGURE 11 - 3

Shoulder Elevation

TABLE 11 - 3

T-Score Norms for Shoulder Elevation

College Men				College Women			
T-Scores	Raw Scores	T-Scores	Raw Scores	T-Scores	Raw Scores	T-Scores	Raw Scores
70	123	49	77	70	123	49	75
69	121	48	75	69	121	48	73
68	119	47	72	68	118	47	70
67	117	46	70	67	116	46	68
66	114	45	68	66	114	45	66
65	112	44	66	65	112	44	63
64	110	43	64	64	109	43	61
63	108	42	61	63	107	42	59
62	106	41	59	62	105	41	56
61	103	40	57	61	102	40	54
60	101	39	55	60	100	39	52
59	99	38	53	59	98	38	50
58	97	37	50	58	96	37	47
57	95	36	48	57	93	36	45
56	92	35	46	56	91	35	43
55	90	34	44	55	89	34	40
54	88	33	42	54	86	33	38
53	86	32	39	53	84	32	36
52	84	31	37	52	82	31	34
51	81	30	35	51	79	30	31
50	79			50	77		

Based on the scores of 99 subjects at N.L.S.C., Monroe, La.   Based on the scores of 100 subjects at N.L.S.C., Monroe, La.

Average Ankle Flexibility [5]

Objective: To measure ability to flex and extend the ankle.

Age Level: Ages 10 through college.

Sex: Satisfactory for both boys and girls.

Reliability: Has been reported as high as .73.

Validity: Face validity was accepted for this test.

Equipment and Materials: Materials needed are paper, long pencils, protractors, thumb tacks, and several cardboard squares about 18″ high and 18″ wide. Several stations may be set up to save time during testing.

Directions: The performer sits on the floor with the back of the knee touching the floor. Keeping the heel stationary, he dorsi-flexes the foot as much as possible. The tester traces the outline of the foot (keeping the pencil horizontal) from just above the ankle to just beyond the big toe on a sheet of paper placed at the side of the foot. The performer then extends (plantar flexes) the foot as far as possible, and the outline is again traced on the same sheet of paper. The angle of each of the lines with the horizontal is measured with a protractor. (See Figure 11 - 4.)

Scoring: The score is the measure taken from the protractor for each foot. An average score for the feet is then figured. (See Table 11 - 4.)

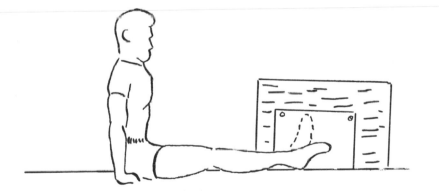

FIGURE 11 - 4

Average Ankle Flexibility

TABLE 11 - 4

T-Score Norms for Average Ankle Flexibility

College Men				College Women			
T-Scores	Raw Scores	T-Scores	Raw Scores	T-Scores	Raw Scores	T-Scores	Raw Scores
75	89	47	51	72	89	48	60
74	87	46	50	71	87	47	58
73	86	45	48	70	86	46	57
72	85	44	47	69	85	45	56
71	83	43	46	68	84	44	55
70	82	42	44	67	83	43	54
69	81	41	43	66	81	42	53
68	79	40	42	65	80	41	52
67	78	39	40	64	79	40	51
66	77	38	39	63	78	39	49
65	76	37	38	62	77	38	47
64	74	36	36	61	75	37	46
63	73	35	35	60	74	36	45
62	71	34	34	59	73	35	44
61	70	33	32	58	72	34	43
60	68	32	31	57	70	33	41
59	67	31	30	56	69	32	40
58	66	30	28	55	68	31	39
57	64	29	27	54	67	30	38
56	63	28	26	53	66	29	36
55	62	27	24	52	64	28	35
54	60	26	23	51	63	27	34
53	59	25	22	50	62	26	33
52	58	24	20	49	61	25	32
51	56	23	19				
50	55	21	16				
49	54	20	15				
48	52						

Based on the scores of 99 subjects at N.L.S.C., Monroe, La.

Based on the scores of 100 subjects at N.L.S.C., Monroe, La.

Front Splits [14]

Objective: To measure the extension of the legs in lowering to a front splits position.

Age Level: Ages 10 through college.

Sex: Satisfactory for both boys and girls.

Reliability: An r of .80282 was found when scores were recorded on separate days and correlated. The reliability can be raised by allowing two trials per testing and recording only the best trial as the test score.

Validity: Face validity was accepted for this test.

Equipment and Materials: The materials needed for this test are yardsticks and rulers. Several testing stations may be set up to save time.

Directions: (See Figure 11 - 5.) The performer slides one foot backward and the other foot forward, lowering the body downward until the crotch is as close to the floor as possible. The position should be held long enough for measurement. While the legs are separating, the tester should get behind the performer and extend a ruler horizontally outward from the edge of the vertical yardstick so that it rests under the crotch of the performer. As the performer lowers, the ruler should lower (sliding down the edge of the yardstick) until the lowest point is reached. A reading from the yardstick is then taken. (See Figure 11 - 5 (B).)

Scoring: The score is the number of inches between the crotch and the floor measured to the nearest quarter of an inch. (See Table 11 - 5.)

Additional Pointers: (1) Clasp the ruler to the yard stick with a firm grip so the reading will not be lost while withdrawing it away from the performer. (2) The performer should be allowed to place a hand on the floor (in front of the crotch) for balance. (3) Make sure that the performer does not let the hips shift away from the vertical during the measurement.

FIGURE 11 - 5

Front Splits

TABLE 11 - 5

T-Score Norms for Front Splits

College Men			College Women		
T-Scores	—	Raw Scores	T-Scores	—	Raw Scores
70	—	0	62	—	0
68	—	1	60	—	1
66	—	2	57	—	2
64	—	3	55	—	3
62	—	4	52	—	4
60	—	5	50	—	5
58	—	6	47	—	6
55	—	7	44	—	7
53	—	8	42	—	8
51	—	9	39	—	9
49	—	10	37	—	10
47	—	11	34	—	11
45	—	12	31	—	12
43	—	13	29	—	13
41	—	14	26	—	14
38	—	15	24	—	15
36	—	16	21	—	16
34	—	17	18	—	17
32	—	18	16	—	18
30	—	19	13	—	19
28	—	20	11	—	20
26	—	21			
24	—	22			
22	—	23			
20	—	24			

Based on the scores of 97 subjects
at N.L.S.C., Monroe, La.

Based on the scores of 125 subjects
at N.L.S.C., Monroe, La.

Side Splits [14]

Objective: To measure the extension of the legs in lowering to a side splits position.

Age Level: Ages 10 through college.

Sex: Satisfactory for both boys and girls.

Reliability: An r of .65335 was found when scores were recorded on separate days and then correlated. This low r indicates that two trials should be allowed for each testing and that only the best score should be recorded as the test score.

Validity: Face validity was accepted for this test.

Equipment and Materials: The materials needed for this test are yardsticks and rulers. Several testing stations may be set up to save time.

Directions: (See Figure 11 - 6.) The performer slides the feet apart and to the sides, lowering the body downward until the crotch is as close to the floor as possible. The position should be held long enough for measurement. When the legs are separating, the tester should get behind the performer and extend a ruler horizontally outward from the edge of the vertical yardstick so that it rests under the crotch of the performer. As the performer lowers, the ruler should lower (sliding down the edge of the yardstick) until the lowest point is reached. A reading from the yardstick is then taken. (See Figure 11 - 5 (B).)

Scoring: The score is the number of inches between the crotch and the floor, measured to the nearest quarter of an inch. (See Table 11 - 6.)

Additional Pointers: (1) Clasp the ruler to the yardstick with a firm grip so the reading will not be lost while withdrawing it away from the performer. (2) The performer should be allowed to place the hands on the floor (in front of the crotch) for balance. (3) Make sure the performer's hips do not lean past the vertical when the measurement is made.

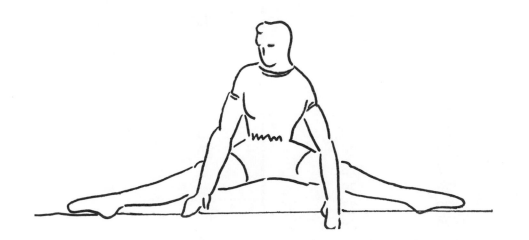

FIGURE 11 - 6

Side Splits

TABLE 11 - 6

T-Score Norms for Side Splits Test

College Men			College Women		
T-Scores	—	Raw Scores	T-Scores	—	Raw Scores
78	—	0	85	—	0
76	—	1	81	—	1
74	—	2	78	—	2
72	—	3	75	—	3
70	—	4	72	—	4
68	—	5	69	—	5
66	—	6	66	—	6
64	—	7	63	—	7
62	—	8	60	—	8
60	—	9	57	—	9
58	—	10	54	—	10
55	—	11	51	—	11
53	—	12	48	—	12
51	—	13	45	—	13
49	—	14	42	—	14
47	—	15	39	—	15
45	—	16	36	—	16
43	—	17	33	—	17
41	—	18	30	—	18
39	—	19	27	—	19
37	—	20	24	—	20
35	—	21	21	—	21
33	—	22	18	—	22
31	—	23	15	—	23
29	—	24			
27	—	25			
25	—	26			
23	—	27			
20	—	28			

Based on the scores of 97 subjects
at N.L.S.C., Monroe, La.

Based on the scores of 125 subjects
at N.L.S.C., Monroe, La.

Trunk Extension [5]

 Objective: To measure ability to extend the trunk backward.

 Age Level: Ages 10 through college.

 Sex: Satisfactory for both boys and girls.

 Reliability: Has been reported as high as .72.

 Validity: Face validity was accepted for this test.

 Equipment and Materials: A string and a yardstick, or a tape measure is required. Several of these are needed if more than one station is to be operated.

 Directions: The performer should lie prone on a mat with his feet and hips held down. He then should raise his trunk as far backward as possible. The tester should measure the vertical distance between the mat and the suprasternal notch. (See Figure 11 - 7.)

 Scoring:[23] The measurement taken (to the nearest quarter of an inch) is multiplied by 100, and the product is divided by trunk length. (See Table 11 - 7.)

 Additional Pointers: (1) The trunk measurement should be taken with the performer seated and back against the wall. The vertical distance between the suprasternal notch and the floor or bench is used to represent trunk length. (2) In getting the measurement of trunk extension, it is helpful to place the zero end of a tape measure on the suprasternal notch. As the lift is made, the tape is pulled taut between the finger tips and the mat so that a quick and accurate reading can be made.

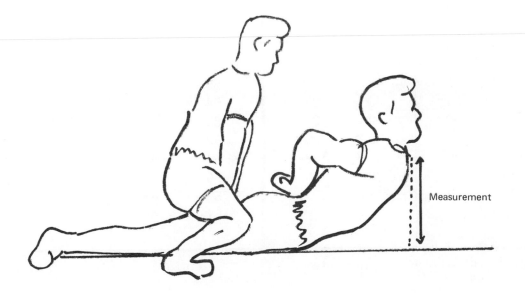

Measurement

FIGURE 11 - 7

Trunk Extension

TABLE 11 - 7

T-Score Norms for Trunk Extension

College Men				College Women			
T-Scores	Raw Scores	T-Scores	Raw Scores	T-Scores	Raw Scores	T-Scores	Raw Scores
80	64	56	45	80	63	55	42
78	63	55	44	79	62	53	41
77	62	54	43	78	61	52	40
76	61	53	42	77	60	51	39
75	60	51	41	75	59	50	38
73	59	50	40	74	58	48	37
72	58	49	39	73	57	47	36
71	57	48	38	72	56	46	35
70	56	47	37	70	55	45	34
69	55	45	36	69	54	44	33
67	54	44	35	68	53	42	32
66	53	43	34	67	52	41	31
65	52	42	33	66	51	40	30
64	51	40	32	64	50	39	29
62	50	39	31	63	49	37	28
61	49	38	30	62	48	36	27
60	48	37	29	61	47	35	26
59	47	36	28	59	46	34	25
58	46			58	45	33	24
				57	44	31	23

Based on the scores of 99 subjects at N.L.S.C.,
Monroe, La.

Based on the scores of 100 subjects at N.L.S.C.,
Monroe, La.

Problems Associated with Flexibility Testing

Concerning flexibility testing, there are several problems and limitations which exist in the laboratory situation. They are identified and briefly discussed below.

1. There is a lack of scientific evidence concerning how much flexibility an individual should possess, or whether too much is more harmful than beneficial. Thus, it appears that flexibility must be evaluated in terms of the activity engaged in and the individual and his specific body parts that require flexibility.

2. Flexibility is specific to the body part involved, and yet, certain motor ability and physical fitness tests fail to take this fact into consideration. Usually such tests include only one or two flexibility items of a specific body part, and thus, results may be distorted. It would seem reasonable to include several flexibility items of similar difficulty and weight and allow the performer to pick the one he can be most successful on.

3. McCloy[23] held that certain tests are unfair because of variations in anthropometeric measures. For example, a person with short legs and long arms may have an unfair advantage over a person with all short extremities on the sit and reach test. Although there is controversy on this point, McCloy's procedure[23] to overcome this problem through mathematical adjustments appears to be a practical safeguard.

4. A frequent criticism of the Scott-French Bobbing Test[30] is that students are afraid to go all out for fear of leaning over too far and falling. Although this limitation prompted Wells and Dillon[34] to develop the sit and reach test, it is suggested by the author that the fear of falling could be overcome by the use of a 3' by 3' plywood board, ¾" thick with a hole cut in the center (large enough for the hands to go through easily). Supported by a bench on each side of the hole, this would give students depth for the reach and also enough surface area to step forward in regaining the balance (when necessary) without danger of falling.

5. There is a need for scoring scales and norms at the elementary, junior high, and high school levels.

Findings and Conclusions From Flexibility Measurement and Research

After studying boys and girls of comparable ages, a number of investigators have concluded that girls are more flexible than boys.[11,10,28,32] Recent laboratory testing by the authors revealed results which further supported the above conclusion.

The research of numerous investigators has made it a well known fact that joint flexibility can be improved.[1,7,15,17,20,24,29,32] In fact, DeVries,[7] Riddle,[29] Kusinitz and Keeney[16] have elicited gains by the use of both static stretch and ballistic or spring stretch methods. Evidence seems to indicate that there is no significant difference between the two methods, although Riddle found both methods superior to a combination of the two.

The layman frequently believes that weight training causes a loss of flexibility or *muscle boundness*. However, studies by Massey[20] and Kusinitz and Keeney[16] revealed that weight training does not reduce joint flexibility. While it is possible that exercises habitually performed over a limited range of motion may cause a permanent shortening of muscles, the condition termed as *muscle boundness* will not occur from weight training when the muscles are stretched by executing each movement through a complete range of motion.[25] To the authors *muscle boundness* is a misnomer. After years of experience and observation in weight training programs, such a condition was never witnessed. However, many cases of inflexibility have been observed to have resulted (seemingly) from a lack of physical activity which placed definite demands upon joint movement.

As mentioned earlier, there is an apparent controversy concerning the relationship between anthropometric measures and flexibility. In two studies by Mathews, one with college women[21] and the other with elementary school boys,[22] the investigator concluded that no significant relationship existed and that flexibility seemed independent of lower limb length. Taking the opposing viewpoint, Broer[2] concluded that for individuals with a longer-trunk-plus-arm measurement and relatively short legs, there is a significant advantage in their favor in the toe-touch test. Moreover, McCloy's quotient[23] was devised to take into account the sizes of the subjects on certain flexibility tests.

While the layman may frequently generalize that a person is very flexible upon observing a display of a wide range of motion in a specific joint, the professional physical educator would be inclined to wait and observe flexibility movements in other joints of the body before making a positive or negative generalization. Since flexibility is specific to the joint involved, as determined by Kingsley,[15] Forbes,[9] and numerous other investigators, a person might be quite flexible in one articulation and rather inflexible in many of the others.

For the most part humans become progressively more flexible from childhood to adolescence and then become progressively less flexible as determined by Hupprich,[12] Phillips,[28] Forbes,[9] and Miller.[26] Forbes[9] has further indicated that although boys lost in flexibility during the adolescent period, that some recovery was made in a number of the joints by the age of eighteen. Both Forbes[9] and Miller[26] noted that hip flexion-extension failed to follow an orderly ascending or descending trend. Another point of interest is that eighteen year old girls have been found to be more flexible than six year old girls in specific areas.[12,28]

Two studies have been conducted for the purpose of comparing athletes and non-athletes, active individuals and inactive individuals, and physical education majors and non-majors. Sigerseth and Haliski[31] found non-athletes in physical education classes to be more flexible than football players in thirteen of twenty-one joints, while McCue[24] found that active individuals were more flexible than the inactive and that significant differences did not exist between physical education majors and non-majors. Although there seems to be some disagreement within the McCue study, it is possible that the non-majors were as active as the physical education majors, or vice-versa.

Flexibility has been found to have little or no relationship to postural divergencies,[6] motor ability,[3,4,27] and the degree of stability of the feet.[18] As previously mentioned, there is controversy as to whether or not it is related to anthropometric measures.

Concerning physical education activities and flexibility, the following findings have been reported: (1) a twenty week tumbling program significantly increased a large number of flexibility measures,[15] (2) modern dance was significantly superior to folk dance in the development of back flexibility,[1] and (3) participation in weight training did not result in a decrease of flexibility.[16,20]

BIBLIOGRAPHY

1. Bennett, Colleen L., "Relative Contributions of Modern Dance, Folk Dance, Basketball, and Swimming to Motor Abilities of College Women," *Research Quarterly,* 27:261, October, 1956.

2. Broer, Marion, and Naomi Galles, "Importance of Relationship Between Various Body Measurements in Performance of the Toe-Touch Test," *Research Quarterly,* 29:262, October, 1958.

3. Burley, Lloyd R., and others, "Relation of Power, Speed, Flexibility, and Certain Anthropometric Measures of Junior High School Girls," *Research Quarterly,* 32:443, December, 1961.

4. Carruth, Wincie A., "An Analysis of Motor Ability and Its Relationship to Constitutional Body Patterns," (Microcarded Doctor's Dissertation, New York University, 1952).

5. Cureton, T. K., Jr., "Flexibility as an Aspect of Physical Fitness," *Research Quarterly Supplement,* 12:388-389, May, 1941.

6. Davies, Evelyn A., "Relationship Between Selected Postural Divergencies and Motor Ability," *Research Quarterly,* 28:4, March, 1957.

7. DeVries, Hebert, "Evaluation of Static Stretching Procedures for Improvement of Flexibility," *Research Quarterly,* May, 1962.

8. Dintiman, George B., "Effects of Various Training Programs on Running Speed," *Research Quarterly,* 35:462, December, 1964.

9. Forbes, Joseph, "Characteristics of Flexibility in Boys," (Microcarded Doctor's Dissertation, University of Oregon, 1950).

10. Hall, D. M., "Standardization of Flexibility Tests for 4-H Club Members," *Research Quarterly,* 27:296-300, October, 1956.

11. Hoffman, Virginia, "Relation of Selected Traits and Abilities to Motor Learning," (Microcarded Doctor's Dissertation, Indiana University, 1955).

12. Hupprich, Florence L., and Peter Sigerseth, "The Specificity of Flexibility in Girls," *Research Quarterly,* 21:32, March, 1950.

13. Hutchins, Gloria Lee, "The Relationship of Selected Strength and Flexibility Variables to the Antero-posterior Posture of College Women," *Research Quarterly,* 36, October, 1965.

14. Johnson, Barry L., "Practical Tests of Flexibility," (Unpublished Study, Northeast Louisiana State College, Monroe, Louisiana, September, 1966).

15. Kingsley, Donald B., "Flexibility Changes Resulting from Participation in Tumbling," (Microcarded Master's Thesis, University of Oregon, 1952).

16. Kusinitz, Ivan, and Clifford E. Keeney, "Effects of Progressive Weight Training on Health and Physical Fitness of Adolescent Boys," *Research Quarterly,* 29:294, October, 1958.

17. Lafuze, Marion, "A Study of the Learning of Fundamental Skills by College Freshman Women of Low Motor Ability," *Research Quarterly,* 22:156, May, 1951.

18. Lawrence, Susan, "A Study of the Flexibility and Stability of the Feet of College Women," (Microcarded Master's Thesis, Smith College, 1955).

19. Leighton, Jack, "A Simple Objective and Reliable Measure of . lexibility," *Research Quarterly,* 13:205-216, May, 1942.

20. Massey, Ben H., and Norman L. Chaudet, "Effects of Systematic, Heavy Resistive Exercise on Range of Joint Movement in Young Male Adults," *Research Quarterly,* 27:50, March, 1956.

21. Mathews, Donald, and others, "Hip Flexibility of College Women as Related to Length of Body Segments," *Research Quarterly,* 28:355, December, 1957.

22. _____ , "Hip Flexibility of Elementary School Boys as Related to Body Segments," *Research Quarterly,* 30:302, October, 1959.

23. McCloy, Charles Harold, and Norma D. Young, *Test and Measurements in Health and Physical Education.* New York: Appleton-Century-Crofts, Inc., 1954, p. 227.

24. McCue, Betty F., "Flexibility Measurements of College Women," *Research Quarterly,* 24:323-324, October, 1953.

25. McMorris, R. O., and E. C. Elkins, "A Study of Production and Evaluation of Muscular Hypertrophy," *Archives of Physical Medicine and Rehabilitation,* 35:420-426, July, 1954.

26. Miller, Charles J., "The Relationship of Flexibility in Boys to Age," (Microcarded Master's Thesis, University of Maryland, 1954).

27. Olsen, Barbara H., "An Investigation of the Relationship of Ankle, Knee, Trunk and Shoulder Flexibility to General Motor Ability," (Microcarded Master's Thesis, University of Oregon, 1956).

28. Phillips, Marjorie, and others, "Analysis of Results from the Kraus-Weber Test of Minimum Muscular Fitness in Children," *Research Quarterly,* 26:322, October, 1955.

29. Riddle, K. S., "A Comparison of Three Methods for Increasing Flexibility of the Trunk and Hip Joints," (Microcarded Doctor's Dissertation, University of Oregon, 1956).

30. Scott, M. Gladys, and Ester French, *Measurement and Evaluation in Physical Education,* Dubuque, Iowa: Wm. C. Brown Company, Publisher, 1959.

31. Sigerseth, Peter O., and Chester Haliski, "The Flexibility of Football Players," *Research Quarterly,* 21:398, December, 1950.

32. Smith, Jean A., "Relation of Certain Physical Traits and Abilities to Motor Learning in Elementary School Children," *Research Quarterly,* 27:228, May, 1956.

33. Tyrance, Herman J., "Relationship of Extreme Body Types to Ranges of Flexibility," *Research Quarterly,* 29:248, October, 1958.

34. Wells, Katherine F., and Evelyn K. Dillon, "The Sit and Reach — A Test of Back and Leg Flexibility," *Research Quarterly,* 23:118, March, 1952.

Chapter XII

THE MEASUREMENT OF RHYTHM AND DANCE

Evaluation in the area of rhythm and dance has depended mainly on rating scales. This dependence on rating scales has been of necessity, since there are very few tests in this area which can be used in the classroom. Authorities in this field have found rhythm as difficult to define as it is to measure. Existing definitions of rhythm from various sources have consistently mentioned such terms as flow, movement, repetition, and beat. Thus, rhythm may be thought of as the flow of movement with the regular repetition of beat in grouping movements for the successful execution of a pattern or a skill. Physical educators frequently think of rhythm as that pattern which makes performance, even difficult performance, look easy and graceful. Rhythm is closely associated with kinesthesis, speed, and agility and is important in any skill which requires a series of successive movements. In the execution of a dance the individual moves his body as he listens to music. Dance is therefore complicated in that movement of the individual is related to a rhythmic pattern of the music. Some instructors insist that the student move in time with the music, while other instructors feel that a student should not be penalized for the inability to pick up a rhythmic pattern of music.*

Uses of Rhythm and Dance Tests

Tests of rhythm and dance may be utilized in physical education in the following ways:
1. As a means to further the learning process by stimulating students to devote their maximum effort toward rhythmic interpretation and performance. This type of use should be followed by a critique so that the student will benefit from his mistakes.
2. As a means to help students recognize rhythmic patterns in sports activities or in improving fundamental skills such as walking, running, and jumping.
3. As a measure for determining achievement and grades in dance classes. Rhythmic action is also a point to consider in grading gymnastics stunts and swimming skills.
4. As a means for evaluating prospective members of physical education exhibition groups in such activities as synchronized swimming, gymnastics, and dance.

Practical Tests of Rhythm and Dance

Since tests of rhythm and dance are quite limited, the author has submitted the following items as the most practical found at the present time. Moreover, the word

*The authors are indebted to Professor I. F. Waglow, University of Florida, Gainesville, Florida, for assistance in writing the above section.

practical is used somewhat apologetically for this section. For directions in each of the various types of dance areas, it is important for the instructor to inform the student as to what the instructor is looking for as he rates the performer. Also, the rating scale to be used should be understood by the student. A few of the criteria and ideas that should be considered in various types of dance were suggested by Waglow* as follows:

1. **Folk Dance.** In folk dancing the following three criteria should be considered in rating students: (a) the style of execution of the movement, (b) the execution of the dance in a pattern as related to the music—in general, the student would have memorized this movement, and (c) the rhythm of the student as related to the music.

2. **Modern Dance.** If the instructor uses set patterns of movement (exercises) in preparing the student for self-expression in modern dance, these movements could be used to evaluate the student. A second area in which the student could be evaluated is in the performance of a dance, whether it be to a poem or music. In judging an original composition of the student, the instructor might look for difficulty, combination of movements, and judge the execution and form. Many instructors find it desirable to bring in other experts in the area of dance to judge the performance of students.

3. **Social Dance.** In social dance the instructor may require students to execute a series of variations while they are being rated. This series of variations is often memorized, and the instructor is provided with a statement as to what variations the students will do. Another way of judging the student would be to require the student to make up variations which were not learned in class, and then as the student performs these variations, he or she could be evaluated. In evaluating the student in social dance, it is important that the student dance in time with the rhythm pattern of the music, and that the style of movement be appropriate for the rhythm that is being played.

4. **Square Dance.** As the student performs square dance movements, the following three criteria should be considered: (a) How well does the performer respond to the caller? (b) How well does the performer execute the movement that is called for? (c) Does the dancer move according to the rhythm pattern of the music? The instructor could make use of a record with a caller on it in evaluating, or the instructor could be the caller and have other instructors do the evaluating.

5. **Tap Dancing.** In evaluating a student in tap dancing, the following three areas should be considered: (a) Are the movements executed properly? (b) Is the memorized routine of the dance performed correctly? (c) Is the dance performed in rhythm with the music that is being played?

Waglow's Social Dance Test [33]

Objective: The objective of this test is to measure the ability of a student to execute a dance step in time with music.

Age Level: Satisfactory for the secondary and college level.

Sex: Satisfactory for both boys and girls.

Reliability: Recent refinements have raised the reliability of this test to $r = .82$. This is considerably higher than the reliability indicated in the original report in the literature.

*Submitted by I. F. Waglow, University of Florida, Gainesville, Florida.

Validity: The validity for this test has been found to be .76 in recent studies. The criterion was the combined subjective ratings of two judges.

Equipment and Materials: In administering the test it is necessary to have music transcribed from records to a tape. Students will need chalk to mark a spot on the floor and also small score cards and pencils for keeping score.

Directions to Tester: The tape is made by indicating the rhythm that is being played. With the tape recorder turned on, the rhythm is identified. It is then indicated how many measures the student will wait before starting to move. For example, the tape would say *waltz,* a short pause, and then *six measures,* a short pause; and then the tape would record the number of measures which are desired. In making the tape the instructor would have to make up his mind as to how many measures of music he would want the students to dance. When that number of measures had gone by, the tape recorder would then cease to record. There would then be a 15 second pause, and the above procedure would then be repeated for another rhythm.

Directions to Students: The students should be instructed to listen for the rhythm that is to be played and also the number of measures they are to wait before beginning to move. As the tape is played, the students are informed that they are not to move until the end of the introductory measures, and then they are to continue moving until the music stops. The forward and backward pattern is to be followed where applicable.

Scoring: The students must be paired up and it doesn't make any difference whether there are two males or two females together. The student performing must make a mark on the floor, and the partner must be seated in front of the performer with a score card and pencil. The scorer should count the number of times that the performer leaves and returns to the chalk mark. Each time the performer returns to the chalk mark he receives a score of one. When the music has stopped, the scorer totals up the score and computes the difference between that score and the correct number of measures for that rhythm. Plus and minus signs are disregarded in scoring. For example, if the correct answer is four and the student performed three steps, the score would be minus one; whereas if the student performed five steps, the score would be plus one. However, the positive and negative scores are added together, disregarding the signs, for a composite score. When the scores are added, the performers with the lowest deviations from the true score would be the better performers. (See Table 12 - 1.)

Additional Pointers: (1) In practicing to take the test, the students should be told to practice doing the steps as neatly as possible so that there will not be any question in the minds of the scorers as to whether the performer left the chalk mark or not. (2) Music used during the teaching of the course should be used to construct the test. (3) It is possible for the performer to finish away from the chalk mark, in which case the score would be at a half count. For example, if there were exactly eight measures of waltz music played and a box step performed, a correct score would be four. If the student performed too fast and completed five box steps, it would indicate that he danced two measures too fast. If he completed three steps, it would indicate that he performed two measures too slow. In such cases one score is as bad as the other.

TABLE 12 - 1

T-Score Norms for the Waglow Social Dance Test
at the College Level

(Raw Scores are based on Performance Deviations)

T-Scores	—	Raw Scores	T-Scores	—	Raw Scores	T-Scores	—	Raw Scores
71	—	.5	48	—	4.5	38	—	8.5
67	—	1.0	47	—	5.0	36	—	9.5
62	—	1.5	45	—	5.5	34	—	10.5
58	—	2.0	43	—	6.0	33	—	11.0
55	—	2.5	42	—	6.5	32	—	11.5
53	—	3.0	41	—	7.0	31	—	12.0
52	—	3.5	40	—	7.5	30	—	12.5
50	—	4.0	39	—	8.0	29	—	13.0

Source: Submitted by I. P. Waglow, University of Florida, Gainesville, Florida.

The Tempo Test [17]

Objective: To measure the ability to repeat a given tempo.

Age Level: Ages 10 through college.

Sex: Satisfactory for both boys and girls.

Reliability: Reliability was not reported for this test. Thus, there is a need for a study on the reliability of the scoring procedure presented below.

Validity: This test was accepted at face validity.

Equipment and Materials: One metronome and either a stop watch or a wrist watch with a second hand are needed.

Directions: Three tempos are sounded on the metronome with settings of 64, 120, and 184 so that the three speeds will give 12, 22, and 32 beats, respectively, in 10 seconds. The performer should listen to the metronome at each speed and then step as nearly as possible in the same tempo while the partner counts the steps for 10 seconds.

Scoring: The score is the total number of deviations from the specified beats for the three speeds.

Ashton's Practical Rhythm Test [2]

Objective: To measure ability to perform rhythmical movement in response to selected musical excerpts.

Age Level: Ages 12 through college.

Sex: Satisfactory for both boys and girls.

Reliability: Has been reported as high as .86.

Validity: Face validity was accepted for this test.

Equipment and Materials: The tester should make a tape recording of the following musical excerpts, or record similar excerpts to those on the following page:

MUSICAL EXCERPTS

Form #1	Meas.	MM.	Time(Sec.)
Section 1			
Walk — Wisconsin Blueprint	12	112	21.9
Skip — Davies	16	192	19.7
Run — Huerter — Fire Dance	24	192	29.3
Section 2			
Skip — Kerry Dance	20	208	21.6
Run — Concone — Study	16	208	24.8
Fast Walk — Prokofieff	32	132	29.0
Slow Walk — Beethoven — Waterman ABC — p. 108	16	104	33.1
Skip — New Mown Hay	24	192	37.2
Run — Reinhold — Gnomes	32	208	27.6
Section 3			
Schottische — Jubilee	16	192	24.7
Slow Waltz — Tschaikowsky — Waltz from Sleeping Beauty	32	138	36.1
Mod. Waltz — Schubert, No. 7	32	168	29.0
Polka — Lichner	32	208	24.3

Form #2	Meas.	MM.	Time(Sec.)
Section 1			
Walk — Davies	12	128	20.3
Skip — Queen of Sheba	16	208	32.5
Run — Wisconsin Blueprint	12	184	14.4
Section 2			
Skip — Schumann — Sicilianish	24	132	21.8
Run — Moszkowski — Scherzino	12	208	22.3
Fast Walk — Handel — Joshua	16	196	21.0
Slow Walk — Hollaender March	17	116	31.6
Skip — Marche Lorraine	32	132	28.8
Run — Delibes — Passapied	24	208	25.5
Section 3			
Schottische — Faust-Up-To-Date	24	168	35.1
Slow Waltz — Gurlitt — First Dance	32	138	35.7
Mod. Waltz — Tschaikowsky — Waltz of the Flowers	32	168	27.2
Polka — Plantation Dance	24	200	25.3

Directions: Students are informed that the first part of the recording has music for walking, running, and skipping. Since each musical excerpt is played twice, students should listen to the first one and perform as it is replayed until the music stops.

During the musical excerpts on the second part of the record, students are to show any movement which they feel will fit the music. Students may restrict their movements to walking, running, and skipping; however, they should show their best movement, since any movement will be accepted and judged for its value.

The third part of the recording has music for the schottische, waltz, and polka with more than one piece of music being played for some movements. Students are told what to do by the tester's voice on the recording.

Scoring: The following rhythm rating scale is used for all parts of the test. The final score is a total of points made on the test.

0 — No response or incorrect response.
        Correct beat and accent only through chance.
        Step and rhythm incorrect.
        Attempts to start self in motion; undecided as to correct step. Starts a
            preliminary faltering movement; then stops.

1 — Correct step but not correct beat (unable to pick up new beat or tempo).
    Correct movement only by imitation of another student.
        Awkward, uncoordinated movement.
        Ability to start self in movement maintained only for a measure or two.
        Difficulty in changing direction.

2 — Step and rhythm pattern correct. Reaction time slow. Movement uncer-
    tain—lapses occasionally into incorrect beat.
        Movements are consistently heavy; she shows tension.
        Maintenance of movement is short; phrase.
        Movement is forced; mechanical. Lacking in style.
        It is prosaic—no variety.

3 — Uses correct step, beat, and accent. If student loses the accent and gets off
    the beat, she is aware of it and able to get back on the beat.
        Ability to maintain movement throughout excerpt.
        Varies direction with effort but is able to maintain movement.
        Student shows ability in simple movement. Movement has direction but
            is not alive and spirited.

4 — Immediate response with correct step, beat, and accent.
        Ability to maintain movement throughout excerpt.
        Ability to vary movement (turns, etc.)
        Confidence shown in her movement. Movements are definite, spirited,
            and easily accomplished. She is relaxed.

Problems and Limitations of Rhythm and Dance Measurement

The problems and limitations that have existed in the measurement of rhythm and dance are identified and briefly discussed below:

1. Most of the testing accomplished in the area of rhythm and dance has pertained to gathering facts and data for research purposes rather than for developing practical tests for the measurement of rhythm and dance ability in the classroom. Thus there appears to be a greater need for objective rhythm and dance tests which are practical for use by the classroom teacher. Graduate students and professional researchers should be encouraged to give greater consideration to the devotion of time and effort for innovating simple tests of rhythm and dance for this purpose.

2. Certain rhythmic tests are limited in use because of the necessity of complicated and/or expensive equipment. Also, since commercial recordings are impractical for use, due to lack of variety and proper arrangement, it has taken considerable time and expense to make recordings for testing purposes. However, greater use should be made of the tape recorder for developing suitable recordings for testing purposes.

3. Some of the well known rhythmic tests require only small muscle response which renders them to limited use in physical education dance classes. Tapping tests and tests which require only a written response fall into this category.

4. Another problem which has been perplexing to the tester is that some students do not do their best when rated in front of a group, due to embarrassment. Also, rating students one at a time takes considerable class time. On the other hand when several students are rated one at a time, the poor student has an opportunity to get cues from the more adept ones.

Findings and Conclusions From Rhythm and Dance Measurement and Research

The Seashore test, a frequently used test of rhythm, has been correlated with various measures of motor performance.[1,4,9,17] Such correlations ranged from -.10 to .48. Two investigators concluded that written sensory tests are not adequate for the type of rhythm emphasized in physical education classes.[17,28]

Several investigators have tested the hypothesis that the rhythm found in music has a positive effect on the learning and performance of physical skills.[9,10,11,18] While the findings of such studies have revealed a positive effect, Nelson[23] found that pure rhythmical tones, or music intensity, had no favorable or unfavorable effect on an endurance performance test.

Two studies have shown that when music is used in conjunction with the presence of other people and with competition, endurance and strength performance is improved.[14,15] Nelson[33] suggested that the same might be true of pure rhythmical tones or musical intensity.

It has been frequently assumed that Negroes are superior to Whites in motor rhythm. Several investigators have tested this hypothesis, and the consensus of results indicates that Negroes show a slight, although not statistically significant, superiority in rhythm to Whites.[16,22,25,26,29]

Concerning the use of rhythm for faster reaction time and movement time, Miles and Graves,[21] Thompson,[32] and Wilson[34] found faster starts when a stimulus was presented in a rhythmic rather than a non-rhythmic series. It was further noted that the speed of movement initiated by reaction is not influenced by rhythmicity or non-rhythmicity.[32]

Controversy exists among investigators concerning the question as to whether rhythm is innate or acquired. McCristal[19] and Swindle[31] concluded that rhythm increases with the amount of training acquired and is not an inherited quality. On the other hand, studies by Haight,[12] and Lemon and Sherbon[17] revealed results which indicated rhythmic ability to be more of the result of innate tendencies. Other studies indicated the importance of practice and development to the improvement of motor rhythm. For example, Muzzey[22] concluded that motor rhythm is a function of school age with each grade showing superiority to the previous one, while Annett[1] found that the earlier a child begins activities related to motor rhythm, everything else being equal, the better he will become as a dancer. Thus, from a study of previous research, it appears that rhythm is innate to a certain extent, but can be greatly improved through consistent practice and training.

Contrary to popular belief, there are tests and measurements instruments which will enable the tester to objectively evaluate a student's rhythm performance. A number of tests involve specially constructed apparatus which is not only complicated, but rarely found in physical education departments.[3,6,7,13,24,28] Other objective tests have been devised which are practical from the standpoint of equipment involved, but take too much time to administer.[20,27]

Benton,[4] testing the hypothesis that dance movement involves more than just rhythm, found that other elements involved are static balance, motor educability, agility, and strength. While no single measure was found of value in predicting dance skill, a combination of several motor tests revealed a high relationship with criterion ratings (sum of three judges' scores for each subject) of dance movement technique.

Bond[6] found that several of the senses (tactile, aural, and visual) are capable of experiencing rhythmic patterns, but failed to find a significant relationship between scores from sensory rhythmic perception tests and measures of motor performance.

BIBLIOGRAPHY

1. Annett, Thomas, "A Study of Rhythmical Capacity and Performance in Motor Rhythm in Physical Education Majors," *Research Quarterly,* 3:190, May, 1932.

2. Ashton, Dudley, "A Gross Motor Rhythm Test," *Research Quarterly,* 24:253-260, October, 1953.

3. Baldwin, B. T., and L. I. Stecher, *The Psychology of the Pre-School Child,* New York: D. Appleton and Company, 1924, pp. 141-145.

4. Benton, Rachel J., "The Measurement of Capacities for Learning Dance Movement Techniques," *Research Quarterly,* 15:139-140, May, 1944.

5. Blake, Patricia Ann, "Relationship Between Audio-Perceptual Rhythm and Skill in Square Dance," *Research Quarterly,* 31:231, May, 1960.

6. Bond, Marjorie H., "Rhythmic Perception and Gross Motor Performance," *Research Quarterly,* 30:259, October, 1959.

7. Buck, Nadine, "A Comparison of Two Methods of Testing Response to Auditory Rhythms," *Research Quarterly,* 7:37-43, October, 1936.

8. Cooper, John M., and Ruth B. Glassow, *Kinesiology,* St. Louis: The C. V. Mosley Company, 1963, pp. 278-279.

9. Dillon, Evelyn K., "A Study of the Use of Music as an Aid in Teaching Swimming," *Research Quarterly,* 23:8, March, 1952.

10. Diserens, C. M., *The Influence of Music on Behavior,* Princeton University, 1926, pp. 224.

11. Estep, Dorothy P., "The Relationship of Static Equilibrium to Ability in Gross Motor Activities," (Unpublished Master's Thesis, University of California, 1958).

12. Haight, Edith C., "Individual Differences in Motor Adaptations to Rhythmic Stimuli," *Research Quarterly,* 15:42, March, 1944.

13. Heinlein, C. P., "A New Method of Studying Rhythmic Responses of Children Together with an Evaluation of the Method of Simple Observation," *Journal of Genetic Psychology,* XXVI: 2, 205-229, June, 1929.

14. Johnson, Barry L., "The Effect of Applying Different Motivational Techniques During Training and in Testing Upon Strength Performance," (Microcarded Doctoral Dissertation, Louisiana State University, 1965).

15. _____, "The Effect of Motivational Testing Situations on an Endurance Test," (Laboratory Experiment, Northeast Louisiana State College, Monroe, 1963).

16. Johnson, Guy B., "A Summary of Negro Scores on the Seashore Music Talent Tests," *Journal of Comparative Psychology,* 11:383393, 1931.

17. Lemon, Eloise, and Elizabeth Sherbon, "A Study of the Relationship of Certain Measures of Rhythmic Ability and Motor Ability in Girls and Women," *Research Quarterly Supplement,* 5:85, March, 1934.

18. Loewenthal, Evelyn, "Rhythm Training," *Journal of Health, Physical Education and Recreation,* 19:7:474, 1948.

19. McCristal, K. J., "Experimental Study of Rhythm in Gymnastics and Tap Dancing," *Research Quarterly,* 4:74-75, May, 1933.

20. McCulloch, Margaret Lorraine, "The Development of a Test of Rhythmic Response Through Movement of First Grade Children," (Microcarded Doctoral Dissertation, University of Oregon, 1955).

21. Miles, W. R., and B. J. Graves, "Studies in Physical Exertion: III. Effect of Signal Variation on Football Charging," *Research Quarterly,* 2:31, October, 1931.

22. Muzzey, Dorothy M., "Group Progress of White and Colored Children in Learning a Rhythm Pattern," *Research Quarterly,* 4:62-70, October, 1933.

23. Nelson, Dale O., "Effect of Selected Rhythms and Sound Intensity on Human Performance as Measured by the Bicycle Ergometer," *Research Quarterly,* 34:488, May, 1963.

24. Patterson, D. G., and others, *Minnesota Mechanical Ability Tests,* Minneapolis: University of Minnesota, 1930.

25. Peterson, J., and L. H. Lanier, "Studies in the Comparable Abilities of Whites and Negroes," *Mental Measurement Monograph 5,* Number 4, 1929, p. 156.

26. Sanderson, Helen E., "Differences in Musical Ability in Children of Different National and Racial Origin," *Journal of Genetic Psychology,* 42:100-120, 1933.

27. Shambaugh, Mary E., "The Objective Measurement of Success in the Teaching of Folk Dancing to University Women," *Research Quarterly,* 6:52, March, 1935.

28. Simpson, Shirley E., "Development and Validation of an Objective Measure of Locomotor Response to Auditory Rhythmic Stimuli," *Research Quarterly,* 29:342, October, 1958.

29. Streep, R. L., "A Comparison of White and Negro Children in Rhythm and Consonance," *Journal of Applied Psychology,* 15:52-71, 1931.

30. Stupp, Lillian L., "A Correlation of Musical Ability and Dancing Ability," (Unpublished Master's Thesis, University of Wisconsin, 1922, p. 43).

31. Swindle, P. F., "On the Inheritance of Rhythm," *American Journal of Psychology,* 24:180203, April, 1913.

32. Thompson, Clem W., and others, "Football Starting Signals and Movement Times of High School and College Football Players," *Research Quarterly,* 29:230, May, 1953.

33. Waglow, I. F., "An Experiment in Social Dance Testing," *Research Quarterly,* 24:100-101, March, 1953.

34. Wilson, Don J., "Quickness of Reaction and Movement Related to Rhythmicity or Nonrhythmicity of Signal Presentation," *Research Quarterly,* 30:109, March, 1959.

35. Young, Glenda Sue, "Teacher-Made Tests of Rhythm," (Unpublished Study, Northeast Louisiana State College, Monroe, Louisiana, 1964).

Chapter XIII

THE MEASUREMENT OF
SPEED AND REACTION

Speed of movement and quick reactions are prized qualities in athletics. Coaches are frequently heard to praise certain players or an entire team for their *quickness*. In football a player who is extremely fast poses a constant threat to break away for the long run; in baseball the fast runner causes hurried throws and adjustments in pitching and defensive strategy; the full-court press is a potent weapon in basketball if a team has the speed to make it effective; and, of course, in track speed is the essence of the sport.

However, despite these commonplace observations, the study of speed of movement and speed of reaction is much more complex than it might appear. Speed of movement, for example, entails much more than mere running speed. The speed with which a wrestler executes a reversal, the lightning flash of a boxer's jab, the explosive spring of the shot putter's move across the throwing circle, and the graceful swiftness of the swimmer and skater are but a few of the many different kinds of movement speeds that are involved in physical performance. Speed of movement shall thus be defined as the rate at which a person can propel his body, or parts of his body, through space.

Reaction time is the interval of time between the presentation of the stimulus and the initiation of the response. While reaction time was initially thought to be a rather simple and easily measured phenomenon, it has been shown to be influenced by a number of variables. Strictly speaking, an individual can not be described as having a single reaction time without specifying the conditions under which he is being tested. Some of the factors which have been found to influence reaction time are the following: the sense organ involved, the intensity of the stimulus, the preparatory set, general muscular tension, motivation, practice, the response required, fatigue, and one's general state of health.

Analysis of speed of movement and reaction time when combined together is even more complex. It has been fairly well established that some individuals react quickly but move slowly; and some react slowly but are able to run or move very rapidly once they get started. However, even though speed of movement and speed of reaction may not show a significant relationship when these traits are measured separately and then correlated with each other, they cannot be separated in actual performance. A linebacker in football, for instance, might react quickly in diagnosing the play, but he still has to move fast enough to be able to make the tackle if he is to be a successful performer.

Therefore, while it may be highly desirable to measure each factor separately for diagnostic purposes and for research, it would seem more practical for the coach and physical educator to measure them together in test situations that duplicate response-movements that are required in the activity in question. Speed and reaction time are considered to be largely innate abilities; however, both can be improved through practice and training. Consequently, it would seem only logical that the practice and training would be performed with reaction time and speed of movement combined in a *gamelike* sequence of movements.

Generally, speed has been measured by short dashes. Distances of over 100 yards are usually not recommended because endurance then becomes a factor. Naturally, the age, sex and characteristics of the subjects should be the major consideration in selecting tests of speed.

Reaction time has usually been more complicated and more expensive to measure because of the timing device that has been employed. The device usually has a stimulus-presenting mechanism, such as a light or buzzer, and a switch that the subject presses or releases in response to the stimulus. A precise timer then measures the interval of time from the stimulus to the response. Recently, Nelson developed a measuring device that is both simple and inexpensive. The Nelson Reaction Timer* is based on the law of constant acceleration of free falling bodies and consists of a stick that is scaled to read in time as computed from the following formula:

$$\text{Time} = \sqrt{\frac{2 \times \text{Distance the stick falls}}{\text{Acceleration due to gravity}}}$$

Utilization of Tests

Speed of movement and reaction time measures may be utilized by physical educators in a number of ways, some of which are suggested below:
1. As a factor in motor ability tests, physical fitness tests, and sport skills tests.
2. For diagnosis prior to specific practice and conditioning work.
3. For classification into homogeneous groups for certain activities.
4. For motivation and information purposes in conjunction with health, safety, and driver education units.

Practical Tests of Speed and Reaction

The physical educator is ordinarily not able to justify the purchase of an expensive timing device. Therefore he is somewhat limited in his measurement of speed of movement and, particularly, in his measurement of reaction time. Nevertheless, armed with only a stop watch and imagination, the physical educator can obtain valuable measures of both of these traits which are both meaningful and sufficiently accurate.

The tests that are presented here include a hand reaction test, a foot reaction test, several dashes, and a choice response-accuracy test. None of the tests require expensive timing devices or elaborate equipment.

The Nelson Hand Reaction Test.[23]
Objective: To measure the speed of reaction with the hand in response to a visual stimulus.
Age Level: Any age from kindergarten upward. The only limiting factor would be the subject's ability to catch the falling stick with the fingers.
Sex: Boys and Girls.
Validity: The validity of the timing device is inherent, since the earth's gravitational pull is consistent; therefore, the timer falls at the same rate of acceleration each time.

*The Nelson Reaction Timer, Model RT-2, Copyright 1965 by Fred B. Nelson, P.O. Box 51987, Lafayette, Louisiana.

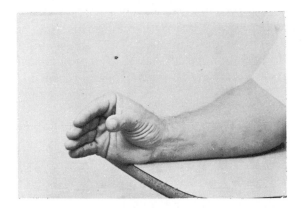

FIGURE 13 - 1

Position of Hand and Fingers for the
Nelson Hand Reaction Test

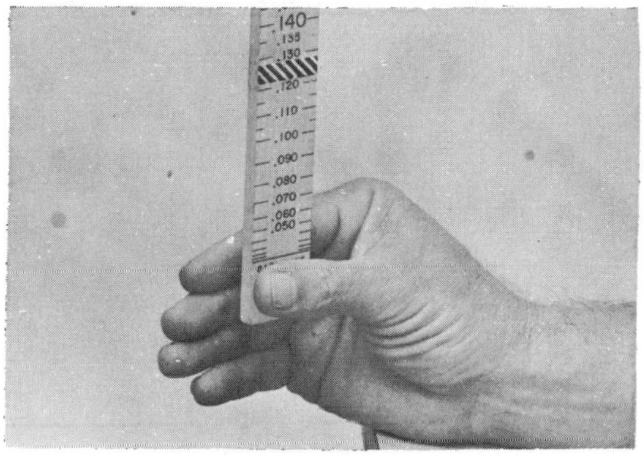

FIGURE 13 - 2

Ready Position with Thumb as Base Line
for Nelson Hand Reaction Test

Reliability: A reliability coefficient of .89 was obtained using average scores taken on two separate test administrations.

Test Equipment and Materials: Nelson Reaction Timer, table and chair, or desk chair.

Directions: The subject sits with his forearm and hand resting comfortably on the table (or desk chair). The tips of the thumb and index finger are held in a *ready to pinch* position about three or four inches beyond the edge of the table. (See Figure 13 - 1.) The upper edges of the thumb and index finger should be in a horizontal position. The tester holds the stick-timer near the top, letting it hang between the subject's thumb and index finger. The Base Line should be even with the upper surface of the subject's thumb (Figure 13 - 2).

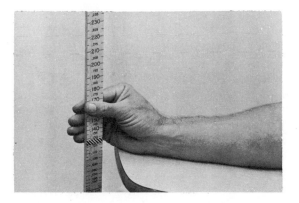

FIGURE 13 - 3

Example of Scoring the Nelson Hand Reaction Test
(.170 seconds in this example)

The subject is directed to look at the *Concentration Zone* (which is a black shaded zone between the .120 and .130 lines) and is told to react by catching the stick (by pinching the thumb and index finger together) when it is released. The subject should not look at the tester's hand; nor is he allowed to move his hand up or down while attempting to catch the falling stick. Twenty trials are given. Each drop is preceded by a preparatory command of *Ready*.

Scoring: When the subject catches the timer, the score is read just above the upper edge of the thumb. (See Figure 13 - 3.) The five slowest and the five fastest trials are discarded, and an average of the middle ten is recorded as the score. Numbers on the timer represent thousandths of a second. Scores may be recorded to the nearest 5/1000 of a second.

Safety Precautions: None.

Additional Pointers: (1) The testing environment should be such that the subject is able to concentrate. (2) Allow the subject three or four practice trials to make sure he understands the procedures and becomes familiar with the task. (3) The interval of time between the preparatory command of *Ready* and the release is extremely important. It should be varied in order to prevent the subject from becoming accustomed to a constant pattern. On the other hand this interval should remain within a range of not less than one-half second nor longer than approximately two seconds. If too short, it catches the subject before he is ready, and if the interval is too long the subject loses his optimal state of readiness. For standardization the tester could have a specific order of these intervals. For example, on the first trial he could say *Ready*, then count to himself 1,001, then release; on the second trial, after *Ready*, he might mentally say, *one*, then release, etc. (4) Obvious anticipations should be discarded and should not be counted as one of the twenty trials. (5) The tester must be careful that the subject's thumb or index finger is not touching the timer. (6) If the subjects are young children, the test should be conducted like a challenging game. (7) The subject's dominant hand should be used if only one hand is to be tested.

Norms are not complete at this time. With college men the average reaction time is around .16 with a range of .13 to .22. With small children (1st graders) the average is about .26.

The Nelson Foot Reaction Test.[23]

Objective: To measure the speed of reaction with the foot in response to a visual stimulus.

Age and Sex: Same as with the hand reaction test.

Validity: Face validity. Same as with the hand reaction test.

Reliability: A reliability coefficient of .85 was obtained with college men as subjects.

Test Equipment and Materials: Nelson Reaction Timer, table or bench, wall space.

Directions: The subject sits on a table (or bench) which is about one inch from the wall. With his shoe off the subject positions his foot so that the ball of the foot is held about one inch from the wall with the heel resting on the table about two inches from the edge. The tester holds the reaction timer next to the wall so that it hangs between the wall and the subject's foot with the Base Line opposite the end of the big toe. The subject looks at the *Concentration Zone* and is told to react, when the timer is dropped, by pressing the stick against the wall with the ball of his foot. Twenty trials are given. (See Figure 13 - 4.)

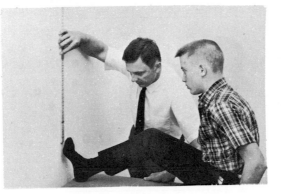

FIGURE 13 - 4

Ready Position with End of Big Toe at Base Line
for Nelson Foot Reaction Test

Scoring: The reaction time for each trial is the line just above the end of the big toe when the foot is pressing the stick to the wall. The slowest five trials and the fastest five trials are discarded, and the average of the middle ten trials is recorded.
Safety Precautions: None.
Additional Pointers: Same as with hand reaction test. Norms are incomplete. The average reaction time for college men is approximately .21.

The Nelson Speed of Movement Test.[23]

Objective: To measure combined reaction and speed of movement of the hands.
Age and Sex: Same as with reaction tests.
Validity: Face validity as long as no attempt is made to separate reaction time and speed of movement.
Reliability: A reliability coefficient for college men was found to be .75.
Test Equipment and Materials: Nelson Reaction Timer, table and chair, chalk or tape and ruler.
Directions: The subject sits at a table with his hands resting on the edge of the table. The palms are facing one another with the inside border of the little fingers along two lines which are marked on the edge of the table twelve inches apart. The tester holds the timer near its top so that it hangs midway between the subject's palms. The Base Line should be positioned so it is level with the upper borders of the subject's hands. (See Figure 13 - 5.)

After the preparatory command *Ready* is given, the timer is released and the subject attempts to stop it as quickly as possible by clapping the hands together. The subject must be careful not to allow his hands to move up or down when he is clapping the hands together. Twenty trials are given.
Scoring: The score for the combined response-movement is read from the timer as the point just above the upper edge of the hand after the catch (Figure 13 - 6). The average of the middle ten trials, after the slowest and fastest five trials have been discarded, are recorded.

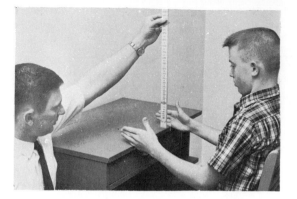

FIGURE 13 - 5

**Ready Position with Hands Twelve Inches Apart
for Nelson Speed of Movement Test**

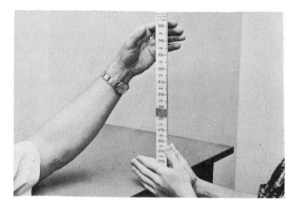

FIGURE 13 - 6

**Example of Scoring the Nelson Speed of Movement Test
(.240 seconds in this example)**

<u>Safety Precautions:</u> None.

<u>Additional Pointers:</u> (1) The pointers listed for the hand reaction time test are applicable for this test. (2) After the subject has his hands in the ready position, a 12 inch ruler should be utilized to make sure the hands are the correct distance apart. (3) A small mark exactly between the two marks should be made to facilitate the positioning of the timer prior to release. (4) The subject should remove any rings to prevent the denting or marring of the timer's surface.

<u>Norms</u> are incomplete at this time. Average time has been found to be about .24 for college men.

4-Second Dash

(See Scott Motor Ability Test, Chapter VIII, for directions.) This test could be utilized for junior high school, high school, and college men.

6-Second Dash [19]

Objective: Although this event has been used as a measure of running endurance, it would seem to be appropriate as a test of speed, at least for older students. Except for the extremely fast high school or college student, the distance covered would rarely be over 50 yards, and endurance should not be a factor.

Age Level: There are only norms for high school boys, but the test could be given for college and junior high school subjects.

Sex: Satisfactory for both boys and girls.

Validity: Face validity is accepted.

Reliability: No figures given.

Test Equipment and Materials: Stop watch, whistle, running space of at least 70 yards to allow for a gradual stop, and approximately 14 markers placed at 2-yard intervals from 34 to 60 yards.

Directions: The subject starts from a standing position with both feet behind the end line. The starter uses the preparatory commands of *get set* and *go*. On the command to go the subject runs in a straight line as fast as possible until the whistle is blown at the end of six seconds. The subject does not have to come to a sudden stop at the sound of the whistle, he merely begins to slow down at his own rate. Two trials are given, five minutes apart.

Scoring: A spotter is assigned to each runner and is positioned about 45 yards from the starting line. At the sound of the whistle the spotter immediately runs to the place where the runner was at the time the whistle was blown. This point is then measured from the nearest marker (or line, if lines are drawn across the running lane). The score is recorded to the nearest yard, and the best of the two trials is used.

Safety: Precautions should be taken to allow sufficient warm-up to avoid strained muscles. Adequate space should be provided along the sides of the running lanes and at the end of the lanes. Proper footwear should be insisted upon.

Additional Pointers: (1) The main advantage of this type of run is that several subjects can be tested with one stop watch. Therefore, it is recommended that more than one runner be tested at a time. Otherwise, running a specific distance for time is a more precise measure. (2) Each spotter must be impressed with the necessity of watching only his runner, and not look to see who is winning. (3) In judging the exact spot at which the runner was when the whistle sounded, the spotter should use the subject's chest as the point of reference. (4) The tester (or timer) should keep his eyes on the watch and not on the runners. He should count loudly the seconds *three, four,* and *five* to alert the spotters as to the approximate point at which their runners will be. (5) Chalk or painted lines across the running lanes at the 2-yard intervals will facilitate scoring, (6) Although a period of five minutes is suggested as the interval between trials, more time should be allowed if fatigue is adjudged to be a possible influence on the second trial.

50-Yard Dash

(See AAHPER Youth Fitness Test, Chapter XVII, for directions and norms.)

TABLE 13 - 1

Scoring Table for 6-Second Run

High School Boys*					
T-Scores	Raw Scores (Yards)	T-Scores	Raw Scores (Yards)	T-Scores	Raw Scores (Yards)
96 —	53	63 —	47	30 —	41
90 —	52	57 —	46	25 —	40
85 —	51	51 —	45	20 —	39
80 —	50	46 —	44	14 —	38
74 —	49	40 —	43	8 —	37
68 —	48	35 —	42	2 —	36

*Source: Charles H. McCloy and Norma D. Young, *Tests and Measurements in Health and Physical Education.* 3rd ed. New York: Appleton-Century-Crofts, Inc., 1954. p. 186.

Nelson Choice-Response-Movement Test.[24]

Objective: To measure ability to react and move quickly and accurately in accordance with a choice-stimulus. It was believed that this type of test simulated movement patterns found in a number of sports.

Age Level: Satisfactory for ages 10 through college.

Sex: Satisfactory for both boys and girls.

Validity: Face validity is accepted.

Reliability: A reliability coefficient of .87 was found for college men, using the test-retest method.

Objectivity: An objectivity coefficient of .83 was obtained with two testers scoring the same individuals. However, much of the disagreement was believed to be due to the difficulty of synchronizing the start with two watches.

Test Equipment and Materials: Stop watch, measuring tape, and marking equipment. See Figure 13 - 7 for diagram of test markings.

Directions: The subject faces the tester while crouching in an on-guard position at a spot exactly between the two side lines. The tester holds the stop watch in his upraised hand. The tester then abruptly waves his arm to either the left or right and simultaneously starts the watch. The subject responds to the hand signal and attempts to run as quickly as possible, in the indicated direction, to the boundary line. The watch is stopped when the subject crosses the correct line. If the subject should start to move in the wrong direction, the watch continues to run until the subject reverses directions and reaches the correct sideline. Ten trials are given, five to each side, but in a random sequence. A rest interval of twenty seconds is provided between each trial.

Scoring: The time for each trial is read to the nearest tenth of a second. The average score is then recorded.

Safety: The teacher should insist upon adequate footwear and should provide warm-up exercises. The testing area must be kept free from obstructions.

Additional Pointers: (1) Several practice trials should be given to acquaint the subjects with the test procedures. (2) The tester should practice the starting signals to attain proficiency in synchronizing his hand signal with the start of the watch. (3) In selecting the sequence of direction, the tester can simply put five slips with *right* on them and five slips with *left* on them in a hat for a random draw. This procedure prevents the subject from anticipating the direction from one trial to the next. However, the subject should not be told that he will have five trials in each direction. In fact, the subject should probably be told that this is not the case — that the distribution of trials is entirely based on random selection and may have more in one direction than another. There should be several prepared sequences so that students waiting to be tested cannot memorize the order of directions. (4) This test could be adapted so as to be more applicable to the specific activity in question. For example, tackling dummies could be placed at each sideline that the subject must hit to stop the clock. (5) As in all speed and reaction tests, the interval between the command, *ready*, and the starting signal should be within a range of approximately one-half to two seconds.

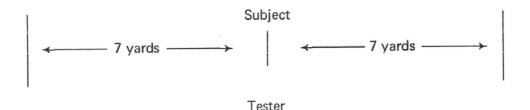

FIGURE 13 - 7

Diagram for Nelson Choice-Response-Movement Test

Problems Associated with Speed of Movement and Reaction Time Testing

Some of the problems and limitations that are associated with speed and reaction time measurement were mentioned in the first part of the chapter. It was pointed out that equipment would be a major obstacle if the physical educator wished to secure very precise measures for a variety of response-movements. Quite obviously the need for elaborate equipment would depend upon the purposes for which the measures were to be used.

When speed of movement and reaction time are to be studied separately, the specificity of each must be considered, as well as how each may operate in relation to the movements involved and the task. In other words it would not make much sense to measure reaction time by having the subject release a telegraph key device upon hearing a buzzer, and speed of movement by the 100-yard dash, and then attempt to make conclusions regarding the reaction and movement speed of a defensive lineman in football. The tasks are too unrelated. It would be much more meaningful and accurate to have the subject react to the movement of the ball on an actual pass from the center; and

TABLE 13 - 2

Norms for Nelson Choice-Response-Movement Test

College Men*					
T-Scores	Raw Scores (Seconds)	T-Scores	Raw Scores (Seconds)	T-Scores	Raw Scores (Seconds)
78 —	1.2	57 —	1.8	37 —	2.4
76 —	1.25	55 —	1.85	35 —	2.45
74 —	1.3	53 —	1.9	33 —	2.5
72 —	1.35	52 —	1.95	32 —	2.55
70 —	1.4	50 —	2.0	30 —	2.6
68 —	1.45	48 —	2.05	28 —	2.65
67 —	1.5	47 —	2.10	27 —	2.7
65 —	1.55	45 —	2.15	25 —	2.75
63 —	1.6	43 —	2.2	24 —	2.8
62 —	1.65	42 —	2.25	22 —	2.85
60 —	1.7	40 —	2.3		
58 —	1.75	38 —	2.35		

*Data gathered from 200 college men, Louisiana State University, Baton Rouge, Louisiana.

have the subject then move to hit a dummy some distance away. To get both reaction and speed of movement on the same trial would require a timing device with two clocks. One clock would start when the ball was moved and would stop when the subject started to move (such as if he lifted his hand from a switch on the ground). This would measure reaction time. A second clock would start when the subject started to move and would stop when contact was made with the dummy, which would measure his movement time.

The meaningfulness and challenge of the test, the testing position, the skill and past experience of the subject are all important points to be considered. The reaction of a football player may be much faster in the above situation than in an artificial setting such as was described earlier using a telegraph key and a buzzer. As in all tests the tester must carefully evaluate the nature of the performance that is being measured. In a great many sports, for example, the crucial speed that is required is but for a very few yards. The abilities to perceive the meaning of the stimulus, react correctly, and move to the required spot just a few feet away are of vital importance in tennis, badminton, handball, football, basketball, baseball, softball and many other sports. The speed at which a person can run 100 yards is not nearly so important in those activities.

The use of a standing start as opposed to the crouched sprinter's stance is ordinarily recommended in physical education class testing. This is due to the fact that persons who have not practiced crouched starts would be at a definite disadvantage. This disadvantage would be even more pronounced if they were given their choice and elected to start from the crouched position without any training. The untrained individual's first move from the sprinter's stance is usually to stand up — then start running — which, of course, is wasted motion.

Concentration and the individual's state of readiness to react are essential for speed and reaction measurement, and therefore the testing situation should be conducive for optimum performance. The importance of the proper interval between the preparatory command and the signal to respond has already been discussed in the descriptions of the tests. The tester must be ever conscious of this foreperiod and guard against the tendency to give the same interval each time. As was recommended earlier, it is best to have a definite sequence established.

The consumption of class time is not a limiting factor if the measures utilized consist only of dashes. However, if the physical educator wishes to measure functional response-movements, then a sufficient number of trials involves considerable time for testing.

Findings and Conclusions from Speed and Reaction Time Measurement and Research

There has been a vast amount of research done in psychology, physiology and physical education on speed of movement and reaction time. Despite the voluminous literature on the subject, much research is still needed.

A misconception held for years by many coaches and physical educators was that strength building exercises would be detrimental to speed of movement. However, research has shown quite convincingly that just the opposite is true. Zorbas and Karpovich,[33] Wilkin,[31] Masley,[18] Endres,[7] and Chui[3] —all found that weight training improved speed of movement. Meadows[20] and Johnson[16] further found that both isotonic and isometric exercises improved speed of movement, while Crowder[5] reported isotonic and isometric exercises produced significant improvement in reaction time. Michael,[21] dealing only with isometric exercises, found significant gains in both speed of movement and reaction time. Dintiman[6] reported that a combination of flexibility and weight training programs, given as supplements to sprint training, improved speed significantly more than the sprint training program alone.

Several studies have reported low correlations between reaction time and movement time. Representative of such studies are those by Owens,[26] Henry,[11] and Clarke.[4] Smith[28] found that reaction time and velocity of the arm when in a state of stretch was not significantly faster than when the arm was relaxed or tensed. But when the prime movers of the limb were stretched, significantly faster performances resulted.

Motivation has been shown to be quite effective in bringing about faster speed of movement and reaction. Henry[12] found that a motivated simple response transferred its increase in speed to a more complex response. Fairclough[8] reported that motivated improvement in speed in one part of the body could be transferred to another body part. The intensity of the stimulus is a factor, as was revealed in Vallerga's[30] study in which a loud sound was found to produce faster speed of movement and more forceful contraction than soft or medium sounds. Studies by Henry,[13] Hipple,[14] Howell[15] and others have shown that devices such as electric shock, suggested failure, etc. result in increased tension and thus increased speed of response. Wilson[32] and Thompson and others[29] reported that rhythmic starting signals improved reaction time performance.

Athletes were found to be superior to non-athletes in reaction time in studies by Keller,[17] Sigerseth and York,[27] Burpee and Stroll,[2] and Olsen.[25] Specific training in sprint starting was found to improve reaction performance in studies by Gibson[9] and Gottshall.[10] A conditioning exercise program was also found to result in improved reaction time in Gottshall's study.

Nakamura[22] studied the foreperiod between the preparatory command and the signal to go and found the optimum time interval to be 1.5 seconds. Bresnahan and others[1] concur and recommend that a foreperiod of 1.4 to 1.6 seconds yields the fastest reaction times.

BIBLIOGRAPHY

1. Bresnahan, George T., W. W. Tuttle, and Francis X. Cretzmeyer. *Track and Field Athletics,* 4th ed., St. Louis: C. V. Mosby, 1956, p. 79; 6th ed., 1964.

2. Burpee, Royal H., and Wellington Stroll, "Measuring Reaction Time of Athletes," *Research Quarterly,* 7:110-118, March, 1936.

3. Chui, Edward, "Effect of Systematic Weight Training on Athletic Power," *Research Quarterly,* 21:188-194, October, 1950.

4. Clarke, David H., "Correlation Between the Strength/Mass Ratio and the Speed of an Arm Movement," *Research Quarterly,* 31:570-574, December, 1960.

5. Crowder, Vernon R., "A Comparison of the Effects of Two Methods of Strength Training on Reaction Time," (Unpublished Master's Thesis, Louisiana State University).

6. Dintiman, George B., "Effects of Various Training Programs on Running Speed," *Research Quarterly,* 35:456-463, December, 1964.

7. Endres, John P., "The Effect of Weight Training Exercise Upon the Speed of Muscular Movements," (Microcarded Master's Thesis, University of Wisconsin, 1953).

8. Fairclough, R. H., "Transfer of Motivated Improvement in Speed of Reaction and Movement," *Research Quarterly,* 23:20-27, March, 1952.

9. Gibson, Dennis A., "Effect of a Special Training Program for Sprint Starting on Reflex Time, Reaction Time and Sargent Jump," (Microcarded Master's Thesis, Springfield College, 1961).

10. Gottshall, Donald R., "The Effects of Two Training Programs on Reflex Time, Reaction Time and the Level of Physical Fitness," (Microcarded Master's Thesis, Springfield College, 1962).

11. Henry, Franklin M., "Reaction Time-Movement Time Correlations," *Perceptual and Motor Skills,* 12:63-66, February, 1961.

12. _____ , "Increase in Speed of Movement by Motivation and by Transfer of Motivated Improvement," *Research Quarterly,* 22:219-228, May, 1951.

13. _____ , "Independence of Reaction and Movement Times and Equivalence of Sensory Motivators of Faster Response," *Research Quarterly,* 23:43-53, March, 1952.

14. Hipple, Joseph E., "Racial Differences in the Influence of Motivation on Muscular Tension, Reaction Time, and Speed of Movement," *Research Quarterly,* 25:297-306, October, 1954.

15. Howell, Maxwell L., "Influence of Emotional Tension on Speed of Reaction and Movement," *Research Quarterly,* 24:22-32, March, 1953.

16. Johnson, Barry L., "A Comparison of Isometric and Isotonic Exercises Upon the Improvement of Velocity and Distance as Measured by the Rope Climb Test," (Unpublished Study, Louisiana State University, January, 1964).

17. Keller, L. F., "The Relation of Quickness of Bodily Movement to Success in Athletics," *Research Quarterly,* 13:146-155, May, 1942.

18. Masley, John W., Ara Hairabedian, and Donald N. Donaldson, "Weight Training in Relation to Strength, Speed, and Coordination," *Research Quarterly,* 24:308-315, October, 1953.

19. McCloy, C. H., and Norma D. Young, *Tests and Measurements in Health, and Physical Education,* 3rd ed., New York: Appleton-Century-Crofts, Inc., 1954, p. 186.

20. Meadows, P. E., "The Effect of Isotonic and Isometric Muscle Contraction Training on Speed, Force, and Strength," (Microcarded Doctor's Dissertation, University of Illinois, 1959).

21. Michael, Charles E., "The Effects of Iosmetric Contraction Exercise on Reaction and Speed of Movement Times," (Unpublished Doctoral Dissertation, Louisiana State University, 1963).

22. Nakamura, H., "An Experimental Study of Reaction Time of the Start in Running a Race," *Research Quarterly Supplement,* 5:33-45, March, 1934.

23. Nelson, Fred B., "The Nelson Reaction Timer," Instruction Leaflet, P. O. Box 51987, Lafayette, Louisiana.

24. Nelson, Jack K., "Development of a Practical Performance Test Combining Reaction Time, Speed of Movement and Choice of Response," (Unpublished Study, Louisiana State University, 1967).

25. Olsen, Einar A., "Relationship Between Psychological Capacities and Success in College Athletics," *Research Quarterly,* 27:79-89, March, 1956.

26. Owens, Jack A., "Effect of Variations in Hand and Foot Spacing on Movement Time and on Force of Change," *Research Quarterly,* 31:75, March, 1960.

27. Sigerseth, Peter O., and Norman N. York, "A Comparison of Certain Reaction Times of Basketball Players and Non-Athletes," *The Physical Educator,* 11:51-53, May, 1954.

28. Smith, Leon E., "Effect of Muscular Stretch, Tension, and Relaxation Upon the Reaction Time and Speed of Movement of a Supported Limb," *Research Quarterly,* 35:546-553, December, 1964.

29. Thompson, Clem W., Francis J. Nagle, and Robert Dobias, "Football Starting Signals and Movement Times of High School and College Football Players," *Research Quarterly,* 29:222-230, May, 1958.

30. Vallerga, John M., "Influence of Perceptual Stimulus Intensity on Speed of Movement and Force of Muscular Contraction," *Research Quarterly,* 29:92-101, March, 1958.

31. Wilkin, Bruce M., "The Effect of Weight Training on Speed of Movement," *Research Quarterly,* 23:361-369, October, 1952.

32. Wilson, Don J., "Quickness of Reaction and Movement Related to Rhythmicity or Non-Rhythmicity of Signal Presentation," *Research Quarterly,* 30:101-109, March, 1959.

33. Zorbas, William S., and Peter V. Karpovich, "The Effect of Weight Lifting upon the Speed of Muscular Contraction," *Research Quarterly,* 22:145-148, May, 1951.

Chapter XIV

THE MEASUREMENT
OF STRENGTH

Strength is frequently recognized by physical educators as the most important factor in the performance of physical skills. While strength may be generally defined as the muscular force exerted against movable and immovable objects, it is best measured by tests which require one maximum effort on a given movement or position. The two types of muscular contraction most frequently measured in physical education classes are dynamic (isotonic) contraction, and static (isometric) contraction. Isotonic contraction takes place when muscular force moves the object of resistance so that contraction takes place over a range of movement. Isometric contraction takes place when muscular force is exerted over a brief period of time (usually six to ten seconds) without movement of the object of resistance or the body joints involved. Both types of contraction may be easily and inexpensively measured by the physical educator in the average school situation. While a certain degree of strength is necessary in performing daily activities and sports skills, a high degree of strength is regarded by the authors as a luxury which makes for greater ease of performance and for a feeling of vitality well worth the effort necessary to acquire and maintain it.

Since strength and power are terms which are often used interchangeably (this is particularly true of isotonic strength), it was felt necessary to present some observations which should help distinguish between them: (1) strength is only a component of power, which also includes the components of time and distance. (2) While in both power and isotonic strength tests an object of resistance is moved through a range of motion, the isotonic strength test differs in the following respects:
1. The object of resistance is always near, if not at, maximum load.
2. The object of resistance is never released with the idea of gaining height or distance.
3. The range of movement is not as exaggerated nor as complete.
4. Measurement is based on the amount of weight moved through a specified range, and not upon distance or time elements.

Uses of Strength Tests

Several ways in which strength tests are utilized in physical education classes are as follows:
1. As a factor in general motor ability tests and physical fitness tests.
2. As a means for determining potential in specific sports activities.
3. As a means for determining achievement and grades in conditioning and weight training classes.
4. As a means of evaluating the possible solutions to overcoming poor postural

positions, or to pin-point areas of weakness which need strengthening for better performance.

5. As a means of motivating students toward a feeling of accomplishment and satisfaction through strength improvement.

Practical Tests of Strength

Only a few of the practical tests of strength in terms of time, equipment, and cost are presented below. In these tests where special testing instruments are necessary, the cost is not unreasonable for most schools. Unfortunately, it was not feasible to present all the strength exercises that are practical for measurement. The following strength tests are presented under the headings of Isotonic Strength Tests, Spring Scale Strength Tests, and Isometric Strength Instruments.

Isotonic Strength Tests.[19]

Objective: To measure strength during a complete range of movement in the following items: (1) Pull-up Test, (2) Dip Test. (3) Bench Squat Test, (4) Sit-up Test, (5) Bench Press, (6) Standing Vertical Arm Press Test.

Age Level: Recommended for ages 12 through college.

Sex: Test items 3, 4, and 5 are recommended for girls, while test items 1, 2, 3, 4, 5, and 6 are recommended for boys.

Reliability: Refer to each individual test item.

Validity: Refer to each individual test item.

Equipment and Materials: Refer to each individual test item.

General Directions: (1) Students should be allowed to become familiar with the isotonic strength tests through the use of similar weight training exercises at least several days prior to testing. When students are not familiar with the tests to be given, it will usually take more than two trials to determine their maximum effort for each test. This, of course, requires a greater amount of time for testing. (2) On each test item the student should be allowed two trials (if he so desires) in which he can move the maximum amount of weight possible for that test. Each student should load his own bar or strap with weight plates, and if he successfully completes the movement on the first trial, he should be given an opportunity to add more weight and try to attain a higher score. If the student was unsuccessful in completing the first trial, he should remove some of the weight, for the second trial. Should the second trial be unsuccessful also, the student should take a short rest and then be retested with a further reduced load. (3) Students should be allowed to warm up before reporting to the testing station, but they should be cautioned not to overwork. (4) Several weight bars and straps should be available so that as one student finishes, the next one will have his weights adjusted and ready for testing. (5) Students should be classified by body weight into the following three weight groups: (a) light weights, (b) middle weights, and (c) heavy weights. Comparisons may then be made between a student's strength/weight score and those of others in his weight group. If grades are to be determined from isotonic strength results, a certain percentage of A's, B's, C's, D's, and F's should be assigned from each of the three weight groups.

Scoring: The best score of two trials is recorded over the student's body weight and then divided and recorded for comparison with other members of his weight class. If the student does not desire to take a second trial, the first trial is recorded over his body weight for subsequent computation.

Isotonic Test Items

Pull-Up Test.[19]

Objective: To measure the strength of the arms and shoulders in the pull-up movement.

Age Level: Ages 12 through college.

Sex: Recommended for boys only.

Reliability: An r of .99 was found for this test when scores were recorded on separate days using students familiar with the exercise.

Validity: Face validity was accepted for this test.

Equipment and Materials: A horizontal bar raised to a height so that all subjects may hang with their feet off the floor should be used. It is also necessary to have several 2½, 5, 10, and 25 pound weight plates available for use. A rope or strap is necessary to secure the weights to the waist of the performer, and one chair should be available to stand on in taking the preliminary position on the bar.

Directions: After securing the desired amount of weight to the waist, the student should step upon the chair and take a firm grasp (palms facing away from face) on the bar. As he assumes a straight arm hang, the chair is removed while the performer pulls upward until the chin is above the bar. As the performer lowers downward, the chair is replaced under his feet. If a second trial is to be taken, the student may step down and readjust the weights before he repeats the exercise. (See Figure 14 - 1.)

Scoring: The best score of two trials is recorded in terms of the amount of extra weight satisfactorily pulled upward. A student who cannot chin with more than his own body weight would, of course, receive zero. (See Table 14 - 1.) The best score is divided by body weight for comparison with other members in his weight class.

Safety: The performer should be assisted to and from the chair as he mounts and dismounts with the extra weight.

Additional Pointers: (1) The performer should refrain from lifting the legs or using a swing action to get upward. (2) The tester may extend his arm horizontally across the performer's thighs to prevent a lifting of the legs during the pull-up. (3) For individuals who cannot chin their own body weight, the following procedure may be used in terms of measurement and motivation: (a) Hang a tape (cloth) measure from the bar so that it bisects the point of the performer's chin as he pulls and slides the chin upward along the tape. (b) Score the performer in terms of the number of inches he gets his chin from the top of the bar. For example, the best non-chinner might get his chin one inch from the top of the bar and consequently score a -1, whereas a weaker performer might lack six inches and receive a -6 as his score.

Dip Strength Test.[19]

Objective: To measure the strength of the arms and shoulders in the dip movement (a vertical lowering and push-up movement).

Age Level: Ages 12 through college.

Sex: Recommended for boys only.

Reliability: An r of .98 was found when scores were recorded on separate days using students familiar with the exercise.

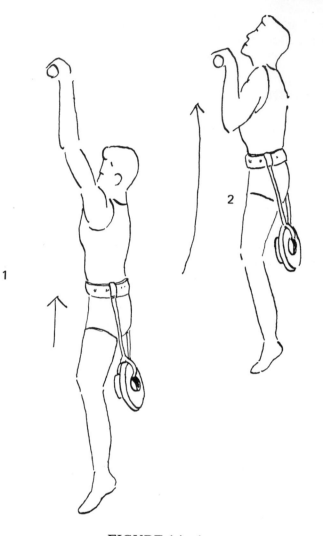

FIGURE 14 - 1

Pull-Up Test

Validity: Face validity was accepted.

Equipment and Materials: Two parallel bars raised to a height so that all subjects are supported freely above the ground (in the lowered bent arm support) are used. Weight plates, straps, and a chair are again required just as in the pull-up test.

Directions: After securing the desired amount of weight to the waist, the student should step upon the chair and take a secure grip on the bars. As he assumes a straight arm support, the chair is removed and the student proceeds to lower himself downward until the elbows form a right angle. As the student pushes up to a straight arm support, the chair is replaced under his feet. If a second trial is to be taken, the student may step down and readjust the weights before he repeats the exercise. (See Figure 14 - 2.)

TABLE 14 - 1

T-Score Norms for Pull-Up Test

Raw scores are figured by dividing body weight into the additional weight successfully used in the test.

College Men					
T-Scores	—	Raw Scores	T-Scores	—	Raw Scores
80	—	.69	52	—	.34
79	—	.67	51	—	.33
78	—	.66	50	—	.32
77	—	.65	49	—	.31
76	—	.64	48	—	.29
75	—	.62	47	—	.28
74	—	.61	46	—	.27
73	—	.60	45	—	.26
72	—	.59	44	—	.25
71	—	.58	43	—	.23
70	—	.56	42	—	.22
69	—	.55	41	—	.21
68	—	.54	40	—	.20
67	—	.53	39	—	.18
66	—	.51	38	—	.17
65	—	.50	37	—	.16
64	—	.49	36	—	.15
63	—	.48	35	—	.14
62	—	.47	34	—	.12
61	—	.45	33	—	.11
60	—	.44	32	—	.10
59	—	.43	31	—	.09
58	—	.42	30	—	.08
57	—	.40	29	—	.06
56	—	.39	28	—	.05
55	—	.38	27	—	.04
54	—	.37	26	—	.03
53	—	.36	25	—	.01
			24	—	.00

Based on a limited number of scores from a men's physical education class at Northeast Louisiana State College, Monroe, Louisiana.

<u>Scoring</u>: Same as for pull-up test. (See Table 14 - 2.)
<u>Safety</u>: Same as for the pull-up test.
<u>Additional Pointers</u>: (1) The performer should refrain from swinging or kicking in returning to the straight arm support position. (2) The tester should extend his fist upward from the bar so that the performer's shoulder will touch it when the elbows form the right angle. (3) For students who cannot push to a straight arm support with their own body weight, the following procedure may be used in terms of measurement and motivation: (a) Attach a scale alongside the parallel bars (marked off in one inch intervals). (b) Mark on the scale the performer's shoulder location (point of the acromion process) while in the straight arm support. (c) Score the performer in terms of the number of inches he gets his shoulders (point of the acromion process) from the straight arm position on the push upward.

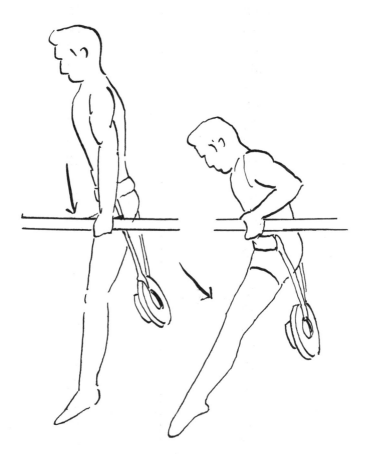

FIGURE 14 - 2

Dip Strength Test

TABLE 14 - 2

T-Score Norms for Dip Strength Test

Raw scores are figured by dividing body weight into the additional weight success-fully used in the test.

College Men					
T-Scores	—	Raw Scores	T-Scores	—	Raw Scores
80	—	.84	48	—	.48
79	—	.83	47	—	.47
78	—	.81	46	—	.46
77	—	.80	45	—	.45
76	—	.79	44	—	.44
75	—	.78	43	—	.43
74	—	.77	42	—	.42
73	—	.76	41	—	.40
72	—	.75	40	—	.39
71	—	.74	39	—	.38
70	—	.73	38	—	.37
69	—	.71	37	—	.36
68	—	.70	36	—	.35
67	—	.69	35	—	.34
66	—	.68	34	—	.33
65	—	.67	33	—	.32
64	—	.66	32	—	.30
63	—	.65	31	—	.29
62	—	.64	30	—	.28
61	—	.63	29	—	.27
60	—	.62	28	—	.26
59	—	.60	27	—	.25
58	—	.59	26	—	.24
57	—	.58	25	—	.23
56	—	.57	24	—	.22
55	—	.56	23	—	.21
54	—	.55	22	—	.20
53	—	.54	21	—	.18
52	—	.53	20	—	.17
51	—	.52	15	—	.12
50	—	.50	10	—	.06
49	—	.49	5	—	.01

Based on a limited number of scores from a men's physical education class at Northeast Louisiana State College, Monroe, Louisiana.

Bench Squat Test.[19]

Objective: To measure the strength of the legs and back in lowering to, and arising from, a sitting position.

Age Level: Ages 12 through college.

Sex: Recommended for both boys and girls.

Reliability: An r of .95 was found when scores were recorded on separate days using students familiar with the exercise.

Validity: Face validity was accepted.

Equipment and Materials: The equipment needed for this test is a bench or chair (15" - 17" in height), a weight bar (5' or 6' in length), and enough weight plates to be more than sufficient for the strongest student. A thick towel is required to pad that part of the bar which rests behind the neck and on the shoulders.

Directions: After adjusting the desired amount of weight on the bar, two assistants place the bar upon the shoulders (and behind the neck) of the student as he stands near the edge of the chair or bench. With the feet a comfortable distance apart and a firm grasp of the hands on the bar, the student lowers to an erect sitting position on the chair or bench. Then, without rocking back and forth, the student returns to the standing position. After the two assistants remove the weight, the performer may readjust the weights if a second trial is to be taken. (See Figure 14 - 3.)

Scoring: The total weight of the barbell (including the collars) satisfactorily raised to the standing position is recorded over body weight. Only the best lift of two trials is recorded. (See Table 14 - 3.) The student's strength score is divided by his body weight for comparison with other members in his weight class.

Safety: The two assistants should stand at each end of the barbell and be ready to catch the bar in the event that the performer over-leans, or starts to fall.

Additional Pointers: The performer should sit on the near edge of the bench or chair so that he will not have to rock back and forth to get up.

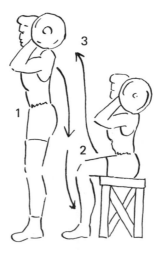

FIGURE 14 - 3

Bench Squat Test

TABLE 14 - 3

T-Score Norms for Bench Squat Test

Raw scores are figured by dividing body weight into the additional weight successfully used in the test.

College Men				College Women			
T Scores	Raw Scores	T Scores	Raw Scores	T Scores	Raw Scores	T Scores	Raw Scores
80	— 2.31	47	— 1.51	80	— 1.72	47	— 1.13
79	— 2.28	46	— 1.48	79	— 1.70	46	— 1.11
78	— 2.26	45	— 1.46	78	— 1.68	45	— 1.09
77	— 2.23	44	— 1.43	77	— 1.66	44	1.08
76	— 2.21	43	— 1.41	76	— 1.65	43	— 1.06
75	— 2.18	42	— 1.38	75	— 1.63	42	— 1.04
74	— 2.16	41	— 1.36	74	— 1.61	41	— 1.02
73	— 2.14	40	— 1.34	73	— 1.59	40	— 1.00
72	— 2.11	39	— 1.31	72	— 1.57	39	— .99
71	— 2.09	38	— 1.29	71	— 1.56	38	— .97
70	— 2.06	37	— 1.26	70	— 1.54	37	— .95
69	— 2.04	36	— 1.24	69	— 1.52	36	— .93
68	— 2.02	35	— 1.21	68	— 1.50	35	— .91
67	— 2.00	34	— 1.19	67	— 1.49	34	— .90
66	— 1.97	33	— 1.17	66	— 1.47	33	— .88
65	— 1.94	32	— 1.14	65	— 1.45	32	— .86
64	— 1.92	31	— 1.12	64	— 1.43	31	— .84
63	— 1.90	30	— 1.09	63	— 1.41	30	— .83
62	— 1.87	29	— 1.07	62	— 1.40	29	— .81
61	— 1.85	28	— 1.05	61	— 1.38	28	— .79
60	— 1.82	27	— 1.02	60	— 1.36	27	— .77
59	— 1.80	26	— 1.00	59	— 1.34	26	— .75
58	— 1.77	25	— .97	58	— 1.33	25	— .74
57	— 1.75	24	— .95	57	— 1.31	24	— .72
56	— 1.72	23	— .92	56	— 1.29	23	— .70
55	— 1.70	22	— .90	55	— 1.27	22	— .68
54	— 1.68	21	— .88	54	— 1.25	21	— .66
53	— 1.65	20	— .85	53	— 1.24	20	— .65
52	— 1.63	15	— .73	52	— 1.22	15	— .55
51	— 1.60	10	— .61	51	— 1.20	10	— .46
50	— 1.58	5	— .49	50	— 1.18	5	— .37
49	— 1.55	0	— .38	49	— 1.16	0	— .29
48	— 1.53			48	— 1.15		

Based on a limited number of scores from a men's physical education class at Northeast Louisiana State College, Monroe, Louisiana.

Based on a limited number of scores from a women's physical education class at Northeast Louisiana State College, Monroe, Louisiana.

Sit-Up Test.[19]

    <u>Objective</u>: To measure the strength of the hip flexors and abdominal muscles.

    <u>Age Level</u>: Ages 12 through college.

    <u>Sex</u>: Satisfactory for both boys and girls.

    <u>Reliability</u>: An r of .91 was found when scores were recorded on separate days using students familiar with the exercise.

    <u>Validity</u>: Face validity was accepted for this test.

    <u>Equipment and Materials</u>: The equipment needed for this test is a mat to lie on, a bar (5' or 6' in length), a dumbbell bar, and an assortment of weight plates.

    <u>Directions</u>: The student may execute the sit-up with either a weight plate, dumbbell, or if necessary, a barbell behind the neck. Should a dumbbell or barbell be used, the attached weight plates must not have a greater circumference than standard five pound plates. After selecting the desired amount of weight, the performer should place it on a mat so that when he assumes the supine position, he can easily grasp the weight and hold it to the back of the neck. While the feet are held down by an assistant, the performer should flex the trunk and touch the elbows to the knees or legs. The knees should be kept straight during the movement. If a second trial is to be taken, the student may readjust the weight and then repeat the exercise. (See Figure 14 - 4.)

    <u>Scoring</u>: Same as for pull-up test. (See Table 14 - 4.)

    <u>Safety</u>: An assistant should be ready to remove the weight at the completion of the lift.

FIGURE 14 - 4

Sit-Up Test

TABLE 14 - 4

T-Score Norms for the Sit-Up Test

Raw scores are figured by dividing body weight into the additional weight successfully used in the test.

College Men				College Women			
T Scores	Raw Scores	T Scores	Raw Scores	T Scores	Raw Scores	T Scores	Raw Scores
85 — .48		52 — .26		80 — .30		49 — .15	
84 — .47		50 — .25		78 — .29		47 — .14	
82 — .46		49 — .24		76 — .28		45 — .13	
81 — .45		47 — .23		74 — .27		43 — .12	
79 — .44		46 — .22		72 — .26		40 — .11	
78 — .43		44 — .21		70 — .25		38 — .10	
76 — .42		43 — .20		68 — .24		36 — .09	
75 — .41		41 — .19		65 — .23		34 — .08	
73 — .40		40 — .18		63 — .22		32 — .07	
72 — .39		38 — .17		61 — .21		30 — .06	
70 — .38		37 — .16		59 — .20		28 — .05	
69 — .37		35 — .15		57 — .19		26 — .04	
67 — .36		34 — .14		55 — .18		24 — .03	
66 — .35		32 — .13		53 — .17		22 — .02	
64 — .34		31 — .12		51 — .16		20 — .01	
63 — .33		29 — .11					
61 — .32		28 — .10					
60 — .31		26 — .09					
58 — .30		25 — .08					
57 — .29		20 — .05					
55 — .28		15 — .02					
54 — .27							

Based on a limited number of scores from a men's physical education class at Northeast Louisiana State College, Monroe, Louisiana.

Based on a limited number of scores from a girls' physical education class at Northeast Louisiana State College, Monroe, Louisiana.

Bench Press Test.[19]

Objective: To measure strength of arm extension in a push-up movement.

Age Level: Ages 12 through college.

Sex: Satisfactory for both boys and girls.

Reliability: An r of .93 was found when scores were recorded on separate days using students familiar with the exercise.

Validity: Face validity was accepted for this test.

Equipment and Materials: The equipment needed for this test is a bench, a weight bar (5′ or 6′ in length) and enough weight plates to be more than sufficient for the strongest student.

Directions: After adjusting the desired amount of weight on the bar, the student assumes a supine position on the bench, and two assistants place the bar in his hands and across the chest. With the hands approximately shoulder width apart, the performer should extend the arms, pressing the bar to a "locked out" (elbows straight) position. The two assistants then remove the bar upon completion of the trial. If a second trial is to be taken, the performer may readjust the weights and then repeat the exercise. (See Figure 14 - 5.)

Scoring: Same as for Bench Squat Test. (See Table 14 - 5.)

Safety: The two assistants should remain ready to catch the barbell at any time during the trial.

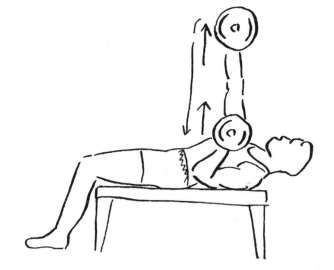

FIGURE 14 - 5

Bench Press Test

TABLE 14 - 5

T-Score Norms for Bench Press Test

Raw scores are figured by dividing body weight into the additional weight successfully used in the test.

College Men				College Women			
T Scores	Raw Scores	T Scores	Raw Scores	T Scores	Raw Scores	T Scores	Raw Scores
85 — 1.77		52 — 1.17		85 — .73		51 — .49	
84 — 1.75		51 — 1.16		84 — .72		49 — .48	
83 — 1.73		50 — 1.14		83 — .71		48 — .47	
82 — 1.71		49 — 1.12		81 — .70		46 — .46	
81 — 1.70		48 — 1.10		80 — .69		45 — .45	
80 — 1.68		47 — 1.08		78 — .68		44 — .44	
79 — 1.66		46 — 1.06		77 — .67		42 — .43	
78 — 1.64		45 — 1.05		75 — .66		41 — .42	
77 — 1.62		44 — 1.03		74 — .65		39 — .41	
76 — 1.61		43 — 1.01		72 — .64		38 — .40	
75 — 1.59		42 — .99		71 — .63		36 — .39	
74 — 1.57		41 — .97		70 — .62		35 — .38	
73 — 1.55		40 — .96		68 — .61		33 — .37	
72 — 1.53		39 — .94		67 — .60		32 — .36	
71 — 1.52		38 — .92		65 — .59		31 — .35	
70 — 1.50		37 — .90		64 — .58		29 — .34	
69 — 1.48		36 — .88		62 — .57		28 — .33	
68 — 1.46		35 — .87		61 — .56		26 — .32	
67 — 1.44		34 — .85		59 — .55		25 — .31	
66 — 1.43		33 — .83		58 — .54		20 — .28	
65 — 1.41		32 — .81		57 — .53		15 — .24	
64 — 1.39		31 — .79		55 — .52		10 — .21	
63 — 1.37		30 — .78		54 — .51		5 — .17	
62 — 1.35		29 — .76		52 — .50		0 — .14	
61 — 1.34		28 — .74					
60 — 1.32		27 — .72					
59 — 1.30		26 — .70					
58 — 1.28		25 — .69					
57 — 1.26		20 — .60					
56 — 1.25		15 — .51					
55 — 1.23		10 — .42					
54 — 1.21		5 — .32					
53 — 1.19		0 — .24					

Based on a limited number of scores from a men's physical education class at Northeast Louisiana State College, Monroe, Louisiana.

Based on a limited number of scores from a girl's physical education class at Northeast Louisiana State College, Monroe, Louisiana.

Standing Vertical Arm Press Test.[19]

Objective: To measure strength of arm extension in a vertical over-head press movement.

Age Level: Ages 12 through college.

Sex: Recommended for boys only.

Reliability: An r of .98 was found for this test with a group of students who were familiar with the exercise. The best score of two trials was recorded as the test score on separate days.

Validity: Face validity was accepted for this test.

Equipment and Materials: The equipment needed is a weight bar (5' or 6' in length) and enough weight plates to be more than sufficient for the strongest student.

Directions: After adjusting the desired amount of weight on the bar, the performer assumes a standing position (feet a comfortable distance apart for balance), and two assistants place the bar in the performer's hands at the front chest position. With a forward grasp (palms facing away) the performer should extend the arms upward pressing the bar to a "locked out" (elbows straight) position. The weight should be held steady for a count of three to show control, after which it it lowered to the floor. If a second trial is to be taken, the performer may readjust the wieghts and then repeat the trial. (See Figure 14 - 6.)

Scoring: Same as for Bench Squat Test.)See Table 14 - 6.)

Safety: The two assistants should remain ready to catch the barbell at any time during the trial.

Additional Pointers: The performer must avoid flexing at the knees and hips during the press.

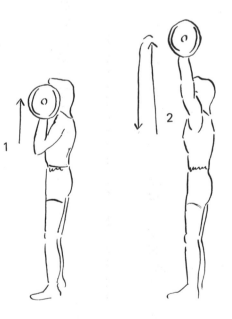

FIGURE 14 - 6

Standing Vertical Arm Press

TABLE 14 - 6

T-Score Norms for Standing Vertical Arm Press

Raw scores are figured by dividing body weight into the additional weight successfully used in the test.

College Men				
T-Scores	Raw Scores		T-Scores	Raw Scores
85	— 1.29		50	— .86
84	— 1.28		49	— .85
83	— 1.26		48	— .84
82	— 1.25		47	— .82
81	— 1.24		46	— .81
80	— 1.23		45	— .80
79	— 1.21		44	— .79
78	— 1.20		43	— .77
77	— 1.19		42	— .75
76	— 1.18		41	— .74
75	— 1.16		40	— .73
74	— 1.15		39	— .72
73	— 1.14		38	— .70
72	— 1.13		37	— .69
71	— 1.11		36	— .68
70	— 1.10		35	— .67
69	— 1.09		34	— .66
68	— 1.08		33	— .65
67	— 1.07		32	— .63
66	— 1.05		31	— .62
65	— 1.04		30	— .61
64	— 1.03		29	— .59
63	— 1.02		28	— .58
62	— 1.00		27	— .57
61	— .99		26	— .56
60	— .98		25	— .54
59	— .97		24	— .53
58	— .95		23	— .52
57	— .94		22	— .51
56	— .93		21	— .50
55	— .92		20	— .48
54	— .91		15	— .42
53	— .90		10	— .36
52	— .89		5	— .29
51	— .87		0	— .24

Based on a limited number of scores from a men's physical education class at Northeast Louisiana State College, Monroe, Louisiana.

Spring Scale Strength Tests.[20]

<u>Objective</u>: To measure strength through a limited range of motion.

<u>Age Level</u>: Ages 12 through college.

<u>Sex</u>: Recommended for girls to correspond to the Pull-Up Test, Dip Test, and Vertical Arm Press Test previously presented for boys only.

<u>Reliability</u>: See each individual test item.

<u>Validity</u>: See each individual test item.

<u>Equipment and Materials</u>: All of the equipment needed for the following spring scale tests can be purchased at most hardware stores for a very reasonable price. The equipment and attachments needed are listed as follows: (1) one 160 lb. spring scale, (2) two heavy-duty eye hooks, (3) two chain links, (4) two 18" chain sections, (5) one 5' section of chain, (6) two S hooks, (7) one screw hook, and (8) one wooden bar (2' length of hickory). (See Figure 14 - 7.)

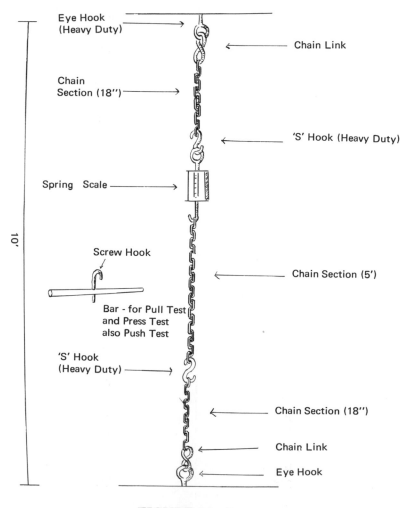

FIGURE 14 - 7

Spring Scale Rig

General Directions: (1) Students should be allowed to become familiar with the three spring scale tests at least several days prior to testing. (2) On each test the student should be allowed two trials (if she so desires) in which she can register the maximum amount of weight possible for that test. (3) The tester should keep his eyes at the same level as the scale in order to determine the maximum amount of weight registered. (4) Students should be allowed to warm up before reporting to the testing station, but they also should be cautioned not to overwork. (5) Foot stance marks should be placed on the floor so that students will assume the same position each time they execute the tests and so that they will be pulling or pushing in a vertical direction. (6) As mentioned under general directions for isotonic testing, students should be divided into three weight groups so that comparisons can be made between a student's score and others in her weight group.

Scoring: The best score of two trials is recorded as the score for each test. The student's best score for each test is then divided by her body weight for comparison with other members of her weight class.

Additional Pointers: If a regular training program is to be conducted, paint marks of different colors along the links of the chain will help each girl to quickly identify her particular link for each exercise.

Spring Scale Test Items

Over-head Pull Test.[20]

Objective: To measure the strength of the arms and shoulders in the pull-up movement.

Age Level: Recommended for ages 12 through college.

Sex: Recommended for girls in place of the pull-up test which was presented for boys only.

Reliability: An r of .98 was found for this test when students were tested, allowed a short rest, and then retested.

Validity: Face validity was accepted for this test.

Equipment and Materials: The equipment needed is the spring scale rig as previously described.

Directions: The tester should hook the bar to that part of the chain which will allow each student to start the pull from a straight arm position, but with all the body weight resting on the feet. The feet should be flat on the floor and about 12" apart. With a forward grasp on the bar (hands about shoulder width apart) the student should pull the bar downward without any bending of the knees, hips, or turning of the body. The student must bend only at the elbows and keep both feet on the floor while maintaining an erect posture. For girls who are strong enough to pull their body weight or more, it is necessary to have an assistant hold the performer's hips so that the feet will not leave the floor. If a second trial is to be taken, the performer may rest a few seconds and then repeat the exercise. (See Figure 14 - 8.)

Scoring: Keeping the eyes on the level of the scale, the tester records the greatest number of pounds reached by means of a steady pull. The best score of two trials is recorded over body weight and divided for comparison with other members of her weight group. (See Table 14 - 7.)

Additional Pointers: Make sure that each student understands that the pull is to be a steady one rather than a hard or fast jerk.

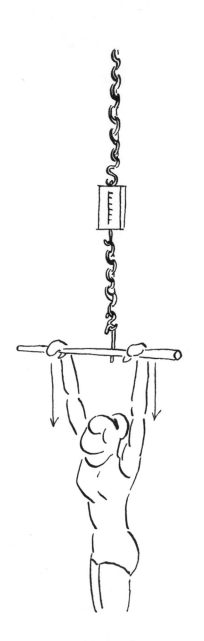

FIGURE 14 - 8

Over-Head Pull Test

TABLE 14 - 7

T-Score Norms for Over Head Pull Test

Raw scores are figured by dividing body weight into the amount of weight registered on the spring scale.

College Women								
T-Scores		Raw Scores	T-Scores		Raw Scores	T-Scores		Raw Scores
100	—	1.36	71	—	1.09	43	—	.82
99	—	1.35	70	—	1.08	42	—	.81
98	—	1.34	69	—	1.07	41	—	.80
97	—	1.33	68	—	1.06	40	—	.79
95	—	1.32	67	—	1.05	38	—	.78
94	—	1.31	66	—	1.04	37	—	.77
93	—	1.30	65	—	1.03	36	—	.76
92	—	1.29	64	—	1.02	35	—	.75
91	—	1.28	63	—	1.01	34	—	.74
90	—	1.27	62	—	1.00	33	—	.73
89	—	1.26	61	—	.99	32	—	.72
88	—	1.25	60	—	.98	31	—	.71
87	—	1.24	59	—	.97	30	—	.70
86	—	1.23	57	—	.96	29	—	.69
85	—	1.22	56	—	.95	28	—	.68
84	—	1.21	55	—	.94	27	—	.67
83	—	1.20	54	—	.93	26	—	.66
82	—	1.19	53	—	.92	25	—	.65
81	—	1.18	52	—	.91	23	—	.64
80	—	1.17	51	—	.90	22	—	.63
79	—	1.16	50	—	.89	21	—	.62
78	—	1.15	49	—	.88	20	—	.61
76	—	1.14	48	—	.87	15	—	.56
75	—	1.13	47	—	.86	10	—	.51
74	—	1.12	46	—	.85	5	—	.46
73	—	1.11	45	—	.84	0	—	.42
72	—	1.10	44	—	.83			

Based on 100 scores secured from physical education classes at Northeast Louisiana State College, Monroe, Louisiana.

Two Hand Push Test.[20]

Objective: To measure the strength of the arms and shoulders in a downward push movement.

Age Level: Ages 12 through college.

Sex: Recommended for girls in place of the dip test which was presented for boys only.

Reliability: An r of .92 was found for this test when students were tested, allowed a short rest, and then retested.

Validity: Face validity was accepted for this test.

Equipment and Materials: Same as for the previous test.

Directions: The tester should hook the bar attachment to that part of the chain which will allow the bar to run horizontally across the navel of the performer. With the body weight distributed equally over the feet, the performer should push the bar vertically downward by attempting to straighten out the arms. The feet must remain flat on the floor during the test. For some girls it may be necessary to have a classmate hold the hips in order to keep the feet down. (See Figure 14 - 9.)

Scoring: Keeping the eyes on the level of the scale, the tester records the greatest number of pounds reached by means of a steady push. The best score of two trials is recorded over body weight and divided for comparison with other members of her weight group. (See Table 14 - 7.)

Additional Pointers: (1) The head of the performer should not be allowed to lean over to the side of the chain, but must remain directly in front and in line with it.

FIGURE 14 - 9

Two Hand Push Test

TABLE 14 - 8

T-Score Norms for Two Hand Push Test

Raw scores are figured by dividing body weight into the amount of weight registered on the spring scale.

College Women			
T-Scores	Raw Scores	T-Scores	Raw Scores
80 — .90		46 — .59	
79 — .89		45 — .58	
78 — .88		44 — .57	
77 — .87		43 — .56	
75 — .86		42 — .55	
74 — .85		41 — .54	
73 — .84		40 — .53	
72 — .83		39 — .52	
71 — .82		38 — .51	
70 — .81		37 — .50	
69 — .80		36 — .49	
68 — .79		35 — .48	
67 — .78		34 — .47	
66 — .77		32 — .46	
65 — .76		31 — .45	
64 — .75		30 — .44	
63 — .74		29 — .43	
61 — .73		28 — .42	
60 — .72		27 — .41	
59 — .71		26 — .40	
58 — .70		25 — .39	
57 — .69		24 — .38	
56 — .68		23 — .37	
55 — .67		22 — .36	
54 — .66		21 — .35	
53 — .65		20 — .34	
52 — .64		15 — .30	
51 — .63		10 — .29	
50 — .62		5 — .20	
49 — .61		0 — .16	
48 — .60			

Based on 100 scores secured from physical education classes at Northeast Louisiana State College, Monroe, Louisiana.

Press Test.[20]

Objective: To measure the strength of arm extension in a vertical overhead press movement.

Age Level: Ages 12 through college.

Sex: Recommended for girls in place of the standing vertical arm press test with a barbell as previously presented for boys only.

Reliability: An r of .93 was found for this test when students were tested, allowed a short rest, and then retested.

Validity: Face validity was accepted for this test.

Equipment and Materials: Same as for previous test.

Directions: The tester should hook the bar to that part of the chain which will allow each student to start the push with the bar located in front of the forehead (between the eyebrows and the hairline). Keeping the feet flat on the floor, the student should press the bar vertically upward by attempting to straighten out the arms. If a second trial is to be taken, the performer may rest a few seconds and then repeat the trial. (See Figure 14 - 10.)

Scoring: Same as for the previous test. (See Table 14 - 10.)

Additional Pointers: The performer should stand facing the back side of the scale so that the tester can simultaneously observe the body position and the score.

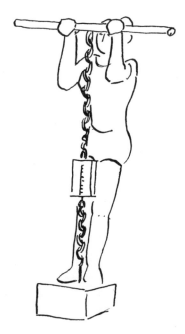

FIGURE 14 - 10

Press Test

TABLE 14 - 9

T-Score Norms for the Press Test

Raw scores are figured by dividing body weight into the amount of weight registered on the spring scale.

College Women					
T-Scores		Raw Scores	T-Scores		Raw Scores
80	—	.64	47	—	.38
79	—	.63	45	—	.37
78	—	.62	44	—	.36
77	—	.61	43	—	.35
75	—	.60	41	—	.34
74	—	.59	40	—	.33
73	—	.58	39	—	.32
71	—	.57	37	—	.31
70	—	.56	36	—	.30
69	—	.55	35	—	.29
68	—	.54	33	—	.28
66	—	.53	32	—	.27
65	—	.52	31	—	.26
64	—	.51	29	—	.25
62	—	.50	28	—	.24
61	—	.49	27	—	.23
60	—	.48	26	—	.22
58	—	.47	24	—	.21
57	—	.46	23	—	.20
56	—	.45	22	—	.19
54	—	.44	20	—	.18
53	—	.43	15	—	.14
52	—	.42	10	—	.10
50	—	.41	5	—	.07
49	—	.40	0	—	.03
48	—	.39			

Based on a limited number of scores from a women's physical education class at Northeast Louisiana State College, Monroe, Louisiana.

Isometric Strength Instruments

<u>Objective</u>: To measure strength without movement of the resistance or the joints involved.

Iso-scale: [11] The equipment required for various tests with the iso-scale includes a nylon strap with numerous slots for the purpose of adjusting two metal bars at any desired distance apart. The slots of the strap also permit the fastening of the iso-scale. The iso-scale indicates the pounds of pressure exerted by each subject on the apparatus. The scale itself is repeatable and measures from 50 up to 750 pounds of pressure. The reliability of various tests with the instrument revealed satisfactory coefficients in the .90's. [18] However, variability between instruments and difficulty of calibration makes it impractical for the construction of norms. (See Figure 14 - 11.)

Tensiometer: [9A] The equipment required for various tests with the tensiometer includes a strap with D ring, a pair of cables with adjusters, a goniometer to establish correct joint angles, and a specially constructed table for various exercise positions. The tensiometer indicates the pounds of pressure exerted up to 300 lbs.; however, a smaller tensiometer (for greater precision) is used when measurements are expected below 30 lbs. due to the inaccuracy of the lower end of the 300 lbs. instrument. The smaller tensiometer measures accurately from 0 to 100 pounds. The reliability of the tensiometer is quite high, since objectivity coefficients for practically all tests were in the .90's. The instrument can be purchased from the Pacific Scientific Co., Inc. of Los Angeles, California. (See Figure 14 - 12.)

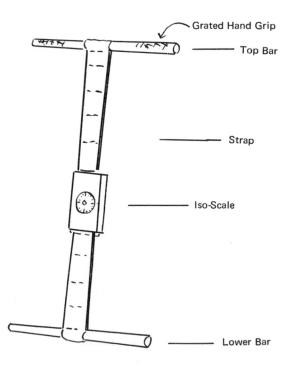

FIGURE 14 - 11

Iso-Scale with Strap and Bar

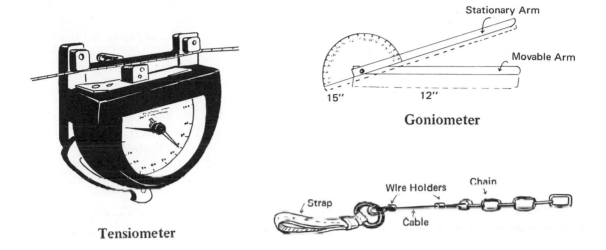

Tensiometer

Goniometer

Tensiometer Attachments

FIGURE 14 - 12

TABLE 14 - 10

Norms of Strength of Grip in Kg. (Smedley)

Age	Boys		Girls	
	Right Hand	Left Hand	Right Hand	Left Hand
6	9.21	8.48	8.36	7.74
7	10.74	10.11	9.88	9.24
8	12.41	11.67	11.16	10.48
9	14.34	13.47	12.77	11.97
10	16.52	15.59	14.65	13.72
11	18.85	17.72	16.54	15.52
12	21.24	19.71	18.92	17.78
13	24.44	22.51	21.84	20.39
14	28.42	26.22	24.79	22.92
15	33.39	30.88	27.00	24.92
16	39.37	36.39	28.70	26.56
17	44.74	40.96	29.56	27.43
18	49.28	45.01	29.75	27.66

Based on 2788 boys in Chicago   Based on 3471 girls in Chicago

Grip Dynamometer: The grip dynamometer is used to secure strength scores of the grip of each hand. It has an adjustable handle to fit the size of the hand and a maximum needle indicator for ease of scoring. The scoring dial is marked off in kilograms. Reliability coefficients have been reported in the .90's, which indicates that there is a satisfactory degree of reliability and that the scale measures from 0 to 100 kg. The instrument may be purchased from the C. H. Stoelting Co. of Chicago, Illinois. (See Figure 14 - 13.) Norms for both boys and girls were established with the use of the Smedley grip dynamometer. (See Table 14 - 10.)

Back and Leg Dynamometer: This instrument consists of a scale which measures from 0 to 2500 pounds in 10 pound increments. It is attached to a strong platform and has a chain and bar attachment for individual adjustments according to height. Satisfactory reliability has been reported for tests with this instrument ranging from .86 into the .90's. The main drawback of this instrument is the expense involved for a limited number of exercises. The instrument may be purchased from the Nissen Corporation of Cedar Rapids, Iowa. (See Figure 14 - 14.)

Heavy Duty Spring Scale: The heavy duty spring scale is seldom used, but can be employed most effectively in a strength testing program. By placing the scale under an isometric rack, accurate measurements can be recorded for the military press, the bench press, the curl, and other exercises. In any exercise where the student is required to push or lift upward, you simply record the maximum amount read on the scale and then subtract body weight from that figure. For the leg press, a bar may be inserted underneath the scale; then a belt is attached to both ends of the bar and is placed over the subject's hips for the lift. The large scale, which provides motivation, can easily be seen by both the tester and the subject. The reliability for this instrument has been reported in the .90's.

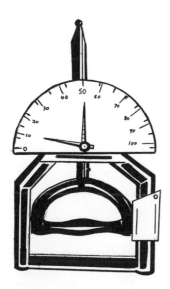

FIGURE 14 - 13

Grip Dynamometer

FIGURE 14 - 14

Back and Leg Dynamometer

Problems Associated with Strength Testing

Several of the problems and limitations associated with the measurement of strength are listed and discussed below:

1. The muscular strength tests most frequently used during the past few decades have included some test items of dubious validity. For example, the inclusion of the lung capacity measure in the Rogers Strength Test has been criticized and defended many times over the years. Also, the inclusion of muscular endurance items, such as pull-ups and dips for maximum repetition, have added to the confusion and misinterpretation concerning strength test results. The test items presented in this chapter are believed to be practical measures of isotonic and isometric strength of the large muscle groups.

2. There are a number of tests which provide accurate strength measurement but require expensive equipment; consequently, many schools have been unable to include such tests in their physical education program. Therefore, the tests presented in this chapter should be of practical value, since all equipment and materials mentioned are well within the budget limits of most schools. Moreover, further attempts should be made to devise inexpensive, but reliable and objective strength tests.

3. At the present time the measurement of abdominal strength has been quite limited. Many of the better known strength tests have avoided this area entirely, although abdominal strength is important in various activities. The situp test with maximum (or near-maximum) resistance behind the neck represents only one attempt at assessing strength in that area. Perhaps another method would be to tie weight to the feet and from a straight arm support on the parallel bars, or from a hang under the horizontal bar, lift the legs to a horizontal position and hold for three counts.

4. In measuring static strength, it is difficult to establish precisely the same position or angle for certain exercises and for all subjects. Differences in the amount of musculature and fatty tissue, and different lengths of body segments pose special problems for accurate testing. Needless to say, it is imperative that such tests start at the same angle for each student, and from the same reference point on each individual. For example, such phrases as "starting with the elbows at a 90° angle" or "starting with the bar between the eyebrows and the hairline" are absolutely necessary if comparisons are to be made within a group or with established norms. Furthermore, in using any type of gauge such as the scale device that does not have a memory pointer (which remains in place after pressure is released) the tester's eyes must be kept at the same level as the scale in order to secure an accurate reading.

Findings and Conclusions from Strength Measurement and Research

Prior to 1950 it was commonly believed by both coaches and athletes that weight training did not produce the type of strength necessary for superior sports performance, and, furthermore, that such training hindered speed of movement. However, starting in 1950 a number of researchers reported that isotonic weight training increased strength and improved speed of movement.[2,6,7,13,30,41,43] As a result of such findings, athletes in practically all sports now use weight training as a valuable adjunct to their sports practice.

Although Elbel,[12] in 1928, was probably the first to note that strength could be increased by short static contraction (isometric) exercises, it was not until the highly publicized experiments of Hettinger and Muller,[16] in 1953, that mass interest was created in this type of training. Since that date numerous studies have indicated that strength can be significantly increased by isometric exercise.[3,14,24,32,36,42]

Once it was clearly understood that both isometric and isotonic exercises could increase strength, investigators turned their attention to a comparison of the two systems. The results of such endeavors have generally revealed that there is no significant difference in the amount of strength developed by the two programs.[1,8,15,23,34] Usually, any difference in the two programs has been specific to the manner in which the strength was tested, either by isotonic means or by isometric measurement.

While one frequently hears of the fantastic strength feats accomplished under hypnosis, a study by Johnson and Kramer[22] failed to reveal that hypnotic conditions were better than non-hypnotic conditions in strength performance.

Concerning the value of strength programs in increasing movement time and reaction time, studies by Meadows,[28] Chui,[8] and Johnson[17] compared isometric and isotonic training programs and found them to be nearly equal insofar as bringing about increases in speed of movement. In contrast, Swegan's study[35] reported that both isometric and isotonic programs slowed down speed of movement. However, in a recent study by Whitley and Smith,[40] it was concluded that regardless of the type of strengthening exercises used, increasing the strength of muscles involved in a particular task makes it possible to execute the movement faster.

Michael[29] found that isometric training increased both speed of movement and reaction time significantly. Crowder* further found that isometric and isotonic strength training were equally effective in improving reaction time when the exercises were performed in the same way in which the reaction time measures were taken.

Several studies have indicated that individuals with greater muscular strength usually have greater muscular endurance, although the development of strength endurance is not directly proportional to maximum strength development.[4,5,38]

Concerning strength and academic achievement, Clarke[9B] found that high strength groups had a consistent tendency to have higher means on standard achievement tests and grade point averages; while two studies[37,39] revealed that persons who had greater strength as measured by grip strength had significantly better grades in physical education courses.

Several studies have indicated the effects of motivation upon strength performance.[21,25,31] For example, Nelson[31] found that students who exerted more effort under the influence of motivational situations had greater strength decrement and recovered more slowly from their strength loss than those less motivated. Johnson[21] found that motivated isometric training groups significantly increased their strength, whereas a non-motivated isometric training group made little or no gain when tested under conditions of no consciously induced motivation. It was further noted that a special motivational testing situation (which included march music, spectators, photographers, and competition) significantly increased the strength scores of training groups over those scores achieved during training. Thus, strength measures seem to be greatly influenced by the level of motivation present during training and testing.

---

*Vernon R. Crowder, "A Comparison of the Effects of Two Methods of Strength Training on Reaction Time," Unpublished Master's Thesis, Louisiana State University, Baton Rouge, 1966.

BIBLIOGRAPHY

1. Adamson, G. F., "Effects of Isometric and Isotonic Exercise on Elbow Flexor and Spine Extensor Muscle Groups," *Health and Fitness in the Modern World,* Chicago: Athletic Institute, 1961, p. 172.

2. Anderson, Robert W., "The Effect of Weight Training on Total Body Reaction Time," (Unpublished Master's Thesis, University of Illinois, 1957, p. 66).

3. Barham, Jerry N., "A Comparison of Two Methods of Isometric Exercises on the Development of Muscle Strength," (Unpublished Master's Thesis, Louisiana State University, Baton Rouge, Louisiana, 1960).

4. Berger, Richard A., "The Effect of Varied Weight Training Programs on Strength and Endurance," (Microcarded Master's Thesis, University of Illinois, 1960).

5. Burke, William E., "A Study of the Relationship of Age of Strength and Endurance in Gripping," (Microcarded Doctor's Thesis, University of Iowa, 1952, p. 49).

6. Capen, Edward K., "The Effect of Systematic Weight Training on Power, Strength, and Endurance," *Research Quarterly,* 21:83-93, May, 1950.

7. Chui, Edward, "Effect of Weight Training on Athletic Power," *Research Quarterly,* 21:188, October, 1950.

8. _____ , "Effects of Isometric and Dynamic Weight-Training Exercises Upon Strength and Speed of Movement," *Research Quarterly,* 35:246-257, October, 1964.

9.(A) Clarke, H. Harrison, "Objective Strength Tests of Affected Muscle Groups Involved in Orthopedic Disabilities," *Research Quarterly,* 19:118-147, May, 1948.

9.(B) _____ , and Boyd O. Jarman, "Scholastic Achievement of Boys 9, 12, and 15 years of Age as Related to Various Strength and Growth Measures," *Research Quarterly,* 32:155, May, 1961.

10. Cureton, T. K., "Analysis of Vital Capacity as a Test of Condition for High School Boys," *Research Quarterly,* 4:80-93, December, 1936.

11. Drury, Francis A., "Strength Through Measurement," Marion, Indiana: Coach's Sporting Goods Corporation, 1963.

12. Elbel, Edwin R., "A Study in Short Static Strength of Muscles," (Unpublished Master's Thesis, International Y.M.C.A. College, Springfield, Massachusetts, July, 1928, p. 64).

13. Endres, John P., "The Effect of Weight Training Exercise Upon the Speed of Muscular Movement," (Microcarded Master's Thesis, University of Wisconsin, Madison, 1953, pp. 29-31).

14. Gardner, Gerald W., "Specificity of Strength Changes of the Exercised and Non-Exercised Limb Following Isometric Training," *Research Quarterly,* 34:99-100, March, 1963).

15. Healy, Alfred, "Two Methods of Weight Training for Children with Spastic Type of Cerebral Palsy," *Research Quarterly,* 29:389-395, December, 1958).

16. Hettinger, Th., and E. A. Muller, "Muskelleistung and Muskeltraining," *Arbeitsphysiologie,* 15, 111-126, 1953.

17. Johnson, Barry L., "A Comparison of Isometric and Isotonic Exercises Upon the Improvement of Velocity and Distance as Measured by a Vertical Rope Climb Test," (Unpublished Master's Thesis, Louisiana State University, 1964).

18. _____ , "Isometric Strength Tests," (Unpublished Study, Northeast Louisiana State College, Monroe, Louisiana, 1966).

19. _____ , "Isotonic Strength Tests," (Unpublished Study, Northeast Louisiana State College, Monroe, Louisiana, 1966).

20. _____ , "Spring Scale Strength Tests: Measuring Strength Through a Limited Range of Motion," (Unpublished Study, Northeast Louisiana State College, Monroe, Louisiana, 1966).

21. _____ , and Jack K. Nelson, "The Effects of Applying Different Motivational Techniques During Training and in Testing Upon Strength Performance," *Research Quarterly,* 38:630-636, December, 1967.

22. Johnson, Warren R., and George F. Kramer, "Effects of Stereotyped Non-hypnotic, Hypnotic, and Post-hypnotic Suggestions upon Strength, Power, and Endurance," *Research Quarterly,* 32:522-529, December, 1961.

23. Lorback, Melvin H., "A Study Comparing the Effectiveness of Short Periods of Static Contraction to Standard Weight Training Procedures in the Development of Strength and Muscle Girth," (Microcarded Master's Thesis, Pennsylvania State University, 1955).

24. Lyne, James, "The Frequency of Static Contraction Exercise Necessary for Strength Level Maintenance," (Microcarded Master's Thesis, Pennsylvania State University, 1958).

25. Marcel, Norman A., "The Effect of Knowledge of Results as a Motivation on Physical Performance," (Unpublished Study, Louisiana State University, Baton Rouge, Louisiana, 1961).

26. Mathews, D. K., and Robert Kruse, "Effects of Isometric and Isotonic Exercises on Elbow Flexor Muscle Groups," *Research Quarterly,* 28:26, Marcy, 1957.

27. McCloy, C. H., and Norma D. Young, *Tests and Measurements in Health and Physical Education,* New York: Appleton-Century-Crofts, Inc., 1954, pp. 130-134.

28. Meadows, P. E., "The Effect of Isotonic and Isometric Muscle Contraction Training on Speed, Force, and Strength," (Microcarded Doctoral Dissertation, University of Illinois, Urbana, 1959, pp. 93-95).

29. Michael, Charles E., "The Effects of Isometric Contraction Exercise on Reaction and Speed of Movement Times," (Unpublished Doctoral Dissertation, Louisiana State University, Baton Rouge, 1963, p. 61).

30. Mosely, John W., and others, "Weight Training in Relation to Strength, Speed, and Coordination," *Research Quarterly,* 24:308-315, October, 1953.

31. Nelson, Jack K., "An Analysis of the Effects of Applying Various Motivational Situations to College Men Subjected to a Stressful Physical Performance," (Microcarded Doctor's Dissertation, University of Oregon, Eugene, 1962).

32. Rarick, Lawrence, and Gene L. Larson, "Observations on Frequency and Intensity of Isometric Muscular Effort in Developing Muscular Strength," *Research Quarterly*, 29:333-341, October, 1958.

33. Rasch, Phillip J., and Lawrence E. Morehouse, "Effects of Static and Dynamic Exercises on Muscular Strength and Hypertrophy," *Journal of Applied Physiology*, 11:25, July, 1957.

34. _____, "Relationship between Maximum Isometric Tension and Maximum Isotonic Elbow Flexion," *Research Quarterly*, 28:85, March, 1957.

35. Swegan, Donald B., "The Comparison of Static Contraction with Standard Weight Training in Effect of Certain Movement Speeds and Endurances," (Microcarded Doctoral Dissertation, The Pennsylvania State University, University Park, 1957, pp. 137-140).

36. Taylor, William E., "A Study Comparing the Effectiveness of Four Static Contraction Training Methods for Increasing the Contractile Strength of Two Body Movements," (Unpublished Master's Thesis, Pennsylvania State University, 1954).

37. Tinkle, Wayne F., and Henry J. Montoye, "Relationship Between Grip Strength and Achievement in Physical Education Among College Men," *Research Quarterly*, 32:242, May, 1961.

38. Tuttle, W. W., and others, "Relation of Maximum Back and Leg Strength to Back and Leg Strength Endurance," *Research Quarterly*, 26:96-106, March, 1955.

39. Wessel, Janet A., and Richard C. Nelson, "Relationship Between Grip Strength and Achievement in Physical Education Among College Women," *Research Quarterly*, 32:244, May, 1961.

40. Whitley, Jim D., and Leon E. Smith, "Influence of Three Different Training Programs on Strength and Speed of a Limb Movement," *Research Quarterly*, 37:142, March, 1966.

41. Wilkin, Bruce M., "The Effect of Weight Training on Speed of Movement," *Research Quarterly*, 23:361369, October, 1952.

42. Wolbers, Charles P., and Frank D. Sills, "Development of Strength in High School Boys by Static Muscle Contraction," *Research Quarterly*, 27:446, December, 1956.

43. Zorbas, William S., and Peter V. Karpovich, "The Effect of Weight Lifting upon the Speed of Muscular Contraction," *Research Quarterly*, 22:145-148, May, 1951.

Chapter XV

THE MEASUREMENT OF MUSCULAR ENDURANCE

Muscular endurance may be either dynamic or static in nature and concerns the ability of a muscle to repeat identical movements or pressures, or to maintain a certain degree of tension over a period of time. Basically there are three types of muscular endurance tests. Each type may be relative or absolute. A relative endurance test is one in which the muscles work with a proportionate amount of the maximum strength load of a particular muscle group, whereas an absolute endurance test requires a set load for all subjects without a definite relationship to the maximum strength of each individual.[49] The three types of muscular endurance tests are identified as follows:

Dynamic Test of Muscular Endurance: The performer executes identical repetitions of a movement through a designated distance and over an unlimited amount of time. The test is scored in terms of the number of correct executions completed. Examples of such tests include barbell exercises with submaximal loads and the frequently used push-ups, pull-ups, and sit-ups.

Repetitive Static Tests of Muscular Endurance: The performer executes repetitions of force against a static measuring device, and the test is scored in terms of the number of times the performer registers a force equal to a certain percent of either the maximum strength of the muscles involved or of body weight. An example would be the number of times a performer can squeeze eighty pounds or more on a grip strength dynamometer. The test is usually stopped when the performer either fails to squeeze the prescribed load or when he falls behind the desired cadence. While some writers identify this type test as a dynamic test, it should be noted that movement over a distance is not a factor.

Timed Static Tests of Muscular Endurance: The performer maintains one continuous muscle contraction rather than a series of repetitive bouts, and the test is scored in terms of the amount of time the weight was held. An example would be the flexed arm hang test for girls.[1]

Tests of muscular endurance are quite practical for the majority of schools and have been widely used in physical fitness testing programs. Such tests differ from strength tests in that the score is based on the number of repetitions executed (or the length of time a set tension was maintained) and not on the maximum amount of weight lifted or force exerted.

While muscular endurance is closely associated with strength, it is also associated with the number of active capillaries within the working muscles. Because of this association muscular endurance tests are sometimes confused with circulorespiratory endurance tests. However, muscular endurance tests primarily tax the skeletal muscles involved; whereas the circulorespiratory endurance items primarily tax the efficiency of the heart and lungs.

Uses of Muscular Endurance Tests

Several ways by which muscular endurance tests are utilized in physical education classes are listed as follows:

1. As a factor in physical fitness and motor ability tests.
2. As a means to motivate students to improve their status within the class.
3. As a measure for determining achievement and grades when improvement in muscular endurance is a specific objective in a physical activity class.
4. As a means to indicate an individual's readiness for vigorous activity.

Practical Tests of Muscular Endurance

Several practical tests of muscular endurance in terms of time, equipment, and cost are presented below:

Chin-ups[1]

Objective: To measure the muscular endurance of the arms and shoulder girdle in pulling the body upward.

Age Level: Ages 10 through college.

Sex: Satisfactory for boys only.

Reliability: An r as high as .87 has been reported for this test when subjects were tested on separate days.

Validity: This test has been accepted for its face validity.

Equipment and Materials: The equipment needed is a horizontal bar (1½ inches in diameter) raised to a height so that the tallest performer cannot touch the ground from the hanging position. If standard equipment is not available, a piece of pipe or the rungs of a ladder can be used.

Directions: The performer should assume the hanging position with the overhand grasp (palms forward) and pull his body upward until the chin is over the bar. After each chin-up he should return to a fully extended hanging position. The exercise should be repeated as many times as possible. (See Figure 15 - 1.)

Scoring: The score is the number of completed chinups. (See Table 15 - 1.)

Additional Pointers: (1) Only one trial is allowed unless it is obvious that the student could do better with a second chance. (2) Swinging and snap-up movements must be avoided. The tester may check this by holding an extended arm across the front of the performer's thighs. (3) The knees must not be flexed during the pull, and kicking motions must be avoided. (4) Although the palms forward grasp is customarily prescribed in physical fitness batteries, there is no logical reason why this, rather than the reverse (palms inward) grasp, should be employed other than it is more difficult. As a matter of fact, since the reverse grip yields more repetitions, it might actually be a better measure in terms of distribution of scores. As McCloy* pointed out, the overhand grip became standard in World War II when the Armed Forces decreed that it was similar to the grip needed in climbing a fence. McCloy adroitly commented that the reverse grip is the one used in the climbing of a rope.

*Charles H. McCloy and Norma D. Young, *Tests and Measurements in Health and Physical Education.* Third Edition, New York: Appleton-Century-Crofts, Inc., 1954, p. 168.

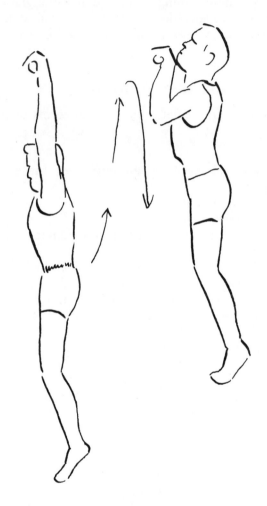

FIGURE 15 - 1

Chin-Up

TABLE 15 - 1

Chin-Ups for Boys[1]

Percentile Scores Based on Age/Test Scores in Number of Chin-Ups

Percentile	Age									Percentile
	10	11	12	13	14	15	16	17	College	
100th	16	20	15	24	20	25	25	32	20	100th
95	8	8	9	10	12	13	14	16	12	95
90	7	7	7	9	10	11	13	14	10	90
85	6	6	6	8	10	10	12	12	10	85
80	5	5	5	7	8	10	11	12	9	80
75	4	4	5	6	8	9	10	10	8	75
70	4	4	4	5	7	8	10	10	8	70
65	3	3	3	5	6	7	9	10	7	65
60	3	3	3	4	6	7	9	9	7	60
55	3	2	3	4	5	6	8	8	6	55
50	2	2	2	3	5	6	7	8	6	50
45	2	2	2	3	4	5	6	7	5	45
40	1	1	1	2	4	5	6	7	5	40
35	1	1	1	2	3	4	5	6	4	35
30	1	1	1	1	3	4	5	5	4	30
25	0	0	0	1	2	3	4	5	3	25
20	0	0	0	0	2	3	4	4	3	20
15	0	0	0	0	1	2	4	4	2	15
10	0	0	0	0	0	1	2	2	1	10
5	0	0	0	0	0	0	0	1	0	5
0	0	0	0	0	0	0	0	0	0	0

Source: AAHPER, Youth Fitness Test Manual, Revised, Washington D.C., 1966, pp. 34, 65.

Flexed Arm Hang.[1]

Objective: To measure the endurance of the arms and shoulder girdle in the flexed arm hang position.

Age Level: Ages 10 through college.

Sex: This test is presented for girls only.*

Reliability: Has been reported as high as .90.

Validity: Face validity was accepted.

Equipment and Materials: The equipment needed is a horizontal bar (1½ inches in diameter) raised to a height so that the tallest girl cannot touch the ground from the flexed arm hang position. If standard equipment is not available, a piece of pipe or a doorway gym bar can be used. A stop watch is also needed for testing.

Directions: With an overhand grasp and the assistance of two spotters, the performer should raise the body off the floor so that the chin is above the bars and the elbows are flexed. The performer should hold this position for as long as possible. (See Figure 15 - 2.)

Scoring: The number of seconds to the nearest second that the performer maintains the proper position is recorded as the score. (See Table 15 - 2.)

Additional Pointers: (1) The time should be started as soon as the subject starts in the flexed hang position. (2) The time should be stopped as soon as the chin touches the bar, tilts backward, or drops below the bar. (3) A variation of this test, which is a little easier to score, is to time the individual from the beginning of the flexed-hang position until the arms are fully extended. There is no difficulty in determining when the person reaches the extended position, and it ordinarily occurs rather suddenly after the subject has hung for a while in a partially flexed position. The time rarely goes over two minutes for men and is usually less than a minute for girls.

FIGURE 15 - 2

Flexed Arm Hang

---

*Although the flexed arm hang test is presented for girls, it can be used quite effectively for boys who cannot chin themselves; thereby enabling the tester to obtain some objective measure of arm and shoulder endurance, as well as providing a record of progress.

TABLE 15 - 2

Flexed Arm Hang For Girls[1]

Percentile Scores Based on Age/Test Scores in Seconds

Percentile	Age								Percentile
	10	11	12	13	14	15	16	17	
100th	66	79	64	80	60	74	74	76	100th
95	31	35	30	30	30	33	37	31	95
90	24	25	23	21	22	22	26	25	90
85	21	20	19	18	19	18	19	19	85
80	18	17	15	15	16	16	16	16	80
75	15	16	13	13	13	14	14	14	75
70	13	13	11	12	11	13	12	12	70
65	11	11	10	10	10	11	10	11	65
60	10	10	8	9	9	10	9	10	60
55	9	9	8	8	8	8	8	9	55
50	7	8	6	7	7	8	7	8	50
45	6	6	6	6	6	6	6	7	45
40	6	5	5	5	5	6	5	6	40
35	5	4	4	4	4	4	4	4	35
30	4	4	3	3	3	3	3	4	30
25	3	3	2	2	2	2	2	3	25
20	2	2	1	2	1	1	1	2	20
15	2	1	0	1	1	0	1	0	15
10	1	0	0	0	0	0	0	0	10
5	0	0	0	0	0	0	0	0	5
0	0	0	0	0	0	0	0	0	0

Source: *AAHPER, Youth Fitness Test Manual*, Revised, Washington, D.C., 1966, pp. 27, 64.

Sit-Ups (Bent-knees).[25]

Objective: To measure the endurance of the abdominal muscles.

Age Level: Ages 10 through college.

Sex: Satisfactory for both boys and girls.

Reliability: Has been reported as high as .94.

Validity: Face validity was accepted for this test.

Equipment and Materials: The only equipment required is a mat.

Directions: From a lying position on the back and with the knees flexed so that the heels are about 10 inches from the seat, the performer should interlace the fingers behind the neck and perform sit-ups alternating the left elbow to a touch of the inside right knee and the right elbow to a touch of the inside left knee. The exercise should be repeated as many times as possible.

Scoring: The total number of repetitions is recorded for the score. However, repetitions should not be counted when fingertips do not maintain contact behind the head, when the knees are not touched, or when the pupil pushes off the floor with the elbow.

Additional Pointers: (1) The feet should rest flat on the floor and may be separated a few inches. (2) The back of the hands should touch the mat each time before curling to the sit-up position.

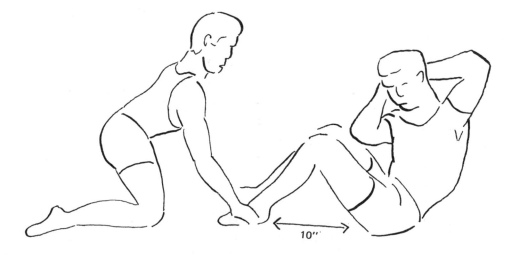

FIGURE 15 - 3

Sit-Ups (Bent Knees)

TABLE 15 - 3

T-Score Norms For Sit-Ups (Bent Knees)

College Men				College Women			
T Scores	Raw Scores	T Scores	Raw Scores	T Scores	Raw Scores	T Scores	Raw Scores
85 — 121		54 — 64		85 — 63		52 — 33	
84 — 119		53 — 62		84 — 62		51 — 32	
83 — 117		52 — 61		83 — 61		50 — 31	
82 — 115		51 — 59		82 — 60		49 — 30	
81 — 113		50 — 57		81 — 59		48 — 29	
80 — 112		49 — 55		80 — 58		46 — 28	
79 — 110		48 — 53		79 — 57		45 — 27	
78 — 108		47 — 51		78 — 56		44 — 26	
77 — 106		46 — 50		77 — 55		43 — 25	
76 — 104		45 — 48		76 — 54		42 — 24	
75 — 102		44 — 46		74 — 53		41 — 23	
74 — 101		43 — 44		73 — 52		40 — 22	
73 — 99		42 — 42		72 — 51		39 — 21	
72 — 97		41 — 40		71 — 50		38 — 20	
71 — 95		40 — 39		70 — 49		36 — 19	
70 — 93		39 — 37		69 — 48		35 — 18	
69 — 92		38 — 35		68 — 47		34 — 17	
68 — 90		37 — 33		67 — 46		33 — 16	
67 — 88		36 — 31		65 — 45		32 — 15	
66 — 86		35 — 30		64 — 44		31 — 14	
65 — 84		34 — 28		63 — 43		30 — 13	
64 — 82		33 — 26		62 — 42		29 — 12	
63 — 80		32 — 24		61 — 41		27 — 11	
62 — 79		31 — 22		60 — 40		26 — 10	
61 — 77		30 — 20		59 — 39		25 — 9	
60 — 75		29 — 19		58 — 38		24 — 8	
59 — 73		28 — 17		57 — 37		23 — 7	
58 — 71		27 — 15		55 — 36		22 — 6	
57 — 70		26 — 13		54 — 35		21 — 5	
56 — 68		25 — 11		53 — 34		20 — 4	
55 — 66							

Based on a limited number of scores from a men's physical education class at Northeast Louisiana State College, Monroe, Louisiana.

Based on a limited number of scores from a women's physical education class at Northeast Louisiana State College, Monroe, Louisiana.

Squat Jumps.

Objective: To measure the endurance of the muscles of the legs.

Age Level: Ages 10 through college.

Sex: Satisfactory for both boys and girls.

Reliability: The author failed to find a reliability coefficient for this test.

Validity: Face validity was accepted for this test.

Equipment and Materials: A mat on the floor.

Directions: With the hands clasped together on top of the head and one foot a step ahead of the other, the performer squats down until the seat nearly touches the rear heel and then jumps upward extending the legs and switching the position of the feet. The exercise is continued for as many repetitions as possible without rest. (See Figure 15 - 4.)

Scoring: One point is scored for each correct repetition. (See Table 15 - 5.)

Additional Pointers: (1) If the performer stops to rest, the score is terminated at that point. (2) The feet must come off the floor on each jump and the legs must be extended. (3) The performer should be cautioned to squat down in a controlled manner and not to *drop* down. By dropping, the ligaments of the knees may possibly be damaged due to the force applied. (4) This exercise produces considerable soreness in the calves and thighs, therefore some conditioning prior to the day of testing is advised.

FIGURE 15 - 4

Squat Jumps

TABLE 15 - 5

T-Score Norms for Squat Jumps

College Men								
	T-Scores	Raw Scores		T-Scores	Raw Scores		T-Scores	Raw Scores
	100 — 95			66 — 68			32 — 34	
	99			65 — 67			31 — 33	
	98 — 94			64 — 66			30 — 32	
	97		Good	63 — 65			29 — 31	
	96 — 93			62 — 64			28 — 30	
	95			61 — 63			27 — 29	
	94 — 92			60 — 62			26 — 28	
	93 —			59 — 61			25 — 27	
	92 — 91			58 — 60			24 — 26	
	91			57 — 59			23 — 25	
	90 — 90			56 — 58			22 — 24	
	89			55 — 57			21 — 23	
Excellent	88 — 89			54 — 56			20 — 22	
	87			53 — 55			19 — 21	
	86 — 88			52 — 54			18 — 20	
	85 — 87			51 — 53			17 — 19	
	84 — 86		Average	50 — 52			16 — 18	
	83 — 85			49 — 51			15 — 17	
	82 — 84			48 — 50		Very	14 — 16	
	81 — 83			47 — 49		Poor	13 — 15	
	80 — 82			46 — 48			12 — 14	
	79 — 81			45 — 47			11 — 13	
	78 — 80			44 — 46			10 — 12	
	77 — 79			43 — 45			9 — 11	
	76 — 78			42 — 44			8 — 10	
	75 — 77			41 — 43			7 — 9	
	74 — 76			40 — 42			6 — 8	
	73 — 75			39 — 41			5 — 7	
	72 — 74		Poor	38 — 40			4 — 6	
	71 — 73			37 — 39			3 — 5	
	70 — 72			36 — 38			2 — 4	
	69 — 71			35 — 37			1 — 3	
	68 — 70			34 — 36				
	67 — 69			33 — 35				

Source: Dept. of the Army, *Physical Training,* Washington D.C.: Headquarters, Dept. of Army, Oct., 1957, pp. 197-201.

Push-Ups.

Objective: To measure the endurance of the arms and shoulder girdle.

Age Level: Ages 10 through college.

Sex: Satisfactory for boys only.

Reliability: The author failed to find a coefficient of reliability reported for this test.

Validity: Face validity was accepted for this test.

Equipment and Materials: A mat on the floor.

Directions: From a straight arm front leaning rest position, the performer lowers the body until the chest touches the mat and then pushes upward to the straight arm support. The exercise is continued for as many repetitions as possible without rest. The body must not sag, nor pike upward, but maintain a straight line throughout the exercise. (See Figure 15 - 5.)

Scoring: The score is the number of correct push-ups executed. (See Table 15 - 6.)

Additional Pointers: (1) The score is terminated if the performer stops to rest. (2) If the chest does not touch or if the arms are not completely extended on an execution, the trial does not count. (3) In order to rigidly supervise the correct execution of the test, the tester or an assistant should lie on the right side of the performer and place his right hand, palm upward, under the performer's chest. The tester's left hand should be placed lightly on the performer's elbow. In this manner the tester can easily determine if the chest was lowered enough and if the arms reached complete extension.

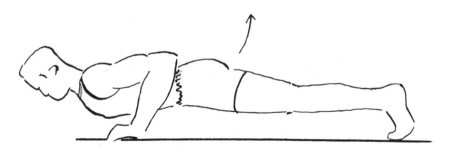

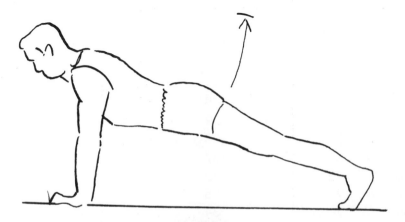

FIGURE 15 - 5

Push-Ups

TABLE 15 - 6

T-Score Norms for Push-Ups

College Men								
	T-Scores	Raw — Scores		T-Scores	Raw — Scores		T-Scores	Raw — Scores
	100 — 60			68 — 44			37	
	99			67			36 — 15	
	98 — 59			66 — 43			35	
	97			65 — 42			34 — 14	
	96 — 58			64 — 41			33	
	95		Good	63 — 40			32 — 13	
	94 — 57			62 — 39			31	
	93			61 — 38			30 — 12	
	92 — 56			60 — 37			29	
	91			59 — 36			28 — 11	
	90 — 55			58 — 35			27	
	89			57 — 34			26 — 10	
Excellent	88 — 54			56 — 33			25	
	87			55 — 32			24 — 9	
	86 — 53			54 — 31			23	
	85			53 — 30			22 — 8	
	84 — 52			52 — 29			21	
	83			51 — 28			20 — 7	
	82 — 51		Average	50 — 27			19	
	81			49 — 26			18 — 6	
	80 — 50			48 — 25		Very	17	
	79			47 — 24		Poor	16 — 5	
	78 — 49			46 — 23			15	
	77			45 — 22			14 — 4	
	76 — 48			44 — 21			13	
	75			43 — 20			12 — 3	
	74 — 47			42 — 19			11	
	73			41 — 18			10 — 2	
	72 — 46			40 — 17			9	
	71			39			8 — 1	
	70 — 45			38 — 16				
	69							

"Reproduced by permission of the Department of the Army."
Source: Dept. of Army, *Physical Training,* Washington, D.C.: Headquarters, Dept. of Army, Oct., 1957, pp. 197-201.

Modified Push-Ups.

Objective: To measure the endurance of the arms and shoulder girdle.

Age Level: Ages 10 through college.

Sex: Satisfactory for girls only.

Reliability: Has been reported as high as .93.

Validity: Has been reported as high as .72 with the Rogers Short Index.[56]

Equipment and Materials: A mat on the floor.

Directions: (See Figure 15 - 6.) With the knees bent at right angles and the hands on the floor (directly under the shoulders), the performer lowers her body to the floor until the chest touches, and then she pushes back to the starting position. The exercise is continued for as many repetitions as possible without rest. The body must not sag but maintain a straight line throughout the trial.

Scoring: The score is the number of correct push-ups executed. (See Table 15 - 7.)

Additional Pointers: (1) The score is terminated if the performer stops to rest. (2) If the chest does not touch or if the arms are not completely extended on an execution, the trial does not count.

FIGURE 15 - 6

Modified Push-Ups

TABLE 15 - 7

Scale Score Norms for Modified Push-Ups

High School Girls	
Scale Scores	Raw Scores
100	61
95	58
90	54
85	51
80	47
75	43
70	39
65	36
60	32
55	28
50	25
45	21
40	17
35	13
30	10
25	6
20	2
15	1
10	0
5	0
0	0

Based upon scores from 25 high schools.

Eleanor Metheny (Chairman, Committee Report): Physical Performance Levels for High School Girls. *Journal of Health & Physical Education,* Vol. 16, No. 6, June, 1945.

Burpee (Squat Thrust).

Objective: To measure the general muscular endurance of the body.

Age Level: Ages 10 through college.

Sex: Satisfactory for both boys and girls.

Reliability: An r of .97 was found for this test when subjects were tested on separate days.

Validity: Face validity was accepted.

Equipment and Materials: Mat on floor.

Directions: (See Figure 15 - 7.) From a standing position (1) bend at the knees and waist and place the hands on the floor in front of the feet, (2) thrust the legs backward to a front leaning rest position, (3) return to the squat position as in the first count, and (4) stand erect. From the signal *go* repeat this exercise at a constant rate of movement for as long as possible.

Scoring: The score is the number of correct repetitions executed. (See Table 15 - 8.) The score is recorded to the nearest whole number.

Additional Pointers: (1) The score is terminated if the performer stops to rest. (2) Repetitions which are incorrect are not counted toward the score.

Start   1   2

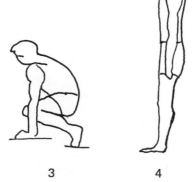

3   4

FIGURE 15 - 7

Burpee (Squat Thrust)

TABLE 15 - 8

T-Score Norms for Burpee (Squat Thrust)

College Men				College Women			
T Scores	Raw Scores	T Scores	Raw Scores	T Scores	Raw Scores	T Scores	Raw Scores
85 — 157		54 — 78		85 — 56		54 — 28	
84 — 155		53 — 76		84 — 55		53 — 27	
83 — 152		52 — 73		83 — 54		52 — 26	
82 — 150		51 — 71		82 — 53		51 — 25	
81 — 147		50 — 68		81 — 52		50 — 24	
80 — 145		49 — 65		79 — 51		49 — 23	
79 — 142		48 — 62		78 — 50		48 — 22	
78 — 139		47 — 60		77 — 49		46 — 21	
77 — 137		46 — 57		76 — 48		45 — 20	
76 — 134		45 — 55		75 — 47		44 — 19	
75 — 132		44 — 52		74 — 46		43 — 18	
74 — 129		43 — 50		73 — 45		42 — 17	
73 — 127		42 — 47		72 — 44		41 — 16	
72 — 124		41 — 44		71 — 43		40 — 15	
71 — 122		40 — 42		70 — 42		39 — 14	
70 — 119		39 — 39		68 — 41		38 — 13	
69 — 116		38 — 37		67 — 40		37 — 12	
68 — 114		37 — 34		66 — 39		36 — 11	
67 — 111		36 — 32		65 — 38		34 — 10	
66 — 109		35 — 29		64 — 37		33 — 9	
65 — 106		34 — 26		63 — 36		32 — 8	
64 — 104		33 — 24		62 — 35		31 — 7	
63 — 101		32 — 21		61 — 34		30 — 6	
62 — 98		31 — 19		60 — 33		29 — 5	
61 — 96		30 — 16		59 — 32		28 — 4	
60 — 93		29 — 14		57 — 31		27 — 3	
59 — 91		28 — 11		56 — 30		26 — 2	
58 — 88		27 — 8		55 — 29		25 — 1	
57 — 86		26 — 6					
56 — 83		25 — 3					
55 — 81							

Based on a limited number of scores from a men's physical education class at Northeast Louisiana State College, Monroe, Louisiana.

Based on a limited number of scores from a women's physical education class at Northeast Louisiana State College, Monroe, Louisiana.

Endurance Dips.

<u>Objective</u>: To measure the endurance of the arms and shoulder girdle.

<u>Age Level</u>: Ages 10 through college.

<u>Sex</u>: Satisfactory for boys only.

<u>Reliability</u>: An r as high as .90 has been reported for this test when subjects were tested on separate days.

<u>Validity</u>: Face validity was accepted for this test.

<u>Equipment and Materials</u>: Two parallel bars raised to a height so that all subjects are supported freely above the ground (in a lowered bent arm support) are used.

<u>Directions</u>: The performer should assume a straight arm support between the bars and lower downward until the elbows form a right angle. He should then push back to a straight arm support and continue the exercise for as many repetitions as possible. (See Figure 15 - 8.)

<u>Scoring</u>: The score is the number of correct repetitions executed. (See Table 15 - 9.)

<u>Additional Pointers</u>: (1) The score is terminated if the performer stops to rest. (2) The performer should refrain from swinging or kicking in returning to the straight arm support position. (3) The tester should extend his fist upward from inside the bar so that the performer's shoulder will touch it notifying both the student and the tester that the elbows reached the right angle. (4) The tester's other arm can be used to hold across the front of the performer's thighs in the event of swinging, and at other times the tester can lightly grasp the performer's elbow to stress full arm extension. (5) If the parallel bars are lower at one end than the other, it facilitates the testing of subjects of different heights.

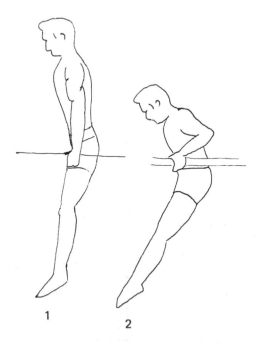

FIGURE 15 - 8

Endurance Dips

TABLE 15 - 9

T-Score Norms for Endurance Dips

Raw Scores	T-Scores
24	77
23	75
22	73
21	71
20	69
19	67
18	65
17	63
16	61
15	59
14	57
13	55
12	53
11	51
10	49
9	47
8	45
7	43
6	40
5	38
4	36
3	34
2	32
1	30
0	28

Based on the scores of 100 male students in physical education classes at East Texas State University, Commerce, Texas.

Repetitive Press Test with Spring Scale.[25]

Objective: To measure the endurance of the arms and shoulders in a mid-military press type exercise.

Age Level: Ages 15 through college.

Sex: Satisfactory for both boys and girls.

Reliability: An r of .92 was found when girls were tested at 1/3 of their body weight.

Validity: Face validity was accepted.

Equipment and Materials: The equipment needed is the spring scale, hook and bar, chains, and a small but sturdy wooden platform to provide better balance during the test. (See Spring Scale Strength Test Items.)

Directions: Same as for the press test under spring-scale strength test items except that the performer is required to register at least ½ of his body weight (1/3 for girls) on the scale at approximately two seconds at a cadence of push-one, push-two, etc. for as many repetitions as possible. The press must be steady each time until it reaches the desired score. The tester should maintain the cadence and reset the dial indicator before each press.

Scoring: The score is the number of repetitions the performer can register the needle indicator above ½ of his body weight or for girls 1/3 of her body weight.

Additional Pointers: (1) The test is terminated on the third successive failure to register the proper score. (2) The score is terminated when the performer is unable to keep up with the cadence. (3) An alternate test would be to use ½ of the performer's maximum strength press (1/3 of maximum for girls). However, maximum strength is much more variable from day to day than is body weight. Also, we never know for certain when we have secured maximum effort from our students.

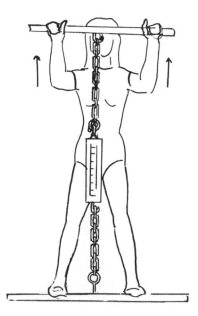

FIGURE 15 - 9

Repetitive Press Test with Spring Scale

TABLE 15 - 10

T-Score Norms for Repetitive Press Test with Spring Scale

College Women					
T-Scores	—	Raw Scores	T-Scores	—	Raw Scores
85	—	88	57	—	41
84	—	87	56	—	39
83	—	85	55	—	38
82	—	83	54	—	36
81		81	53		34
80		80	52	—	32
79	—	78	51	—	31
78		76	50	—	29
77	—	75	49	—	27
76	—	73	48	—	26
75	—	71	47	—	24
74	—	70	46	—	22
73	—	68	45	—	21
72	—	66	44	—	19
71	—	65	43	—	17
70	—	63	42	—	16
69	—	61	41	—	14
68	—	60	40	—	12
67	—	58	39	—	11
66	—	56	38	—	9
65	—	54	37	—	7
64	—	53	36	—	5
63	—	51	35	—	4
62	—	49	34	—	3
61	—	48	33	—	2
60	—	46	31	—	1
59	—	44			
58	—	43			

Based upon a limited number of scores from a women's physical education class at Northeast Louisiana State College, Monroe, Louisiana.

Problems Associated with Muscular Endurance Testing

Several of the problems associated with muscular endurance testing are listed as follows:

1. Definite guide lines must be followed when scoring muscular endurance tests, since slight deviations from the correct form and procedure may greatly affect the final results.

2. Since motivational factors greatly influence results, it is most important that the tester standardize as much as possible the presence of motivation during endurance testing so that all students are scored on the same basis. Furthermore, if the scores are to be used as norms, a notation should be made if a special type of motivation was utilized.

3. Certain muscular endurance tests take a considerable amount of time to administer, and as a result, a time limit is sometimes placed on them. However, this is not always justifiable, since low correlations are often found between the timed and untimed tests. Perhaps a better approach would be to use barbell plates in terms of a certain percent of each performer's body weight so that the repetitions will not be so numerous. Clarke* suggested, in his studies on ergography, that a load and cadence that will accomplish the most work in a relatively short amount of time be considered as a criterion.

4. On some occasions testers have used dynamic muscular endurance exercises in a training program, but have measured their effectiveness with a static endurance test and vice versa. However, it should be recognized that the most valid measure of dynamic endurance training is a dynamic endurance test, and that, likewise, the most valid measure of static endurance training is a static endurance test.

5. Many of the norms presently used are out of date or were set up on a limited number of cases. Thus, there is a need for the construction of new norms for both old and new tests.

Findings and Conclusions from Muscular Endurance Measurement and Research

Muscular endurance has been measured and studied in various ways. For example, it has been studied by the following methods: (1) repetitive static method where maximal or submaximal contractions are repeated in cadence (usually every two or three seconds) for maximum repetitions;[10,17,45] (2) the dynamic method by varying the load in proportion to maximum isotonic strength and then performing repetitive isotonic movements;[20,38,54] (3) the dynamic method by varying the load in proportion to maximum isometric strength and then performing isotonic movements;[4,12,37,41] (4) the timed static method by varying the load in porportion to maximum isometric strength and then holding for as long as possible.[19,38,48,49,52]

At the present time conflicting concepts exist concerning the value of isometric exercises in increasing muscular endurance. One concept indicates that muscle endurance is associated with capillarization, and that capillarization is enhanced by rapid contraction movements so that the blood flow in the muscle is increased. Therefore, researchers have

---

*H. Harrison Clarke, and others, "Precision of Elbow Flexion Ergography Under Varying Degrees of Muscular Fatigue," *Archives of Physical Medicine,* Vol. 33 (May, 1952), pp. 279-288.

indicated that since isometric contraction restricts the flow of blood to the muscle, it is not effective in producing capillarization and the development of endurance.[2,3,9,11] A second concept indicates that while endurance is dependent to some extent upon circulation, muscular endurance is also influenced by strength and will improve no matter how strength is developed. There are several studies which support this concept.[4,14,23,34,42]

Research in various exercise programs reveals the following findings concerning muscular endurance:

1. Weight training (dynamic overload) programs will improve performance on muscular endurance exercises.[5,6,8,33] Moreover, muscular endurance performance is influenced by the strength of the individual.[7,13,28,51]

2. Isotonic exercises are more effective than isometric exercises in the development of muscular endurance.[37,44,50,53] Furthermore, a faster rate of repeated contractions produces the greater endurance.[32,37]

3. In contradiction to the above finding, several researchers have found both isometric and isotonic programs to be equally effective in improving muscular endurance.[4,14,23,34,42] While Meadows[42] found both methods significantly increased dipping and chinning endurance, he found the isotonic method superior in the chinning test. In addition Swegan[50] found that isotonic exercises increased muscular endurance significantly on eight tests, whereas isometric exercises significantly increased such performance in only one of the eight tests.

4. Various types of motivational techniques employed during testing periods will significantly increase muscular endurance performance.[16,18,24,26,27,43] Two interesting studies by Johnson and Kramer[26,27] revealed improved endurance performance during hypnosis.

5. Concerning the effect of warming up before endurance performance, no significant effect was observed as a result of passive heating of the muscle,[46] or as a result of active warm-ups using hypnosis to control the psychological variable.[39]

6. There are conflicting reports concerning the effect of the cross transfer of training on muscular endurance. One study found that both the exercised and non-exercised arm improved in strength, while only the exercised arm significantly improved in endurance.[40] However, a more recent study found that when endurance in the trained limb was increased to a high level, the endurance in the untrained limb increased about 28% of that level.[22]

7. Several studies have indicated that muscular endurance is not directly proportional to the development of maximum strength.[36,55,51] Thus, a great increase in muscular endurance is not necessarily accompanied by an equal increase in strength itself.

8. Excess weight is a handicap to students in performing endurance exercises such as push-ups, pull-ups, and squat jumps.[35,47]

Several studies have been conducted to determine proper procedures for endurance testing. The following points should be noted:

1. Since reverse grasp chin-ups give greater results than regular grasp chin-ups, they must not be used interchangeably on chin-up tests.[15,31] Also, hip or kick action should not be allowed, since they will increase chin-up scores.[15]

2. Karpovich found low correlations between leg lifts and sit-ups,[29] and between timed sit-ups and untimed sit-ups,[30] indicating that such items should not be used interchangeably in test batteries.

3. The AAHPER Youth Fitness Test Committee found the flexed arm hang test more efficient and reliable than the modified pull-up test for girls.[1]

BIBLIOGRAPHY

1. AAHPER: *Youth Fitness Test Manual,* Revised ed., Washington, D.C., AAHPER, 1965.

2. Asmussen, E., "Positive and Negative Muscular Work," *Acta Physiol Scandinavica,* 28:364-382, 1952.

3. _____, "Training of Muscular Strength by Static and Dynamic Activity," Kongressen *Voredrog, Lingiaden,* Stockholm, 11:22-23, 1949.

4. Baer, Adrian D., and others, "Effects of Various Exercise Programs on Isometric Tension, Endurance, and Reaction Time in the Human," *Arch. Phy. Med. and Rehab.,* 36:495-502, 1955.

5. Berger, Richard A., "The Effect of Varied Weight Training Programs on Strength and Endurance," (Microcarded Master's Thesis, University of Illinois, 1960).

6. Bready, Charles F., "A Study of the Effects of Heavy Resistance Training Upon the Pattern of Muscular Development as Indicated by Strength, Endurance, and Girth of the Right Elbow Flexors," (Microcarded Master's Thesis, University of Maryland, 1961).

7. Burke, William E., "A Study of the Relationship of Age of Strength and Endurance in Gripping," (Microcarded Doctor's Thesis, University of Iowa, 1952, p. 49).

8. Capen, Edward K., "The Effect of Systematic Weight Training on Power, Strength, and Endurance," *Research Quarterly,* 21:83-94, May, 1950.

9. Clarke, David H., "Energy Cost of Isometric Exercise," *Research Quarterly,* 31:3-6, March, 1960.

10. _____, "Strength Recovery from Static and Dynamic Muscular Fatigue," *Research Quarterly,* 33:349-355, October, 1962.

11. Clarke, H. Harrison, "Development of Volitional Muscle Strength as Related to Fitness," *Exercise and Fitness,* Chicago: The Athletic Institute, 1959.

12. _____, and others, "Strength and Endurance (Conditioning) Effects of Exhaustive Exercise of the Elbow Flexor Muscles," *Journal Assoc. Phy. Ment. Rehabilitation,* 8:184188, 1954.

13. Cook, Ellsworth B., and Robert J. Wherry, "Statistical Evaluation of Physical Fitness," *Research Quarterly,* 21:94-111, May, 1950.

14. Dennison, J. D., and others, "Effect of Isometric and Isotonic Exercise Programs Upon Muscular Endurance," *Research Quarterly,* 32:348-353, October, 1961.

15. DeWitt, R. T., "A Comparative Study of Three Types of Chinning Tests," *Research Quarterly,* 15:240-248, October, 1944.

16. Gerdes, Glen R., "The Effects of Various Motivational Techniques Upon Performance in Selected Physical Tests," (Microcarded Doctor's Dissertation, Indiana University, 1958, pp. 88-92).

17. Grose, Joel E., "Depression of Muscle Fatigue Curves by Heat and Cold," *Research Quarterly,* 29:19-31, March, 1958.

18. Hall, D. M., "Endurance Tests for 4-H Club Members," *Research Quarterly,* 22:48, March, 1951.

19. Hansen, J. W., "The Effect of Sustained Isometric Muscle Contraction on Various Muscle Functions," *Int. Z. Angew, Physiol. Einschl. Arbeilphysiol.,* 19:430-434, 1963.

20. _____ , "The Training Effect of Dynamic Maximal Resistance Exercises," *Int. Z. Angew. Physiol. Arbeilphysiol.,* 19:420-424, 1963.

21. Hellebrandt, F. A., and S. J. Hautz, "Mechanisms of Muscle Training in Man," *Physical Therapy Review,* 36:371-383, 1956.

22. Hodgkins, J., "Influence of Unilateral Endurance Training on Contri-lateral Limb," *Journal of Applied Physiology,* 16:991-993, 1961.

23. Howell, Maxwell L., and others, "Effect of Isometric and Isotonic Exercise Programs Upon Muscular Endurance," *Research Quarterly*, 33:539, December, 1962.

24. Johnson, Barry L., "The Effect of Motivational Testing Situations on an Endurance Test," (Laboratory Experiment, Northeast Louisiana State College, Monroe, Louisiana, 1963).

25. _____ , "Practical Tests of Muscular Endurance," (Unpublished Study, Northeast Louisiana State College, Monroe, Louisiana, 1967).

26. Johnson, Warren R., and Kramer, George F., "Effects of Different Types of Hypnotic Suggestions upon Physical Performance," *Research Quarterly,* 32:522-529, December, 1961.

27. _____ , "Effects of Stereotyped Non-Hypnotic, Hypnotic, and Post-hypnotic Suggestions upon Strength, Power, and Endurance," *Research Quarterly,* 32:522-529, December, 1961.

28. Karpovich, Peter V., "Fatigue and Endurance," Supplement to the *Research Quarterly,* 12:416, May, 1941.

29. _____ , and others, "Relation Between Leg-Lift and Sit-Up," *Research Quarterly,* 17:21-24, March, 1946.

30. _____ , "Studies of the AAF Physical Fitness Test: Selection of a Time Limit for Sit-ups," Project No. 245, Report No. 3, AAF School of Aviation Medicine, Randolph Field, Texas, July, 1944.

31. _____ , "The Effect of Reverse and Forward Grips Upon Performance in Chinning," Project No. 178, Report No. 1, AAF School of Aviation Medicine, Randolph Field, Texas, October, 1943.

32. Kincaid, Don. G., "The Specificity of Muscular Endurance Following Different Rates of Training," (Microcarded Master's Thesis, Pennsylvania State University, 1959, p. 53).

33. Kusinitz, Ivan, and Clifford E. Keeney, "Effects of Progressive Weight Training on Health and Physical Fitness of Adolescent Boys," *Research Quarterly,* 29:294, October, 1958.

34. Lawther, John E., "The Pennsylvania State University Studies on Strength Decrement, Maintenance, and Related Aspects," *61st Annual Proceedings,* College Physical Education Association, 1958.

35. Loveless, James C., "Relationship of the War-Time Navy Physical Fitness Test to Age, Height, and Weight," *Research Quarterly,* Vol. 23: October, 1952, p. 347.

36. McCloy, C. H., "A New Method of Scoring Chinning and Dipping," *Research Quarterly,* 2:132-143, December, 1931.

37. McCraw, Lynn V., and Stan Burnham, "Resistive Exercises in the Development of Muscular Strength and Endurance," *Research Quarterly,* 37:81, March, 1966.

38. Martens, Rainer, and Brian J. Sharkey, "Relationship of Phasic and Static Strength and Endurance," *Research Quarterly,* 37:435-436, October, 1966.

39. Massey, Benjamin, and others, "Effect of Warm-up Exercise Upon Muscular Performance Using Hypnosis to Control the Psychological Variable," *Research Quarterly,* 32:63-71, March, 1961.

40. Mathews, Donald K., and others, "Cross Transfer Effects of Training on Strength and Endurance," *Research Quarterly,* 27:206-212, May, 1956.

41. _____ , and Robert Kruse, "Effects of Isometric and Isotonic Exercises on Elbow Flexor Muscle Groups," *Research Quarterly,* 28:26-37, 1957.

42. Meadows, P. E., "The Effect of Isotonic and Isometric Muscle Contraction Training on Speed, Force, and Strength," (Microcarded Doctoral Dissertation, University of Illinois, Urbana, 1959).

43. Nelson, Jack K., "An Analysis of the Effects of Applying Various Motivational Situations to College Men Subjected to a Stressful Physical Performance," (Microcarded Doctoral Dissertation, University of Oregon, Eugene, 1962).

44. Petersen, Flemming B., "Muscle Training by Static, Concentric, and Eccentric Contraction," *Acta Physiol. Scandinavica,* 48:406-416, 1960.

45. Rich, George Q. III, "Muscular Fatigue Curves of Boys and Girls," *Research Quarterly,* 31:485-498, October, 1960.

46. Sedgwick, A. W., and H. R. Wahalen, "Effect of Passive Warm-up on Muscular Strength and Endurance," *Research Quarterly,* 35:45-59, March, 1964.

47. Sills, Frank D., and Peter W. Everett, "The Relationship of Extreme Somatotypes to Performance in Motor and Strength Test," *Research Quarterly,* 21:223-228, May, 1953.

48. Start, K. B., and Rosemary Holmes, "Local Muscle Endurance with Open and Occluded Intramuscular Circulation," *Journal of Appl. Physiology,* 18:804-807, 1963.

49. _____ , and J. S. Graham, "Relationship Between the Relative and Absolute Isometric Endurance of an Isolated Muscle Group," *Research Quarterly,* 35:193-194, May, 1964.

50. Swegan, Donald B., "The Comparison of Static Contraction with Standard Weight Training in Effect on Certain Movement Speeds and Endurances," (Microcarded Doctoral Dissertation, The Pennsylvania State University, University Park, January 1957, pp. 137-140).

51. Tuttle, W. W., and others, "Relation of Maximum Back and Leg Strength to Back and Leg Strength Endurance," *Research Quarterly,* 26:96-106, March, 1955.

52. _____, "Relation of Maximum Grip Strength to Grip Strength Endurance," *Journal of Appl. Physiology,* 2:663-670, 1950.

53. Wallace, Joseph, "The Development of Muscular Strength and Muscular Endurance through Isotonic and Isometric Exercise," *New Zealand Journal of Physical Education,* 14:3-9, 1958.

54. Walters, C. Etta, and others, "Effect of Short Bouts of Isometric and Isotonic Contractions on Muscular Strength and Endurance," *Am. J. Physical Med.,* 39:131-141, 1960.

55. Wedemeyer, Ross, "A Differential Analysis of Sit-ups for Strength and Muscular Endurance," *Research Quarterly,* 17:40-47, March, 1946.

56. Wilson, Marjorie, "Study of Arm and Shoulder Girdle Strength of College Women in Selected Tests," *Research Quarterly,* 15:258, October, 1944.

Chapter XVI

THE MEASUREMENT OF CARDIOVASCULAR CONDITION

To most people being in *good shape* is exemplified by such feats as climbing several flights of stairs without being red in the face and breathing hard; or the ability to comfortably resume hiking, or cycling, or jogging after a scant few minutes rest. To put it in slightly more technical language, it means the ability of the circulatory and respiratory system to adjust to and recover from the effects of exercise or work. It is unquestionably one of the key components of physical fitness, and to some physical educators it is the single most indicative measure of a person's physical condition. The most accurate measure of this quality is generally considered to be maximal oxygen uptake, which measures the amount of oxygen consumed per kilogram of body weight per minute of exercise. However, this measurement requires expensive equipment, and the testing is time-consuming and rigorous. Therefore, these factors place such a measuring technique out of reach of most schools and colleges.

There have been a number of tests devised to measure cardiovascular function. Some tests simply require the subject to perform a task that calls for sustained total body movement. Usually these tests involve running a prescribed distance; and the subject's cardiovascular endurance is measured by the elapsed time required to cover the distance. This pragmatic approach has been commonly employed in physical fitness test batteries. Some of these test items are described in Chapter XVII.

Other tests have sought to determine cardiovascular fitness through measures of pulse rate and blood pressure under various conditions involving changes in body position and before and after different degrees of work. Such tests are based on the accepted principle that a physically fit person has more efficient circulatory and respiratory systems than an untrained person. The conditioned individual has a greater stroke volume which enables more blood to be pumped each stroke, thus enabling fewer strokes per minute to do the work. The trained person is also able to achieve fuller oxygen-carbon dioxide exchange resulting in more available oxygen taken from the air; a slower rate of breathing; and a lower rate of lactic acid formation than is found in the average individual.

Moreover, while heart rate will, of course, increase with exercise, the pulse of the person in poor condition will increase much faster than in the trained person. The pulse of the untrained individual increases considerably upon moving from a reclining to standing position, whereas the person in good condition will show a very slight increase, if any. The systolic pressure of the trained person rises when he stands, and the poorly trained person's systolic pressure does not, and, in fact, may even fall.[8] The heart rate, blood pressure, and breathing rate of the person in good physical condition return to the pre-exercise levels more quickly after exercise than the rates do of the individual in poor condition.

Utilization of Cardiovascular Tests

Cardiovascular tests may be given for any of several purposes within the school setting. One purpose, and probably the most common, is as part of a physical fitness test battery in classifying and rating students for assessing status and improvement. In this capacity the test is generally in the form of a distance run or endurance exercise rather than of physiological measurements.

Another purpose may be for screening. A note of caution should be sounded here. Certainly such a test should not be one which requires the subject to exert maximal effort. Furthermore, such a test should not be considered as a substitute for a medical examination.

Cardiovascular tests may be utilized by the physical educator for the purpose of research. This may be in the form of observational research in which measures are taken of status or for establishing norms; or, tests may be given before and after a training program in order to measure improvement.

Perhaps one of the most important uses of cardiovascular tests in which pulse rate and blood pressure are measured is as an educational device. The tests may be given in conjunction with a health unit, a biology class or as a special physical education activity. In any case such tests can be very effective for their motivational properties and for the information that is derived concerning the circulatory and respiratory systems.

While there are quite a number of tests of cardiovascular condition, only a very few will be presented here. The reasons for this are simply that most of the tests are either too involved, or too time-consuming for use in physical education classes, or require expensive equipment. The tests presented in this first section can all be administered to students in groups.

Harvard Step Test.[5,6]

Objective: The Harvard Step Test was developed by Brouha for the purpose of measuring physical fitness for muscular work and the ability to recover from work.

Sex and Age Level: The test was originally designed for young men of college age.

Validity: Brouha tested 2,200 male students at Harvard in the original validation of the step test. Athletes were found to score considerably higher than non-athletes and their scores improved with training and decreased after training. Taddonio and Karpovich[30] also found supporting evidence as to its validity.

Test Equipment and Materials Needed: A stable bench or platform 20 inches high and a watch with a second hand are the only equipment needed. A large wall clock with a second hand may be used effectively for group testing.

Directions: The subject stands before the bench and on the command to begin steps onto the bench with one foot, then the other; on the third count he steps down with one foot, then the other. The cadence is 30 steps per minute, which means that he mounts the bench and steps down 30 times in one minute. The cadence for the placement of each foot would be 120 times per minute. The body should be erect when he steps onto the bench. There is no regulation regarding which foot the subject should lead off with, nor is there any requirement to alternate the feet periodically. This is left up to the individual who may or may not alternate. The subject continues to exercise at the prescribed cadence for 5 minutes, unless he feels that he must stop before then because of exhaustion. As soon as he stops exercising, he sits down and remains seated and quiet throughout the pulse counts.

There are two forms of the test, the long form and the short form. In the long form the pulse is counted 1 to 1½, 2 to 2½, and 3 to 3½ minutes after exercise. In the short form the pulse is taken only once, 1 to 1½ minutes after exercise.

Scoring: For the long form a Physical Efficiency Index (PEI) is computed with this formula:

$$\text{PEI} = \frac{\text{Duration of exercise in seconds} \times 100}{2 \times \text{sum of pulse counts in recovery}}$$

Example: A subject exercises for the full five minutes (300 seconds). His pulse counts are 83 for 1 to 1½ min.; 67 for 2 to 2½ min.; and 50 for 3 to 3½ minutes after exercise. His PEI score is:

$$\text{PEI} = \frac{300 \times 100}{2 \times 200} = \frac{30,000}{400} = 75$$

The following standards of performance were established after testing approximately 8,000 college students.

Below 55 . . . . . . Poor
55 to 64 . . . . . . Low Average
65 to 79 . . . . . . High Average
80 to 89 . . . . . . Good
Above 90 . . . . . . Excellent

For the short form the scoring formula is as follows:

$$\text{PEI} = \frac{\text{Duration of exercise in seconds} \times 100}{5.5 \times \text{pulse count for 1 to 1½ minutes after exercise}}$$

A table (Table 16 - 1) for scoring the short form of the Harvard Step Test has been developed. The score in arbitrary units is based on duration of exercise and the rate of the recovery pulse. The following norms have been established for interpretation:

Below 50 . . . . . . Poor
50 - 80 . . . . Average
Above 80 . . . . . . Good

Additional Pointers: (1) The short form correlates very highly with the long form[24] and in the interest of time may be preferable to the long form. (2) The pulse may be taken at either the radial artery or the carotid artery. In both cases three fingers should be used to feel the pulse, and not one's thumb due to the possible confusion arising from feeling one's own pulse rate transmitted through the thumb. The carotid pulse is located below the ear at the base of the neck. The radial pulse is found in the hollow on the thumb side of the wrist. (3) An arrangement for mass testing that has been found to work effectively is to divide the class into groups of three. Three test administrations are of course required. While one of each group is exercising, the other two serve as counters. If each counter records the pulse rate separately without consultation, an objectivity coefficient can be obtained, if desired. (4) When utilizing the above system of testing, it is well to establish some criteria to follow in cases where the two counters disagree. The tester may set an arbitrary number such as 5 or 7, for example, which would be the maximum difference allowable. If the difference is more than that, the subject is retested. A practical exception to the latter would be when one of the counters admitted that he simply lost the count. (5) Obviously, the key to accurate testing of this kind requires a period of orientation and practice. This orientation period is not only beneficial for the purposes of counting but also for the students for becoming accustomed to the cadence and nature of the exercise. (6) It must be stressed that the person exercising and the counters remain silent throughout the counting period. (7) During the exercise the tester can help the subjects to maintain the cadence by calling out UP, UP, DOWN, DOWN. Even more effective is to make a tape recording of the cadence. This allows the tester to supervise all aspects of the testing more closely. (8) When a subject is forced to stop prior to the end of the five minutes, it is imperative that his duration of exercise be recorded and that the timing for the pulse taking after exercise be started. A large wall clock with a second hand is very valuable in these cases. It is a simple matter for the counters to record the time at the start of the exercise, record the time at which the subject is forced to stop, and to begin taking the pulse a minute afterwards for 30 seconds, and so on. Trained assistants may also serve in this capacity.

Safety Precuations: (1) The principal safety factor is inherent in the test itself — which is, that the test is rather strenuous and might be dangerous for someone in poor health. This underlines the importance of medical examinations for all students and cautions against giving the step test to persons known to have some abnormalities. (2) About the only other safety precaution involves the possibility of the subject missing his footing and hitting his knee against the bench. Padding of some kind is recommended. Sometimes a mat folded over a bench or bleacher will provide for the exact 20 inch height as well as will serve as protective padding.

Gallagher and Brouha Test for Secondary School Boys.[12]

Gallagher and Brouha experimented with different heights of benches to be used for testing boys 12 to 18 years of age in order to account for the differences in body size. The body surface area in square meters is determined by use of the nomographic chart shown in Figure 16 - 1.

Boys having a body surface area of less than 1.85 square meters use an 18 inch bench; boys with body surface areas of 1.85 and over utilize a 20 inch bench. Example: A 14 year old boy is 5′4″ tall and weighs 125 pounds. The body surface area is obtained by placing a ruler on the nomographic chart connecting his height and weight. In this case the point at which the ruler crosses the middle column is 1.58 square meters. Consequently, this boy should use the 18 inch bench.

The cadence is 30 steps per minute for a maximum of four minutes. The score is determined by the same formula as in the Harvard Step Test as follows:

$$\frac{\text{Duration of exercise in seconds} \times 100}{2 \times \text{sum of pulse counts}}$$

The following norms were obtained from 600 boys:

50 and below . . . . Very poor
51 - 60 . . . . Poor
61 - 70 . . . . Fair
71 - 80 . . . . Good
81 - 90 . . . . Excellent
91 and above . . . . Superior

It is suggested that an arbitrary score of 45 be given to any boy who cannot finish the 4 minute duration. A score of 55 is suggested for a boy who does not keep cadence or *loafs.*

Nomogram for Calculating the Basal Metabolic

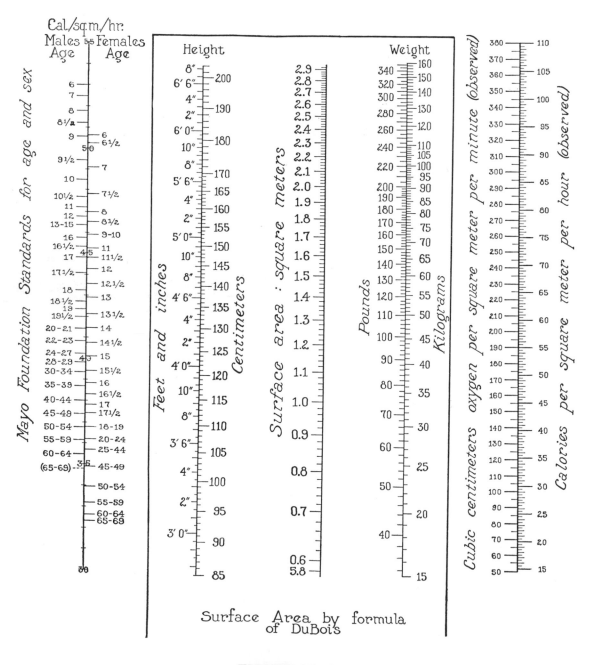

Surface Area by formula
of DuBois

FIGURE 16 - 1

(By Permission of Mayo Clinic, Rochester, Minn.)

Rate and Determining the Probability of Normality

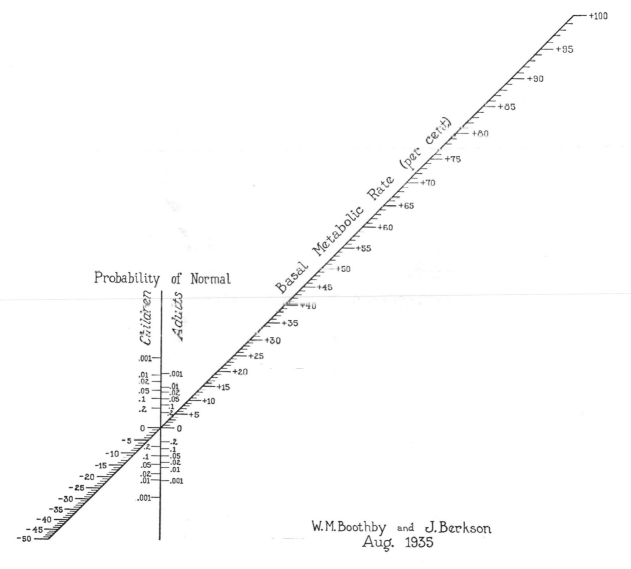

W.M.Boothby and J.Berkson
Aug. 1935

MC-817

TABLE 16 - 1

Scoring for the Harvard Step Test*

Duration of Effort (minutes)	Total Heart Beats 1½ Minutes in Recovery											
	40-44	45-49	50-54	55-59	60-64	65-69	70-74	75-79	80-84	85-89	90-94	95-99
	Score (Arbitrary Units)											
0 − ½	6	6	5	5	4	4	4	4	3	3	3	3
½−1	19	17	16	14	13	12	11	11	10	9	9	8
1 −1½	32	29	26	24	22	20	19	18	17	16	15	14
1½−2	45	41	38	34	31	29	27	25	23	22	21	20
2 −2½	58	52	47	43	40	36	34	32	30	28	27	25
2½−3	71	64	58	53	48	45	42	39	37	34	33	31
3 −3½	84	75	68	62	57	53	49	46	43	41	39	37
3½−4	97	87	79	72	66	61	57	53	50	47	45	42
4 −4½	110	98	89	82	75	70	65	61	57	54	51	48
4½−5	123	110	100	91	84	77	72	68	63	60	57	54
5	129	116	105	96	88	82	76	71	67	63	60	56

*From *Physiological Measurements of Metabolic Function in Man,* by Conzolazio, C. F., Johnson, R. E., and Pecora, L. J., 1963. Used by permission of McGraw-Hill Book Company.

Cardiovascular Efficiency Test for Girls and Women.[28,15,29]

Skubic and Hodgkins conducted extensive research with junior and senior high school girls and college women throughout the United States. National norms for cardiovascular efficiency were established.

Sex and Age Level: The test is designed for junior high school girls, senior high school girls, and college women.

Validity and Reliability: The norms were prepared from 686 junior high school girls and 1,332 senior high school girls from 55 secondary schools, and from 2,360 college women from 66 colleges. The test successfully differentiated among the sedentary, active, and well-trained subjects. A reliability coefficient of .82 was reported using the test-retest method.[28]

Test Equipment and Materials: An 18 inch bench and a stop watch or wall clock with second hand are all the equipment needed for this test.

Directions: The same basic directions are followed as were described in the Harvard Step Test. The differences are that the cadence is 24 steps per minute instead of 30; the bench is 18 inches instead of 20; and the maximum duration of exercise is 3 minutes instead of 5. Only one pulse count is taken. The pulse rate is felt at the carotid artery and is counted from 1 to 1½ minutes after exercise. The same procedures apply for a subject who stops before the end of the 3 minutes, as in the Harvard Test: the time is noted and the pulse is counted for 30 seconds, starting 1 minute after cessation of stepping.

Scoring: The following formula is employed in computing the subject's cardiovascular efficiency score:

$$\frac{\text{Number of seconds completed} \times 100}{\text{Recovery pulse} \times 5.6}$$

Example: A junior high school girl exercises for the full 3 minutes (180 seconds). Her recovery pulse count measured from 1 to 1½ minutes after exercise is 55. Her cardiovascular efficiency score is:

$$\frac{180 \times 100}{5.6 \times 55} = \frac{18,000}{308} = 58.4 \text{ (round off to 58)}$$

Norms for junior high school girls, senior high school girls, and college women are presented in Table 16 - 2.

Additional Pointers: Same as for Harvard Step Test.

Safety Precautions: Same as for Harvard Step Test.

Other Cardiovascular Tests

Some additional measures of cardiovascular condition are mentioned here. These tests have limited application for use in physical education classes. However, this does not mean that these tests are of little or no value in physical education. The physical education teacher may wish to use one of these tests in an adaptive program, for screening, or as a supplement to the medical examination.

TABLE 16 - 2

Norms for Cardiovascular Efficiency Test
for Girls and Women (15) (29)

Rating	Junior H.S. Age Girls		Senior H.S. Age Girls		College Age Girls	
	Cardio-vascular Efficiency Score	30-sec. Recovery Pulse	Cardio-vascular Efficiency Score	30-sec. Recovery Pulse	Cardio-vascular Efficiency Score	30-sec. Recovery Pulse
Excellent	72-100	44 or less	71-100	45 or less	71-100	43 or less
Very Good	62- 71	45-52	60- 70	46-54	60- 70	46-54
Good	51- 61	53-63	49- 59	55-66	49- 59	55-66
Fair	51- 50	64-79	40- 48	67-80	39- 48	67-83
Poor	31- 40	80-92	31- 39	81-96	28- 38	84-116
Very Poor	0- 30	93 and over	0- 30	96 and above	0- 27	117-120

Tuttle Pulse-Ratio Test.[31]

In this test the ratio between resting pulse and pulse rate after exercise is studied. The subject's score is the amount of exercise needed to increase the pulse rate 2.5 times above the resting pulse. The assumption, of course, is that the physically fit individual can work with greater physiological efficiency than the unfit individual.

Directions:
1. The subject is seated and his pulse rate taken until it remains constant. Then his resting pulse is taken for 30 seconds and doubled to represent his resting pulse rate.
2. The subject then stands and steps up and down on a 13 inch bench for one minute at 20 steps per minute for men, 15 steps per minute for women. The exercise is performed in 4 counts similar to the Harvard Step Test (up, up, down, down) with the subject standing erect on the bench each time.
3. The number of steps is recorded as S^1 (this should be 20, but it may vary slightly).
4. The subject sits down and the tester immediately begins the pulse count. This pulse count for two minutes is recorded.
5. The first pulse ratio (r_1) can now be computed by dividing resting pulse into the pulse for two minutes after exercise.
6. The subject remains in a sitting position until his pulse returns to normal.
7. The subject exercises again for 1 minute, but at a cadence of 40 steps per minute for men, 35 steps per minute for women. (It isn't essential that the exact cadence be followed as long as it is a rapid cadence.) The number of steps is recorded (S_2) and the second pulse ratio (r_2) may be computed.

8. The values can now be substituted into the formula to compute the number of steps required for a 2.5 ratio (S_0).

$$S_0 = S_1 + \frac{(S_2 - S_1)(2.5 - r_1)}{r_2 - r_1}$$

Example:

Resting pulse rate	= 72
Number of steps in 1 minute for first test	= 20 (S_1)
Pulse rate for 2 minutes following first test	= 163
First pulse ratio (2-minute pulse after exercise ÷ resting pulse = 163 ÷ 72 = 2.26)	= 2.26 (r_1)
Number of steps in second exercise	= 40 (S_2)
Pulse rate for 2 minutes after second exercise	= 216
Second pulse ratio $\left(\frac{216}{72}\right)$	= 3.00 (r_2)

$$S_0 - 20 + \frac{(40 - 20)(2.5 - 2.26)}{3.00 - 2.26} = 20 + \frac{4.8}{.74} = 20 + 6.5 = S_0 = 26.5$$

The following means for this test have been found:

Boys 10 to 12 years of age ....= 33 steps
Boys 13 to 18 years of age ....= 30 steps
Adult Males ....= 29 steps
Adult Females ....= 25 steps

Using a criterion of 50 steps per minute as representing a person in excellent condition, an efficiency rating (ER) can be computed.

$$ER = \frac{100 \text{ (Number of steps for 2.5 ratio)}}{50}$$

In the above example the individual's efficiency rating would be:

$$ER = \frac{100 \times 26.5}{50} = 53\%$$

A simplified version consisting of only one exercise bout of one minute at 40 steps per minute was reported by Tuttle and Dickenson to correlate .957 with the original test.[32]

Much research has been done concerning the tuttle Pulse-Ratio test and the results have, in general, led to the conclusion that this test has merit as a screening device. However, it should be used as a supplement to a thorough medical examination.

Schneider Test.[26]

The Schneider Test was originally developed to determine the physical condition of aviators in World War I. Pulse rate and systolic blood pressure are measured while the subject is reclining, after rising, and after a mild stepping exercise.

Directions:
1. The subject lies quietly for five minutes.
2. The pulse rate is taken for 20 seconds. This is repeated until consecutive counts

agree, and then this number is multiplied by 3 to represent reclining, resting pulse rate.

3. Systolic pressure readings are taken two or three times for reliability. The average reading is recorded.
4. The subject stands for two minutes. The pulse is measured for 15 seconds (and repeated to obtain consistency). The number is multiplied by four and recorded.
5. The difference between the reclining and standing pulse is determined.
6. The systolic pressure is recorded while standing, and the difference between the readings for reclining and standing positions is recorded.
7. The subject then steps up on a chair 18½ inches high 5 times in 15 seconds. This is timed with a stop watch.
8. Immediately after exercise the pulse rate is counted for 15 seconds and multiplied by 4.
9. The pulse rate is counted at 15 second intervals (while the subject remains standing) until the pulse has returned to normal. The total number of seconds elapsed is recorded. If, after two minutes, the pulse has still not returned to normal, the number of beats above normal pulse at this time is recorded.

Norms are provided in the original source. They are not reproduced here because it is generally agreed that this test has very little value for physical education. There are conflicting reports as to the reliability in administering the test, as well as in its predictive ability. It may have some value in supplementing the medical examination.

Barach Index.[3]

The Barach Energy Index has been utilized for over fifty years. This test was devised to measure the amount of energy expended by the heart. The items measured are the pulse rate, the systolic pressure, and the diastolic pressure. These measures are taken while the subject is seated and after consistent consecutive readings have been obtained.

The readings are inserted in the formula

$$\text{Energy Index} = \frac{(\text{Systolic pressure} - \text{Diastolic pressure}) \times \text{Pulse rate}}{100}$$

Example: An individual has a blood pressure reading of 124/82 and a resting pulse rate of 75. His energy index is:

$$\text{Energy Index} = \frac{(124 + 82) \times 75}{100} = 154.5$$

Barach indicated that healthy persons could be expected to have scores of about 110 to 160. Individuals scoring over 200 were considered to be hypertensed, and persons scoring below 90 were considered hypotensed. Hunsicker[17] found the Barach Energy Index to correlate fairly well with a measure of cardiac output, which consisted of heart stroke volume for an all-out run on a treadmill divided by body surface area.

Crampton Blood Ptosis Test.[8]

Crampton's test of general cardiovascular condition is based on the changes in heart rate and systolic blood pressure upon standing from a reclining position.

Directions:

1. The subject lies in a comfortable position until his pulse rate is stabilized. This is determined when two consecutive 15 second readings are the same.

2. The pulse rate is then counted for 1 minute.
3. The systolic pressure is also measured at this time.
4. The subject stands, and 15 second pulse counts are taken until the count is steady.
5. The systolic blood pressure is recorded.

The score is the difference between the reclining and standing pulse rates and the reclining and standing blood pressure measurements. A table is then consulted to obtain the test score. This table can be found in the original source.

The main criticism of this test is that the exercise is too mild and that it does not appear to differentiate among more athletic subjects as to relative degrees of fitness.[22] It does appear to have some value for persons of very low fitness and for hospital patients.

Blood Pressure Measurement

The measurement of systolic and diastolic blood pressure is relatively simple; however, like most testing, it requires considerable practice to become proficient. The cuff of the sphygmomanometer is wrapped around the bare arm above the elbow. With the earphones of the stethoscope in the tester's ears, the bell of the stethoscope is placed on the brachial artery just above the hollow of the elbow. The cuff is pumped up until the artery has been collapsed i.e., no pulse beat can be heard. Pressure is then slowly released as the tester watches the gauge or mercury column. When the first sound of the pulse is heard, the reading in millimeters of mercury at that instant is recorded as the systolic pressure. The tester continues to slowly release pressure until a very dull, weak beat is noted. At that instant the pressure in millimeters of mercury is noted which represents the diastolic pressure. The measures are recorded with the systolic pressure first, then the diastolic pressure. A typical reading might be 120/80 or 125/75, etc.

Problems Associated with Cardiovascular Fitness Testing

There are so many variables which can affect the pulse rate and blood pressure that it is very difficult to obtain an *average* or *typical* measurement on any given day. Emotions, for example, have a very noticeable effect on cardiorespiratory functions. Physicians often allow for this when they are taking patients' pulse rate and blood pressure during medical examinations.

Besides nervousness, tension, and other emotional manifestations, it has been found that temperature, time of day, exercise, changes in body position, altitude, humidity, digestion, and current state of health also may influence cardiovascular measurements. Consequently, reliability and objectivity coefficients are often low.

The main influencing factors mentioned above dictate that great care should be taken in the measurement of pulse rate and blood pressure. If a resting or normal pulse rate is desired, the subject should be allowed to rest for several minutes until the count has stabilized. As has been suggested before, this can be determined by taking consecutive readings until they are similar. It has been observed that a subject's pulse rate is sometimes lower after mild exercise than when he first entered the laboratory.

Of course, one of the foremost problems associated with cardiovascular fitness testing in physical education classes is the time required for testing. This problem in turn relates to the purposes for which the tests may be used. The group tests, such as the Harvard Step Test and its modifications, are not overly time-consuming. Furthermore, these tests are generally most effective in differentiating among normal students; in other words, athletes as opposed to non-athletes, etc. For the most part the other tests are more appropriate for adaptive programs and as screening devices because they are of an individual nature and are geared more toward identifying those persons in poor condition.

A Brief Summary of Research Findings
Concerning Cardiovascular Fitness Tests

There have been differences of opinion expressed concerning the significance of pulse rate measurements before, during, and after exercise. Tuttle[31] contended that it was necessary to obtain a ratio of resting pulse rate to the pulse rate after exercise. Brouha,[5] in developing the Harvard Step Test, stated that initial or pre-exercise pulse rate is relatively unimportant, and only the recovery pulse rate need be considered. Henry[14] concluded that a decrease in heart rate is an effective measure of changes in athletic conditioning, and that the resting pulse rate has validity as an indirect indication of condition.

In general, the correlations among various tests of cardiovascular condition have been quite low. Several explanations for this have been suggested, such as the fact that the scoring systems are different. In addition, some use pre-exercise pulse rates, some post-exercise, and some employ both. The differing relations of pre-exercise pulse rate and post-exercise pulse rate following different degrees of work have also been suggested as possible cause for the lack of relationship among tests.[9,10] Clark,[7] in studying the relationships of initial and recovery pulse rate and recovery index, found similar relationships for both male and female subjects. The main finding of her study was that recovery pulse rate increased in proportion to the duration of exercise up to two minutes of exercise. After that point the increase in recovery pulse rate diminished markedly in magnitude.

Numerous studies have shown that conditioning programs improve scores on cardiovascular fitness. This improvement has been in the form of lowered pulse rates, higher resting stroke volumes, and increased resting cardiac output. Among the studies reporting such findings have been Holloszy,[16] Henry,[14] Faulkner,[11] and King.[19]

There have also been many studies undertaken to investigate the comparative contributions of different activities in improving cardiovascular fitness. Kozar[20] studied the relative strenuousness of six sports, as measured by telemetered heart rates. It was found that while there were no differences among handball, paddleball, tennis, and badminton, these four activities were superior to volleyball and bowling. Volleyball, in turn, produced higher heart rates than bowling.

King[19] compared two training programs, bicycle riding and running, as to changes in pulse rate, respiration rate and amplitude, minute volume of respiration, and oxygen consumption at base level and after exercise. In general, no differences were found between the programs with regard to the amount of cardiovascular improvement.

Although many persons stated that isometric exercises could have no beneficial effect in improving one's cardiovascular condition, there have been quite a number of studies conducted recently that have shown isometrics to be of value. Alost[2] compared a training program consisting of one minute of running each day with a program of sixty seconds of isometric exercises. Other variables involved different levels of condition and number of days per week of exercise. Both exercise programs were equally effective in producing significant improvement in the Harvard Step Test scores.

Life[21] studied the effects of swimming and golf, with and without supplementary isometric exercises, in improving cardiovascular efficiency scores and in the Rogers Physical Fitness Test. All groups except golf alone improved in cardiovascular efficiency.

Hamilton[13] investigated the effects of isometric and isotonic exercise programs on cardiovascular fitness test scores when junior high school girls were classified according to initial fitness and body weight. Isometric exercises were found to be more beneficial when all classifications were combined, but isotonic exercises were better for girls classified as having low cardiovascular fitness.

Shvartz[27] compared isotonic and isometric exercises on heart rate. He found that isometric exercise performed for 45 seconds at one-half maximum resistance stimulated heart rate to the same extent as isotonic exercise of similar intensity and duration. He also reported that maximum isometric tension resulted in nearly a twofold increase in heart rate.

Milton,[23] using 463 subjects, compared four training programs as to their effectiveness in improving cardiovascular fitness, as measured by the Harvard Step Test. One group ran for 10 minutes, one group for 20 minutes, and one group for 30 minutes a day, four days a week. The fourth group participated only in isometric exercises. All groups gained significantly, although the running groups' gains were generally superior to the gains of the isometric group. Overall, the amount of running did not result in differences in amount of cardiovascular improvement.

Being overweight has been shown to be detrimental to step test performance,[1,13] and Bookwalter[4] presented evidence that height and age may be influencing factors in the Harvard Step Test.

While studies have shown smoking to produce higher pulse rate and blood pressure readings, the results have been inconclusive regarding physical performance on the step test and other endurance measures.[25,33,18]

Dr. Kenneth Cooper* did extensive research in an attempt to establish a rating scale for measuring relative values of activities in terms of circulorespiratory conditioning. His research showed the importance of such activities as running, swimming, cycling, walking, handball, basketball, squash and others in the development of circulorespiratory endurance. Cooper provides a simple 12 minute run-walk scoring scale for people to evaluate their own condition. As this has received such widespread publicity, the scoring scale is presented in Appendix C.

*Kenneth H. Cooper, *Aerobics,* (New York: Bantam Books, Inc., 1968).

BIBLIOGRAPHY

1. Abdou, Samia H. A., "Leg Strength and Height-Weight Factors in Relation to Cardiovascular Efficiency of College Women," (Doctoral Dissertation, Louisiana State University, 1965).

2. Alost, Robert A., "A Study of the Effect of Initial Cardiovascular Condition Type of Training Program and Frequency of Practice Periods Upon the Cardiovascular Development of College Men," (Unpublished Doctoral Dissertation, Louisiana State University, 1963).

3. Barach, J. H., "The Energy Index," *Journal of American Medical Association,* 62:525-530, February 14, 1914.

4. Bookwalter, Karl W., "A Study of the Brouha Step Test," *The Physical Educator,* 5:55, May, 1948.

5. Brouha, Lucian, "The Step Test: A Simple Method of Measuring Physical Fitness for Muscular Work in Young Men," *The Research Quarterly.* 14:31-36, March, 1943.

6. _____, Norman W. Fradd, and Beatrice M. Savage, "Studies in Physical Efficiency of College Students," *Research Quarterly,* 15:211-244, October, 1944.

7. Clark, Jean W., "The Relationship of Initial Pulse Rate, Recovery Pulse Rate, Recovery Index and Subjective Appraisal of Physical Condition After Various Deviations of Work," (Unpublished Master's Thesis, Louisiana State University, 1966).

8. Crampton, C. Ward, "A Test of Condition: Preliminary Report," *Medical News,* 87:529-530, September, 1905.

9. Elbel, Edwin R., "The Relationship Between Pre-Exercise and Post-Exercise Pulse Rate," *Research Quarterly,* 19:222-228, October, 1948.

10. _____, Kenneth M. Reid, and Donald E. Ormond, "Comparison of Certain Tests of Physical Fitness and Certain Body Measurements," *Journal of Applied Physiology,* 12:37-41, January, 1958.

11. Faulkner, J. A., "Effect of Cardiac Conditioning on the Anticipatory, Exercise, and Recovery Rates of Young Men," *Journal of Sports Medicine and Physical Fitness,* 4:79-86, June, 1964.

12. Gallagher, J. Roswell, and Lucien Brouha, "A Simple Method of Testing the Physical Fitness of Boys," *Research Quarterly,* 14:24-30, March, 1943.

13. Hamilton, Xandra L., "The Effects of Isometric and Isotonic Endurance Exercises on the Development of Cardiovascular Efficiency of Eighth Grade Girls Classified According to Initial Cardiovascular Efficiency and Weight," (Unpublished Doctoral Dissertation, Louisiana State University, 1966).

14. Henry, Franklin M., "Influence of Athletic Training on the Resting Cardiovascular System," *Research Quarterly,* 25:28-41, March, 1954.

15. Hodgkins, Jean, and Vera Skubic, "Cardiovascular Efficiency Scores for College Women in the United States," *Research Quarterly,* 34:454-461, December, 1963.

16. Holloszy, John V., "Effect of Physical Conditioning on Cardiovascular Function," *American Journal of Cardiology,* 14:761-770, December, 1964.

17. Hunsicker, Paul A., "A Validation of Cardiovascular Tests by Cardiac Output Measurements," (Microcarded Doctoral Dissertation, University of Illinois, 1950).

18. Johnstone, John A., "A Comparative Study of the Cardiovascular Fitness of Smokers and Nonsmokers," (Unpublished Master's Thesis, San Diego State College, San Diego, California).

19. King, Louise C., "An Investigation of the Effects of Two Training Programs on Selected Cardio-Respiratory Variables of College Women" (Microcarded Master's Thesis, Women's College, University of North Carolina, Greensboro, 1962).

20. Kozar, Andrew J., and Paul Hunsicker, "A Study of Telemetered Heart Rate During Sports Participation of Young Adult Men," *Journal of Sports Medicine and Physical Fitness,* 3:1-5, March, 1963.

21. Life, Mary Louise, "The Effects of Supplementary Isometric Exercises with Swimming and Golf on Selected Physiological Factors of College Women," (Unpublished Doctoral Dissertation, Louisiana State University, 1964).

22. McCloy, Charles H., and Norma D. Young, *Tests and Measurements in Health and Physical Education,* 3rd ed., New York: Appleton-Century-Crofts, Inc., 1954, p. 292.

23. Milton, George C., "The Effects of Three Programs of Long Distance Running and an Isometric Exercise Program on the Development of Cardiovascular Efficiency," (Unpublished Doctoral Dissertation, Louisiana State University, 1966).

24. Moore, Robert W., "The Relationship of the Harvard Step Test to a Vertical Jump Test of Short Duration in Measuring Cardiovascular Efficiency," (Unpublished Master's Thesis, Louisiana State University, 1965).

25. Moutis, Nicholas P., "Cardiovascular Measurement on College-Age Smokers and Non-Smokers," *Research Quarterly,* 26:454-460, December, 1955.

26. Schneider, E. C., "A Cardiovascular Rating as a Measure of Physical Fitness and Efficiency," *Journal of the American Medical Association,* 74:1506-1507, May 29, 1920.

27. Shvartz, Esar, "Effect of Isotonic and Isometric Exercises on Heart Rate," *Research Quarterly,* 37:121-125, March, 1966.

28. Skubic, Vera, and Jean Hodgkins, "Cardiovascular Efficiency Test for Girls and Women," *Research Quarterly,* 34:191-198, May, 1963.

29. _____ , "Cardiovascular Efficiency Test Scores for Junior and Senior High School Girls in the United States," *Research Quarterly,* 35:184-192, May, 1964.

30. Taddonio, Dominick A., and Peter V. Karpovich, "Endurance as Measured by the Harvard Step Test," *Research Quarterly,* 22:381384, October, 1951.

31. Tuttle, W. W., "The Use of the Pulse-Ratio Test for Rating Physical Efficiency," *Research Quarterly,* 2:5-17, May, 1931.

32. _____ , and Russell E. Dickenson, "A Simplification of the Pulse-Ratio Technique for Rating Physical Efficiency and Present Condition," *Research Quarterly,* 9:73-80, May, 1938.

33. Wenner, George J., "The Effects of a Moderate Physical Conditioning Program on Cigarette Smokers and Nonsmokers as Measured by Heart Rate Response to a Standard Bicycle Ergometer Test," (Unpublished Master's Thesis, Temple University, 1964).

Chapter XVII

THE MEASUREMENT OF
MOTOR FITNESS

Distinction Between Physical Fitness and Motor Fitness

Since the days of the early Greeks, physical fitness has been an important objective of physical education. In fact, the desire to establish a scientific approach to the development of physical fitness was the primary reason for the meeting of physical educators in 1885 that resulted in the birth of our profession.[19] Through the years interest in physical fitness has been somewhat cyclic in nature, being affected by draft statistics, the emphasis on fitness during time of war, and the Kraus-Weber Test in which American youth were found to be inferior when compared with children of other countries with regard to minimum muscular fitness.[15] The latter, of course, resulted in President Eisenhower establishing in 1956 the President's Council on Youth Fitness which launched the recent wave of concern for physical fitness.

Yet, despite the long standing concern for physical fitness and the vast amount of research on the subject, there is evidently considerable difference of opinion within the profession as to what elements constitute physical fitness. Perhaps this is typical of any concept within the disciplines that attempts to study human behavior. For example, members of the medical profession do not always agree on what is the definition of health. The lack of agreement regarding the concept of physical fitness basically centers around whether or not items involving skill and ability should be included in such a battery. Some authors list only the relatively basic elements, such as strength, muscular endurance and cardiovascular endurance. Others build from this base and include items of agility, flexibility, power, balance, speed, and neuromuscular coordination.

Definitions are largely matters of opinion. Consequently, we certainly cannot settle the issue. For the record this text endorses the concept of physical fitness which includes the elements of strength, muscular endurance, circulo-respiratory endurance and flexibility. The other qualities, we feel, are abilities which underlie motor performance but are not essential for basic physical fitness. In other words, a person does not have to possess speed, agility, power, etc. which make for success in athletics in order to be physically fit. If the reverse were true, then a person who is slow of foot, poorly coordinated, or who is crippled could never be physically fit. We might add that we include the element of flexibility primarily because it is important in preventing injury while carrying on one's daily activities, and it is an indicator of regularity of exercise and fitness. We do not wish to imply that everyone should be able to do the splits, or to be able to tie themselves into knots. Tests for measuring the components of physical fitness as viewed by your authors may be found in the respective chapters devoted to strength, muscular endurance, cardiovascular efficiency, and flexibility.

The term _motor fitness_, while often used synonymously with physical fitness, was coined to include elements which involve more abilities than those basic physical fitness components, yet was not to encompass the various neuromuscular coordination skills which make up general motor ability. Motor fitness thus takes into account efficiency of basic movements, and therefore would involve such elements as power, agility, speed, and balance. It is readily apparent that none of the tests described in this chapter would be classified as strictly measures of physical fitness, as outlined above. They tend to fall much more so into the category of motor fitness. Even then, there are items that definitely would be more appropriately classed as general motor ability test items, such as those items that call for skill in throwing a ball.

It seems important that we should not be too careless in the use of the various terms. It well may be that it is more desirable to develop (and measure) motor fitness than basic physical fitness in the schools. The objectives of physical education include the development of efficiency in the fundamental movements, as well as the development of neuromuscular skills and organic efficiency. However, the distinction between skill and organic fitness should be made clear to the student. Two examples that represent opposite but equally unfortunate misconceptions come to mind. One, the student with poor skills should be made to realize that he still can be physically fit. Secondly, it is just as important that the individual who excels at throwing a softball for distance understands that this does not make up for scoring lowest in the 600 yard run, insofar as physical fitness is concerned. As usual, proper interpretation is imperative in order for the maximum worth of a test to be realized.

Ways of Using Motor Fitness Tests

Motor fitness tests can provide valuable information to the physical educator. Some of the uses of such tests are as follows:

1. To evaluate the effectiveness of the physical education program in developing and maintaining motor fitness.
2. To measure achievement in the elements of motor fitness that are represented by the different test items.
3. To diagnose strengths and weaknesses of the individual students with regard to motor fitness, and thus better meet their needs.
4. As one means of interpreting the physical education program to parents, the administration, and the public.

Practical Tests of Motor Fitness

There are so many motor fitness test batteries that it would be fool-hardy to attempt to provide descriptions of all of them in one chapter of one book. It would also be highly repetitious, since a great many of the test items are the same.

A number of the state departments of education, state colleges and universities, and city and county school systems have their own fitness batteries, as do the Armed Forces and the military academies. Organizations such as the American Association for Health, Physical Education and Recreation, the President's Council on Physical Fitness, the Amateur Athletic Union, and the Division of Girl's and Women's Athletics have proposed fitness tests for screening and evaluation. Finally, certain individuals have also developed fitness batteries that have received widespread recognition.

In the following section several test batteries will be briefly described. These tests are considered to be representative of the majority of such batteries. The AAHPER Youth Fitness Test is given the most coverage, since it is probably employed by more physical education teachers across the country than any other single test battery. For the most part the items that comprise the various test batteries have been described in detail in other parts of this text. Therefore, in order to avoid excessive repetition and to conserve space, the reader will be referred to other chapters in those instances.

AAHPER Youth Fitness Test.[1]

The AAHPER Youth Fitness Test Project represented the first attempt by the physical education profession to establish national norms. The test battery was originally developed in 1957 by a special committee of the AAHPER Research Council.

In selecting the test items the committee was guided by the following criteria: the tests should be reasonably familiar; the tests should require little or no equipment; the tests could be administered to the entire age range of grades 5 - 12; the tests should measure different components of fitness; and the tests could be given to both boys and girls. The exception to the last criterion is the pull-ups test.

Validity and Reliability: It was emphasized that in selecting the tests the major consideration was placed on what each test item indicated rather than in the test item itself. The planning committee agreed upon the seven-item battery as representing measures of strength, endurance, and agility and proficiency in running, jumping, and throwing. The intercorrelations among the items are low, indicating that they are measuring separate elements.

Test Items: Pull-ups (for boys), flexed-arm hang (for girls), sit-ups, shuttle-run, standing broad jump, 50-yard dash, softball throw for distance, and the 600-yard run-walk. Three aquatic test items were selected but not used on a national scale because of the general lack of swimming facilities or instruction.

PULL-UPS FOR BOYS. To measure arm and shoulder girdle strength. (See pages 273-275.)

Equipment: A metal or wooden bar approximately 1½ inches in diameter is recommended. However, a ladder, a doorway gym bar, or a piece of pipe could be used.

Directions: The subject assumes a hanging position using the overhand (palms forward) grip. His arms and legs should be fully extended. Regular chinning procedures are followed. No swinging or kicking or kipping motions are allowed. One trial is given unless it is obvious that the student has not had a fair chance.

Scoring: The number of completed pullups to the nearest whole number is recorded.

Additional Pointers are discussed in Chapter XV.

FLEXED-ARM HANG FOR GIRLS. This item replaced the modified pull-ups that were included in the original battery, as it was believed to be a more reliable and efficient measure of arm and shoulder girdle strength. (See pages 276-277.)

Equipment: A bar, or doorway gym bar, or piece of pipe and a stop watch are needed for this test.

Directions: The bar should be adjusted to about the same height as the subject. The subject uses the overhand grip and, with the help of two spotters, raises her body off the floor so that her chin is just above the bar. The spotters are positioned in front and behind the subject. The subject then attempts to hold this position with her chin above the bar, her arms flexed, and her chest close to the bar for as long as possible. The time is started as soon as the subject attains this position and continues until the chin falls below the level of the bar, touches the bar, or in the event that the subject tilts her head back in an effort to keep the chin above the bar.

<u>Scoring</u>: The time to the nearest second that the subject maintains the correct hanging position is recorded.

SIT-UPS. To measure the efficiency of the abdominal and hip flexor muscles.
<u>Equipment</u>: Mat or floor.
<u>Directions</u>: The subject lies on his back with his legs straight and about two feet apart. His hands are placed behind his neck with the fingers interlaced. A partner holds the subject's ankles so that his heels are in contact with the floor or mat at all times. The subject sits up, twisting his trunk to the left to touch his right elbow to the left knee. He then returns to the starting position, making sure that his elbows are flat on the mat or floor before sitting up again. The subject sits up and twists to the right in order to touch his right knee with his left elbow. The subject then repeats the exercise, alternating to the right or left each time. The fingers must remain in contact throughout the exercise, and the back should be rounded with head and neck leading so as to *curl* up. The knees should remain on the mat or floor as the subject sits up, but they may bend slightly when the elbow touches the knee.
<u>Scoring</u>: Each movement of sitting up, touching elbow to knee, and returning to the mat counts one point. The maximum number of sit-ups is 100 for boys and 50 for girls. Any sit-up in which the fingertips come apart, or the knees are bent, or the subject pushes off the mat from an elbow is not counted, and the subject should be told of the infraction.
<u>Additional Pointers</u> are discussed in Chapter XV.

SHUTTLE RUN. To measure speed and change of direction.
<u>Equipment</u>: Each station needs two blocks of wood, 2 X 2 X 4 inches, and a stop watch. A 30 foot running area is needed. The width of a volleyball court is appropriate.
<u>Directions</u>: The subject starts from a standing position behind one of the lines. Behind the other line are placed two blocks of wood. At the starting signal the subject races to the blocks, picks one up, and runs back to the starting line. He places (not throws) the wooden block behind the starting line, runs back and picks up the remaining wooden block, then carries it across the starting line. In all, the distance is crossed four times making a total distance of 120 feet, or 40 yards. Two trials are given with some rest between trials.
<u>Scoring</u>: The time to the nearest tenth of a second of the better of two trials is the score for this event.
<u>Additional Pointers</u>: (1) To facilitate testing, the runners should be divided so half start from one side and half from the other side. Starting them alternately eliminates carrying the blocks of wood back each time. (2) The tester should standardize procedures for the placement of the first block by the subject. He should not be allowed to drop it or throw it. (3) If a watch with a split-second timer is used, or if two stop watches are available, the tester can run two subjects at a time. (4) Other additional pointers for agility testing are given in Chapter VII.
<u>Safety Precautions</u>: Most of the safety precautions have been mentioned in Chapter VII. However, the importance of adequate footwear should be stressed again, as well as the need to keep the running lanes clear.

STANDING BROAD JUMP. To measure explosive power of the leg extensors.
<u>Equipment</u>: A mat, or outdoor jumping pit, or perhaps simply the floor itself may be used. A tape measure or marked surface is needed also.

<u>Directions</u>: The subject stands behind the take-off line, swings the arms backward and bends the knees, then jumps as far forward as possible. The usual directions for this event apply. Three trials are given.

<u>Scoring</u>: The distance is measured from the take-off line to the point of contact by the heel or other part of the body that is nearest the take-off line. The distance of the best of the three trials to the nearest inch is recorded.

<u>Additional Pointers and Safety Precautions</u> are discussed in Chapter VIII.

50-YARD DASH. To measure speed.

<u>Equipment</u>: Two stop watches, or a watch with a split-second timer is needed. A suitable running area to allow the 50-yard run plus extension for stopping is also required.

<u>Directions</u>: It is advised that two subjects run at the same time. Both start from a standing position. The commands, *Are you ready?* and *Go!* are given. At the command to go the starter drops his arm so that the timer at the finish line can start the timing. The subjects run as fast as possible across the finish line.

<u>Scoring</u>: The elapsed time from the starting signal until the runner crosses the finish line is measured to the nearest tenth of a second.

<u>Additional Pointers and Safety Precautions</u> for dashes are described in Chapter XIII.

SOFTBALL THROW FOR DISTANCE. To measure skill and coordination.

<u>Equipment</u>: Softball (preferably several in good condition), tape measure, and small metal or wooden marking stakes are needed. A football field that is marked in five-yard intervals serves nicely for this event.

<u>Directions</u>: The subject must throw from within a 6 feet restraining area which is drawn parallel to the five-yard field markers. The ball's point of contact is marked. If his second or third throw is farther, the marker is moved. Three trials are given. It is advised that a group of approximately five students be tested together, and after completing the third throw, the subject should jog out and stand at his marker while the measurements are being taken. In this way the possibility of recording the wrong score is reduced.

<u>Scoring</u>: The distance to the nearest foot of the best of three trials is the score. The measurement is made at right angles from the point of landing to the restraining line. In other words, the tape is not swung in an arc for each throw.

<u>Additional Pointers and Safety Precautions</u> are the same as in Barrow's Test in Chapter VIII.

600-YARD RUN-WALK. To measure cardiovascular efficiency.

<u>Equipment</u>: A stop watch is needed and a track, football field, or similar open area to accommodate this test. <u>The AAHPER</u> Youth Fitness Test Manual shows diagrams of three suggested areas: (1) A football field on which four flags are placed at the end line of the end zone thirty yards apart. These markers make a rectangular course 120 X 30 yards, and twice around equals 600; (2) Any open area in the form of a square measuring 50 yards on each side can be used. Twice around measures 600 yards; and (3) The inside circumference of a 440 yard track may be used. In this arrangement the tester might start the runners, then walk 160 yards down the track to the finish line.

<u>Directions</u>: It is possible to have as many as a dozen runners at a time in this event. Each runner is assigned a spotter. The subject uses a standing start. The tester gives the commands, *Ready? Go!* The subject is told that he may walk whenever he feels it is necessary. Each spotter positions himself at the finish line where he can hear the timer

who begins counting aloud the times every second as the runners cross the finish line. The spotter watches his partner and remembers his announced time. The spotters must be impressed with the importance of paying close attention and not talking to anyone until they give their partners' time to the recorder.

Scoring: The time in minutes and seconds are recorded as the score.

Additional Pointers: (1) The same partners should not score each other. (2) Some practice in spotting should be given. (3) The timer must guard against the tendency to stop the watch as soon as the first runner finishes. (4) Each runner should be

EXAMPLE

	Pupil A				Pupil B	
		Exponent				Exponent
Age 13 yrs. (156 mos.)		7		Age 13 yrs. (156 mos.)		7
Ht. 64 in.		14		Ht. 64 inc.		14
Wt. 100 lbs.		8		Wt. 127 lbs.		14
	Total	29 = Class E			Total	35 = Class G

Test Item	Pupil A			Pupil B	
	Raw Score	Percentile Score (Norm for Class E)	Percentile Score Based on Age (13)	Raw Score	Percentile Score (Norm for Class G)
Pull-ups	4	70	60	4	55
Sit-ups	75	65	60	75	55
Shuttle Run	10.5 sec.	65	55	10.5 sec.	50
Standing Broad Jump	6'3''	80	70	6'3''	55
50-Yd Dash	7.2 sec.	75	65	7.2 sec.	55
Softball Throw	159 ft.	90	70	159 ft.	55
600-Yd Run	2'15''	60	40	2'15''	30

Note: Pupil A achieves considerably higher scores when norms are based on Classification Index than when norms are based only on age.

Pupil B, on the other hand, with the same raw scores as Pupil A scores higher when norms are based on age than when based on Classification Index.

FIGURE 17 - 1

Comparison of Percentile Scores When Norms are Based on Age with Percentile Scores Based on Classification Index.

instructed to listen for his own time as a safeguard against the possibility of a spotter forgetting the time.

Safety Precautions: (1) The subjects should be given adequate training and practice. Too often the students are made to run without prior training, and this frequently results in nausea, soreness, and exhaustion. Then the same situation is repeated at the end of the year. (2) The medical condition and history of each subject should be known. (3) It is sometimes advisable to caution students who are unaccustomed to running not to attempt to maintain the same space utilized by some student who is fast and in good condition.

Norms: New national norms are presented in the revised *Manual*. The percentile scores were determined as a result of nationwide sampling in 1964-65. Two sets of scoring tables are provided. One set is based on age and one set is based on the Neilson-Cozens Classification Index.

The procedures for translating age, height, and weight into the exponents for the Classification Index were discussed in Chapter V. Basically, the smaller or lighter person benefits most from being scored on tables based on the Classification Index. The example in Figure 17 - 1 demonstrates the different results obtained by using the two sets of norms. In the example the performance of the two boys was exactly the same, and they were identical in age and height. Only their body weight differed.

The following tables of norms are based only on age. The reader is referred to the revised *Manual* for norms based on the Neilson-Cozens Classification Index. Space does not permit the inclusion of all the tables in this test.

When consulting the following tables, the age is expressed in the number of birthdays the subject has had. For example, a pupil who is 12 years, 11 months is still considered as a 12-year-old. Norms for ages 10 through 17 are presented in Tables 17 - 1 through 17 - 7.

Norms have also been constructed for college men and women. These norms are shown in Table 17 - 8.

TABLE 17 - 1
AAHPER Youth Fitness Test*

PULL-UP FOR BOYS
Percentile Scores Based on Age/Test Scores in Number of Pull-Ups

| Percentile | Age | | | | | | | | Percentile |
	10	11	12	13	14	15	16	17	
100th	16	20	15	24	20	25	25	32	100th
95th	8	8	9	10	12	13	14	16	95th
90th	7	7	7	9	10	11	13	14	90th
85th	6	6	6	8	10	10	12	12	85th
80th	5	5	5	7	8	10	11	12	80th
75th	4	4	5	6	8	9	10	10	75th
70th	4	4	4	5	7	8	10	10	70th
65th	3	3	3	5	6	7	9	10	65th
60th	3	3	3	4	6	7	9	9	60th
55th	3	2	3	4	5	6	8	8	55th
50th	2	2	2	3	5	6	7	8	50th
45th	2	2	2	3	4	5	6	7	45th
40th	1	1	1	2	4	5	6	7	40th
35th	1	1	1	2	3	4	5	6	35th
30th	1	1	1	1	3	4	5	5	30th
25th	0	0	0	1	2	3	4	5	25th
20th	0	0	0	0	2	3	4	4	20th
15th	0	0	0	0	1	2	3	4	15th
10th	0	0	0	0	0	1	2	2	10th
5th	0	0	0	0	0	0	0	1	5th
0	0	0	0	0	0	0	0	0	0

FLEXED-ARM HANG FOR GIRLS
Percentile Scores Based on Age/Test Scores in Seconds

| Percentile | Age | | | | | | | | Percentile |
	10	11	12	13	14	15	16	17	
100th	66	79	64	80	60	74	74	76	100th
95th	31	35	30	30	30	33	37	31	95th
90th	24	25	23	21	22	22	26	25	90th
85th	21	20	19	18	19	18	19	19	85th
80th	18	17	15	15	16	16	16	16	80th
75th	15	16	13	13	13	14	14	14	75th
70th	13	13	11	12	11	13	12	12	70th
65th	11	11	10	10	10	11	10	11	65th
60th	10	10	8	9	9	10	9	10	60th
55th	9	9	8	8	8	8	8	9	55th
50th	7	8	6	7	7	8	7	8	50th
45th	6	6	6	6	6	6	6	7	45th
40th	6	5	5	5	5	6	5	6	40th
35th	5	4	4	4	4	4	4	4	35th
30th	4	4	3	3	3	3	3	4	30th
25th	3	3	2	2	2	2	2	3	25th
20th	2	2	1	2	1	1	1	2	20th
15th	2	1	0	1	1	0	1	0	15th
10th	1	0	0	0	0	0	0	0	10th
5th	0	0	0	0	0	0	0	0	5th
0	0	0	0	0	0	0	0	0	0

*AAHPER Youth Fitness Test Manual, Revised Edition. Washington, D. C.: AAHPER, 1965.

TABLE 17 - 2
AAHPER Youth Fitness Test

SIT-UP FOR BOYS
Percentile Scores Based on Age/Test Scores in Number of Sit-Ups

Percentile	Age								Percentile
	10	11	12	13	14	15	16	17	
100th	100	100	100	100	100	100	100	100	100th
95th	100	100	100	100	100	100	100	100	95th
90th	100	100	100	100	100	100	100	100	90th
85th	100	100	100	100	100	100	100	100	85th
80th	76	89	100	100	100	100	100	100	80th
75th	65	73	93	100	100	100	100	100	75th
70th	57	60	75	99	100	100	100	100	70th
65th	51	55	70	90	99	100	99	99	65th
60th	50	50	59	75	99	99	99	85	60th
55th	49	50	52	70	77	90	85	77	55th
50th	41	46	50	60	70	80	76	70	50th
45th	37	40	49	53	62	70	70	62	45th
40th	34	35	42	50	60	61	63	57	40th
35th	30	31	40	50	52	54	56	51	35th
30th	28	30	35	41	50	50	50	50	30th
25th	25	26	30	38	45	49	50	45	25th
20th	23	23	28	35	40	42	42	40	20th
15th	20	20	25	30	36	39	38	35	15th
10th	15	17	20	25	30	33	34	30	10th
5th	11	12	15	20	24	27	28	23	5th
0	1	0	0	1	6	5	10	8	0

SIT-UP FOR GIRLS
Percentile Scores Based on Age/Test Scores in Number of Sit-Ups

Percentile	Age								Percentile
	10	11	12	13	14	15	16	17	
100th	50	50	50	50	50	50	50	50	100th
95th	50	50	50	50	50	50	50	50	95th
90th	50	50	50	50	50	50	50	50	90th
85th	50	50	50	50	50	50	50	50	85th
80th	50	50	50	50	49	42	41	45	80th
75th	50	50	50	50	42	39	38	40	75th
70th	50	50	50	45	37	35	34	35	70th
65th	42	40	40	40	35	31	31	32	65th
60th	39	37	39	38	34	30	30	30	60th
55th	33	34	35	35	31	29	28	29	55th
50th	31	30	32	31	30	26	26	27	50th
45th	30	29	30	30	27	25	25	25	45th
40th	26	26	26	27	25	24	24	23	40th
35th	24	25	25	25	23	21	22	21	35th
30th	21	22	22	22	21	20	20	20	30th
25th	20	20	20	20	20	19	18	18	25th
20th	16	19	18	19	18	16	16	16	20th
15th	14	16	16	15	16	14	14	15	15th
10th	11	12	13	12	13	11	11	12	10th
5th	8	10	7	10	10	8	7	9	5th
0	0	0	0	0	0	0	0	0	0

TABLE 17 - 3
AAHPER Youth Fitness Test

SHUTTLE RUN FOR BOYS
Percentile Scores Based on Age/Test Scores in Seconds and Tenths

Percentile	Age								Percentile
	10	11	12	13	14	15	16	17	
100th	9.0	9.0	8.5	8.0	8.3	8.0	8.1	8.0	100th
95th	10.0	10.0	9.8	9.5	9.3	9.1	9.0	8.9	95th
90th	10.2	10.1	10.0	9.8	9.5	9.3	9.1	9.0	90th
85th	10.4	10.3	10.0	9.9	9.6	9.4	9.2	9.1	85th
80th	10.5	10.4	10.2	10.0	9.8	9.5	9.3	9.2	80th
75th	10.7	10.5	10.3	10.1	9.9	9.6	9.5	9.3	75th
70th	10.8	10.7	10.5	10.2	9.9	9.7	9.5	9.4	70th
65th	10.9	10.8	10.6	10.3	10.0	9.8	9.6	9.5	65th
60th	11.0	10.9	10.7	10.4	10.0	9.8	9.7	9.6	60th
55th	11.0	11.0	10.9	10.5	10.2	9.9	9.8	9.7	55th
50th	11.2	11.1	11.0	10.6	10.2	10.0	9.9	9.8	50th
45th	11.4	11.2	11.0	10.8	10.3	10.0	10.0	9.9	45th
40th	11.5	11.3	11.1	10.9	10.5	10.1	10.0	10.0	40th
35th	11.6	11.4	11.3	11.0	10.5	10.2	10.1	10.0	35th
30th	11.8	11.6	11.5	11.1	10.7	10.3	10.2	10.1	30th
25th	12.0	11.8	11.6	11.3	10.9	10.5	10.4	10.4	25th
20th	12.0	12.0	11.9	11.5	11.0	10.6	10.5	10.6	20th
15th	12.2	12.1	12.0	11.8	11.2	10.9	10.8	10.9	15th
10th	12.6	12.4	12.4	12.0	11.5	11.1	11.1	11.2	10th
5th	13.1	13.0	13.0	12.5	12.0	11.7	11.5	11.7	5th
0	15.0	20.0	22.0	16.0	16.0	16.6	16.7	14.0	0

SHUTTLE RUN FOR GIRLS
Percentile Scores Based on Age/Test Scores in Seconds and Tenths

Percentile	Age								Percentile
	10	11	12	13	14	15	16	17	
100th	8.5	8.8	9.0	8.3	9.0	8.0	8.3	9.0	100th
95th	10.0	10.0	10.0	10.0	10.0	10.0	10.0	10.0	95th
90th	10.5	10.2	10.2	10.2	10.3	10.3	10.2	10.3	90th
85th	10.8	10.6	10.5	10.5	10.4	10.5	10.4	10.4	85th
80th	11.0	10.9	10.8	10.6	10.5	10.7	10.6	10.5	80th
75th	11.0	11.0	10.9	10.8	10.6	10.9	10.8	10.6	75th
70th	11.1	11.0	11.0	11.0	10.8	11.0	10.9	10.8	70th
65th	11.4	11.2	11.2	11.0	10.9	11.0	11.0	11.0	65th
60th	11.5	11.4	11.3	11.1	11.0	11.1	11.0	11.0	60th
55th	11.8	11.6	11.5	11.3	11.1	11.2	11.2	11.1	55th
50th	11.9	11.7	11.6	11.4	11.3	11.3	11.2	11.2	50th
45th	12.0	11.8	11.8	11.6	11.4	11.5	11.4	11.4	45th
40th	12.0	12.0	11.9	11.8	11.5	11.6	11.5	11.5	40th
35th	12.1	12.0	12.0	12.0	11.7	11.8	11.8	11.6	35th
30th	12.4	12.1	12.1	12.0	12.0	11.9	12.0	11.8	30th
25th	12.6	12.4	12.3	12.2	12.0	12.0	12.0	12.0	25th
20th	12.8	12.6	12.5	12.5	12.3	12.3	12.2	12.0	20th
15th	13.0	13.0	12.9	13.0	12.6	12.5	12.5	12.3	15th
10th	13.1	13.4	13.2	13.3	13.1	13.0	13.0	13.0	10th
5th	14.0	14.1	13.9	14.0	13.9	13.5	13.9	13.8	5th
0	16.6	18.5	19.8	18.5	17.6	16.0	17.6	20.0	0

TABLE 17 - 4
AAHPER Youth Fitness Test

STANDING BROAD JUMP FOR BOYS
Percentile Scores Based on Age/Test Scores in Feet and Inches

Percentile	Age								Percentile
	10	11	12	13	14	15	16	17	
100th	6' 8"	10' 0"	7'10"	8' 9"	8'11"	9' 2"	9' 1"	9' 8"	100th
95th	6' 1"	6' 3"	6' 6"	7' 2"	7' 9"	8' 0"	8' 5"	8' 6"	95th
90th	5'10"	6' 0"	6' 4"	6'11"	7' 5"	7' 9"	8' 1"	8' 3"	90th
85th	5' 8"	5'10"	6' 2"	6' 9"	7' 3"	7' 6"	7'11"	8' 1"	85th
80th	5' 7"	5' 9"	6' 1"	6' 7"	7' 0"	7' 6"	7' 9"	8' 0"	80th
75th	5' 6"	5' 7"	6' 0"	6' 5"	6'11"	7' 4"	7' 7"	7'10"	75th
70th	5' 5"	5' 6"	5'11"	6' 3"	6' 9"	7' 2"	7' 6"	7' 8"	70th
65th	5' 4"	5' 6"	5' 9"	6' 1"	6' 8"	7' 1"	7' 5"	7' 7"	65th
60th	5' 2"	5' 4"	5' 8"	6' 0"	6' 7"	7' 0"	7' 4"	7' 6"	60th
55th	5' 1"	5' 3"	5' 7"	5'11"	6' 6"	6'11"	7' 3"	7' 5"	55th
50th	5' 0"	5' 2"	5' 0"	5'10"	6' 4"	6' 9"	7' 1"	7' 3"	50th
45th	5' 0"	5' 1"	5' 5"	5' 9"	6' 3"	6' 8"	7' 0"	7' 2"	45th
40th	4'10"	5' 0"	5' 4"	5' 7"	6' 1"	6' 6"	6'11"	7' 0"	40th
35th	4'10"	4'11"	5' 2"	5' 6"	6' 0"	6' 6"	6' 9"	6'11"	35th
30th	4' 8"	4'10"	5' 1"	5' 5"	5'10"	6' 4"	6' 7"	6'10"	30th
25th	4' 6"	4' 8"	5' 0"	5' 3"	5' 8"	6' 3"	6' 6"	6' 8"	25th
20th	4' 5"	4' 7"	4'10"	5' 2"	5' 6"	6' 1"	6' 4"	6' 6"	20th
15th	4' 4"	4' 5"	4' 8"	5' 0"	5' 4"	5'10"	6' 1"	6' 4"	15th
10th	4' 3"	4' 2"	4' 5"	4' 9"	5' 2"	5' 7"	5'11"	6' 0"	10th
5th	4' 0"	4' 0"	4' 2"	4' 5"	4'11"	5' 4"	5' 6"	5' 8"	5th
0	2'10"	1' 8"	3' 0"	2' 9"	3' 8"	2'10"	2' 2"	3' 7"	0

STANDING BROAD JUMP FOR GIRLS
Percentile Scores Based on Age/Test Scores in Feet and Inches

Percentile	Age								Percentile
	10	11	12	13	14	15	16	17	
100th	7' 0"	7'10"	8' 2"	7' 6"	7' 4"	7' 8"	7' 5"	7' 8"	100th
95th	5' 8"	6' 2"	6' 3"	6' 3"	6' 4"	6' 6"	6' 7"	6' 8"	95th
90th	5' 6"	5'10"	6' 0"	6' 0"	6' 2"	6' 3"	6' 4"	6' 4"	90th
85th	5' 4"	5' 8"	5' 9"	5'10"	6' 0"	6' 1"	6' 2"	6' 2"	85th
80th	5' 2"	5' 6"	5' 8"	5' 8"	5'10"	6' 0"	6' 0"	6' 0"	80th
75th	5' 1"	5' 4"	5' 6"	5' 6"	5' 9"	5'10"	5'10"	5'11"	75th
70th	5' 0"	5' 3"	5' 5"	5' 5"	5' 7"	5' 9"	5' 8"	5'10"	70th
65th	5' 0"	5' 2"	5' 4"	5' 4"	5' 6"	5' 7"	5' 7"	5' 9"	65th
60th	4'10"	5' 0"	5' 2"	5' 3"	5' 5"	5' 6"	5' 6"	5' 7"	60th
55th	4' 9"	5' 0"	5' 1"	5' 2"	5' 4"	5' 5"	5' 5"	5' 6"	55th
50th	4' 7"	4'10"	5' 0"	5' 0"	5' 3"	5' 4"	5' 4"	5' 5"	50th
45th	4' 6"	4' 9"	4'11"	5' 0"	5' 1"	5' 3"	5' 3"	5' 3"	45th
40th	4' 5"	4' 8"	4' 9"	4'10"	5' 0"	5' 1"	5' 2"	5' 2"	40th
35th	4' 4"	4' 7"	4' 8"	4' 8"	5' 0"	5' 0"	5' 0"	5' 0"	35th
30th	4' 3"	4' 6"	4' 7"	4' 6"	4' 9"	4'10"	4'11"	5' 0"	30th
25th	4' 2"	4' 4"	4' 5"	4' 6"	4' 8"	4' 8"	4'10"	4'10"	25th
20th	4' 0"	4' 3"	4' 4"	4' 4"	4' 6"	4' 7"	4' 8"	4' 9"	20th
15th	3'11"	4' 1"	4' 2"	4' 2"	4' 3"	4' 6"	4' 6"	4' 7"	15th
10th	3' 9"	3'11"	4' 0"	4' 0"	4' 1"	4' 4"	4' 4"	4' 5"	10th
5th	3' 6"	3' 9"	3' 8"	3' 9"	3'10"	4' 0"	4' 0"	4' 2"	5th
0	2' 8"	2'11"	2'11"	2'11"	3' 0"	2'11"	3' 2"	3' 0"	0

TABLE 17 - 5
AAHPER Youth Fitness Test

50-YARD DASH FOR BOYS
Percentile Scores Based on Age/Test Scores in Seconds and Tenths

| Percentile | Age | | | | | | | | Percentile |
	10	11	12	13	14	15	16	17	
100th	6.0	6.0	6.0	5.8	5.8	5.6	5.6	5.6	100th
95th	7.0	7.0	6.8	6.5	6.3	6.1	6.0	6.0	95th
90th	7.1	7.2	7.0	6.7	6.4	6.2	6.1	6.0	90th
85th	7.4	7.4	7.0	6.9	6.6	6.4	6.2	6.1	85th
80th	7.5	7.5	7.2	7.0	6.7	6.5	6.3	6.2	80th
75th	7.6	7.6	7.3	7.0	6.8	6.5	6.3	6.3	75th
70th	7.8	7.7	7.5	7.1	6.9	6.6	6.4	6.3	70th
65th	8.0	7.8	7.5	7.2	7.0	6.7	6.5	6.4	65th
60th	8.0	7.8	7.6	7.3	7.0	6.7	6.5	6.5	60th
55th	8.1	8.0	7.8	7.4	7.0	6.8	6.6	6.5	55th
50th	8.2	8.0	7.8	7.5	7.1	6.9	6.7	6.6	50th
45th	8.3	8.0	7.9	7.5	7.2	7.0	6.7	6.7	45th
40th	8.5	8.1	8.0	7.6	7.2	7.0	6.8	6.7	40th
35th	8.5	8.3	8.0	7.7	7.3	7.1	6.9	6.8	35th
30th	8.7	8.4	8.2	7.9	7.5	7.1	6.9	6.9	30th
25th	8.8	8.5	8.3	8.0	7.6	7.2	7.0	7.0	25th
20th	9.0	8.7	8.4	8.0	7.8	7.3	7.1	7.0	20th
15th	9.1	9.0	8.6	8.2	8.0	7.5	7.2	7.1	15th
10th	9.5	9.1	8.9	8.4	8.1	7.7	7.5	7.3	10th
5th	10.0	9.5	9.2	8.9	8.6	8.1	7.8	7.7	5th
0	12.0	11.9	12.0	11.1	11.6	12.0	8.6	10.6	0

50-YARD DASH FOR GIRLS
Percentile Scores Based on Age/Test Scores in Seconds and Tenths

| Percentile | Age | | | | | | | | Percentile |
	10	11	12	13	14	15	16	17	
100th	6.0	6.0	5.9	6.0	6.0	6.4	6.0	6.4	100th
95th	7.0	7.0	7.0	7.0	7.0	7.1	7.0	7.1	95th
90th	7.3	7.4	7.3	7.3	7.2	7.3	7.3	7.3	90th
85th	7.5	7.6	7.5	7.5	7.4	7.5	7.5	7.5	85th
80th	7.7	7.7	7.6	7.6	7.5	7.6	7.5	7.6	80th
75th	7.9	7.9	7.8	7.7	7.6	7.7	7.7	7.8	75th
70th	8.0	8.0	7.9	7.8	7.7	7.8	7.9	7.9	70th
65th	8.1	8.0	8.0	7.9	7.8	7.9	8.0	8.0	65th
60th	8.2	8.1	8.0	8.0	7.9	8.0	8.0	8.0	60th
55th	8.4	8.2	8.1	8.0	8.0	8.0	8.1	8.1	55th
50th	8.5	8.4	8.2	8.1	8.0	8.1	8.3	8.2	50th
45th	8.6	8.5	8.3	8.2	8.2	8.2	8.4	8.3	45th
40th	8.8	8.5	8.4	8.4	8.3	8.3	8.5	8.5	40th
35th	8.9	8.6	8.5	8.5	8.5	8.4	8.6	8.6	35th
30th	9.0	8.8	8.7	8.6	8.6	8.6	8.8	8.8	30th
25th	9.0	9.0	8.9	8.8	8.9	8.8	9.0	9.0	25th
20th	9.2	9.0	9.0	9.0	9.0	9.0	9.0	9.0	20th
15th	9.4	9.2	9.2	9.2	9.2	9.0	9.2	9.1	15th
10th	9.6	9.6	9.5	9.5	9.5	9.5	9.9	9.5	10th
5th	10.0	10.0	10.0	10.2	10.4	10.0	10.5	10.4	5th
0	14.0	13.0	13.0	15.7	16.0	18.0	17.0	12.0	0

TABLE 17 - 6
AAHPER Youth Fitness Test

SOFTBALL THROW FOR BOYS
Percentile Scores Based on Age/Test Scores in Feet

Percentile	Age								Percentile
	10	11	12	13	14	15	16	17	
100th	175	205	207	245	246	250	271	291	100th
95th	138	151	165	195	208	221	238	249	95th
90th	127	141	156	183	195	210	222	235	90th
85th	122	136	150	175	187	204	213	226	85th
80th	118	129	145	168	181	198	207	218	80th
75th	114	126	141	163	176	192	201	213	75th
70th	109	121	136	157	172	189	197	207	70th
65th	105	119	133	152	168	184	194	203	65th
60th	102	115	129	147	165	180	189	198	60th
55th	98	113	124	142	160	175	185	195	55th
50th	96	111	120	140	155	171	180	190	50th
45th	93	108	119	135	150	167	175	185	45th
40th	91	105	115	131	146	165	172	180	40th
35th	89	101	112	128	141	160	168	176	35th
30th	84	98	110	125	138	156	165	171	30th
25th	81	94	106	120	133	152	160	163	25th
20th	78	90	103	115	127	147	153	155	20th
15th	73	85	97	110	122	141	147	150	15th
10th	69	78	92	101	112	135	141	141	10th
5th	60	70	76	88	102	123	127	117	5th
0	35	14	25	60	31	60	30	31	0

SOFTBALL THROW FOR GIRLS
Percentile Scores Based on Age/Test Scores in Feet

Percentile	Age								Percentile
	10	11	12	13	14	15	16	17	
100th	167	141	159	150	156	165	175	183	100th
95th	84	95	103	111	114	120	123	120	95th
90th	76	86	96	102	103	110	113	108	90th
85th	71	81	90	94	100	105	104	102	85th
80th	69	77	85	90	95	100	98	98	80th
75th	65	74	80	86	90	95	92	93	75th
70th	60	71	76	82	87	90	89	90	70th
65th	57	66	74	79	84	87	85	87	65th
60th	54	64	70	75	80	84	81	82	60th
55th	52	62	67	73	78	82	78	80	55th
50th	50	59	64	70	75	78	75	75	50th
45th	48	57	61	68	72	75	74	74	45th
40th	46	55	59	65	70	73	71	71	40th
35th	45	52	57	63	68	69	69	69	35th
30th	42	50	54	60	65	66	66	66	30th
25th	40	46	50	57	61	64	63	62	25th
20th	37	44	48	53	59	60	60	58	20th
15th	34	40	45	49	54	58	55	52	15th
10th	30	37	41	45	50	51	50	48	10th
5th	21	32	37	36	45	45	45	40	5th
0	8	13	20	20	25	12	8	20	0

TABLE 17 - 7
AAHPER Youth Fitness Test

600-YARD RUN-WALK FOR BOYS
Percentile Scores Based on Age/Test Scores in Minutes and Seconds

Percentile	10	11	12	13	14	15	16	17	Percentile
100th	1'30"	1'27"	1'31"	1'29"	1'25"	1'26"	1'24"	1'23"	100th
95th	1'58"	1'59"	1'52"	1'46"	1'37"	1'34"	1'32"	1'31"	95th
90th	2' 9"	2' 3"	2' 0"	1'50"	1'42"	1'38"	1'35"	1'34"	90th
85th	2'12"	2' 8"	2' 2"	1'53"	1'46"	1'40"	1'37"	1'36"	85th
80th	2'15"	2'11"	2' 5"	1'55"	1'48"	1'42"	1'39"	1'38"	80th
75th	2'18"	2'14"	2' 9"	1'59"	1'51"	1'44"	1'40"	1'40"	75th
70th	2'20"	2'16"	2'11"	2' 1"	1'53"	1'46"	1'43"	1'42"	70th
65th	2'23"	2'19"	2'13"	2' 3"	1'55"	1'47"	1'45"	1'44"	65th
60th	2'26"	2'21"	2'15"	2' 5"	1'57"	1'49"	1'47"	1'45"	60th
55th	2'30"	2'24"	2'18"	2' 7"	1'59"	1'51"	1'49"	1'48"	55th
50th	2'33"	2'27"	2'21"	2'10"	2' 1"	1'54"	1'51"	1'50"	50th
45th	2'36"	2'30"	2'24"	2'12"	2' 3"	1'55"	1'53"	1'52"	45th
40th	2'40"	2'33"	2'26"	2'15"	2' 5"	1'58"	1'56"	1'54"	40th
35th	2'43"	2'36"	2'30"	2'17"	2' 9"	2' 0"	1'58"	1'57"	35th
30th	2'45"	2'39"	2'34"	2'22"	2'11"	2' 3"	2' 1"	2' 0"	30th
25th	2'49"	2'42"	2'39"	2'25"	2'14"	2' 7"	2' 5"	2' 4"	25th
20th	2'55"	2'48"	2'47"	2'30"	2'19"	2'13"	2' 9"	2' 9"	20th
15th	3' 1"	2'55"	2'57"	2'35"	2'25"	2'20"	2'14"	2'16"	15th
10th	3' 8"	3' 9"	3' 8"	2'45"	2'33"	2'32"	2'22"	2'26"	10th
5th	3'23"	3'30"	3'32"	3' 3"	2'47"	2'50"	2'37"	2'40"	5th
0	4'58"	5' 6"	4'55"	5'14"	5'10"	4'10"	4' 9"	4'45"	0

600-YARD RUN-WALK FOR GIRLS
Percentile Scores Based on Age/Test Scores in Minutes and Seconds

Percentile	10	11	12	13	14	15	16	17	Percentile
100th	1'42"	1'40"	1'39"	1'40"	1'45"	1'40"	1'50"	1'54"	100th
95th	2' 5"	2'13"	2'14"	2'12"	2' 9"	2' 9"	2'10"	2'11"	95th
90th	2'15"	2'19"	2'20"	2'19"	2'18"	2'18"	2'17"	2'22"	90th
85th	2'20"	2'24"	2'24"	2'25"	2'22"	2'23"	2'23"	2'27"	85th
80th	2'26"	2'28"	2'27"	2'29"	2'25"	2'26"	2'26"	2'31"	80th
75th	2'30"	2'32"	2'31"	2'33"	2'30"	2'28"	2'31"	2'34"	75th
70th	2'34"	2'36"	2'35"	2'37"	2'34"	2'34"	2'36"	2'37"	70th
65th	2'37"	2'39"	2'39"	2'40"	2'37"	2'36"	2'39"	2'42"	65th
60th	2'41"	2'43"	2'42"	2'44"	2'41"	2'40"	2'42"	2'46"	60th
55th	2'45"	2'47"	2'45"	2'47"	2'44"	2'43"	2'45"	2'49"	55th
50th	2'48"	2'49"	2'49"	2'52"	2'46"	2'46"	2'49"	2'51"	50th
45th	2'50"	2'53"	2'55"	2'56"	2'51'	2'49"	2'53"	2'57"	45th
40th	2'55"	2'59"	2'58"	3' 0"	2'55"	2'52"	2'56"	3' 0"	40th
35th	2'59"	3' 4"	3' 3"	3' 3"	3' 0"	2'56"	2'59"	3' 5"	35th
30th	3' 3"	3'10"	3' 7"	3' 9"	3' 6"	3' 0"	3' 1"	3'10"	30th
25th	3' 8"	3'15"	3'11"	3'15"	3'12"	3' 5"	3' 7"	3'16"	25th
20th	3'13"	3'22"	3'18"	3'20"	3'19"	3'10"	3'12"	3'22"	20th
15th	3'18"	3'30"	3'24"	3'30"	3'30"	3'18"	3'19"	3'29"	15th
10th	3'27"	3'41"	3'40"	3'49"	3'48"	3'28"	3'30"	3'41"	10th
5th	3'45"	3'59"	4' 0"	4'11"	4' 8"	3'56"	3'45"	3'56"	5th
0	4'47"	4'53"	5'10"	5'10"	5'50"	5'10"	5'52"	6'40"	0

TABLE 17 - 8
AAHPER Youth Fitness Test

PHYSICAL FITNESS TEST NORMS
Percentile Scores for College Men

Percentile	Pull-Up	Sit-Up	Shuttle Run	Standing Broad Jump	50-Yard Dash	Softball Throw	600-Yard Run-Walk
100th	20	100	8.3	9' 6"	5.5	315	1:12
95th	12	99	9.0	8' 5"	6.1	239	1:35
90th	10	97	9.1	8' 2"	6.2	226	1:38
85th	10	79	9.1	7'11"	6.3	217	1:40
80th	9	68	9.2	7'10"	6.4	211	1:42
75th	8	61	9.4	7' 8"	6.5	206	1:44
70th	8	58	9.5	7' 7"	6.5	200	1:45
65th	7	52	9.5	7' 6"	6.6	196	1:47
60th	7	51	9.6	7' 5"	6.6	192	1:49
55th	6	50	9.6	7' 4"	6.7	188	1:50
50th	6	47	9.7	7' 3"	6.8	184	1:52
45th	5	44	9.8	7' 1"	6.8	180	1:53
40th	5	41	9.9	7' 0"	6.9	176	1:55
35th	4	38	10.0	6'11"	7.0	171	1:57
30th	4	36	10.0	6'10"	7.0	166	1:59
25th	3	34	10.1	6' 9"	7.1	161	2:01
20th	3	31	10.2	6' 7"	7.1	156	2:05
15th	2	29	10.4	6' 5"	7.2	150	2:09
10th	1	26	10.6	6' 2"	7.5	140	2:15
5th	0	22	11.1	5'10"	7.7	125	2:25
0	0	0	13.9	4' 2"	9.1	55	3:43

Percentile Scores for College Women

Percentile	Modified Pull-Up	Sit-Up	Shuttle Run	Standing Broad Jump	50-Yard Dash	Softball Throw	600-Yard Run-Walk
100th	40	50	7.5	7'10"	5.4	184	1:49
95th	39	43	10.2	6' 6"	7.3	115	2:19
90th	38	35	10.5	6' 3"	7.6	103	2:27
85th	33	31	10.7	6' 1"	7.7	96	2:32
80th	30	29	10.9	5'11"	7.8	90	2:37
75th	28	27	11.0	5'10"	7.9	86	2:41
70th	26	25	11.1	5' 8"	8.0	82	2:44
65th	24	24	11.2	5' 7"	8.1	79	2:48
60th	22	22	11.3	5' 6"	8.2	76	2:51
55th	21	21	11.5	5' 5"	8.3	73	2:54
50th	20	20	11.6	5' 4"	8.4	70	2:58
45th	18	19	11.7	5' 3"	8.6	67	3:01
40th	17	18	11.9	5' 2"	8.7	65	3:05
35th	16	16	12.0	5' 0"	8.8	62	3:08
30th	15	15	12.1	4'11"	9.0	59	3:13
25th	13	14	12.2	4'10"	9.1	57	3:18
20th	12	13	12.4	4' 8"	9.2	54	3:23
15th	11	11	12.6	4' 7"	9.4	51	3:29
10th	9	9	12.9	4' 5"	9.7	47	3:38
5th	7	7	13.4	4' 1"	10.1	42	3:53
0	0	0	17.3	2' 3"	13.7	5	5:29

JCR Test.[20]

Objective: The JCR Test is a three-item test battery designed to measure ability to perform fundamental motor skills such as jumping, climbing, running, and dodging. The test is intended to assess total ability rather than the basic elements which make up total ability.

Sex and Age Level: College Men. Could be also used for high school. Test was developed using men from the United States Air Force.

Reliability and Validity: Reliability coefficients of .91 and .94 were obtained for the total battery, using different groups. Individual item reliability coefficients ranged from .80 to .95. Validity was established using a 25-variable criterion in which an R of .81 was obtained. An R of .90 was found for the test with a 19-item criterion of physical fitness.

Test Equipment Materials Needed: A vertical jump board, or wall surface, chalk for the fingers, chinning bar, stop watch, and bankboards for the shuttle run are needed to administer this test. The bankboards are about 12 inches wide and set at an angle of 40 degrees with the floor. The bankboards are 10 yards apart with each lane measuring 6 feet in width. Exact instructions are given in the original reference.

VERTICAL JUMP.

Directions: The jump is performed in the typical manner. Three trials are given. The best of three trials is used for scoring.

CHINNING.

Directions: The usual directions for chinning are followed. Half chins do not count.

SHUTTLE RUN.

Directions: The subject's starting position is standing inside the starting line with one foot in contact with the bankboard. On the signal to begin he runs as fast as he can to the opposite bankboard, touches it, and runs back to the starting bankboard. He should spring from the bankboards and not bounce off them. Five complete round trips are made for a total distance of 100 yards. He thus finishes at the same line from which he started, stepping over the board at the finish.

Scoring: The elapsed time to the nearest half-second is recorded as the score for this event.

Additional Pointers: (1) Several lanes can be constructed to facilitate group testing. Several students can be tested with only one watch as follows: the tester begins counting aloud in half seconds (*20-hup, 21-hup, 22-hup,* etc.) as the first runner nears the finish line and continues counting until the last runner has finished. Students or assistants are assigned a subject to watch and listen for his time as he crosses the finish line. (2) The tester should practice counting this way silently for a few seconds before he counts aloud in order to establish the proper rhythm. (3) The subject must touch the bankboard each time. If he does not, he should be stopped and given a brief rest, then retested. (4) The subjects should be given a short practice period in which to become accustomed to the bankboard turns. (5) The subjects should be told the number of laps they have completed as they are running and be given additional instructions, such as *two more to go,* etc.

Safety Precautions: (1) The floor surface should be smooth and free from obstructions. (2) The bankboards should be well braced to prevent movement or collapse. (3) The subjects should be given ample warm-up. (4) It must be stressed that each runner stay within his running lane.

Norms are provided in the original reference. It is suggested that each tester construct his own norms.

Division of Girls' and Women's Athletics (DGWS) Physical Performance Test.[17]

Objective: The Research Committee of the National Section on Women's Athletics (NSWA), now the Division of Girl's and Women's Athletics (DGWS), selected eight tests for the purpose of assessing muscular control and coordination, speed and agility, and strength.

Sex and Age Level: High school girls.

Validity: The items were selected by the Research Committee on an empirical basis. Therefore, the items are assumed to have face validity. Some of the items were chosen to evaluate general motor ability, such as the standing broad jump, the basketball throw, and the potato race. Agility measures include the ten-second squat thrust as well as the potato race. The strength of the arm and shoulders is represented by performance in the pull-ups or push-ups, and the abdominal muscle strength is measured by sit-ups. Endurance is assessed by the thirty-second squat thrust. No reliability figures were given; however, the test items were administered to over twenty thousand girls, and scoring scales were constructed based on data gathered from the twenty-five schools showing the best performances.

Test Items: The eight items are as follows: standing broad jump, basketball throw, potato race, pull-ups, push-ups, sit-ups, 10-second squat thrust, and 30-second squat thrust. The Committee recommends that if it is not feasible to administer all eight of the tests, the battery may be shortened to the following:

> Standing broad jump
> Basketball throw
> Potato race or 10-second squat thrust
> Sit-ups
> Push-ups or pull-ups

STANDING BROAD JUMP.

Directions: Performed in the usual manner, scored in feet and inches.

BASKETBALL THROW.

Directions: The floor should be marked off in 5-foot intervals to facilitate scoring. The subject stands behind the restraining, or zero line, and throws a regulation basketball as far as possible. She may take one step in throwing, but she must not step over the restraining line. Any method of throwing may be used. Two trials are given.

Scoring: Spotters are employed to stand along the throwing lanes at a distance the girl has thrown in practice. As soon as the ball hits, the spotters immediately stand at that point. The marked zone is noted and the distance to the nearest foot is recorded. The best of two trials is the score.

POTATO RACE.

Directions: The same procedures are followed as were described for the shuttle race in the AAHPER Youth Fitness Test. Two trials are given.

Scoring: The best score of the two trials to the nearest fifth of a second is recorded.

SIT-UPS.

Directions: Same as for AAHPER Youth Fitness Test, except that the girls do not stop at 50.

Scoring: The maximum number is recorded.

PUSH-UPS.

Directions: The girl assumes a position in which the hands are placed on the mat, shoulder width apart; the knees are in contact with the mat with feet raised; and the

body is kept straight from head to knees. The subject bends her arms to touch the chest to the floor and pushes up again keeping the body as straight as possible throughout. The arms must come to complete extension, and only the chest is allowed to touch the floor. The subject repeats the exercise with no rest for as long as possible.
Scoring: The maximum number of repetitions is recorded.

PULL-UPS.
Directions: A horizontal bar is adjusted at a height of 3½ feet from the floor. The subject grips the bar and moves under it so that her arms are completely extended, her knees are bent to right angles, and her body is straight from the shoulders to the knees and parallel with the floor. All of her weight should be borne by hands and feet. The subject then pulls upward, using only her arms (no leg action) until her chest touches the bar. The body moves from the knees with no bending at the hips or rounding of the back, nor is resting allowed. The arms must be completely extended after each touching of the chest.
Scoring: The maximum number of repetitions is recorded.

SQUAT THRUSTS.
Directions: The squat thrusts are performed in the usual manner as described in Chapter VII. Emphasis is placed on making each of the four parts of the exercise distinct – (1) squat, (2) front leaning rest, (3) squat, (4) return to standing position – and the subject's body should be straight with no sway or bend when in the front leaning rest position.
Scoring: The number of complete movements, plus extra quarter movements performed in the ten-second or thirty-second time period.
Additional Pointers for the DGWS Test Battery: (1) The Committee recommends that the test should not be given to any students who have not been given medical approval for strenuous exercise, and no girl should be tested during her menstrual period. (2) Form should be stressed instead of all out maximum performance. Not more than two tests should be given in one day; furthermore, not more than two tests that are to be used for official records should generally be given in one week. (3) The test scores should be employed to evaluate the program with respect to selecting activities which provide balanced development. (4) Girls who score very poorly on the tests should be given special attention as to cause and remedial work.
Norms: The scoring table with the scale based on three standard deviations above and below the mean is given in Table 17 - 9.

Oregon Motor Fitness Test.[18]

The Oregon State Department of Education provides a manual of motor fitness test batteries and norms for three age groups: intermediate boys and girls, grades 4, 5, 6; junior high school boys and girls, grades 7, 8, 9; and senior high school boys and girls, grades 10, 11, and 12. For boys in grades four through six the items include the standing broad jump, floor push-ups, and sit-ups. The junior and senior high school tests are pull-ups, jump and reach, and the 160-yard potato race. All of the foregoing test items, except the potato race, have been described previously.

The 160-yard potato race is conducted in an area requiring 70 feet for running, plus some space for finishing. Three circles are drawn on the floor in a line; each circle is one foot in diameter. The first circle is drawn immediately behind the starting line. The second circle is 50 feet, and the third is 70 feet away. A small block or eraser 2″ X 4″ is placed in circle two and another in circle three. The subject runs to circle two, picks up

TABLE 17 - 9

Norms for DGWS Physical Performance Test*

Scale Score	Standing Broad Jump	Basket-Ball Throw	Potato Race	Pull-Ups	Push-Ups	Sit-Ups	10-Second Squat Thrust	30-Second Squat Thrust	Scale Score
100	7-9	78	8.4	47	61	65	9-1	24	100
95	7-7	75	8.6	45	58	61	9	23	95
90	7-4	72	8.8	42	54	57	8-3	22	90
85	7-2	68	9.0	39	51	54	8-1	21	85
80	6-11	65	9.4	37	47	50	8	20	80
75	6-9	62	9.6	34	43	46	7-3	19	75
70	6-7	59	10.0	32	39	43	7-1	18-2	70
65	6-4	56	10.2	29	36	39	7	18	65
60	6-2	53	10.4	26	32	36	6-2	17	60
55	6-0	50	10.8	24	28	33	6-1	16	55
50	5-9	46	11.0	21	25	29	6	15	50
45	5-7	43	11.2	18	21	25	5-2	14-2	45
40	5-5	40	11.6	16	17	22	5-1	14	40
35	5-2	37	11.8	13	13	18	4-3	13	35
30	5-0	34	12.0	10	10	15	4-2	12	30
25	4-9	31	12.4	8	6	11	4	11	25
20	4-7	27	12.6	5	2	7	3-3	10	20
15	4-4	24	13.0	3	1	3	3-2	9	15
10	4-2	21	13.2	1	0	1	3	8-2	10
5	4-0	18	13.4	0	0	0	2-3	7-2	5
0	3-9	15	13.6	0	0	0	2-2	7	0

*Eleanor Metheny, Chairman, "Physical Performance Levels for High School Girls," *Journal of Health and Physical Education,* June, 1945. p. 309.

the block and runs to place it in the first circle. He then runs to circle three, picks up the block and places it in circle one. As soon as he has placed it in the circle, he grabs the first block and returns it to circle two, runs back and gets the remaining block and carries it to circle three. He finishes the race by dashing across the finish line. The score is in seconds.

The Girls' Battery also contains three items. They are: the <u>standing broad jump</u>, <u>hanging in arm-flexed position</u>, and <u>crossed-arm curl-ups</u>. The <u>hanging in arm-flexed position test</u> is similar to the Flexed-Arm Hang for girls in the AAHPER Youth Fitness Test except that the timing continues as long as there is some flexion in the elbow. The time stops as soon as the elbow straightens.

The <u>crossed-arm curl-ups</u> are done with the knees bent at about a ninety degree angle and with the soles of the feet flat on the floor. The feet are held down by a partner. The subject folds her arms across her chest and raises to a sitting position without using the arms in any way to help. The subject then returns to a lying position and repeats the exercise as many times as possible. It is not permissable to bounce back up, nor to rest at any time.

California Physical Performance Tests.[2]

There are five test items for boys and girls from 10 to 18 years of age in the California Physical Performance Tests. The items are: <u>pull-ups for boys</u>, <u>knee push-ups for girls</u>, <u>standing broad jump</u>, <u>knee bent situps for time</u>, <u>50-yard dash</u>, and <u>softball throw</u> for distance. Nearly all the test items have been described previously. It should be noted that several of the AAHPER Youth Fitness Test items were taken from this test. The knee push-ups are performed as outlined in the NSWA Test except that the maximum is 50. Some of the unique features of the knee-bent sit-ups for time should be mentioned.

KNEE-BENT SIT-UPS FOR TIME. The sit-up is accomplished in the manner described in Chapter XV for the curl-ups. The hands are clasped behind the head, and the subject raises the trunk by lifting first the head, then the shoulders, and then the back. Each student must show that he or she can do this exercise by performing five sit-ups for the testers before proceeding with the time trials. The following time limits are observed: 30 seconds for boys and girls 10 and 11; 60 seconds for boys 12, 13, and 14 and for all girls 12 and over; and 90 seconds for boys 15 and above.

The revised norms for the test battery are in percentiles and are based on only sex and age. Espenschade[7] found that height and weight did not significantly affect performance any more than age alone.

The Navy Standard Physical Fitness Test.[21]

The Navy Standard Physical Fitness Test is an example of the type of motor fitness tests used by the armed forces. It has also had widespread utilization by colleges and universities. The five test items in the battery are the following: <u>squat thrusts</u> for one minute, <u>sit-ups</u> as given in the AAHPER test, <u>push-ups</u>, <u>pull-ups</u>, and <u>squat jumps</u>. Norms in the form of T-scores are available, based on the performance of well-conditioned Navy men.

The Rogers Physical Fitness Index.[22]

The Rogers Physical Fitness Index (PFI) is more of a test of physical fitness than motor fitness. It is made up of muscular strength and endurance items that were selected because they were not amendable to improvement due to skill. Rogers adapted this test from an earlier battery devised by Sargent. The test items include the following ones: right and left grip strength, back lift, leg lift, pull-ups, push-ups (dips), and lung capacity.

The test can be given to both sexes from age eight to thirty-eight. A strength index is found by calculating an arm strength score in which the number of pull-ups and push-ups are added and then multiplied by the value obtained from the following formula:

$$\frac{Weight\ (in\ lbs.)}{10} + Height\ (in\ inches)\ - 60$$

The resulting arm strength score is then added to the scores in pounds for the grip strength tests, the back and leg lifts, and the lung capacity score in cubic inches. This total is the *Strength Index*. The score in itself is supposed to be a measure of general athletic ability and not a measure of physical fitness nor of skill in any particular sport. The physical Fitness Index is determined by consulting a table of strength index norms based upon sex, weight, and age. The formula for computing the PFI is as follows:

$$PFI = \frac{Achieved\ Strength\ Index}{Normal\ Strength\ Index}\ \times\ 100$$

Therefore, a person who is *average* in physical fitness would have a PFI of 100. The PFI score marking the lowest quartile is 85, and 115 denotes the upper quartile.

This test has excellent credentials and has been utilized extensively for screening and for research purposes. The dynamometers needed for the measurement of grip strength and for measuring back and leg strength are quite expensive. The test also demands trained testers. This is particularly true for the leg strength test where an error in adjustment of the belt and chain needed for the lift of only an inch or so can make a difference of several hundred pounds. The test takes considerable time to administer unless there are several back and leg dynamometers and numerous testers available. Generally speaking, the test is not likely to be used in most high schools. For the above reasons, this test was not presented here. Clarke[5] gives a thorough description of the administration of the test, and a comprehensive discussion of the validity of the PFI, suggested revisions of the battery and implications for its use.

Problems Associated with Motor Fitness Testing

As in the discussion of the measurement of motor ability, the problems associated with motor fitness tests pertain primarily to the unique problems concerning the individual test items. For example, in running tests of agility the kind of footwear and the condition of the running surface are important considerations which will greatly influence performance. Regarding this particular point, perhaps more utilization could be made of bankboards such as are used in the JCR Test. They certainly prevent the excessive sliding that typifies many agility testing situations.

A number of authorities in the areas of anatomy and kinesiology have objected to the performance of sit-ups with straight legs. Sit-ups done in this manner are said to involve the iliopsoas more so than the abdominal muscles, and it has been observed that the iliopsoas muscle does not ordinarily require additional exercise. More important, however, is the possible harm that can be done to the back in persons with weak abdominal muscles. Because of the attachment of the iliopsoas to the lumbar vertebrae, straight leg sit-ups are said to cause excessive pull and possible strain in the lumbar area.

Thus, bent knee sit-ups are recommended since they reduce the effects of the iliopsoas and are directed more to the abdominal muscles. Despite these objections many motor fitness tests, including the AAHPER test, use the straight leg sit-ups.

Most of the motor fitness tests require very little equipment, which is a good point in their favor. They are also relatively easy to administer. Each local setting, whether it be a single school or county or state, should strive to establish standardized testing procedures. Through clinics and workshops the various fine points of administration that are not covered in the directions should be agreed upon. This is, of course, the principal value of the laboratory portion of a class in tests and measurements. Without actually going through the tests and discussing the procedures, it is impossible to attain the rigid standardization that is necessary for accurate and worthwhile results. For the same reasons the teacher should exercise good judgment in using national norms. These norms are intended only for general reference. It should be obvious that under the varied conditions for testing that are allowable in a test such as the AAHPER Youth Fitness Test the results will also vary. For example, if some testers administer the shuttle race out of doors and others use a gymnasium floor, their scores would hardly be comparable. Similarly, if the 50-yard dash is given in one instance on a track and another on the grass, variation in scores will result. In most cases the makers of tests recommend that local norms be constructed. In any case the norms should be made available to the students so as to have maximum interpretative and motivational values. We repeat once more, a test should be used for evaluation on the part of the teacher, the students, the parents, the administration and the general public.

Brief Summary of Research Findings Concerning Motor Fitness

The literature in the area of motor fitness is so extensive it would fill volumes. There have been numerous studies reported on constructing tests, on the contribution of various activities in developing fitness, and the relationship of fitness to other traits and types of performance. In this brief review of literature the term physical fitness is sometimes used by the writers of the studies, but the measuring devices employed are motor fitness tests as the term is used in this text.

Wilbur[24] compared two types of activity programs, a sports program and an apparatus program, in developing motor fitness. The sports program was found to be superior for developing arm and shoulder strength, body coordination, agility and control. The programs were equal in improving leg speed and strength and endurance. In a somewhat similar study Landiss[16] investigated the contributions of eight selected physical education activities in developing fitness. It was found that the combined activities of tumbling and gymnastics were most effective in developing motor fitness and motor ability, and that tennis, swimming, and boxing ranked lowest.

Davis[6] found that a training and conditioning program for the 200-yard crawl stroke in swimming brought about significant improvement in motor fitness tests. Campbell[3] studied the effects of supplemental weight training given to members of football, basketball, and track squads with regard to improving motor fitness performance. His findings showed that weight training produced a significantly greater increase in fitness than the normal conditioning program alone. A program of creative activities was found by Estes[8] to produce increases in muscular fitness, strength, balance and flexibility.

Keough[12] compared a daily physical education program with a program which met twice a week on the development of motor fitness in third and fifth grade children. The actual time spent in class was the same for both programs, since the daily program lasted for four weeks and the two-day-a-week program continued for ten weeks. Both programs were equally effective in improving motor fitness. Fabricus[9] found that a physical education program for fourth grade boys and girls in which calisthenics were added to the normal program improved fitness, as measured by the Oregon Motor Fitness Test, to a greater degree than the program without added calisthenics. Wireman[25] concluded from his study that a knowledge of results of performance in calisthenics, games, and sports facilitated improvement in motor fitness.

Harkness[10] compared the physical education program with an ROTC program on improvement in motor fitness as measured by the JCR Test. The physical education program was significantly superior to the ROTC program in the development and maintenance of motor fitness.

A number of studies have shown that programs of conditioning will produce gains in fitness.[11,14,23] In contradiction to this, Campney and Wehr[4] concluded that a ten week training period utilizing the exercises advocated by the President's Council on Physical Fitness was not likely to produce significant improvements in any of the fitness components studied except in flexibility. Kirby[13] investigated the effects of different amounts of extra exercise performed in addition to the regular physical education activities on improvement of college men on the JCR Test. He found that the gains in the JCR scores were inversely proportional to the number of additional exercises. He concluded that the intensity of performing the exercises in a short time was more influential than the number of exercises performed.

BIBLIOGRAPHY

1. *AAHPER Youth Fitness Test Manual,* Revised ed., Washington, D.C.: American Association for Health, Physical Education and Recreation, 1965.

2. *California Physical Performance Tests,* Sacramento, California: Bureau of Health Education, Physical Education, and Recreation, California State Department of Education, 1962.

3. Campbell, Robert L., "Effects of Supplemental Weight Training on the Physical Fitness of Athletic Squads," *Research Quarterly,* 33:343-355, October, 1962.

4. Campney, Harry K., and Richard W. Wehr, "Effects of Calisthenics on Selected Components of Physical Fitness," *Research Quarterly,* 36:393-402, December, 1965.

5. Clarke, H. Harrison, *Application of Measurement to Health and Physical Education,* 4th ed., Englewood Cliffs, New Jersey: Prentice-Hall, Inc., 1967, Chapter 7.

6. Davis, J. F., "Effects of Training and Conditioning for Middle Distance Swimming Upon Various Physical Measures," *Research Quarterly,* 30:399-412, December, 1959.

7. Espenschade, Anna S., "Restudy of Relationships Between Physical Performances of School Children and Age, Height, and Weight," *Research Quarterly,* 34:144-153, May, 1963.

8. Estes, Mary M., "The Role of Creative Play Equipment in Developing Muscular Fitness," (Microcarded Doctoral Dissertation, State University of Iowa, 1959).

9. Fabricius, Helen, "Effect of Added Calisthenics on the Physical Fitness of Fourth Grade Boys and Girls," *Research Quarterly,* 35:135-140, May, 1964.

10. Harkness, William W., "The Contributions of AFROTC and Physical Education Experiences to Selected Components of Fitness of College Men," (Microcarded Doctoral Dissertation, Stanford University, 1957).

11. Hughes, B. O., "Test Results of the University of Michigan Physical Conditioning Program June 15 through September 26, 1942," *Research Quarterly,* 13:498511, December, 1942.

12. Keough, Betty J., "The Effects of a Daily and Two Day Per Week Physical Education Program Upon Motor Fitness of Children," (Microcarded Doctoral Dissertation, State University of Iowa, 1962).

13. Kirby, Ronald F., "The Effects of Various Exercise Programs Involving Different Amounts of Exercise on the Development of Certain Components of Physical Fitness," (Unpublished Doctoral Dissertation, Louisiana State University, 1966).

14. Kistler, Joy W., "A Study of the Results of Eight Weeks of Participation in a University Physical Fitness Program," *Research Quarterly,* 15:23-28, March, 1944.

15. Kraus, Hans, and Ruth Hirschland, "Minimum Muscular Fitness Tests in School Children," *Research Quarterly,* 25:178188, May, 1954.

16. Landiss, C. W., "Influence of Physical Education Activities on Motor Ability and Physical Fitness of Male Freshmen," *Research Quarterly,* 26:295-307, October, 1955.

17. Metheney, Eleanor, "Physical Performance Levels for High School Girls," *Journal of Health and Physical Education,* 16:32-35, June, 1945.

18. *Motor Fitness Tests for Oregon Schools,* Salem, Oregon: State Department of Education, 1962.

19. Nixon, Eugene, and Frederich W. Cozens, *An Introduction to Physical Education,* 5th ed., revised by John E. Nixon and Florence S. Frederickson, Philadelphia: W. B. Saunders Company, 1959, p. 209; 6th ed., 1964.

20. Phillips, B. E., "The JCR Test," *Research Quarterly,* 18:12-29, March, 1947.

21. *Physical Fitness Manual for the U.S. Navy,* Bureau of Naval Personnel, Training Division, Physical Section, 1943, Chapter 4.

22. Rogers, Frederick Rand, *Physical Capacity Tests in the Administration of Physical Education,* New York: Bureau of Publications, Teachers College, Columbia University, 1926.

23. Sills, F. D., "Special Conditioning Exercises for Students with Low Scores on Physical Fitness Tests," *Research Quarterly,* 25:333-337, October, 1954.

24. Wilbur, E. A., "A Comparative Study of Physical Fitness Indices as Measured by Two Programs of Physical Education: The Sports Method and the Apparatus Method," *Research Quarterly,* 14:326-332, October, 1943.

25. Wireman, Billy O., "Comparison of Four Approaches to Increasing Physical Fitness," *Research Quarterly,* 31:658-666, December, 1960.

Chapter XVIII

THE MEASUREMENT OF
SPORTS SKILLS

One of the major objectives of physical education is the development of neuro-muscular skills. It naturally follows then that physical educators should strive to construct precise and meaningful measuring devices to help evaluate the extent to which this objective is being met. Much of the total physical education program is devoted to the acquisition of sports skills. Thus, it is doubly important that continued efforts be made to scientifically construct valid, reliable, and objective tests in the various sports activities.

Utilization of Sports Skills Tests

There are many ways in which the teacher and the student may use skill tests. Some of these purposes of measurement are the same as for tests in other areas. But again, because sports activities represent such a major part of the physical education program, these performance tests are especially applicable to the instructional phase. Some specific uses of skills tests are suggested below:

1. The tests may be used to measure achievement in the particular sports activity.
    a. This information may be used to help evaluate the instructional program in terms of the effectiveness of the teaching methods and the strengths and weaknesses of the course's content.
    b. Achievement measures may also be utilized, in conjunction with other information, for grading purposes.
2. Skill tests can, and should, play an important role as a teaching aid to supplement instruction and to be used for practice. This would apply to the coach as well as to the teacher.
3. Skill tests enable each student to objectively plot his individual progress throughout the course and, conceivably, from one year to the next.
4. Skill tests can be used for diagnostic purposes by pointing out needs for special emphasis at each particular grade level in which a sport is taught. This is one way to avoid the needless repetition and lack of progression that characterizes many physical education programs.
5. In some cases skill test items can, in themselves, be used for competition in intramural programs and for rainy day activities.
6. Skill tests have been used effectively as one of the means of interpreting the program to the administration, the parents, and the public.
7. Skill tests can and should serve as excellent motivational devices.

Some Practical Sports Skills Tests

In this section some practical tests for measuring sports skills are presented. The reader is cautioned not to rely too heavily on one test or any battery of tests. Except in those sports such as archery, bowling, golf, certain track events, etc. in which the actual score itself is essentially an objective measure of achievement, skill tests can only measure certain aspects of performance in a particular sport. Furthermore, even in those sports mentioned above there are many factors such as environmental conditions, emotional *pressure,* and daily variations in performance that greatly influence one's score. It is suggested that the teacher think of skills tests more as instructional aids and motivational devices for the students, rather than as valid measures of the students' ability to play a particular sport. In addition, the teacher should be especially alert to use these tests in developing local norms which are applicable and meaningful to the individual situation with regard to the factors of age, sex, interests, and socio-economic setting.

Sound tests have not been constructed for all sports. The authors have selected the following tests on the basis of their practicability in terms of the time required to administer them, the limited equipment needed, the ease of scoring, and their ability to measure at least certain aspects of performance in that sport. In some cases only one or two items have been taken from a particular battery; in other cases the entire battery is briefly described. The reader should consult the original reference if a more complete description in a specific test is desired.

Archery

Hyde Archery Test.[17]

Hyde constructed standards of performance for college women in the Columbia Round, which is a standard event in archery. This event consists of 24 arrows shot at 50 yards, 24 at 40 yards, and 24 at 30 yards.

The standard 48-inch target face is used. The target has a gold center worth 9, an adjacent red circle worth 7, a blue circle worth 5, a black circle worth 3, and an outside white circle worth 1. The center of the gold circle is 4 feet from the ground.

The directions are as follows:

1. It is suggested that an initial test be given after a minimum of practice, such as 120 arrows shot at each of the three distances. Then a final test should be given near the end of the course to adequately measure achievement.
2. The arrows should be shot in ends of 6 arrows each. Only one practice end is to be allowed for each distance. Twenty-four arrows must be shot at each distance.
3. The entire test, or round, does not have to be completed in one day, but testing at least one distance should be finished each session.
4. In scoring an arrow which cuts two colors the higher value is given. If an arrow goes completely through the target, or if it bounces off from the target, an arbitrary score of 5 is given for that arrow.

There are three parts to the achievement scale.[18]

1. There is a scale for the first test, or round.
2. There is a scale for the final test, or round, which indicates achievement after much practice.
3. There is an achievement scale given for each of the distances of 50, 40, and 30 yards. It should be noted that these scales were taken from the final round scores, thus beginners would be expected to be fairly low on the scale.

Badminton

French Short Serve Test.[29]

<u>Purpose</u>: To measure accuracy of placement and ability in the low, short serve in badminton.

<u>Age and Sex</u>: College women (but can be used equally well with men).

<u>Validity</u>: With tournament rankings as a criterion, coefficients from .41 to .66 have been reported.

<u>Reliability</u>: Reliability coefficients from .51 to .89 have been obtained by using the odd-even method and the Spearman-Brown Prophecy Formula. The amount of playing experience apparently inversely influences the size of the reliability coefficient.

<u>Equipment and Floor Markings</u>: A clothesline rope should be stretched above the net, on the same standards, at a distance of 20 inches from the top of the net. A tightly strung badminton racket is needed and at least 5 serviceable shuttles should be available for each player. Markings 2 inches wide in the form of arcs are drawn on the floor at distances of 22, 30, 38, and 46 inches from the midpoint of the intersection of the center line and the short service line of the right service court. (See Figure 18 - 1.) The distances include the width of the 2-inch lines.

<u>Directions</u>: The subject stands in the service court diagonally opposite from the target. Twenty serves are attempted, either consecutively or in groups of ten. The subject tries to send the shuttle <u>between</u> the net and the rope. The scorer stands nearer the center of the left service court, facing the target (designated as B in Figure 18 - 1). The subject tries to hit the the target area nearest the intersection of the center line and short service line. Shuttles which hit on a line are given the higher point value.

<u>Scoring</u>: The zones are given point values of 5, 4, 3, 2, and 1 as indicated in Figure 18 - 1. The value of the area in which each shuttle hits is recorded as the score for each trial. Any trial which does not pass between the net and rope counts as zero; similarly, any trial landing out of bounds, either to the side or short of the short service line is zero. If the shuttle hits the rope, it is reserved and no trial counted.

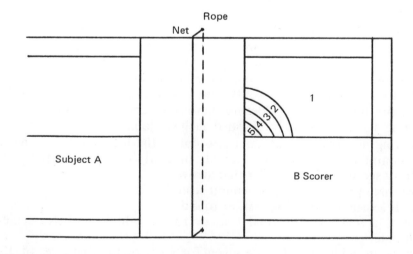

FIGURE 18 - 1

Court Markings for French Short Serve Test

Additional Pointers: (1) It is recommended that the test not be given until the students have had adequate practice. The test tends to be unreliable for beginning players until a certain degree of skill has been attained. (2) It is time-consuming to administer unless there are several courts so that the testing does not interfere with regular play. (3) In keeping with a realistic game situation the subject should probably be instructed to serve from a point no closer than 2 or 3 feet from the short service line in his court.

Scott and Fox Long Serve Test.[29]

Purpose: To measure ability to serve high and deep to the rear of the court.

Age and Sex: May be used for both sexes. College and/or high school level.

Validity: The test correlated .54 with subjective ratings by judges on forty-five university women.

Reliability: Reliability coefficients of .68 and .77 were obtained by Scott and Fox using the odd-even trials method and the Spearman-Brown Prophecy formula.

Equipment and Floor Markings: Extra standards are needed from which a rope can be stretched across the court at a height of 8 feet and at a distance of 14 feet from the net. A tightly strung racket and at least 5 shuttles in good condition are needed for the test.

Using chalk or washable paint arcs are drawn outward from the intersection of the left singles side line and the long service line. The arcs are drawn at distances of 22, 30, 38, and 46 inches from the midpoint. Each distance includes the width of the 2-inch lines. (See Figure 18 - 2.)

Directions: The subject (A) stands in the service court diagonally opposite the target and attempts to serve over the rope into the corner of the court containing the target zones. The shuttle must pass over the rope in order to score points. Only legal serves count as trials. The target zones are marked according to the point values shown in Figure 18 - 2. Twenty shuttles are served.

Scoring: Any shuttle falling on a line is given the higher point value. The score for the entire test is the total of the 20 trials. Fouls are repeated. The scorer (B) should stand so that he can determine whether or not the shuttle passed over the rope as well as to see where the shuttles hit. Scores are called out to a recorder.

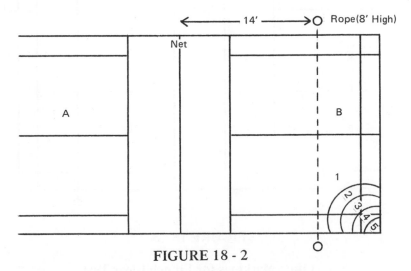

FIGURE 18 - 2

Court Markings for Scott and Fox Long Serve Test

French Clear Test.[29]

   Purpose: To measure power necessary to successfully execute the clear shot in badminton.

   Age and Sex: College women (but can be used with men).

   Validity: The validity coefficient was reported to be .60 when correlated with tournament rankings.

   Reliability: The odd-even method stepped up by the Spearman-Brown Prophecy formula resulted in a correlation of .96.

   Equipment and Materials Needed: A clothesline rope is stretched across the court at a height of 8 feet, at a distance of 14 feet from the net. At least 5 shuttlecocks, a tightly strung racket, and floor markings with lines 1½ inches wide drawn on the floor as shown in Figure 18 - 3.

   Directions: The subject (A) stands behind the short service line on the court opposite the target. Small marks are drawn in each service court 11 feet from the net and 3 feet from the center line. An experienced player (B) (or perhaps the instructor) serves to the subject who stands between the two marks. A total of 20 shuttles are served to each subject who attempts to return each shuttle with a clear shot that goes over the rope and, preferably, lands near the end line. The twenty shuttles may be given consecutively or in groups of ten. The serves to the subject should fall between the two marks. If it does not go that far, or falls outside the marks, the subject is not supposed to return it. Thus, the subject does not have to play a poorly placed shuttle; only those shuttles played by the subject count as trials. The subject repeats any trial in which a foul is committed, such as when a stroke is *carried* or *slung,* or in the event that the shuttle hits the rope. The instructor demonstrates, and two practice trials are then given. The target extends from side to side, thus the subject does not have to confine his shots to one-half the court. The point values are shown in Figure 18 - 3.

   Scoring: The server also acts as the scorer, calling out the point value for each shuttle. The score is the total points for the 20 trials. An assistant records the scores. Any shuttle landing on a line receives the higher point value. Only those shuttles passing over the rope count for score.

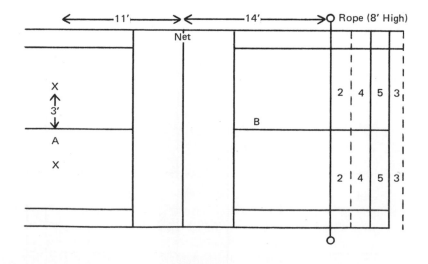

FIGURE 18 - 3

Court Markings for French Clear Test

<u>Additional Pointers</u>: (1) Sometimes it is difficult to ascertain whether the shuttle passed over or under a rope. Consequently, it has sometimes been found effective to use a regular badminton net in place of a rope. (2) It may be necessary for the instructor to determine whether or not the subject should have played a shuttle. In some cases the subject tends to be too selective. (3) The server should strive to standardize as much as possible the placement of his serves for the 20 trials for each subject. He may wish to serve a specified number to particular spots so that the subject would be required to clear from different positions. (4) If desired two subjects can be tested at the same time. When this is done, a mark is placed in each service court 11 feet from the net and 6 feet from the center line. The serves then must carry to the area between the center line and the mark in order for the subject to attempt to play it. One recorder can write down the scores of two subjects with no difficulty.

Basketball

The AAHPER Basketball Skill Test.[1,2]

As part of the AAHPER Sports Skills Tests Project (Frank D. Sills, Chairman), a battery of basketball skills tests has been developed for boys and girls. David K. Brace was test consultant for this sport.

The following criteria guided the selection of test items for the sports skills tests project:

1. The test should have face validity in that the test should duplicate as nearly as possible the skill being measured.
2. Reliability coefficients should be .80 and higher for test items that are scored on the basis of distance, and not lower than .70 for items scored on form and accuracy.
3. Items that could be scored objectively in terms of distance and accuracy were preferred to items that have to be scored on the basis of form.
4. The tests should also serve as practice drills.
5. Items scored for accuracy should provide a normal distribution of scores and differentiate between various levels of ability.
6. Factors other than the subject's skill should be held constant. For example, the test should not be influenced by the skill of someone else as an opponent.
7. The instructions should be explicit and the tests should not require a great deal of equipment, space, time, and expense.

The nine test items for both boys and girls are the (1) front shot, (2) side shot, (3) foul shot, (4) under basket shot, (5) speed pass, (6) jump and reach, (7) overarm pass for accuracy, (8) push pass for accuracy, and (9) dribble. (See Norms in Appendix.)

The only differences in the test items for boys and girls are in the distances for the two passing for accuracy tests and for the side shot. A brief description of each test item follows:

Front Shot. The subject shoots from a marked spot to the left of the free throw line just outside the circle. Any method of shooting is permitted, and the player attempts to make the shot without hitting the backboard. A total of 15 trials are given in series of 5 at a time. He must leave the spot after each 5 shots. <u>Scoring</u>: A basket made counts 2 points; 1 point is awarded for a shot that hits the rim but does not go in (provided that it does not hit the backboard before it hits the rim). A total of 30 points is possible.

Side Shot. Line is drawn near the corner of the court at each side of the basket — 20 feet for boys, 15 feet for girls — measured from the center of the basket. The subject shoots 10 shots from each side, using any type shot. Scoring: Each basket counts 2 points, and 1 point is given for balls that hit the rim but do not go in. In this case it doesn't matter whether or not the backboard is hit. A total of 40 points is possible.

Foul Shot. The subject shoots 20 free throws in series of 5 at a time. He must leave the spot after each 5 shots. Any method of shooting is permitted. Scoring: One point is given for each basket made regardless of how it goes in. A total of 20 points is possible.

Under Basket Shot. The subject stands with the ball under the basket. On the signal to begin he starts making as many lay-up shots as possible within 30 seconds. Any method of shooting is permitted; the subject must recover the ball each time. Two complete trials are given. Scoring: One point is given for each basket made. The number of baskets made in 30 seconds in the better of the two trials is the score.

Speed Pass. The subject stands behind a line drawn 9 feet from the wall. On the signal to begin he passes the ball against the wall as rapidly as possible until 10 passes have hit the wall. All passes have to be made from behind the line, and the subject must recover his pass each time. Two complete trials are given. Scoring: The watch is started as soon as the first pass hits the wall and is stopped when the tenth ball hits. The time to the nearest tenth of a second of the better of the two trials is recorded as the score.

Jump and Reach. The usual procedures for this test are followed. The subject holds a piece of chalk ¾ inch long to make the standing and jumping marks. Two trials are given. Scoring: The score is the difference between the standing and jumping marks of the better of two trials to the nearest inch.

Overarm Pass for Accuracy. The subject, using a one-armed throw, passes the ball at a distance — 35 feet for boys, 20 feet for girls — away from the target which is circular and consists of three circles. The inner circle is 18 inches in diameter; the second circle is 38 inches, and the outer circle is 58 inches in diameter. The bottom of the outer circle is 3 feet from the floor. Ten passes are made, and all must be made from behind the restraining line. Scoring: The point values for the inner, middle, and outer circles are 3, 2, and 1, respectively. Any pass hitting a line is given the higher score. A maximum of 30 points is possible.

Push Pass for Accuracy. The subject passes from behind a line — 25 feet for boys, 15 feet for girls — from the same target as used in the overarm pass. A two-hand push pass is used. Ten trials are given. Scoring: The same scoring procedures are used as in the overarm pass. A total of 30 points is possible.

Dribble. Six chairs are placed in a straight line. The first chair is 5 feet from the starting line; the rest of the chairs are 8 feet apart. The subject stands behind the starting line, and on the command to *go* he begins to dribble around the right side of the first chair, then to the left of the second, and so on alternately around the rest of the chairs and back to the starting line. He may dribble the ball with either hand, but he must use only legal dribbles. He must dribble at least once as each chair is passed. Two trials are allowed. Scoring: The better score of the two trials to the nearest tenth of a second is recorded. The time starts at the signal *go* and stops as the subject crosses the starting line on his return.

LSU Basketball Passing Test.[24]

Purpose: To measure ability to pass and recover the ball accurately while moving.

Equipment and Floor Markings: A basketball, stop watch, smooth wall surface, and tape or paint for marking are required for this test. Six squares are painted or marked by tape as shown in Figure 18 - 4. The bottoms of the low targets are 3 feet from the floor; the bottoms of the high targets are 5 feet from the floor. Each target is 2 × 2 feet (the dimensions include the widths of the lines). The targets are spaced 2 feet apart. A restraining line is drawn 10 feet from the wall. Note: The height of the targets should be lowered for upper elementary and junior high school players. The bottoms of the low and high targets are 2 and 4 feet, respectively, and the restraining line is drawn 7 feet from the wall.

Directions: The subject stands with the ball behind the restraining line facing the target on the far left. On the signal to begin, he passes the ball to the target, recovers the rebound, passes to the second target as he moves to the right. After passing at the last target at the right, he passes again at that target and begins moving to his left. He does this as many times as possible in 30 seconds. He must keep moving, and he is not allowed to pass at any target twice in succession, except for the targets at either end while changing directions. He must pass from behind the restraining line, although he may go in front to retrieve a loose ball. Two trials are given. If the ball gets completely away from the subject, a new trial is given. This only is allowed once. Scoring: The time starts when the first pass hits the wall and stops at the end of 30 seconds. Each target that is hit counts 1 point. Any part of the target that is hit by the ball counts. The score is the total number of points for both trials.

Additional Pointers: (1) Variations can be added. The teacher or coach may want to have the players pass with the right hand while moving to the right and with the left hand while moving to the left. (2) The scoring of the test can be modified in that the subject must hit each target in turn until three or four trips are traversed and the score then is in elapsed seconds. In this version the subject may have to pass at one target several times before being able to move along.

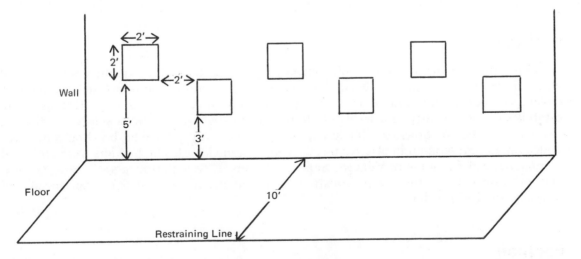

FIGURE 18 - 4

Wall Markings for LSU Basketball Passing Test

LSU Long and Short Test.[24]

Purpose: To measure the ability to shoot long and short shots in basketball, and, to a certain extent, ball handling and dribbling skills.

Equipment and Floor Markings: The equipment needed include a basketball, stop watch, regulation basket and backboard, and a string and chalk for marking the floor. A string is stretched from directly under the basket to the top of the free throw circle. Keeping the string taut, an arc is made with chalk from the top of the free throw circle to the end line on either side of the basket. This is the restraining line for the long shots.

Directions: The subject stands with the ball in back of the restraining line. On the signal to begin he shoots from behind the restraining line, then rushes in to get the rebound, and shoots a short shot. After attempting the lay-up, he runs back behind the restraining line and shoots a long shot, recovers the ball and shoots a short shot. He thus continues, alternating a long and short shot until the whistle blows at the end of one minute. He cannot run with the ball, he must dribble it regardless of how far he must go to retrieve it. He may shoot the short shot from anywhere — it does not have to be a lay-up; the long shot has to be shot from behind the restraining line. Two complete trials are given with a short rest in between the trials.

Scoring: The watch is started on the signal to begin and is stopped at the end of one minute. A long shot counts 2 point and a short shot counts 1 point. The score is the total number of points made in the two trials.

Additional Pointers: (1) The distance from the basket for the long shot can be varied depending upon the age level and the type of shot being stressed. (2) The type of shot may be varied; for example, the teacher or coach may want the subjects to shoot a jump shot, then rush in and recover and shoot a lay-up or a short jump shot. (3) Or, the arc may be shortened to test shooting left-handed, then right-handed, or vice-versa, depending upon the particular student's dominant hand, with the higher point value given for baskets made with the non-dominant hand. (4) The test works well as a drill and provides for individual competition among the players while practicing, much like the familiar game of *21.*

Bowling

The game of bowling is, in itself, objective measurement. Consequently, most of the work done in this area has been the construction of norms. Phillips and Summers[27] developed norms for college women based on initial levels of ability. Ratings were established for the different levels of ability as to progress at various stages up through twenty-five lines of bowling. Martin and Keogh[23] recently published bowling norms for college men and women in elective physical education classes. The bowlers were classified as experienced or non-experienced. Separate norms as to superior, good, average, poor, and inferior performance were constructed for men and women for experienced and non-experienced bowlers.

Football

The AAHPER Football Skills Tests.[3]

Ten tests have been presented as part of the AAHPER Sports Skills Tests Project to measure the fundamental skills of football. Each test purports to measure a single basic skill.

The tests are the following ones: (1) Forward Pass for Distance, (2) 50-Yard Dash with Football, (3) Blocking, (4) Forward Pass for Accuracy, (5) Football Punt for Distance, (6) Ball Changing Zigzag Run, (7) Catching the Forward Pass, (8) Pull-out, (9) Kick-off, and (10) Dodging Run. All the tests except the blocking test may also be used to evaluate basic skills in touch or flag football. (See Norms in Appendix.)

Forward Pass for Distance. The test is administered and scored in the same manner as the softball throw for distance in the *Youth Fitness Manual* and the *Softball Skills Test Manual.* (Best of three trials, 6-foot restraining area, distance measured to the last foot passed, and measured at right angles to the throwing line—not arcing from the point from which the throw was made.

50-Yard Dash with Football. The subject runs as fast as he can for 50 yards carrying a football. Two trials are given with a rest in between the two trials. Scoring: When the starter shouts *go* and simultaneously swings a white cloth down with his arm, the timer starts the watch. The time is stopped when the runner crosses the finish line. The score is to the nearest tenth of a second. The better score of the two trials is used as the score.

Blocking. On the signal to *go,* the subject runs forward and executes a cross-body block against a blocking bag. He immediately recovers and charges toward a second bag placed 15 feet directly to the right of the first bag. After cross-body blocking that bag clear to the ground, he scrambles to his feet and races toward the third bag. The third bag is 15 feet away in the direction of the starting line, but at a 45 degree angle to the line from bags 1 and 2. (This places the bag about 5 feet from the starting line.) The subject blocks this third bag to the ground with a cross-body block and then runs across the starting line. Two trials are given. The blocking bags must be blocked clear to the ground. (See Figure 18 - 5 for diagram of bag placement.) Scoring: The time from the signal *go* until he crosses back over the line is measured to the nearest tenth of a second. The better of the two trials constitutes the subject's score.

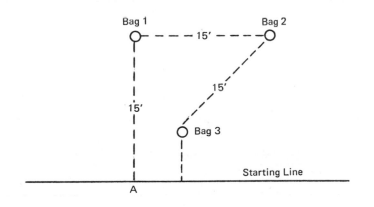

FIGURE 18 - 5

Diagram for AAPHER Football Blocking Test

Forward Pass for Accuracy. A target is painted on a 8 X 11 ft. canvas which is hung from the cross bar of the goal posts. The center circle is 2 feet in diameter, the middle circle 4 feet, and the outer circle 6 feet in diameter. The bottom of the outer circle is 3 feet from the ground. It is recommended that a wooden or metal bar be inserted in a channel sewn along the bottom of the canvas, and then the channel be tied to the goal posts to keep the canvas stretched taut. A restraining line is drawn 15 yards from the target. The player takes two or three small running steps along the line, hesitates, then throws at the target. The player may go either to the right or to the left, but he must stay behind the restraining line. He should pass the ball with good speed. Ten trials are given. <u>Scoring</u>: The target circles score 3, 2, and 1 for the inner, middle, and outer circles, respectively. Passes hitting on a line are given the higher value. The point total for the 10 trials is the score.

Football Punt for Distance. The player takes one or two steps within the 6-foot kicking zone and punts the ball as far as possible. The administration and scoring are the same as for the Forward Pass for Distance. (See also Softball Throw for Distance in *Youth Fitness Manual.*)

Ball Changing Zigzag Run. Five chairs are placed in a line, 10 feet apart, and all facing away from the starting line. (See Figure 18 - 6.) The first chair is 10 feet in front of the starting line. Holding a football under his right arm, the subject starts from behind the starting line on the signal *go.* He runs to the right of the first chair, then changes the ball to his left arm as he runs to the left of the second chair. He continues running in and out of the chairs in this manner, changing the position of the ball to the outside arm as he passes each chair. The inside arm should be extended as in stiff-arming. He circles around the end chair and runs in and out of the chairs back to the starting line. He is not allowed to hit the chairs. Two timed trials are given. <u>Scoring</u>: The time from the signal *go* until he passes back over the starting line is recorded to the nearest tenth of a second. The better of the two trials constitutes the subject's score for this test.

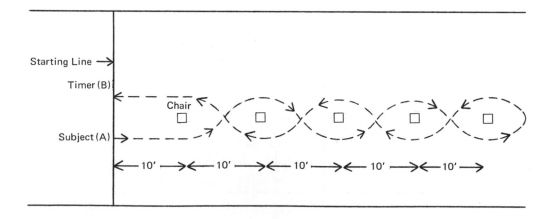

FIGURE 18 - 6

Diagram for AAHPER Football Ball Changing Zigzag Run Test

Catching the Forward Pass. A scrimmage line is drawn with two *end* marks located 9 feet to the right and to the left of the center. (See Figure 18 - 7.) At a distance of 30 feet in front of these marks are *turning points.* The subject lines up on the right *end* mark facing the *turning point* 30 feet directly in front of him. On the signal *go* he runs straight ahead, cuts around the *turning point,* and runs to receive the pass 30 feet away at the *passing point.* On the signal *go* the center snaps the ball 15 feet to the passer who takes one step, then passes the ball directly over the *passing point* above head height. The passer must be able to pass the ball in a mechanical manner to the passing point without paying attention to the receiver. A similar passing point is located 30 feet to the left of the left turning point. Ten trials are given to the right and ten trials are given to the left. The player need not try for poorly thrown passes, but he must go around the turning point before proceeding to the passing point. Scoring: One point is scored for each pass caught. The sum of passes caught from both sides is recorded as the score for this test. Note: Considerable practice and skill are needed on the part of the passer to be able to time his pass so as to enable the subject to reach the passing point in a controlled manner and get his hands on the ball.

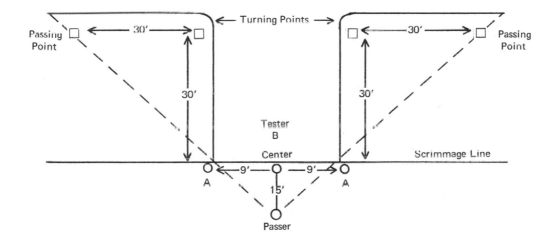

FIGURE 18 - 7

Diagram for AAHPER Football Forward Pass Catching Test

Pull-out. The subject lines up in a set position halfway between two goal posts. On the signal *go* he pulls out and runs parallel to the imaginary line of scrimmage, cuts around the right hand goal post and races straight ahead across a finish line 30 feet from and parallel to the goal posts. Two timed trials are given. Scoring: The score is the better of the two trials, measured from the signal *go* until he crosses the finish line in seconds and tenths of seconds.

Kick-off. A kicking tee is placed in the center of one of the lines running across the field. The ball is positioned so that it tilts slightly back toward the kicker. The player takes as long a run as he wants and kicks the ball as far as possible. Three trials are given. Scoring: Same as for the forward pass and the punt for distance.

Dodging Run. The Frederick W. Cozens Dodging Test is used, with the only exception being that the subject carries a football. The course is laid out as is shown in Figure 18 - 8. The player starts from behind the line to the right of the first hurdle which is on the starting line. On the signal *go* he runs to the left of the second hurdle and follows the course as shown in the diagram. Two complete round trips constitute a run; two runs are given. The ball does not have to be changed from side to side. Scoring: The time is measured to the nearest tenth of a second. The better of the two runs is recorded as the score.

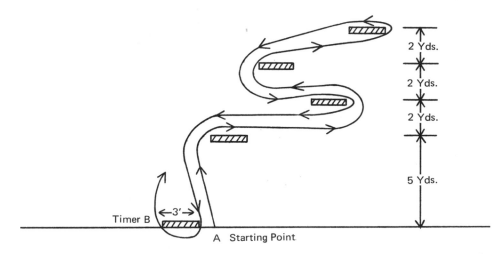

FIGURE 18 - 8

Diagram for AAHPER Dodging Run Test

Golf

Clevett's Putting Test.[9]

Clevett devised four tests of golf utilizing the brassie, midiron, mashie, and putter. The putting test is described here.

Equipment and Materials: A smooth carpet 20 feet long and 27 inches wide is marked as shown in Figure 18 - 9. Each zone is 9 inches square. The *10* square represents the hole. A putter and at least ten golf balls in good condition are required.

Directions: The subject putts at a distance of 15 feet from the *hole*. It can be seen in Figure 18 - 9 that the subject is encouraged to putt for the hole rather than leave it short. Ten trials are given.

Scoring: The point at which the ball stops is the score for that putt. The total of the ten trials is the score. Balls resting on a line are given the higher point value.

Additional Pointers: (1) The test can be decidedly improved by cutting an actual hole in the carpet. Several movable putting surfaces can be constructed using carpeting stretched over plywood, thus enabling a hole to be formed. The scoring areas should then be altered slightly reducing somewhat the point values for going beyond the hole. (2) To make the test more functional, the distances could be varied. (3) The use of synthetic grass would undoubtedly improve the test also.

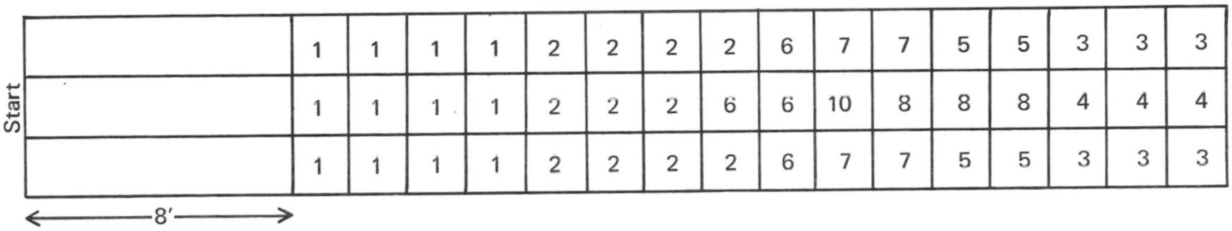

Start		1	1	1	1	2	2	2	2	6	7	7	5	5	3	3	3
		1	1	1	1	2	2	2	6	6	10	8	8	8	4	4	4
		1	1	1	1	2	2	2	2	6	7	7	5	5	3	3	3

←———— 8' ————→

FIGURE 18 - 9

Markings for Clevett's Golf Putting Test

The Nelson Pitching Test.[25]

Purpose: To measure the ability of a golfer to use the short irons in pitching close to the pin.

Age and Sex: Suitable for both boys and girls at the secondary and college levels.

Validity: A correlation of .86 was obtained with judges' ratings of ability. An r of .79 was found between the test scores and golf scores.

Reliability: Using odd-even trials and the Spearman-Brown Prophecy Formula, a coefficient of reliability of .83 was found with men and women college students.

Equipment and Materials: The equipment needed include the following items: the appropriate golf club that is being used, usually the 8 iron, 9 iron or wedge; preferably four baskets each with 13 balls in good condition (although two baskets will suffice if only one person is being tested at a time); a flag stick for the center of the target, two flags or markers for the restraining line; tape measure and lime or other field markings materials. The target is marked as shown in Figure 18 - 10. The inner circle is 6 feet in diameter. Proceeding out from the center, each circle's radius is 5 feet wider than the previous one. The diameters are 6, 16, 26, 36, 46, 56, and 66 feet. The target is divided into equal quadrants. A restraining line is marked 20 yards from the flag and the hitting line is 40 yards from the flag. The numbers for the particular sectors of each circle are as shown in the figure.

Directions: Preferably 2 students are tested at a time, taking turns hitting. A spotter is assigned for each subject. The instructor acts as the recorder. The instructor and the spotters stand near the target. The subject is given three practice shots, then ten trials, attempting to have each ball come to rest as near the flag as possible. The ball must be airborne until it passes the restraining line in order to be a good shot and to prevent rolling the ball all the way. If the subject swings and misses, it counts as a trial. Any swing, regardless of how far the ball goes, counts as a trial. After the subjects have finished, they retrieve their balls, and the spotters prepare to be tested next. Two new spotters are then called.

<u>Scoring</u>: The point value for the area in which the ball comes to rest is called out to the recorder. The spotter calls out his subject's name and score—for example, *Smith, 7*. The recorder enters each score. It is not difficult for the recorder to see every score, but the spotters aid in double checking and in avoiding errors in entering scores for the proper person. A ball resting on a line is given the higher point value. The score is the total point value for the ten trials.

<u>Additional Pointers</u>: (1) Using different colored golf balls, three subjects can easily be tested at a time without requiring the services of spotters. The instructor then stands back at the hitting line. After all have finished, he goes to the target area to record the scores for each subject by noting the zone in which each particular colored ball is resting. (2) The subjects must take turns hitting so as not to bother one another. If a subject is particularly slow in hitting, he may be tested by himself at the end or with another equally slow player. (3) Balls that hit before passing the restraining line are immediately removed so that they will not be mistakingly counted if they should roll onto the target. (4) It sometimes aids the subject to call out his score if, because of uneven ground, he cannot see the exact position of the previous shot. (5) The test works well as a practice drill, enabling each student to have an objective record of his progress. For this reason it is best to have the circles permanently marked by burning the lines in the grass or etching the lines in the ground. (6) The hitting distance can be varied for more functional practice and more effective testing. (7) If time is pressing, very little reliability is lost by having the student hit 10 balls and the instructor discarding the three lowest trials from them, and then totaling the remaining seven.

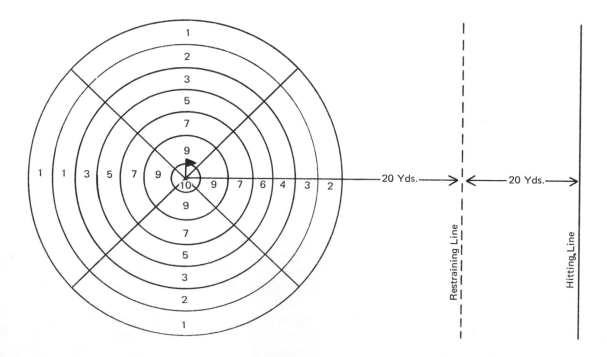

FIGURE 18 - 10

Target for the Nelson Pitching Test

Handball

Cornish Handball Test.[11]

Cornish constructed a test for the measurement of handball ability. Five test items were selected: the 30-second volley, the front-wall placement, the back-wall placement, the service placement, and the power test.

Age and Sex: College men.

Validity: A criterion consisting of the total points scored by each student minus the points scored by his opponents was used in the statistical procedures for test selection. The R for the five tests with the criterion was .694. The power test singly correlated highest with the criterion (r = .58). This test along with the 30-second volley correlated nearly as high with the criterion (.667) as did the five items. Consequently, in the interests of time and ease of administration, these two tests are recommended.

Equipment and Court Markings: Only the power test and 30-second volley will be described here. Other markings are needed for the three placement tests. Several handballs in good condition are required. All should be comparable with regard to their liveliness. The service line is all the markings necessary for the volley test. For the power test a line is drawn on the front wall at a height of 6 feet. Lines are also drawn on the floor as follows: the first line is 18 feet from the front wall; the second line is 5 feet behind the first; the third, fourth, and fifth lines are each 5¾ feet apart. These lines form six scoring zones. The area from the front wall to the first line scores 1 point, as does the first of the five zones behind. The second, third, fourth, and fifth zones score 2, 3, 4, and. 5 points, respectively. A stop watch is needed for the volley test.

Directions:

Power Test. The subject stands in the service zone and throws the ball against the front wall, letting it hit the floor on the rebound before striking it. He then hits the ball as hard as possible, making sure that it strikes the front wall below the 6 foot line. He throws the ball against the wall prior to each power stroke. Five trials are given with each hand. A retrial is allowed for any attempt in which the subject steps into the front court or fails to hit the wall below the 6 foot line.

Scoring: The value of the scoring zone in which each trial first touches the floor is recorded. The score is the total points for the ten trials.

30-Second Volley. The subject stands behind the service line, drops the ball, and begins volleying it against the front wall for 30 seconds. The subject should hit all strokes from behind the service line. In case the ball fails to return past this line, the subject is allowed to step into the front court to hit the ball, but he must get back behind the line for the succeeding stroke. If he should miss the ball, he is handed another ball by the instructor, and he continues volleying.

Scoring: The score is the total number of times the ball hits the front wall in 30 seconds.

Pennington and others[26] constructed a test of handball ability consisting of service placement, a total wall volley score, and back-wall placement tests. These were selected by the Wherry-Doolittle test selection method from seventeen strength, motor ability, and handball skill test items. This test was constructed while using a larger ball than regulation, with fewer rebound characteristics, and on a smaller than regulation court. For this reason it is not described here. However, because of its high validity coefficient, it is recommended that these items be studied as to their applicability with the regulation court and ball.

Soccer

McDonald Soccer Test.[22]

> Purpose: To measure general soccer ability.
>
> Age and Sex: College men.
>
> Validity: Validity coefficients were computed for college varsity players, junior varsity players, freshman varsity players, and for the combined groups. The scores of the above groups were correlated with coaches' ratings and the resulting coefficients were .94, .63, .76, and .85, respectively.
>
> Equipment and Materials: A wall or backboard 30 feet wide and 11½ feet high is needed. A restraining line is drawn 9 feet from the wall. A stop watch and three soccer balls, properly inflated and in good condition, are required.
>
> Directions: At the signal *go,* the subject begins kicking the ball from behind the 9 foot restraining line against the wall as many times as possible in 30 seconds. The subject may kick it on the fly or on the bounce. He may retrieve the ball using his hands or by kicking it, but in order to count as a hit, the kick must be made from behind the restraining line. If the ball gets out of control, the subject has the option of playing one of the spare balls instead of retrieving the loose ball. He may use his hands in getting a spare ball in position. The two spare balls are placed 9 feet behind the restraining line. Four trials are allowed.
>
> Scoring: The score is the highest number of legal kicks in any of the four trials.

Johnson Soccer Test.[19]

> Purpose: To measure general soccer ability by a single-item test.
>
> Age and Sex: College men.
>
> Validity: A coefficient of correlation between test scores and ratings by the investigator of .98 was found for physical education service class students; an r of .94 was obtained for physical education majors; and correlations of .58, .84, and .81 were found for varsity players on the first, second, and third teams.
>
> Reliability: A reliability coefficient of .92 was found for consecutive trials.
>
> Equipment and Materials: Soccer balls, stop watch, and a backboard 24 feet wide and 8 feet high are required. This target has the same dimensions as a regulation soccer goal. A restraining line is marked 15 feet from the wall. A ball box for spare balls is located 15 feet in back of the restraining line.
>
> Directions: The subject holds a soccer ball while standing behind the restraining line. On the signal to begin, the subject kicks the ball against the backboard (either on the fly or after bouncing it). He attempts to kick the ball against the backboard as many times as possible in 30 seconds. The ball must be kicked from behind the restraining line; regulation soccer rules pertaining to kicking the ball are followed. Assistants retrieve the loose balls if the subject elects to use a spare ball instead of chasing the loose ball. Three 30-second trials are given.
>
> Scoring: The score is the total number of legal hits on the three trials.

Softball

Generally, the tests suggested for the AAHPER Softball Skill Tests represent items that have been employed in previous tests. Test descriptions, diagrams, and percentile norms are provided by the *Manuals.* The items are briefly presented here.

AAHPER Softball Skills Test.[4,5]

Purpose: To measure fundamental skills of softball for boys and girls.

Validity and Reliability: Evidently, face validity was accepted. In the criteria for the sports skills test project, it was decided that the reliability coefficients should not be less than .80 on events scored on distance and not less than .70 for events scored on the basis of accuracy and form.

Test Items: (1) Throw for distance, (2) overhand throw for accuracy, (3) underhand pitching, (4) speed throw, (5) fungo hitting, (6) base running, (7) fielding ground balls, (8) catching fly balls. The items are identical for both boys and girls except that the throwing distances for the throw for accuracy and underhand pitching are shorter for girls. (See Norms in Appendix.)

Throw for distance. Same as in *AAHPER Youth Fitness Test Manual.*

Overhand throw for accuracy. The subject throws ten throws from a distance of — 65 feet for boys, 40 feet for girls — at a target with the following dimensions: three concentric circles with 1-inch lines, the center circle measuring 2 feet in diameter; the next circle is 4 feet; and the outer circle is 6 feet in diameter. The bottom of the outer circle is 3 feet from the floor. The target may be marked on a wall, or, preferably, in order to conserve softballs, on canvas against a mat hung on the wall. (This target is the same as used in the AAHPER Football battery.) The subject is given one or two practice throws prior to the ten trials. Scoring: The center circle counts 3 points, the second circle counts 2 points, the outer circle counts 1 point. The total points made on 10 throws is the score. Balls hitting a line are given the higher point value.

Underhand pitching. The target is rectangular in shape, representing the strike zone. The bottom of the target is 18 inches from the floor. The outer lines are 42 inches long and 29 inches wide. An inner rectangle is drawn 30 inches by 17 inches. A 24-inch pitching line is drawn — 46 feet for boys, 38 feet for girls — from the target. The subject takes one practice pitch, then pitches 15 underhand trials to the target. He must keep one foot on the pitching line while delivering the ball, but he can take a step forward. Only legal pitches are scored. A mat behind the target helps prevent damage to the softballs. Scoring: Balls hitting the center area or its boundary line count 2 points, balls hitting the outer area count 1 point. The score is the sum of the points made on 15 pitches.

Speed throw. The subject, holding a softball, stands behind a line drawn on the floor 9 feet from a smooth wall. On the signal to *go* he throws the ball overhand against the wall and catches the rebound and repeats this as rapidly as possible until 15 hits have been made against the wall. Balls that fall between the wall and the restraining line can be retrieved, but the subject must get back of the line before continuing. If the ball gets entirely away, the subject may be given one new trial. A practice trial is allowed and two trials are then given for time. Scoring: The watch is started when the first ball hits the wall, and is stopped when the fifteenth throw hits the wall. The score is in time to the nearest tenth of a second on the better of the two trials.

Fungo hitting. The subject selects a bat and stands behind home plate with a ball in his hand. When ready, he tosses the ball up and tries to hit a fly ball into right field. He then hits the next ball into left field. He alternates hitting to right and left fields until ten balls have been hit in each direction. Every time the ball is touched by the bat it is considered as a trial. Regardless of where the ball goes, he must hit the next ball to the opposite (right or left) field. Practice trials are allowed to each side. Hits to a specific side must cross the base line between second and third, or first and second base. Scoring: If a player completely misses two balls in a row, it is considered as a trial; otherwise a complete miss is not counted. A fly ball that goes to the proper field counts 2 points, a ground ball counts 1 point. No score is given for a ball that lands in the wrong field. The point value for each trial is recorded and summed at the end. The maximum is 40 points.

Base running. All subjects stand holding a bat in the right hand batter's box. On the signal to *hit,* the subject swings at an imaginary ball, then drops the bat and races around the bases. He must not throw or carry the bat, and he must take a complete swing before beginning to run. Each base must be touched in proper sequence. A practice and two timed trials are given. Scoring: The watch is started on the signal *hit* and is stopped when the runner touches home plate. The better time of the two trials to the nearest tenth of a second is the score.

Fielding ground balls. A rectangular area 17 X 60 ft. is marked off as shown in Figure 18 - 11. Two lines are drawn across the area 25 and 50 feet from the front, or throwing, line. This results in 3 areas being drawn. The subject stands in the 17 X 10 ft. area at the end of the rectangle. The thrower stands behind the throwing line with a basket of 10 balls. On the signal to begin the thrower begins throwing ground balls at exactly 5-second intervals into the first 17 X 25 ft. zone. The throw is made in an overhand manner with good speed. Each throw must hit the ground inside the first area for at least one bounce. Some variation in direction is desirable, but the thrower should not try to deliberately make the subject miss. A throw that does not land as specified should be taken over. The subject attempts to field each ball cleanly, holds it momentarily, then tosses it aside. The subject starts back of the 50-foot line, but thereafter he may field the ball anywhere in back of the 25-foot line. A practice trial and then 20 trials for score are given. Scoring: The scoring is on a pass or fail basis. Each throw scores 1 point or zero. The maximum score is 20.

Catching fly balls. This test involves catching balls thrown out of a second story window. It is described in the manual.

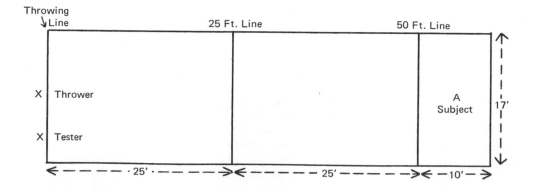

FIGURE 18 - 11

Diagram for AAHPER Fielding Ground Balls Test

The O'Donnell Softball Test for High School Girls.[28]

O'Donnell established a test for softball which included the following six items:

Speed Throw. When the signal is given, the subject throws from behind a restraining line at a wall 65 feet away. The score is the elapsed time from the signal until the ball hits the wall. The best of three trials is taken as the score.

Fielding Fly Balls. The subject stands behind a line, 6 feet from the wall, holding a softball. Upon the signal the subject throws against the wall and catches it in the air as many times as possible in thirty seconds. The ball must strike the wall on or above a line drawn 12 feet from the floor. The balls must be thrown from behind the restraining line but may be caught ahead of it. One practice and then one trial is given. The number of legal catches made is the score.

Throw and Catch. A rope is stretched 8 feet above a starting line drawn on the floor. The subject throws a ball over the rope and runs to catch it in the air. She attempts to cover the maximum distance and still catch the ball. The distance from the starting line to the heel of the front foot is measured to the nearest foot. One practice is given. The score is the best of three trials.

Repeated Throws. The subject, when told to begin, throws the ball from behind a restraining line, drawn 15 feet from the wall, against a wall on or above a line 7½ feet above the floor. She catches the rebound and repeats throwing as many times as possible in 30 seconds. The score is the number of legal hits in that time period.

Fungo Batting. From the batter's box the subject tosses the ball in the air and attempts to hit it into the outfield. Only tosses which are swung at count as trials. Balls that land in the outfield count 5 points; balls that hit in the infield count 3 points; and foul balls count 1 point. Ten trials are given, and the score is the total points.

Overhand Accuracy Throw. A target is drawn on a wall, consisting of concentric circles. The center of the target is 3 feet from the floor. The inner circle has a radius of 3 inches; the next, 11 inches; the next, 21 inches; and the outer circle 33 inches. The scoring is 4, 3, 2, and 1, respectively. The subject throws from behind a restraining line 45 feet from the target. The score is the total points in ten trials.

Equations are given for the six-item battery, a three-item battery (tests 3, 4 and 6), and a two-item battery (tests 3 and 4). Norms for each test and each battery are limited, and it is recommended that local norms be constructed.

Speedball

Buchanan[8] developed a four-item test designed to measure the fundamental skills in speedball. The four items are the following: lift to others, throwing and catching, dribbling and passing, and kick-ups. A complete description, along with diagrams and achievement scales, may be found in Weiss and Phillips.[30]

Lift to Others. A net (volleyball, tennis, or badminton) is stretched between two standards so that the top of it is 2½ feet from the ground. Standing behind a line 6 feet from the net, the subject attempts to lift the ball with either foot and pass it so that it crosses the net and lands within a 3 foot square diagonally opposite from the subject. Ten trials are given, one point being scored for each pass that lands in the proper square. The test is designed for partners to score one another and alternate turns from each side of the net.

Throwing and Catching. A restraining line is drawn 6 feet from, and parallel to, an unobstructed wall space. On the signal *ready, go,* the subject throws the ball and catches the rebound as many times as possible in 30 seconds. The score is the average number of catches made in five trials.

Dribbling and Passing. A starting line is marked 60 yards from the end line of the field. Five Indian clubs or other objects are placed in a line 10 yards apart. At the end line two goal areas are marked, one to the right and one to the left of the dribbling course. The goal areas are 6 yards long, and their inner borders are 4 feet to the left and 4 feet to the right of the dribbling line. The subject stands behind the starting line, and on the signal *ready, go* starts dribbling down the field. The subject dribbles to the right of the first Indian club and to the left of the second, etc. Immediately after dribbling to the right of the last club, the subject attempts to kick the ball to the left into the goal area. Ten trials are given, five to the right and five to the left. Three scores are obtained: the combined score is the sum of the scores in seconds on the 10 trials minus 10 times the number of accurate passes to the goal on the 10 trials; the dribbling score is the sum of the 10 trials in seconds; the passing score is the number of accurate passes made in 10 trials.

Kick-Ups. Each testing station for this test item consists of a 2-foot square, with the inner side 3 feet from the side line. A starting line is drawn 4 feet from the outside corner of the square following an imaginary extension of the diagonal of the square. Partners are used for this test whereby one student throws the ball from behind the side line directly opposite the square. The thrower tosses the ball from overhead so that it lands in the 2-foot square. The subject stands behind the starting line until the thrower releases the ball; at that instant the subject runs forward and executes a kick-up to herself. The score is the number of successful kick-ups in 10 trials.

Swimming

Hewitt constructed achievement scales for college men[13] and for high school boys and girls[14] for the purposes of classifying students into homogenous swimming groups and measuring improvement in performance. The test items for the College Swimming Achievement Scales are as follows:

15-minute endurance swim: The subject swims for 15 minutes, counting the number of lengths of the pool covered. The lengths are converted into yards. No score is given if subject fails to swim for 15 minutes.

20 and 25 yard underwater swims: From a regulation start, using any type of stroke, the subject swims the entire distance underwater. Time is to the nearest tenth of a second.

25-yard and 50-yard swims using the crawl, breast, and back-crawl strokes: From a regulation start the swims are scored to the nearest tenth of a second.

50-yard glide relaxation swims using elementary back stroke, side stroke, and breast stroke: The scores for each of these events is the number of strokes taken to cover the distance. All starts are made in the water.

The items for the High School Swimming Achievement Scales are as follows:
1. **50-yard crawl:** Using a racing dive, this crawl stroke event is scored in time to the nearest second.
2. **25-yard flutter kick with polo ball:** The subject holds onto the side with one hand and the ball with the other until given the signal to go. He then pushes off and kicks to the other end (25 yards) of the pool. The score is timed to the nearest tenth of a second.

3. **25-yard glide relaxation using the elementary back stroke, side stroke and breast stroke:** Same testing procedures as in the college test except for the distance. The score is the number of strokes taken.

Fox Swimming Power Test.[12]

Purpose: To measure the power of swimmers in the side stroke and front crawl.

Age and Sex: College women.

Validity: Coefficients of .83 and .69 were found for correlations between test and form ratings for the side stroke and crawl stroke, respectively.

Reliability: Reliability coefficients of .97 for the side stroke and .95 for the front crawl were reported.

Equipment and materials: A rope is needed that measures about 20 feet longer than the width of the pool. This should be firmly tied on one end at a distance of 2 feet from the end of the pool. The other end of the rope remains free. A weight is fastened to the rope in the middle so that the rope will drop to the bottom when the free end is released. Adhesive tape, masking tape, or some other material is used for markers which start at the rope and are placed at 5-foot intervals for a distance of 55 feet.

Directions: The rope is pulled so that it is about 1 foot under water at the starting point. The subject assumes a floating position (either on her side or face down for the crawl stroke) with her ankles resting on the rope. On the signal to go the rope is dropped, at which time the subject starts from a motionless floating position and takes six strokes.

Scoring: For the side stroke the distance from the starting line to the position of the ankles at the beginning of the recovery of the sixth stroke is measured to the nearest foot. For the front crawl stroke, the score is the distance, to the nearest foot, from the starting line to the point where the ankles were when the fingers were entering the water at the beginning of the sixth stroke.

Additional Pointers: (1) Scott and French[29] include the side stroke, back stroke, crawl, and breast stroke for measurement by this test. (2) The subjects should be given opportunity to practice starting a few times from the rope position. (3) Kicks taken before the arm movements or while gliding count as strokes. This is rather difficult to standardize and must be observed closely.

Tennis

Hewitt's Revision of the Dyer Backboard Tennis Test.[15]

Purpose: For classification of beginning and advanced tennis players.

Age and Sex: May be used for both sexes at the college and high school levels.

Validity: Rank order correlations were computed using the results of round robin tournaments and scores made on the Hewitt revision test for beginning and advanced tennis players. Rho's were converted to r's and were found to range from .68 to .73 for the beginner classes, and .84 to .89 for the advanced classes.

Reliability: Using the test-retest method, the reliability coefficients were .93 for the advanced players and .82 for the beginners.

Equipment and Materials: A wall 20 feet high and 20 feet wide is needed for the test. The required equipment includes a tennis racket, a stop watch, a basket with at least a dozen new tennis balls, and masking tape for marking lines. A line 1-inch wide is marked on the wall at a height of 3 feet and 20 feet long to simulate the net. A restraining line 20 feet long and 1 inch wide is marked 20 feet from the wall.

Directions: The subject starts with two tennis balls behind the 20 foot restraining line, and serves the ball against the wall. Any type of serve may be used. The watch is started when the served ball hits above the net line on the wall. The subject then rallies from behind the restraining line against the wall using any type of stroke. If the ball should get away from the student, he may take another ball from the basket. However, each time he takes a new ball, it must be started with a serve again. The hitting continues for 30 seconds. Three trials are given.

Scoring: One point is counted for each time the ball hits above the 3 foot net line. No score is counted when the subject steps over the restraining line, or for balls that hit below the net line. Balls that hit the line are counted. The average of the three trials is the score.

Hewitt's Tennis Achievement Test.[16]

Hewitt constructed an achievement test for measuring the service and forehand and backhand drives. Beginners, advanced, and varsity tennis players were utilized in validating the test and establishing achievement scales.

Validity coefficients ranged from .52 to .93, and reliability coefficients from .75 to .94. It was found that the service placement test had the highest predictive value for the varsity players; the revised Dyer wall test had highest validity for the advanced players; and the speed of service test had the highest validity coefficient for beginners.

Hewitt recommends the revised Dyer test as being the best test because of its simplicity and ease of administration. Its validity coefficients were .87, .84, and .73 for varsity, advanced and beginning players, respectively. If no wall is available, Hewitt suggests that the Hewitt Tennis Achievement Test be used.

The service placement test, the speed of service test, and the forehand and backhand drive tests are briefly described here. Complete descriptions are provided in the original reference.

Hewitt's Service Placement Test. This test was found to have the highest validity coefficient for varsity players.

Court Markings: The right service court is marked as shown in Figure 18 - 12. The point values from 1 to 6 are also shown in the figure. A one-quarter inch rope is stretched above the net at a height of 7 feet.

Directions: After a demonstration by the instructor and a 10-minute warm-up on another court, the subject serves 10 balls into the marked right service courts. He must serve the ball between the net and the rope.

Scoring: The point value for the zone in which each ball hits constitutes the score. The points are added for the 10 trials. Balls going over the rope are given a score of zero.

Hewitt's Speed of Service Test. Hewitt found that the distance the ball bounced after it hit the service court to be a good indication of the speed of service. The type of serve had little effect on this distance. This test had the highest validity coefficient for beginners.

Court Markings: Four zones are formed. Zone 1 is the backcourt area to the baseline; zone 2 is the area 10 feet beyond the baseline; zone 3 consists of the area from 10 to 20 feet beyond the baseline; and zone 4 is the area 20 feet beyond the baseline or the fence in most courts. (See Figure 18 - 12.)

Directions: This test can be scored at the same time as the serve placement test. For each of the good serve placements (in other words, those that hit in the service court) the zone in which the ball hits on the second bounce is noted.

<u>Scoring</u>: The point values for zones 1, 2, 3, and 4 are 1 point, 2 points, 3 points, and 4 points, respectively.

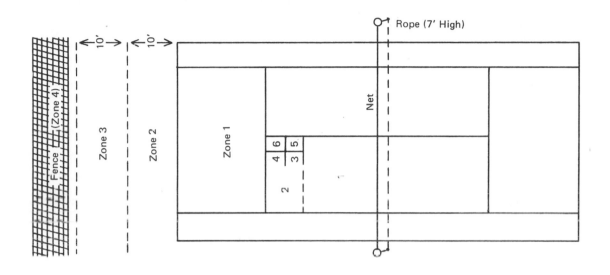

FIGURE 18 - 12

Court Markings for Hewitt's Service Placement and Speed of Service Test

Hewitt's Forehand and Backhand Drive Tests.

<u>Court Markings</u>: Using the service line as one of the lines for the test, three chalk lines are drawn 4½ feet apart between the service line and the baseline. Figure 18 - 13 shows the court markings and the point value for each zone. A one-quarter inch rope is stretched above the net at a height of 7 feet.

<u>Directions</u>: The subject stands at the center mark of the baseline. With a basket of balls the instructor takes a position across the net at the intersection of the center line and the service line. The instructor hits 5 practice balls to the student just beyond the service court. Then 10 trials are given for the forehand and 10 for the backhand. The student may choose which 10 balls to hit forehand and backhand. The student tries to hit the ball between the net and the rope so that the ball goes deep into the court. The same instructor should hit to all students to standardize the testing as much as possible. A ball-throwing machine, if available, would be very effective. Net balls are repeated.

<u>Scoring</u>: The point values for the scoring zones in which the forehand and backhand trials hit are recorded. Balls that pass over the rope receive half the point value of the respective zones.

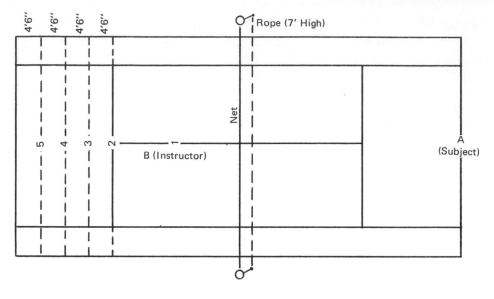

FIGURE 18 - 13

Court Markings for Hewitt's Forehand and Backhand Drive Tests

Volleyball

Brady Wall Volley Test.[6]

Purpose: To measure volleyball playing ability of college men for the purposes of classification, improvement of teaching, measurement of improvement of skill and for grading.

Age and Sex: College men.

Validity: A coefficient of .86 was reported for the correlation between test scores and subjective ratings by qualified judges.

Reliability: Using test-retest in the same testing period, a reliability coefficient of .93 was obtained.

Equipment and Materials: The equipment needed includes a stop watch, a volleyball, and a smooth wall with the following markings: a horizontal chalk line 5 feet long and 11½ feet from the floor; vertical lines extending upward at the ends of the 5 foot line toward the ceiling.

Directions: The subject stands with the ball near the wall and, on the signal to begin, throws the ball against the wall. He plays the rebound with a legal volleyball hit and attempts to volley it against the wall within the boundaries of the chalk lines as many times as possible. Only legal volleys count. If he loses control of the ball, or catches it, he starts it again with a throw as at the beginning of the test.

Scoring: The number of successful volleys that hit within the target area in 60 seconds constitutes the score. The thrown balls do not count.

Modification of Brady Test for High School Boys.[20]

Kronqvist and Brumbach devised a wall volley test for high school boys after critically analyzing and experimenting with the following factors: need for a restraining line, height of the line on the wall, target size, and the time limit and number of trials.

The final form of the test utilized a 5-foot line 11 feet from the floor. At each of the ends of this line vertical lines are extended upward at least 4 feet. Three 20-second trials are given. The test is started on the command *ready, go* by the subject throwing the ball against the wall within the rebound area and then volleying the ball as many times as possible until told to stop. Only legal volleys within the target area are counted. Any time the volley is interrupted, it must be started again with a throw. The time between trials is approximately 30 seconds.

A validity coefficient of .767 was found for all subjects between their test scores and subjective ratings by three experienced volleyball teachers. The test-retest method of determining reliability resulted in a coefficient of .817.

Clifton's Single Hit Volley Test for Women [10]

Purpose: To evaluate the volleying ability of college women students in volleyball.

Age and Sex: College women.

Validity: A coefficient of correlation between test scores from two trials and ratings in volleying by five experienced judges was .70.

Reliability: Using test-retest, a reliability coefficient of .83 was reported.

Equipment and Materials: The test requires a stop watch, a properly inflated volleyball, and wall and floor space to permit the following markings: a line on the wall 7½ feet from the floor and 10 feet long; a restraining line on the floor 10 feet long parallel to the wall and at a distance of 7 feet from the wall. The wall should be high enough to permit ample space above the 7½ foot line for volleying.

Directions: On the signal *ready, go* the subject, standing behind the 7-foot restraining line, tosses the ball underhand against the wall. She then volleys the ball as many times as possible above the 7½ foot line on the wall. All volleys must be legal hits and made from behind the restraining line in order to count. If she loses control of the ball, she must restart it with an underhand toss from behind the restraining line. At the end of the first 30-second trial a rest of 2 minutes is allowed, and then another 30-second trial is given.

Scoring: The score is the number of successful volleys touching on or above the 7½ foot line on the wall. No scores are allowed for hits made while the subject was standing on or over the restraining line, or for illegal hits. The sum of trials 1 and 2 is used as the total score.

Brumbach Service Test.[7]

Purpose: To measure the ability to serve the volleyball low and deep into the opponent's court.

Equipment and Floor Markings: Tall standards (or means for making extensions to the regular standards) are needed from which a rope is stretched 4 feet above and parallel to the top of the net. The floor is marked by chalk as shown in Figure 18 - 14. There should be several properly inflated volleyballs.

Directions: The subject stands behind the rear boundary line and attempts to serve the ball so that it crosses the net without touching it, but goes under the rope, and lands in the opposite court. He attempts to have the ball hit as near the other court's rear boundary line as he can. No practice trials are allowed. Twelve trials are given in two sets of six. The best 10 count for score.

Scoring: Balls that successfully pass between the rope and the net are given the higher of the two values for the particular zone in which the ball hits. Balls going over the rope receive the smaller value. Balls which hit the rope are reserved and not counted as trials. Balls which hit the net are scored zero; foot faults score zero; and balls which hit out-of-bounds, except for the two-foot extension zone at the end of the court, score zero. The subject's score is the total point value for the ten trials. A perfect score would be 30.

Additional Pointers: (1) The squad system of six students in a squad makes for efficient administration of this test. (2) One squad is placed behind the serving line waiting to be tested. The other squad helps with the test administration and retrieving of the balls. (3) Two students are placed at the net to note whether the ball goes over or under the rope. To avoid confusion they are instructed to only call out when the ball goes over the rope and to remain silent when the ball passes between the rope and net. (4) One student stands at the serving line and calls out if the server foot faults. (5) Another student records the scores as the tester calls them out. The tester should call them out loudly so that the server may hear also. (6) The other two students in that squad retrieve the balls. (7) After one squad has been tested, the positions are reversed and the other squad is tested while the first squad assists in administering the test.

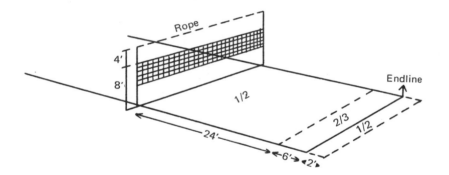

FIGURE 18 - 14

Court Markings for the Brumbach Volleyball Service Test

Liba-Stauff Test for the Volleyball Pass.[21]

Liba and Stauff reported a test for measuring the ability to execute a volleyball chest pass that appears to have excellent possibilities. It is based on the premise that desirable trajectories can be identified for the sex and age level and the pass situation. The test can thus be adapted to the desired trajectory.

Age and Sex: In developing the test, college women and junior high school girls were utilized in establishing reliability. However, it would seem adaptable to either sex and to any age level.

Validity: Logical validity was claimed as a measure of the ability to execute a volleyball chest pass. No attempt was made to determine the extent to which this test measures general volleyball playing ability.

<u>Reliability</u>: Reliability was studied by analysis of variance procedures. Several reliability estimates were reported. Good reliability estimates were obtained for both age levels when 10 trials were recorded on each of two days. These estimates for the college groups were .90 and .88, they were .84 for the seventh grade, and they were .90 for the eighth grade.

<u>Equipment and Materials</u>: <u>For college women</u> the desired vertical height for the pass was approximately 15 feet, and 20 feet was chosen for the horizontal distance. By specifying a particular height and distance it is possible to determine the velocity and direction of the projected ball. The authors constructed a table for various horizontal passer-receiver distances from which the vertical height, range to the floor, velocity, and angle of projection can be read. Consequently, from the table for 20 feet passer-receiver distance and approximately 15 feet vertical height the exact vertical height of 14.66 feet was determined, and the horizontal range to the floor for the 20-foot pass was 22.92 feet. Ropes are placed at heights of 13 feet and 11 feet and located 10½ feet from the restraining line. The top rope allows for adequate clearance of the ball. A target in the form of a canvas strip 2 feet by 30 feet is suggested to determine the horizontal distance the ball travels. The canvas is placed so that the center of target area 8, which is the desired point of landing, is 23½ feet away from the passer (the extra ½ foot allows for a slightly forward position of the hands relative to the feet while passing). Each zone on the target measures 2 feet square. (See Figure 18 - 15.)

For the <u>junior high school girls</u> the desired vertical height was chosen to be 13 feet and the horizontal range to the floor for the selected 12 foot pass was 15 feet. Ropes are placed 12 feet and 10 feet above the floor and are located 6½ feet from the restraining line. The target for this test is a canvas 2 X 28 feet with the desirable landing point being 7 instead of 8.

<u>Directions</u>: The subject is given two practice trials and then takes the desired number of trials for score. Each pass is started from a self-toss. The subject tries to pass the ball over the top rope and onto the desired target square (8 for college, 7 for junior high). If the pass is clearly interfered with by a rope, it is taken over. Each pass must be a legal volleyball hit in order to count for score. If the ball lands to either side of

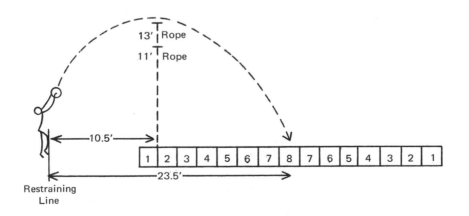

FIGURE 18 - 15

Diagram for the Liba-Stauff Volleyball Passing Test

the target within 5 or 6 feet, it is still given a distance score, since the test authors contended that a receiver could easily take a step in either direction and handle the pass. Ten trials on two separate days provide for good reliability. Fifteen or twenty trials on one day also give acceptable reliability.

Scoring for Vertical Height: 3 points are given for a ball that goes over the 13 foot rope (12 feet for junior high school); 2 points are given for a ball that goes between the two ropes; 1 point is given for a ball that goes under the low rope; 0 points if the ball fails to reach the ropes.

Scoring for Horizontal Height: The number of the zone on the target is also recorded for each trial. The score for the passing test is the sum of the vertical height score multiplied by the horizontal distance score for each trial. For example, a college player whose pass goes over the 13-foot rope and lands on zone 8 receives a score of 24 for that trial (3 for going over the top rope times 8 for the zone). No fouls are counted for stepping over the restraining line; however, the subjects should be cautioned to stay behind the line.

Problems in Sports Skills Measurement

In any sport there are a number of skills and abilities involved which make for successful performance. Even though the fundamental components can be identified, they can never be measured separately and then summed up to represent actual performance. Here, as in many phases of human performance, the whole is greater than the sum of the parts. The successful teacher must recognize this and strive to select those tests which will provide the student and the teacher with the most accurate information of the student's progress and achievement.

The basic concepts and criteria of test construction and selection which were discussed in Chapter IV are especially pertinent in the area of sports skills measurement. Criteria such as ease of administration, needed equipment, time required to administer the tests, need for trained testers, the meaningfulness of the test items, and the ease and objectivity of scoring are all very much interrelated. Singly and in combination, they also greatly contribute to or detract from the basic concepts of validity, reliability and objectivity. Much of the discussion in Chapter IV utilized skill tests in the examples; therefore it would be redundant to discuss these problems again. However, there are a few points that appear to the authors to be so crucial that they deserve some reiteration. One of these concerns objective scoring versus realism and validity. Test makers frequently attempt to eliminate the influence of a second person on the performance of the subject being measured. Consequently, in tennis, for example, some test items require the subject to drop the ball, then stroke it; rather than to stroke a ball that has been hit to him by another person. Similarly, in softball tests, the subject is tested by throwing at a target instead of a person, and he bats the ball from a batting tee, or tosses the ball to himself instead of hitting a pitched ball. Furthermore, when a second person is involved in certain test items, that person's role is often out of content with regard to actual performance. Using tennis and softball again as examples, the second person in some tests may stand at the net and throw tennis balls to the subject; and in softball, the second person is sometimes used to throw ground balls and/or fly balls to the subject being tested.

Obviously, the reasons for using test items such as these relate to the objectivity of scoring and, presumably, greater consistency in the test administration. But let us examine these practices with regard to the performance they are supposed to measure.

First, though, we should hasten to say that tennis and softball are certainly not the only sports in which these problems exist. All sports skills tests are faced with the problem of including only realistic, functional test items.

In some tennis tests there is a definite skill involved in being able to drop the ball and then successfully hit it with a forehand (and particularly a backhand) stroke that is not called for in the actual game of tennis. The perception, timing, and footwork that are necessary in being able to execute a forehand or backhand drive are not involved in such a test.

In softball and similar sports, throwing at a target may be viewed as violating the well-established teaching and coaching point that the player should not *aim* his throw. The height of the target should also be examined. The softball and baseball player usually throws to a relatively low target, such as when the first baseman stretches to meet the throw, or to the catcher who must make the tag low on the sliding runner. In batting, hitting from a tee is quite different from hitting a pitched ball. A batting tee is usually just employed in practice to help correct *hitches* in the swing and other fundamental faults in the stance and swing. The validity of fungo hitting as a measure of batting skill may also be questioned. During practice sessions the pitchers spend a large amount of time hitting fly balls to other players, but as a group they are notoriously poor hitters. There does not seem to be much point in continuing to question other test items, such as whether or not fielding ground balls or catching fly balls is different when the ball is thrown or batted, etc. The question essentially becomes that of how much deviation from the actual skill the teacher is willing to sacrifice in order to increase the objectivity of the test item.

It is hoped that the test items would be usable for practice drills and serve as motivation and provide indications of progress for the student. This is one very important way in which tests may serve several functions and thereby justify their use in terms of time spent for testing. Permanent testing stations and mobile test equipment are extremely valuable in this respect.

The scoring of the test should be such that it is able to distinguish among persons of different levels of ability. Decisions must be made as to target size, whether or not to give a score for hitting just behind the boundary lines, and whether or not the nature of the test encourages poor form. While it is of considerable value and interest for a test to possess national norms, the physical education teacher should always be urged to construct and utilize local norms.

Finally, the teacher should exercise great care insofar as the proportion of a student's grade that is determined by performance in skills tests. The teacher must continually evaluate the degree to which performance on a specific test reflects the ability to play the game. Certain activities, of course, lend themselves to more precise evaluation than others. The performance in some sports like golf, bowling, etc. is measured by the scores themselves. Relative ability in certain activities like handball, badminton, and others can be assessed quite accurately through round-robin tournaments. While in still others, such as in swimming, diving, and gymnastics, the performance must almost always involve subjective judgment. Performance in team sports like touch football, basketball, volleyball, and others is sometimes more difficult to determine. Here, as in all sports, skills tests can be used to good advantage for grading, provided that they are combined with careful subjective evaluation of the subject's actual performance in that sport.

BIBLIOGRAPHY

1. *AAHPER Skills Test Manual: Basketball for Boys,* David K. Brace, Test Consultant, Washington, D.C.: American Association for Health, Physical Education and Recreation, 1966.

2. *AAHPER Skills Test Manual: Basketball for Girls,* David K. Brace, Test Consultant, Washington, D.C.: American Association for Health, Physical Education and Recreation, 1966.

3. *AAHPER Skills Test Manual: Football,* David K. Brace, Test Consultant, Washington, D.C.: American Association for Health, Physical Education and Recreation, 1965.

4. *AAHPER Skills Test Manual: Softball for Boys,* David K. Brace, Test Consultant, Washington, D.C.: American Association for Health, Physical Education and Recreation, 1966.

5. *AAHPER Skills Test Manual: Softball for Girls,* David K. Brace, Test Consultant, Washington, D.C.: American Association for Health, Physical Education and Recreation, 1966.

6. Brady, George F., "Preliminary Investigations of Volleyball Playing Ability," *Research Quarterly,* 16:14-17, March, 1945.

7. Brumbach, Wayne, *Beginning Volleyball, A Syllabus for Teachers.* Eugene, Oregon: Wayne Baker Brumbach, (Distributed by University of Oregon Cooperative Store), Revised edition, 1967.

8. Buchanan, Ruth E., "A Study of Achievement Tests in Speedball for High School Girls," (Unpublished Master's Thesis, State University of Iowa, 1942).

9. Clevett, Melvin A., "An Experiment in Teaching Methods of Golf," *Research Quarterly,* 2:104-106, December, 1931.

10. Clifton, Marguerite A., "Single Hit Volley Test for Women's Volleyball," *Research Quarterly,* 33:208-211, May, 1962.

11. Cornish, Clayton, "A Study of Measurement of Ability in Handball," *Research Quarterly,* 20:215-222, May, 1949.

12. Fox, Margaret G., "Swimming Power Test," *Research Quarterly,* 28:233-237, October, 1957.

13. Hewitt, Jack E., "Swimming Achievement Scale Scores for College Men," *Research Quarterly,* 12:282-289, December, 1948.

14. _____, "Achievement Scale Scores for High School Swimming," *Research Quarterly,* 20:170-179, May, 1949.

15. _____, "Revision of the Dyer Backboard Tennis Test," *Research Quarterly,* 36:153-157, May, 1965.

16. _____, "Hewitt's Tennis Achievement Test," *Research Quarterly,* 37:231-237, May, 1966.

17. Hyde, Edith I., "National Research Study in Archery," *Research Quarterly,* 7:64-73, December, 1936.

18. _____, "An Achievement Scale in Archery," *Research Quarterly,* 8:109-116, May, 1937.

19. Johnson, Joseph R., "The Development of a Single-Item Test as a Measure of Soccer Skill," (Microcarded Master's Thesis, University of British Columbia, 1963).

20. Kronqvist, Robert A., and Wayne B. Brumbach, "A Modification of the Brady Volleyball Skill Test for High School Boys," *Research Quarterly,* 39:116-120, March, 1968.

21. Liba, Marie R., and Marilyn R. Stauff, "A Test for the Volleyball Pass," *Research Quarterly,* 34:56-63, March, 1963.

22. McDonald, Lloyd G., "The Construction of a Kicking Skill Test as an Index of General Soccer Ability" (Unpublished Master's Thesis, Springfield College, 1951).

23. Martin, Joan and Jack Keogh, "Bowling Norms for College Students in Elective Physical Education Classes," *Research Quarterly,* 35:325-327, October, 1964.

24. Nelson, Jack K. "The Measurement of Shooting and Passing Skills in Basketball," (Unpublished Study, Louisiana State University, 1967).

25. _____, "An Achievement Test for Golf," (Unpublished Study, Louisiana State University, 1967).

26. Pennington, G. Gary, James A. P. Day, John N. Drowatsky, and John F. Hanson, "A Measure of Handball Ability," *Research Quarterly,* 38:247-253, May, 1967.

27. Phillips, Marjorie, and Dean Summers, "Bowling Norms and Learning Curves for College Women," *Research Quarterly,* 21:377-385, December, 1950.

28. O'Donnell, Doris J., "Validation of Softball Skill Tests for High School Girls," (Unpublished Master's Thesis, Indiana University, 1950).

29. Scott, M. Gladys, and Esther French, *Measurement and Evaluation in Physical Education,* Dubuque, Iowa: Wm. C. Brown Company Publishers, 1959, Chapter VI.

30. Weiss, Raymond A., and Marjorie Phillips, *Administration of Tests in Physical Education,* St. Louis: The C. V. Mosby Company, 1954, pp. 253-257.

Chapter XIX

THE MEASUREMENT
OF POSTURE

The evaluation of posture has been a problem for tests and measurements people for nearly a century. The problem has been attacked in a variety of ways using rating charts, posture screens, photographs, silhouettes, plumb lines, aluminum pointers, angle irons, and adhesive tape. Unfortunately, even the most sophisticated techniques of photographic analysis with body landmarks, angles, etc. have not met with a great deal of success. Primarily, this failure is because posture experts can not agree on what constitutes good posture. This is not meant as criticism; instead, it merely points up the fundamental complexity of the problem — what is good posture?

This text cannot presume to answer the question; it can only adopt a working concept from which to base our approach to measurement. It is generally recognized that posture involves mechanical considerations, such as the alignment of body segments, the strength and stress of the muscles and ligaments, and the effects of gravity on the body parts. It is also acknowledged that posture is of an esthetic nature as well as being a reflection of the individual's total being, his self-image, his physical state, and his concept of himself in relation to his environment. Above all, it should be realized that posture, like all human characteristics, not only involves differences among individuals, but also differences within the individual. Posture is not just the ability of the individual to stand in one position in front of a plumb line while someone examines him from various angles. The evaluation of an individual's posture should include the appraisal of his posture while walking, running, climbing, descending, sitting, and standing. Moreover, the appraisal should be in accordance with the individual's skeletal architecture and body build.[17]

Utilization of Posture Tests

Primarily, posture tests are employed for (a) remedial work in an adaptive program; or (b) as a means of providing information and motivation for the student in a planned program of posture improvement. Adaptive work requires a specialist. In analyzing a student's posture a tester must be able to identify abnormalities and be able to determine whether or not improvements can be made by strengthening and stretching certain muscles. If the person is not well prepared in this area, there are no objective tests that will enable him to intelligently evaluate posture. If he is well qualified, it is doubtful that any objective measuring devices will give him any more information than his own eyes and hands.[22] However, he may well want to utilize objective devices as teaching aids in attempting to motivate the student to strive for improvement.

In selecting posture tests the physical education teacher should be guided primarily by the needs of the program, his own preparation and competency, and, of course, the cost and administrative feasibility of the test.

Measures of Posture

Iowa Posture Test.*

This test is recommended for use in classes. Groups of ten students can be rated at a time. The posture ratings are subjective, but the examiner has specific criteria on which to evaluate the elements in posture while standing, walking, running, sitting and stair climbing. This test represents a practical approach to the problem of assessing posture of the individual when he is moving and performing daily activities rather than just standing in a fixed position.

Validity and Reliability: No coefficients are given, although Moriarity[19] reported a reliability coefficient of .965 using dual but independent ratings.

Test Equipment and Floor Space: Ten chairs are arranged in a row about two feet apart. Open floor space is needed for the students to be able to walk ten or more steps away from the chair. Stairs may be constructed, or real ones utilized. The stairs should be sufficiently wide to accommodate two students at a time. The subjects should be dressed in swim suits or leotards and should also be barefoot.

Foot Mechanics Test.

Directions: The students take turns walking approximately ten steps forward and then back to their chairs. The examiner stands at the side and rates each subject on heel contact, weight transfer, and toe drive.

The examiner then stands in front of each subject, who walks first toward the examiner and then away as the examiner assesses foot alignment and the absence or presence of pronation.

Scoring: The suggested three-point scoring scale is primarily based on ratings of good, fair, and poor, which are given point values of 3, 2, and 1, respectively. More specific criteria for making each rating are presented here, as provided by McCloy.[17]

Criteria for foot mechanics test.

1. Heel-toe walking
    a. Heel contacts the ground first.
    b. The weight is transferred through the outside of the foot and then diagonally across to the ball of the foot.
    c. Toes are used in gripping action.
    d. Spring in the walk.

Scoring: Good = 3, Fair = 2, Poor = 1.

2. Absence of pronation
    a. No bony bulge in front of and below the medial malleolus.
    b. No noted inward protrusion of the navicular.
    c. Heel cord is not noticeably turned outward.

Scoring: No pronation = 3, Some pronation - 2, Marked pronation - 1.

3. Feet parallel
    a. A slight angle of toeing out is considered good.
    b. Some degree of toeing in may be permissible, but unattractive.

Scoring: Normal = 3, Moderate toeing out = 2, Marked toeing out = 1.

---

*Mimeographed form published by The Department of Physical Education for Women, University of Iowa. The test and scoring charts is also presented in Scott and French, *Measurement and Evaluation in Physical Education.*[21]

Standing Position Test.

Directions: The subjects stand with their left side toward the front of their chairs. The tester, viewing from the side, rates the alignment of the body segments and the weight distribution.

Criteria for correct alignment of body segments:

1. An axis approximating a straight line running through the head, neck, trunk, and legs.
2. The head and neck are erect (although there may be some slight forward inclination).
3. Chest high, abdomen flat.
4. Slight roundness of the upper back and slight hollow of lower back (i.e. normal curves).
5. Over-all impression of ease and balance.

Scoring: Good alignment = 3, Slight general deviation = 2, Marked general deviation = 1.

Walking Test.

Directions: The subjects walk around the row of ten chairs, keeping five or six feet from one another. The tester stands to the side and checks for body alignment, weight distribution, stiffness, and unnecessary movements while walking.

Criteria for walking test:

1. Alignment of body segments while walking. The rating is the same as for standing.
   Scoring: Same as for walking—3, 2, and 1.
2. Weight distribution. The weight should be carried farther forward than in standing position, but only slightly. There should be no forward or backward deviation from the perpendicular.

Scoring: Good weight distribution = 3, Some deviation = 2, Marked deviation = 1.

Sitting Test.

Directions: The examiner stands at the side and rates each subject in the sitting position. The subject then is instructed to lean forward about thirty degrees and is rated in this position. After this rating the subject rises and walks forward a few steps. Body mechanics and carriage while rising from a sitting position is assessed during this movement. If desired, the tester could rate the subject's performance in sitting down as well.

Criteria for sitting test:

1. Sitting position.
   a. Upper trunk balanced over pelvis.
   b. Head erect, chest high, shoulders back (but not stiff).
   c. Abdomen controlled and normal upper-back curve.
   d. Hips should be well back, and back of chair utilized for support.
   Scoring: Correct position = 3, Some deviation = 2, Marked deviation = 1.
2. Rising from a sitting position
   a. One foot slightly under the chair, the other foot slightly in advance. The trunk is inclined from the hips and the arms relaxed.

    b. The hips should be kept well under the body when rising, with no appreciable bending of the back or dropping of the head.

    c. The movement should be smooth and graceful with no stiffness.

Scoring: Good = 3, Fair = 2, Poor = 1.

Stooping to Pick up Light Object Test.

Directions: A small object is placed on the floor a few feet in front of the subject. The subject is instructed to walk to the object, pick it up, and then return it to the floor. The examiner views the subject from the side.

Criteria for picking up light object test:

1. The subject should bend mainly at the knees and a slight bend from the hips.
2. The feet and hips are kept well under the body with one foot slightly ahead of the other.
3. Trunk forms a relatively straight line, but arms are relaxed and back controlled, avoiding a stiff appearance.
4. The object is picked up (and replaced) slightly ahead of the foot. The movement should be smooth with good balance maintained throughout.

Scoring: Good = 3, Fair = 2, Poor = 1.

Ascending and Descending Stairs Test:

Directions: Each subject ascends and descends eight or ten stairs. The examiner stands at the side and rates the subject's carriage for ascending and descending separately.

Criteria for ascending and descending stairs test:

1. Ascending
       a. The weight should be only slightly forward, and the bend should be from the ankles, not the hips.
       b. The push-up is from the ankles and knees with no swinging of the hips.

   Scoring: Good = 3, Fair = 2, Poor = 1.

2. Descending
       a. Weight is lowered in a controlled manner (not a relaxed drop).
       b. Movement is smooth with no bobbing.

   Scoring: Good = 3, Fair = 2, Poor = 1.

Additional Pointers: (1) If desired, the physical educator could include running, picking up and carrying heavy objects, jumping, etc. (2) The desired mechanics for each test may be explained, or they may not, depending upon whether the teacher wishes to evaluate the students' normal behavior, or whether the teacher wishes to observe their performance after instruction. (3) The teacher may also wish to devise a system in which each subject is evaluated covertly, as, for example, while another student is performing, or during a pause between tests.

Woodruff Body Alignment Posture Test.*

An inexpensive device for measuring body alignment was developed by Woodruff at the University of Oregon. By the use of a wooden frame (see Figure 19 - 1)

*Janet Woodruff, School of Health, Physical Education, and Recreation, University of Oregon, Eugene, Oregon. Described in H. Harrison Clarke's *Application of Measurement to Health and Physical Education,* 4th Ed. Englewood Cliffs, New Jersey: Prentice-Hall, Inc., 1967, pp. 123-124.

containing nine strings running lengthwise, three-fourths of an inch apart, an objective score can be obtained of deviations in the alignment of body segments. The inventor believed this test represented a more reliable means of assessing body alignment than subjective ratings, and, at the same time, is less time consuming and less expensive than most of the objective devices.

Directions: The subject stands between the wall and the frame. The subject's left side is toward the frame, and the left foot is placed at the 1½ inch line that is marked on the floor. The tester then directs the subject to adjust the foot position until the base line is directly under the instep. The tester stands ten feet from the frame and, looking through the strings, aligns the center string with the 1 inch line drawn on the wall. The subject is instructed to stand in a *normal* position.

Scoring: This test is basically a plumb line test. The tester starts at the alignment of the ankle with the center string and proceeds upward, scoring each body segment's deviation from the one below it (not from the center line). In other words, the prescribed points at the ankle, knee, hip, shoulder, and ear are scored in terms of the number of strings each segment is found to deviate in either direction from the segment below it. A perfect score is 25, and one point is subtracted for each deviation.

Norms: There are no published norms, although Clarke reported a mean of 20, and a range of 16 to 25 had been obtained for college women.[2]

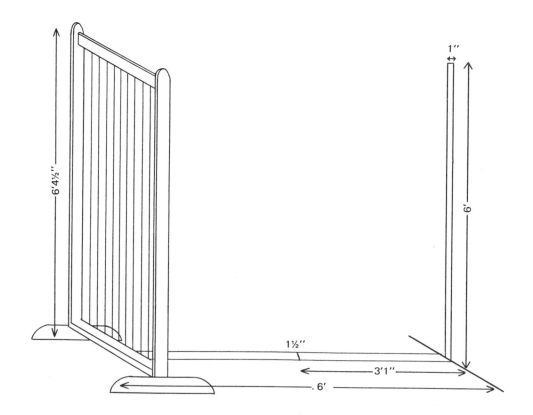

FIGURE 19 - 1

Objective Posture Tests

Brief mention is made here of some of the objective tests that have been devised in attempting to analyze and evaluate posture. Readers who desire more information and detailed descriptions of the tests are referred to the original sources. Considerable effort was expended during the thirties and forties in developing objective devices. Since then there has not been a great deal of work done in the way of invention.

Cureton-Gunby Conformateur.[4]

Cureton was an early leader in the attempt to develop objective, reliable instruments for measuring anteroposterior spinal curvature. Unsatisfied with the errors of exaggeration in using silhouettes, Cureton and Gunby devised the conformateur. This instrument utilizes metal rods which slide through holes placed in an upright. The subject stands with his back toward the upright, and the metal rods are pushed through the holes so that they make contact with the subject from his head down the entire length of the spine. The rods are locked in place, thus presenting an outline of the spinal curvature. Cureton recommends that it be used in conjunction with silhouettographs in order to facilitate interpretation and allow for a personal record for student motivation.

Wellesley Posture Test.[15]

Utilizing aluminum markers taped on the subject's sternum and spine, a method of objective measurements from photographs was developed by MacEwan and Howe. The pointers were attached at the lower end of the sternum, and on the spinous process of the seventh cervical and every other vertebra down to the sacrum. After photographing the subject the actual position of the spine and the chest could be drawn on the photograph from knowing the actual length of the pointers. In this way certain body parts such as the arms, breasts, back muscles and projecting scapulae would not mask the true spinal curvature, which had heretofore been a noted weakness of silhouettes and photographs. Three measurements were taken and weighted to make up the posture grade of each subject.

The Wickens and Kiphuth Posture Test.[24]

Wickens and Kiphuth developed a test by which the anteroposterior curvature of the spine could be measured objectively from photographs by using aluminum pointers and flesh pencil markings. Markings are made on the points of the body through which the plumb line should pass by a black flesh pencil, and five pointers are utilized to capture the true spinal curvature and chest position. After making tiny holes in the picture at the sites of the pointer attachments, at the flesh pencil markings, and at the most protuberant part of the abdomen, the picture is placed face down on an illuminated mimeoscope. Measurements are then drawn on the back of the picture.

Using a vernier caliper and protractor, the position of the head and neck, the amount of kyphosis and lordosis, and the positions of the chest, abdomen, shoulders, trunk, hips, and knees are measured and evaluated.

Massey Posture Test.[18]

Massey developed a technique of assessing posture from silhouettes in which the following measurements are determined: I, angle of the head and neck with the trunk; II, trunk with the hips; III, hips with thighs; and IV, thighs with legs. The angles are in degrees away from a straight line. The sum of the angles are converted to a letter grade.

Howland Alignometer.[12]

The alignometer, designed by Howland, consists of two sliding pointers which are calibrated and attached to a vertical rod. These pointers are adjusted so as to fix the position of the center of the sternum and the superior border of the symphysis pubis. Howland determined from research that the structural balance of the trunk approximated the line of gravity when the upper trunk and tilt of the pelvis were in vertical alignment. Disalignment is noted on the alignometer by the difference in the readings of the two calibrated pointers. If the subject's alignment is balanced, the difference in readings will be zero.

Problems Associated with the Measurement of Posture

The problems and limitations of posture appraisal have been discussed at length in various meetings, in professional journals, and in books. While there is considerable disagreement about various aspects of posture measurement, there is consensus that posture is difficult to measure. Some of the problems of posture appraisal are listed below:

1. Probably first and foremost has been the inability of workers in this area to establish standards of posture that will take into account individual differences.
2. Individuals tend to assume an unnatural pose when they know they are being tested for posture.
3. Problems are sometimes encountered in retesting and scoring because of the difficulty of standing in exactly the same pose as before.
4. In terms of administration and analysis the techniques for posture appraisal are generally quite time-consuming, and some of the devices are expensive.
5. The use of photographs and silhouettes have in the past required considerable skill in lighting and lens adjustment, etc. in order to obtain clear and well-defined pictures. However, recent advances in photographic equipment, such as polaroid cameras and equipment with automatic adjustments, have alleviated this problem considerably.
6. The subjective ratings of posture have generally been criticized for low reliability and objectivity.
7. Because of the many variables involved, doubts have often been expressed concerning the accuracy of the measures. Even more basic have been the questions raised as to the real significance of the measures once they are obtained.

Despite the many problems associated with posture appraisal, there is much that a skilled and imaginative teacher can do to help students to become conscious of posture and to strive for improvement. To conclude that posture work is a waste of time because of the problems of measurement is just as indefensible as concluding that social adjustment is not important because it too does not lend itself readily to measurement.

The evidence, while contradictory, does tend to indicate that posture is related to certain physiological and emotional factors which make up the general health status of the individual. Clarke[2] suggests that perhaps many of the contradictory findings in the literature could be due to the lack of precision of the measuring instruments. Nevertheless, even if there were no relationship whatsoever between posture and physical health, a posture improvement program could well be justified for esthetic purposes alone. Physical education has the same basic goals as general education, and the program should thus be based on the needs of the student. Not everyone can have the physique of a superb athlete or the looks of a glamorous movie star. However, everyone does have the opportunity and perhaps even the obligation to do the best with what he has. Physical education should profit from the subtle teachings of movies and television concerning the importance of posture and graceful carriage for good appearance.

Perhaps herein lies the key to the rather difficult task of fostering posture consciousness. For some students it may be effective for them simply to be led to the realization that frequently persons who make a very attractive appearance are actually quite plain — their grace, poise, and beauty of movement completely overshadows any flaws in face or form. For other students a more direct and personal approach is needed. One of the most powerful and effective motivating techniques is the use of motion pictures. In most cases the student has no idea what he or she looks like while moving.

A modified version of *candid camera* was employed in a high school health class wherein motion pictures were secretly taken of each class member and then shown during class for analysis and discussion of posture. In each instance the student was unaware of the picture taking. Some of the pictures were even taken away from the school grounds. Needless to say, there was a great deal of interest in the project. There was no appreciable expense involved as the camera was borrowed and the class members each contributed a small amount for film. While no drastic changes were brought about, the project was very effective in calling attention to posture, and considerable value was derived from the discussions. As a result of the unit three class members began exercise programs in an attempt at re-education of posture habits, and two individuals began dieting.

The elementary grades are undoubtedly the most important in terms of being able to identify and then help to remedy faulty posture. This is where concentrated efforts should be made to install posture screening programs. Well planned motivational devices should be employed to create favorable attitudes toward good posture and body mechanics, rather than relying on the typical nagging admonition to *sit up straight.*

In conclusion, the ratings and objective measuring devices used for posture evaluation have not met with a great deal of success insofar as being generally accepted by the profession. Despite the problems, however, it is felt that posture and body mechanics are important facets of physical education. Until better measuring tools are developed, the logical approach would seem to be to begin planned posture screening and improvement programs early in the elementary grades, and to strive to diagnose and evaluate posture in relation to each individual's structure and capacity for improvement.

Findings and Conclusions from Posture Measurement and Research

In an early study Maple[16] reported some observations concerning the influence of chronological age on certain postural characteristics. Among the conclusions were that the head is not held completely erect until the age of six or seven; that the scapulae do not lie flat until after ten years of age; that the sacral angle increases markedly from three to six or seven; and that the infant is more erect than the child. In another early study Korb[14] found the comparograph, in which an outline of good posture was placed on the subject's picture, to be a valid, reliable, and inexpensive method for grading posture. Cureton and others[4] in 1935 concluded that objective measurement was more precise than subjective methods.

Flint[8] studying the relationship between flexibility and strength to lumbar posture assessment, found no significant correlation between lordosis and strength of the abdominal muscles or the back extensor muscles, or between lordosis and hip, or hip-trunk flexibility. The position of the center of gravity was not found to be affected by lordosis or pelvic inclinations. Flint and Diehl[9] had previously found trunk-strength balance, abdominal strength, and back extensor strength all to be significantly related to anteroposterior alignment. In a recent study Hutchins[13] found supporting evidence to the above and concluded that the balance of strength between trunk-flexor and trunk-extensor muscles and other muscle groups was an important factor in anterio-posterior alignment. She further reported that the results of her study provided evidence in support of the current posture-training methods which involve specific strength and flexibility exercises.

Coppock[3] reported that tightness of the pectoral muscles did not correlate significantly with round shoulders. Fox[10] concluded that faulty pelvic tilt was not associated with any appreciable weakness in the abdominal muscles, nor was sway-back related to weak abdominal musculature. She did report that dysmenorrhea was more severe among women having sway-back than among the control group.

DiGiovanna,[7] in an early investigation, studied the relationship of athletic achievement and posture. The results, although not statistically treated, indicated a fairly definite relationship between the two variables. Davies,[6] however, found little or no relationship between motor ability and judges' ratings of postural divergencies.

Several individuals have studied the gravitational line of the body and have recommended specific points on the different segments of the body along which a plumb line should fall. Basically, the line passes through the lobe of the ear, the tip of the shoulder, the greater trochanter of the hip, behind the knee cap, and in front of the external malleolus. There has been some disagreement concerning the exact location of these body sites. For example, Phelps, Kiphuth, and Goff[20] objected to the criterion that the mastoid bone be in line with the acromion process because of individual variations in the mobility of the shoulders. Minor differences have also been noted with regard to the point at which the gravitational line passes through the ankle. Fox and Young[11] concluded that the line of gravity lay anterior to the center of the ankle joint and near enough to the anterior border of the tibia to be considered on line with it.

Various investigators have attempted to relate posture to health and to certain physiological and emotional characteristics. In 1931 Alden and Top[1] studied the relationship of posture to the factors of weight, vital capacity, and intelligence. There was no relationship between posture and any of the variables studied. Cyriax[5] stated that poor dorso-cervical posture which induces cardiac impairment may cause sudden heart failure, angina, and functional heart troubles. Moriarity and Irwin[19] reported a significant relationship between poor posture and certain physical and emotional factors, including self-consciousness, fidgeting, restlessness, timidity, fatigue, underweight, disease, heart defects, hearing problems and asthma. After studying the association between physical defects and functional disorders, Spindler[23] concluded that there was a need for corrective and remedial work, and that an increased emphasis in postural work was necessary.

BIBLIOGRAPHY

1. Alden, Florence D., and Hilda Top, "Experiment on the Relation of Posture to Weight, Vital Capacity and Intelligence," *Research Quarterly,* 2:38-41, October, 1931.

2. Clarke, H. Harrison, *Application of Measurement to Health and Physical Education,* 4th ed., Englewood Cliffs, New Jersey: Prentice-Hall, Inc., 1967, Chapter 6.

3. Coppock, Doris E., "Relationship of Tightness of Pectoral Muscles to Round Shoulders in College Women," *Research Quarterly,* 29:146-153, May, 1958.

4. Cureton, Thomas K., J. Stuart Wickens, and Haskell P. Elder, "Reliability and Objectivity of Springfield Postural Measurements," *Research Quarterly Supplement,* 6:81-92, May, 1935.

5. Cyriax, E., "The Relation of Dorso-Cervical Postural Deficiencies to Cardiac Disease, Especially from Middle Life Onwards," *Research Quarterly,* 7:74-79, December, 1936.

6. Davies, Evelyn A., "Relationship Between Selected Postural Divergencies and Motor Ability," *Research Quarterly,* 28:1-4, March, 1957.

7. DiGiovanna, Vincent G., "A Study of the Relation of Athletic Skills and Strengths to Those of Posture," *Research Quarterly,* 2:67-79, May, 1931.

8. Flint, M. Marilyn, "Lumbar Posture: A Study of Roentgenographic Measurement and the Influence of Flexibility and Strength," *Research Quarterly,* 34:15-20, March, 1963.

9. _____ , and Bobbie Diehl, "Influence of Abdominal Strength, Back Extensor Strength and Trunk Strength Balance upon Antero-Posterior Alignment of Elementary School Girls," *Research Quarterly,* 32:490-498, December, 1961.

10. Fox, Margaret G., "Relationship of Abdominal Strength to Selected Posture Faults," *Research Quarterly,* 22:141-144, May, 1951.

11. _____ , and Olive G. Young, "Placement of the Gravital Line in Antero-Posterior Standing Posture," *Research Quarterly,* 25:277-285, October, 1954.

12. Howland, Ivalclare Sprow, *Body Alignment in Fundamental Motor Skills,* New York: Exposition Press, 1953, p. 78.

13. Hutchins, Gloria Lee, "The Relationship of Selected Strength and Flexibility Variables to the Antero-Posterior Posture of College Women," *Research Quarterly,* 36:253-269, October, 1965.

14. Korb, Edward M., "A Method to Increase the Validity of Measuring Posture," *Research Quarterly,* 10:142-149, March, 1939.

15. MacEwan, Charlotte G., and Eugene C. Howe, "An Objective Method of Grading Posture," *Research Quarterly,* 3:144-147, October, 1932.

16. Maple, Katherine N., "Chronological Variations in the Posture of Children Ages One to Seven and Ten to Thirteen," *Research Quarterly,* 1:30-33, March, 1930.

17. McCloy, Charles H., and Norma D. Young, *Tests and Measurements in Health and Physical Education,* 3rd ed., New York: Appleton-Century-Crofts, Inc., 1954, Chapter 21.

18. Massey, Wayne W., "A Critical Study of Objective Methods of Measuring Antero-Posterior Posture with a Simplified Technique," *Research Quarterly,* 14:3-10, March, 1943.

19. Moriarity, Mary J., and Leslie W. Irwin, "A Study of the Relationship of Certain Physical and Emotional Factors to Habitual Poor Posture Among School Children," *Research Quarterly,* 23:221-225, May, 1952.

20. Phelps, W. W., R. J. H. Kiphuth, and C. W. Goff, *The Diagnosis and Treatment of Postural Defects,* 2nd ed., Springfield, Illinois: Charles C. Thomas, Publisher, 1956, pp. 118-138.

21. Scott, M. Gladys, and Esther French, *Measurement and Evaluation in Physical Education,* Dubuque, Iowa: Wm. C. Brown Company, Publishers, 1959, pp. 414-421.

22. Smithells, Philip A., and Peter E. Cameron, *Principles of Evaluation in Physical Education,* New York: Harper & Brothers, Publishers, 1962, pp. 334-340.

23. Spindler, Evelyn B., "Prevalence of and Correlations Between Physical Defects and Their Coincidence with Functional Disorders," *Research Quarterly,* 2:36-56, May, 1931.

24. Wickens, J. Stuart, and Oscar W. Kiphuth, "Body Mechanics Analysis of Yale University Freshmen," *Research Quarterly,* 8:38-44, December, 1937.

25. Woodruff, Janet, School of Health, Physical Education, and Recreation, University of Oregon.

Chapter XX

THE MEASUREMENT OF SOCIAL QUALITIES AND ATTITUDES
Part I – Social Qualities

Introduction

Social development is considered by most physical educators to be one of the major objectives of physical education. Unfortunately, social qualities such as character, sportsmanship, social adjustment, personality, and attitudes are very difficult to measure objectively. Because these traits cannot be easily measured, some critics have argued that this area should not be included as one of our objectives. However, as we have mentioned before, attempts at developing scientific measures in this area are still in a relatively immature stage. It is certainly logical to assume that better evaluative techniques will be developed.

It seems appropriate to also point out that these traits do indeed exist and that they can be appraised. It is too often assumed that desirable changes automatically come about through athletics and physical education participation. We must also remember that games and other physical activities under poor or no leadership can breed undesirable social changes. Therefore, irregardless of the fact that our measuring tools are somewhat crude, a systematic, conscientious effort should be made to evaluate this aspect of the student's development just as in the more tangible areas of organic efficiency and skills.

Uses of Social Measurement

Social adjustment measures are utilized in physical education in the following ways:
1. To assist in the evaluation of character and personality.
2. To determine the social status of individuals within the group.
3. To assist the teacher in pin-pointing those students in need of guidance or in need of referral to professional personnel.

Practical Measurements of Social Factors

Several practical measurements of social factors are listed as follows:

Breck's Sociometric Test of Status.[6]
    Objective: To measure the status of students within a group concerning acceptance for team membership and friendship.
    Age Level: Satisfactory for ages 12 through college.
    Sex: Satisfactory for both boys and girls.
    Reliability: The reliability of the skill status test was reported as $r = .894 \pm .01$. The reliability of the friendship status test was reported as $r = .79 \pm .01$.

Validity: Face validity has been accepted for the two items.
Materials: Cards or paper and pencils are needed for this test.
Directions: Students are asked to print in order of preference the names of five students they would most prefer to have as members of their team, and the five they would least like to have as members of their team. Also, the students are directed to list the names they would most prefer to have as friends and the five they would least like to have as friends.
Scoring: For team membership the number of choices received by each student, minus the number of rejections by classmates, is calculated. For friendship the number of choices received by each student is merely tabulated.

Blanchard Behavior Rating Scale.[3]

Objective: To measure the character and personality of students.
Age Level: Satisfactory for ages 12 through 17.
Sex: Satisfactory for both boys and girls.
Reliability: The reliability has been reported as high as $r = .711$.
Validity: A validity of .930 was found when intercorrelations of one trait action were made with the rest of the items in its category.
Directions: The teacher rates each student on the basis of the following scale items. Individual items are then analyzed for specific weaknesses.
Scoring: With 120 points possible, the higher scores indicate better general evaluations of character and personality. (See Rating Scale on page 385.)

Cowell's Social Adjustment Index.[10]

Objective: To determine the degree of social adjustment or mal-adjustment of students within their social groups.
Age Level: Satisfactory for ages 12 through 17.
Sex: Satisfactory for both boys and girls.
Reliability: The reliability was reported as high as .82.
Validity: With Pupil Who's Who Ratings as the criterion, an r of .628 was obtained with the Social Adjustment Index.
Direction: The teacher rates each student on the basis of the following scale items for Form A and Form B.
Scoring: The total score for Form A minus the total score for Form B is computed to give the raw score. High (+) scores indicate good social adjustment, whereas low (-) scores indicate mal-adjustment. (See Rating Scale on pages 386-388.)

Cowell's Personal Distance Scale.[10]

Objective: To determine a student's degree of acceptance by his social group.
Age Level: Satisfactory for ages 12 through college.
Sex: Satisfactory for both boys and girls.
Reliability: The reliability has been reported as high as .93.
Validity: With Pupil's Who's Who Rating as the criterion, an r of .844 was obtained with Pupil's Personal Distance Scale.
Direction: Each student is directed to rate fellow students on the basis of the following scale items. (See pages 389-391.)

BLANCHARD BEHAVIOR RATING SCALE

School _____

Name of Person Rated _____ Grade _____ Age _____

Name of Rater _____ Date _____

Personal Information:	No Opportunity to Observe	Never	Seldom	Fairly Often	Frequently	Extremely Often	Score
LEADERSHIP							
1. He is popular with classmates		1	2	3	4	5	
2. He seeks responsibility in the classroom		1	2	3	4	5	
3. He shows intellectual leadership in the classroom		1	2	3	4	5	
POSITIVE ACTIVE QUALITIES							
4. He quits on tasks requiring perseverance		5	4	3	2	1	
5. He exhibits aggressiveness in his relationship with others		1	2	3	4	5	
6. He shows initiative in assuming responsibility in unfamiliar situations		1	2	3	4	5	
7. He is alert to new opportunities		1	2	3	4	5	
POSITIVE MENTAL QUALITIES							
8. He shows keenness of mind		1	2	3	4	5	
9. He volunteers ideas		1	2	3	4	5	
SELF-CONTROL							
10. He grumbles over decisions of classmates		5	4	3	2	1	
11. He takes a justified criticism by teacher or classmate without showing anger or pouting		1	2	3	4	5	
COOPERATION							
12. He is loyal to his group		1	2	3	4	5	
13. He discharges his group responsibilities well		1	2	3	4	5	
14. He is cooperative in his attitude toward the teacher		1	2	3	4	5	
SOCIAL ACTION STANDARDS							
15. He makes loud-mouthed criticisms and comments		5	4	3	2	1	
16. He respects the rights of others		1	2	3	4	5	
ETHICAL SOCIAL QUALITIES							
17. He cheats		5	4	3	2	1	
18. He is truthful		1	2	3	4	5	
QUALITIES OF EFFICIENCY							
19. He seems satisfied to "get by" with tasks assigned		5	4	3	2	1	
20. He is dependable and trustworthy		1	2	3	4	5	
21. He has good study habits		1	2	3	4	5	
SOCIABILITY							
22. He is liked by others		1	2	3	4	5	
23. He makes a friendly approach to others in the group		1	2	3	4	5	
24. He is friendly		1	2	3	4	5	

COWELL'S SOCIAL ADJUSTMENT INDEX

FORM A

Date: _____ Grade: _____

School: _____ Age: _____

_____ Describer: _____
Last Name   First Name

INSTRUCTION: Think carefully of the student's behavior in group situations and check <u>each behavior trend</u> according to its degree of descriptiveness.

Behavior Trends	Descriptive of the Student			
	Markedly (+3)	Somewhat (+2)	Only Slightly (+1)	Not at All (+0)
1. Enters heartily and with enjoyment into the spirit of social intercourse _____				
2. Frank; talkative and sociable, does not stand on ceremony _____				
3. Self-confident and self-reliant, tends to take success for granted, strong initiative, prefers to lead _____				
4. Quick and decisive in movement, pronounced or excessive energy output _____				
5. Prefers group activities, work or play; not easily satisfied with individual projects _____				
6. Adaptable to new situations, makes adjustments readily, welcomes change _____				
7. Is self-composed, seldom shows signs of embarrassment _____				
8. Tends to elation of spirits, seldom gloomy or moody _____				
9. Seeks a broad range of friendships, not selective or exclusive in games and the like _____				
10. Hearty and cordial, even to strangers, forms acquaintanceships very easily _____				

COWELL'S SOCIAL ADJUSTMENT INDEX

FORM B

Date: _____ Grade: _____

School: _____ Age: _____

_____ Describer: _____

Last Name   First Name

INSTRUCTION: Think carefully of the student's behavior in group situations and check each behavior trend according to its degree of descriptiveness.

Behavior Trends	Descriptive of the Student			
	Markedly (−3)	Somewhat (−2)	Only Slightly (−1)	Not at All (−0)
1. Somewhat prudish, awkward, easily embarrassed in his social contacts _____				
2. Secretive, seclusive, not inclined to talk unless spoken to _____				
3. Lacking in self confidence and initiative, a follower _____				
4. Slow in movement, deliberative or perhaps indecisive. Energy output moderate or deficient _____				
5. Prefers to work and play alone, tends to avoid group activities _____				
6. Shrinks from making new adjustments, prefers the habitual to the stress of reorganization required by the new _____				
7. Is self-conscious, easily embarrassed, timid or "bashful" _____				
8. Tends to depression, frequently gloomy or moody _____				
9. Shows preference for a narrow range of intimate friends and tends to exclude others from his association _____				
10. Reserved and distant except to intimate friends, does not form acquaintanceships readily _____				

Percentile Scale—Cowell Social Adjustment Index

Raw Score	%ile Score	Raw Score	%ile Score	Raw Score	%ile Score
88	99.55	60	90.09	43	73.42
81	99.10	59	89.19	42	72.97
80	98.65	58	88.29	41	72.52
79	98.20	57	86.49	40	72.07
78	97.75	56	86.04	38	71.17
77	97.30	55	85.14	37	69.37
75	96.85	54	84.23	36	68.47
74	96.40	52	83.33	35	67.12
73	95.94	51	82.88	34	65.32
72	95.50	50	82.43	33	64.41
70	95.04	49	81.08	32	63.51
68	94.59	48	80.18	31	61.26
65	92.79	47	79.28	30	59.91
63	92.34	46	78.38	29	59.01
62	91.44	45	77.03	28	57.21
61	90.54	44	74.77	27	56.31
26	55.40	2	32.43	−28	12.16
25	54.95	1	30.63	−29	11.71
24	53.60	−1	29.73	−35	10.81
23	52.70	−2	28.38	−36	9.91
22	51.80	−3	27.48	−39	8.56
21	50.90	−5	26.00	−40	8.11
20	50.45	−6	25.22	−42	7.66
18	48.65	−7	23.87	−43	7.21
17	46.85	−8	23.42	−44	6.76
16	45.94	−9	22.97	−45	6.31
15	45.50	−12	22.52	−46	5.40
14	45.04	−15	21.62	−47	4.50
13	43.24	−16	21.17	−49	4.05
12	41.44	−17	20.72	−50	3.60
11	40.54	−18	19.82	−54	3.15
10	40.09	−19	18.92	−55	2.70
9	38.74	−20	18.47	−58	1.80
8	37.84	−21	17.51	−61	1.35
7	36.94	−23	16.22	−62	.90
6	35.59	−25	15.32	−71	.45
4	34.68	−26	13.96	−73	.00
3	33.33	−27	12.36		

n = 222

COWELL PERSONAL DISTANCE BALLOT

What To Do:

I would be willing to accept him:

If you had full power to treat each student on this list as you feel, just how would you consider him? How near would you like to have him to your family? Check each student in one column as to your feeling toward him. Circle your own name	Into my family as a brother	As a very close "pal" or "chum"	As a member of my "gang" or club	On my street as a "next-door neighbor"	Into my class at school	Into my school	Into my city
	1	2	3	4	5	6	7

1. _____

2. _____

3. _____

4. etc. _____

Scoring: See page 391.

Percentile Scale—Cowell Personal Distance

Raw Score	%ile Score	Raw Score	%ile Score	Raw Score	%ile Score
159	99.34	260	82.78	319	62.91
161	98.68	265	82.12	321	61.59
173	98.01	266	81.46	327	60.93
196	97.35	267	80.79	329	60.26
200	96.69	271	79.47	331	59.60
205	94.04	274	78.81	333	58.94
210	93.38	281	76.16	335	57.62
211	92.71	282	75.50	336	56.29
219	92.05	283	74.17	344	54.97
220	91.39	284	73.51	347	54.30
222	90.73	285	72.85	351	53.64
233	90.07	289	72.18	352	52.98
237	89.40	294	70.20	369	45.70
240	88.74	295	68.87	371	45.03
252	88.08	300	68.21	375	44.37
256	86.75	311	65.56	376	43.71
257	84.10	312	64.90	377	43.05
259	83.44	315	64.24	378	41.06
379	40.40	395	31.79	431	13.91
353	51.66	396	31.12	433	13.24
354	50.33	398	30.46	434	12.58
355	49.67	400	29.80	435	11.92
357	49.01	405	26.49	439	11.25
359	48.34	412	25.83	445	10.60
361	47.68	415	25.16	455	9.93
363	47.02	416	24.50	457	9.27
366	46.36	417	23.84	469	7.95
380	39.74	418	23.18	470	7.28
381	38.41	419	21.19	471	6.62
382	37.75	420	20.53	482	5.96
384	37.09	421	19.87	495	5.30
385	36.76	422	19.20	496	4.64
386	35.10	423	17.22	500	3.97
389	34.44	425	16.56	503	1.99
390	33.77	426	15.89	509	1.32
391	33.11	428	15.23	541	.66
392	32.45	429	14.57	636	.00

n = 151

<u>Scoring</u>: Add each subject's total weighted scores given by fellow students and divide by the total number of respondents. Division is carried to two places and the decimal point is dropped. The lower the score, the greater the degree of acceptance. (See pages 389-390.)

Problems Associated with Social Measurement

Several of the problems associated with social measurement are listed as follows:

1. Since many physical educators are not trained observers of character and personality traits, the validity of their evaluations may be questioned. Thus, it seems most important for such measurement to include pupil evaluations in conjunction with teacher evaluation.

2. The physical and mental condition of the teacher frequently affects the type of ratings students get. For example, a teacher who is ill or unduly tired at the time of the rating may not give the same ratings as would be given at a time when the same teacher was feeling well or in high spirits. Also, the personality of the teacher may have a bearing on the ratings in that the teacher may rate students who exhibit behavior patterns similar to their own as *good* and students of an opposite nature as *poor*.

3. Although sociometric tests are quite reliable and valid for the purpose they serve, they are limited in the types of information they can provide.

4. Results may not be too valid when sociometric tests are given without consideration for feelings toward the opposite sex. Usually it is best to have boys rate boys, girls rate girls, and then have each to rate members of the opposite sex. Otherwise, certain students may indicate only members of the opposite sex as the ones they would like to work with or have as friends.

Findings and Conclusions From Social Measurement and Research

Numerous studies have found that various physical measures (motor ability, physical fitness, physically active, athletic ability, height, weight, health, etc.) were significantly related to social measures (leadership ability, well-adjusted, popularity, etc.).[1,28,30,32,33,37]

Concerning the characteristic of being physically active, Cowell,[9] Tryon,[35] Kuhlen and Lee,[21] and Hanley[16] all found it to be an important factor in social acceptance.

Physical educators have long contended that physical education activity participation brings about desirable traits or closer social integration within the group. Several studies have found support for such a contention.[4,8,31,38] While desirable changes in social status have been reported, it is feasible that physical activity participation under the wrong leadership could breed undesirable social change. Perhaps differences in leadership or in emphasis on social goals was the reason why Blanchard[4] found girls' activity classes to be significantly superior to boys' activity classes in the acquisition of wholesome character and personality traits.

Two studies have investigated the effects of motivated activity participation upon social acceptance.[24,36] Walters[36] found motivated groups to be more closely knit than non-motivated groups in bowling classes, and that students became more closely integrated socially as a result of acquaintance and group participation. Nelson and Johnson[24] further found that motivated participation brought about positive changes in social ratings when anti-cohesive pairs were induced to work together.

Several studies have found that individuals do not radically shift from one position to a very different position concerning social standings, thus revealing the stability of sociometric testing.[5,17,24] Such testing has been used to show objective relationships between physical education and the development of groups,[5,18,40] and the closer integration of individuals constituting those groups.[5,23,29] Moreover, some studies have concerned themselves with the relationships between sociometric status and skill in specific activities such as volleyball, swimming, and dancing.[6,14,31]

Members of athletic teams were found to have higher social status than boys who could not make the team or were not members of a team.[13,25,22,2,11] Trapp,[34] Cowell, and Ismail[12] further noted that social integration in a football squad was positive and remained so, or increased as the playing time together increased.

Concerning the relationship of physical fitness and strength to social prestige, Clarke,[7] Yarnell,[39] Jones,[19,20] and Popp[26] found that boys who scored higher in strength and physical fitness enjoyed greater social prestige than those who did not. However, Haines[15] did not find such a relationship with fifth grade students. On the other hand, Cowell and Ismail[11] and Rarick[27] found that students who scored high in physical measures and motor achievement to be the most popular.

BIBLIOGRAPHY

1. Betz, Robert L., "A Comparison Between Personality Limits and Physical Fitness Tests of Males 26 - 60," (Unpublished Master's Thesis, University of Illinois, Urbana, 1956).

2. Biddulph, Lowell G., "Athletic Achievement and Personal-Social Adjustment of High School Boys," *Research Quarterly,* 25:1-7, 1954.

3. Blanchard, B. E., "A Behavior Frequency Rating Scale for the Measurement of Character and Personality in Physical Education Classroom Situations," *Research Quarterly,* May, 1936, pp. 56-66.

4. _____ , "A Comparative Analysis of Secondary School Boys' and Girls' Character and Personality Traits in Physical Education Classes," *Research Quarterly,* March, 1946, 17:33-39.

5. Breck, Sabina June, "A Sociometric Measurement of Status in Physical Education Classes," *Research Quarterly,* May, 1950, 21:75-82.

6. Breck, June, "A Sociometric Test of Status as Measured in Physical Education Classes," (Unpublished Master's Thesis, University of California at Los Angeles, 1947).

7. Clarke, H. Harrison, and David H. Clarke, "Social Status and Mental Health of Boys as Related to their Maturity, Structural, and Strength Characteristics," *Research Quarterly,* 32:326, October, 1961.

8. Clevett, Melvin A., "An Experiment in Physical Education Activities Related to the Teaching of Honesty and Motor Skills," *Research Quarterly,* 3:121-127, March, 1932.

9. Cowell, Charles C., "An Abstract of a Study of Differentials in Junior High School Boys Based on the Observation of Physical Education Activities," *Research Quarterly,* 6:129-136, December, 1935.

10. _____ , "Validating an Index of Social Adjustment for High School Use," *Research Quarterly,* March, 1958, pp. 7-18.

11. _____ , and A. H. Ismail, "Relationships Between Selected Social and Physical Factors," *Research Quarterly,* 33:42, March, 1962.

12. _____ , "Validity of a Football Rating Scale and Its Relationship to Social Integration and Academic Ability," *Research Quarterly,* 32:461-467, December, 1961.

13. Flowtow, Ernest A., "Charting Social Relationships of School Children," *The Elementary School Journal,* 46:498, May, 1946.

14. Fulton, Ruth E., "Relationship Between Teammate Status and Measures of Skill in Volleyball," *Research Quarterly,* 21:274-276, October, 1950.

15. Haines, James E., "The Relationship of Kraus-Weber Minimal Muscular Fitness and Rogers' Physical Fitness Index Tests with Social Acceptance, Teacher Acceptance, and Emotional Stability in Selected Fifth Grade Pupils," (Unpublished Doctoral Dissertation, Springfield College, 1957).

16. Hanley, Charles, "Physique and Reputation of Junior High School Boys," *Child Development,* 22:247, 1951.

17. Jennings, Helen H., "Sociometry and Social Theory," *American Sociological Review,* 6:512-522, 1941.

18. Johnson, Alvin D., "An Attempt at Change in Inter-Personal Relations," *Sociometry,* 2:43-49.

19. Jones, Harold E., "Motor Performance and Growth," Berkeley: University of California Press, 1949.

20. _____ , "Physical Ability as a Factor in Social Adjustment in Adolescence," *Journal of Educational Research,* 4:287, 1946.

21. Kuhlen, Raymond G., and Beatrice J. Lee, "Personality Characteristics and Social Acceptability in Adolescence," *Journal of Educational Psychology,* 34:321, 1943.

22. McCraw, L. N., and J. W. Tabert, "Sociometric Status and Athletic Ability of Junior High School Boys," *Research Quarterly,* 24:72-78, 1953.

23. McKenna, Helen M., "The Effects of Two Methods of Grouping in Physical Education Upon the Social Structure of the Group," (Unpublished Master's Thesis, University of California at Los Angeles, 1948).

24. Nelson, Jack K., and Barry L. Johnson, "Effects of Varied Techniques in Organizing Class Competition Upon Changes in Sociometric Status," *Research Quarterly,* 39:634-639, 1968.

25. Ondrus, Joseph, "A Sociometric Analysis of Group Structure and the Effect of Football Activities on Inter-personal Relationships," (Unpublished Doctoral Dissertation, New York University, New York, 1953).

26. Popp, James, "Case Studies of Sophomore High School Boys with High and Low Physical Fitness Indices," (Unpublished Master's Thesis, University of Oregon, 1959).

27. Rarick, G. Lawrence, "A Study of Twenty Third-Grade Children Exhibiting Extreme Levels of Achievement on Tests of Motor Proficiency," *Research Quarterly,* 20:142-152, May, 1949.

28. Reaney, M. Jane, "The Correlation Between General Intelligence and Play Ability as Shown in Organized Group Games," *British Journal of Psychology,* 7:226-252, 1914.

29. Robinson, Virginia Ruth, "A Study of the Effects of Two Methods of Teaching Physical Education as Measured by a Sociometric Test," (Unpublished Master's Thesis, University of California at Los Angeles, 1948).

30. Signorella, Michael, "Social Adjustment and Athletic Participation," (Unpublished Study, Purdue University, Lafayette, 1963).

31. Skubic, Elvera, "A Study in Acquaintanceship and Social Status in Physical Education Classes," *Research Quarterly,* 20:80-87, March, 1947.

32. Sperling, A. P., "The Relationship Between Personality Adjustment and Achievement in Physical Education Activities," *Research Quarterly,* 13:351-363, October, 1942.

33. Stogdill, Ralph M., "Personal Factors Associated with Leadership: A Survey of Literature," *Journal of Psychology,* 25:35-71, 1948.

34. Trapp, William G., "A Study of Social Integration in a College Football Squad," Washington, D.C.: *56th Annual Proceedings,* College Physical Education Association, 1953.

35. Tryon, Caroline C., "Evaluation of Adolescent Personality by Adolescents," *Monograph of the Society for Research in Child Development,* Vol. 4, 1939.

36. Walters, C. Etta, "A Sociometric Study of Motivated and Non-Motivated Bowling Groups," *Research Quarterly,* 26:107-112, March, 1955.

37. Wells, Harold P., "Relationship Between Physical Fitness and Psychological Variables," (Unpublished Doctoral Dissertation, University of Illinois, Urbana, 1958).

38. Whilden, Peggy P., "Comparison of Two Methods of Teaching Beginning Basketball," *Research Quarterly,* 27:235-242, May, 1956.

39. Yarnell, C. Douglas, "Relationship of Physical Fitness to Selected Measures of Popularity," *Research Quarterly,* 37:287, May, 1966.

40. Zeleny, Leslie Day, "Status: Its Measurement and Control in Education," *Sociometry,* 4:193-204.

Part II – Attitudes

Introduction

Attitudes are ideas or feelings that one may have about something as a result of past experience, or as a result of imaginative likes and dislikes. Moreover, attitudes may change as often as we sometimes hear that a woman may change her mind. When conditions or changes in the environment occur, whether for better or worse, we can usually expect to see a change in attitudes. In physical education we are concerned with the attitudes of students toward the physical education activity program as well as toward individual activities within the program. It is important to measure attitudes to see what effect various types of programs, administrative procedures, and methods of instruction have upon a student's feelings. When such measurement is objectively conducted, avenues of approach are opened up so that desirable changes can be logically brought about.

Uses of Attitude Tests

Several ways by which attitude tests may be utilized in physical education classes are listed as follows:
1. To assist in determining whether objectives are being reached or not.
2. As a means for assembling information in a survey for administrative planning and curriculum development, and
3. To evaluate the effectiveness of teaching methods in helping students to enjoy physical education.

Attitude Scales

Several practical attitude scales are included below:

Wear's Attitude Scale with Equivalent Forms.[17]
<u>Objective</u>: To measure changes in attitude toward physical education as a result of special experiences to which students might be involved.
<u>Age Level</u>: College.
<u>Reliability</u>: The reliability of Form A was reported as .94 and the reliability of Form B was .96. The product correlation between scores on the two forms was .96.
<u>Validity</u>: Face validity has been accepted for the two scales.
<u>Directions</u>: Students are directed to consider physical education only from the standpoint of its place as an activity course taught during a regular class period and to check the response which best expresses the feeling about each statement. Students

are also told to let their own personal experiences determine their answers and that their answers will in no way affect their grade in any course.

Scoring: The five possible responses to each inventory item are as follows: strongly agree, agree, undecided, disagree, and strongly disagree. The responses are scored 5-4-3-2-1 when the item is worded positively and 1-2-3-4-5 when worded negatively. Thus, a high score would indicate a favorable attitude toward physical education.

FORM A

1. If for any reason a few subjects have to be dropped from the school program, physical education should be one of the subjects dropped.
2. Physical education activities provide no opportunities for learning to control the emotions.
3. Physical education is one of the more important subjects in helping to establish and maintain desirable social standards.
4. Vigorous physical activity works off harmful emotional tensions.
5. I would take physical education only if it were required.
6. Participation in physical education makes no contribution to the development of poise.
7. Because physical skills loom large in importance in youth, it is essential that a person be helped to acquire and improve such skills.
8. Calisthenics taken regularly are good for one's general health.
9. Skill in active games or sports is not necessary for leading the fullest kind of life.
10. Physical education does more harm physically than it does good.
11. Associating with others in some physical education activity is fun.
12. Physical education classes provide situations for the formation of attitudes which will make one a better citizen.
13. Physical education situations are among the poorest for making friends.
14. There is not enough value coming from physical education to justify the time consumed.
15. Physical education skills make worthwhile contributions to the enrichment of living.
16. People get all the physical exercise they need in just taking care of their daily work.
17. All who are physically able will profit from an hour of physical education each day.
18. Physical education makes a valuable contribution toward building up an adequate reserve of strength and endurance for everyday living.
19. Physical education tears down sociability by encouraging people to attempt to surpass each other in many of the activities.
20. Participation in physical education activities makes for a more wholesome outlook on life.
21. Physical education adds nothing to the improvement of social behavior.
22. Physical education class activities will help to relieve and relax physical tensions.
23. Participation in physical education activities helps a person to maintain a healthful emotional life.
24. Physical education is one of the more important subjects in the school program.
25. There is little value in physical education as far as physical well-being is concerned.
26. Physical education should be included in the program of every school.
27. Skills learned in a physical education class do not benefit a person.
28. Physical education provides situations for developing desirable character qualities.
29. Physical education makes for more enjoyable living.
30. Physical education has no place in modern education.

FORM B

1. Associations in physical education activities give people a better understanding of each other.
2. Engaging in vigorous physical activity gets one interested in practicing good health habits.
3. The time spent in getting ready for and engaging in a physical education class could be more profitably spent in other ways.
4. A person's body usually has all the strength it needs without participation in physical education activities.
5. Participation in physical education activities tends to make one a more socially desirable person.
6. Physical education in schools does not receive the emphasis that it should.
7. Physical education classes are poor in opportunities for worthwhile social experiences.
8. A person would be better off emotionally if he did not participate in physical education.
9. It is possible to make physical education a valuable subject by proper selection of activities.
10. Developing a physical skill brings mental relaxation and relief.
11. Physical education classes provide nothing which will be of value outside the class.
12. There should not be over two one-hour periods per week devoted to physical education in schools.
13. Belonging to a group, for which opportunity is provided in team activities is a desirable experience for a person.
14. Physical education is an important subject in helping a person gain and maintain all-round good health.
15. No definite beneficial results come from participation in physical education activities.
16. Engaging in group physical education activities is desirable for proper personality development.
17. Physical education activities tend to upset a person emotionally.
18. For its contributions to mental and emotional well-being physical education should be included in the program of every school.
19. I would advise anyone who is physically able to take physical education.
20. As far as improving physical health is concerned, a physical education class is a waste of time.
21. Participation in physical education class activities tends to develop a wholesome interest in the functioning of one's body.
22. Physical education classes give a person an opportunity to have a good time.
23. The final mastering of a certain movement or skill in a physical education class brings a pleasurable feeling that one seldom experiences elsewhere.
24. Physical education contributes little toward the improvement of social behavior.
25. Physical education classes provide values which are useful in other parts of daily living.
26. Physical education should be required of all who are physically able to participate.
27. The time devoted to physical education in schools could be more profitably used in study.
28. The skills learned in a physical education class do not add anything of value to a person's life.
29. Physical education does more harm socially than good.

Wear's Physical Education Attitude Scale.[18]

Objective: To determine the individual and group attitude toward physical education as an activity course.

Age Level: High school and college.

Sex: Satisfactory for both boys and girls.

Reliability: A reliability as high as .98 has been reported for this scale.

Validity: Face validity has been accepted.

Directions: Students are directed to consider physical education only from the standpoint of its place as an activity course taught during a regular class period and to check the response which best expresses the feeling about each statement. Students are also told to let their own personal experiences determine their answers, and that their answers will in no way affect their grade in any course.

STATEMENTS

1. If for any reason a few subjects have to be dropped from the school program, physical education should be one of the subjects dropped.
2. Associations in physical education activities give people a better understanding of each other.
3. Physical education activities provide no opportunities for learning to control the emotions.
4. Engaging in vigorous physical activity gets one interested in practicing good health habits.
5. Physical education is one of the more important subjects in helping to establish and maintain desirable social standards.
6. The time spent in getting ready for and engaging in a physical-education class could be more profitably spent in other ways.
7. Vigorous physical activity works off harmful emotional tensions.
8. A person's body usually has all the strength it needs without participation in physical education activities.
9. I would take physical education only if it were required.
10. Participation in physical education activities tends to make one a more socially desirable person.
11. Participation in physical education makes no contribution to the development of poise.
12. Physical education in schools does not receive the emphasis that it should.
13. Because physical skills loom large in importance in youth, it is essential that a person be helped to acquire and improve such skills.
14. Physical education classes are poor in opportunities for worthwhile social experiences.
15. Calisthenics taken regularly are good for one's general health.
16. A person would be better off emotionally if he did not participate in physical education.
17. Skill in active games or sports is not necessary for leading the fullest kind of life.
18. It is possible to make physical education a valuable subject by proper selection of activities.
19. Physical education does more harm physically than it does good.
20. Developing a physical skill brings mental relaxation and relief.
21. Associating with others in some physical education activity is fun.

22. Physical education classes provide nothing which will be of value outside the class.
23. Physical education classes provide situations for the formation of attitudes which will make one a better citizen.
24. There should not be over two one-hour periods per week devoted to physical education in schools.
25. Physical education situations are among the poorest for making friends.
26. Belonging to a group, for which opportunity is provided in team activities, is a desirable experience for a person.
27. There is not enough value coming from physical education to justify the time consumed.
28. Physical education is an important subject in helping a person gain and maintain all-round good health.
29. Physical education skills make worthwhile contributions to the enrichment of living.
30. No definite beneficial results come from participation in physical education activities.
31. People get all the physical exercise they need in just taking care of their daily work.
32. Engaging in group physical education activities is desirable for proper personality development.
33. All who are physically able will profit from an hour of physical education each day.
34. Physical education activities tend to upset a person emotionally.
35. Physical education makes a valuable contribution toward building up an adequate reserve of strength and endurance for everyday living.
36. For its contributions to mental and emotional well-being physical education should be included in the program of every school.
37. Physical education tears down sociability by encouraging people to attempt to surpass each other in many of the activities.
38. I would advise anyone who is physically able to take physical education.
39. Participation in physical education activities makes for a more wholesome outlook on life.
40. As far as improving physical health is concerned, a physical education class is a waste of time.

SCORING

As previously explained there are five possible responses to each Inventory item: strongly agree, agree, undecided, disagree, and strongly disagree. The response considered most favorable to physical education receives a score of 5. Thus the above responses would be scored 5-4-3-2-1 or 1-2-3-4-5, depending on whether the item was worded positively or negatively. A subject's score on the Inventory is the sum of the scores made on the individual items. According to this method of scoring, a high score would indicate a favorable attitude toward physical education.

Table 4 gives normalized T-scores which were derived from the Short Form raw scores of the population of 472 college men, 332 of whom were beginning freshmen. After being calculated, the T-scores were plotted against the corresponding raw scores. A curve was then fitted to the plotted points and smoothed. The T-scores given in the table were read from this smoothed curve.

TABLE 4

T-Scores Corresponding to Given Raw Scores

R	T	R	T	R	T	R	T	R	T	R	T
200	78	175	60	150	47	125	38	100	31	75	26
199	77	174	59	149	47	124	38	99	31	74	25
198	76	173	59	148	46	123	37	98	30	73	25
197	75	172	58	147	46	122	37	97	30	72	25
196	74	171	58	146	46	121	37	96	30	71	25
195	73	170	57	145	45	120	36	95	30	70	25
194	72	169	56	144	45	119	36	94	30	69	25
193	72	168	56	143	44	118	36	93	29	68	24
192	71	167	56	142	44	117	36	92	29	67	24
191	70	166	55	141	43	116	35	91	29	66	24
190	69	165	54	140	43	115	35	90	29	65	24
189	68	164	54	139	43	114	35	89	28	64	24
188	68	163	53	138	42	113	34	88	28	63	24
187	67	162	53	137	42	112	34	87	28	62	23
186	66	161	52	136	42	111	34	86	28	61	23
185	66	160	52	135	41	110	34	85	28	60	23
184	65	159	51	134	41	109	33	84	27	59	23
183	64	158	51	133	41	108	33	83	27	58	23
182	64	157	50	132	40	107	33	82	27	57	23
181	63	156	50	131	40	106	33	81	27	56	23
180	63	155	50	130	40	105	32	80	27	55	22
179	62	154	49	129	39	104	32	79	26	54	22
178	62	153	49	128	39	103	32	78	26	53	22
177	61	152	48	127	39	102	32	77	26	52	22
176	60	151	48	126	38	101	31	76	26	51	22

Carr Physical Education Attitude Scale.[5]

    <u>Objective</u>: To determine the attitudes of girls as they relate to physical education.

    <u>Age Level</u>: High school.

    <u>Sex</u>: Satisfactory for girls.

    <u>Reliability</u>: Reliability was not reported for this scale.

    <u>Validity</u>: Face validity was accepted in addition to following selected criteria in establishing the scale.

    <u>Directions</u>: The student is directed to indicate her attitude by either agreeing or disagreeing with each statement.

    <u>Scale</u>: Place a check mark in the desired space before each statement.

AGREE   DISAGREE

1. Being a leader is a fine responsibility.
2. I feel as if I am learning something when I play with someone who plays better than I do.
3. I prefer playing outdoors when the weather is good.
4. I like to bathe after playing hard.
5. I like to set a goal for my own improvement and want to practice until I reach that goal.
6. I like to talk to my teachers as that makes them seem like friends.
7. I prefer to play in a playsuit as I feel I can play more freely.
8. I like games that have lots of vigorous activity in them.
9. I like to have a place to keep my own things.
10. Playing games with a group is more fun than playing alone.
11. I like to try new things just to see if I can do them.
12. Teachers are friendly and helpful if I try to do my work.
13. Dancing is a necessary part of every girl's education.
14. I like to be a leader in a group if I feel that the whole group wants me.
15. I like to be given suggestions as to how to improve myself.
16. I like to be able to do things as well as my friends do.
17. Teachers usually have very good advice to offer.
18. Taking a shower after playing hard is a necessary precaution against taking cold.
19. I am uncomfortable if I have to wear clothes that have been worn by someone else.
20. There is more than a small chance of catching a disease in the shower room.
21. There is no reason why I should not take a shower when I am menstruating.
22. There is a chance that I might catch some skin infection if I wear other girls' clothes.
23. I would not mind having other girls around while I take a shower.
24. I do not mind having other girls around while I take a shower.
25. I like to play games in which one team tries to outdo the other team in playing ability.
26. I never wear clothes that belong to other girls.

AGREE   DISAGREE

_____   _____   27. I do not mind having my mother or sister around while I bathe.

_____   _____   28. Games with running and jumping are healthful for most girls.

_____   _____   29. It is probably a good thing to bathe after playing hard.

_____   _____   30. I would be willing to play with girls of another race or color, especially if they had no one else to play with.

_____   _____   31. To take a shower with others around is no worse than to take a shower alone.

_____   _____   32. I feel sure that taking a shower after playing hard will prevent me from taking a cold.

_____   _____   33. My friends will like me better if I take a shower after playing hard.

_____   _____   34. Disease caught in the shower room might be caught any place else.

_____   _____   35. The chance of catching a disease in a shower room is very small.

_____   _____   36. I feel much better in a room with light walls than in one with dark walls.

_____   _____   37. I can keep my clothes neat and orderly if I have to.

_____   _____   38. It makes me feel very bad if I am the last one to be chosen in a game.

_____   _____   39. I have about as much fun playing alone as I do in a group.

_____   _____   40. I usually want to be my own boss.

_____   _____   41. Games played with boys are more fun than games played with girls.

_____   _____   42. I am uncomfortable if I have to wear clothes that are not like those other girls are wearing.

_____   _____   43. It makes no difference to me whether I win or lose in a game.

_____   _____   44. One kind of game is as good as another.

_____   _____   45. I usually am satisfied with the way I do things.

_____   _____   46. It would make me very uncomfortable to have anyone around while I take a shower.

_____   _____   47. I do not like to play games in which I try to win over an opponent.

_____   _____   48. Playing games with boys is not fun as they are too rough.

_____   _____   49. One teacher is as good as another.

_____   _____   50. I like quiet games with no running or jumping.

_____   _____   51. Girls should play games that are not very strenuous.

_____   _____   52. If there is a chance of being hurt in a game I would rather not play.

_____   _____   53. Keeping things in order all the time takes too much time from other things.

_____   _____   54. I like to play with only one or two girls.

_____   _____   55. Keeping score in a game bothers me.

_____   _____   56. Being a leader in a group is not important.

_____   _____   57. I like to play indoors better than outdoors.

_____   _____   58. I do not mind if my clothes are worn by someone else.

_____   _____   59. It makes very little difference in the prevention of colds whether or not I take a shower.

AGREE   DISAGREE

_____ _____   60. I feel that it makes no difference what kind of clothes one plays in.

_____ _____   61. Taking a shower after playing hard is an unnecessary precaution against taking cold.

_____ _____   62. I dislike wearing playsuits.

_____ _____   63. I like to play with just the girls in my neighborhood.

_____ _____   64. I do not enjoy playing with girls who can play better than I can.

_____ _____   65. I feel that I should play with only girls of my own race or color.

_____ _____   66. Taking a shower after playing hard may give me a cold.

_____ _____   67. I would rather take a low grade if it is passing than to work hard for a high one.

_____ _____   68. It is dangerous for most girls to take a shower during the menstrual period.

_____ _____   69. I feel that other people have no right to tell me what to do.

_____ _____   70. It makes no difference to me whether I bathe after playing hard.

_____ _____   71. I usually will do what my friends do although it is against my better judgment.

_____ _____   72. I like best to play alone.

_____ _____   73. I do not like to bathe after playing hard.

_____ _____   74. The leader of a group does all the work and has no fun.

_____ _____   75. It is a waste of time to bathe after playing hard.

_____ _____   76. Teachers are like dictators because they want to boss us.

_____ _____   77. Taking showers with other girls is a sure way of catching a disease.

_____ _____   78. I feel that I should never take a shower during my menstrual period.

_____ _____   79. It is dangerous to swim with other girls in a pool.

_____ _____   80. I feel that I would be lowering myself if I took part in a dance.

_____ _____   81. Teachers make rules just to make us behave the way they want us to.

_____ _____   82. It is a waste of time to change clothes in which to play.

_____ _____   83. We are born to be as we are. There is no use to try to improve.

_____ _____   84. Being beaten in a game is disgraceful.

Scoring: The first 37 statements are indicated as desirable attitudes and the remaining 47 statements as undesirable attitudes. The final score is determined by subtracting the percentage of undesirable attitudes indicated from the percentage of desirable attitudes checked.

Lakie's Attitudes Toward Athletic Competition Scale.[11]

Objective: To determine to what degree the "win-at-any-cost" attitude exists among students and groups.

<u>Age Level</u>: College level.
<u>Sex</u>: Satisfactory for both men and women.
<u>Reliability</u>: A reliability of .81 was reported.
<u>Validity</u>: Face validity was accepted for this scale.
<u>Directions</u>: Students are directed to circle the category that indicates their feelings toward the behavior described in each of the situations below:

(1) Strongly Approve (2) Approve (3) Undecided (4) Disapprove (5) Strongly Disapprove

1 2 3 4 5   1. During a football game team A has the ball on its own 45-yard line, fourth down and 1 yd. to go for a first down. The coach of team A signals to the quarterback the play that he wants the team to run.

1 2 3 4 5   2. Team A is the visiting basketball team and each time a member of the team is given a free shot the home crowd sets up a continual din of noise until the shot has been taken.

1 2 3 4 5   3. Tennis player A frequently calls out, throws up his arms, or otherwise tries to indicate that his opponent's serve is out of bounds when it is questionable.

1 2 3 4 5   4. In a track meet team A enters a man in the mile run who is to set a fast pace for the first half of the race and then drop out.

1 2 3 4 5   5. In a football game team B's quarterback was tackled repeatedly after handing off and after he was out of the play.

1 2 3 4 5   6. Sam, playing golf with his friends, hit a drive into the rough. He accidently moved the ball with his foot; although not improving his position, he added a penalty stroke to his score.

1 2 3 4 5   7. A basketball player was caught out of position on defense, and rather than allow his opponent to attempt a field goal he fouled him.

1 2 3 4 5   8. Player A during a golf match made quick noises and movements when player B was getting ready to make a shot.

1 2 3 4 5   9. School A has a powerful but quite slow football team. The night before playing a smaller but faster team, they allowed the field sprinkling system to remain on, causing the field to be heavy and slow.

1 2 3 4 5   10. A basketball team used player A to draw the opponent's high scorer into fouling situations.

1 2 3 4 5   11. The alumni of College A pressured the Board of Trustees to lower the admission and eligibility requirements for athletes.

1 2 3 4 5   12. Team A, by use of fake injuries, was able to stop the clock long enough to get off the play that resulted in the winning of the touchdown.

1 2 3 4 5   13. A tennis player was given the advantage of a bad call in a close match. He then *evened up* the call by intentionally hitting the ball out of bounds.

1 2 3 4 5   14. The coach of basketball team A removed his team from the floor in protest to an official's decision.

1 2 3 4 5   15. Between seasons a coach moved from College A to College B, and he then persuaded three of College A's athletes to transfer to College B.

1 2 3 4 5   16. After losing a close football game, the coach of the losing team publicly accused the game officials of favoritism when the game movies showed that the winning touchdown had been scored by using an illegal maneuver.

1 2 3 4 5   17. College C lowered the admission requirements for boys awarded athletic scholarships.

1 2 3 4 5   18. Team A's safety man returned a punt for a touchdown. Unseen by the officials, he had stepped out of bounds in front of his team's bench. His coach notified the officials of this fact.

1 2 3 4 5   19. A college with very few athletic scholarships to offer gives athletes preference on all types of campus jobs.

1 2 3 4 5   20. Several wealthy alumni of College C make a monthly gift to several athletes who are in need of financial assistance.

1 2 3 4 5   21. College K has a policy of not allowing any member of a varsity squad to associate with the visiting team until the contest or meet is completed.

1 2 3 4 5   22. The Board of Trustees at College C fired the football coach and gave as the reason for his dismissal his failure to win a conference championship during the past five years.

Scoring: Except for items 6, 13, and 18 where points should be figured in reverse order, add the points as scored. The scoring range is from 22 to 110 and the lower the score the greater the student agrees with a "win-at-any-cost" attitude.

Problems Associated with Attitude Testing

Several of the problems associated with attitude testing are listed as follows:
1. Each statement must be worded carefully to secure the actual attitude response and to avoid giving away the desired response.
2. There is an obvious lack of stability of attitudes of young people, especially those below the high school level. It is quite common for students to change their attitudes rapidly after exposure to new experiences. Therefore, attitude results must not be regarded as permanent.
3. The validity associated with attitude scales is sometimes questionable. If students have had limited experience with certain aspects of a program, obviously they cannot make intelligent responses concerning them.

Findings and Conclusions from Attitude Measurement and Research

Numerous studies have reported that students generally have favorable attitudes toward physical education as an activity course.[1,2,3,4,8] Brumbach[4] further found that students who participated in a high school athletic program or who attended a small school (enrollment under 300) were apt to have a wholesome attitude toward physical education. Moreover, both Bell[2] and Brumbach[4] found that the university students with the most favorable attitudes toward physical education were the ones who had had more years of physical education in high school.

Physical educators who are concerned with the social and ethical values of activities often question the contributions of varsity athletics toward such values. Both Kistler[10] and Richardson[14] found that varsity athletes had poorer attitudes about sportsmanship than did those students who had either not participated at the varsity level, or who had engaged in the less publicized sports.

While Kistler[10] found that only a small number of students were aware of the benefits concerning social and ethical values received from participation in physical education classes, Keogh[9] reported that students endorsed the social, physical, and emotional values of physical education, and Vincent[16] found that college women expressed greatest appreciation for the physiological-physical values of physical education.

Carr[5] and Vincent[16] found that attitudes held by girls do influence their success in physical education. Wessel and Nelson[19] further found that strength among college women is significantly related to attitudes toward physical activity.

Several studies have measured attitudes of various groups toward athletic competition. The results of such studies are listed as follows:

1. Scott[15] found that a majority of the parents, teachers, and administrators surveyed tended to favor intensive competition at the elementary school level.
2. McGee[13] found that parents and coaches are significantly more in favor of intensive athletic competition for high school girls than are administrators.
3. Leyhe[12] reported that a majority of the women members of AAHPER believed that girl participants in varsity sports are happier and better adjusted than non-participants.

BIBLIOGRAPHY

1. Baker, Mary C., "Factors Which May Influence the Participation in Physical Education of Girls and Women," *Research Quarterly,* 11:126-131, 1940.

2. Bell, Margaret, and C. Etta Walters, "Attitudes of Women at the University of Michigan Toward Physical Education," *Research Quarterly,* 24:379, December, 1953.

3. Broer, Marion, and others, "Attitudes of University of Washington Women Students Toward Physical Education Activity," *Research Quarterly,* 36:378-384, December, 1955.

4. Brumbach, Wayne B., and J. A. Cross, "Attitudes Toward Physical Education of Male Students Entering the University of Oregon," *Research Quarterly,* 36:10, March, 1965.

5. Carr, Martha G., "The Relationship Between Success in Physical Education and Selected Attitudes Expressed by High School Freshman Girls," *Research Quarterly,* 16:176-191, October, 1945.

6. Drinkwater, Barbara L., "Development of an Attitude Inventory to Measure the Attitudes of High School Girls Toward Physical Education as a Career for Women," *Research Quarterly,* 31:575-580, December, 1960.

7. Jaeger, Eloise, "An Investigation of a Projective Test in Determining Attitudes of Prospective Teachers of Physical Education," (Unpublished Doctoral Dissertation, State University of Iowa, 1952).

8. Kappes, Eveline E., "Inventory to Determine Attitudes of College Women Toward Physical Education and Student Services of the Physical Education Department," *Research Quarterly,* 25:429-438, December, 1954.

9. Keogh, Jack, "Analysis of General Attitudes Toward Physical Education," *Research Quarterly,* 33:239-248, May, 1962.

10. Kistler, J. W., "Attitudes Expressed About Behavior Demonstrated in Certain Specific Situations Occurring in Sports," *60th Ann. Proc.* Nat. College Phy. Educ. Assn., pp. 55-59, 1957.

11. Lakie, William L., "Expressed Attitudes of Various Groups of Athletes Toward Athletic Competition," *Research Quarterly,* 35:497-503, December, 1964.

12. Leyhe, Naomi L., "Attitudes of the Women Members of the American Association of Health, Physical Education and Recreation Toward Competition in Sports for Girls and Women," (Microcarded Dissertation, University of Iowa, 1955), p. 99.

13. McGee, Rosemary, "Comparison of Attitudes Toward Intensive Competition for High School Girls," (Microcarded Dissertation, University of Iowa, June, 1954), pp. 18, 72.

14. Richardson, Deane E., "Ethical Conduct in Sport Situations," *66th Ann. Proc.* Nat. Coll. Phy. Educ. Assn., pp. 98-104, 1962.

15. Scott, Martha P., "Attitudes Toward Athletic Competition in the Elementary School," *Research Quarterly,* 24:352-361, October, 1953.

16. Vincent, Marilyn F., "Attitudes of College Women Toward Physical Education and Their Relationship to Success in Physical Education," *Research Quarterly,* 38:130, March, 1967.

17. Wear, C. L., "Construction of Equivalent Forms of an Attitude Scale," *Research Quarterly,* 26:113-119, March, 1955.

18. _____ , "The Evaluation of Attitudes Toward Physical Education as an Activity Course," *Research Quarterly,* 22:114-126, March, 1951.

19. Wessel, Janet, and Richard Nelson, "Relationship Between Strength and Attitudes Toward Physical Education Activities Among College Women," *Research Quarterly,* 35:562-568, December, 1964.

Chapter XXI

THE MEASUREMENT
OF KNOWLEDGE

The measurement of knowledge in physical education activity classes is just as important as knowledge measurement in other subject areas. When the physical educator elects not to secure a measure of knowledge, he has ignored one of the major objectives of our field and has failed to capitalize on the potential of such tests to further the learning process. Evaluation of the students' knowledge of rules, strategy, etiquette and other pertinent information should be considered as an integral and vital part of every teaching unit.

The tools employed in the measurement of knowledge should be so designed that the teacher can easily determine what the students have learned in laboratory participation and from facts and materials presented within the unit. Knowledge tests consist of several types. The most common and practical type used in the classroom is the teacher-made test which may be either objective or subjective in nature. The objective test calls for a brief response and, if properly constructed, has higher reliability and objectivity than the subjective or essay test which usually calls for a long and detailed response.

A standardized test is merely one that has been subjected to rigorous steps and procedures in construction and usually is accompanied by norms. Most standardized tests are of the objective type consisting of true-false, matching, and multiple choice questions. Standardized tests have not had widespread use in physical education, at least not on the national level.

Uses of Knowledge Tests

Several ways in which knowledge tests in physical education classes may be utilized are listed as follows:
1. To determine the needs of the students as to what information should be imparted.
2. To evaluate student achievement and form the basis for determining grades at the end of an instructional unit.
3. To evaluate teaching effectiveness in that when a class (as a whole) fails to respond properly, some inadequacy on the part of the teacher may be noted.
4. To motivate students to learn the information deemed important by the teacher and perhaps stimulate the students to undertake more comprehensive study on the subject.
5. To further the learning process by providing a knowledge of the results. When immediate results are provided, the desired responses are more apt to be learned than when the results are delayed, or when the tests are not returned at all.

Practical Test Items for Knowledge Measurement

The most common types of test questions are the completion, multiple choice, matching, true-false, and the essay. Each of these methods are discussed briefly by presenting some sample questions and listing strong points and weak points of each.

Completion Items.

These items require that the student supply a word or phrase in a blank to complete a sentence. Obviously, only key words or phrases should be asked for since trivial information serves little instructional purpose.

Directions: Complete each sentence by writing in the correct answer in the blank to the extreme left.

Samples:

_____ 1. The __(1)__ event is conducted in a square area approximately 40 X 40 on the floor.

_____ 2. The two American gymnastics events which are not contested as

_____ 3. part of the all-around competition are __(2)__ and __(3)__

_____ 4. __(4)__ refers to assisting or helping someone during the performance of a stunt.

_____ 5. Strength is a term used to denote __(5)__ being exerted against a resistance.

Strong Points:
1. It reduces the problem of guessing.
2. Completion items can be used in a variety of ways to obtain the desired answers.
3. It requires intensive study on the part of the student in that he must recall and reproduce material rather than merely recognize it.
4. Completion items are relatively easy to prepare.

Weak Points:
1. Subjective judgment on the part of the teacher as to what specific items are most important may be a weakness.
2. It is easy to get different answers, each of which could be appropriate due to the wording of the statement.
3. There is a tendency to test on isolated facts in order to confine the answers to one word.

Multiple Choice Items.

Questions of this type consist of an incomplete statement which is followed by several answers, one of which is the correct one. In some cases the student may be directed to pick the only incorrect answer from among several correct responses, or to pick the one best answer from among all correct responses.

Directions: Place the letter of the correct response for each statement on the line at the left.

Samples:

——————————— 1. Tonus is decreased by:
                          a. Worry   d. Colds
                          b. Exercise   e. Inactivity
                          c. Lack of sleep

——————————— 2. The normal college student needs:
                          a. Light exercise   d. Mainly team sports
                          b. Vigorous exercise   e. Infrequent exercise
                          c. No exercise

——————————— 3. One of the best measurements of physical fitness is through:
                          a. Mental tests   d. Tests of agility
                          b. Blood tests   e. Tests of balance
                          c. Muscular strength tests

——————————— 4. The inability of a muscle to contract as a result of continual contraction indicates:
                          a. Nervous block   d. Destruction of end plate
                          b. Poor nutrition   e. Fatigue
                          c. Malfunction of nerve impulse

——————————— 5. A person develops neuromuscular skill through:
                          a. Occasional sports activity   d. Repeated practice of skills
                          b. Studying films of movement e. A corrective program of
                          c. Watching others perform   physical education

Strong Points:
1. Multiple choice items can be applied to most types of material and information.
2. Such items are easy to score.
3. Such items can be used at practically all educational levels.
4. Guessing is discouraged if the questions are well constructed.

Weak Points:
1. Good multiple choice items are relatively difficult to prepare.
2. Too much emphasis is frequently placed on isolated facts, and it is difficult to avoid ambiguity when the tester tries to confine the choices to short statements.

Matching Items.

A matching item usually consists of two columns of words or partial sentences, and the student is directed to correctly associate the responses of one column with those of the other. Letters by the responses in the right hand column are usually placed in blanks by the numbers along the left hand column.

Directions: Indicate in the space at the left by letter which muscle action is associated with each muscle.

Sample:

——————————— 1. Rectus abdominis   a. Flexion of neck

——————————— 2. Trapezius   b. Flexion of ankle

——————————— 3. Rhomboid   c. Trunk flexion

                                                   d. Upward rotation of scapula

_____ 4. Pectoralis major   e. Downward rotation of scapula

_____ 5. Biceps   f. Abduction of humerus

_____ 6. Triceps   g. Flexion of forearm

     h. Extension of the hip

_____ 7. Sternocleidomastoid   i. Extension of forearm

_____ 8. Biceps femoris   j. Abduction of femur

Strong Points:
1. The matching items are usually quick and relatively easy to prepare.
2. Such items usually cover a maximum amount of material in a minimal amount of space.
3. It is easy to score.

Weak Points:
1. It is time-consuming on the part of students if the lists are lengthy.
2. It is limited in that it measures only recognition.
3. The choices should out-number the questions, or else the students may be able to achieve the correct match through a process of elimination.

True-False Items.

Questions of this type consist of statements which confront the student with two possible answers (either negative or positive).

Directions: Place a T in the blank before all true statements and an F before all false statements.

Samples:

_____ 1. Walking in a handstand is considered as a weakness or fault in gymnastics competition.

_____ 2. In performing a headstand, most of the weight should rest on top of the head.

_____ 3. In performing a backward roll the hands should be placed on the mats so that the little fingers are next to the ears.

_____ 4. Static balance is directly proportional to the area of the base on which the body is supported.

_____ 5. A body will turn faster when the length of the radius of rotation about the center of gravity is increased.

Strong Points:
1. It is possible to cover a wide range of topics in a short period of time.
2. It provides coverage of material which does not lend itself to coverage by other test items.
3. It is objective and easy to score.

Weak Points:
1. It encourages guessing.
2. There is a tendency to test on isolated facts and to insert *trick* words which tend to trap students who actually knew the material.

3. The better students tend to read things into such statements and consequently may do worse than weaker students on true-false sections.
4. Students can develop a certain *knack* in taking true-false tests by identifying certain *keys* that are typical of this form of questions. For example, short sentences are more apt to be false and long sentences true, and questions containing words such as *never* and *always* are almost always false.

Essay Questions.

Essay Questions consist of statements which direct the student to discuss with some detail and organization the pertinent information related to a particular topic. They are often referred to as short question-long answer items. Such questions usually direct the student to summarize, contrast, compare, describe, or explain some subject.

Samples:
1. Summarize the contributions of early German gymnastic instructors to the development of the sport of gymnastics.
2. Compare the Swedish system of gymnastics with the German system.
3. Name four organizations which have contributed to the development of gymnastics in the U.S.A. and discuss the importance of each organization's contributions.
4. Identify the present Olympic gymnastic events and briefly summarize their description, characteristics, and values.
5. List and explain four scientific principles of balance.

Strong Points:
1. Essay questions are quickly constructed.
2. Essay tests require the learning of larger units of subject matter rather than isolated facts.
3. Essay items are effective in testing such skills as synthesizing pertinent information, organizing, and relating the facts and material that have been learned.
4. Guessing is held to a minimum in essay items.
5. Essay items allow for greater freedom of response and permit variety in expression.

Weak Points:
1. Essay tests have low objectivity and reliability.
2. Essay tests require considerable time to grade.
3. Bluffing and rambling are inherent dangers in essay tests. Also, students who write slowly or have difficulty organizing their answers are severely penalized.

Physical Education Knowledge Tests

The following list of knowledge tests represents the majority of studies conducted for the purpose of constructing test items for use in physical education activity classes. Although a number of tests are now out of date, they may still be valuable in giving teachers ideas about new test items as well as serving as examples of procedures utilized in constructing the tests. The knowledge tests are presented in alphabetical order according to activities.

Archery.

Ley, Katherine L., "Constructing Objective Test Items to Measure High School Levels of Achievement in Selected Physical Education Activities," (Microcarded Doctoral Dissertation, University of Iowa, 1960).

Snell, Catherine, "Physical Education Knowledge Tests," *Research Quarterly,* 6:83-86, October, 1935.

Badminton.

Fox, Katherine, "Beginning Badminton Written Examinations," *Research Quarterly,* 24:135-146, May, 1953.

French, Esther, "The Construction of Knowledge Tests in Selected Professional Courses in Physical Education,"*Research Quarterly,* 14:406-424, 1943.

Goll, Lillian M., "Construction of Badminton and Swimming Knowledge Tests for High School Girls," (Microcarded Master's Thesis, Illinois State Normal University, 1956, pp. 65-75).

Hennis, Gail M., "Construction of Knowledge Tests in Selected Physical Education Activities for College Women," *Research Quarterly,* 27:301-309, October, 1956. (Also, see Physical Education Microcards.)

Ley, Katherine L., "Constructing Objective Test Items to Measure High School Levels of Achievement in Selected Physical Education Activities," (Microcarded Doctoral Dissertation, University of Iowa, 1960).

Phillips, Marjorie, "Standardization of a Badminton Knowledge Test for College Women," *Research Quarterly,* 17:48-63, March, 1946.

Scott, Gladys M., "Achievement Examination in Badminton," *Research Quarterly,* 12:242-253, May, 1941.

Baseball.

Goldberg, Isidor H., "The Development of Achievement Standards in Knowledge of Physical Education Activities," (Microcarded Doctoral Dissertation, New York University, 1953).

Hemphill, Fay, "Information Tests in Health and Physical Education for High School Boys," *Research Quarterly,* 3:82, December, 1932.

Rodgers, E. G., and Marjorie L. Heath, "An Experiment in the Use of Knowledge and Skill Tests in Playground Baseball," *Research Quarterly,* 2:128-130, December, 1931.

Snell, Catherine, "Physical Education Knowledge Tests," *Research Quarterly,* 7:87-91, May, 1936.

Basketball.

Bliss, J. G., *Basketball,* Philadelphia: Lea & Febiger, 1929.

Fisher, Rosemary B., "Tests in Selected Physical Education Service Courses in a College," (Microcarded Doctoral Dissertation, State University of Iowa, 1950, pp. 158-181).

French, Esther, "The Construction of Knowledge Tests in Selected Professional Courses in Physical Education," *Research Quarterly,* 14:406-424, 1943.

Goldberg, Isidor H., "The Development of Achievement Standards in Knowledge of Physical Education Activities," (Microcarded Doctoral Dissertation, New York University, 1953).

Hemphill, Fay, "Information Tests in Health and Physical Education for High School Boys," *Research Quarterly,* 3:82, December, 1932.

Hennis, Gail M., "Construction of Knowledge Tests in Selected Physical Education Activities for College Women," *Research Quarterly,* 27:301-309, October, 1956. (Also, see Physical Education Microcards.)

Ley, Katherine L., "Constructing Objective Test Items to Measure High School Levels of Achievement in Selected Physical Education Activities," (Microcarded Doctoral Dissertation, University of Iowa, 1960).

Schwartz, Helen, "Knowledge and Achievement Tests in Girls' Basketball on the Senior High School Level," *Research Quarterly,* 8:153-156, March, 1937.

Snell, Catherine, "Physical Education Knowledge Tests," *Research Quarterly,* 7:79-82, March, 1936.

Body Mechanics.

French, Esther, "The Construction of Knowledge Tests in Selected Professional Courses in Physical Education," *Research Quarterly,* 14:406-424, 1943.

Bowling.

Hennis, Gail M., "Construction of Knowledge Tests in Selected Physical Education Activities for College Women," *Research Quarterly,* 27:301-309, October, 1956.

Ley, Katherine L., "Constructing Objective Test Items to Measure High School Levels of Achievement in Selected Physical Education Activities," (Microcarded Doctoral Dissertation, University of Iowa, 1960).

Canoeing.

French, Esther, "The Construction of Knowledge Tests in Selected Professional Courses in Physical Education," *Research Quarterly,* 14:406-424, 1943.

Dance and Rhythm.

French, Esther, "The Construction of Knowledge Tests in Selected Professional Courses in Physical Education," *Research Quarterly,* 14:406-424, 1943.

Murry, Josephine K., "An Appreciation Test in Dance," (Unpublished Master's Thesis, University of California, 1943).

Football.

Goldberg, Isidor H., "The Development of Achievement Standards in Knowledge of Physical Education Activities," (Microcarded Doctoral Dissertation, New York University, 1953).

Hemphill, Fay, "Information Tests in Health and Physical Education for High School Boys," *Research Quarterly,* 3:82, December, 1932.

Fundamentals.

Snell, Catherine, "Physical Education Knowledge Tests," *Research Quarterly,* 6:79-83, October, 1935.

Golf.

French, Esther, "The Construction of Knowledge Tests in Selected Professional Courses in Physical Education," *Research Quarterly,* 14:406-424, 1943.

Ley, Katherine L., "Constructing Objective Test Items to Measure High School Levels of Achievement in Selected Physical Education Activities," (Microcarded Doctoral Dissertation, University of Iowa, 1960).

Snell, Catherine, "Physical Education Knowledge Tests," *Research Quarterly,* 7:79-80, May, 1936.

Waglow, I. F., and C. H. Rehling, "A Golf Knowledge Test," *Research Quarterly,* 24:463-470, December, 1953.

Gymnastics.

Fisher, Rosemary B., "Tests in Selected Physical Education Service Courses in a College," (Microcarded Doctoral Dissertation, State University of Iowa, 1950, pp. 145-156).

French, Esther, "The Construction of Knowledge Tests in Selected Professional Courses in Physical Education," *Research Quarterly*, 14:406-424, 1943.

Gershon, Ernest, "Apparatus Gymnastics Knowledge Test for College Men in Professional Physical Education," *Research Quarterly*, 28:332, December, 1957.

Nipper, John, "A Knowledge Test of Tumbling and Gymnastics," (Unpublished Study, Northeast Louisiana State College, 1966).

Handball.

Phillips, Bernath E., *Fundamental Handball*, New York: A. S. Barnes and Company, 1937.

Hockey.

Dietz, Dorthea, and Beryl Trech, "Hockey Knowledge Test for Girls," *JOHPER*, 11:366, 1940.

French, Esther, "The Construction of Knowledge Tests in Selected Professional Courses in Physical Education," *Research Quarterly*, 14:406-424, 1943.

Grisier, Gertrude J., "The Construction of an Objective Test of Knowledge and Interpretation of the Rules of Field Hockey for Women," *Research Quarterly Supplement*, 5:79-81, March, 1943.

Hennis, Gail M., "Construction of Knowledge Tests in Selected Physical Education Activities for College Women," *Research Quarterly*, 27:301-309, October, 1956. (Also, see Physical Education Microcards.)

Kelly, Ellen D., and Jane E. Brown, "The Construction of a Field Hockey Test for Women Physical Education Majors," *Research Quarterly*, 23:322-329, October, 1952.

Snell, Catherine, "Physical Education Knowledge Tests," *Research Quarterly*, 6:86-89, October, 1935.

Horseback Riding.

Snell, Catherine, "Physical Education Knowledge Tests," *Research Quarterly*, 7:80-84, May, 1936.

Physical Fitness.

Stradtman, Alan D., and T. K. Cureton, "A Physical Fitness Knowledge Test for Secondary School Boys and Girls," *Research Quarterly*, 21:53-57, March, 1950.

Recreational Sports.

Fisher, Rosemary B., "Tests in Selected Physical Education Service Courses in a College," (Microcarded Doctoral Dissertation, State University of Iowa, 1950, pp. 285-319).

French, Esther, "The Construction of Knowledge Tests in Selected Professional Courses in Physical Education," *Research Quarterly*, 14:406-424, 1943.

Soccer.

Fisher, Rosemary B., "Tests in Selected Physical Education Service Courses in a College," (Microcarded Doctoral Dissertation, State University of Iowa, 1950, pp. 123-143).

French, Esther, "The Construction of Knowledge Tests in Selected Professional Courses in Physical Education," *Research Quarterly,* 14:406-424, 1943.

Heath, Marjorie L., and E. G. Rodgers, "A Study in the Use of Knowledge and Skill Tests in Soccer," *Research Quarterly,* 3:33-53, October, 1932.

Knighton, Marion, "Soccer Questions," *Journal of Health and Physical Education,* Vol. 1, October, 1930.

Ley, Katherine L., "Constructing Objective Test Items to Measure High School Levels of Achievement in Selected Physical Education Activities," (Microcarded Doctoral Dissertation, University of Iowa, 1960).

Snell, Catherine, "Physical Education Knowledge Tests," *Research Quarterly,* 7:76-79, March, 1936.

Softball.

Fisher, Rosemary B., "Tests in Selected Physical Education Service Courses in a College," (Microcarded Doctoral Dissertation, State University of Iowa, 1950, pp. 254-270).

French, Esther, "The Construction of Knowledge Tests in Selected Professional Courses in Physical Education," *Research Quarterly,* 14:406-424, 1943.

Hennis, Gail M., "Construction of Knowledge Tests in Selected Physical Education Activities for College Women," *Research Quarterly,* 27:301-309, October, 1956. (Also, see Physical Education Microcards.)

Ley, Katherine L., "Constructing Objective Test Items to Measure High School Levels of Achievement in Selected Physical Education Activities," (Microcarded Doctoral Dissertation, University of Iowa, 1960).

Waglow, I. F., and Foy Stephens, "A Softball Knowledge Test," *Research Quarterly,* 26:234-237, May, 1955.

Sportsmanship.

Haskins, Mary J., "Problem-Solving Test of Sportsmanship," *Research Quarterly,* 31:601-605, December, 1960.

Swimming.

Fisher, Rosemary B., "Tests in Selected Physical Education Service Courses in a College," (Microcarded Doctoral Dissertation, State University of Iowa, 1950, pp. 182-253).

French, Esther, "The Construction of Knowledge Tests in Selected Professional Courses in Physical Education," *Research Quarterly,* 14:406-424, 1943.

Goll, Lillian M., "Construction of Badminton and Swimming Knowledge Tests for High School Girls," (Microcarded Master's Thesis, Illinois State Normal University, 1956).

Scott, M. Gladys, "Achievement Examinations for Elementary and Intermediate Swimming Classes," *Research Quarterly,* 11:104-111, May, 1940.

Team-Game Activities.

Rodgers, Elizabeth G., "The Standardization and Use of Objective Type Information Tests in Team Game Activities," *Research Quarterly,* 10:103, March, 1939.

Tennis.

Broer, Marion R., and Donna M. Miller, "Achievement Tests for Beginning and Intermediate Tennis," *Research Quarterly,* 21:303-313, October, 1950.

Fisher, Rosemary B., "Tests in Selected Physical Education Service Courses in a College," (Microcarded Doctoral Dissertation, State University of Iowa, 1950, pp. 271-284).

French, Esther, "The Construction of Knowledge Tests in Selected Professional Courses in Physical Education," *Research Quarterly*, 14:406-424, 1943.

Hennis, Gail M., "Construction of Knowledge Tests in Selected Physical Education Activities for College Women," *Research Quarterly*, 27:301-309, October, 1956. (Also, see Physical Education Microcards.)

Hewitt, Jack E., "Comprehensive Tennis Knowledge Test," *Research Quarterly*, 8:74-84, October, 1937.

_____ , "Hewitt's Comprehensive Tennis Knowledge Test," *Research Quarterly*, 35:149-154, May, 1964.

Miller, Wilma K., "Achievement Levels in Tennis Knowledge and Skill for Women Physical Education Major Students," *Research Quarterly*, 24:81-89, March, 1953.

Scott, M. Gladys, "Achievement Examination for Elementary and Intermediate Tennis Classes," *Research Quarterly*, 12:43-49, March, 1941.

Snell, Catherine, "Physical Education Knowledge Tests," *Research Quarterly*, 7:84-87, May, 1936.

Track and Field.

French, Esther, "The Construction of Knowledge Tests in Selected Professional Courses in Physical Education," *Research Quarterly*, 14:406-424, 1943.

Volleyball.

Fisher, Rosemary B., "Tests in Selected Physical Education Service Courses in a College," (Microcarded Doctoral Dissertation, State University of Iowa, 1950, pp. 82-122).

French, Esther, "The Construction of Knowledge Tests in Selected Professional Courses in Physical Education," *Research Quarterly*, 14:406-424, 1943.

Hennis, Gail M., "Construction of Knowledge Tests in Selected Physical Education Activities for College Women," *Research Quarterly*, 27:301-309, December, 1957.

Langston, Dewey F., "Standardization of a Volleyball Knowledge Test for College Men Physical Education Majors," *Research Quarterly*, 26:60-66, March, 1955.

Ley, Katherine L., "Constructing Objective Test Items to Measure High School Levels of Achievement in Selected Physical Education Activities," (Microcarded Doctoral Dissertation, University of Iowa, 1960).

Snell, Catherine, "Physical Education Knowledge Tests," *Research Quarterly*, 7:73-76, March, 1936.

Problems and Limitations of Knowledge Measurement

1. Most standardized knowledge tests in physical education are not available on a commercial basis and consequently must be located from various sources and be prepared for distribution. There appears to be a definite need for the encouragement of commercial interest in physical education knowledge tests.

2. Standardized tests do not always fit the local situation. They may cover materials which are not covered in some schools due to limited time, equipment, facilities or emphasis.

3. Knowledge tests require careful security measures to insure that all students are exposed to the test at the same time. Students sometimes use ingenious methods to gain an unfair advantage in order to insure success on knowledge tests. There is also the problem of students passing on information about the test from one class to another.

4. Norms for standardized knowledge tests are of doubtful value since they are dependent upon such specific factors as age group, unit of instruction, length of unit, and content presented. Since these factors can vary so greatly, such norms are seldom applicable to many groups.

5. The standardized test frequently encourages the teacher to emphasize certain information while leaving out other information which is important, but not covered in the standardized test. This practice is often referred to as *teaching for testing* with the obvious purpose of helping the students, and thus the teacher, look good on norm comparisons.

6. The construction of good tests is a much more difficult task than it might appear. The tests must be valid; and the teacher must continually ask himself whether the questions are fair and pertinent to the material covered in class.

7. The writing of good test questions requires skill in expression which, unfortunately, many physical educators lack.

8. The physical educator must guard against the temptation to make the questions too comprehensive and difficult in an unconscious attempt to prove that physical education is not a *snap* course.

Findings and Conclusions From Knowledge Measurement and Research

Numerous tests of knowledge in physical education activities have been available for years; however, test constructors have been quick to point out that such tests should only be used in situations where the distribution of factual information is in relatively close agreement with the specifications of the published test.[21,26] Many knowledge tests are presented in their entirety in professional publications and can serve as guides for constructing teacher-made tests.[13,14,15,17,22]

A number of test constructors have established norms which may be used for comparative purposes when the test is used in its entirety.[16,20,21,23,25,28,40] However, as previously pointed out, there are so many specific factors involved that norms are seldom applicable.

Concerning a possible relationship existing between knowledge about an activity and skill in the activity, Scott[36] noted that a direct relationship did not exist in tennis measurement. However, Hewitt[23] found a high relationship between knowledge in tennis and playing experience in tennis. The author has often noted that students who are highly skilled in an activity frequently take for granted their knowledge of the activity and do not do as well on the activity knowledge test as students who are less skilled in the activity.

In 1960 Ley[26] studied objective knowledge test items in selected physical education activities, and some of her comments might prove valuable to future test constructors. They are listed as follows:

1. Test constructors since 1940 have not used any particular method of determining the relevance level of individual items.

2. The knowledge tests studies contained too many factual items while neglecting items in the generalization, understanding, application, and interpretation categories.

3. Examinations by committee groups were not found to be superior to those by an individual in regard to topical content, relevance level, and the worth of the individual items.

4. Rules of play have dominated physical education knowledge tests, and it is doubtful that such a practice can be justified in many situations.

5. If accurate, pictures and diagrams are of value in developing test items.

6. Highly relevant items can be written for all topical areas found in physical education activity knowledge tests.

Ley[26] found physical education major students significantly higher than non-major students in only one out of six physical activity knowledge tests. If this finding is characteristic of the knowledge of physical education majors across the nation, then greater emphasis should be placed on a more thorough understanding of *what is what* in physical activities for majors.

Several investigators have researched the effect of knowledge on learning to perform skills in various activities or tasks. Operating on the hypothesis that exposing students to an understanding and application of mechanical principles will bring about greater improvement than instruction without reference to these principles, Mohr,[29] Broer,[7] Ruger,[35] and Colville[11] found such knowledge to be beneficial.

Numerous investigators have used such knowledge measures as grade point average, standard achievement test scores, and intelligence scores to determine the relationship between mental ability and physical ability. Most studies of such relationships have varied with some reports indicating little or no relationship,[3,6,8,24,38] while others indicated a low but positive relationship.[24,12,27,41] However, Clarke[9] has pointed out that most of the investigations which showed little or no relationship did not allow variances in the intelligence of the subjects. Along this line the authors would like to stress the fact that one needs extremes in the variables concerned in order to obtain a high coefficient of correlation. If the sample is too homogeneous in the variables, such as is the case concerning most traits possessed by students in a typical class, it is simply mathematically unrealistic to expect high correlations even though a significant relationship could exist.

Through the years various physical educators and researchers have held the belief that physical fitness improves the effectiveness of the individual's mental capabilities. Research which supports this contention is presented as follows:

1. Studying two groups of college men with nearly equal intelligence quotient averages, Rogers[34] found the scholarship in the physically stronger group to be considerably higher than that of the low strength group.

2. Terman[39] noted that symptoms of general weakness were reported 30% less frequently for gifted students than for non-gifted students.

3. Brace[5] has reported studies from England which revealed that only 2.35% of students who were above average in scholarship were below average in body build as compared to 39.7% of students with poor scholarship who were below average in body build.

4. A report from Massachusetts[33] revealed that the average physical fitness index for 126 high school honor students attending Brookline public schools was 117, which is two points above the national third quartile score.

5. Studying one high group and one low group of children in motor proficiency, Rarick[32] found that the high motor group demonstrated better scholastic adjustment than the low group in reading, writing, and comprehension.

6. Two studies noted that male freshmen at large universities with low physical indexes were also low in scholastic accomplishment, as compared to other students, in spite of the fact that these same low fitness students were above average in scholastic aptitude.[10,30]

7. Shaffer[37] found that as intelligence increased, failures on the Kraus-Weber Test decreased.

8. Popp[31] compared boys of low physical fitness with boys of high physical fitness and noted that eight out of twenty in the low fitness group failed to graduate from high school, whereas only two out of twenty in the high fitness group failed to graduate.

9. Clarke[9] found that subjects high in physical measures had a consistent and significant tendency to have higher means on knowledge measures than subjects low in physical measures. The groups were previously equated by intelligence scores.

10. Two studies indicated that physical fitness is an important factor in the improvement of mental tasks.[18,19]

BIBLIOGRAPHY

1. Barrow, Harold M., and Rosemary McGee, *A Practical Approach to Measurement in Physical Education,* Philadelphia: Lea & Febiger, 1964, p. 358.

2. Berk, Robert, "Comparison of Performance of Subnormal, Normal, and Gifted Children on the Oseretsky Tests of Motor Ability," (Unpublished Doctoral Dissertation, Boston University, 1957).

3. Bond, M. H., "Rhythmic Perception and Gross Motor Performance," *Research Quarterly,* 30:259-265, October, 1959.

4. Brace, D. K., "Motor Learning of Feeble-Minded Girls," *Research Quarterly,* 19:269-275, December, 1948.

5. _____, "Some Objective Evidence of the Value of Physical Education," *Journal of Health and Physical Education,* 4:36, April, 1933.

6. _____, "Studies in the Rate of Learning Gross Bodily Skills," *Research Quarterly,* 12:181-185, May, 1941.

7. Broer, Marion, "Effectiveness of a General Basic Skills Curriculum for Junior High School Girls," *Research Quarterly,* 29:379-388, December, 1958.

8. Burley, L., and R. L. Anderson, "Relation of Jump and Reach Measures of Power to Intelligence Scores and Athletic Performance," *Research Quarterly,* 30:259-265, March, 1959.

9. Clarke, H. Harrison, and Boyd O. Jarman, "Scholastic Achievement of Boys 9, 12, and 15 Years of Age as Related to Various Strength and Growth Measures," *Research Quarterly,* 32:155, May, 1961.

10. Coefield, John R., and Robert H. Collum, "A Case Study Report of Seventy-eight University Freshmen Men with Low Physical Fitness Indices," (Microcarded Master's Thesis, University of Oregon, 1955).

11. Colville, Frances, "The Learning of Motor Skills as Influenced by a Knowledge of General Principles of Mechanics," (Unpublished Doctoral Dissertation, University of Southern California, 1956).

12. Distefano, M. K., and others, "Motor Proficiency in Mental Defectives," *Percep. Mot. Skills,* 8:231-234, 1958.

13. Fisher, Rosemary B., "Tests in Selected Physical Education Service Courses in a College," (Microcarded Dissertation, State University of Iowa, 1950, p. 72).

14. Fox, Katherine, "Beginning Badminton Written Examination," *Research Quarterly,* 24:135, May, 1953.

15. French, Esther, "The Construction of Knowledge Tests in Selected Professional Courses in Physical Education," *Research Quarterly,* 14:406-424, December, 1943.

16. Gershon, Ernest, "Apparatus Gymnastics Knowledge Test for College Men in Professional Physical Education," *Research Quarterly,* 28:332, December, 1957.

17. Goll, Lillian M., "Construction of Badminton and Swimming Knowledge Tests for High School Girls," (Microcarded Master's Thesis, Illinois State Normal University, 1956, p. 54).

18. Gutin, Bernard, "Effect of Increase in Physical Fitness on Mental Ability Following Physical and Mental Stress," *Research Quarterly,* 37:211, May, 1966.

19. Hart, Marcia E., and Clayton T. Shay, "Relationship Between Physical Fitness and Academic Success," *Research Quarterly,* 35:445, October, 1964.

20. Hemphill, Fay, "Information Tests in Health and Physical Education for High School Boys," *Research Quarterly,* 3:82, December, 1932.

21. Hennis, Gail M., "Construction of Knowledge Tests in Selected Physical Education Activities for College Women," *Research Quarterly,* 27:301-309, October, 1956.

22. Hewitt, Jack E., "Comprehensive Tennis Knowledge Test," *Research Quarterly,* 8:74-84, October, 1937.

23. _____ , "Hewitt's Comprehensive Tennis Knowledge Test," *Research Quarterly,* 35:147-155, May, 1964.

24. Johnson, G. B., "Study of the Relationship that Exists Between Physical Skill as Measured, and the General Intelligence of College Students," *Research Quarterly,* 13:57-59, March, 1942.

25. Langston, Dewey F., "Standardization of a Volleyball Knowledge Test for College Men Physical Education Majors," *Research Quarterly,* 26:60-66, March, 1955.

26. Ley, Katherine L., "Constructing Objective Test Items to Measure High School Levels of Achievement in Selected Physical Education Activities," (Microcarded Dissertation, University of Iowa, 1960, p. 25).

27. McMillan, Betty Jo, "A Study to Determine the Relationship of Physical Fitness as Measured by the New York State Physical Fitness Test to the Academic Index of High School Girls," (Unpublished Master's Thesis, Springfield College, 1961).

28. Miller, Wilma K., "Achievement Levels in Tennis Knowledge and Skill for Women Physical Education Major Students," *Research Quarterly,* 24:18-89, March, 1953.

29. Mohr, Dorothy R., and Mildred E. Barrett, "Effect of Knowledge of Mechanical Principles in Learning to Perform Intermediate Swimming Skills," *Research Quarterly,* 33:574, December, 1962.

30. Page, C. Getty, "Case Studies of College Men with Low Physical Fitness Indices," (Unpublished Master's Thesis, Syracuse University, 1940).

31. Popp, James, "Case Studies of Sophomore High School Boys with High and Low Physical Fitness Indices," (Microcarded Master's Thesis, University of Oregon, 1959).

32. Rarick, Lawrence G., and Robert McKee, "A Study of Twenty Third Grade Children Exhibiting Extreme Levels of Achievement on Tests of Motor Efficiency," *Research Quarterly,* 20:142, May, 1949.

33. "Report of the School Committee and Superintendent of Brookline, Massachusetts," December 31, 1941.

34. Rogers, Frederick R., "The Scholarship of Athletes," (Unpublished Master's Thesis, Stanford University, 1922).

35. Ruger, Henry A., "The Psychology of Efficiency," *Archives of Psychology,* 2:85, 1910.

36. Scott, M. Gladys, "Achievement Examinations for Elementary and Intermediate Tennis Classes," *Research Quarterly,* 12:40-49, March, 1941.

37. Shaffer, G., "Interrelationship of Intelligence Quotient to Failure of Kraus-Weber Test," *Research Quarterly,* 30:75-86, March, 1959.

38. Start, K. R., "Relationship Between Intelligence and the Effect of Mental Practice on the Performance of a Motor Skill," *Research Quarterly,* 31:644-649, 1960.

39. Terman, Lewis M., ed., "Genetic Studies of Genius I. Mental and Physical Traits of a Thousand Gifted Children," Stanford, California: Stanford University Press, 1925.

40. Waglow, I. F., and Foy Stephens, "A Softball Knowledge Test," *Research Quarterly,* 26:234-237, May, 1955.

41. Weber, John R., "Relationship of Physical Fitness to Success in College and to Personality," *Research Quarterly,* 24:471, December, 1954.

Chapter XXII

GRADING IN PHYSICAL EDUCATION
Part I – Philosophical Concepts of
Grading in Physical Education

Educators are in close agreement concerning the importance of basing measurement and evaluation upon the objectives which guide the educative process. However, they differ considerably concerning what objectives should be measured and how they should be measured.

Considering Educational Objectives.

The objectives which are most commonly listed as worthy of pursuit in physical education are (1) Neuromuscular Skill; (2) Physical Fitness; (3) Social Development; and (4) Acquisition of Knowledge. While some educators in the field would measure each objective as nearly equal as possible in determining grades, others would support the use of only two or three which they considered to be unique to the field of physical education. For example, Duncan[6] supports sports and dance skills and physical development as the unique objectives in our field. From this viewpoint social and mental fitness objectives are still important; however, the physical educator's primary emphasis is not directed toward them. Unfortunately, other less informed physical educators tend to completely ignore measurement and evaluation from the standpoint of our more widely recognized objectives, but concern themselves with awarding grades based upon such administrative details as the number of absences, the number of times the student failed to dress out, whether the student took showers after activity or not, the number of times tardy, improper uniforming, etc. Rather than grade on the number of absences, it might be a wiser administrative procedure to require students to repeat any course which has been missed a certain number of times. Otherwise students who are penalized for missing a few classes as such may be penalized twice in that they may make a poor showing on test days due to previous absences. On the other hand, students who miss a few classes, not enough to have to repeat, but who still do well on test days should not be penalized at all. This is the usual situation in other subject areas. As educators we should be primarily concerned with measuring educational objectives, not administrative objectives.

Improvement Vs. Status.

Some physical educators become quite concerned as to whether we should grade on improvement or on class status. While some teachers feel that improvement (the progress made between the initial test and final test) is of utmost importance in determining grades, other educators support grades based on class status because of their traditional acceptance among teachers of other subject areas. A third view seems to possess a middle of the road approach to the issue. Supporters for this view indicate that to arrive at a grade completely on improvement, testing must be conducted prior to the instructional unit; obviously, in certain activities students will not know enough to take an initial test safely and with any degree of validity. In such courses as swimming and gymnastics beginning students should not be expected to execute basic skills safely enough to be tested without some detailed instruction and practice. Thus, the skill grade would primarily evolve from class status at the end of the course. On the other hand this same view holds that it might be quite safe to give an initial test in other activities, in which case, both improvement and class status might be considered in the skill grade. However, it should be pointed out that where improvement alone is the basis for skill grading, many students will hold back on the initial test in order to show great improvement on the final test. Even if all the students do their best on both tests, the weaker student has a definite advantage when improvement alone is considered, since it is easier for him to improve when he is at the bottom end of the scale than when he starts out already near the top. Moreover, some educators feel that since life is made up of one competitive situation after another that there is little need in measuring improvement (especially since there are inherent problems involved) when all that is really necessary is to determine the status of the student within his group. For educators with this view grading is quite simple. Those students with the highest class status would get the A's and those who were next would get B's and so on down to the F group. This concept has been strictly adhered to in many academic subject areas. It should also be noted that some physical educators support the use of two grades; one based on improvement and the other on grade status. However, this practice has not been widely followed since most schools require only one grade for each course.

Future Growth Vs. Present Status.

Another point of philosophical contemplation is whether to consider a student's future growth and development or to consider only his present status for grading purposes. It has been said that whatever exists in any amount can be measured, but by the same reasoning it must be recognized that what does not yet exist cannot be measured. However, education is fundamentally interested in the student's future growth and development, although it does not yet exist.[3] Thus, this type of measurement evolves into evaluation which is not only different, but more difficult than that measurement which is concerned with the student *here and now* as the finished product.[4] While some educators would tend to follow the *here and now* method in a strict sense, others would place primary emphasis on the student as they see him *here and now,* but make adjustments where there is no denying that future growth and development is inevitable. Such adjustments are merely qualitative judgments.

Ability to Repeat Vs. Ability to Work With or Change.

Still another point of interest is whether we should evaluate the student's ability to repeat that which has been presented, or should we be concerned with what he can do with what he has learned. One of the most widely held views is that learning is the successful acquisition of material or skill which has been set out to be learned. This is sometimes called the *input* method, where the teacher is the transmitter of the information or skill and the student's mind is a sort of storage reservoir until such time as he is called upon to reproduce it on a test.[3] However, there are others who support the *output* method and who strive to present students with important concepts or general ideas and then grade on how well the student can work with what he has learned insofar as showing initiative, new ideas, improved concepts, patterns, skills, or movement is concerned.

Quantitative Movement.

At this point it seems essential to call attention to the fact that quantitative measurement flourishes where factors of the educative process can be isolated, as in the case of learning specific motor skills or special bodies of information. The isolation of variables is the very basis of scientific control; whereas the more numerous and interdependent these variables become, the less the possibility for establishing validity.[5] Many measurement people recognize this limitation and consequently try to measure only that which can be measured quantitatively.[1] Moreover, teachers tend to teach only those facts and skills which can be isolated for scientific measurement and grading. When this situation exists, it is unfortunate, for there are many other things which need to be covered. However, it cannot be denied that there is a tremendous social significance attached to the movement to measure educational results scientifically. Our social structure has demanded that educators learn to handle large numbers of students with all due regard to their individualities. Therefore, statistics have become a *must* in learning about large numbers of people through careful sampling. The results of such information are necessary in directing and guiding the action of future plans.

Conservative Vs. Liberal.

To briefly summarize, the more conservative view in measurement and evaluation has been to grade on class status concerning essential subject matter. Other qualities such as citizenship, values, attitude, and appreciation are considered important, but since these qualities are difficult to measure scientifically for the *here and now* or otherwise, they are not to be included as a part of the grade. On the other hand, the more liberal view supports grading on improvement and status concerning essential subject matter, plus including the additional qualities of citizenship, attitude, and appreciation. This view would include an estimate of future growth and development and not depend entirely on that which can be measured easily by scientific means. For those who support this view, learning is not just storing information and skills, but improving and re-creating that which has been learned into new forms and patterns; and if this form of learning has to be evaluated subjectively, then they feel they are qualified to make such judgments.

BIBLIOGRAPHY

1. Bayles, Ernest E., "The Philosophical Approach to Educational Measurement," *Educational Administration and Supervision.* 26:455-461, September, 1940.

2. Bovard, John F., Frederick W. Cozens, and E. Patricia Hagman, *Tests and Measurements in Physical Education,* 3rd ed., Philadelphia: W. B. Saunders Co., 1950, pp. 3-4.

3. Brubacher, John S., *Modern Philosophies of Education,* 3rd ed., New York: McGraw-Hill Book Co., Inc., 1962, p. 253.

4. Dewey, John, "Progressive Education and the Science of Education," *Progressive Education,* 5:200, August, 1928.

5. _____, *The Sources of a Science of Education,* New York: Liveright Publishing Co., 1929, pp. 64-65.

6. Duncan, Ray O., "Fundamental Issues in Our Profession," *JOHPER,* May, 1964.

7. Kilpatrick, William H., *A Reconstructed Theory of the Educative Process,* New York: Teachers College, Columbia University, 1935, pp. 29-30.

8. Larson, Leonard A., and Rachael D. Yocom, *Measurement and Evaluation in Physical, Health, and Recreation Education,* St. Louis: C. V. Mosby Co., 1951.

Part II – Determining Grades in Physical Education

Determining grades in physical education classes is one of the most perplexing problems that physical educators face. Since grades should be the result of accurate evaluations of the student's achievement toward the major objectives, varied evidence must be collected and weighted to assure validity and fairness. The primary purpose of grading is to report to the student, the parents, and interested educational administrators an evaluation of the student's achievement. The logical steps which are necessary for effectively determining grades in physical education are discussed below.

Selecting and Loading Course Objectives.

In physical education classes the instructor must rely upon logic and philosophy to determine what objectives are most important in accordance with the nature of the activity and the needs of the student. The emphasis varies from one instructor to another and from course to course. Thus, one instructor may select and load the objectives in a particular course as follows: physical fitness, 50%; skill, 25%; and knowledge, 25%. In this case the area of social development was not considered in terms of making up part of the grade; but instead the teacher might elect to use the results of social measurement for guidance purposes. Another instructor might feel that skills should make up 40% of the grade; physical fitness, 25%; knowledge, 25%; and social development, 10%. As can be seen from these examples, the amount of weight an objective carries in evaluation depends upon the philosophy of the teacher as well as on the particular course that is being taught.

Selecting and Administering Tests for the Instructional Unit.

If an instructional unit covers a six weeks period, then an adequate but reasonable number of tests should be selected to assess student progress within this period. The selection of tests should be made on the basis of the weighted objectives for the course and the type of activity in which the students engaged during the instructional unit. The data in Table 22 - 1 represent scores of eight tests that were administered during a six weeks softball unit. Four tests are skill items (representing 50% of the unit grade), two tests are physical fitness items (representing 25% of the unit grade), one test is for knowledge (representing 12.5% of the unit grade), and one test is for social measurement (representing 12.5% of the unit grade). In the illustration each test item is considered to have equal weight; therefore, each item would be worth 12.5%. Consequently, once raw scores have been converted to T-scores, the teacher merely can average the T-scores and convert them into letter grades. Obviously, this would not always be the case. Some items may be weighted more heavily than others, so they would be multiplied by that weighting before averaging.

It is important to note that when only a single letter grade is used on a report card per course, it should not be influenced by administrative practices such as the number of absences, tardies, or failures to dress out. While the physical educator may be concerned with such details, he should not confuse the report by attempting to include them in only one grade. Therefore, the grade should indicate achievement toward unit and course objectives only, while other non-germane factors should be either reported separately or handled in some other way.

Converting Raw Scores to T-Scores.

Since raw scores from different tests are not directly comparable, it becomes necessary to use some type of score which will reduce such variables as time, distance, and rating scores to a common denominator. (See Chapter 3.) Thus, T-scores are frequently used so that all tests can be added or compared. The T-score has the advantage of always being positive and in whole numbers between 0-100.

While converting raw scores into T-scores may seem like excessive work, it soon becomes as familiar as other less acceptable scoring systems. A major advantage of the T-score method is that it shows the arithmetical distance of each score from the mean of the distribution, thus avoiding a distortion of differences. See Chapter 3 for greater detail concerning T-scores.

It should be noted that while other methods may be used for converting raw scores into standards and common denominators, it was not within the scope of this book to cover them.

Converting Average T-Scores into Letter Grades.

Once all the important evidence has been numerically collected, treated, and combined into average T-scores, it becomes necessary to convert such scores into letter grades of A, B, C, D, and F for the report. Converting final scores into letter grades may involve any one or more of several methods. The methods of curve grading, grading by absolute standards, and grading by observation of scores are discussed below with examples given for each using the average T-scores shown in Figure 22 - 1.

Grading on an Absolute Standard.

In this method, the teacher or the school sets up standards whereby each student's final score must fall into a scale such as: 95-100 = A; 85-94 = B; 76-84 = C; 66-75 = D; and below 65 = F. For this system to work satisfactorily, the measuring instruments must be right, or the teacher will end up adjusting the difficulty of tests so that the majority of students will not end up with extremely high or low grades. Table 22 - 2 shows the computations that are necessary to convert the average T-scores into percentages for the scale. Notice that the highest average T-score of 65 must be treated as the highest possible score in order to bring the other scores up high enough to fit into the scale.

Other obvious disadvantages to absolute grading are the following: (1) that frequently additional computations must be made after final average scores have been computed in order to satisfactorily fit such scores into the absolute scale pattern, and (2) that allowances are not made when differences as slight as one score inhibits the next higher grade from being assigned.

TABLE 22 - 1

Six Week Softball Unit

NAME	Accuracy Throw	T-Score	Fungo Hitting	T-Score	Speed Throw	T-Score	Fielding Ground Balls	T-Score	Softball Throw	T-Score	50-Yard Dash	T-Score	Knowledge Test	T-Score	Social Test	T-Score	Total T-Score	Average T-Score	Observation Method	Curve Method	Absolute Method
					6 Weeks Skill Test—50% (AAHPER Items)						Phy. Fit.—25% (AAHPER Items)		Know. 12½%		So.D. 12½%		Compu-tations		Grading Methods*		
1 A.L.	25	72	39	66	14.2	57	20	63	291	80	6.3	55	97	68	89	62	523	65	A	A	A
2 A.D.	16	54	34	60	17.6	45	18	57	176	46	6.8	49	80	53	96	68	432	54	B	B	C
3 A.J.	12	46	28	53	15.6	48	14	43	195	51	6.5	52	65	39	78	52	384	48	C-	C	D
4 B.B.	11	44	19	41	15.3	53	18	57	180	47	6.4	53	90	62	68	42	399	50	C	C	C
5 B.C.	17	56	28	53	13.9	58	17	53	190	50	6.6	51	66	40	87	60	421	53	B-	C	C
6 B.D.	14	50	21	44	18.3	43	20	63	249	64	6.9	48	72	45	77	51	408	51	C	C	C
7 C.C.	23	68	17	39	14.5	56	15	47	171	45	6.5	52	88	60	93	65	432	54	B	B	C
8 C.D.	15	52	37	63	15.6	52	18	57	185	49	6.7	50	64	38	65	40	401	50	C	C	C
9 C.E.	10	42	26	50	13.2	60	17	53	163	43	7.0	47	78	51	79	53	399	50	C	C	C
10 D.E.	13	48	15	36	14.8	45	16	50	235	63	6.0	58	96	67	72	46	413	52	C	C	C
11 D.I.	13	48	32	58	18.9	41	20	63	155	40	7.0	47	71	44	95	67	408	51	C	C	C
12 D.K.	21	64	11	31	14.8	55	12	37	190	50	6.7	50	77	50	74	48	385	48	C-	C	D
13 E.E.	14	50	26	50	14.9	54	16	50	150	39	5.6	62	87	59	71	45	409	51	C	C	C
14 E.L.	9	40	40	68	12.8	61	10	30	226	60	7.1	45	68	42	86	59	405	51	C	C	C
15 E.M.	12	46	29	54	19.9	38	20	63	195	51	6.5	52	76	49	56	32	385	48	C-	C	D
16 F.G.	8	38	14	35	16.2	50	17	53	141	36	7.7	39	95	66	76	50	367	46	D	D	D
17 F.H.	4	30	31	56	14.9	46	9	27	218	58	6.0	58	75	48	63	47	370	49	C	C	D
18 F.P.	19	60	25	49	16.7	48	19	60	198	52	6.4	53	85	57	83	56	435	54	B	B	C
19 G.G.	13	48	36	63	16.2	50	6	17	117	29	6.6	51	58	33	70	44	335	42	F	D	F
20 G.Z.	7	36	13	34	12.1	64	17	53	213	57	6.1	57	75	48	66	40	389	49	C	C	D
21 G.J.	12	46	30	55	21.2	33	17	53	185	49	10.6	7	84	56	73	47	346	43	F	D	D
22 H.I.	18	58	23	46	15.3	47	19	60	180	47	6.7	50	60	35	61	36	379	47	D	D	D
23 H.M.	6	34	35	61	26.1	17	9	27	207	55	6.2	56	73	46	85	58	354	46	D	D	D
24 H.O.	11	44	21	44	17.2	47	16	50	198	52	6.7	50	63	37	72	46	370	46	D	D	D
25 I.K.	17	56	29	54	10.0	71	19	60	203	54	6.3	55	75	48	58	34	442	54	B	B	C

*Note that the observation method rendered the nearest approximation to the normal curve with the 25 Av. T-Scores.

TABLE 22 - 2

Converting Average T-Scores into Percentages for the Absolute Scale

$\frac{65}{65}(100) = 100$ $\frac{54}{65}(100- = 83$ $\frac{51}{65}(100) = 80$ $\frac{42}{65}(100) = 65$

$\frac{54}{65}(100) = 83$ $\frac{50}{65}(100) = 77$ $\frac{51}{65}(100) = 80$ $\frac{49}{65}(100) = 75$

$\frac{48}{65}(100) = 74$ $\frac{50}{65}(100) = 77$ $\frac{48}{65}(100) = 74$ $\frac{43}{65}(100) = 66$

$\frac{50}{65}(100) = 77$ $\frac{52}{65}(100) = 80$ $\frac{46}{65}(100) = 71$ $\frac{47}{65}(100) = 73$

$\frac{53}{65}(100) = 82$ $\frac{51}{65}(100) = 78$ $\frac{40}{65}(100) = 75$ $\frac{46}{65}(100) = 71$

$\frac{51}{65}(100) = 78$

$\frac{48}{65}(100) = 74$

Absolute Scale	Frequency	Grade
95 — 100	1	A
85 — 94	0	B
76 — 84	13	C
66 — 75	10	D
0 — 65	1	E
N = 25		

$\frac{54}{65}(100) = 83$

$\frac{46}{65}(100) = 71$

$\frac{54}{65}(100) = 83$

*Note that with this particular set of scores, grading by absolute standards resulted in too many C's and D's and in no B's.

Curve Grading.

Curve grading is based upon the mean and standard deviation found for a group of scores. Although many teachers indicate that they grade on a curve, very few actually find the mean and standard deviation which are needed for true curve grading.

The steps necessary for curve grading are presented as follows:
1. Set up a frequency distribution and compute the mean and standard deviation for a set of scores. Table 22 - 3 shows this step using the average T-scores from a six weeks softball unit.
2. Divide the number of letter grades to be used into the sigma spread of 6 (since 3σ's above the mean and 3σ's below the mean contain practically all the scores). Example: Using the 5 letter grades of A, B, C, D, and F, we divide $6\sigma/5$ and get 1.2σ per letter grade.[2]

TABLE 22 - 3

Frequency Distribution, Mean, and Standard Deviation
for Final Scores of a Volleyball Unit*

Interval	Tallies	f	d	fd	fd²	Computations
64-65	1	1	8	8	64	$C = \dfrac{\Sigma fd}{N} = \dfrac{21}{25} = .84$
62-63	0	0	7	0	0	
60-61	0	0	6	0	0	$Ci = .84 \times 2 = 1.68$
58-59	0	0	5	0	0	$AM = 48.50$
56-57	0	0	4	0	0	$M = AM + Ci = 48.50 + 1.68$
54-55	| | | |	4	3	12	36	$M = \underline{50.18}$
52-53	| |	2	2	4	8	$\sigma = \sqrt{\dfrac{\Sigma fd^2}{N} - C^2}$
50-51	⊬⊬⊤ | |	7	1	7	7	$\sigma = \sqrt{\dfrac{137}{25} - .84^2} \times 2$
48-49	⊬⊬⊤	5	0	0	0	
46-47	| | | |	4	–1	–4	4	$\sigma = \sqrt{5.48 - .7056} \times 2$
44-45	0	0	–2	0	0	$\sigma = \sqrt{4.7744} \times 2$
42-43		2	–3	–6	18	$\sigma = 2.19 \times 2$
						$\sigma = \underline{4.38}$
	N = 25			$\Sigma fd = 21$	$\Sigma fd^2 = 137$	

*A detailed explanation of how to set up a frequency distribution and find the mean and standard deviation is presented in Chapter 3.

3. Figure the sigma range per letter grade with the mean at the mid-point of the C range. Example: See Figure 22 - 1.

   C range = Mean ± .6σ (Since the mean splits the 1.2σ area of the C range, we have .6σ above and below the mean.)
   B range = .6σ to 1.8σ above the mean (.6σ + 1.2σ = upper limit of 1.8σ).
   A range = 1.8σ and above
   D range = .6σ to 1.8σ below the mean
   F range = 1.8σ and below

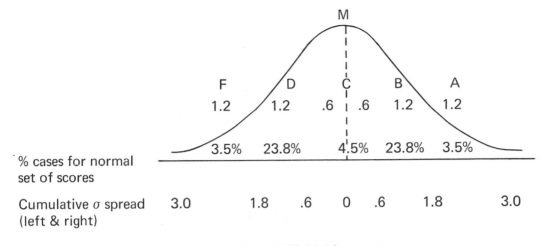

% cases for normal set of scores

Cumulative σ spread (left & right)

FIGURE 22 - 1

The Normal Curve Showing Letter Grade Areas with Sigma Values

4. Figure the score range per letter grade. From our previous computations on the softball grading unit (Table 22 - 3), we found a true mean of 50.18 and a standard deviation of 4.38. Thus, we have the information necessary for the computations in Table 22 - 4.
5. Figure the frequency of scores in each grade range as shown in the f column of Table 22 - 4.
6. Plot the curve for the group. See Figure 22 - 2.

TABLE 22 - 4

Computing the Score Range Per Letter Grade

Grade	σ Value X Standard Dev. ± Mean	Grade Scale (Rounded)	Frequency
A		59 & above	1
B	1.8 X SD of 4.38 = 7.884 + M of 50.18	54-58	4
C	0.6 X SD of 4.38 = 2.628 ± M of 50.18	48-53	14
D	1.8 X SD of 4.38 = 7.884 – M of 50.18	42-47	6
F		41 & below	0
			N = 25

*Computations for the A and F range are not necessary when the C, B, and D ranges are computed first.

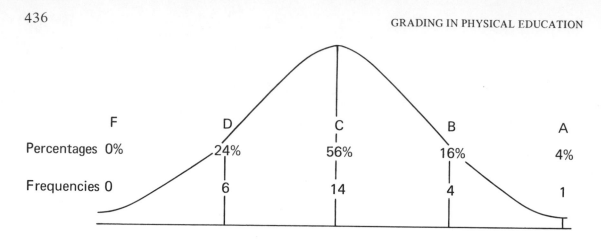

FIGURE 22 - 2

Curve Grading Based on 25 Final Scores

The above application of curve grading to the final scores of 25 students in a 6 week softball unit yielded 4% A's, 16% B's, 56% C's, 24% D's, and no F's. The deviation between the percentages elicited here and those cited earlier in Figure 22 - 1 where scores were normally distributed is due to a lack of normality of scores for this small classroom size group.

By comparing the sample grading curve (Figure 22 - 2) with the ideal grading curve (Figure 22 - 1), any one or more of the following implications may become evident to the teacher as he evaluates the testing situation:

1. The test factors making up the final composite score average were too hard for the group.
2. The group was a little below average in comparison with past groups who had taken the same tests.
3. The teacher failed to cover certain skills and knowledges thoroughly before testing.
4. There perhaps were not enough cases to exhibit normality.

While curve grading is a scientific approach to assigning grades and enables the teacher to evaluate the testing results in terms of what should be normal, it has the following disadvantages:

1. It is more applicable to groups larger than those found in the average classroom.
2. It requires additional computations after final average scores have been computed.
3. It may distinguish between two scores when there is only as slight a difference as one point, resulting in one score getting a lower grade than the other.
4. When strictly followed, it frequently allows above-average students to *coast* and still get a high grade, while weak students may work exceedingly hard and never get higher than a D or F.

See Chapter 3 for additional information on the normal curve.

Grading by Observation of Scores.

This method is quite simple in that final scores are merely listed down a page in a high-to-low order. After closely observing the scores, lines are drawn between the natural breaks in scores which frequently separate upper and lower groups from the large average

TABLE 22 - 5

Grading by Observation of Scores

Six Weeks Average T-Scores (Softball)

$$\underline{\frac{65}{54}} = A$$

$$\frac{54}{54} = B$$

$$\underline{54}$$

$$\underline{53} = B-$$

52

51

51

51

$$\frac{51}{50} = C$$

50

50

49

$$\underline{49}$$

48

$$48 = C-$$

$$\underline{48}$$

47

$$\frac{46}{46} = D$$

$$\underline{46}$$

$$\frac{43}{42} = F$$

group. If a break does not appear within a reasonable distance, keen judgment must be used in determining where the cut-off point is, say between a B and a C. In cases where scores run close together, some teachers find it satisfactory and fair to designate the top score of what they would normally consider to be in the C group as a B- (although it may eventually be recorded as a B), and the next lower score would be considered as a C. This procedure is shown in Table 22 - 5.

Assigning grades by observation of scores allows the teacher to use the performance of a student in relation to that of classmates who have been through the same procedure, plus, the teacher is free to use his keenest insight in assigning grades with both individual capacity and standards in mind. Another advantage of this method is that additional computations are not necessary once the average T-scores have been computed.

Summary

To briefly summarize the important points concerning grading in physical education classes, it must be remembered that the grade should reflect achievement toward the objectives for the unit of instruction. Administrative policies such as tardies and absences should not be scored and figured as a factor in the grade.

The steps to grading for a unit of instruction are listed as follows:
1. Establish sound objectives or goals for the unit.
2. Determine the importance or weight of each objective before the unit of instruction begins.
3. Select and administer a practical number of tests during the unit of instruction.
4. Convert raw scores for all tests into T-scores, and total and average T-scores for the final scores.
5. Convert final scores into letter grades by one of the following methods:
   a. absolute standards
   b. curve grading
   c. observation of scores

Although there are many varied methods of grading, there is probably no one best method to fit all situations. However, the physical educator should make every effort to have a fair and sound method of testing and grading which will fit into the evaluation pattern of the school.

Selected Readings

1. Barrow, Harold M., and Rosemary McGee, *A Practical Approach to Measurement in Physical Education,* Philadelphia: Lea & Febiger, 1964, pp. 436-453.

2. Garrett, Henry E., *Statistics in Psychology and Education,* New York: David McKay Company, Inc., 1958, pp. 87-119.

3. Mathews, Donald K., *Measurement in Physical Education,* Philadelphia: W. B. Saunders Company, 1963, pp. 313-328.

4. Remmers, H. H., and others, *A Practical Introduction to Measurement and Evaluation,* New York: Harper & Row, Publishers, 1965, pp. 286-302.

5. Smith, Fred M., and Sam Adams, *Educational Measurement for the Classroom Teacher.* New York: Harper & Row, Publishers, 1966, pp. 194-199.

APPENDIXES

APPENDIX A
STATISTICAL DATA

PUSH-UP SCORES AND HARVARD STEP TEST SCORES OF
60 COLLEGE MEN IN THE ILLUSTRATION OF THE
PRODUCT-MOMENT METHOD OF CORRELATION
USING A SCATTERGRAM (Figure 3 - 2)

Push-ups	HST	Push-ups	HST	Push-ups	HST	Push-ups	HST	Push-ups	HST	Push-ups	HST
30	81	20	68	22	65	13	57	28	59	27	77
17	66	18	66	22	69	27	80	24	64	20	60
12	55	47	69	37	66	35	88	17	55	21	70
41	98[h]	32	71	53[h]	68	5[l]	49	25	73	15	57
36	91	25	88	26	67	31	72	25	80	34	69
24	72	12	81	20	80	26	69	38	61	28	84
25	70	9	50	6	48[l]	22	73	32	68	30	70
18	73	31	90	16	83	15	85	10	59	16	63
26	65	38	85	29	69	29	84	17	80	23	74
30	79	34	70	42	75	37	61	27	68	25	68

PRACTICE DATA
ISOMETRIC PRESS SCORES AND ISOTONIC PRESS SCORES OF
25 JR. HIGH BOYS

SUBJECT	ISOMETRIC SCORES	ISOTONIC SCORES
1	63	76
2	78	80
3	46	92
4	82	102
5	74	73
6	103	87
7	78	70
8	103	85
9	87	79
10	73	93
11	95	82
12	82	90
13	89	83
14	73	81
15	92	85
16	85	72
17	80	81
18	81	96
19	90	81
20	78	85
21	86	90
22	78	75
23	101	73
24	65	90
25	84	86

APPENDIX B
AAHPER SPORTS SKILL TEST NORMS

AAHPER BASKETBALL

FRONT SHOT (BOYS)

Percentile Scores Based on Age/Test Scores in Points

Percentile	Age								Percentile
	10	11	12	13	14	15	16	17-18	
100th	23	26	27	27	27	29	29	30	100th
95th	17	17	18	21	22	22	22	24	95th
90th	15	16	18	19	20	21	21	22	90th
85th	13	15	17	18	20	20	20	21	85th
80th	12	14	16	17	19	20	20	20	80th
75th	11	13	15	16	18	19	19	19	75th
70th	10	12	14	16	17	18	18	18	70th
65th	9	12	14	15	17	17	17	18	65th
60th	9	11	13	15	16	17	17	17	60th
55th	8	10	12	14	16	16	16	17	55th
50th	7	9	11	14	15	16	16	16	50th
45th	7	9	11	13	15	15	15	16	45th
40th	6	8	10	12	14	15	15	15	40th
35th	5	7	9	12	13	14	14	14	35th
30th	4	6	9	11	12	14	14	14	30th
25th	4	6	8	10	12	13	13	13	25th
20th	3	5	7	10	11	12	12	12	20th
15th	2	4	6	8	10	11	11	11	15th
10th	1	2	5	7	9	10	10	10	10th
5th	0	1	3	5	7	7	8	8	5th
0	0	0	0	0	0	3	3	3	0

FRONT SHOT (GIRLS)

Percentile	Age							Percentile
	10-11	12	13	14	15	16	17-18	
100th	21	21	30	30	30	30	30	100th
95th	14	15	17	18	18	18	18	95th
90th	12	13	15	16	16	17	17	90th
85th	11	12	14	15	15	15	16	85th
80th	10	11	13	14	14	14	15	80th
75th	9	10	12	13	13	14	14	75th
70th	8	9	11	12	13	13	13	70th
65th	7	9	10	11	12	12	13	65th
60th	6	8	9	10	11	12	12	60th
55th	6	8	9	9	10	11	11	55th
50th	5	7	8	9	9	10	11	50th
45th	4	6	7	8	9	9	10	45th
40th	3	6	6	8	8	9	9	40th
35th	3	5	6	7	7	8	9	35th
30th	2	4	6	6	7	8	8	30th
25th	1	4	5	5	6	7	7	25th
20th	1	3	4	4	5	6	6	20th
15th	1	2	3	3	4	5	5	15th
10th	0	1	2	2	3	4	4	10th
5th	0	0	1	1	2	2	3	5th
0	0	0	0	0	0	0	0	0

SIDE SHOT (BOYS)

Percentile Scores Based on Age/Test Scores in Points

Percentile	Age								Percentile
	10	11	12	13	14	15	16	17-18	
100th	27	29	32	33	35	35	35	36	100th
95th	17	18	21	25	26	26	26	26	95th
90th	14	16	20	21	24	24	25	25	90th
85th	13	14	17	20	22	22	22	24	85th
80th	11	13	17	19	21	21	21	22	80th
75th	9	12	15	17	20	20	20	21	75th
70th	8	11	14	16	19	19	19	21	70th
65th	7	10	13	15	18	18	18	20	65th
60th	6	9	12	14	17	17	17	19	60th
55th	5	8	12	14	16	16	16	18	55th
50th	5	7	11	13	16	16	16	18	50th
45th	4	6	10	12	15	15	15	17	45th
40th	3	5	9	11	15	15	15	16	40th
35th	3	5	8	10	14	14	14	15	35th
30th	2	4	7	9	13	13	13	14	30th
25th	1	3	6	8	12	12	12	13	25th
20th	1	2	5	7	11	11	11	12	20th
15th	0	2	4	6	10	10	10	11	15th
10th	0	2	3	5	7	7	9	9	10th
5th	0	2	2	3	5	5	7	7	5th
0	0	0	0	1	1	2	2	2	0

SIDE SHOT (GIRLS)

Percentile	Age							Percentile
	10-11	12	13	14	15	16	17-18	
100th	25	26	29	30	31	31	32	100th
95th	16	16	19	21	22	23	22	95th
90th	13	15	17	18	20	20	20	90th
85th	12	13	15	17	18	18	18	85th
80th	11	12	14	16	17	17	17	80th
75th	9	11	13	15	16	16	16	75th
70th	8	10	12	14	15	15	15	70th
65th	7	9	11	13	14	14	14	65th
60th	6	8	11	12	13	13	13	60th
55th	5	7	10	11	12	12	12	55th
50th	4	6	9	11	12	12	12	50th
45th	4	6	8	10	11	11	11	45th
40th	3	5	7	9	10	10	10	40th
35th	2	4	6	8	9	9	9	35th
30th	1	3	6	8	8	8	8	30th
25th	1	3	5	7	7	7	7	25th
20th	0	2	4	6	6	6	6	20th
15th	0	1	3	5	5	5	5	15th
10th	0	0	1	3	3	3	3	10th
5th	0	0	0	1	2	1	1	5th
0	0	0	0	0	0	0	0	0

FOUL SHOT (BOYS)

Percentile Scores Based on Age/Test Scores in Number of Baskets Made

Percentile	Age								Percentile
	10	11	12	13	14	15	16	17-18	
100th	13	16	17	20	20	20	20	20	100th
95th	7	8	10	12	13	16	16	16	95th
90th	5	7	8	10	11	13	13	13	90th
85th	4	6	7	9	10	12	12	12	85th
80th	4	5	7	8	10	11	11	11	80th
75th	3	5	6	7	9	10	10	10	75th
70th	3	4	6	7	8	9	9	9	70th
65th	3	4	5	6	8	8	8	9	65th
60th	2	3	5	6	7	8	8	8	60th
55th	2	3	4	5	7	8	8	8	55th
50th	2	3	4	5	6	8	8	8	50th
45th	2	3	4	5	6	7	7	7	45th
40th	1	2	3	4	5	7	7	7	40th
35th	1	2	3	4	5	6	6	6	35th
30th	1	1	3	3	4	5	5	5	30th
25th	0	1	2	3	4	5	5	5	25th
20th	0	1	2	2	4	4	4	4	20th
15th	0	1	1	2	3	4	4	4	15th
10th	0	0	1	1	2	3	3	3	10th
5th	0	0	0	1	2	2	2	2	5th
0	0	0	0	0	0	0	0	0	0

FOUL SHOT (GIRLS)

Percentile	Age							Percentile
	10-11	12	13	14	15	16	17-18	
100th	20	20	20	20	20	20	20	100th
95th	7	8	9	9	9	10	10	95th
90th	5	6	7	7	8	9	9	90th
85th	4	5	6	6	7	8	8	85th
80th	4	5	5	5	6	7	7	80th
75th	3	4	5	5	6	6	6	75th
70th	3	4	4	4	5	6	6	70th
65th	2	3	4	4	5	5	5	65th
60th	2	3	3	3	4	5	5	60th
55th	2	2	3	3	4	4	5	55th
50th	1	2	3	3	4	4	4	50th
45th	1	2	2	3	3	4	4	45th
40th	1	2	2	2	3	3	4	40th
35th	0	1	2	2	3	3	3	35th
30th	0	1	1	2	2	3	3	30th
25th	0	1	1	2	2	2	3	25th
20th	0	1	1	1	2	2	2	20th
15th	0	0	1	1	1	1	2	15th
10th	0	0	0	1	1	1	2	10th
5th	0	0	0	0	0	0	1	5th
0	0	0	0	0	0	0	0	0

UNDER BASKET SHOT (BOYS)

Percentile Scores Based on Age/Test Scores in Number of Baskets Made

Percentile	Age								Percentile
	10	11	12	13	14	15	16	17-18	
100th	14	23	23	23	23	29	33	34	100th
95th	10	11	13	15	16	18	19	20	95th
90th	9	10	11	13	15	17	17	18	90th
85th	7	9	10	12	14	16	17	17	85th
80th	7	8	10	12	14	15	15	16	80th
75th	6	8	9	11	13	15	15	15	75th
70th	6	7	9	10	12	14	14	15	70th
65th	6	6	8	10	12	13	14	14	65th
60th	6	6	8	10	12	13	14	14	60th
55th	5	6	7	9	11	13	13	14	55th
50th	5	6	7	8	10	11	12	13	50th
45th	4	5	7	8	10	11	12	12	45th
40th	4	5	5	6	9	10	11	11	40th
35th	4	4	5	6	9	9	10	11	35th
30th	3	4	5	6	8	9	9	10	30th
25th	3	4	4	5	8	8	9	10	25th
20th	3	3	4	5	7	8	8	9	20th
15th	2	3	4	5	6	7	7	8	15th
10th	2	2	3	3	4	6	6	7	10th
5th	1	1	2	2	3	4	5	6	5th
0	0	1	1	1	1	1	1	1	0

UNDER BASKET SHOT (GIRLS)

Percentile	Age							Percentile
	10-11	12	13	14	15	16	17-18	
100th	15	15	16	16	18	19	20	100th
95th	8	10	10	11	11	13	13	95th
90th	7	8	8	10	10	11	11	90th
85th	6	7	8	9	9	10	10	85th
80th	5	7	7	8	8	9	9	80th
75th	5	6	7	8	8	8	8	75th
70th	5	6	7	7	7	8	8	70th
65th	5	5	6	7	7	7	7	65th
60th	4	5	6	6	6	7	7	60th
55th	4	5	6	6	6	6	6	55th
50th	4	4	5	6	6	6	6	50th
45th	4	4	5	5	5	5	5	45th
40th	3	4	5	5	5	5	5	40th
35th	3	4	4	5	5	5	5	35th
30th	3	3	4	4	4	4	4	30th
25th	2	3	4	4	4	4	4	25th
20th	2	3	3	4	4	4	4	20th
15th	2	2	3	3	3	3	3	15th
10th	1	2	2	3	3	3	3	10th
5th	1	1	1	2	2	2	2	5th
0	0	0	0	1	1	1	1	0

SPEED PASS (BOYS)

Percentile Scores Based on Age/Test Scores in Seconds and Tenths

Percentile	Age								Percentile
	10	11	12	13	14	15	16	17-18	
100th	10.0	8.5	5.5	5.5	5.5	4.5	4.5	4.5	100th
95th	11.6	10.5	8.5	7.8	7.6	7.4	7.3	6.8	95th
90th	11.6	11.2	9.7	8.3	8.0	7.8	7.7	7.2	90th
85th	12.2	11.6	10.1	8.8	8.3	8.0	7.9	7.5	85th
80th	12.5	11.9	10.4	9.3	8.6	8.3	8.1	7.8	80th
75th	12.8	12.2	10.7	9.8	8.9	8.5	8.4	8.0	75th
70th	13.1	12.4	11.1	10.0	9.0	8.7	8.6	8.2	70th
65th	13.3	12.7	11.4	10.3	9.2	8.9	8.7	8.3	65th
60th	13.6	12.9	11.7	10.6	9.4	9.1	8.9	8.6	60th
55th	13.9	13.2	11.7	10.8	9.6	9.3	9.1	8.8	55th
50th	14.2	13.4	12.2	11.1	9.9	9.4	9.2	9.0	50th
45th	16.6	13.7	12.5	11.4	10.2	9.6	9.4	9.2	45th
40th	14.9	14.0	12.7	11.8	10.4	10.0	9.6	9.4	40th
35th	15.2	14.3	13.0	12.2	10.6	10.2	9.9	9.6	35th
30th	15.6	14.6	13.3	12.6	11.0	10.5	10.2	9.9	30th
25th	16.0	14.9	13.6	13.0	11.3	10.9	10.5	10.2	25th
20th	16.5	15.3	14.2	13.4	11.7	11.3	11.1	10.5	20th
15th	17.3	15.7	14.9	14.2	12.2	12.0	11.6	11.1	15th
10th	18.1	16.3	15.5	15.1	13.0	12.8	12.5	11.9	10th
5th	19.3	17.5	16.9	16.6	14.4	14.1	14.0	13.4	5th
0	26.0	26.5	25.0	21.4	20.4	20.4	20.3	20.0	0

SPEED PASS (GIRLS)

Percentile	Age							Percentile
	10-11	12	13	14	15	16	17-18	
100th	7.5	7.5	7.5	7.5	7.5	6.5	6.5	100th
95th	11.9	10.5	10.4	10.0	9.5	9.5	9.5	95th
90th	12.6	11.1	11.1	10.7	10.2	10.1	10.0	90th
85th	12.9	11.7	11.7	11.1	10.7	10.6	10.4	85th
80th	13.2	12.0	12.0	11.5	11.0	10.9	10.7	80th
75th	13.5	12.4	12.4	11.8	11.3	11.2	11.0	75th
70th	13.9	12.8	12.7	12.1	11.6	11.5	11.3	70th
65th	14.2	13.1	13.0	12.4	11.9	11.8	11.6	65th
60th	14.5	13.4	13.2	12.7	12.2	12.1	11.9	60th
55th	14.9	13.7	13.5	13.0	12.5	12.4	12.2	55th
50th	15.3	14.0	13.8	13.4	12.8	12.7	12.5	50th
45th	15.6	14.4	14.2	13.7	13.1	13.0	12.8	45th
40th	15.9	14.8	14.5	14.0	13.5	13.4	13.1	40th
35th	16.3	15.1	14.9	14.4	13.9	13.6	13.4	35th
30th	16.7	15.5	15.3	14.8	14.3	14.1	13.8	30th
25th	17.2	16.1	15.8	15.1	14.8	14.5	14.4	25th
20th	17.7	16.8	16.4	15.5	15.3	15.1	15.0	20th
15th	18.3	17.6	17.1	16.2	16.1	15.7	15.7	15th
10th	19.1	18.4	18.2	17.3	17.0	16.6	16.6	10th
5th	20.3	21.1	20.0	19.2	18.6	18.0	17.9	5th
0	25.5	25.4	25.4	25.4	25.4	25.4	24.4	0

JUMP AND REACH (BOYS)

Percentile Scores Based on Age/Test Scores in Inches

Percentile	10	11	12	13	14	15	16	17-18	Percentile
100th	18	22	25	29	29	31	31	34	100th
95th	14	16	18	20	22	24	24	26	95th
90th	13	15	17	19	21	22	23	25	90th
85th	13	14	16	18	21	21	22	24	85th
80th	12	14	16	17	20	21	21	24	80th
75th	12	13	15	17	19	20	21	23	75th
70th	12	13	15	17	19	20	21	23	70th
65th	11	12	14	16	18	19	20	22	65th
60th	11	12	14	16	18	19	20	22	60th
55th	11	12	13	15	17	18	19	21	55th
50th	10	11	13	15	17	18	19	20	50th
45th	10	11	13	14	16	17	18	20	45th
40th	10	11	13	14	16	17	18	19	40th
35th	10	10	12	14	15	17	18	19	35th
30th	9	10	12	13	15	16	17	18	30th
25th	9	10	11	13	14	16	17	18	25th
20th	9	9	10	11	13	14	15	16	20th
15th	8	9	10	11	13	14	14	15	15th
10th	8	8	10	11	13	13	14	15	10th
5th	6	7	9	9	12	12	13	14	5th
0	4	4	5	5	7	7	8	13	0

JUMP AND REACH (GIRLS)

Percentile	10-11	12	13	14	15	16	17-18	Percentile
100th	18	21	24	24	25	25	25	100th
95th	15	16	17	18	18	18	18	95th
90th	14	15	16	16	17	17	17	90th
85th	13	14	15	15	16	16	16	85th
80th	12	14	15	15	16	16	16	80th
75th	12	13	14	14	15	15	15	75th
70th	11	13	14	14	15	15	15	70th
65th	11	13	13	14	14	14	14	65th
60th	11	12	13	13	14	14	14	60th
55th	10	12	12	13	14	14	14	55th
50th	10	12	12	13	13	13	13	50th
45th	10	11	12	12	13	13	13	45th
40th	10	11	11	12	13	13	13	40th
35th	9	11	11	12	12	12	12	35th
30th	9	10	11	11	12	12	12	30th
25th	9	10	10	11	11	11	12	25th
20th	9	9	10	10	11	11	11	20th
15th	8	9	9	10	10	10	11	15th
10th	8	9	9	9	10	10	10	10th
5th	7	8	8	9	9	9	9	5th
0	5	5	5	5	7	7	7	0

OVERARM PASS FOR ACCURACY (BOYS)
Percentile Scores Based on Age/Test Scores in Points

Percentile	Age								Percentile
	10	11	12	13	14	15	16	17-18	
100th	18	27	27	27	29	31	31	31	100th
95th	14	18	20	20	22	24	24	25	95th
90th	13	15	18	19	21	22	22	23	90th
85th	11	14	17	18	20	21	21	22	85th
80th	10	12	16	17	19	20	20	21	80th
75th	8	11	15	16	18	19	19	20	75th
70th	7	11	14	16	18	19	19	19	70th
65th	6	10	13	15	17	17	18	18	65th
60th	6	9	12	15	17	17	17	17	60th
55th	5	8	12	14	16	17	17	17	55th
50th	4	7	11	13	16	16	16	16	50th
45th	3	6	10	12	15	15	15	15	45th
40th	2	5	10	12	14	15	15	15	40th
35th	2	4	9	11	14	14	14	14	35th
30th	1	3	8	10	13	13	13	13	30th
25th	0	2	7	9	12	12	12	12	25th
20th	0	2	6	9	10	11	11	11	20th
15th	0	1	5	8	10	10	11	11	15th
10th	0	1	3	6	9	9	9	9	10th
5th	0	0	2	4	7	7	8	8	5th
0	0	0	0	0	0	0	0	0	0

OVERARM PASS FOR ACCURACY (GIRLS)

Percentile	Age							Percentile
	10-11	12	13	14	15	16	17-18	
100th	27	29	30	30	30	30	30	100th
95th	23	24	25	25	26	26	26	95th
90th	22	23	24	24	25	25	25	90th
85th	21	22	23	23	24	24	24	85th
80th	19	21	22	22	23	23	23	80th
75th	18	20	21	21	22	22	22	75th
70th	17	19	20	20	22	22	22	70th
65th	16	18	19	20	21	21	21	65th
60th	14	17	18	19	20	21	20	60th
55th	13	16	18	18	20	20	19	55th
50th	12	15	17	18	19	19	19	50th
45th	11	15	17	17	18	18	18	45th
40th	10	14	15	16	17	17	17	40th
35th	8	13	14	15	17	17	15	35th
30th	7	12	13	15	16	16	14	30th
25th	5	11	12	14	15	15	13	25th
20th	4	9	11	13	13	14	11	20th
15th	2	7	9	11	12	12	10	15th
10th	0	4	7	9	9	9	8	10th
5th	0	1	4	6	6	6	5	5th
0	0	0	0	0	0	0	0	0

PUSH PASS FOR ACCURACY (BOYS)

Percentile Scores Based on Age/Test Scores in Points

Percentile	Age							Percentile
	11	12	13	14	15	16	17-18	
100th	29	29	29	29	29	30	30	100th
95th	19	22	24	25	27	27	29	95th
90th	17	20	22	24	25	26	28	90th
85th	14	18	21	23	24	25	28	85th
80th	12	16	20	21	23	24	27	80th
75th	11	14	19	21	23	23	27	75th
70th	9	13	18	20	22	23	26	70th
65th	8	12	17	19	21	22	26	65th
60th	7	11	16	18	21	21	26	60th
55th	5	10	15	18	20	21	25	55th
50th	4	9	13	17	19	20	24	50th
45th	3	8	13	16	19	19	24	45th
40th	2	7	12	15	18	18	23	40th
35th	1	5	11	14	17	18	23	35th
30th	1	4	10	14	16	17	22	30th
25th	1	3	9	12	15	16	21	25th
20th	1	2	7	11	14	15	20	20th
15th	0	2	5	10	13	14	18	15th
10th	0	1	2	8	11	12	17	10th
5th	0	1	1	4	6	9	14	5th
0	0	0	1	1	2	4	5	0

PUSH PASS FOR ACCURACY (GIRLS)

Percentile	Age							Percentile
	10-11	12	13	14	15	16	17-18	
100th	29	30	30	30	30	30	30	100th
95th	26	27	28	28	29	29	29	95th
90th	24	26	27	28	28	28	28	90th
85th	23	25	26	27	27	27	27	85th
80th	22	24	25	26	27	27	27	80th
75th	21	23	24	25	26	26	26	75th
70th	21	22	24	25	25	26	26	70th
65th	20	22	23	24	25	25	25	65th
60th	19	21	22	23	24	25	25	60th
55th	18	20	22	23	24	24	24	55th
50th	17	19	21	22	23	24	24	50th
45th	16	19	21	22	23	23	23	45th
40th	15	18	20	21	22	22	23	40th
35th	13	17	19	20	22	22	22	35th
30th	12	16	18	19	21	21	21	30th
25th	10	14	17	18	20	20	20	25th
20th	8	12	15	17	19	19	19	20th
15th	7	10	13	15	18	17	17	15th
10th	4	8	11	13	16	12	13	10th
5th	2	4	7	10	12	8	9	5th
0	0	0	0	0	0	0	0	0

DRIBBLING (BOYS)
Percentile Scores Based on Age/Tests Scores in Seconds and Tenths

Percentile	\multicolumn{8}{c}{Age}	Percentile
	10	11	12	13	14	15	16	17-18	
100th	12.0	10.5	6.5	6.5	6.5	5.5	5.5	5.5	100th
95th	13.0	12.0	10.3	9.8	9.7	9.5	9.5	8.8	95th
90th	13.7	12.8	11.3	10.4	10.1	9.8	9.8	9.5	90th
85th	14.1	13.0	11.7	10.8	10.7	10.1	10.0	9.9	85th
80th	14.6	13.3	12.1	11.2	10.9	10.3	10.3	10.3	80th
75th	14.8	13.6	12.3	11.6	11.1	10.6	10.5	10.5	75th
70th	15.1	13.9	12.6	11.9	11.3	10.9	10.8	10.8	70th
65th	15.3	14.1	12.9	12.2	11.5	11.1	11.0	11.0	65th
60th	15.5	14.4	13.2	12.4	11.8	11.4	11.3	11.2	60th
55th	15.8	14.7	13.4	12.7	12.0	11.7	11.5	11.5	55th
50th	16.0	15.0	13.7	13.0	12.3	12.0	11.8	11.7	50th
45th	16.3	15.3	14.1	13.3	12.6	12.3	12.1	11.8	45th
40th	16.5	15.6	14.4	13.6	12.9	12.6	12.3	12.0	40th
35th	16.9	16.0	14.7	13.9	13.2	12.9	12.6	12.3	35th
30th	17.2	16.3	15.0	14.2	13.6	13.2	12.9	12.6	30th
25th	17.6	16.8	15.3	14.4	13.9	13.5	13.2	13.0	25th
20th	18.0	17.2	15.8	14.9	14.3	14.0	13.4	13.3	20th
15th	18.4	17.9	16.5	15.3	14.8	14.5	13.8	13.7	15th
10th	19.4	18.8	17.3	16.1	15.6	15.2	14.2	14.2	10th
5th	21.4	20.4	18.7	18.3	17.4	16.5	14.7	14.6	5th
0	26.0	26.5	26.5	23.0	22.0	22.0	21.6	21.5	0

DRIBBLING (GIRLS)

Percentile	\multicolumn{7}{c}{Age}	Percentile
	10-11	12	13	14	15	16	17-18	
100th	9.5	9.5	9.5	9.5	9.5	8.5	7.5	100th
95th	13.7	12.0	11.7	11.7	11.7	10.9	10.8	95th
90th	14.5	12.9	12.8	12.6	12.3	11.7	11.7	90th
85th	14.9	13.5	13.3	13.0	12.8	12.1	12.0	85th
80th	15.2	14.0	13.7	13.4	13.1	12.5	12.4	80th
75th	15.6	14.3	14.0	13.7	13.4	12.7	12.7	75th
70th	15.9	14.6	14.4	14.0	13.6	13.0	13.0	70th
65th	16.2	14.9	14.7	14.3	13.8	13.2	13.2	65th
60th	16.5	15.2	14.9	14.5	14.0	13.5	13.4	60th
55th	16.8	15.5	15.1	14.8	14.2	13.7	13.6	55th
50th	17.1	15.8	15.4	15.0	14.5	14.0	14.0	50th
45th	17.5	16.2	15.7	15.2	14.7	14.3	14.3	45th
40th	17.8	16.5	16.1	15.5	15.0	14.6	14.5	40th
35th	18.2	16.9	16.4	15.8	15.3	14.9	14.7	35th
30th	18.5	17.3	16.7	16.2	15.6	15.2	15.0	30th
25th	19.0	17.7	17.1	16.5	16.0	15.5	15.2	25th
20th	19.5	18.2	17.5	17.0	16.3	16.0	15.5	20th
15th	20.4	18.7	18.0	17.5	16.9	16.5	16.3	15th
10th	21.1	20.5	18.2	17.8	17.2	17.1	17.0	10th
5th	22.4	21.2	20.6	19.8	18.9	18.4	18.0	5th
0	29.0	24.5	24.5	24.5	24.5	24.5	24.5	0

AAHPER FOOTBALL TEST

FORWARD PASS FOR DISTANCE

Percentile Scores Based on Age/Test Scores in Feet

Percentile	Age								Percentile
	10	11	12	13	14	15	16	17-18	
100th	96	105	120	150	170	180	180	180	100th
95th	71	83	99	115	126	135	144	152	95th
90th	68	76	92	104	118	127	135	143	90th
85th	64	73	87	98	114	122	129	137	85th
80th	62	70	83	95	109	118	126	133	80th
75th	61	68	79	91	105	115	123	129	75th
70th	59	65	77	88	102	111	120	127	70th
65th	58	64	75	85	99	108	117	124	65th
60th	56	62	73	83	96	105	114	121	60th
55th	55	61	71	80	93	102	111	117	55th
50th	53	59	68	78	91	99	108	114	50th
45th	52	56	66	76	88	97	105	110	45th
40th	51	54	64	73	85	94	103	107	40th
35th	49	51	62	70	83	92	100	104	35th
30th	47	50	60	69	80	89	97	101	30th
25th	45	48	58	65	77	85	93	98	25th
20th	44	45	54	63	73	81	90	94	20th
15th	41	43	51	61	70	76	85	89	15th
10th	38	40	45	55	64	71	79	80	10th
5th	33	36	40	46	53	62	70	67	5th
0	14	25	10	10	10	20	30	20	0

50-YARD DASH WITH FOOTBALL

Percentile Scores Based on Age/Test Scores in Seconds and Tenths

Percentile	Age								Percentile
	10	11	12	13	14	15	16	17-18	
100th	7.3	6.8	6.2	5.5	5.5	5.8	5.5	5.0	100th
95th	7.7	7.4	7.0	6.4	6.4	6.2	6.0	6.0	95th
90th	7.9	7.6	7.2	6.8	6.6	6.3	6.1	6.1	90th
85th	8.1	7.7	7.4	6.9	6.8	6.4	6.3	6.2	85th
80th	8.2	7.8	7.5	7.0	6.9	6.5	6.4	6.3	80th
75th	8.3	7.9	7.5	7.1	7.0	6.6	6.5	6.3	75th
70th	8.4	8.0	7.6	7.2	7.1	6.7	6.6	6.4	70th
65th	8.5	8.1	7.7	7.3	7.2	6.8	6.6	6.5	65th
60th	8.6	8.2	7.8	7.4	7.2	6.9	6.7	6.6	60th
55th	8.6	8.3	7.9	7.5	7.3	7.0	6.8	6.6	55th
50th	8.7	8.4	8.0	7.5	7.4	7.0	6.8	6.7	50th
45th	8.8	8.5	8.1	7.6	7.5	7.1	6.9	6.8	45th
40th	8.9	8.6	8.1	7.7	7.6	7.2	7.0	6.8	40th
35th	9.0	8.7	8.2	7.8	7.7	7.2	7.1	6.9	35th
30th	9.1	8.8	8.3	8.0	7.8	7.3	7.2	7.0	30th
25th	9.2	8.9	8.4	8.1	7.9	7.4	7.3	7.1	25th
20th	9.3	9.1	8.5	8.2	8.1	7.5	7.4	7.2	20th
15th	9.4	9.2	8.7	8.4	8.3	7.7	7.5	7.3	15th
10th	9.6	9.3	9.0	8.7	8.4	8.1	7.8	7.4	10th
5th	9.8	9.5	9.3	9.0	8.8	8.4	8.0	7.8	5th
0	10.6	11.0	12.0	12.0	12.0	11.0	10.0	10.0	0

BLOCKING
Percentile Scores Based on Age/Test Scores in Seconds and Tenths

Percentile	10	11	12	13	14	15	16	17-18	Percentile
100th	6.9	5.0	5.5	5.0	5.0	5.0	5.0	5.0	100th
95th	7.5	6.6	6.6	5.9	5.8	6.0	5.9	5.5	95th
90th	7.7	7.1	7.3	6.5	6.2	6.2	6.1	5.7	90th
85th	7.9	7.5	7.6	6.7	6.6	6.3	6.3	5.8	85th
80th	8.1	8.0	7.7	6.9	6.8	6.5	6.5	6.0	80th
75th	8.3	8.3	7.9	7.2	7.0	6.7	6.7	6.2	75th
70th	8.5	8.6	8.1	7.4	7.1	6.9	7.0	6.3	70th
65th	8.9	9.1	8.4	7.6	7.3	7.0	7.2	6.5	65th
60th	9.3	9.5	8.6	7.7	7.5	7.2	7.4	6.7	60th
55th	9.6	9.7	8.8	7.9	7.7	7.4	7.6	7.0	55th
50th	9.8	9.9	9.0	8.1	7.8	7.5	7.8	7.2	50th
45th	10.1	10.2	9.2	8.3	8.0	7.8	8.0	7.4	45th
40th	10.5	10.4	9.4	8.4	8.1	7.9	8.3	7.6	40th
35th	10.7	10.6	9.6	8.6	8.3	8.2	8.6	7.8	35th
30th	11.0	10.9	9.7	8.9	8.5	8.3	8.8	8.0	30th
25th	11.3	11.1	9.9	9.1	8.7	8.5	9.1	8.2	25th
20th	11.6	11.3	10.2	9.4	9.0	8.8	9.5	8.5	20th
15th	12.0	11.6	10.5	9.8	9.2	9.0	9.0	9.0	15th
10th	12.8	12.0	10.9	10.2	9.5	9.4	10.6	9.4	10th
5th	14.4	13.1	11.6	11.2	10.3	10.4	10.7	10.8	5th
0	17.5	18.0	15.0	15.0	15.0	13.0	15.0	14.0	0

FORWARD PASS FOR ACCURACY
Percentile Scores Based on Age/Test Scores in Points

Percentile	10	11	12	13	14	15	16	17-18	Percentile
100th	18	26	26	28	26	26	28	28	100th
95th	14	19	20	21	21	20	21	22	95th
90th	11	16	18	19	19	19	20	21	90th
85th	10	15	17	18	18	18	18	19	85th
80th	9	13	16	17	17	17	17	18	80th
75th	8	12	15	16	16	16	16	18	75th
70th	8	11	14	15	15	15	15	17	70th
65th	6	10	13	14	14	14	15	16	65th
60th	5	9	12	13	13	13	14	15	60th
55th	4	8	11	13	13	13	13	15	55th
50th	3	7	11	12	12	12	13	14	50th
45th	2	6	10	11	11	11	12	13	45th
40th	2	5	9	11	10	11	12	12	40th
35th	1	5	8	10	9	9	11	12	35th
30th	0	4	7	9	8	9	10	11	30th
25th	0	3	6	8	8	8	9	10	25th
20th	0	2	5	7	7	7	8	9	20th
15th	0	1	4	5	5	6	7	8	15th
10th	0	0	3	4	4	5	6	7	10th
5th	0	0	1	2	2	3	4	5	5th
0	0	0	0	0	0	0	0	0	0

FOOTBALL PUNT FOR DISTANCE

Percentile Scores Based on Age/Test Scores in Feet

Percentile	Age								Percentile
	10	11	12	13	14	15	16	17-18	
100th	87	100	115	150	160	170	160	180	100th
95th	75	84	93	106	119	126	140	136	95th
90th	64	77	88	98	110	119	126	128	90th
85th	61	75	84	94	106	114	120	124	85th
80th	58	70	79	90	103	109	114	120	80th
75th	56	68	77	87	98	105	109	115	75th
70th	55	66	75	83	96	102	106	110	70th
65th	53	64	72	80	93	99	103	107	65th
60th	51	62	70	78	90	96	100	104	60th
55th	50	60	68	75	87	94	97	101	55th
50th	48	57	66	73	84	91	95	98	50th
45th	46	55	64	70	81	89	92	96	45th
40th	45	53	61	68	78	86	90	93	40th
35th	44	51	59	64	75	83	86	90	35th
30th	42	48	56	63	72	79	83	86	30th
25th	40	45	52	61	70	76	79	81	25th
20th	38	42	50	57	66	73	74	76	20th
15th	32	39	46	52	61	69	70	70	15th
10th	28	34	40	44	55	62	64	64	10th
5th	22	27	35	33	44	54	56	53	5th
0	11	9	10	10	10	10	10	10	0

BALL CHANGING ZIGZAG RUN

Percentile Scores Based on Age/Test Scores in Seconds and Tenths

Percentile	Age								Percentile
	10	11	12	13	14	15	16	17-18	
100th	7.2	7.4	7.0	6.0	6.5	6.0	6.0	6.0	100th
95th	9.9	7.7	7.8	8.0	8.7	7.7	7.7	8.4	95th
90th	10.1	8.1	8.2	8.4	9.0	8.0	8.0	8.7	90th
85th	10.3	8.6	8.5	8.7	9.2	8.3	8.4	8.8	85th
80th	10.5	9.0	8.7	8.8	9.4	8.5	8.6	8.9	80th
75th	10.7	9.3	8.8	9.0	9.5	8.6	8.7	9.0	75th
70th	10.9	9.6	9.0	9.2	9.6	8.7	8.8	9.1	70th
65th	11.1	9.8	9.1	9.3	9.7	8.8	8.9	9.2	65th
60th	11.2	10.0	9.3	9.5	9.8	8.9	9.0	9.3	60th
55th	11.4	10.1	9.5	9.6	9.9	9.0	9.1	9.4	55th
50th	11.5	10.3	9.6	9.7	10.0	9.1	9.3	9.6	50th
45th	11.6	10.5	9.8	9.8	10.1	9.2	9.4	9.7	45th
40th	11.8	10.6	10.0	10.0	10.2	9.4	9.5	9.8	40th
35th	11.9	10.9	10.1	01.2	10.4	9.5	9.7	9.9	35th
30th	12.2	11.1	10.3	10.3	10.5	9.6	9.9	10.1	30th
25th	12.5	11.3	10.5	10.3	10.7	9.9	10.1	10.3	25th
20th	12.8	11.6	10.8	10.8	10.9	10.1	10.3	10.5	20th
15th	13.3	12.1	11.1	11.1	11.2	10.3	10.6	10.9	15th
10th	13.8	12.9	11.5	11.4	11.5	10.6	11.2	11.4	10th
5th	15.8	14.2	12.3	12.1	12.0	11.5	12.2	12.1	5th
0	24.0	15.0	19.0	20.0	14.5	20.0	17.0	15.0	0

CATCHING THE FORWARD PASS
Percentile Scores Based on Age/Test Scores in Number Caught

Percentile					Age					Percentile
	10	11	12	13	14	15	16	17-18		
100th	20	20	20	20	20	20	20	20		100th
95th	19	19	19	20	20	20	20	20		95th
90th	17	18	19	19	19	19	19	19		90th
85th	16	16	18	18	18	19	19	19		85th
80th	14	15	18	17	18	18	18	18		80th
75th	13	14	16	17	17	18	18	18		75th
70th	12	13	16	16	16	17	17	17		70th
65th	11	12	15	15	15	16	16	16		65th
60th	10	12	14	15	15	16	16	16		60th
55th	8	11	14	14	14	15	15	15		55th
50th	7	10	13	13	14	15	15	15		50th
45th	7	9	12	13	13	14	14	14		45th
40th	6	8	12	12	12	13	13	13		40th
35th	5	7	11	11	11	12	12	13		35th
30th	5	7	10	10	10	11	11	12		30th
25th	4	6	10	9	9	10	10	11		25th
20th	3	5	8	8	8	9	9	10		20th
15th	2	4	7	7	8	8	8	9		15th
10th	1	3	6	6	6	7	6	8		10th
5th	1	1	5	4	4	6	4	6		5th
0	0	0	0	0	0	0	0	0		0

PULL-OUT
Percentile Scores Based on Age/Test Scores in Seconds and Tenths

Percentile					Age					Percentile
	10	11	12	13	14	15	16	17-18		
100th	2.5	2.2	2.2	2.4	2.2	2.0	2.0	1.8		100th
95th	2.9	2.5	2.8	2.8	2.7	2.5	2.5	2.6		95th
90th	3.2	2.7	3.0	2.9	2.8	2.6	2.6	2.7		90th
85th	3.3	2.8	3.0	3.0	2.9	2.7	2.7	2.8		85th
80th	3.4	2.9	3.1	3.0	3.0	2.8	2.9	2.8		80th
75th	3.5	2.9	3.1	3.1	3.0	3.0	2.9	2.9		75th
70th	3.5	3.0	3.2	3.1	3.0	3.0	3.0	2.9		70th
65th	3.6	3.1	3.3	3.2	3.1	3.0	3.0	3.0		65th
60th	3.6	3.2	3.3	3.2	3.1	3.1	3.1	3.0		60th
55th	3.7	3.3	3.4	3.3	3.2	3.1	3.1	3.1		55th
50th	3.8	3.4	3.4	3.3	3.2	3.2	3.2	3.1		50th
45th	3.8	3.5	3.5	3.4	3.3	3.2	3.2	3.1		45th
40th	3.9	3.6	3.5	3.4	3.3	3.3	3.3	3.2		40th
35th	3.9	3.7	3.6	3.5	3.4	3.3	3.3	3.2		35th
30th	4.0	3.8	3.7	3.5	3.4	3.4	3.3	3.2		30th
25th	4.0	3.9	3.8	3.6	3.5	3.5	3.4	3.3		25th
20th	4.1	4.0	3.9	3.7	3.5	3.6	3.5	3.4		20th
15th	4.2	4.1	3.9	3.8	3.6	3.7	3.7	3.5		15th
10th	4.3	4.2	4.1	3.9	3.7	3.9	3.9	3.6		10th
5th	4.4	4.4	4.2	4.0	4.0	4.1	4.3	3.9		5th
0	5.5	5.0	5.0	5.0	5.0	5.0	5.0	5.0		0

KICK-OFF
Percentile Scores Based on Age/Test Scores in Feet

Percentile	Age								Percentile
	10	11	12	13	14	15	16	17-18	
100th	88	110	120	129	140	160	160	180	100th
95th	69	79	98	106	118	128	131	138	95th
90th	64	72	83	97	108	120	125	129	90th
85th	59	68	78	92	102	114	119	124	85th
80th	58	64	74	86	97	108	114	119	80th
75th	55	60	70	81	94	104	108	113	75th
70th	53	58	67	78	90	100	104	108	70th
65th	50	56	65	75	86	96	99	105	65th
60th	47	54	64	72	84	93	97	103	60th
55th	46	52	60	69	81	90	95	98	55th
50th	45	50	57	67	77	87	93	95	50th
45th	43	48	54	64	74	83	90	92	45th
40th	40	46	52	62	71	79	87	88	40th
35th	39	44	48	59	68	76	83	84	35th
30th	37	42	45	56	65	72	79	79	30th
25th	35	40	42	52	62	69	75	74	25th
20th	32	37	38	48	58	64	70	70	20th
15th	30	34	34	42	52	59	65	64	15th
10th	26	30	29	36	45	50	60	57	10th
5th	21	24	22	26	38	40	47	43	5th
0	5	10	0	0	0	10	10	10	0

DODGING RUN
Percentile Scores Based on Age/Test Scores in Seconds and Tenths

Percentile	Age								Percentile
	10	11	12	13	14	15	16	17-18	
100th	21.0	18.0	18.0	17.0	16.0	16.0	16.0	16.0	100th
95th	24.3	20.4	23.8	23.3	22.6	22.4	22.3	22.2	95th
90th	25.8	21.6	24.6	24.2	23.9	23.5	23.3	23.2	90th
85th	26.3	22.5	25.0	24.8	24.6	24.1	23.9	23.7	85th
80th	26.4	23.5	25.2	24.9	24.7	24.6	24.3	24.1	80th
75th	27.5	24.0	25.3	25.3	25.2	24.9	24.7	24.4	75th
70th	27.8	25.0	25.8	25.7	25.2	25.2	25.0	24.7	70th
65th	28.1	25.7	26.3	26.1	26.1	25.5	25.3	25.0	65th
60th	28.4	26.3	26.6	26.5	26.3	25.8	25.5	25.3	60th
55th	28.7	26.9	26.9	26.8	26.6	26.1	25.8	25.6	55th
50th	28.9	27.4	27.3	27.2	26.9	26.4	26.1	26.0	50th
45th	29.3	28.0	27.6	27.5	27.2	26.7	26.3	26.3	45th
40th	29.7	28.3	27.9	27.9	27.5	27.0	26.7	26.6	40th
35th	30.1	28.8	28.4	28.3	27.9	27.4	27.0	26.9	35th
30th	30.5	29.2	28.8	28.7	28.3	27.8	27.3	27.2	30th
25th	30.9	29.8	29.2	29.1	28.7	28.2	27.7	27.6	25th
20th	31.3	30.4	29.8	29.5	29.3	28.6	28.1	28.0	20th
15th	31.8	31.1	30.4	30.1	29.9	29.1	28.8	28.7	15th
10th	32.7	32.0	31.3	30.8	30.7	29.8	29.6	29.2	10th
5th	33.6	33.5	33.0	32.3	31.8	31.0	30.6	30.4	5th
0	40.0	40.0	41.0	40.0	36.0	36.0	36.0	36.0	0

AAHPER SOFTBALL TEST

SOFTBALL THROW FOR DISTANCE (BOYS)

Percentile Scores Based on Age/Test Scores in Feet

Percentile	Age							Percentile
	10-11	12	13	14	15	16	17-18	
100th	200	208	200	230	242	247	255	100th
95th	154	163	185	208	231	229	229	95th
90th	144	152	175	203	205	219	222	90th
85th	127	146	167	191	198	213	216	85th
80th	121	140	160	184	192	208	213	80th
75th	118	135	154	178	187	202	207	75th
70th	114	132	150	173	182	196	204	70th
65th	111	129	145	168	178	193	199	65th
60th	109	125	142	163	174	190	196	60th
55th	106	122	138	159	170	186	192	55th
50th	103	118	135	154	167	183	188	50th
45th	100	115	131	152	165	180	185	45th
40th	98	113	128	148	161	174	182	40th
35th	95	109	125	144	157	171	178	35th
30th	92	106	122	140	154	167	173	30th
25th	91	102	117	137	148	164	169	25th
20th	85	98	113	133	143	159	163	20th
15th	80	93	107	129	138	152	153	15th
10th	72	85	101	123	133	146	147	10th
5th	62	76	97	113	119	140	140	5th
0	24	31	60	105	93	135	90	0

SOFTBALL THROW FOR DISTANCE (GIRLS)

Percentile	Age							Percentile
	10-11	12	13	14	15	16	17-18	
100th	120	160	160	160	200	200	200	100th
95th	99	113	133	126	127	121	120	95th
90th	84	104	112	117	116	109	109	90th
85th	76	98	105	109	108	103	102	85th
80th	71	94	98	104	103	98	97	80th
75th	68	89	94	99	97	94	93	75th
70th	66	85	90	95	93	91	89	70th
65th	62	81	86	92	88	87	87	65th
60th	60	77	83	88	85	84	84	60th
55th	57	74	81	85	80	81	82	55th
50th	55	70	76	82	77	79	80	50th
45th	53	67	73	79	75	76	77	45th
40th	50	64	70	76	72	73	74	40th
35th	48	61	68	73	70	70	72	35th
30th	45	58	64	69	67	67	69	30th
25th	43	55	62	66	64	63	66	25th
20th	41	51	60	61	61	60	63	20th
15th	38	48	56	57	58	56	60	15th
10th	34	43	51	52	54	51	55	10th
5th	31	37	43	43	49	45	50	5th
0	20	20	20	20	20	10	10	0

OVERHAND THROW FOR ACCURACY (BOYS)

Percentile Scores Based on Age/Test Scores in Points

| Percentile | Age | | | | | | | Percentile |
	10-11	12	13	14	15	16	17-18	
100th	22	22	23	25	25	27	25	100th
95th	14	17	18	19	20	20	21	95th
90th	12	15	16	17	17	18	19	90th
85th	11	13	15	16	16	17	18	85th
80th	9	12	13	15	15	16	17	80th
75th	8	11	12	14	14	15	16	75th
70th	8	11	12	13	13	14	15	70th
65th	7	10	11	12	12	14	15	65th
60th	6	9	10	11	11	13	14	60th
55th	5	9	10	11	11	12	13	55th
50th	5	8	9	10	10	11	13	50th
45th	4	7	8	10	10	11	12	45th
40th	4	6	7	9	9	10	11	40th
35th	3	6	7	8	9	9	11	35th
30th	3	5	6	8	8	8	10	30th
25th	2	4	5	7	7	8	9	25th
20th	1	3	4	6	7	7	8	20th
15th	1	3	3	6	6	6	7	15th
10th	0	2	2	5	5	5	6	10th
5th	0	0	1	3	3	4	4	5th
0	0	0	0	0	0	1	0	0

OVERHAND THROW FOR ACCURACY (GIRLS)

| Percentile | Age | | | | | | | Percentile |
	10-11	12	13	14	15	16	17-18	
100th	24	26	26	26	30	30	26	100th
95th	17	17	18	19	19	22	20	95th
90th	14	16	16	17	18	20	18	90th
85th	13	14	15	15	16	18	17	85th
80th	12	13	14	14	15	17	16	80th
75th	11	12	13	13	14	16	15	75th
70th	10	11	12	12	13	15	14	70th
65th	9	10	11	11	12	13	13	65th
60th	8	9	10	11	11	12	12	60th
55th	7	9	9	10	11	12	11	55th
50th	6	8	9	9	10	11	10	50th
45th	5	7	8	9	9	10	9	45th
40th	4	6	7	8	8	9	8	40th
35th	4	5	6	7	8	8	7	35th
30th	3	4	6	6	7	7	6	30th
25th	2	4	5	5	6	6	5	25th
20th	1	3	4	4	5	5	4	20th
15th	1	2	3	3	3	4	3	15th
10th	0	1	1	2	2	2	2	10th
5th	0	0	0	1	1	1	1	5th
0	0	0	0	0	0	0	0	0

UNDERHAND PITCH (BOYS)
Percentile Scores Based on Age/Test Scores in Points

| Percentile | Age | | | | | | | Percentile |
	10-11	12	13	14	15	16	17-18	
100th	18	23	21	22	24	25	25	100th
95th	12	14	15	16	18	19	19	95th
90th	10	12	13	15	16	17	17	90th
85th	9	11	11	14	15	15	16	85th
80th	8	9	10	12	14	14	15	80th
75th	7	9	10	12	13	13	14	75th
70th	7	8	9	11	12	12	13	70th
65th	6	7	8	10	11	12	12	65th
60th	6	7	8	9	10	11	12	60th
55th	5	6	7	9	10	10	11	55th
50th	4	6	7	8	9	9	10	50th
45th	4	5	6	7	8	9	10	45th
40th	3	4	5	7	7	8	9	40th
35th	3	4	5	6	7	8	8	35th
30th	2	3	4	6	6	7	8	30th
25th	2	3	4	5	5	6	7	25th
20th	1	2	3	4	4	5	6	20th
15th	1	2	3	4	4	4	5	15th
10th	1	1	2	3	3	3	4	10th
5th	0	0	1	2	2	2	3	5th
0	0	0	0	0	0	0	0	0

UNDERHAND PITCH (GIRLS)

| Percentile | Age | | | | | | | Percentile |
	10-11	12	13	14	15	16	17-18	
100th	23	22	24	24	26	27	26	100th
95th	12	14	16	17	16	19	21	95th
90th	10	13	14	15	15	16	18	90th
85th	8	11	12	14	13	14	17	85th
80th	7	10	11	13	12	12	15	80th
75th	6	9	10	12	11	12	14	75th
70th	6	8	9	11	10	11	13	70th
65th	5	7	9	10	9	10	12	65th
60th	5	6	8	9	8	10	11	60th
55th	4	6	7	8	7	9	10	55th
50th	4	5	7	8	6	8	9	50th
45th	3	5	6	7	6	8	9	45th
40th	3	4	6	6	5	7	8	40th
35th	2	4	5	5	4	6	7	35th
30th	2	3	4	5	4	5	6	30th
25th	1	2	4	4	3	5	5	25th
20th	1	2	3	3	2	4	5	20th
15th	0	1	2	3	2	3	4	15th
10th	0	0	2	2	1	2	3	10th
5th	0	0	1	1	0	0	2	5th
0	0	0	0	0	0	0	0	0

SPEED THROW (BOYS)

Percentile Scores Based on Age/Test Scores in Seconds and Tenths

Percentile				Age				Percentile
	10-11	12	13	14	15	16	17-18	
100th	13.1	11.0	10.0	9.0	13.0	10.0	10.0	100th
95th	16.1	15.3	14.9	13.0	13.5	12.5	12.1	95th
90th	17.1	16.1	14.9	14.0	13.8	13.2	12.8	90th
85th	17.6	16.8	15.7	14.6	14.2	13.7	13.2	85th
80th	18.0	17.3	16.2	15.1	14.5	14.1	13.3	80th
75th	18.6	17.6	16.8	15.6	14.9	14.5	13.9	75th
70th	19.1	18.0	16.9	15.9	15.6	14.8	14.2	70th
65th	19.7	18.4	17.3	16.3	15.9	15.1	14.5	65th
60th	20.2	18.9	17.6	16.6	16.0	15.5	14.8	60th
55th	20.8	19.5	17.9	17.1	16.4	15.8	14.9	55th
50th	21.3	19.8	18.4	17.3	16.7	16.4	15.3	50th
45th	21.8	20.4	19.1	17.7	17.1	16.6	15.6	45th
40th	22.6	21.0	19.3	18.1	17.5	17.1	16.2	40th
35th	23.6	21.5	19.8	18.5	17.9	17.4	16.7	35th
30th	24.6	22.2	20.6	19.0	18.3	18.2	17.2	30th
25th	25.7	23.1	12.2	19.5	18.9	18.8	17.6	25th
20th	26.7	23.9	21.9	20.2	19.5	19.4	18.3	20th
15th	28.2	25.4	23.0	21.3	20.2	19.9	18.9	15th
10th	30.1	27.8	24.2	22.5	20.9	20.9	19.9	10th
5th	34.7	29.5	26.4	25.1	22.2	23.0	21.2	5th
0	43.1	36.0	29.3	28.2	24.9	25.5	26.1	0

SPEED THROW (GIRLS)

Percentile				Age				Percentile
	10-11	12	13	14	15	16	17-18	
100th	10.0	12.0	12.0	12.0	12.0	14.0	14.0	100th
95th	20.1	13.8	13.0	13.0	15.6	15.8	15.0	95th
90th	21.4	15.8	16.3	13.9	16.6	16.9	15.0	90th
85th	22.8	17.7	17.8	15.3	17.6	17.6	15.6	85th
80th	24.1	18.8	18.6	16.5	18.1	18.1	16.1	80th
75th	25.2	19.8	19.4	17.6	18.6	18.5	17.6	75th
70th	26.0	20.8	20.0	18.2	19.1	18.9	18.0	70th
65th	27.0	21.6	20.6	18.7	19.6	19.4	18.5	65th
60th	27.4	22.3	21.3	19.3	20.1	20.0	18.9	60th
55th	28.8	23.1	21.9	19.9	20.6	20.7	19.3	55th
50th	29.8	24.1	22.7	20.7	21.1	21.4	19.8	50th
45th	30.9	25.2	23.4	21.1	21.7	22.2	20.3	45th
40th	31.9	26.2	24.3	21.8	22.6	22.9	20.8	40th
35th	33.0	27.5	25.4	22.5	23.3	23.7	21.4	35th
30th	34.1	28.6	26.4	23.5	24.3	24.8	22.3	30th
25th	35.9	29.8	27.5	24.6	25.4	26.1	23.3	25th
20th	38.0	31.3	28.9	25.8	26.9	27.8	24.1	20th
15th	41.0	33.1	30.9	27.4	28.7	30.4	25.0	15th
10th	46.1	36.7	33.0	30.2	31.5	33.0	26.1	10th
5th	55.2	40.8	38.5	33.5	37.4	36.9	28.9	5th
0	105.0	66.0	52.0	50.0	50.0	52.0	40.0	0

FUNGO HITTING (BOYS)
Percentile Scores Based on Age/Test Scores in Points

Percentile	Age							Percentile
	10-11	12	13	14	15	16	17-18	
100th	40	40	39	36	40	40	40	100th
95th	35	36	38	35	39	38	39	95th
90th	32	33	34	35	37	36	37	90th
85th	29	31	33	33	34	34	36	85th
80th	27	30	31	31	33	33	35	80th
75th	26	29	30	30	31	33	34	75th
70th	24	28	29	29	30	32	32	70th
65th	22	27	28	28	29	30	31	65th
60th	21	26	27	27	28	29	30	60th
55th	20	25	25	26	26	28	29	55th
50th	19	23	24	24	24	26	28	50th
45th	17	22	23	23	23	25	26	45th
40th	16	20	21	21	21	23	25	40th
35th	14	19	19	19	19	21	23	35th
30th	13	17	18	18	17	19	21	30th
25th	11	15	16	16	16	17	19	25th
20th	10	13	15	15	14	15	17	20th
15th	8	11	14	13	12	13	15	15th
10th	6	10	12	12	11	11	13	10th
5th	3	7	9	11	9	9	11	5th
0	0	0	1	9	1	0	3	0

FUNGO HITTING (GIRLS)

Percentile	Age							Percentile
	10-11	12	13	14	15	16	17-18	
100th	30	38	38	38	38	38	38	100th
95th	21	28	30	31	30	30	31	95th
90th	18	24	26	30	27	27	28	90th
85th	15	22	23	26	25	25	26	85th
80th	14	20	22	23	23	24	25	80th
75th	13	18	20	21	22	22	23	75th
70th	12	17	19	20	20	21	22	70th
65th	12	16	18	19	19	19	20	65th
60th	11	15	17	18	18	18	19	60th
55th	9	14	16	17	17	17	18	55th
50th	9	13	14	15	16	16	17	50th
45th	8	12	13	14	15	15	16	45th
40th	7	11	13	13	14	14	15	40th
35th	6	10	12	12	13	13	14	35th
30th	6	9	11	11	12	12	14	30th
25th	5	8	10	10	11	11	13	25th
20th	4	7	8	9	10	10	12	20th
15th	3	5	7	8	8	9	10	15th
10th	2	4	6	6	7	8	8	10th
5th	0	2	4	3	4	5	6	5th
0	0	0	0	0	0	0	0	0

BASE RUNNING (BOYS)

Percentile Scores Based on Age/Test Scores in Seconds and Tenths

Percentile	Age							Percentile
	10-11	12	13	14	15	16	17-18	
100th	10.1	9.6	9.4	9.7	10.0	10.0	10.0	100th
95th	12.9	12.4	11.7	11.5	11.6	11.3	11.1	95th
90th	13.5	12.5	12.2	11.9	11.9	11.6	11.4	90th
85th	13.9	13.3	12.7	12.2	12.2	11.8	11.6	85th
80th	14.1	13.5	12.9	12.5	12.4	12.0	11.8	80th
75th	14.3	13.7	13.2	12.7	12.5	12.1	11.9	75th
70th	14.5	13.9	13.4	12.9	12.7	12.3	12.0	70th
65th	14.8	14.1	13.6	13.0	12.8	12.4	12.2	65th
60th	14.9	14.3	13.8	13.1	13.0	12.5	12.3	60th
55th	15.1	14.5	13.9	13.3	13.1	12.6	12.4	55th
50th	15.2	14.7	14.1	13.4	13.2	12.8	12.6	50th
45th	15.4	14.8	14.3	13.5	13.3	12.9	12.7	45th
40th	15.6	15.0	14.5	13.7	13.5	13.0	12.8	40th
35th	15.8	15.2	14.7	13.9	13.6	13.2	12.9	35th
30th	16.0	15.4	14.9	14.1	13.7	13.3	13.0	30th
25th	16.2	15.7	15.1	14.2	13.9	13.6	13.2	25th
20th	16.5	15.9	15.4	14.5	14.0	13.8	13.4	20th
15th	17.0	16.2	15.7	14.8	14.3	14.1	13.6	15th
10th	17.4	16.5	15.9	15.2	14.5	14.4	13.9	10th
5th	18.2	17.4	16.7	15.8	15.0	15.3	14.9	5th
0	23.0	20.6	17.2	17.2	16.8	18.0	17.8	0

BASE RUNNING (GIRLS)

Percentile	Age							Percentile
	10-11	12	13	14	15	16	17-18	
100th	11.0	11.0	12.0	12.0	12.0	12.0	12.0	100th
95th	13.1	13.4	12.6	12.7	12.9	13.2	13.6	95th
90th	13.8	13.7	13.1	13.1	13.5	13.7	13.9	90th
85th	14.3	14.0	13.5	13.5	13.7	14.0	14.3	85th
80th	14.7	14.3	13.7	13.7	13.9	14.4	14.6	80th
75th	14.9	14.5	13.9	13.8	14.1	14.6	14.8	75th
70th	15.2	14.7	14.1	14.0	14.3	14.8	14.9	70th
65th	15.4	14.9	14.3	14.2	14.5	14.9	15.1	65th
60th	15.6	15.0	14.5	14.4	14.7	15.1	15.3	60th
55th	15.8	15.2	14.7	14.5	14.9	15.3	15.5	55th
50th	16.0	15.3	14.8	14.8	15.0	15.5	15.7	50th
45th	16.2	15.5	15.0	14.9	15.2	15.6	15.9	45th
40th	16.4	15.7	15.2	15.1	15.4	15.8	16.1	40th
35th	16.7	15.8	15.4	15.3	15.5	15.9	16.3	35th
30th	17.0	16.0	15.6	15.5	15.8	16.0	16.5	30th
25th	17.3	16.2	16.0	15.7	16.1	16.2	16.9	25th
20th	17.7	16.5	16.3	16.0	16.3	16.3	17.1	20th
15th	18.2	16.9	16.6	16.4	16.7	16.4	17.6	15th
10th	18.8	17.4	17.2	16.9	17.3	17.8	18.2	10th
5th	19.9	18.2	18.0	17.8	18.1	18.4	19.2	5th
0	27.0	20.0	22.0	23.0	28.0	31.0	32.0	0

FIELDING GROUND BALLS (BOYS)

Percentile Scores Based on Age/Test Scores in Points

Percentile	Age							Percentile
	10-11	12	13	14	15	16	17-18	
100th	20	20	20	20	20	20	20	100th
95th	19	20	20	20	20	20	20	95th
90th	18	19	19	19	19	20	20	90th
85th	18	19	19	19	19	20	20	85th
80th	17	18	18	18	18	19	19	80th
75th	17	18	18	18	18	19	19	75th
70th	16	17	17	17	18	19	19	70th
65th	16	17	17	17	17	18	18	65th
60th	15	16	16	16	16	18	18	60th
55th	15	16	16	16	16	17	17	55th
50th	14	15	15	15	15	17	17	50th
45th	13	15	14	14	15	16	17	45th
40th	13	14	14	14	14	16	16	40th
35th	12	14	13	13	13	15	16	35th
30th	11	13	13	12	12	14	15	30th
25th	10	12	12	10	11	13	14	25th
20th	9	11	11	10	10	10	12	20th
15th	8	9	10	9	9	9	10	15th
10th	6	8	8	8	8	9	9	10th
5th	4	6	6	6	7	8	9	5th
0	0	0	1	1	1	5	6	0

FIELDING GROUND BALLS (GIRLS)

Percentile	Age							Percentile
	10-11	12	13	14	15	16	17-18	
100th	20	20	20	20	20	20	20	100th
95th	18	20	20	20	20	20	20	95th
90th	17	19	19	19	20	20	20	90th
85th	16	19	19	19	19	19	19	85th
80th	15	18	19	19	19	19	19	80th
75th	15	18	18	18	18	19	19	75th
70th	14	17	18	18	18	18	18	70th
65th	13	16	17	17	18	18	18	65th
60th	13	15	17	17	17	18	18	60th
55th	12	15	16	17	17	17	17	55th
50th	11	14	16	16	16	17	17	50th
45th	10	13	15	15	16	17	17	45th
40th	10	12	15	15	15	16	16	40th
35th	9	10	14	14	15	16	16	35th
30th	8	10	13	13	14	15	15	30th
25th	8	9	12	12	13	14	14	25th
20th	7	9	11	10	12	13	14	20th
15th	6	8	10	10	11	12	13	15th
10th	5	7	9	9	10	10	11	10th
5th	3	5	8	8	9	8	9	5th
0	0	0	0	0	0	0	0	0

CATCHING FLY BALLS (BOYS)

Percentile Scores Based on Age/Test Scores in Points

Percentile	Age							Percentile
	10-11	12	13	14	15	16	17-18	
100th	20	20	20	20	20	20	20	100th
95th	20	20	20	20	20	20	20	95th
90th	20	20	20	20	20	20	20	90th
85th	19	19	19	19	20	20	20	85th
80th	19	19	19	19	19	19	19	80th
75th	19	19	19	19	19	19	19	75th
70th	18	19	18	19	19	19	19	70th
65th	18	18	18	18	18	19	19	65th
60th	17	18	17	18	18	18	18	60th
55th	17	17	17	18	17	18	18	55th
50th	16	17	16	16	17	17	18	50th
45th	15	16	16	16	16	16	17	45th
40th	14	15	15	15	15	15	16	40th
35th	12	14	14	13	14	13	15	35th
30th	10	12	13	12	12	10	14	30th
25th	9	10	11	10	11	10	11	25th
20th	8	10	10	10	10	10	10	20th
15th	7	8	9	9	9	9	10	15th
10th	6	7	8	8	8	9	9	10th
5th	3	5	6	7	7	8	9	5th
0	0	0	0	0	0	0	0	0

CATCHING FLY BALLS (GIRLS)

Percentile	Age							Percentile
	10-11	12	13	14	15	16	17-18	
100th	15	17	19	19	20	20	20	100th
95th	13	15	17	17	19	19	19	95th
90th	10	13	15	16	18	19	19	90th
85th	9	11	13	15	18	18	18	85th
80th	9	10	12	14	17	17	17	80th
75th	8	9	11	13	16	16	16	75th
70th	7	8	10	12	15	15	16	70th
65th	7	7	9	11	14	14	15	65th
60th	6	7	8	10	13	13	15	60th
55th	6	6	7	9	12	13	14	55th
50th	5	6	6	9	11	12	13	50th
45th	4	5	5	8	10	11	12	45th
40th	4	5	5	8	9	10	11	40th
35th	3	4	4	7	8	9	10	35th
30th	3	3	3	6	7	8	9	30th
25th	2	3	3	5	6	7	8	25th
20th	2	2	2	4	5	6	7	20th
15th	1	2	2	3	4	5	6	15th
10th	1	1	1	2	3	4	5	10th
5th	0	0	0	1	2	3	4	5th
0	0	0	0	0	0	0	0	0

APPENDIX C
THE TWELVE MINUTE RUN-WALK TEST

The Twelve Minute Run-Walk Test[1]

This test represents a simple method of self evaluation as to one's level of fitness, or unfitness as the case may be. Naturally, it is assumed that the individual will be in good health, with no known heart defects or other abnormalities.

The test consists of running, or running and walking, as great a distance as possible in 12 minutes. The route could be measured by using the odometer in your car, or by carrying a pedometer, etc. The score is the distance covered in 12 minutes. The individual can then check his general fitness level by consulting the table.

Doolittle and Bigbee[2] reported a test-retest reliability coefficient of .94 and a validity coefficient of .90 when maximum oxygen intake was used as the criterion.

12 Minute Run-Walk — Scoring Scale*

Distance Covered	Fitness Level
Less than 1 mile	Very Poor
1 to 1¼ miles	Poor
1¼ to 1½ miles	Fair
1½ to 1¾ miles	Good
1¾ miles or more	Excellent

*For men over 35, 1.4 miles is good; for women, 1.3.

[1] Kenneth H. Cooper, *Aerobics,* New York: Bantam Books, Inc., 1968.

[2] T. L. Doolittle and Rollin Bigbee, "The Twelve-Minute Run-Walk: A Test of Cardiorespiratory Fitness of Adolescent Boys." *Research Quarterly* 39:491-495, October, 1968.

INDEX